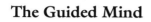

The Guided Mind

The Guided Mind

A Sociogenetic Approach to Personality

Jaan Valsiner

Harvard University Press

Cambridge, Massachusetts, and London, England | 1998

Library of Congress Cataloging-in-Publication Data

Valsiner, Jaan.
    The guided mind : a sociogenetic approach to personality / Jaan Valsiner.
        p.   cm.
    Includes index.
    ISBN 0-674-36757-X
    1. Personality—Social aspects.
    2. Personality and culture.
    I. Title.
    BF698.9.S63V35   1997
    155.2—dc21   97-30564

Contents

Figures

Preface

The writing of this book has been a torturous process. Since my previous substantive effort (*Culture and the Development of Children's Action* [Chichester, England: Wiley, 1987]), I have moved away from issues of child development to those of psychological development of adults. In this field, different kinds of discourses can be encountered. First, there is the "traditional" personality psychology, which has generated many empirical investigations and rather little basic understanding of the ways in which human personality functions. Most of this "knowledge base" is purposefully overlooked in the present book. I focus on the universal processes that organize human psychological functioning rather than describe the variety of interindividually unique structural forms of personality. The latter are described—in one form or another—by the so-called individual differences research in empirical psychology. Personality psychology has become overly concerned by description (which is often masked by the prestigious label of "measurement") of individual differences. That concern is directly opposite to my task here. My aims in this book are theoretical—how to make sense of the social nature of human psychology in general, using the tradition of different semiotic approaches. From that standpoint, summarizing the accumulated "research literature" in personality psychology would have been counterproductive. Furthermore, our contemporary talk of "research literatures" in any area does not add to our understanding of issues but rather lets general understanding become drowned in the ocean of empirical details. Sometimes it is better to pretend that these kinds of "literatures" do not exist at all—a rather ambivalent commentary upon the results of empiricist fashions in psychology.

Second, the realm of developmental psychology has rarely included adult personality organization. The sociogenetic traditions in developmental psychology have never become tired of repeating the maxim that "human personality is social"—yet they usually fail to explain what that means. Trying to answer that question by elaborating processes of internalization and externalization of semiotic constraint systems required a renewed look at the discourse on dualisms. Instead of continuing the fight with the windmills of dualisms, here I distinguish dualisms and dualities (chapter 1). The latter not only are existing, but constitute a desirable starting point for a theory of human development.

Third, the frequent claim that human psychology has to consider the meaningful nature of psychological phenomena led me into making sense of some roots of the discipline of semiotics—the science of signs. Semiotics has mostly looked at signs in their static forms, while in making sense of personality organization it is the immediate, dynamic role of signs that is of relevance. Signs are constantly being constructed (and reconstructed) by persons in their immediate life-worlds. Previously constructed, by others, signs are imported into persons' "here-and-now" life situations through constructive internalization/externalization process.

The goal I had set myself in the present book was to give a theoretical consideration of personality in terms of the core concepts of "bounded determinacy" and "constraining." I had not tried to return to these ideas for a number of years, since their systematic presentation in 1987 (and re-publication in 1997). I was afraid of creating a form of talk where the use of constraint terminology becomes overwhelming. Nevertheless, some papers written since 1987 included an effort to carry the notion of constraining to the realm of adult mental activity, as well as to the domain of social regulation of the thought processes in sciences (particularly in psychology). However, I avoided overusing the constraining terminology. It seemed utterly uninteresting to find myself (or anybody else) suddenly reformulating all (or even some) psychological problems in the language of "constraints." Furthermore, extended uses of general concepts can easily lead to the inflation of these concepts, as often happens in the social sciences. For example, people who are fascinated by Lev Vygotsky may easily see the whole world as being (or being filled with) "zones of proximal development"—yet such relabeling of complex phenomena by another complex label does not solve our theoretical problems.

So it took nine years before I dared to try again to take up the "zonology" of constraining ideas and apply them to the intrapsychological (yet social) processes. The result—for better or worse—is the present book. What I have tried to emphasize here is the basic unity of the realms of thinking, feeling, and acting. For all these domains, the constraining principles can apply. The resulting general picture is that of active persons who construct meanings and strive themselves—and attempt to guide others—toward some constructed meaningful future objectives. Teleology in some form is part and parcel of any account of personality that emphasizes its regulatory organization.

In this focus on personal teleology, I also found some powerful allies in the history of psychological, sociological, and linguistic thought. In my previous understanding, I had overlooked the contributions of personologies of William Stern and Gordon Allport in their dynamic-organizational sense. But so has the whole discipline of psychology. Furthermore, the constructive work of Karl Bühler in explaining the psychology of speaking constitutes a powerful parallel to his criticisms of the state of psychology in the 1920s. His (as well as Lev Vygotsky's) criticisms of meaningfulness-avoiding traditions of psychology still stand in the 1990s. In fact, these criticisms may perhaps be even more fitting in our day. Integration of the meaningful nature of human psychological phenomena into the existing research schemes of psychology is more than a simple task. Nor is it solved by the use of magical words, such as an emphasis on "interdisciplinarity."

The empirical examples used in this book are all borrowed from others and are reconstructed within the theoretical framework of this book. I hope that these reconstructions bring home the simple idea of any data being constructed by the researcher—by deriving abstracted information from the richness of phenomena on the basis of one's theoretical system. Psychology is very rich in different kinds of data yet sufficiently poor in making sense of them.

Different parts of the book benefited from critical readings by a number of persons. Joint work with René van der Veer over many years has had its beneficial role in building up a number of ideas in this work. It has given me the pleasure of intellectual companionship that defies the usual competitive jealousies that so often make collaboration in psychology very difficult. In Berlin, in our discussions held in a similar atmosphere, Kurt Kreppner has challenged my thinking by pointing out the importance of William Stern and the whole "Hamburg tradition" (of Ernst Cassirer and others) as a theoretical heritage that is perhaps too well known to be adopted in our present science. Dietmar Görlitz's always colorful expositions of pictures and cultural life forms of humanity have challenged me over the past years not to stop at the usual boundaries of my own limits of knowledge.

In Chapel Hill, I have over years benefited from close intellectual exchange with Bob Cairns, with whom we have had chances to escape from the everyday routine of the university for "beer-drinking sessions." During those sessions, we have spent less time consuming beer than discussing ideas of development in ways that go beyond the usual stories psychologists tell one another. In a similar vein, Maria Lyra has challenged my mechanistic tendencies in theory building by constantly pushing me toward considering the poetry of the process of highlighting in human development, as well as in science. Discussions of issues of development with Terry Winegar over the past decade have been important in the formulation of many of the present ideas. The always curious critical questions raised by Ingrid E. Josephs while reading my work have contributed to the formulation of ideas and recognition of my own intellectual constraints in a productive way. A number of theoretical extensions of previous ideas that appear in this book were born in the process of discussions within the "Gruppa V" context in Chapel Hill (which was indebted to the organizational energies of Vera Vasconcellos and Helena Hurme), and in various seminars at the University of Brasilia and University of São Paulo at Ribeirão Preto. Different versions of the manuscript were read and critically commented upon by numerous colleagues: Angela Branco, Agnes Dodds, Sumi Gupta, Jeanette Lawrence, Simone Lima, Gorjana Litvinovic, Eleonora Magomedova, Teresa Mettel, Zilma M. R. de Oliveira, and Clotilde Rossetti-Ferreira. I remain indebted to them for all their input to the manuscript, as well as their understanding of the complexities of human personality in its fullness. Nevertheless, I reserve the dubious privilege not to have accepted some of the advice—for better or worse.

I am grateful to the copyright holders for permission to reprint the following:

Gordon Allport: Excerpts from *Letters from Jenny* by Gordon W. Allport, copyright © 1965 by Harcourt Brace & Company and renewed 1993 by Robert P. Allport, reprinted by permission of the publisher. Excerpts from *Personality*, copyright © 1937 by Henry Holt & Co. Reprinted with permission of the publisher.

E. Boesch: Excerpts from "Cultural Psychology in Action" from *Growth and Progress in Cross-Cultural Psychology*, edited by C. Kagitçibasi (The Netherlands: Swets & Zeitlinger, 1989).

Karl Bühler: Excerpt from *Theory of Language: The Representational Function of Language*. Translated by Frasier Goodwin (Philadelphia: John

Benjamins Publishing, 1990). Reprinted by permission of John Benjamins Publishing.

Louis Dumont: Excerpt from *Homo Hierarchicus: The Caste System and Its Implications.* Copyright © 1980 by The University of Chicago Press. Reprinted with permission of The University of Chicago Press.

R. Engler: Figure from *Ferdinand de Saussure, Cours de Linguistique Génerale: Edition Critique* (Wiesbaden, Germany: Otto Harrasowitz Verlag, 1968).

D. B. Harris: Excerpts from *The Concept of Development.* Copyright © 1957 by University of Minnesota Press. Reprinted with permission of University of Minnesota Press.

G. Hornstein: Excerpts from Chapter 9 in *The Rise of Experimentation in American Psychology,* edited by Jill G. Morawski (New Haven, Conn.: Yale University Press, 1988).

W. M. Kurtines & J. L. Gewittz: Excerpt from *Moral Development through Social Interactions,* copyright © 1987. Reprinted by permission of John Wiley & Sons, Inc.

Alfred Lang: Excerpt from "Non-Cartesian Artifacts in Dwelling Activities—Steps Towards a Semiotic Ecology," *Schweizerische Zeitschrift für Psychologie, 52 (2),* 1993.

F. Marglin: Excerpts from "Refining the Body: Transformative Emotion in Ritual Dance," in *Divine Passions: The Social Construction of Emotion in India,* edited by Owen Lynch. Copyright © 1990 by The Regents of the University of California. Reprinted with permission from The University of California Press.

W. McGuire: Excerpt from Chapter 3 of *Personality and the Prediction of Behavior,* edited by R. A. Zucker, J. Aronoff, and A. I. Rabin (San Diego: Academic Press, 1984).

Gananath Obeyesekere: Excerpts from *Medusa's Hair: An Essay on Personal Symbols and Religious Experience.* Copyright © 1981 by The University of Chicago. Excerpts from *The Work of Culture: Symbolic Transformation in Psychoanalysis and Anthropology.* Copyright © 1990 by The University of Chicago. Excerpt from *The Cult of the Goddess Pattini.* Copyright © 1984 by The University of Chicago. Reprinted with permission of The University of Chicago Press.

Rayna Rapp: Excerpts from Chapter 11 from *Women and Prenatal Testing,* edited by K. Rothenberg and E. J. Thomson (Columbus, Oh.: Ohio State University Press, 1994).

Alan Roland: Excerpts from *In Search of Self in India and Japan*. Copyright © 1988 by Princeton University Press. Reprinted by permission of Princeton University Press.

Lee Siegel: Excerpt from *Sacred and Profane Dimensions of Love in Indian Traditions as Exemplified in the Gitagovinda*. Copyright © 1978 by Lee Siegel. Reprinted with permission from Lee Siegel.

Jaan Valsiner: Excerpts from "Devadasi Temple Dancers and Cultural Construction of Persons-in-Society" from *Dimensions of Human Society and Culture*, edited by M. K. Raha (New Delhi: Gyan Publishing House, 1996). Reprinted by permission of M. K. Raha.

H. Werner and B. Kaplan: Excerpts from *Symbol Formation* (Mahwah, N.J.: Lawrence Erlbaum Associates, 1984).

Figure 16: from *The Collected Papers of Charles Sanders Peirce*, edited by Charles Hartshorne and Paul Weiss. Copyright © 1935 by the President and Fellows of Harvard College. Reprinted by permission of Harvard University Press.

Figure 6.2: from *Cours de Linguistique Génerale* (Paris: Payot Editions, 1949).

The writing of the book benefited from support from the Fulbright Foundation (in the form of a serial grant to teach in Brazil over a period of three years), and from the Alexander von Humboldt *Forschungspreis*, which I was awarded in Germany for 1995. The University of Leiden invited me to stay at its Graduate School on Human Development in 1995. These sources made it possible to write parts of the book outside of the hassles of my home university. Because the whole book was written while I was traveling, I consider myself a kind of a naive wanderer in the landscape of human phenomena.

The Guided Mind

Introduction: Why a Sociogenetic Approach to Personality?

The issue of human personality organization has been one of the oldest in psychology. Making sense of the integrated whole of a person is as central to human inquiry into the nature of the world as is investigation of other planets, microparticles, or viruses. All of these, as well as human personality, can be viewed from a contextualized or decontextualized point of view. In psychology, it has usually been the latter that has guided investigations into personality. The primary research question has been phrased within an individualistic perspective. Personality is usually considered to be a phenomenon that "belongs" inherently to the person and is not causally related to the social context. The glory of the person becomes a myth that overrides the person's linkages with the social world.

Even when such relation of the personality with the social world is allowed, it is seen as taking the form of one-sided causal influences rather than a bidirectional process of interdependence. For instance, it may be assumed that the individual personality is "shaped" or "molded" by the social world. Surely such views are built on the folk models of society that consider the social world to be an external force that superimposes its rule over persons rather than the context within which persons develop. In contrast, the sociocultural direction within developmental psychology has adamantly emphasized the "social basis" of human personality. Because society participates in the process of persons' construction of themselves, it is thus an "insider" in this process rather than an "external force."

This book outlines a sociogenetic approach to personality. Personality is viewed as emerging in ontogeny through social relations and their cultural organization. In its established forms, socially emerged personality becomes relatively autonomous from the very social world within which it has emerged. Thus, personality is *simultaneously* socially dependent and individually independent, with both parts of this whole being mutually interdependent.

1

Goals of the Book: Synthesis of Personology and Sociogenesis

In line with this general perspective, the present approach synthesizes the individual-focused traditions of personalistic psychology with the semiotic orientations of the cultural-historical perspective (of James Mark Baldwin, George Herbert Mead, and Lev Vygotsky) and its contemporary sematology of Karl Bühler. Personological and sociocultural perspectives have habitually been viewed as opposites—an approach that is quite unproductive for making sense of either. The difference between these two views of personality is one of emphasis on either the personal or the social part of the whole. In one case, the focus is on the *ontology* of the person as a unique autonomous individual (i.e., the personological view). In the other case, it is the social *origins* of such autonomy that are emphasized. Yet both stories—those of ontology and of origins—belong to the same object of investigation: the person. The person simultaneously *is* and maintains his or her autonomy relative to the given social context, and *has become* the way he or she is through the history of such relations. Both foci of investigation—the personal and the social—are thus complementary yet distinct.

More specifically, the goals of this book are as follows:

1. To outline a sociogenetic theory of personality that is constructed on an explicitly sociogenetic basis, with an emphasis on the *semiogenetic* (sign-constructing and sign-using) nature of human psychological processes);
2. To demonstrate this theory's historical and intellectual continuities and discontinuities with classic approaches to personality (especially those of William Stern and Gordon Allport);
3. To provide selective empirical case histories to illustrate the theoretical system; and
4. To outline some directions for a developmental methodology that is adequate for a sociogenetic approach to personality.

Personality as Co-Constructed Whole of Hierarchical Organization

The focus in this book is on the developmental mechanisms of personality formation, and the intricate relations between the personality and its social context. Personality emerges through *co-construction* of human development jointly by the social world and the active, developing person. In the history of personality psychology, the traditions of personalism of William Stern and Gordon Allport are closest to the sociogenetic foundations upon which this book will be built. Specifically, Stern's concept of the person as *unitas multiplex* (i.e., heterogeneity of the psychological functions within the personality structure, which corresponds to the heterogeneity of the flow of lived-through encounters with the world) will be put to use in the present construction of a theory of human development that is an extension of the focus on "bounded indeterminacy" (Valsiner, 1987, 1997b). In this perspective, the process of development is organized by the constant construction and reconstruction of constraints upon the stream of conduct in any corresponding context.

In the previous version of this theory, the dynamic constraining perspective was applied to the development of children's actions within meaningfully structured everyday settings. In the present book, it is extended to the intrapsychological (i.e., internalized) processes that are regulated by semiotic devices. The latter are viewed as constraining the flow of feeling, thinking, and acting. They are loci for the construction of new semiotic means that prepare the person for possible encounters with novel life situations in the future.

Structure of the Book

The structure of the book is quite complex. It moves from an outline of the technicalities of the suggested theoretical system to an analysis of its antecedent ideas in the history of the social sciences and finally presents analyses of selected empirical materials. A historically oriented reader may benefit from beginning at Part II before delving into the intricacies of the proposed theoretical system in Part I.

The theoretical system is outlined in Part I. The notion of *constraint systems* is elaborated in chapter 2, with a focus on the dynamic nature of building (and rebuilding) these systems in irreversible time. This focus on constraints differs from the talk about absolute constraints upon basic psychological processes (e.g., on learning, or on cognitive processing capacities). Whereas the latter emphasize the limits of the particular (learning or cognitive system) as it exists in its static form, the perspective espoused in this book emphasizes the role of constraining as the main mechanism of human development in always specific here-and-now contexts. Constraints as depicted in the present book are *temporary organizational devices,* constructed in action and ideation, in dialogue between persons, between persons and contextual expectations, or between personal sense and collec-tive-cultural meanings.

The linkage between the domains of constraining of (and by) actions and constraining by semiotic devices is created through the notions of constructive internalization and externalization. These mutually interde-pendent processes are contrasted with the notion of appropriation, dis-missing the latter as a theoretical impasse. It is through internalization and externalization that human personality can become the autonomous or-ganizing structure of personal lives, yet retaining its interdependence with the social world and resulting from transactions with that world in onto-geny.

The ethos of this book is clearly historical in its totality. No theoretical system is without its intellectual interdependence, and a thorough analysis of the history of relevant ideas is a necessary component of a system. Therefore, three domains of theoretical thought are analyzed in Part II. Chapter 4 presents an analysis of sociogenetic and cultural-psychological perspectives that are relevant for making sense of personality. Most of the ideas utilized in the present theoretical system have their predecessors in specific classical thinking of James Mark Baldwin, William James, Pierre Janet, George Herbert Mead, Lev Vygotsky, and Jean Piaget—as well as in the work of our contemporary thinkers Ernest Boesch, Gananath Obeye-sekere, Michael Cole, Richard Shweder, James Wertsch, and others. In the history of personological thought, the work of William Stern and Gordon Allport is seminal for the present perspective (see chapter 5). However, perhaps the most relevant addition to the constraining perspective (since its previous form—Valsiner, 1987) is the substantive working through of the history of ideas in the area of sign-related (semiotic, semiological, or sematological) perspectives (see chapter 6). These perspectives illustrate previous efforts to create explanatory accounts of human psychological phenomena that do not avoid the centrality of meanings, and—more im-portant—of the *constant reconstruction of meanings* that occurs in human lives.

Human beings create parallel constraint systems in two domains—extra-mental (actions within contexts) and intramental (construction of hierar-chies of meanings, with each new level setting constraints both for itself and for lower levels). The potentially infinite possibility of reconstructing one's *meaningful position relative to any given context* through semiotic devices is perhaps the greatest freedom that *Homo sapiens* has.

Toward Meanings-Respecting Methodology

However, human freedom for meaningful constraint of one's subjective world is an inevitable nuisance for psychological research methodology. Admission of the flexibility of personal semiotic construction makes it necessary to reorder many aspects of methodology. Directions for such reformulation are outlined in chapter 7; I have also dealt with them in greater depth elsewhere (Valsiner, 1997b).

A theoretical system always needs an empirical counterpart of relevant analyses of phenomena. Part III of the present book is devoted to selected examples of how the present theoretical system deals with what is habitually called "data" in psychology. In clear defiance of the received practices in contemporary psychology, two rather unusual phenomena are analyzed (or reanalyzed) from the perspective of the present theory. First, a selective reanalysis of Gordon Allport's key empirical case—a sequence of letters from the mother of his college roommate—is meant to indicate how existing personal documents can be analyzed through the prism of constraint systems (see chapter 8). In chapter 9, phenomena that are describable only through secondary (historical and anthropological) sources are likewise subjected to scrutiny from the present perspective. Although these examples appear diverse, nevertheless they are unified by the focus on the cultural heterogeneity of possible trajectories of human personality development. Within the myriad of cross-cultural differences, visible on the surface, exist basic human tendencies for cultural construction of human life courses, in all their variety. It is the unity within diversity that needs theoretical explanation.

1

Personality and Psychology: Commonsense and General Assumptions

How is human personality culturally constituted, and how do personal actions participate in social change? These fundamental questions have been asked by social sciences for at least a century, but answering them proves to be a very difficult task. Basic assumptions within the existing social sciences—borrowed from the limited basis of European cultural traditions—may have complicated the search for adequate answers to these questions, in part because of the linguistic guidance of thought (as will be described in chapter 6). Human languages guide their users toward some—rather than other—ways of conceptualizing the distinctions between the individual person and his or her culturally structured life-world. Active users of ordinary languages are thus led toward either emphasizing the *distinction of* the person (as an active agent) from the environment or—alternatively—*fusing* the person with the social context. The latter emphasis has prevailed in contemporary Western "deconstruction" of self-concepts, as well as in ancient Chinese Taoist views of the self (Ho, 1995).

Distinguishing the self from the context and fusing the self with the context are often presented as mutually exclusive, irreconcilable alternatives. The person is either independent from *or* identical with the social environment. These two directions have been widespread in occidental thought, on which psychology as a science has based its efforts to conceptualize its phenomena (see Shweder and Bourne, 1984, illustrating the contrast between "egocentric contractual" and "sociocentric organic" views of the person). This can be combined with researchers' human-made contrast of their own versus other societies: "we" are X ("individualist," "ego-centered," etc.), while "they" are Y ("collectivistic," "sociocentric," etc.). As a result of such attribution, the focus of interest is on cultural *organization* of personality (which is a question of systemic integration—

6

see Bühler, 1968) rather than on the realm of direct cross-cultural comparisons which homogenize the complex reality.

In contrast, within other traditions of cultural history, the focus on personality may be built on the notion of *relationship between* person and environment. As an example, in the system of Hindu logic (Gupta, 1895; Vidyabhusana, 1970), the conceptual focus has been on relationships and not on object properties. The focus on relationships does not deny separation of subject and object (this separation remains as central for locating relationships) but instead directs the investigator to look at the ways in which the parts are functioning within the whole. Conceptualizing such processes is no simple matter, since human languages are known to promote the construction of static representations of dynamically changing phenomena.

This contrast between static and dynamic orientations guided by language does not mean that a simple turn from occidental language uses to those projected onto the oriental mind-set (or from static to dynamic descriptions) solves our conceptual problems in psychology. Instead, such contrasts merely indicate the necessity for careful conceptual analyses of the meanings that psychologists elevate from ordinary to scientific language. Even as our everyday ways of speaking in any language might entail intricate reflection upon psychological phenomena (e.g., as claimed by Siegfried, 1994), an enrichment of the theoretical realm of the discipline by learning from the "common person" does not necessarily lead to better conceptualizations of issues. Psychology's concepts often carry the unavoidable baggage of connotations of the same term as used in ordinary language, thus making theoretical precision a rare achievement in the discipline. Borrowing language terms of "greater richness" from the common language may lead to further lack of precision in topics where such precision is both possible and theoretically desirable. The semantic richness of ordinary language may be an obstacle for psychological conceptualizations.

The notion of personality is one such term of ill fate. Psychology of personality has been largely the hostage of the multiple meanings that have been given to that term in common language. Furthermore, the propensity of common language to provide stable accounts of ever-flowing psychological processes has guided personality psychology toward the construction of static, ontological depictions of personality. At the same time, the phenomena that constitute the basis for such ontological depictions can be complex and hyperrelational. Consider the following self-description:

> *Question:* Tell us about yourself.
>
> *Answer* [by a seventh-grade American boy]: I am a kid that has nothing and gets nothing. When I born I born trouble. My mother said to me that I was born just for trouble. I was born in New York. I used to think myself that I should be dead. I never had a good time for long. When I come home I just get fust at. I was born just to be born. I am a kid that is hardly known to the world. I am a human just like everybody you know and should be treated like one. Please be my friend.
>
> . . .
>
> *Question:* Tell us some things you are not.
>
> *Answer:* I am not a hero or prince or king. But I can do some things well maybe better than anybody. Some people can do things better than me but I can top people in sports. I am not a prince, hero, or king. But I am a kid that lives. (McGuire, 1984, pp. 113–114)

This self-presentation is clearly complex, yet it is not easily analyzable into unitary personality characteristics. It involves contrasts over time and across persons, affective valuation of the contrasts, and expression of desire that corresponds to the act of presenting this self-description. From phenomena like this, it is a long way to the usual talk of psychologists, which generally concentrates on issues of personality "traits," "dimensions," or other characteristics that are assumed to exist as stable and semicontinuous entities. These supposed entities are a result of abstraction from the complex flow of human psychological life events that take place under varied conditions. It is the person who proceeds through all these varied conditions, demonstrating both continuity and discontinuity in conduct and reflection. The complexity of persons' self-presentations is the starting point for psychology's efforts at inductive generalizations.

Meanings of "Personality" and "Self" In the History of Psychology

The concept of "personality" (and its various synonyms, such as "self") has a complicated fate in the terminological confusion of psychology. That confusion seems to result from psychology's tumultuous history as a sociopolitical discipline that touches upon sociomoral issues in any society that maintains it. It could be argued that the need to talk about the self or personality emerged in the context of social argumentation (and political fighting between rival groups) in the history of occidental societies. Construction of goal-oriented moralistic narratives about persons who have acted in socially valued ways has led to the separation of descriptions of persons from their social contexts and idealization of their actions (e.g., the construction of stories about "saints" in the emerging Christian reflections of persons in the second through fourth centuries A.D.—Drijvers, 1994). The persons were described not as persons per se but as bearers of specific social roles—saints, warlords, kings, and so on. Differentiation of persons from their social contexts was first (and foremost) an act of construction of myth-stories (in the sense of Boesch, 1991), which were goal-directed by the social institutions that needed to legitimize their own political actions. This practice is no different in our own day (see Rose, 1996).

DIFFERENT MEANINGS   Gordon Allport's analysis of fifty different meanings of personality reveals how human beings have tried to make sense of themselves through the use of the word "personality" and its closest sister terms—"self," "person," "persona," "character," and so forth (Allport, 1937c, chapter 2). The word "personality" came into use in English in the fourteenth century (Allport, 1937c, p. 36), Likewise, the first use of the term "self" in English as a reference to the autonomous nature of personality-in-itself has been attributed to David Hume (Hughes, 1906)—as a "bundle" or *collection of* different perceptions. In contrast, the French tradition of thought (from Descartes to Binet, Janet, and Piaget) emphasizes *dynamic coordination* of meanings, operations, and goals that constitute personality (Fisher, 1995). Gordon Allport, borrowing from Continental European thought models, defined personality as "the *dynamic organization* within the individual of those psychophysical systems that *determine his unique adjustments to his environment*" (Allport, 1937c, p. 48; emphasis added).

Under "dynamic organization" Allport (1937c, pp. 48–50) emphasized the constantly evolving system of psychological organizers, which is active and motivating. Allport's notion of "psychophysical systems" refers to "traits or groups of traits in a latent or active condition." The "psychophysical" label emphasized for him that personality is not mental or "neural," but rather the unity of body and mind—"inextricably fused into a personal unity." Furthermore, the personality acts as a "mode of survival" by mastering the environment, as well as considering its demands. This latter dynamic of adaptation leads to the question of "real" versus "pretense" ways of being.

The Mask and the Real In Personality

The opposition of reality and appearance in the depiction of personality has long plagued efforts to make sense of persons. The terminology used to depict persons in their psychological characteristics entails the notions of "mask" (of the "true person"), as well as of the "truth" about the person:

> Cicero . . . asked, "Why should I walk around like a *persona?*"—why, that is, should he assume an appearance false to his nature, pretending to be that which he was not? . . . *persona* means not only what a man is . . . but likewise precisely the opposite: what he is *not*. This ambiguity has never been overcome even in modern definitions of personality. In Latin it was somewhat lessened in certain contexts through the adoption of the derivative participle *personatus* to mean exclusively wearing a *false appearance*. In English, we have the verb "to personate"; more commonly, "to impersonate." (Allport, 1937c, p. 39)

The unity of what a person is and what she or he is not (or is not yet) creates the general content domain of a sociogenetic perspective on personality. Within the sociogenetic view, it is possible to overcome the "being" and "nonbeing" dichotomy by emphasizing the developmental unity of moving from a state of "not-yet-being" toward the one of "being." Thus, an individual who impersonates a certain social role may take over that role and become it. Furthermore, any state of "being" simultaneously constitutes a state of "not-yet-being"; hence, the tension between "being" and "appearance" can be viewed as the continuous duality between what the person currently is and the future state toward which the person is moving in the present. An inquisitive child of eleven years can be viewed (simultaneously) as "being inquisitive" (as the eleven-year-old), as moving away from "having been a child," and as moving toward becoming "a troublesome adolescent" (if such characteristic is assumed, socially, to guide adolescents' conduct). The child acts as if he or she is a child no more but already is an adolescent. Yet in reality the child is in the process of developing his or her self through different "as-if" modes of conduct.

Human conduct can be seen in terms of "as-if" kinds of realities that lead to the emergence of actual individual organization. Personality becomes socially guided and individually constructed in the course of human life. People are born as potential persons, and the process of becoming actual persons takes place through individual transformation of social experience (Harré, 1995, p. 372). By making (or assuming) different "masks" of social roles or pretense self-presentations, personality becomes "true" through internalization-externalization processes. Both the tension between internal (e.g., "true self") and external (e.g., a "mask") and the individual versus social nature of personality are captured by these meanings. As Takeo Doi has elaborated:

> Why do actors wear masks in the first place? Because the mask makes the actor's role clear at a single glance. The mask expresses the actor's role even more directly than an elaborate costume or skillfully contrived makeup. It is for this reason that the list of characters in a play (not the actors) is still called the *dramatis personae*. In this way, *persona,* the actor's mask, came to mean "a role in a play," and then, in English, became "person," a human being. (Doi, 1985, p. 25)

If this reconstruction of the history of the meaning of personality is correct, then the whole emergence of personal distinctiveness depends upon the generalization and individualization of the roles (masks) that a person takes and enacts in his or her drama of life. That drama may at times be a comedy, a parody, or a tragedy—depending upon the social roles that are created within a society, in the form of rituals and under suggestion of myth-stories. These stories may be abstracted from the lives of real persons and turned into narratives of how other persons are expected to think and act.

Thus, personality is far from being a "private matter": "Personality is gained through interaction and communication with persons and objects of the social and material environment and is based on the structures of the organism. Personality, in other words, is the result of the processing and managing of external reality (environment) and internal reality (organism) at all points in time during the life span" (Hurrelmann, 1988, p. 45).

What follows from this explanatory effort is a recognition that personality is *a means* for the individual to relate to the environment, and not an end in itself. As such, it is necessarily dependent upon the environment yet simultaneously autonomous from it. It becomes a subject that relates to the environment as the object of one's actions. Such an emerging agentive role is important for some social processes and unnecessary for others. The emergence of the subject-object differentiation in the case of the notion of personality can be viewed as a version of constructing "in-group" and "out-group" distinctions (and counterpositions) in relations between social groups (Sherif et al., 1961). In the case of the person, however, the "in-group" consists of one person (oneself), who is set up to relate to the "out-group" (the environment, with all "social others" included) in ways similar to the dynamics of social groups.

Persons As Independently Dependent Autonomous Actors

Persons are always interrelated with their immediate life environments. This means that any person is *at the same time* inevitably embedded in some semiotically organized environmental context and relatively autonomous in relation to it. The context entails social predefinition of the role of the person as a result of his or her location in the kinship network (e.g., via naming practices—Geertz, 1975), within the social stratification system (e.g., caste—Davis, 1983; Raheja, 1990), or by particular religious context (Young, 1942). Still, the psychological phenomena that the person "lives through" in his or her goal-oriented ways remain the person's subjective characteristic—available directly only to him- or herself—even if the personal self is intricately interdependent with the sociocultural matrix of meanings and practices (see Parish, 1994, for a concrete analysis). The bases for such separation of one's self from the environment are perceptual-kinesthetic (Neisser, 1991), in which the structure of language builds its further structured ways of referring to the person-environment relations (Bühler, 1990).

The developing person is active in one's construction of the personal world. Through sign-mediated imagination, fantasy, and internal self-dialogues, a person can transcend the immediate social confines of any particular context of the here and now. Human minds are constantly involved in the imaginary construction of scenarios of events of "there and then"— be those their present reconstructions of the past or their present preconstructions of possible (desired or dreaded) futures. This flexibility is made possible by their construction (and constant reconstruction) of signs—semiotic mediating devices that both present and represent some aspects of the person-environment relation (see chapter 6).

The process of human development takes place in the present. Inevitably all semiotic construction takes place in the present of the constructor (i.e., within the here and now). Transcending the here and now is possible in semiotic imagination and in play, both of which are dependent upon the here-and-now situation, yet that dependency makes it possible to transcend it (Cole, 1992, 1995; Winegar, Renninger, and Valsiner, 1989). Or, as was pointed out by James Mark Baldwin (see chapter 4), it is exactly the personal psychological autonomy that proves the claim of sociogenetic origins of human psychological functioning. The human personality is social insofar as it is uniquely individual in its different individual forms. This stance includes a focus on existing processes of relating with the culturally organized environments. As Harré has claimed: "Psychology, as an account of the mentation of human beings, must be rooted in an ontology of activities, skills, and powers, not in an ontology of substances. There is thinking, but, in a deep sense, there are no thoughts. There is believing, but there are no beliefs. . . The ultimate ontological 'unit' is the *person,* a being equipped with all sorts of properties and powers" (Harré, 1995, p. 369).

The focus on the person *in terms of processes of relating* to the environment has proven to be a complication for psychology's theoretical constructions. There is a tendency to turn reflections of such processes into assumed ideal substances. Such ideal assumed substances (e.g., starting from "mind"-"body" separation) lead to the difficult problem of handling dualities within psychological discourse.

A conceptual refusal to view person and environment as differentiated parts of the same whole—which is a necessary stance of the exclusive separation thought model—eliminates the notion of structure from consideration, reducing the dynamic processes of development to cycles of functionalist terms. The latter, however, carry the inherent danger of becoming entified—a label that is initially given to a process, shifts its meaning in the course of use, and begins to depict that process *as if it were an entity.* Practices of psychologists' talk demonstrate that a number of functionalist labels—applied initially to processes or relationships (e.g. "attachment," "affordance," "cognition," "appropriation," "coordination")—become used as essentialistic properties of parts of the implied relationship (e.g., "attachment" *of* the child, "affordance" *of* the object, "cognition*s*" about something, "appropriation" *of* something, "coordination*s*" in general). On the one hand, this translation of relationship-oriented labels into static entities and properties of one of the related parts in a whole may be a universal process in language use (Bloom, 1981; Valsiner, 1994d).

However, in the case of scientific knowledge, we can observe social reconstruction of metatheoretical boundaries upon the construction of terminology. "Deconstructionist efforts" in psychology in recent decades may have resulted in an unfortunate "side effect": together with demolishing the "positivist castle" of the traditions of previous psychology, the efforts toward increased precision in conceptual constructions may have been eliminated. As a result, psychologists' language use is often unbounded, and close to mythological construction of meanings (Boesch, 1991). Focus on "dialogicality," "narrative nature of knowledge," or "sociocultural research" does not replace the theoretical efforts of previous traditions with new contents but can simply provide new ways of talking about old problems. If extensions from some commonsensically legitimate explanatory terms to others are unconstrained in a science, the latter has the power of illusionary explanations of everything, through the omniscopous nature of language (which is used by fortune-tellers—Aphek and Tobin, 1990) and along the lines of traditional mythologies. As is explained in the following, promotion of unlimited conceptual creativity constrains the agent in one's construction of knowledge.

Crusades Against Dualisms In Psychology

Psychology has been filled with claims against "dualisms" (e.g., "mind"-"body" dualism, person-society dualism), and it has been customary for psychologists to accept the negative connotation of dualisms as a conceptual given (Dewey, 1895, 1896). Contemporary psychology's trends of "social constructionism" and "discursive psychology" claim to eradicate dualisms between the person and the social world (Fisher, 1995; Gergen, 1994). At the same time, claims for "dialectical" or "dialogic" approaches need to construe the world of personality in terms of opposites. At times that need leads to the treatment of similar phenomena as if they were different (and related—see Hermans, 1995a, p. 378). Dialogic views require the making of contrasting opposites—or recognition of duality of the phenomena.

Nevertheless, crusades against dualisms may easily destroy the view on dualities, and the best-meaning crusaders may be left without the phenomena that had interested them. In the atmosphere of war against dualisms, it is easy to deny *any* separation of person and environment. The argument proceeds as follows: since it is inadmissible to consider person and environment as separate from each other, we need to consider them as *united*. However, the ways in which the two can be united are hostages to the poverty of language's descriptive lexicon of such relationships, as well as to the suggestion inherent in the notion of unity that it must entail an undifferentiated communion of the person with the environment. Thus, talk about "socially situated activities," "direct perception," or "socially aided learning" implies an immersion of the person in the undifferentiated environment. In a similar way, person and context are at times conceived of as being in a "mutually constituted" or "seamless" relation. This illustrates the complexity of reflecting *processes* that *separate and unite* different parts of the same whole in simultaneous terms.

Exclusive and Inclusive Separation: Distinction between Dualism and Duality

The problem of *how* human beings—in all their subjective, psychological complexity—relate to the environment remains the core of understanding personality. As has been pointed out elsewhere (Valsiner, 1989, chapter 3; Valsiner and Cairns, 1992), the metaconceptual orientation toward *exclusive separation* of the person and the social world sets the stage for the conceptual difficulty in making sense of person-environment relationships. It entails treating the person as an entity that is completely separate from the environment (and, conversely, the environment is treated as separate from the person). The "relation" between them may be conceptualized in terms of inclusion of one object within the other (the person exists within an environment), and questions of direct linear causality can be asked (e.g., What are the "effects" of the environment on the person, or of the person on the environment?). Within this framework, dualisms abound. It is against the use of the exclusive separation strategy that the crusades against dualisms are oriented, and for good reason. It is not possible to study the processes in person-environment relations once those relationships are eliminated from our focus of attention by their axiomatic forgetting.

In contrast, the metaconceptual strategy of *inclusive separation* maintains the relationship between the separated parts of the system. Even if person and environment are distinguished from each other (i.e., they are separated), the separation is the background upon which their relationship can be investigated. Thus, inclusive separation entails distinction of three facets of the phenomenon (P, E, and relation $P<<>>E$), whereas exclusive separation includes only two (P, E). Kurt Lewin's formula $B = f(P \times E)$ (behavior = function of person and environment) clearly belonged to the world of inclusive separation.

STRUCTURES OF DISJUNCTION   The contrast between exclusive and inclusive separation is related to the distinction between disjunctive and conjunctive disjunction ("or") in classical logic. Thus, "X or Y" can be interpreted in classical logic in exclusively separating terms (i.e., "if X then not Y" and "if Y then not X"). However, the disjunction "or" is also given a conjunctive meaning in classical logic. In this designation, "X *or* Y" means "X *and* Y"—in the sense that one of the two options necessarily takes place, while no third alternative exists.

It is easy to see that these two interpretations of disjunction are readings from the general Boolean notion of summativity of the two opposites into unity (i.e., $X + Y = 1$). Thus, it entails a *twofold* exclusive separation:

1. The whole becomes delineated from its context (e.g., the latter can be Z, P, Q) by defining the X and its complementary ("all of the other"—be it designated as "non-X" or Y). This results in separating the two components from any linkages beyond this designated whole (that entails X and Y). All there is in this "field" of argumentation is X and Y, which "fill in" the whole "field": X or Y, *but not* Z, P, Q.
2. The opposites (X and Y) are *mutually* exclusively separated: if X then not Y, if Y then not X.

The result of such twofold exclusive separation is an atomistic view of the world that does not allow further linking of the separated parts, other than by purely formal linkages of summative ("and") or correlative kind. Exclusive separation eliminates any possibility of viewing the existing processual relation between the separated elements: $X + Y$ reflects summation of the two separated parts into a *formal* reconstructed whole (e.g., "head" + "body" = "whole animal"), from where functional wholeness of the separated parts cannot be retrieved (e.g., after successfully separating the head and the body of a Robespierre by way of the advanced technology of the guillotine, well-meaning and humanitarian social actors of the time of the French Revolution would still have failed in bringing that remarkable politician back to his life and deeds, no matter how advanced surgical technology might be).

The inclusive separation strategy leads to a different view on disjunctive structures. As Rychlak (1995, pp. 524–525) has demonstrated, a non-Boolean (dialectical, or "soft") disjunction entails the *unity of the opposites in terms of mutual delimitation of each other.* Thus, A delimits the boundaries of non-A, and vice versa; yet *both are assumed to exist simultaneously* (and cannot exist separately from each other). This amounts to the preservation of the existing systemic relations between the parts in the whole (i.e., A, non-A, and their relation), while contrasts of exclusive separation may be delegated to comparisons between the systems. The latter can be labeled by making a distinction between *non-A* and *not-A:* non-A is the *complementary part of the system,* while not-A refers to other systems (B, C, etc.), each of which entails its own internal systemic organization (B and non-B; C and non-C, etc.; see Figure 1.1).

This figure takes its beginning in a depiction of dialectical disjunction offered by Rychlak (1995, p. 525, Figure 6). The disjunction here specifies the *difference* between A and the class of systemic phenomena with which it is contrasted: not-A. It is given in terms of exclusive separation—both A and not-A are separated from anything else.

Within this disjunction, both parts (A and "not-A") entail inclusively separated interdependent *oppositions.* Opposition here is different from difference; the latter is detected by exclusive separation, the former via inclusive separation. Thus, A and non-A, B and non-B, and C and non-C constitute systemic oppositions that can be investigated as such, while the difference between A and the class not-A is merely a nonfunctional device for delimiting the field of operation to a contrast between detecting either A or not-A.

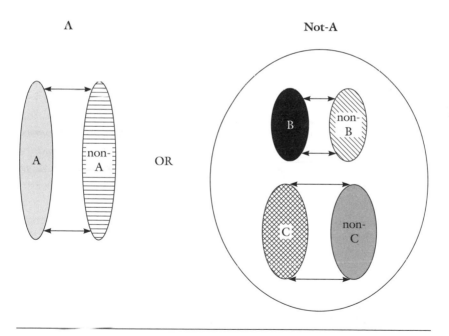

Figure 1.1. Distinction between dialectical opposition (A and non-A) and its differences with disjunctive difference (A and not-A).

THE TIME FLOW AND ITS ROLE   No notion of time is included in the logical exercise depicted in Figure 1.1. This fits with the axioms of classical logic, where time is not considered as being of relevance. For this reason, classical logic is a poor formal tool for any developmental perspective. However, even mere change over time entails a focus on the relevance of time. Let us consider von Wright's example:

> Consider a process such as rainfall. It goes on for some time and then it stops. It does not stop suddenly, let us assume, but gradually. . . during a certain stretch of time it is first definitely raining (p), later definitely not raining (~p), and between these two states in time there is a "zone of transition" when a few drops may be falling—too few to make us say that it is raining then but too many to prevent us from saying that rain has definitely stopped. In this zone the proposition p is neither true nor false. . . One could, however, also take the view that as long as some drops of rain are falling then it is *still* raining— but also the view that when there are only a few drops of rain falling, then it is *no longer* raining. When viewing the situation from these points of view one includes the intermediate zone of transition or vagueness both under the rain and under not-rain . . . Then instead of saying that it is neither raining nor not-raining in the zone, one would say that it is both raining and not-raining in this area. (Von Wright, 1986, pp. 12–13)

This example illustrates the nonapplicability of the disjunctive operation to phenomena that change over time. Yet there is still a large gap between these and developmental phenomena. The latter include the emergence of a new form from previous ones. The "zone of transition" in the example of rain stopping is a permanent state of the externally visible side of development (e.g., what can be observed *is* no longer A, *nor is it yet* a version of not-A). The actual emergence entails the transformation of an internal opposition within A (i.e., A and non-A) into a form previously assumed to be in not-A (e.g., B and non-B).

DAVID HERBST'S "CO-GENETIC LOGIC"   Inclusive separation of differentiating structures was the starting point for Herbst's system (Herbst, 1995; Figure 1.2). Each emergence entails a coordinated arrival of a form (n) and its environment (m), thus defining its boundary (p). In this scheme, n refers to the distinguished inside, m to the distinguished outside, and p to the boundary between them. This triadic unit has clearly specified properties:

1. it is *co-genetic:* the three parts of the unit come into being together;
2. it is *non-separable:* the three parts cannot be "taken out" of the unit without losing the unit itself;
3. it is *non-reducible:* the whole of the triadic unit cannot be reduced to any of the three parts;
4. it is *contextual:* if any of the parts disappears, the whole unit disappears with it. (Herbst, 1995, pp. 67–68)

Since all developmental processes entail the becoming of new, previously not existing phenomena and the disappearance of some of the previous states, the areas of unity of A and non-A are the focus of developmental analysis. The methodological problems posed by this focus have been outlined elsewhere (Valsiner, 1994a; see also chapter 7). Developmental analysis targets processes of becoming that (by their nature of becoming) provide the investigator with a picture of semiorganized, transitory, and often vague transitional forms that bridge the movement of the developing system from its present to the immediate future (i.e., next present) state.

INCLUSIVE SEPARATION, OPEN SYSTEMS, AND REDUN-DANCY IN DEVELOPMENT   All biological, psychological, or sociological developmental phenomena are necessarily open systems in the sense that they can exist only thanks to their constant interdependence with their

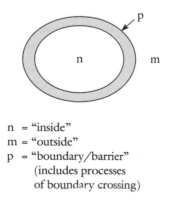

n = "inside"
m = "outside"
p = "boundary/barrier"
    (includes processes
    of boundary crossing)

Figure 1.2. Making of distinctions (in David Herbst's co-genetic logic).

environments (Bertalanffy, 1950). The crucial feature of open systems is their *continuous exchange relationship* between the organism and the environment. All living systems are open systems, hence the impossibility of reasoning about development in terms of classical (Boolean) logic. From the viewpoint of open systems, this conjunctive interpretation of disjunction fits with the notion of *redundancy:* a conjunctive disjunction "A [or = and] B" entails the inclusion of both A and B among the set of possibilities, and the recognition of the use of either A, or B, or both in the case of a developing system X. The systemic processes both within the organism (A and non-A) and within the environment (B and non-B) contribute to the organism's development. The mutual interdependence of these processes is also observable if we use the tactic of inclusive separation: the whole of a person-environment relation (P and non-P) entails two inclusively separated subprocesses—one "inside" the person (A and non-A), the other in the environment (B and non-B)—the unity of which is characterized (at their metalevel) by inclusive separation of P (= A and non-A) and non-P (= B and non-B). Talking about separation of genetic and environmental factors in development is possible only in terms of their unity of functioning in the developmental process, not in terms of their exclusive separation and "weighing" of their "relative contributions," independently of each other.

MULTILINEARITY OF DEVELOPMENT   A particular psychological function may come into being in ontogeny through a variety of routes or trajectories. Individual human beings may develop along different routes yet arrive at the same outcome state (which is obviously a base for further development). For some of these individual trajectories, the personal resources are sufficient for the arrival in that (equifinal) state, with minimal support from the interdependent environment. Yet for others, the dominant role in reaching the same state may be taken over by environmental guidance, and the interdependent person follows the lead of this guidance.

DUALITY AND DUALISM   The contrast between inclusive and exclusive separation strategies at the metatheoretical level can bring some distinction to the issue of duality versus dualism. Surely the duality of organization—the separability of complex systems into mutually linked opposite parts—does not amount to dualism as the latter has been chased in psychology. *Separation of the opposites in terms of exclusive separation does amount to the construction of dualisms.* From that point of view, the dualism-fighting squads of psychologists—ranging from early pragmatists to our contemporaries—have been involved in an entirely justifiable holy war on intellectually unproductive concepts in psychology.

From the standpoint of inclusive separation, the dangers of dualism are eliminated a priori. The person and the environment are *both separate and united;* separation makes it possible to study their actual relationship as a process. The notion of unity here becomes explicitly available for study, since the duality of the person-environment structure entails both unity and separation. The very differentiation of the person and the environment makes it possible to study the ways in which they are interdependent. Duality—copresence and relation—of differentiated parts that function within the same whole is not dualism but a form of systemic organization.

DUALITIES AS NECESSARY BASES FOR ANY "DIALECTICAL APPROACH"   A most ironic conceptual confusion occurs in the efforts to fight dualism when talk about dialectical perspectives is imported into the dualism-bashing discourse. By its very nature, dialectical thought entails the separation of opposites and consideration of the contradictory relationships between the separated opposites. Both of these acts of analysis would be completely ruled out from the exclusive separation model of thought, yet when the concept of dialectics is evoked within that framework, it is applied indiscriminately as a generic term, creating a "black box" to cover the indeterminate fusion state of the person-environment relations. Thus, we may see claims about "dialectics" of the relation of the person with the "situated activity contexts" *without any effort to elaborate* which kinds of contradictions, and between which opposites, are involved in the given case. Even beyond that, one can hear the entified version ("dialectics" as objects; e.g., "There are *a number of dialectics* involved in X").

It is obvious that entification of dialectical thought systems—turning processes into entities—does not constitute a productive direction in psychological theorizing. If the focus on dynamics of contradictory relationships is proclaimed within a theory, it needs to be translated into methodological criteria that fit the concepts, rather than used as mere "umbrella concepts" to allow any kind of (mostly unfitting) empirical investigation. In this book, consistency between basic assumptions, their methodological translation, theorizing, and empirical work is presented as the core of sociogenetic personality research. But what does such a claim entail for the theoretical and methodological repertoire of psychology as science (i.e., a thought system oriented toward constructing general knowledge)?

Empiricism and Pseudoempiricism

By the end of the twentieth century, psychology has become thoroughly empirical in its orientation. Even as empirical evidence is of central relevance for any science, however, extensive proliferation of empirical emphasis for its own sake can lead a discipline to counterproductive results. This is certainly the case in personality research. Issues of methodology in general are discussed further in chapter 7. Here, however, it is worthwhile to set the stage for what constitutes "empirical science" in psychology. The use of the qualifier "empirical," as long as it is appropriate, is applied to the notion of "science" as a complementary part of the knowledge construction system. In my terms, it amounts to inclusive separation of "empirical" and "nonempirical" (e.g., "theoretical") sides of the system of processes called "science" and the unity of the two parts within the latter complex (see also Overton, 1997). However, an exclusive separation tactic often is involved when "empirical" is used as a qualifier to "science": "empirical" is viewed as the (good) opposite pole to the "nonempirical" ("theoretical"), with the former considered superior to the latter. This case of exclusive separation of the empirical from the theoretical leads to the social proliferation of empiricism (decontextualized religion of "the data"—Valsiner, 1995b).

When empiricism begins to govern interpretative thought, it simultaneously sets up a framework of meanings that legitimizes such change. Therefore, voices of caution, like Gordon Allport's, are often forgotten: "Galloping empiricism, which is our present occupational disease, dashes forth like a headless horseman. It has no rational objective; uses no rational method other than mathematical; reaches no rational conclusion. It lets the discordant data sing for themselves" (Allport, 1966, pp. 3–4).

Psychology's problems are primarily theoretical and conceptual (Smedslund, 1988, 1994, 1995) and secondarily empirical. However, this verdict is certainly not a received wisdom in contemporary psychology. The result of this oversight is that empirical investigations often are conducted to reveal meanings that are already encoded in language concepts, and thus are in no need of empirical verification. An empirical study of the hypothesis "bachelors are male and unmarried" (i.e., Smedslund's example—Smedslund, 1995, p. 196), using a comparison of a sample of male and female subjects and "discovering" that all the male subjects who were bachelors were also unmarried, while the number of bachelors among the males is significantly higher than in the sample of females (where is found to be zero), would be a caricature (yet a realistic one!) of a pseudoempirical study.

Pseudoempiricism in psychology can be viewed as an adaptation of the discipline to its ambiguous state between the natural sciences (from where most of its methodology is appropriated) and research questions that bear the mark of psychology's sociopolitical interdependence with social institutions. Psychology is not alone in such status; anthropology's history as a "colonial science" (Kuklick, 1991) and the emergence of "tropical medicine" (Naraindas, 1996) on the basis of the politics of sociomoral concerns in an occidental society are examples of a similar social construction. In its effort to get free from the political-theological guidance of how psychology should approach its subject matter, reification of the purity of "empirical evidence" made good sense. Yet it replaced a religious dogma with a secular, socially constructed value system. The further move from careful empirical work to empirical investigations conducted for their own sake (and for the sake of "symbolic capital" accumulation of academics—in the form of an increased number of publications) was not difficult.

Empiricism creates its own consensually validated social norms for its activities. Central to this is the question of generalization: How can empirical investigations that are *necessarily particular* and limited in space and time lead to basic knowledge of whatever is being studied? One simple yet treacherous solution is to deny the possibility of such generalization altogether. This position is popular at times when the notions of "modularization of the mind" and "context-dependency of phenomena" gain popularity. Such a solution promotes the value of a locally situated empiricism that need not pretend to generalize at all. Yet if such a solution is not accepted, the question of how generalization can happen can be answered in two alternative ways.

Two Ways of Arriving at Generalizations

The first of these tactics of generalization entails transfer of findings from a limited sample of phenomena to the whole class—or "population"—of such phenomena. As a result of proliferation of this approach, *pseudopopulationalization* has become a methodological habit. It derives from the socially conventionalized belief that generality of knowledge is obtainable only if the specific empirical evidence can be generalized to be true of "populations" of the specimens under study. This direction has gradually eliminated careful analyses of individual cases from the empirical practices of psychology. Instead, large samples are used to arrive at empirical (or often pseudoempirical) claims that are made in the hope of arriving at generalizability.

The notion of "population" as a viable target of generalization may be upheld if it is constituted as a strict finite set, where all members consistently belong to it in a stable and steady manner. First of all, the boundaries of a "population" are assumed to exist in ways that investigators believe in but cannot access in full (hence the need for "sampling" from a "population"). In reality, these boundaries may be considered to be constantly ill defined, or not to exist at all. All members of a set ("population") are vulnerable to death or birth. In both ways, the membership limits within the set are necessarily open; hence, population is an abstract concept that cannot be defined in a static manner. Population is an abstraction of illusionary stability, the reality of which is constantly in flux. Consequently, generalization efforts from samples to populations entail abstractive infinite unclarity.

The second tactic of generalization entails abstraction from single systems to systems in a generic sense and is free of any reference to populations. The indeterminate nature of populations no longer is an obstacle, since the generic model of a system is tested on the basis of concrete specimens. Evidence about samples of systems may be helpful in deciding about the existence of possible parallel forms of organization of the same functions, but it would never replace generalization by abstraction from studied cases to abstract case models. The generalizing problem here is different. It is a priori possible to assume the existence of different equally functional generic models. This follows from the assumptions of an open-systemic kind: those of equifinality and redundancy of developmental mechanisms. Yet it is not certain in the case of discovery of a new model in an individual case whether that amounts to one of those equifunctional forms or is merely an aberration of the previously known form. Nevertheless, generalization from single cases to generic models treats each new single subject as an empirical study on its own (where the "sample" size is 1) and tests specific propositions that stem from the model on empirical materials.

Personality psychology has been at the forefront of the "battle for the legitimacy of the individual case." Gordon Allport's emphasis on the systemic analysis of single cases as the core of psychology's scientific orientation remains a basic insight into how psychology can be scientific (Valsiner, 1986). Recent analyses of personal profiles (in contrast with variables-oriented approaches—Magnusson, 1988, 1990; Magnusson and Törestad, 1993) have been aimed at working out a reasonable compromise between individual-focused and sample-focused traditions of research.

MEANINGS OF PROBABILITY IN PSYCHOLOGY   A basic issue is at stake in psychology's methodology—the applicability of different notions of probabilistic thinking in its theoretical discourse. Of the three models of probability—frequentistic, subjective, and propensity—only the first two are amply utilized by psychologists. The notion of frequentistic probability is most widely used (because it allows for the use of inductively accumulated knowledge of frequencies of events) and is often translated into *the* probability notion. An example of such translation was criticized by Allport in the context of prediction of personality: "A fatal non sequitur occurs in the reasoning that if 80 per cent of the delinquents who come from broken homes are recidivists, then *this* delinquent from a broken home has an 80 per cent chance of becoming a recidivist. The truth of the matter seems to be that *this* delinquent has either 100 per cent certainty of becoming a repeater or 100 per cent certainty of going straight" (Allport, 1942, p. 156).

The logic of Allport's argument can be followed if we look at his arguments from a strictly defined developmental perspective—of irreversibility of time in the lives of organisms (Valsiner, 1994d). From that viewpoint, it becomes reasonable to reject the habitual transfer of frequentistic probability notions from nondevelopmental psychologies to the life course-oriented study of personality. In the case of a set of multilinear possible life course trajectories, the knowledge of any number of previous cases (N) cannot provide researchers with adequate information about the actual construction of the next ($N + 1$) case. The actual construction of the person's life experience takes place in irreversible time and concrete life contexts as those emerge during that time period. Each possible next step in this course is predictively equifinal from the vantage point of the present (e.g., a person who has committed a delinquent act either does it again—i.e., has "100 per cent certainty" for that—or does not). Whether the person actually reaches either one of the states depends on the actual living through of the ongoing life experiences, and on the person's active construction of one (or the other) outcome. Predictive speculations based on sample-based quantifications of chances do not reflect any aspect of this time-dependent constructive process of the particular person's actual life course. The unique world of the person contains influences that will always remain unknown to the investigator (and possibly overlooked in actual importance by the person him- or herself). Certainly that side of the person remains unknown to the sample-accumulating statistician (see Allport, 1962, pp. 411–412; Allport and Vernon, 1933, p. 134ff.) and thus remains beyond the data that are accumulated according to the sacredness of the belief in the "law of large numbers."

Undoubtedly it is helpful to *know* the previous occurrence distribution of the different outcomes in the population, but such knowledge is of only orientational, not substantive, value for the actual understanding of the processes in personality development. Or, as Allport (1942, p. 157) has emphasized, *psychological causation is always personal and never actuarial.* This claim acquires the status of an imperative for knowing the phenomenological reality—if it is viewed in a developmental context. In contrast, from the viewpoint of the traditional discourse about "nomothetic" versus "idiographic" orientations, it can easily be misinterpreted as a call for personalistic recognition of voluntarism. As will be shown later in this book, it is not the case that a move to a personalistic focus in psychology entails elimination of basic scientific issues. Quite the contrary. The personalistic focus has been oriented toward explaining the universality that makes it possible for unique personal forms of organization to come into being and to exist in their uniqueness. The usual distinction between nomothetic and idiographic perspectives has been misleading; in personalistic accounts, we encounter the nomothetic analysis of idiographically described phenomena.

A CENTRAL METHODOLOGICAL AXIOM   The focus on variability brings us to the central methodological axiom: the definitive empirical base for psychological investigations at large (and for the study of personality in particular) is the single case, analyzed in the process of its relations with the immediate environment. This follows from the open-systemic nature of development. The reality of development is that of individual human beings—and any conglomerate of such beings (ranging from organized social groups to randomly assembled "samples") constitutes a grouping of such persons. Some groupings (e.g., natural social groups like families, peer networks, or work teams) can be treated as developing individuals. The persons involved are considered parts of the individual system (i.e., group) that develops in constant interaction with its environment.

This focus on the centrality of the individual case is not another exposition of the much-discussed idiographic versus nomothetic contrast in psychology (Valsiner, 1986). That separation in psychological discourse constitutes another example of exclusive separation tactics, in which the nomothetic approach is habitually equated with the "large-N" kind of sample-based research and given a positive value, while the idiographic label is linked with "$N = 1$" and by contrast is undervalued. The analysis of single cases in systemic terms is nomothetic (in the sense of looking for general knowledge), and specific posited forms of organization of the issues under study can be tested on another single case. Sample-based empirical work equals $N = 1$ study if the sample is the specimen under study (e.g., a social group, or crowd, or the whole of a social institution, in social psychology or sociology).

Sociogenetic Approaches, Co-Constructionism, and Its Basic Assumptions

Human personality is possible only because of the *semiogenetic* (i.e., sign-constructing) nature of human development. Therefore, an analysis of the social processes that guide the development of personality, and the latter's personal construction of social means (signs), constitutes the core of personality. The sociogenetic approach that lays the foundation for the perspective in this book has been called *co-constructionist* (Valsiner, 1988b, 1994b, 1994c). Even as the co-constructionst label has been used in similar ways (e.g., Kurtines et al., 1995; Wozniak, 1986, 1993), in our sociogenetic context it entails a systemic unity of the social guidance of development, on the one hand, and individually unique construction of novelty in relating to the world, on the other. The co-constructionist process takes place in irreversible time (emphasized by Bergson and Prigogine—see Valsiner, 1994d), with all the limits that time sets up for human lives (e.g., individual and context-specific uniqueness of concrete phenomena).

The co-constructionist perspective entailed in this book is based on the bidirectional model of cultural transmission (Lawrence and Valsiner, 1993; Valsiner, 1988b, 1989, 1994a). This model focuses on the reconstruction of cultural messages by recipients in ways that include construction of novelty at each transmission episode. Thus, cultural transmission necessarily leads to heterogeneity of cultural construction, both intrapsychologically (within a person's life course) and between personalities within any social group or population. Although the bidirectional model is rarely made explicit in the social sciences, it has been explicated on a number of occasions (Bartlett, 1920a, 1920b, 1932; Groeben and Christmann, 1995; Wertsch, 1991; Youniss, 1987). It constitutes a synthesis of personal-constructivist and sociogenetic orientations.

PROCESS OF CONSTRUCTION MOVING TOWARD A FUTURE
The focus in this book is on the dynamic, processual facet of the development and existence of personality. We will look upon the processes of constraining that operate both within the field of actions (as outlined in Valsiner, 1987) and in the semiotic domains of meaning. The constraining-based perspective focuses on future-oriented modulation of possibilities for acting, feeling, and thinking, which are constructed in the present, by the person who is interdependent with the environment. Such a person—who is being constrained by the circumstances, and who constrains oneself in anticipation of future circumstances—is the personality that interests us here. This personality is sociogenetic (i.e., socially based) in its origin and is semiautonomous in relation to any social context at any given time and place. This personality *actively constructs its future*—by setting goals, attempting to reach them, and abandoning them. The perspective on personality that is outlined in this book differs from most other accounts in its emphasis on the developmental nature of the actively self-constraining person who is constantly interdependent with the cultural context, which enables the person to be autonomous within relationships, by way of constructing ever-changing hierarchical control systems of a semiotic kind. These control mechanisms can be of a temporary nature, either vanishing or becoming instantly reconstructed. The functions of such constructed mechanisms of the self are in the feed-forward organization of psychological processes, which have been described as follows: "Feedforward processes are anticipatory; they prepare the system for future action. They involve predictive processes about how to produce desired results rather than just interpretive processes about current circumstances . . . it is feed-forward processes that make human proactive, goal-directed functioning possible" (Ford and Lerner, 1992, p. 100).

This perspective attempts to unite the sociogenetic and personological approaches to personality. If the notion of irreversibility of time in development is taken seriously, no feed*back* processes are theoretically possible, and all information that is "fed back" (in a manner of speaking) is actually "fed forward" so as to be functional in the *new present* state in which the (already further changed) organism encounters a novel environment. Different forms of such feed-forward functionality can be assumed (e.g., ranging from determination of the encounter with the environment to neutrality or blocking of an encounter). Thanks to the variety of such feed-forward signals, the developing organism can be both "conservative" and "innovative"—relative to its own past—at the same time.

This view—*teleogenetic* and feed-forward-based—differs cardinally from the usual conceptualizations of personality in the history of psychology. The latter have emphasized personality in terms of its being (ontology of personality characteristics), while the perspective elaborated here is oriented toward understanding personality's *constant process of becoming*—while maintaining relative temporal stability. This process is increasingly emphasized in contemporary psychology in the thought models of dynamic systems theory (Fogel, 1993; Krech, 1950).

Currently there exists a fashion to talk about development in terms of "chaos theory" or "dissipative structures." This constitutes an interesting story in the transition of basic ideas. The focus on irreversibility of time advocated by Henri Bergson (Valsiner, 1994d) was largely based on the developmental biological and psychological thought of the 1890s (see also chapter 4 in this book). This focus led to some further uses in developmental psychology (e.g., Jean Piaget's theoretical elaborations), but in general it became extinct. However, the notion of irreversible time proved to be revolutionary in physical chemistry (Prigogine, 1973, 1978; Prigogine, Allen, and Herman, 1977), from where—under the halo effect of emanating from the so-called hard sciences—it is reentering developmental psychology.

MULTILINEARITY OF DEVELOPMENTAL TRAJECTORIES AND THE UNIQUENESS OF INDIVIDUAL DEVELOPMENT The dynamic systems perspective leads both developmental and personality psychologies to consider the problem of multilinear emergence of similar forms in development. On the one hand, each person's individual development is uniquely constructed within an irreversible lifetime. However, such uniqueness is possible when in principle there exists a multitude of possible developmental trajectories for the given species. When the personally unique life course is created, this multiple possibility is turned into unique actuality. At the same time, the set of possibilities at any junction of a particular life course is itself limited. Hence, it is not surprising that individual personalities, while unique in their development, still can be viewed as being similar to one another—within some speciesspecific limits. This similarity is not sameness; it constitutes an abstraction of the general mechanisms of personality organization that can provide for all the versions of individual uniqueness. Aside from the obvious species-specific biological frame of human development, the cultural processes between the person and the social world limit the set of possibilities, keeping them within a relatively stable range.

Personality as Personal Culture

The theoretical perspective utilized here emerges from the developmental traditions within European science (e.g., the work of Jean Piaget, Lev Vygotsky, Heinz Werner, Pierre Janet) and in some respects converges with contemporary efforts to build "cultural psychology" (e.g., Boesch, 1993; Cole, 1990, 1995; Krewer, 1992; Miller, 1994; Shweder, 1990, 1995). However, it differs from these contemporary tendencies in cultural psychology in its insistence on preserving the *duality* of the personal-cultural and social-cultural worlds. The present cultural-historical perspective is outlined elsewhere (Valsiner, 1987, 1994b, 1994c). The central aim of co-constructivist developmental psychology is to explain the processes that are involved in the construction of *personal culture* under the canalizing directions of the *collective culture* (Valsiner, 1989, pp. 47–48). This heuristic distinction is analogous to Georg Simmel's (1908) distinction between "subjective" and "objective" culture.

The collective culture entails communally shared meanings, social norms, and everyday life practices, all united in a heterogeneous complex. On the basis of this complex, individual persons construct their personally idiosyncratic semiotic systems of symbols, practices, and personal objects, all of which constitute the *personal culture*. The relation between the collective and personal cultures is conceptualized as persons' active and constructive internalization-externalization process.

What does it mean when claims about "socially shared" entities (e.g., those of meanings, norms, practices) are made? What is the form of such sharing? Sharing of material objects differs from that of ideational objects—for example, material objects can be physically controlled by a person and offered to others in exchange, or for temporary relinquishing of control. Sharing of immaterial entities—norms and meanings—entails the internalization-externalization process: two (or more) persons can "share" meanings only by externalizing their personal sense into the communication process. Everyday life practices can be "shared" by participation—via distribution of roles in the structure of joint action. Thus, there are at least three types of sharing: of control over objects, of communication about meanings, and of participation in activities.

As a result, the collective culture is inherently heterogeneous. It consists of structures that are either semipermanent in the environment (e.g., culturally meaningful architectural spaces, styles of objects of fashions), or that constitute transitory aspects of a person's encounters with others (e.g., allusions made by persons in public places that are overheard by another person). Likewise, constructed local social norms within a group (that need not generalize beyond that group—Sherif, 1936), advertisements, conduct practices, and so on belong to collective culture. The central focus of the collective culture is the particular person, in relation to whom the particular heterogeneous and dynamic conglomerate of meaningful objects, various social suggestions from different persons and institutions, and occasional or regular ritualistic behavior settings can be described as a collective culture. Thus, *collective culture is person-anchored* and not a "property" of social units. It is of no use to speak of "American collective culture" or "the collective culture of high school No. 4," but it is possible to speak of the collective culture that organizes the life of John or Sally who studies in high school No. 4 in a town in the United States. The functional structure of persons (in their social roles) and social institutions, and the semiotic organization of the environment of that high school, its surroundings, and Sally's or John's hometown constitute the heterogeneous complex of the collective culture.

Collective culture may include its "focal points" (where the same meaning is promoted and channeled for internalization through varied forms of semiotic messages and by different agents, all in parallel), alongside unstructured areas (fields) that may be occasionally structured by few and inconsistent social suggestions. At any time this pattern of heterogeneity can be changed, with the "focal areas" relocated to new areas of the previously unstructured field. In child development, such change in the structure of collective culture can be observed in the case of the step-by-step introduction of the child into new systems of meanings (e.g., Herdt, 1980, 1981) in the course of initiation rituals. Likewise, such changes are introduced by age-specific social institutions in the lives of developing children (e.g., entrance into school or into the workforce) that necessarily reorganize the heterogeneous structure of the collective culture. The collective culture can be described in terms of Bronfenbrenner's "nested system" model (Bronfenbrenner, 1977, 1979, 1989; Bronfenbrenner and Ceci, 1994) or in terms of any other systemic model that allows for consideration of the hierarchical and heterogeneous nature of the collective culture.

Personal cultures emerge *on the basis of* the collective culture, yet they do so in ways that do not necessarily reflect the exact forms of the collective culture. Since the function of personal culture is to organize intra- and interpersonal worlds to provide personal sense to encounters with the world, a person constructs an understanding of the world that goes beyond the collective culture in idiosyncratic ways. This personal understanding can lead to efforts to change some aspects of the collective culture, starting from one's own immediate life contexts. For example, an adolescent girl who receives an encyclopedia as a present may use the knowledge in that encyclopedia as a beginning for breaking out of her immediate collective-cultural world (Lawrence, Benedikt, and Valsiner, 1992). Similarly, Nepali women construct new meanings within the collective culture by externalizing their desires for social role changes as they insert new contents into the frame of ritual song construction and into the public presentation of such songs (Skinner, Basnet, and Valsiner, 1993). An existing collective-cultural form for public actions is used to express personal desires, becomes part of the reorganized collective-cultural world for the others, and thus participates in the transformation of the personal worlds of those others. The relation between collective and personal cultures is bidirectional. Innovation in the personal culture, when externalized, may play a role in the transformation of the collective culture.

Human development within collective-cultural contexts proceeds through feed-forward-type constraints that delimit the range of immediately possible novel forms of action or intrapsychological semiotically organized affect and thought. Such delimiting at any particular time guarantees that human development is *simultaneously* continuous and discontinuous (or conservative and opportunistic), structured (by way of constraints), and fluid (because the constraints allow for a range of possibilities), only one of which will become actualized (since real life proceeds in irreversible time). Personal cultures always are expected to transcend the expectations inherent in the collective culture (by way of constructive externalization), and they provide the basis for the introduction of person-initiated novelties into the collective culture. This is possible because of the internalization-externalization processes involved in human development (as will be described in chapter 3).

Intersubjectivity and Personality

The open-endedness of human development is made possible by the renegotiability of the semiotic constraint systems that persons use to organize their present experiences. However, in order to open the possibilities for such renegotiability, the interacting persons need to establish a temporary basis—a jointly shared domain—within which any negotiation can take place. In contemporary discussions about communication, this domain is labeled *intersubjectivity*.

When persons enter into communication with one another, an actual form of intersubjectivity is being constructed by transcending their "private worlds." However, the starting point for such construction is built up by personal senses. In order to make actual intersubjectivity possible, persons need

> *capacity for decentered categorization and attribution, reciprocal role-taking* and *complementarity of intentions*. Reciprocity and complementarity may indeed be conceived of as generative "pragmatic postulates" in the construction of intersubjectivity. *I have, for instance, to assume that my partner in dialogue is trying to answer my question in order to make sense of his response to it.* This is also the case when his response sounds odd. My faith in him, however, will make me search for some *by him* potentially taken-for-granted aspect of our only partially shared HERE-and-NOW *which may confirm my faith.* (Rommetveit, 1979b, p. 160)

Intersubjectivity is a metaprocess of reflexivity that constantly leads to creating, maintaining, and changing of the persons' sense-backgrounds of the (foreground) dialogic activity. Human reasoning operates on the primary basis of lived-through experience, on the basis of which abstractions emerge. Intersubjectivity is assumed not only between persons but also—in a similar vein—between levels of semiotic functioning. Thus it is not a concept that would denote some nebulous state of affairs that is assumed to exist, like "sharing." Instead, it is a process of person-centered metacommunicative activity. That process itself is co-constructive: the person acts "as if" the others are oriented in way X in the dialogue, monitors the actual acts of the others (X'), and modifies the "as-if" determination in accordance with X' or by one's own momentary intention (i.e., by another personally constructed "as-if" state).

Intersubjectivity As an "As-If" Construction

The history of the issue of intersubjectivity in this century has followed different developmental pathways: from the traditions of "as-if" (als-ob) philosophy of Hans Vaihinger (see Vaihinger, 1920), the aesthetic theory of Einfühlung (Lipps, 1903, 1923), and the philosophy of irreversible lifetime (dureé) of Henri Bergson (Bergson, 1911a). Human beings are necessarily involved in "as-if" psychological constructions: viewing the present world in terms of its desired state, trying to "take the role" of another person, and so on.

Any reflection upon intersubjectivity starts from a personal (subjective) basis. The basis for any construction of intersubjectivity is a set of fundamental axioms for the social world taken for granted by at least two persons:

> First, the existence of intelligent (endowed with consciousness) fellow-men and, second, the experienceability (in principle similar to mine) by my fellow-men of the objects in the life-world. . . I know that "the same" Object must necessarily show different aspects to each of us. First, because the world in my reach cannot be identical with the world in your reach, etc.; because my here is your there; and because my zone of operation is not the same as yours. And, second, because my biographical situation with its relevance systems, hierarchies of plans, etc., is not yours and, consequently, the explications of the horizon of objects in my case and yours could take entirely different directions. (Schütz and Luckmann, 1973, p. 59)

On the basis of these axioms, two idealizations can be constructed: that of interchangeability of standpoints and congruence of relevance systems (Schütz and Luckmann, 1979, p. 60). Notice that both originate in the subjectivity of persons and lead to contrasting of different subjectivities, rather than the reverse. The referential anchor point for any perception and action relative to the external world is the person's ego-centered point of existence (see Bühler, 1990; see also chapter 6). It is only by way of extension outward from that ego center through Einfühlung with others, or taking the perspective of the others, that intersubjectivity becomes possible.

The heterogeneity of intersubjectivity is based on the social roles assumed by the intersubjectivity constructor. These roles are normatively asymmetrical, both in their embeddedness in the social structure and in the dynamic flow of dialogues. The static and dynamic ways of looking at intersubjectivity become encoded in the distinction of different kinds of intersubjectivity. Markova (1994) distinguishes the "as-if" and "strived-for" kinds of intersubjectivity and recognizes the tension between them. The former sets up the (static and imaginary) perspective that intersubjectivity already exists (i.e., constitutes an ontological postulate), whereas the latter entails the process of the actual construction of mutual understanding in irreversible time.

STRIVED-FOR INTERSUBJECTIVITY   The central characteristic of intersubjectivity is the interdependent relation between the *subjectivities* involved in the shared activity (and of codes of communication). It is the persons who, on the basis of their (life)-historically constructed personal cultures at the given moment, enter into communication with each other. Human beings endure the uncertainty that the entrance into communication entails by creating an "as-if" image of intersubjectivity, which is pre-structured by the social roles that the participants assume or construct in the process of communication (Oliveira and Rossetti-Ferreira, 1996). Even when alone, the person creates an "as-if" reflection of the world that operates as a practical, productive "error" (Vaihinger, 1920, p. 165) in the process of forward-oriented preadaptation to the next momentary context. Development is based upon such "as-if" apperception; in other words, by creating such "practical errors," the organism participates in its own development. Or, in other terms, when preadaptation to possible future conditions is considered, the meaning of "error" becomes indeterminate. Specific patterns of action in a present context can be viewed as "error" only in relation to the present context, while such consideration relative to potential future contexts is not possible.

THE DIALOGIC PERSPECTIVE UPON SUBJECTIVITY   Dialogic dynamics can be approached in a number of ways (see also the discussion of "voices of the mind" in chapter 3). For the sake of simplicity, let us look at *equilibrational* and *disequilibrational* perspectives on the dynamic flow of dialogue.

The equilibrational perspective treats a dialogue process from the angle of maintenance of a certain equilibrium state of intersubjectivity as it was assumed before (but proven to be absent). Thus, in conversational analysis, the so-called third turn repair (Schegloff, 1987, 1991) describes the correction of the partner's previously indicated misunderstanding as an equilibrational act. Likewise, different pro-terms (i.e., reduced forms of speech, pronouns in particular, that replace their full versions mentioned previously by the interactants—Schegloff, 1989, p. 146) are used to maintain the flow of dialogue within relatively open fields of meanings of the participants, with substantial overlap between the fields. This intersubjectivity is defended by a number of strategies (Schegloff, 1992, pp. 1337–1341).

At the fringes of dialogue repair, actions by the interactants begin to introduce novelty. Yet within the equilibrational perspective, such novelty may take the form of introduction of a new stylistic element (e.g., a joke—Schegloff, 1987; an ironic comment or emphasis—Schegloff, 1989), which may constitute a new equilibrium state of the dialogic process (e.g., shift from "serious" to "joking" talk). The process of transition between these states remains unanalyzed, even if the outcome—that is, the shift in state—is clearly documented.

The disequilibrational perspective entails a look at the emergence of novel meaningfulness on the basis of the opposition between the parts of the dialogic system. This perspective on mutualities between opposing parts of a whole has notable traditions in the history of occidental natural sciences and language sciences; it amounts to the specification of dialectical philosophical perspectives in the context of dialogue analyses (Markova, 1994). Synthesis of novelty in dialogue needs to be elaborated within the dialogic perspective, as Markova has accomplished in her analysis of dialogic events into three-step process units of codevelopment (Markova, 1990b). Such three-step units entail an opposition of two parts at time 1 (e.g., A claims X, B claims the opposite of X), which leads to the emergence of novelty of at least one of the parts at time 2 (e.g., now A claims Z and B claims not-Z; both parties in the dialogue have overcome the previous "X versus not-X" contradiction and created a new opposition). Consider a dialogue within the mind of a very diet-conscious person:

Time 1
Internal voice 1: This cake looks delicious!
Internal voice 2: I should not eat so much.
Time 2 (at which the cake is consumed)
Internal voice 1: Today is a special day.
Internal voice 2: Good that my mother doesn't see me.

This example illustrates the emergence of novelty in dialogue: a decision to act grows out of a dialogue, leading to further dialogue about the ongoing action. However, such novelty is constructed in any present process of a dialogue with two orientations considered simultaneously. It emerges from the oppositions of the (immediate or not so immediate) past, but it also takes into account the expectable future. In the latter case, dialogic processes entail a *teleogenetic* (i.e., goal-creating) orientation, as goal orientations by any parts of the dialogic whole may guide the oppositions toward some future desired state. Human communication is preemptively strategic, aside from being immediately constructive on the basis of the past events.

Strategic Communication:
Goal Orientations and Intersubjectivity

Interestingly, the emergence of novelty as a result of dialogic processes leads to constant undermining of actual intersubjectivity. This may happen as a result of a novel sense emerging at the intersection of partners in dialogue. However, it may likewise—and probably more substantially—depend upon the goal-oriented nature of the dialogic processes (Branco and Valsiner, 1997; Kindermann and Valsiner, 1989; see also the teleological personalism of William Stern, described in chapter 5). At any moment in the dialogic process, the agents involved are capable of setting up their general goal orientations, acting in accordance with those orientations, and changing those orientations dynamically. These goal orientations are set up on the basis of subjectivities of the interlocutors and therefore create constant challenges for any status of intersubjectivity.

General goal orientations may lead to ways of transforming assumed intersubjectivity. This set of forms may entail intentional misunderstanding (by way of alternative interpretations—see Schegloff, 1987, pp. 213–214), purposeful transgression of sociolinguistic norms (e.g., see the separation of breakable and implicitly marked taboos—Ohnuki-Tierney, 1994), or making use of a minimal range of possible individuality in the case of rule-governed creativity (Arima, 1991). The teleogenetic nature of human communication entails the presence of multiple and dynamically changing objectives:

> Communicative action is purposive. But here the teleology of the individual action plans and of the operations for carrying them out is *interrupted* by the action-coordinating mechanism of mutual un-

derstanding. Orientations and action processes are at first egocentrically tailored to the various actors, but communicative "switching" via candidly executed illocutionary acts places them under the structural limitations of an intersubjectively shared language. The telos of reaching understanding, inherent in linguistic structures, compels the communicative actors to alter their perspective; this finds expression in the necessity of going from the objectivating attitude of success-oriented action, which seeks to *effect* something in the world, over to the performative attitude of a speaker who seeks to *reach an understanding* with a second person about something. (Habermas, 1992b, pp. 80–81)

Habermas underestimates the coordinative possibilities of various goal orientations within a dialogue (by denying "dual intention" of both understanding and influencing—Habermas, 1992b, p. 79). It is possible to envisage a highly effectual dialogic process that builds on the arrival at understanding, and vice versa. Habermas's own goal orientations seem to have constrained his view of the strategic nature of communication.

SOCIAL ROLE RELATIONSHIPS AND INTERSUBJECTIVITY
The strategic nature of communication in the domains of claimed intersubjectivity leads us to the necessary consideration of how personal subjectivities (which include both understanding and goal-oriented facets) and intersubjectivity are united within a differentiated whole. Thus, in communication a purposeful agent attempts to set up a field of intersubjectvity by meanings of fusion of the participants' closeness (Example 1) or by setting up a shared asymmetrical intersubjective state (expert-novice relation, as in Example 2). In both cases, however, the communication that follows is aimed at accomplishing the goals of the intersubjectivity setter (obtaining a desired object in Example 1 and a desired answer in Example 2).

Example 1 (interaction of two friends)
A: We are very good friends, aren't we? We would do anything for each other.
B: Yes, that is true. I would do anything for you, and I know you'd do the same.
A: Will you give me this nice X of yours?
B: (gives the X)
Example 2 (teacher to student)
T: Anand and Kenesh always drink tea together. Anand is drinking tea now. What is Kenesh doing?

S: Drinking tea.

T: Why?

S: Because they always drink tea together.

Example 2 is built on the asymmetrical setting of intersubjectivity (where both participants share the notion that the claims of the dominant one—the teacher—are not to be questioned). If the teacher gives a particular "fill-in" to the major premise of the syllogism tested here (which is modeled on widespread uses of syllogistic reasoning tasks in cross-cultural psychology—e.g., Luria, 1976; Tulviste, 1991), the student accepts the given premise without further questioning (because the teacher "knows better"). The teacher receives the desired ("correct") answer on the basis of the asymmetrically constructed intersubjectivity, which allows for the premise of the syllogism to be taken for granted.

In sum, human beings can construct intersubjectivity through the exercise of their subjectivities. Thus, it may be impossible to fully describe the dynamic process of intersubjectivity, since its subjective cocreators are constantly undergoing change. As Fogel has commented, "Relationships must have a mystique: there must be something not quite known, something that may never be understood or even articulated, something that entices the mind and body and renews the meaning in the relationship" (1993, p. 90).

Thus the intersubjectivity in any relationship is a dynamic process that is constantly "moving on" through the subjectivities of the persons involved in it. These subjective worlds—personal cultures—are the locus for *breaking* of the assumed intersubjectivity in accordance with one's set goals. Thus, it can be said that human personality emerges on the basis of—and through—establishing contradistinctions to the personal cultures of others. Intersubjectivity is relevant insofar as it serves as a temporary basis for idiosyncratic personal constructions of one's subjective world and its goal-directed strategic actions.

Summary: Cultural Processes of Personality

Personality is a loosely defined complex phenomenon that refers to a semiotically constructed holistic labeling of the person's reflection on him- or herself. It can be seen as a result of elevating an ordinary language term to the status of a central concept in psychology's terminology. The heterogeneity of the abstract term "personality"—including a variety of semantic nuances that range from a "mask" to "true self"—provides for the popu-

larity of the term and the impossibility of its clear definition. Yet its usefulness may prevail through efforts to elaborate the processes involved in the
differentiation of the "self" (be it "true," "false," "unknown," or any
other kind) and the person's reflection upon it in its complexity.

Personality is viewed as a general notion of the person that the person
has constructed in the context of his or her life-world. It can be described
in terms of context-dependent complexes of ideas (e.g., the "relational"
versions of "the self," often attributed to persons in oriental societies) or in
terms of abstracted and decontextualized listing of "personality characteristics." In both cases, the main questions remain the same: How do
human beings construct their reflections upon their own selves? And how
do such constructed notions feed into further development of the persons? This process of construction entails two sign-mediated processes: the
guidance of the development of the person's self-construction through
social direction (collective-cultural canalization) and the corresponding
active construction of the unique self-presentation for him- or herself, as
well as for others.

Two core ideas are elaborated in the inherently cultural theory of human
personality that is undertaken in the rest of this book: that of constraining
of the intrapsychological processes and the construction of semiotic means
for such constraining. In the next part, which outlines the contraints-based
viewpoint on the dynamics of personality processes, an effort is made to
make sense of personality in dynamic and semiotically constructing terms.

Human personality is a cultural process—first, at the level of the constant construction of personal culture by the developing person, and, second, as a way of reflecting upon one's self as socially suggested by the
collective culture. However, mere declarations of the social nature of personality are not sufficient. In order to make a developmental, systemic
account of personality as cultural process work as a theory, specific mechanisms that represent the processes between the person and the environment, and within the person's subjective world, need to be elaborated.
Part I of this book undertakes this task, followed in Part II by a tracing of
the histories of the ideas used for such elaboration.

I

A THEORETICAL FRAMEWORK: "BOUNDED INDETERMINACY" IN PERSONALITY ORGANIZATION

2

Constraining of Acting, Feeling, and Thinking: Semiotic Regulation of Personality

The present theoretical system is based on the duality of partitioning of the world by active persons who construct meaning. Relationships between person and environment require the distinction between the two (as discussed in chapter 1) and lead to further distinctions in both the person and the environment. Partitioning creates the figure-ground distinction already at the level of basic perceptual processes. At the level of experience as a whole, oppositional relations between "what is" (i.e., what is brought into focus through constraining) and "what is not" (i.e., the other possibilities that remain outside of focus) are defined through partitioning. When viewed developmentally, partitioning of a field—or making a distinction—creates duality (see Herbst, 1995; see also Figure 1.2). This created duality in its turn—due to the processes that link its opposing parts—is the basis of further development.

The notion of making distinctions has been at the heart of all developmental thought in science, starting with Karl Ernst von Baer's focus on differentiation of the embryo (von Baer, 1828) and reaching our contemporary developmental psychology through the "orthogenetic principle" of Heinz Werner—with an emphasis on differentiation and hierarchical integration (see later analysis). Differentiation is a continuous process of emergence, growth, and elimination of distinctions. It is through distinctions that what is distinguished can be conceptualized—either in contrast with other distinguished structures or in contrast with the undistinguished part of the scene. For example, in the process of making a figure-ground distinction, both the "figure" and the "ground" are necessary for each other (see Figure 1.2).

Similarly, making distinctions is at the heart of all semiotic mediation of the human lived-through personal worlds. Construction of signs creates the duality between experience and the (constructed) reflection upon these experiences. Since awareness of personal subjective worlds entails an act of interpretation of these worlds, the question of a reference system for the distinctions made can be itself a matter of making distinctions. When one creates a sign to refer to something, the sign becomes the highlighted "figure" observable on the basis of the "ground" of experience. However, as the sign is evoked, it becomes the "ground" from which further experiential life events become highlighted when they take place, and constructed purposefully. For example, once concepts like "fairness" or "abuse" have become constructed by a person, based on some complex background experience, they become the background for evaluation and selection of further personal experiences.

The Beginning of Distinctions: Nothingness and Non-Nothingness

In the case of developmental processes—where *emergence* is our focus of attention—the primary contrast that can be made is between "nothingness" (nonbeing) and "non-nothingness" (being). Development entails detection of the emergence of the latter from the former in irreversible time. Thus, our first reference system is a "zero case"—a state wherein the given process has not yet emerged. This "ground" is the basis on which the emergence of novelty is detected, at a next time moment. Nevertheless, such "ground" is inherently ambiguous, since the basis for the emergence of the "figure" (new phenomenon) from such a basis entails philosophical complications that force researchers to rethink methodology (as will be analyzed in chapter 7).

The contrast of "being" and "nonbeing" is ontological. Developmentally speaking, this opposition of linked parts (A and *non*-A) guides the emergence of the A from *not*-A (see Figure 1.1)—that is, from another previously existing opposition of B and non-B, C and non-C, and so forth. The use of the nonexistence of something at a time previous to the emergence of that something provides theoretical discourse with a number of very interesting challenges. It forces us to operate with a general, undefinable concept—"not-yet-ness." This has created numerous difficulties for developmental concepts (e.g., Vygotsky's notion of the "zone of proximal development"—Valsiner and Van der Veer, 1993). If a concept is created so as to reference developmental phenomena, it has to "capture" the emergence of something out of something else. Yet that emergence can be inherently unpredictable—hence the difficulty for the concept.

Philosophically, it is not possible to conceptualize "nothing" (Bergson, 1906). Nevertheless, development entails the emergence of novelty from *its* previous absence, yet on the basis of the previous presences of something else. A simple solution for developmental approaches is to consider the emergence of something (X at time 1) from *something else* at a previous time (e.g., from Y at time t − 1). This solution has been widely used in received research practices (e.g., ranging from microlevel Markovian analysis of developmental phenomena to macrolevel stage accounts—where the next "something," or a new stage, is assumed to develop from a previous "something," or another stage). Nevertheless, the process of becoming (of X) remains a movement from a state of absence of X at a previous time to its subsequent presence. Other emerged "somethings" of previous times (Y) may play some role in this emergence, yet that role is not predefined. Furthermore, absence of something in some context may itself indicate a presence of something else. In the process of development, the emerged something may disappear, which in itself is a case of progression in development (e.g., the disappearance of the Moro reflex in infancy).

It may be possible to claim that developmentally the boundaries of emergence and disappearance of phenomena are the domains where developmental processes take place (Valsiner, 1994a). In this case, the focus of developmental research is necessarily directed upon heterogeneous and semiformed phenomena—phenomena that are "no longer X" and "not yet Y." The complications this focus brings to developmental methodology are substantial (see chapter 7). Both presences and absences of observable phenomena may be important for analyses of development.

The Uses of Absences by Culture

The notion of nothingness has been utilized in human cultural histories as a relevant contrast frame (e.g., Japanese *mu*—see Ohnuki-Tierney, 1994; or *sunyata* [emptiness] doctrine in Mahayana Buddhism—Much and Harré, 1994). There is a theoretical benefit in using open general concepts in a science as well (Löwy, 1992), so the use of nothingness in cultural histories is a symbolization effort similar to sciences. In linguistics, the concept of zero phoneme (*absence* of a phoneme in locations where it *could* be present but is not) and Barthes's (1979) zero sign (a sign that "creates meaning out of nothing"), are constructive theoretical uses of the opposition between nothingness and emergent somethingness. In a similar vein, Markova (1994) has called for the conceptualization of "A and non-A" oppositions in the construction of units of dialogic analysis of interaction processes. The "meaning of silence" is a powerful communication device both in cultural history (Baumann, 1983) and for information construction in face-to-face interaction (e.g., the use of decisions *not* to speak in Apache interaction—Basso, 1970). In principle, all semiotic mediation devices can become reconstructed as abstract means of cultural process, leaving their original reflexive functions behind in their own history (Ohnuki-Tierney, 1981).

The distinction-making power of "zero signifiers" is most effectively demonstrated in the intentional uses of the *opposites* of these cultural tools for purposes of meaningful transgression of the presently existing cultural order. Thus, breaking silence in situations where refraining from speaking is the established cultural consensus and construction of affective relations with the world through swearing *in specific ways* constitute such transgressions that explicate the role of such signifiers:

> If the most sacred is too powerful to be objectified, its/their objectification is a blasphemous transgression, which, in turn, is purposely used not only to defy the sacred but also to use them for secular insults . . . Curse words in American English center on sex and religion, many of which are objectifications in words of the unmentionables and those not to be mentioned. In either case, the taboo against verbalization dictates that the most powerful must remain as zero signifiers whose meanings are of extreme cultural significance. In Japanese culture neither sex nor religion constitute a focal point of significance, yielding to the paucity of curse words involving those cultural institutions. The deliberate misuse of the discourse of politeness and deference as the most frequent weapon of insult testifies to the centrality accorded to the *social relationship* or *sociality* in Japanese culture. (Ohnuki-Tierney, 1994, p. 68)

Zero signifiers are constructed semiotic devices that utilize the *absence of* something *as if this is* something in itself. Such contextually meaningful "nothingness" is "somethingness." In terms of Figure 1.1, both opposites of an A↔non-A linkage can be observable, or not. In the former case, an explicit "dialogical state of affairs" ("dialogue" between A and non-A) may be observed. However, equally likely is the case in which one of the opposites (A or non-A) is unobservable. If the non-A part of the whole is the unobservable (invisible) part of the functioning whole, the dialogical state of affairs becomes a manifestly "monological" state. Nevertheless, there is actual dialogicality present in such manifest monologicality—the epic myth-stories can carry their psychological function on the basis of dialogic oppositions between the *manifest A* that is in opposition with the *concealed non-A* (Gupta and Valsiner, 1996). The reverse construction of manifest monologicality—in this case by way of visibility of the non-A— occurs in case of zero signifiers. Zero signifiers can be considered to be implicitly marked and breakable taboos—they are officially not to be broken, but if they are transgressed, the power of such transgressions is enhanced exactly due to their implicit nature or their culturally constructed "nothingness" (Ohnuki-Tierney, 1994, p. 71). The implicitness of the framework of such taboos (the A) is linked with the explicitness of the absences (the non-A). In general, dialogicality (unity of A and non-A) exists in both forms: when both opposites within a whole are manifest, and when one of them is concealed. Monological-looking semiotic phenomena—be they seemingly unitary sign uses or equally unitary-looking "silences"—entail an oppositional counterpart that maintains the manifest monologue. A person who is constantly attempting to indicate "I am X" is operating by the tension generated through a X ↔ non-X opposition.

Construction of Meta-Levels of Wholes

As has been shown, distinctions are being made in the process of experiencing, through the use of perceptual distinctions and semiotic (signs-based) differentiation of the experience. At each junction of such developmental process a new level—a meta-level (relative to its preceding state) is constructed. Construction of a meaning Z to refer to the X ↔ non-X opposition establishes a meta-level semiotic reflection upon the original opposition: Z {X ↔ non-X}. However, the meaning Z evokes its opposite (non-Z) to maintain the new distinction at the level of meanings. Thus, the opposition [Z ↔ non-Z] is the means of reflection upon {X ↔ non-X}. Following the distinction of the first meta-level, a next (meta-meta) level of reflection (P) can be constructed. That reflection evokes its counterpart (non-P), which may lead to further construction of increasingly abstracted general meanings. In general terms, the following open-ended hierarchy may be constructed:

etc.
|
[next meta-level opposition]
|
P ↔ non-P
|
Z ↔ non-Z
|
X ↔ non-X

Each emerging level of reflexivity leads to a reorganization of the semiotic constraint system that regulates itself, the next level lower to itself, and gives rise to the potential construction of the next level above itself. Each next level is constructed semiotically, in terms of signs that are feelings-full and referential at the same time (see elaborations in chapter 6). Given such growth into the "semiosphere" (Lotman, 1992), the whole of human personality is a cultural process. It is a self-organizing whole that becomes differentiated and hierarchically integrated.

This hierarchical growth of levels of semiotic regulation can help us understand how both presences and absences of signs in specific contexts can be functional in human psychological processes. A previously made distinction at a previous level (e.g., naming) can serve as the ground for subsequent construction of the absence of the named entity (i.e., the uttering of the name can be ruled out). That absence functions as a semiotic regulator of specific psychological functions. On the basis of such constructed, meaningful absence, a new distinction can be made by the reappearance of the semiotic device—but now on the background of the previous meaningful absence. Thus, a developing child's acting "inappropriately" in public (e.g., a preschool girl proudly showing her genitals to her peers) may lead to social regulation of the action by way of a "zero signifier" (not just suppressing the action but also making clear that any reference to it is "out of place"), followed (later) by explicit general talk about "modesty." Uses of meanings at different levels of generality, and in different forms (explicit and implicit), constitute a flexible and multilevel social regulatory system of human feeling, thinking, and acting.

AN EXAMPLE: CO-CONSTRUCTION OF THE MEANING SYS-
TEM   The construction of the semiotic social regulation system is a
constant process. It is so pervasive that in our ordinary lives we may pay no
attention to it. However, a brief look at some ordinary dialogues may
illustrate how that system is constantly in the making, while existing already in some form. David and Rosa Katz recorded some of their bedtime
"confession talks" with their sons (Theodor and Julius). The following
excerpt indicates how secondary meta-level "framing" by the mother sets
up the use of primary meta-level reflection upon (completed) actions:

> *Mother:* Did you do *anything good* today? *Perhaps you handed*
>   Grandmother a chair?
> *Julius:* There was a chair and Grandmother sat down in it herself.
> *Mother: Perhaps you picked up* Grandmother's handkerchief for her?
> *Julius:* No, Theodor did that.
> *Mother:* Did you *clean up* the playroom?
> *Julius:* Yes.
> *Mother:* Did you *put the chairs away?*
> *Julius:* Yes.
> *Theodor:* Mamma, I struck everybody today and I bit the baby.
> *Mother:* Why did you strike at them?
> *Theodor:* They would not let me come to you from the playroom.
> *Mother:* Why did you bite the baby? [baby = Julius]
> *Theodor:* Well, Mamma, you know he changed the locomotive and cars
>   around and you know that won't do. The car is shorter and the
>   locomotive is longer.
> *Mother:* Well, is that *so bad* that you *had* to bite him?
> *Theodor:* No. You must *always explain* it. You must *have a school.*
> *Mother:* How do you come to think that?
> *Theodor:* Yes, you must *always say, "Theodor, don't bite."* Mamma, I also
>   pinched Baby's fingers in the drawer.
> (Katz, 1928, p. 339; emphasis added)

The emphasized parts of this trialogue indicate the ways in which meanings are used at different levels of social regulation of children's reasoning
of their own actions. The mother brings in two secondary meta-level
notions ("good" and "bad"), working upon the children's linking of their
specific themes of reflection upon action (primary meta-level) with these
general meanings. She does it by suggesting immediate connections with

the primary meta-level meanings ("perhaps you did X," "did you X?").
The younger child (Julius) is "working through" the list of mother's ideas
for "good deeds" while the older displays reflection (confession) of his
"wrongdoings" (while "breaking in" the interaction), together with reflection upon internalization of semiotic action prevention means ("Theodor, don't bite"). Constraining of action occurs both intrapsychologically
(in a person's suggestions for one's own action or its inhibition) and
interpsychologically (mother's implications of a boundary between legitimate and not-legitimate actions: "was it really *so bad* . . ."

The notion of constraining is theoretically a special kind of a term. It
entails partitioning of a field (the time-free facet of the term) together with
direction of the time-dependent process toward some future state.

Constraining As Direction-Providing

Constraining is the enabling of the process of emergence of novel phenomena through creation of temporary partitions (limits) within a field of
(previously) indeterminate possibilities. It does not carry negative connotations (e.g., of "suppression" or "repression") but is a neutral term used
in the present theoretical context solely to indicate the construction of di-
rective order within emerging phenomena. Constraining creates bounded
indeterminacy of developmental processes:

> Psychological development, both in ontogeny and in history, can
> be considered deterministically indeterministic. This deterministic
> (bounded) indeterminacy guarantees the developing organism the
> possibility of developing novel ways of acting *within a strictly deter-
> mined range of options* at every time in development. The flexibility of
> the developing organism within that constrained range of possibilities
> may be of crucial significance in situations where the organism has to
> continue existing under changing environmental conditions. (Valsi-
> ner, 1987, p. 238)

When the notion of bounded indeterminacy was introduced, it was
intended as a conceptual vehicle to overcome the opposition between
determinacy and indeterminacy that has plagued the conceptual worlds of
psychologists (Fogel, Lyra, and Valsiner, 1996). The notion specified that
indeterministic, deterministic, and ambiguous "zones" coexist in the case
of regulation of developmental processes. In other words, the world of
developmental phenomena is heterogeneous as to its determinacy. In some

parts of the field it is strictly—even if temporarily—determined, while in adjacent parts the actual organizaton of development may be ambiguous. Thus, to ask the question in "either-or" fashion (Is development deterministic or not?) would be an a priori conceptual blinder. Development is both deterministic and indeterministic at the same time, in different domains (or parts of the field). The notion of probabilistic epigenesis (Gottlieb, 1976, 1992, 1997) has reflected this principle in developmental biology. However, the same principle of bounded indeterminacy applies at the level of microgenetic events (Branco and Valsiner, 1997), and the process of communication can be viewed as entailing "bounded randomness" (Weissert, 1995).

ORDINARY-LANGUAGE CONSTRAINING OF THE NOTION OF CONSTRAINT   The unfortunate ordinary-language connotations of the term *constraint* could not be avoided in the previous presentation of the concept. As a scientific term, *constraint* is value-free—*it indicates a specific partition of a field.* The only conceivable case of absence of some constraint is a fully homogeneous field. Any distinction within a field, any separation of a figure from the ground, is possible only through the creation of constraints.

Furthermore, constraints are constantly in the process of being created and becoming obsolete. Constraints exist as *temporary* means of organization of the process of development. They are created by persons for the solution of specific tasks in their here-and-now situation, with the involvement of goal orientations to reach some future set objective (*Soll-Wert*—or desired-value-state—according to Boesch, 1991, pp. 103–105). However, once created, *some* of the constraints may become relatively fixed in their "steady state," hence creating the relative endurance of the constraints over irreversible time. It is usually those persevering constraints that are most easily detectable by investigators and, given their "steady-state" stability, are describable *as if* those were static entities. The development of sign construction proceeds from the establishment of transient referential behavioral forms—gestural signs—that refer to the target (in phylogeny: Valsiner and Allik, 1982; in ontogeny: Moro and Rodriguez, 1994) to relative fixation of the referential function in the case of consensual lexicon.

Since some constraints can become structurally fixed entities, they may become encoded in some fixed form in the environment of the developing person. Not surprisingly, the terminology of constraining in psychology emerged via Kurt Lewin's transposition of the notion of environmentally fixed constraints ("barriers") to the realm of the psychological life-space. In the case of the bounded indeterminacy view on development, Lewin's notion of barriers (as relatively static organizers of the life-space) was extended in the dynamic direction, with an emphasis on the temporary functional and constructed nature of these regulational devices. Thus, in the present terminology *constraint* differs from the ordinary-language connotations by being "a regulator of the move from the present to the immediate future state of the developing organism-environment system, which delimits the full set of possible ways of that move, thus enabling the developing organism to construct the actual move under a reduced set of possibilities."

This way of looking at constraints in the process of constant construction of the immediate future eliminates the term's negative connotation (of "suppression") in ordinary-language use (Valsiner, 1987, pp. 90–95). Constraints are co-constructed both externally (parents' attempts to regulate children's actions, given goal orientations, and children's actions toward these efforts) and—in parallel—internally (a person's self-constraining of acting, feeling, or thinking, in dialogue with different meanings). If they are encoded in the fixed aspects of the environment (e.g., architectural forms of buildings of symbolic relevance, such as churches and temples) or in constantly maintained semiotic forms (e.g., myth-stories and fairy tales—Bühler, 1918; Boesch, 1991; Gupta, 1995), their organizational roles can be passed on over generations—with appropriate reconstructions due to the internalization/externalization process (as will be analyzed in chapter 3).

CONSTRAINTS AS TEMPORAL (AND TEMPORARY) REGULATORS OF DIFFERENTIATION PROCESSES The term *constraint* denotes a dynamic, temporary regulator of development (a device to partition the field of possibilities), which under some conditions may become statically represented in the environment or within the person's psychological system (e.g., fixed ideas, relatively stable personal senses). Constraint in this theoretical system is a *primarily dynamic* and secondarily (potentially) *relatively* stable organizational device. In ordinary language, the notion of constraint is usually cast in static terms—yet the functions of language terms entail regulation of the flow of psychological phenomena.

The notion of differentiation of the meaning of terms and their hierarchical integration between scientific and ordinary-language terms is consistent with Werner's orthogenetic principle (Werner, 1940a, 1957) and has been illustrated by empirical work on symbol construction (Werner and Kaplan, 1984). Human semiotic activity is oriented toward both *vertical generalization* of the meanings of ordinary-language terms (either by mapping them upon other terms or by raising them to a more general level) and *lateral extension* of their meanings. In both directions the construction of the scientific concept is coordinated with the ordinary-language use of the given terms. However, the range of acceptable ordinary uses of the term is no obligatory limit for the construction of the semantic fields of scientific terms.

The Conceptual System of Zones: ZFM, ZPA, and ZPD

The bounded indeterminacy principle of development was elaborated through the invention and borrowing of three zone concepts and setting them up in a mutual systemic relation (Valsiner, 1987). A zone does not necessarily constitute a fixed and closed area (as implied in ordinary-language use) but can entail partially differentiated domains, or even definition of zone by exclusion. Examples of this kind are depicted in Figure 2.1.

For instance, zone X may be definable by indicating a solid boundary between it and whatever remains beyond the boundary (zone Y in Figure 2.1). This remains the case if the boundary is not solid (Figure 2.1) or is only partly evident (Figure 2.1). Finally, a zone can be defined in terms of exclusion; in case of Figure 2.1, the zone x is defined to include *all but* areas a, b, and c. For instance, the distinctions made by "zero signifiers" as described earlier constitute a zone of the latter kind. The field, the boundaries of which are defined by a zero signifier, includes all of the possible versions of the meanings, *except* for the ones included in the particular zero signifier.

In a similar vein, Karl Büher's speech theory (see chapter 6) includes zones of the uneven extension of the boundary of the zones from the center of the field (e.g., the notion of "I") to include different others ("we") at different dynamic moments of speaking. Authors of scientific publications often extend the boundary of "I" to the indeterminate "we," which may include anybody ranging from "I" to the immediate interlocutors, to the whole of humankind. The specific boundary setting of where "we" ends (and its opposite, "they," begins) is always flexible, redefinable at a moment, yet at any moment it can be fixated in a strict form.

The zones are not fixed but are dynamically changing partitioning devices. The zone of "they" is defined at any moment by the specific range of inclusion into "we"; in this respect, "they" becomes defined by way of exclusion of everybody else from "we." The condition of *relative stability* of a zone is the result of a steady state in the development of an open system. In the case of exclusionary zone construction (as in the case of "we"-"they"), the fluidity of boundaries can always be brought into action in social life, when necessary. Such phenomena as in-group/out-group distinctions, prejudice, and social stigmatization are made possible by the modulation and valuation of the limits between "we" and "they."

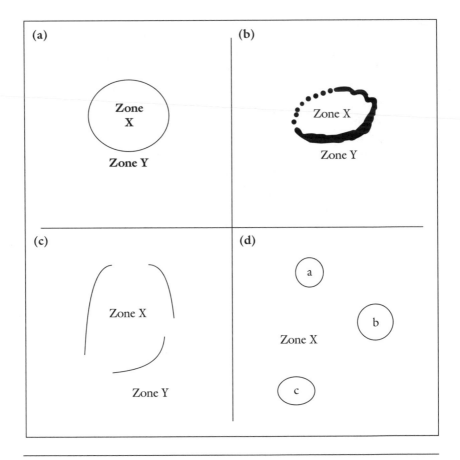

Figure 2.1. Schematic illustrations of different kinds of "zones" (from Valsiner, 1987, p. 96).

The Zone of Freedom of Movement (ZFM)

The first of the zone concepts—*zone of freedom of movement* (ZFM)—was borrowed from Kurt Lewin's field theory. It denoted "an inhibitory psychological mechanism" (Valsiner, 1987, p. 99), a set of constraints that

> structures the child's (1) access to different areas in the environment, (2) availability of different objects within an accessible area, and (3) ways of acting with available objects in the accessible area. As a result of development the child learns *to set up ZFMs in his personal thinking and feeling*—the ZFMs become internalized. In the internalized case, the Zone of Free Movement *provides a structural framework for the child's cognitive activity and emotions. . . .* The ZFM is simultaneously a structure of the child's actions within the environment at the given time, and *the structure of the thinking of the child.* (Valsiner, 1987, pp. 97–98; emphasis added)

Aside from regulating the activities of persons within environments, the ZFM organizes the *intra*psychological functions of the person, through internalized semiotic mediating devices that set up boundaries for possible ways of thinking and feeling. The existence of such boundaries can be experienced introspectively on any occasion where a person's ideational system generates a specific way of reflection that is instantly forced out of the range of possibilities by way of a feeling-laden boundary marker (e.g., "That is horrible! I can't think *this* way" or "I would never do *that*"—in one's intrapsychological dialogue within the self in which some out-of-ZFM option is contemplated). These ZFM boundaries of a *possible and personally allowable* set of scenarios of thinking and feeling partition that set from their possible but personally nonallowable counterparts at the given time. The self-reflection of horror described above speaks of the intrapsychological *semiotic boundary-contact action* in a field of meanings. As a result of this, the boundaries of ZFM can be changed or maintained. If we (i.e., I!) were to use set-theoretic denotation, then a ZFM at a given time can be given as follows:

$$ZFM(t1) = \{a^*, b^*, c, d, e, f, ?, ??, g^*, h^*\}$$

where a through h constitute specified areas of the zone, ? and ?? denote existing but unspecified areas, and the addition of * to some members of the set denote those members that are in immediate contact with the boundaries of the zone. The notion of *bounded indeterminacy* exists in two ways in this depiction. First, the *-marked set members (which are involved in boundary negotiation) and the "in"-members constitute the set of uncertainty. The given ZFM is constantly in an uncertain state, since it is being reorganized as it exists. Second, the unspecified areas (? and ??) denote the part of the set that at the given time is not yet specified—hence uncertain.

Modulation of the ZFM system is expected to take place first at the areas of the zone that interact with a particular constraint (i.e., the *-marked members). If, in our previous example, the contemplated "out-of-ZFM" phenomenon could be denoted as j (and be adjacent to h*), then the self-constraining by the notion of "how horrible a thought!" indicates boundary negotiation between h* (which is in the ZFM) and j (which is not). Surely, dramatic constraints effectively maintain the given boundary of ZFM. Yet other ways of conceptualizing the same negotiation process— for instance, the out-of-ZFM phenomenon j is thought of, together with a qualifier "what a good idea, and others have not thought of it!"—which would lead to the incorporation of the j into the ZFM:

$$ZFM(t2) = \{a^*,b^*,c,d,e,f,?,??,g^*,h,j^*\}$$

In this case, the boundaries of the ZFM are extended, and the new member of the set j becomes (instead of h) one of the boundary-marked members of the ZFM set.

In parallel to such boundary-contact action, most of the present ZFM contents are even not known to the actors (e.g., as depicted by ? and ??). Human beings encounter their ZFMs—set up in joint construction in an intrapersonal or interpersonal dialogue—not by exhaustive sampling of all of their contents but by detecting boundary areas in some unsystematic way. The experiencing of the ZFM boundaries is episodic, and the inner region of the ZFM provides for only one subarea (or a few) to be experienced at the given time. Hence, persons are necessarily ignorant of numerous subareas—those not experienced contemporaneously—of their ZFMs. This ignorance constitutes a "reserve" area for possible experiences, if the ZFM remains in a steady state for a while.

ANALOGUES OF ZFM   In a parallel terminology to that of the present theory and developed on the basis of Lewin's zone of free movement concept, Boesch (1991, pp. 103–104) speaks of *ranges of tolerance* that are set up at the intersection of *Ist-Wert* (the value of the existing state of affairs) and *Soll-Wert* (the value of desired state of affairs). Personal generalized sense systems ("fantasms" in Ernest Boesch's terminology—see chapter 4) regulate the boundaries of the range of tolerance. Thus the meaning of instrumental cultural objects—for instance, money—may encounter specific boundaries of tolerance limits (or ZFM in the present terminology); for instance, "Money can buy many things, even status or love, and if it cannot buy happiness it can at least eliminate many reasons for unhappiness. Yet all this is subject to the condition that things are for sale. A coveted object may have a market value of a hundred dollars, but if the owner refuses to sell it, even a thousand dollars would be worthless as far as it is concerned" (Boesch, 1991, p. 196).

The boundary of ZFM of the meaning of monetary value is thus socially negotiated and personally internalized. The latter can lead to construction of "no-sale" conditions as applied to specific objects or activities. Specific meanings can be brought into relation with a particular reflection so as to set up boundaries of the ZFM, and such construction of ZFM boundaries within the field of reflection can become a regulator of the field of acting. Furthermore, it can lead to the construction of Nth rank meta-level of social-regulatory fields that constrains reasoning and feeling at their subordinate levels, as well as (eventually) action.

GENERAL MEANINGS AS SPECIFYING ZFM BOUNDARIES   As was pointed out earlier, the semiotic creativity of human beings makes it possible to reorganize person-environment relationships in a flexible way. Aside from the relative fixedness of such organizational forms, the system of sign regulation of the boundaries of the zones of acting, feeling, and thinking needs to be flexible for quick reorganization.

Let us consider the meaning of "dirt" as it can be observed to exist to set ZFM boundaries. Introspective phenomena such as the recognition *"Oh, this is dirty!"* indicate the ZFM boundary–maintenance function of the notion of dirt. Yet the meaning "dirt" can be utilized by human self- (and other-) regulatory systems in flexible ways, ranging from the first level of reflection (upon action), to Nth meta-level discourse about the world. At the intermediate level of sign construction, "dirt" can be viewed

as matter out of place . . . It implies two conditions: a set of ordered relations and a contravention of that order. Dirt then, is never a unique, isolated event. Where there is dirt there is system. Dirt is the by-product of a systematic ordering and classification of matter, in so far as ordering involves rejecting inappropriate elements . . . We can recognize in our own notions of dirt that we are using a kind of omnibus compendium which includes all the rejected elements of ordered systems. It is a relative idea. Shoes are not dirty in themselves, but it is dirty to place them on the dining table; food is not dirty in itself, but it is dirty to leave cooking utensils in the bedroom, or food bespattered on clothing, bathroom equipment in the drawing room; clothing lying on chairs; out-door things in-doors . . . under-clothing appearing where over-clothing should be. (Douglas, 1966, pp. 35–36)

Douglas's view on "dirty" starts from the ontological, culturally set view of whole-part relationships, while the focus in the present book is on the developmental side. It is the exactly personal use of the collective-culturally suggested meaning of "dirt" in regulation of action that stops many of us, under ordinary circumstances, from putting shoes onto the dining table, or eating up leftover food from the plates of our guests at the end of a dinner. However, we may quite ordinarily "finish up" food left on the plate by our own child. The notion of "dirty" thus regulates the boundaries of the wholes of ZFM, stopping our actions at the boundary of the ZFM by creating an affective block for acting and thinking. Douglas's focus on the relativity of the notion of "dirt" takes the form of the changed context of applicability of such a boundary-regulating device, once the whole of ZFM changes. This happens by way of renegotiation of the boundaries of ZFM for action, often by way of personally introduced change in the semiotic regulatory system. As has been shown elsewhere (Josephs and Valsiner, 1996), each basic meaning (such as "dirt") evokes a family of potential strategies to circumvent its boundary-maintaining role. The flexibility of relating to the realm of personal experience is thus guaranteed, together with the inflexibility of affective restriction of the ZFM boundary.

Simultaneously with the establishment of the flexibility/inflexibility of the semiotic regulators of ZFM boundaries close to the realm of immediate actions, generalized meanings operate at ever-abstracted meta-levels of the control system. The meaning of "dirt" becomes related with other generalized meanings at these higher regulation levels, creating discourse about the phenomena that acquires relative autonomy from the action level. Thus, "Dirt is matter which breeds *disease,* especially in our more enlightened modern times. But it also denotes *low social status:* the laborer in the fields, the coal miner, the blacksmith and many other "lower" occupations *exhibit a dirty appearance,* as would also the vagabond or tramp.

Cleanliness, then, symbolically—or really—protects against *moral defilement,* against the threats of disease, and against social abasement" (Boesch, 1991, p. 232; emphasis added).

The linkage of "dirt" with "disease" and "low social status" is certainly a semiotic overgeneralization, the function of which is symbolic ZFM boundary maintenance at some Nth order meta-level of discourse construction. The same meaning—dirt—can be brought to guide persons' thinking and feeling about social class boundaries (or gender distinctions—Hershman, 1974), thus creating the difference that at any time can be extended to other areas of thinking or acting (Bourdieu, 1985, 1988, 1991). The use of "dirt" as a marker of boundaries of *moral* "cleanliness" is closely intertwined in the history of occidental societies with religious purification efforts (for a history of cleanliness in U.S. history, see Bushman and Bushman, 1988; Wilkie, 1986).

As a ZFM-setting meaning, any generalized meaning ("dirt," "fairness," "justice," etc.) delimits the person's feeling, thinking, and acting to a range of possibilities of a specifiable direction (i.e., in contrast with its opposite direction, or other specifiable orientations). It sets up the functional fields for feeling, thinking, and acting, within which further differentiation takes place. The social regulatory fields develop into a hierarchy of semiotic control systems, allowing for flexible over- and undercontrol of the action field.

There is a specific theoretical benefit to using ZFM terminology: it defines the area of interest for the study of development. If the latter process entails renegotiation of ZFM boundaries, it becomes obvious that the location of such boundaries—rather than sampling of the entire contents of the ZFM—is important. ZFM boundaries can be located on the basis of evidence for boundary renegotiation—in external or internal dialogue. Domains of such renegotiation may be marked by specific meanings that distinguish between the options within ZFM and those outside. Thus, the meaning of "dirty" may be a marker to distinguish between the actions with the same object (e.g., a piece of bread) if it is taken from a plate and eaten (= not dirty) or if it falls on the floor, is picked up, and then is eaten (= dirty).

The Zone of Promoted Actions (ZPA)

The notion of *zone of promoted actions* (ZPA) was invented as a subzone of the ZFM, which provides further structure to the ZFM by highlighting some parts of it, guiding the person's actions, feeling, and thinking toward those, rather than other, areas of the ZFM. A ZFM can include any number of ZPAs, each of which may be strictly or approximately defined, as described in Figure 2.2.

Figure 2.2a depicts the simple case of two ZPAs (x and y) located within a ZFM. One of these (x) is well defined, whereas the other (y) remains a nebulous orientation of some subpart of the ZFM as distinct from others. In Figure 2.2b we have a more provocative case where the ZPA is located at the ill-defined region of the ZFM boundary. It is in these latter cases

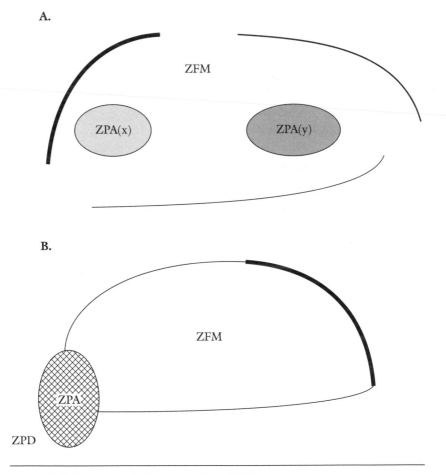

Figure 2.2. Different relations of ZFM and ZPAs.

that the ZPA can operate as a vehicle for changing the ZFM boundaries, as well as their becoming better defined.

The concept of ZPA allows us to consider the activities of the co-constructing agents (the developing person, his or her "social other") in terms of their efforts to direct the actions toward some objectives within the ZFM, rather than others. The ZPA can be viewed as a promotion device because it has a direction in the form of some goal orientation. The promoted orientation, however, lacks obligatory power. Here lies the difference between the ZPA and the ZFM. For the latter, the marked boundaries are obligatory (unless they become renegotiated by the next time moment), whereas for the ZPA the directions suggested remain orientational devices that can be resisted or neglected without extended negotiations.

Thus, the ZPA is "a set of activities, objects, or areas in the environment, in respect of which the child's actions are promoted . . . Once a ZPA is set up but the child does not follow the lead of the parents' promotion effort, but acts with other objects (in other ways) . . . there is no way in which the child *can be made to act* within the ZPA (Valsiner, 1987, pp. 99–100; emphasis added).

The nonbinding nature of the ZPA as described in the case of the action field is similar if we apply the concept of ZPA to the intrapsychological semiotic constraining systems. Specific meanings can be utilized by the person within the stream of consciousness in ways that *promote some direction of thinking and feeling, without obligating the person's intrapsychological stream to move further in that direction.* These are general attention-directing, or pacemaking semiotic feed-forward signals used as "occasional happenstance guidance devices" of a kind. Thus, in one's intrapsychological dialogue, a person might remark that "thinking X may be *the right thing* to do," while the actual flow of reflecting does not follow in that direction within the field of possible scenarios of the thinking-feeling field. The meaning "the right thing" is temporarily appropriated as a ZPA device. It lacks immediate "effect" upon the person's reflecting on whatever it is about, yet it maintains the possible directionality of that reflection process over personal duration (à la Bergson—see chapter 4). It also promotes the generalization of the notion (that there are "right" and "not-right" ways to think) in parallel—yet, again, not determining the next step in the flow of the reflection.

Fritz Heider's analysis of everyday thought brings to us many elaborated versions of semiotic ZPA complexes (Heider, 1958). The meaning of "ownership" of a particular domain may lead a person to view something in one light, while there is no obligation for it. For instance, "One might enjoy the noise of one's own son (how full of spirits the boy is), but the same noise produced by the child of a disliked person would be perceived with displeasure" (Heider, 1958, p. 149).

The meaning of "ownership" can guide one's feelings to turn a "glass half empty" into one "half full" (Heider, 1958, p. 157). Likewise, specific meanings can set up ambiguous ZPAs, setting up promotions for acting and feeling in ways that chart out a possibility that is immediately curbed by impossibility. The latter may entail construction of symbolic barriers that are *desired* by the person, and followed so as to delay or give up actions (see also the analysis of Janet's "fear of action" phenomena in chapter 4). Heider's example (of Benchley) is illustrative:

> That afternoon you look up the dentist's number in the telephone book. A wave of relief sweeps over you when you discover it isn't there. How can you be expected to make an appointment with a man who hasn't a phone? The thing is impossible! . . .
>
> Bright and early Monday morning you make another try at the telephone book and find, to your horror, that some time between now and last Tuesday the dentist's name and number have been inserted. Fortunately the line is busy, which allows you to put it over until Tuesday. . . (Heider, 1958, p. 228)

The setup ZPA at the level of reflection (and at any meta-level of any rank) can entail *direct orientations* (one could think/feel about A in ways X, Y, or Z) or *bounded orientations* (one could think/feel about A in way X if condition x applies, or in way Y if condition y applies, or Z if both x and y apply). The ZPA is mapped upon the ZFM as its background; hence it is appropriate to consider the ZFM and ZPA as a system of related concepts.

The ZFM/ZPA System

In the original presentation of these zone concepts, it was claimed that the ZFM and the ZPA are mutually intermapped and constitute a functioning system (Valsiner, 1987, pp. 101–107). While the ZFM keeps the person's acting or thinking-feeling within the field of acceptable possibilities, the ZPA provides suggestions for further differentiation of the field. Yet these suggestions are mere orientations, not obligations.

To continue the set depiction of the zones:

$$\text{ZFM/ZPA(tX)} = \{a^*, b^*, c, d, e, f, ?, ??, g^*, h, j^*\}$$

where the set members are denoted as above, with the addition of the specification of the ZPAs within the set by way of italics. The ZFM/ZPA complex here is specified to *negotiate potential change* in two boundary areas (b^* and j^*), as well as within one nonboundary area (e). Again, the principle of bounded indeterminacy is shown here; the process under question is canalized both by the set of ZFM-included options and by the ZPA highlights. For the latter, it is still not determined which of the highlighted areas (if any) actually leads to the change into the next nearest state of the ZFM/ZPA system. Change can come into being in other areas of the ZFM/ZPA complex as well, without the ZPA functions (or despite them)—for instance, via specification of the ? or ?? areas.

"JUMPS" OF CANALIZATION FROM ONE LEVEL TO ANOTHER   The relative form of the ZPA (to the ZFM) may provide canalization of the process within the level of action—by narrowing the ZFM boundaries to the absolute minimum (of *two* possibilities—to act/think *or not*, using the ZFM that includes just X), paired with equating the ZPA with that narrowly defined ZPA (e.g., it is best to act or think-feel X) is likely to lead to the expected outcome.

Nevertheless, the multilevel semiotic control system is open. It is always possible to counteract the narrowly prescribed ZFM/ZPA complex at the level of actions by constructing a wide ZFM/ZPA complex at the next level of semiotic reflection upon action. Once that system becomes fixed in narrow ways, a "jump" of the meaning-making to the next meta-level can liberate the thinking-feeling process by way of generalized ZFM/ZPA system construction. The hierarchy of semiotic meta-levels extending beyond the action level makes such "jumps" possible. Even when the ZFM/ZPA system is overconstrained in one field, the co-constructive process can be transposed to another related field and become open-ended again. This usually happens between the domains of action and reflection. Our sct-descriptive example may be modified as follows:

$$\text{ZFM/ZPA(tX+1)} = \{a^*, Bb^*, c, d, e, f, ?, ??, Gg^*, h, Jj^*\}$$

Here we add denotations of emerging sign-mediated reflections upon parts of the ZFM/ZPA complex by capital letters (B, G, J), adjacent to the particular areas of the ZFM action subzones. This description shows that *not all parts* of the ZFM/ZPA complex need to be semiotically mediated (i.e., could be reflected by use of signs). Furthermore, not all such mediational devices themselves become highlighted by the ZPA (e.g., highlighting is the case for Jj^* but not for Bb^* or Gg^*). Furthermore, a particular sign mediator may become attached to different parts of the ZFM/ZPA complex, such as:

$$ZFM/ZPA(tX+2) = \{a^*,Bb^*,c,d,Be,f,?,B??,Bg^*,h,Bj^*\}$$

For instance, the general designation "this is good to do" can be applied to different parts of the ZFM/ZPA set, in some cases fortifying the ZPA function (Bb^*, Be, Bj^*) and in others just marking the action area in these terms (Bg*). In fact, the complicated set description is merely a compression of phenomena at two parallel levels. It can also be written as follows:

$$ZFM/ZPA \{\text{meta-level } 1\}(tX+2) =$$
$$\{. . .,B, . . ,. . .,B,. . .,B, B,. . .,B\}$$
$$\quad | \quad | \quad | \quad |$$
$$|ZFM/ZPA\{\text{action}\}(tX+2) = \{a^*,b^*,c,d,e,f,?,??,g^*,h,j^*\}$$

where the | indicates the specific connections between the two levels— reflection and action.

HIERARCHY OF ZFM/ZPA FIELDS: TRANSPOSITIONS FROM ACTIONS TO REFLECTIONS   If a person's action domain is over-constrained, the domain of semiotic construction of personal-cultural sense of his or her relation with the given context can be constrained only by the active participation of the person. In the domain of feelings-full reflection, the person is the dominant constructor of the personal sense system (and the social suggestions from collective culture are subdominant in this process).

Let us consider as an example a set of "strict" disciplinary rules in a school—to act in way X only (i.e., ZFM including only {no-X; X} possibilities), together with equal promotional marking (ZPA = {"right way" = X; "not-right way" = no-X}), may lead students to construct the meaning of "I act X as I must, and as they say is right, *yet I just do it and do not care.*" The action performed under these conditions is not "serious"; it is psychologically distanced (see chapter 3) by the co-constructing student who has no other way to reorganize the ZFM/ZPA complex than by changing its personal sense for his- or herself. The possibility for personal construction of such alienated relation to the socially constrained action may be the reason collective-cultural constraining systems attempt to provide ZPA/ZFM systems redundantly at both the levels of acting and reflecting. Thus, aside from the strict disciplinary practices, the social environment of the school includes parallel ZPA/ZFM construction in terms of "moral duties," demands for "liking" one's actions, and so on. Since the intrapersonal (personal-cultural) world can be constrained by the internalization/externalization processes (and not directly by the social context), redundant control efforts at both action and reflection level are the best strategy for the collective culture to constrain personal development. Nevertheless, given the open-endedness of the personal-cultural construction process, such redundancy can never guarantee success.

The latter possibility of semiotic reorganization of the action/meaning complex (ZFM/ZPA) by the co-constructing person is the resistance to the ZFM/ZPA complex that leads to its reorganization on behalf of the person. The ZFM/ZPA structure is constantly being reconstructed through semiotic remediation, with corresponding psychological distancing and construction of integrated ambivalence structures (Giordano, 1989; Giordano and Valsiner, forthcoming; also Rogers, 1951, pp. 528, 530). Integrated ambivalence is a structure of duality, where two opposite-valenced feelings-full reflections are unified into a whole with abstracted (generalized) personal sense (see also Bühler's "principle of abstractive relevance" in chapter 6).

RELATIVE AUTONOMY OF ACTION AND REFLECTION DO-MAINS   The flexibility of ZPA construction in the domain of reflection can lead to establishment of reflective foci that effectively maintain the person in a state of perpetual reflection and disconnect the semiotic level of functioning from that of actual actions. Chapter 4 contains examples from Pierre Janet's psychiatric patients whose reflection led them to "fear of action." In these cases, the semiotic means were used to *block* action (i.e., mark the boundaries of self-set ZFM). Simultaneously, however, such means can be used to enhance the process of reflection about something (ZPA) within a wider field of possibilities that include connecting thinking and acting (ZFM), so that the action itself becomes de facto forgotten. For example, a person may construct for him- or herself the ZPA in the domain of thinking (and talking) about the need to "save time" (or "save poor children"). The person can then be observed talking (and thinking) about that topic (i.e., setting up one's ZPA) and not utilizing possibilities that may actually be available (within the present state of ZFM) to act in accordance with the ideas that are talked (and thought) about. The person is overoccupied by the self-promoted meaning domain for talking, thinking, and feeling, which results in the lack of action due to concentration in the sphere of reflection. The phenomena of "empty talking" (or, likewise, "thoughtless involvement in activities," e.g., fusing one's actions with those of a crowd) indicate the strategic functioning of the ZPA/ZFM mechanisms in the ego-defense processes (as will be shown in chapter 3).

Levels of Constraining by ZFM/ZPA Mechanisms

In human organization of psychological processes, constraining can take place interdependently at different levels (or fields), starting from the person's actions-field and gradually relating to it semiotic fields of meanings of different generality: (1) field of meanings to reflect upon actions; (2) field of meanings to reflect upon reflections upon actions, and so on. In principle, the hierarchy of fields that are made functional for the person can be infinite (in other terms, human interpretations allow for infinite reinterpretations), yet in reality limits are set upon how far in this field construction the person is expected to proceed. The ZFM/ZPA complexes can be seen at work at all functioning fields of that kind. Constraining at the higher-level (semiotic) fields usually guides the field of action, and vice versa.

However, it is possible to separate different fields for specific purposes. Dissociation of the acting and reflecting domains of personality functioning is often a target of collective-cultural guidance efforts. Displacement of action by talking about action is a simple way of guaranteeing nonaction. A certain collective-cultural system may set up a social context that enhances talking (and thinking) about issue X, thus redirecting the talkers about X away from acting about X. Such "displacement" of the focus of practice from the sphere of action to the sphere of talk about action is a widespread means of social regulation. Within the latter sphere, the participants are not only allowed but *constantly encouraged* to construct ever-new solutions to "problems," reconstruct existing meanings, and make plans for "improvement." This may be encouraged through public events that focus the attention to the issue at stake (e.g., ritualistic "world conferences" on important topics, like those on "global ecology"—Little, 1992; Ribeiro, 1994). Such dissociated semiotic activity can also be promoted by meta-level semiotic canalization devices used to regulate the activity of reflecting upon the reflector (e.g., "we stand for *progress,*" or apply the notion of "creativity" to the collective-culturally canalized flow of semiotic construction).

By providing the public with domains of promoted reflection—be these vicarious participation in gladiator fights, football games, discussions of politics, or soap operas—the collective-cultural system directs (but cannot determine) the reflexive processes of persons toward nonaction through exaggeration of the semiotic self-processes. Since the ZPA is related to the ZFM (because it is based on the latter), other constraints may be set so that practical action in the given sphere also becomes unavailable (i.e., outside the ZFM), thus redundantly guaranteeing that persons would shy away from action (blocked by ZFM boundaries) and personally legitimize it through reference to their reflection.

THE ZFM/ZPA COMPLEX AND THE USE OF ZERO SIGNIFI-
ERS   Within the dynamic structure of ZFM/ZPA, the use of zero signifiers can be functionally linked with ZPA construction. Thus, domains of discourse that are constructed to be outside of the ZFM (e.g., explicit talk about sex, money, and religious feelings among acquaintances in U.S. middle-class society) can be used via implicit allusions, which in turn may semiotically mark the specific emphasis that is being promoted. Thus, while talking about some object, a person may make an indeterminate comment ". . . and it was *so* expensive!"—thus focusing the interaction (or one's own internal dialogue) on the referenced object in the next moment (at least). The person may expect the interlocutor not to follow up the exclamation by matter-of-fact questions about the actual price, nor would the person (in internal dialogue) launch into a consideration of exact prices. Rather, the allusion to the value using the background of out-of-ZFM domain creates the power of personal emphasis. It is a form of semiotic "boundary behavior" (transgressing, yet not transgressing, the ZFM boundary) that serves as a device to set up a ZPA focus.

Furthermore, goal-oriented transgressions of the existing ZFM boundaries of the field of appropriate meanings can be utilized for setting up ZPAs. A person can purposefully set up her interlocutor by forcing the latter to transgress the ZFM boundary, thus creating tension. That tension can be used for the purposes of ZPA focus. In the following dialogue between a health-promoting female nurse and a middle-aged man, the nurse sets up the transgression "subzone," followed by its resolution through making it work for marking ZPA directions:

> *Nurse:* What about sex? Do you have regular sex?
> *Patient:* Yes.
> *Nurse:* Good, good. How long does that last for? Thirty minutes, forty-five?
> *Patient* (blushes and shifts in his chair)
> *Nurse:* Oh, longer, eh? [Laughs]. Well, that's good. I bet your wife's pleased. *No, but the point is that physical exercise is very good for the heart and sex is very good physical exercise.* And don't forget, the fitter you are . . . (conversation continues on the topic of exercise programmes)
> (O'Brien, 1994, p. 405; emphasis added)

The patient's tension, created by transgression of the ZFM boundary, is immediately linked with the goal-oriented promotion of the notion of "health." It is a basic process of triggering a disequilibrated state in the psychological system, which is then guided to a new state of the ZFM/ZPA complex. The power of zero signifiers—which reference domains outside of ZFM—is brought into action to move the *current* ZFM/ZPA structure to a new state.

The Zone of Proximal Development (ZPD)

Finally, the notion of *zone of proximal development* (ZPD) was borrowed from the intellectual heritage of Lev Vygotsky but was reconstructed in an attempt to fit it with the other two zone concepts (ZFM/ZPA). The actual history of the emergence of the ZPD concept in the intellectual history of Vygotsky's thought was not known to me ten years ago, and even after its clarification (Valsiner and Van der Veer, 1993; Van der Veer and Valsiner, 1991) it still contains unresolved mysteries and difficulties for theoretical conceptualization.

Since the ZPD refers to possibilities that are relative to the given present state, in principle it cannot be used empirically in terms of "measurement" (Valsiner, 1987, p. 109; Valsiner, 1995b). In its original uses by Vygotsky, the term was merely a metaphor meant to persuade educators to transcend the limits of their fashion for testing children's IQs and academic performance and to instead guide children's potentials (Van der Veer and Valsiner,

1991). Vygotsky did not mean to build a systematic theoretical system around the notion of ZPD; rather, his main theoretical contribution of cultural-historical orientation was already constructed by the time he turned to talk about ZPD (in the last two years of his life—Valsiner and Van der Veer, 1993).

While Vygotsky used ZPD as a convenient metaphor in his disputes with educators of his time, later efforts have been in the direction of treating it as a theoretical concept. Numerous efforts exist to provide concrete elaborations for the ZPD concept. A number of investigators have attempted to measure differences between different posited "zones" of action (e.g., Calil, 1994; Cole, 1985; Ignjatovic-Savic et al., 1988; Moll, 1990; Newman, Griffin, and Cole, 1989; Portes, Smith, and Cuentas, 1994). Others have attempted to clarify the relations of that concept with other similar concepts (e.g., "scaffolding"—Rojas-Drummond and Rico, 1994; "situated cognitive representations"—Saada-Robert, 1994). Extensions of the ZPD model into the domain of semiotic mediation by concepts and reconstruction of external environment led to relating ZPD with the meaningfulness of everyday life contexts (Alvarez, 1994; Del Rio and Alvarez, 1992).

I also attempted to elaborate the ZPD notion (Valsiner, 1987), with considerable unresolved difficulties. The notion of ZPD as it was used was a narrowed-down version of Vygotsky's concept that was made subservient to the ZFM/ZPA complex. Thus, ZPD entailed the *set of possible next states* of the developing system's relationship with the environment, *given the current state* of the ZFM/ZPA complex and the system. Thus, "The ZPD is a term that helps us to capture those aspects of child development that have not yet moved from the sphere of the possible into that of the actual, but are currently in the process of becoming actualized" (Valsiner, 1987, p. 107).

When taken to the realm of semiotic mediation, the ZPD would entail the *set of possible new meanings (or personal senses)* that could become constructed given the present person-environment relationship and the ZFM/ZPAs involved in it. The example of a student's acting in accordance with the narrowly set ZFM/ZPA complex and constructing the meaning ". . . but I don't care" indicates the openness for semiotic reconstruction of the situation by the person. Some directions of construction of new meanings of the person-environment situation are open as possibilities for the co-constructing person (and those belong to the ZPD—a set of potential semiotic reconstructions). To continue with the set-theoretic depiction, the ZPD can be defined as a family of possible novel forms of change, given particular areas of the ZFM/ZPA complex:

CR/TAB\ZFM/ZPA(t)   ZPD (t+1)

$\{a*\}$	$\to$	$\{a,a*,Aa,Aa*,A,?\}$
$\{Bb*\}$	$\to$	$\{b,b*,Bb*,Bb,B,?\}$
$\{c\}$	$\to$	$\{c,c*,Cc,C,?\}$
$\{d\}$	$\to$	$\{d,d*,Dd,D,?\}$
$\{Be\}$	$\to$	$\{e,e*,Be,Ee,E,?\}$
$\{f\}$	$\to$	$\{f,f*,Ff,F,?\}$
$\{?\}$	$\to$	$\{?,?*,X?,X,??\}$
$\{B??\}$	$\to$	$\{??,??*,B??,X??,???\}$
$\{Bg*\}$	$\to$	$\{g,g*,Bg*,Bg,B,?\}$
$\{h\}$	$\to$	$\{h,h*,Hh,H,?\}$
$\{Bj*\}$	$\to$	$\{j*,j,Bj*,Jj,J,?\}$

This formal example specifies that the set of ZPD options is dependent upon the ZFM/ZPA in a number of ways: the nearest future can include maintenance of the previous ZFM/ZPA area (the depiction in the left column is included in the right column sets). In the ZPD case, possible new ZPA forms are not included (no italicized members in the sets in the right column). The novelty can be constructed in the nearest future by altering the boundary status of the areas (leaving or adding *), by constructing signs (capital letters), or by a further open-ended option (?, ??, or ???). Again, the crucial point is the notion of bounded indeterminacy—the range of possibilities within the ZPD, given the previous ZFM/ZPA complex, is defined, yet *which of those options* is going to become actualized remains to be negotiated in the actual development.

LACK OF DIFFERENTIATION OF MICROGENETIC AND ON-TOGENETIC LINES OF DEVELOPMENT IN THE ZPD   The narrowed-down version of the ZPD as it was used in the previous theoretical system included an interesting oversight: fusion of immediate (microgenetic) developmental events with those of ontogenetic relevance. It was clear that the ZFM/ZPA complex was microgenetically oriented, and the ZPD linked with it was primarily elaborated in terms of *immediate* future possibilities (i.e., also in terms of microgenetic process). Yet, at the same time, the longer time perspective of ontogenetic progression was implied:

> The relationship between ZFM, ZPA and ZPD is *constantly "filled in" with new content* that depends on what is important in the life of the particular child at a given time. For example, a toddler starts to climb different objects in the home. This constitutes a new motor skill which is canalized through ZFM and ZPA . . . If the given toddler's previous motor development has created a basis onto which the new skill of climbing stairs can easily be integrated, with instructions from the adults, then *ZPA fits into ZPD, and the new skill is learned relatively quickly and without difficulty.* (Valsiner, 1987, p. 108; emphasis added)

Here I was caught in the usual trap of equating microgenetic and ontogenetic perspectives, a problem that is rampant throughout developmental psychology. If the ZFM/ZPA complex is clearly an organizing device of the here-and-now context, and ZPD is added to it as the mechanism for microgenetic "stretching" of the process to the next immediate set of possibilities, the discourse remains appropriately in the microgenetic sphere. In this respect, the ongoing action process can indeed lead to "filling ZPD in" with new content—for example, a next object for the toddler to climb. However, the discourse switches to the ontogenetic plane ("old" and "new" skills, learned "relatively quickly"), and it thus becomes assumed that microgenesis equals ontogenesis. This assumption constitutes a conceptual trap. On the one hand, it opens the processes involved in the ZPD for empirical analysis. Such analysis is necessarily microgenetic—for instance, analysis of mother-child interaction in the process of solving a puzzle (Hoogsteder, 1994; Wertsch, 1979). On the other hand, the dynamic regulatory processes of interaction (or of introspective intra-action or self-reflection in adults in microgenetic experiments) may—but need not—be of ontogenetic importance. These microgenetic processes may also be *idioadaptations,* to borrow Severtsov's term from phylogenetic analysis (Sewertzoff, 1929). Such idioadaptations are temporary constructions to fit the expectations of the present setting, which do not lead to progression at the more general level (for Severtsov—phylogenesis; for us—ontogenesis). Thus, a "microscopic" view on the ZPD process in conjunction with the ZFM/ZPA complex may allow an adequate view on how person's action A becomes action B, but how that transition is participating in the person's ontogenetic progression is not immediately obvious from this level of analysis.

Constraining within Dynamic Fields

Field theories have had their relevant role in the history of physical, biological and psychological sciences (Lewin, 1933; following him Boesch, 1991). In cases where field-theoretic notions have been applied to the study of development, it is the time parameter that necessarily is encountered in the appropriate conceptualizations (Waddington, 1966). The fields of constraining processes that we will consider are all constructed fields—they come into existence (as well as disappear) within irreversible time.

The irreversibility of time was the main obstacle in the way of Kurt Lewin's field theory becoming appropriately developmental. As is well known, Lewin operated from the notion of the field at a given time (Lewin, 1943) and could not integrate ontogenesis into his microgenetic field-theoretic scheme. Modeling his field notion after theoretical constructions in physics, Lewin could not conceptualize the forward-oriented nature of many aspects of ontogeny. A "field at a given time" is a field for the possible future. However, that future is being constructed in the here-and-now hierarchical structure of fields, where the domain of action within the field is the basis for the construction and operation of concurrent semiotic fields.

Emerging Hierarchies of Fields

Developmentally, we can think of *constantly emerging fields* and their hierarchical relations. Semiotic fields do not exist in the personal culture prior to the person's co-construction of any here-and-now episode of personal experience. That co-construction is *pre*structured by the collective-cultural organization of the structure of the meaningful environment (which is entered by the person) and the goal-oriented social inputs from other persons (e.g., see the notion of "developmental niche" in Harkness and Super, 1994). On the basis of a previous structure of the fields, their new structures are constructed through joint efforts of the person and his or her social others.

A similar field terminology was evident in Karl Bühler's sematology (see chapter 6). By uniting Lewinian and Bühlerian traditions here, we could posit the existence of parallel—yet mutually episodically interdependent—fields of action, reflection upon action (i.e., meta-level field, relative to that of actions), reflection upon reflections (i.e., meta-level field, relative to reflection), and so on. Semiotic fields can emerge on the basis of previous ones, as domains the constraining of which can both constrain the dynamics of the other fields, and of themselves.

In Figure 2.3, the field of primary representations ("primary field") is regulated by a superordinate field of secondary representations (which, in line with Bühler's ideas, entails episodic personal memories and personal senses). Both of these may be subordinate to the field of goal-oriented "speech acts"—indicated desires for future outcomes. The move from primary to secondary to tertiary fields at time 1 is followed by reorganiza-

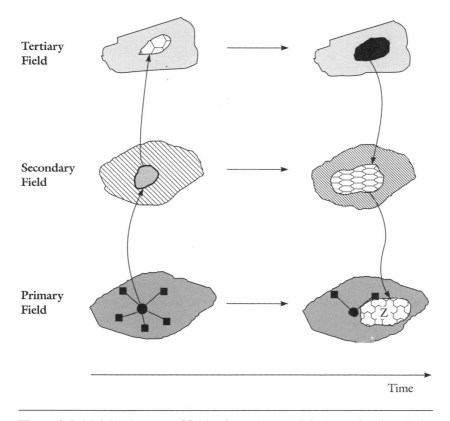

Tertiary Field

Secondary Field

Primary Field

Time

Figure 2.3. Multilevel system of fields of meanings, with horizontal and vertical constraining processes (after Bühler).

tion of the primary field (new zone form Z) as the two higher levels "feed into" the primary field (see Bühler's hierarchy of fields as extended in chapter 6).

CONSTRAINING BY EXAGGERATEDLY WIDE CONSTRAINTS
This case of unboundedness of the use of general terms gives us an example of constraining of the scientific discourse by the constraint of *absence* of limits. At first glance, the notion of no-limits as a constraint may seem counterintuitive (e.g., constraint of no-constraint). Furthermore, such constraint is clearly indeterminate—the limits of no-limits cannot be determined. Nevertheless, the case of no-limits can be viewed as a constraint that enables the potentially endless proliferation of constructed phenomena in some domain, while blocking such constructivity in an adjacent domain. Consider a hypothetical example:

> *Adult to child:* You can do *everything you want.*
> *Child:* Hmh. . . what do I want?. . . Can I do X?
> *Adult:* Yes, you can do X. You can do everything you want.
> *Child:* But can I do Y?
> Etc.

In this invented dialogue, the constraints of "*everything* you want" are exaggeratedly wide and are made conditional to the creation of the desires of the child. The adult creates an illusion for the child of boundless freedom—leaving it to the child to "fill in" particulars. In fact, this co-constructive situation becomes constrained by the child's construction of the set of those particulars, under the illusory meaning that "everything" is possible. Surely that illusion would be modified by the adult, were the child to include in the set of "everything" something that the adult would actually not let happen (for whatever reasons).

UNLIMITED ACTION OR REFLECTION AS A CONSTRAINING DEVICE   The talk about "everything"—as implied in the previous example—can be seen as a constraining device that creates the illusion of limitless freedom. Such created illusion (at the level of reflection) may lead to dissociation of reflection and action by way of a ZFM/ZPA system where persons may be guided to continuous talking and thinking, and away from possible courses of action (which also are within the ZFM). However, such proliferation of semiotic constructivity creates new constraints as it becomes escalated. The promotion of such constructions—an "anything goes" orientation—leads to a reiterative cycle of constructs that set up limits on human thinking and feeling—by way of recurrent ways of reasoning—while the person continues in the process of promoted "unlimited" ways of thinking. For instance, the general ordinary-language meaning of "freedom" (as an unbounded field for action or thought) guides a person to construct other ways of thinking, feeling, and acting that bound his or her psychological phenomena. The idea of "feeling completely free" guides one as a constraint, since it evokes the opposite (non-X, or "nonfree") and creates a constraining force via the uncertainty involved in the "free field." The declared freedom leads to uncertainty, which operates as a partitioning force upon the field.

Examples of *constraining by declared denial of constraints* can be found in sociopolitical discourse in a society, or science. Constraining by denying the existence of constraints can be observed in cases of transitional periods in a science. Thus, moves from one to another accepted worldview (e.g., the move from behaviorist traditions to the "cognitive revolution" in North America or efforts to build "Marxist psychology" in the Soviet Union in the 1920s—Valsiner, 1988a) can entail proliferation of semiotic constructions of the meaning of the move itself, leaving the actual changes in practice without attention.

A similar scenario for the proliferation of talk about issues that are semiotically marked in unbounded ways is the case of various "dialectical approaches" in psychology. A researcher who takes the dialectical approach and then can state about any aspect of the investigated phenomenon that it includes some "dialectic" (not elaborating which and how) is involved in the unbounded translation process of the previous description of the phenomena into the new "language of dialectics." This translation practice may proceed extensively, and eventually the researcher may be able to claim that *all* possible psychological phenomena entail *some* kind of "dialectic." Nevertheless, no new knowledge about the phenomena under study is created. It may be the case that psychology's easy access to the richness of common language allows for many possibilities for such unbounded translations.

Personality Development through Constraining

The nature of the internalized construction of psychological functions remains that of *enabling* our cognitive-affective processes by way of constraining their *directions* of *possible* further movement. Thus, in the intrapsychological sphere of a developing person the emergence of new personal senses (based on collective-cultural meanings) and concepts of different (hierarchically organized) levels of abstraction allows for reorganization of the dynamic flow of affective/mental processes. That reorganization can lead to further differentiation (or, episodically, to states of fusion or dedifferentiation) of these internal processes that are mostly available to investigators through the use of some form of introspection. Hence a different (self-) canalizing system is constructed in the course of internalization/externalization in ontogeny, which allows for relative inconsistency between what people understand and talk about, and what they do. The view of constraints as hierarchically organized fields that regulate the processes of development guarantees that there is inconsistency between these fields.

Relations between the semiotic field and that of actions are not of one-to-one but *one-to-many* kind. A particular meaning constructed within the semiosphere constrains multiple specific actions, allowing different (even seemingly contradictory) actions to be justified by the same meanings. Similarly, every act of conduct (within the field of actions) is polysemous in its meanings—it constrains the construction of multiple personal senses at the semiotic level. Given the hierarchical fields notion adopted here, it is no surprise that human personality is necessarily heterogeneous in its self-structure and inconsistent between the domains of thinking-feeling and acting. Consistency in the latter may be an episodic phenomenon—contrary to the efforts of traditional personality researchers, who have been trying to find such consistency (e.g., Bem and Allen, 1974; Bem and Funder, 1978). In the systemic organization of personality, the principles of *redundancy, hierarchical temporary order,* and *dissociability* of actions, thinking, and feeling give the system a very high potential degree of heterogeneity and flexibility.

Redundancy As a Vehicle of Goal-Directed Control Efforts

All open systems are characterized by redundancy. Redundancy refers to parallel constraining of the same functions within the same present time, and the construction of feed-forward regulation devices for possible future occasions. In human ontogeny, such redundancy is visible first in the multitude of different-in-form (but similarly goal-oriented) constraint systems of multiple kinds (e.g., the ZFM/ZPA complex as described in conjunction with action development—Valsiner, 1987). Furthermore, the redundancy of external social constraints amounts to the copresence of action constraints and semiotic expressions of the meanings of such constraints (i.e., constraining in the sphere of communication by meanings).

For example, consider parents who not only stop the toddler from X and try to redirect her attention to Y (action constraining via ZFM/ZPA) but also simultaneously (or successively) *explain their reasons* for their actions to the child. Such explanation of reasons may happen in a variety of ways, ranging from elaborate ones to generic "this is not good" blanket suggestions. Nevertheless, it is the unity of actions and meanings constraining that guarantees the redundancy in the sociogenetic process of personality development. This semiotic constraining of the meanings of action need not lead to immediate (microgenetic) results. Rather, it may guide the child's constructive internalization of the meanings and lead to the development of intrapsychological self-constraining mechanisms later in ontogeny. Through redundancy of the action and meaning constraining, the immediate and longer-term goals of the parents may be sought in parallel.

Another focus on redundancy in personality development entails the overlap between personal (intramental) and social (extramental) constraint systems. Once the intramental constraint systems—cognitive-affective schemata and personal sense (i.e., the personal-cultural counterpart of meanings)—have become established, the constraining of the self both by the self and by others begins to constitute a partially overlapping process. The social world around the person continues to entail a variety of constraining efforts by the others. In the myriad of such—less or more explicit or forceful—efforts, it is the person's internalized self-constraining mechanisms that make it possible to be both autonomous from, and aligned with, the realm of social constraining efforts. The parallel presence of external and internal social regulation systems constitutes a basis for redundancy in regulation.

Finally, we find redundant functioning within the intramentally constructed self-constraining mechanisms. Different schemata of action constraining may have partially overlapping functions; different personal senses may overlap in the constraining of a person's feeling-thinking fields. As in the case of external social constraining, the redundancy within the personal constraining system can entail coordination of action and interpretation systems: the person may act in way X and explain to him- or herself why and how that action is either necessary or desirable (i.e., creating the ZPA) or possible (e.g., within the "rules" applicable in the given situation, within the ZFM).

VARIETIES OF REDUNDANCY   Within these redundancies, one can find various specific forms, not all of which constitute a case of constraints' similarity between levels of action and reflection upon action, or within each of these levels. Redundancy also (and most often) entails *coordinated differences* between constraint systems, from the operation of which psychological tension of developmental significance may arise.

For example, a purposeful difference between constraining of a child's action and the opposite set of constraining at the level of interpretations of the child's oppositional action indicates how such psychological tension may be productive in ontogeny. A description from an Inuit context may illustrate this:

> A mother and her 3-year-old daughter are visiting in a tent where there are a number of other people. The 3-year-old's sister, aged 4, is outside, playing with other children.
>
> Mother (hands candy to the 3-year-old daughter and says in exaggeratedly happy-excited-secret-persuasive voice): *Eat it quickly and don't tell your sister, because it is the last one!*
>
> Three-year-old (breaks the candy into two pieces, eats one and takes the other outdoors to her sister)
>
> Mother (says to the audience, with a pleased (and perhaps amused) smile): *She never keeps things for herself; she always shares.* (Briggs, 1979, p. 396)

The suggestion here is given as simultaneously creating a ZPA in ways that include both possible courses of action—one of them at the level of manifest contents, the other by exaggeration of it, which indicates the opposite to the demand by the mother. Further redundancy can be added by semiotic marking of the suggestions by joking or teasing (e.g., parents teasing the child around the meanings of "sharing"), or evoking the power of "zero signifiers" (see earlier discussion) and marking some important issue by silences to fortify the desired socialization objectives. Redundancy involves the possible use of all these semiotic means in parallel or in some sequence—and the social experience of the persons is thus filled with the same goal-oriented socialization objective in always-novel forms.

REDUNDANCY IN MEANINGFUL OVERDETERMINATION OF CONDUCT   At the level of the personal culture, similar coordinated differences can occur in the case of dilemmas of affective thought. Such dilemmas—most often explicated in psychology by Kohlberg's moral reasoning tasks—are made possible if the constraints of two (or more) meaning systems are set up in ways of irreconcilable oppositions. Thus, the meanings of "stealing" and "helping" another person in a life-threatening state are set up in such way in the well-known "Heinz dilemma"—what the semantic field of one prescribes is beyond the ZFM boundary of the other, and vice versa. The constraining of one's moral reasoning becomes even more complicated if further meanings are imported into a given situation. In a detailed case described by Shweder and Much (1987, pp. 235–244), a number of meanings-based regulations of the person's moral reasoning are being used as he tries to explain his viewpoint to the Western interviewer. The person—Babaji, a male Oriya adult in his thirties—is a member of a high-status caste, of primary-school education, earning his living by repairing cars. In the dialogue about the "Heinz" dilemma (adjusted to the context as the "Ashok dilemma"), jointly constructed (with Shweder) a line or argument that illustrates the ZFM/ZPA complex in action:

Interviewer: Why doesn't Hindu dharma permit stealing?

Babaji: If he steals, it is a *sin*—so what virtue is there in saving a life. Hindu *dharma keeps man from sinning.* [1]

Interviewer: Why would it be a sin? Isn't there a saying "One must jump into fire for others"? [2]

Babaji: That is there in our dharma—*sacrifice, but not stealing.* [3]

Interviewer: But if he doesn't provide the medicine for his wife, she will die. *Wouldn't it be a sin to let her die?* [4]

Babaji: That's why, according to the capacities and powers which God has given him, he should try to give her shamanistic instructions and advice. Then she can be cured.

Interviewer: But, that particular medicine is *the only way* out. [5]

Babaji: There is *no reason to necessarily* think that that particular drug will save her life. [6]

Interviewer: Let's suppose she can only be saved by that drug, or else she will die. Won't he face *lots of difficulties* if his wife dies? [7]

Babaji: No.

Interviewer: But his *family will break up.* [8]

Babaji: He *can marry other women.* [9]

Interviewer: But he has no money. How can he remarry?

Babaji: Do you think he should steal? If he steals, he will be sent to jail. Then what's the use of saving her life to keep the family together. She has enjoyed the days destined for her. But stealing is bad. *Our sacred scriptures tell that sometimes stealing is an act of dharma.* If by stealing for you I can save your life, then it is an act of dharma. But one cannot steal for his wife or his offspring or for himself. If he does that, it is simply stealing. [10]

Interviewer: If I steal for myself, then it's a sin?

Babaji: Yes.

Interviewer: But *in this case I am stealing for my wife, not for me.* [11]

Babaji: But your *wife is yours.* [12]

Interviewer: Doesn't Ashok *have a duty or obligation to steal* the drug? [13]

Babaji: He may not get the medicine by stealing. He *may sell himself.* He may sell himself to someone for say 500 rupees for 6 months or 1 year. [14]

Interviewer: Does it make a difference whether or not he *loves his wife?* [15]

Babaji: So what if he loves his wife? When the husband dies, the wife does not die with him or vice versa. We have come into this world alone and we will leave it alone. Nobody will accompany us when we leave this world. It may be a son or it may be a wife. Nobody will go with us. (from Shweder and Much, 1987, p. 236; emphasis added)

If we were to analyze this dialogue from the viewpoint of semiotic constraining of the efforts to construct joint understanding of the issue (given by the Heinz/Ashok dilemma), we can observe the use of meanings of various generality (ranging from "sin," "duty," "obligation," "love," and "dharma" to concrete "difficulties," "selling oneself," etc.) that are expected to set up ZFM/ZPA structures to guide the argumentation by the other interlocutor. However, the worldviews of the two interlocutors maintain their respective positions. The interviewer was doing everything possible to persuade Babaji to accept the occidental framing of the dilemma (as a tension produced by equivalence of two opposite tendencies—to steal for moral cause versus the immorality of stealing). This included an effort to narrow the realm of possible actions to the question of stealing, which was rejected by Babaji [5–6].

For Babaji, the "Heinz/Ashok dilemma" failed to become a dilemma. This failure was organized by a semiotic ZFM/ZPA structure that ruled out stealing for oneself (as the wife is included in oneself—see [10]–[12] in the transcript)—by creating a ZFM through the semiotic marker of "sin." What Babaji's ZFM/ZPA structure includes—selling oneself [14]—is ruled out from the interviewer's ZFM system. The interviewer tried to set up specific ZPAs within Babaji's meanings-ZFM by suggesting special conditions—that stealing equals sacrifice in this case (which was vehemently denied—[3]), or that it is a sin to let the wife die (again denied—[4]), as well as by pointing to "difficulties" of "family breakdown" [7–8]. However, the latter ZPA focus was rejected by Babaji [9], whose argumentation moved in the direction of providing alternative solutions—shamanistic cures or selling oneself to slavery to earn the necessary money [14]—which failed to change the interviewer's understanding of the context. The interviewer returned to generic terms ("duty," "obligation"—as linked to stealing [13]; and "love"—[15]) to direct Babaji's reasoning but was counteracted by reference to the basic reality of individual existence in human transition through life and rebirth. The only subarea of intersubjectivity in this case was jointly constructed in this interview around the issue of stealing being potentially legitimate under some conditions (stealing for saving the life of "the other"), yet who might belong to the status of that "other" immediately revealed basic disagreement [10–12].

Even if this example may be discounted as utilizing collective-cultural materials that are generally poorly understood by Western psychology (see also chapter 9), similar processes of negotiation of different subjectivities occur constantly as most ordinary inter- and intrapersonal processes in our everyday lives. These processes entail the construction, use, and dismantling of hierarchical semiotic regulatory systems. The semiotic constraining in ontogeny starts within the domain of collective-cultural processes, where changes in interpersonal relations (as well as in-between social-institutional roles within a society) are regulated by specific boundaries of meanings used in discourse (e.g., Danet, 1980—fight in the United States about an aborted fetus being nameable as "baby" or "fetus"). Likewise, social discourse that regulates the distinction of "insider" and "established outsider" (e.g., those of homosexuals or women) roles (Elias and Scotson, 1965) within a society modulates the meaning boundaries that frame the very same reality of relations in different ways. The collective-culturally suggested change in meanings can be observed in cases of persons in crisis:

A woman of about fifty told us that you used to be thought lucky if the man you married turned out to be a good one. If he was a bad man it was just *your bad luck*. The woman used the term *"bad luck"* . . . to indicate her previous attitude to her husband. In the crisis department of the women's home her ideas changed: what she had previously accepted as bad luck, she now regarded as *wrong against herself which she resisted*. She was not the only one—all the women we spoke to felt they had been *unjustly* treated. The bad-luck phase, the period of resignation to an unpleasant fate, was most noticeable in the life histories of older women. (Van Stolk and Wouters, 1987, p. 479; emphasis added)

Changes in collective-cultural canalization reorganize the meanings of specific aspects of relations. In the preceding example, we see cases of age-cohort changes in the prevailing meanings that cover marital relations. Certainly each wife (and husband) creates his or her own set of meanings about their relations. Institutional efforts at semiotic recanalization constrain the given personality's structure of control beliefs (see Rothbaum, Weisz, and Snyder, 1982; Eastman, Weisz, and McCarthy, 1996). In some domains of everyday life the person may maintain the orientation of relinquishing control (e.g., guaranteed by "bad luck" attribution), while in others the primary control or secondary control beliefs may become prominent. A social institution canalizes personality change by providing a ZFM/ZPA structure that rules out doubt in the provider. For instance, an institution that promotes a woman's move from "bad luck" to "being unjustly treated" understanding will never allow the woman to believe that this change of relating to the husband might be a takeover of control of her loyalties from the husband to a form of "feminism" as an institutional social force. The latter (entirely possible) way of giving meaning to the institution's activities is clearly beyond the ZFM boundary; within the ZFM boundary are all versions of positive-supportive meanings related to the institution. The meanings of "unjust treatment" and "resistance" may be seen as specially set-up ZPA areas within the ZFM, with the ZPD expectation of creating and maintaining psychological distance with any male, thus leading to a social boundary creation in everyday life of *both* women and men. Such boundary constructions between social groups have been targets for classic studies of intergroup relations in social psychology (Sherif et al., 1961). What has not been pointed out sufficiently clearly is the role of the semiotic modulation of meaning boundaries as the psychological vehicle for such construction of social boundaries (see also Penuel and Wertsch, 1995a; Shi-xu, 1995, 1996).

Collective-cultural canalization of personal-cultural meaning fields often entails specification of the direction toward internalization through the use of the meaning of a person's "own free will." Wouters (1987) has analyzed the history of collective-cultural guidance in the recent cultural history of the Netherlands, demonstrating a pattern of disappearance of "cultural etiquette books" in the period 1966 to 1979 and their subsequent return to the collective-cultural sphere in the 1980s. Their disappearance can be viewed as a case of *formalization of informalization* of social relations (i.e., their place was taken by "liberation and self-actualization" literature, which *prescribed* to persons the style of relating to others by *un*prescribed ways). Thus, suggestions for internalized personal reconstruction of the "etiquette" were emphasized. For example, the literature at the time of the return to the "etiquette" notion included suggestions like these: "In order to feel comfortable with the etiquette of the eighties, all *we really need* is *just one thing*. It is the capacity, *without forcing ourselves*, to have *understanding for other people* in the most widely divergent situations, based on *essential respect* for whoever the other person might be" (Wouters, 1987, p. 413; emphasis added); "Whereas *we* used to be pleasant and polite because etiquette required it, now we are because we *ourselves want to be*" (Wouters, 1987, p. 416; emphasis added).

In these examples, notice the construction of illusory intersubjectivity (in the form of "we"—see further chapter 6, Bühler's speech act theory), which creates the "joint field" of meanings between the author and the assumed reader of the books. Furthermore, the author sets up a focused ZPA within undetermined boundaries of ZFM, through the notion of "really need" (i.e., there may be N different needs within the unspecified ZFM, but one is moved into focus of the ZPA—through "really"). That ZPA is revealed to include anything that can be denoted by "understanding" (for others); what is to be included within that meaning field is left unclear, except for the qualifying condition (ZPA) that this *must* come without "forcing ourselves." The fuzzy meaning of "understanding" is further rooted within the ZFM boundaries of another fuzzy meaning, hierarchically declared to be superior to it—"essential respect." The ZFM boundaries of applicability of the latter are declared to be maximally wide ("whoever the other person might be"). In the second example, a similar illusory intersubjectivity basis is used to suggest that the person is "polite" (another fuzzy general meaning) not because it is "required" (which is outside of the ZFM) but because of the person's own "free will"—"we ourselves want to be." Through the use of multilevel meaning systems with boundary conditions (of ZFM or ZPA) defined strategically, the recipient is expected to be guided toward feeling, thinking (and, eventually, acting) in ways that are collective-culturally expected, yet eradicating the history of the socially suggested nature of these expectation by promoting the meanings that indicate the person's own agency. The person begins to believe that he (or she) is the independent decision maker, even if the decisions are made within the realm of collective-culturally acceptable options. Semiotically, the "independent dependence" of the personal culture in relation to the collective culture is being cultivated through such socially guided forgetting of the origins of these decisions.

CO-CONSTRUCTION IN THE CONTEXT OF CULTURAL CANALIZATION   Collective-cultural semiotic canalization efforts of personal cultures become reflected upon by the recipient active co-constructors of such messages. The histories of personal cultures provide for the actual co-construction of the meaning system of personal cultures.

It is often the case that technological innovations bring with them novel opportunities for knowing—as well as challenges to the personal-cultural systems of meaning. A good example is the opportunity to know about the genetic health (or lack of it) of fetuses before they are born. Modern amniocentesis opens new possibilities for prospective parents to know about the possible biological future life courses of the babies. Given the potential to abort a genetically defective fetus at an early stage of pregnancy (in the case of the United States, including a homogeneous collective-cultural expectation that this is what parents might do), it is interesting to look at different personal-cultural bases for any decision (aborting or not) in such cases:

> In two cases of the same diagnosis (the sex chromosome anomaly, Klinefelter syndrome), the same decision to end the pregnancy was made. But in one case, a middle-class professional couple said they "didn't want the pregnancy if he can't have a shot at growing up to be president," while a recently immigrated working-class couple said, "it isn't fair to impose this burden, too, on a child." A young Puerto Rican welfare mother continued her pregnancy after a prenatal diagnosis of Klinefelter. When I interviewed her four years later, during a second amniocentesis for a subsequent pregnancy, she was confident about her growing son's abilities, stressing that Klinefelter syndrome was not a physical disability. "As long as he looks normal, I'll be there for him," she told me. It is important not to romanticize her reactions; initially sent for amniocentesis because she had a sister disabled by spina bifida, she would have aborted for that diagnosis . . .

. . . A Colombian manicurist, . . . married to a Dominican factory worker, received a fetal diagnosis of Klinefelter. At their counselling session, they did not express much concern about the 10–20% risk of learning disabilities or mental retardation that accompanies this syndrome, and they listened to discussions of gynecomastia (male breast enlargement) and micropenises without intense distress. But the husband asked, "Is this going to make him homosexual? I don't want that." And the wife said. "He won't be able to have children—I wonder if he'll blame us." Both expressed concern about knowing something hidden that the son wouldn't know about himself, at least until he was older. (Rapp, 1994, pp. 225–226)

The same diagnosis led to vastly different ways of personal-cultural construction of its meaning—both for the parents and (in their projection) for the future children who would have to live with the realities of Klinefelter syndrome. Notice the use of general meanings as meta-level organizers of the feelings and thoughts of the parents—from the "nothing less than president" image to not wanting the child being homosexual, as well the comment that all is fine if there is no obvious physical disability. Furthermore, the evocation of such general meanings leads to the domination of the whole hierarchy of meanings that has been (or is being) constructed around the new information. Thus, the general meaning of "homosexual" instantly evoked a hierarchy of meanings for the Dominican father that framed all the medical information, in ways that expressed his personal-cultural horror. The affective favor of meanings can reverberate through a hierarchically construed meaning system, with profound results.

Hierarchical Organization: Constructed, Temporary, and Intransitive

The theoretical constructions in the contemporary social sciences seem to be guided by the collective-cultural constraints of the value-laden notion of "hierarchy" in the context of "modern" or "postmodern" societies—which are often considered to be "egalitarian" and "democratic." As Louis Dumont has emphasized, "It is appropriate to keep in mind our aversion to hierarchy. Not only does this aversion explain our difficulty in deepening our understanding of hierarchy, but we are facing a kind of taboo, an unmistakable censure, and caution requires the adoption of a circumspect approach, the avoidance of any provocative statements or premature judgments" (Dumont, 1980, p. 239).

In the context of a desired state of egalitarianism in the construction of personal externalizations, the reality that nonegalitarian states of distinctions are constantly and inevitably made in nature, psyche, and society may easily become hidden. Theoretical foci using the notion of hierarchical organization have been natural constructions in our efforts to understand biological or social systems (Bourdieu, 1991; Crick, 1988; Gottlieb, 1992). However, what is a hierarchy and how it functions in psychological systems has been a topic of much conceptual confusion and intense ideological infighting.

FROM DIFFERENTIATION TO HIERARCHICAL ORDER: MINIMAL FORM   In its minimal form, any hierarchy entails the definition of nonsameness distinction between A and B. Before such nonsameness relation is established, we do not distinguish A from B. Hence, the basis for any construction of hierarchical structure is the process of differentiation. However, mere distinction of A from B does not equal hierarchical relationship (as the distinction can be made in terms of "A is not B" without specification of any kind of comparison).

Thus, hierarchical relations emerge if, instead of the distinction by negation of sameness (i.e., "A is not B"), we set up a specific comparison between them. Thus, the relations "bigger than" (e.g., A > B) or "smaller than" (A < B) indicate specific forms of dominance relationship between two entities. Thus, a claim that "A is <dominant over> B" (in whatever sense this dominance relationship is elaborated) allows us to speak of a dominance hierarchy A > B. In the discourse about personality trait structure as expressed by Gordon Allport (see chapter 5), the hierarchy of "cardinal traits" (radixes) over ordinary traits indicated the emergence of dominance hierarchy. Likewise, Pierre Janet's descriptions of hierarchical control relations between thinking and acting (chapter 4) provided concrete examples of the emergence and functioning of hierarchical relations within the psychological system.

However, the nature of dominance hierarchies—in both their structural and dynamic sides—provides us with a great complexity of forms. These can be distinguished by way of their structure (i.e., transitivity, intransitivity, or mixed forms) and dynamic perseverance (temporary versus temporarily fixed hierarchies).

TRANSITIVE AND INTRANSITIVE HIERARCHIES   Any hierarchical relationship can be of two possible general kinds: *linear hierarchy,* which is based on the logical relation of *transitivity* (i.e., if A > B and B >

C then A > C), or *cyclical hierarchy,* which is based on intransitive relations (i.e., A > B and B > C *and* C > A).

Usually when "hierarchy" is used in psychology, it is the first kind of hierarchy that is being considered. Linear hierarchy fits with "top-down" kinds of control systems and represents a deterministic view of the phenomena it describes. It is the second kind of hierarchy—that based on intransitivities—that would dominate the regulatory processes in the biological and psychological worlds. Most of the biological regulatory processes are of a basic cyclical structure. Likewise, social relations entail cyclical order. An example of intransitivity hierarchies can be seen in chapter 9, where power relationships in the Hindu temple form a cycle of king >> priests >> *devadasi* >> king.

Based largely on discussions about the supposed status of *Homo hierarchicus* in the Hindu context, Dumont was led to explicate the meaning of hierarchy in ways that entail the intransitivities-based kind of hierarchy form as it is discussed here: "The hierarchical relation is, very generally, that between a whole (or a set) and an element of this whole (or set): the element belongs to the set and is in this sense consubstantial or identical with it; at the same time, the element is distinct from the set and stands in opposition to it. This is what I mean by the expression 'the encompassing of the contrary'" (Dumont, 1980, p. 240).

This set-theoretic elaboration entails the notion of a dominance relationship between the whole set and its distinguished members. However, Dumont moves toward adopting a systemic-organismic perspective on the hierarchical organization:

At the superior level there is unity; at the inferior level there is distinction, there is . . . complementariness or contradiction. Hierarchy consists in the combination of these two propositions concerning different levels. In hierarchy thus defined, complementariness or contradiction is contained in a unity of superior order. But as soon as we intermingle the two levels, we have a logical scandal, because there is identity and contradiction at the same time. No doubt this fact has contributed to the movement of modern thought away from the idea of hierarchy, to the neutralization or repression of this idea in the modern mind. At the same time, it evokes a formidable neighbour, the Hegelian undertaking that consists of transforming obstacle into instrument, in using contradiction as a base for superior understanding. (Dumont, 1980, p. 242)

Dumont's effort to clarify the nature of *Homo hierarchicus* leads to the importance of distinguishing levels of organization and viewing hierarchical relations in their process of change. Hierarchical opposition (see also Hage, Harary, and Milicic, 1995) entails hierarchical coexistence of opposites—the unity of A and non-A (refer to chapter 1) is here located at adjacent levels of hierarchy.

TEMPORARY AND TEMPORARILY STABLE HIERARCHIES   In both kinds of hierarchies—transitive and intransitive—plasticity is embedded in the possibility that change in any particular relationships can proliferate to change the whole structure. Undoubtedly it is the cyclical (intransitive) hierarchies that can escalate the process of change, starting from the subdominant parts but leading to change in the dominant ones. In biological systems, we can argue that the normal state of hierarchies is transitory—by their functioning they themselves become transformed. Such dynamic/temporary hierarchies cannot be described in their ontology, as such descriptions entail the ancient Heraclitan problem of being unable to "step into the same river twice."

However, under some conditions of functioning, the dynamic hierarchical processes enter into a relatively steady state, during which it is possible to describe the functioning of such temporarily stable hierarchies. All our examples of personality as a hierarchical semiotic system in subsequent chapters (e.g., Janet in chapter 4, Allport in chapter 5) and our empirical reanalyses (chapters 8–9) rely on cases where the hierarchical control systems have temporarily become fixed in some relatively steady state. Hence there is always a temptation to take the descriptions of temporary being as if they were representations of their normal nature. This temptation—natural for ordinary cognition (see Avrahami and Kareev, 1994)—is misleading for the construction of a dynamic model of personality self-regulation.

Differentiation As Construction of Hierarchical Forms

Processes of differentiation have been emphasized for over two centuries in developmental biology and psychology, yet there have been few consistent efforts to give them theoretical elaboration. An exception is the legacy of Heinz Werner. In Werner's area of interests, the processes of semiotic construction have occupied a central place. The question of construction of meanings of words in the context of sentences, and changes in meanings, were a target of his investigations while he still worked in William Stern's institute in Hamburg (Werner, 1930, 1931, 1954; Werner and Kaplan, 1984; see coverage of Stern's ideas in chapter 5). Likewise, the emergence of structure in the flow of melodies (Werner, 1926, 1940b) was consistently in Werner's focus of interests. However, it was the basic principle of differentiation that underlay all his interests.

WERNER'S "ORTHOGENETIC PRINCIPLE" REEXAMINED
For English-language psychology, the received version of Werner's general view is usually given as follows: "Developmental psychology postulates one regulative principle of development; it is an orthogenetic principle which states that wherever development occurs it proceeds from a state of relative globality and lack of differentiation to a state of increasing differentiation, articulation, and hierarchical integration (Werner, 1957, p. 126).

In order to understand Werner's intentions, his elaborations of the idea must be considered. First, it is important to emphasize Werner's focus on the emergence of the polarity (= differentiation) of the subject (of action) and its object:

> Increasing subject-object differentiation involves the corollary that the organism becomes increasingly less dominated by the immediate concrete situation; the person is less stimulus-bound and less impelled by his own alternative states. A consequence of this freedom is the clearer understanding of goals, the possibility of employing substitutive means and alternative ends. There is hence a greater capacity for delay and planned action. The person is better able to exercise choice and willfully rearrange a situation. In short, he can manipulate the environment rather than passively respond to the environment. This freedom from the domination of the immediate situation also permits a more accurate assessment of others. (Werner, 1957, p. 127)

This focus on increased person-environment differentiation reflects Baldwin's earlier argument about the best proof of sociogenetic origins of psychological functions being their *autonomy from the immediate field* of social demands (see chapters 1 and 4). It constitutes an example of how inclusive separation (of subject and object) is a necessary step in theorizing about structure. Furthermore, the core of differentiation is hierarchical integration of the developing system.

The orthogenetic law was not meant to be a unilinear principle. At the level of concrete developmental phenomena, Werner recognized the multilinearity of developmental trajectories (Werner, 1957, p. 137). He viewed differentiation as including dedifferentiation as its complementary part (Werner, 1957, p. 139). The process of hierarchical integration involves qualitative reorganization of the "lower" (i.e., previously established) levels of organization, when the higher levels emerge in their specificity:

> Development . . . tends towards stabilization. Once a certain stable level of integration is reached, the possibility of further development must depend on whether or not the behavioral patterns have become so automatized that they cannot take part in reorganization . . . The individual, for instance, builds up sensorimotor schemata [à la Piaget] . . . these are the goal of early learning at first, but later on become instruments or apparatuses for handling the environment. Since no two situations in which an organism finds itself are alike, the usefulness of these schemata in adaptive behavior will depend on their stability as well as on their pliability (a paradoxical "stable flexibility").
>
> . . . if one assumes that the emergence of higher levels of operations involves hierarchic integration, it follows that lower-level operations will have to be reorganized in terms of their functional nature so that they become subservient to higher functioning. A clear example of this is the change of the functional nature of imagery from a stage where images serve only memory, fantasy, and concrete conceptualization, to a stage where images have been transformed to schematic symbols of abstract concepts and thought. (Werner, 1957, pp. 139–140)

Werner's perspective on subject-object differentiation consistently led to the notion of psychological mediating devices emerging as human-made organizers of the mental and affective processes (e.g., his reference to the transformation of imagery to symbols). In this, there exists a clear parallel with other semiotic approaches (see chapter 6). In Werner's terms, these mediating devices emerge in the differentiation process:

> Development from a lower to a higher type of action—in terms of differentiation—is marked by the appearance of circuitous approaches, that is, means of action, instruments of mediation. On the level of the most primitive action, object (stimulus) and subject (response) are

not separated by the devices of mediation; that is, the interaction is *immediate*. Development in the mode of action is further determined by a growing specificity of the personal and subjective as against the objective aspect of the action involved. The growth and differentiation of the personal factor in action are demonstrated in the emergence of a specifically personal *motivation*. The growing recognition of a self-dependent objectivity is reflected in the development of *planful behavior.* (Werner, 1940a, p. 191)

Werner's inclusion of motivation among the emerging set of mediating devices serves as an example of theoretical alleys in psychology that have been suggested and then forgotten. Persons as constructors of their own motivation (see Allport in chapter 5)—via construction of cultural meanings (see chapter 6)—allow ever-new forms of self-regulation to emerge in ontogeny, and innovation of cultural meaning systems (as well as differentiation of language forms, e.g. metaphoric devices) in human history. Furthermore, differentiation allows for temporary dissociability of subparts of the hierarchical system.

DISSOCIABILITY   Dissociability refers to the possible (albeit temporary) differentiation of constraint systems within the personality. This makes it possible for a particular person to act inconsistently with one's stated thinking but not noticing it. This heterogeneity within the constraint structures is possible thanks to the prevalence of nonstrict (and ambiguous) hierarchical ordering. The nature of ego-defense mechanisms (see chapter 3) is likewise based on the differentiation process within personality.

Ontogenetically, dissociability results from the "fossilization of behavior" (a term used by Vygotsky)—the loss of the history of the development of a given form in the final product, except for a few traces. In other words, dissociability of differentiated forms allows for their further abbreviation of actions to become recombined in a new action process (Dewey, 1895, pp. 26–27). At the level of symbolic functioning, the abbreviation of symbolic forms in the process of their emergence allows for extension of the reality of here-and-now toward the future (Lyra and Rossetti-Ferreira, 1995, p. 76). Dissociability of parts of the hierarchy is the basis for functional autonomy (along the lines of Allport—chapter 5) of internalized semiotic mediating devices that dissociate themselves from their historical past and begin to function as personal motives.

Cultural Constraining by the Unity of Affective and Cognitive Constructions

The whole field of human feelings is the ultimately personal subjective phenomenon, which is not directly accessible to extrospective analyses. However, already within persons' subjective intrapsychological world, the field of feelings is constantly being differentiated by the use of semiotic mediation (Hochschild, 1983; Holland and Eisenhart, 1990; Lutz, 1988; O'Brien, 1994; Wikan, 1989, 1990). The flow of sentiments within the intrapersonal feelings field becomes reorganized by collective-culturally provided emotion terms, which become connected with different areas of the feelings field and provide it with a temporary hierarchical structure.

DOUBLE REGULATION OF THE FEELINGS FIELD   The semi-otically structured feelings field constitutes the semantic field of the personal sense at the given moment and may become externalized by the person in a communicative effort. That effort is regulated by the person's self-reflection on the one hand and by social norms of discourse on the other. On the side of personal subjectivity, the feelings field is intimately based upon the physiological processes, upon which internalized personal sense constructs act as hierarchically superior organizers of the intrapersonal world. In the realm of extrapersonal regulators, one can easily point to the relevance of societal control of the person's social roles within kinship networks (e.g., wife, daughter-in-law, husband, or mother-in-law), vocational roles (e.g., nun, courtesan, or nurse), and situation-appropriate conduct rules. This amounts to double cultural canalization of human development: human conduct is redundantly organized by cultural meanings and corresponding activity constraints. Both relatively long-standing differentiated "person complexes" (e.g., those of occidental Christianity-organized societies versus Buddhism-based societies—Much and Harré, 1994) and specific collective-cultural meanings (e.g., role expectations for women who enter "health promotion"–oriented occupations—O'Brien, 1994) set up constraint systems on meanings within which the particular social role–centered sets of meanings and personal identification with the assumed roles are co-constructed (see Ho, 1995). The feelings are semiotically marked in linkage with the meanings—nurses are expected to be "caring" and "competent," with benevolent feeling-tone surrounding these meanings. Likewise, in parenting practices the meaning of "punishment" can be embedded within the feeling-tone field of either "unconditional" or "conditional" "love" (Benigni and Valsiner, 1995), which provides a different orientation for the use of the meaning of "punishment" in parent-child interaction. Thus we can distinguish two roles of the affective phenomena—those of targets for being constrained and the role of constraining devices themselves. Feelings are both culturally regulating thinking and themselves being culturally regulated.

AFFECTIVE SCENARIOS AS CONSTRAINING DEVICES   It could be claimed that the duality of affective and mental parts exists in any semiotic constraining device that regulates personal culture. This axiomatic claim renders the "purely rational" constraints to be ones where the affective counterpart is either minimal or hidden. An example used by William Stern (see chapter 5 for his theoretical elaboration) illustrates how the affective-cognitive duality operates as a self-constraining device. The *thought* "Careless handling of benzine can result in fire and death," however clearly entertained, may not, in its abstractness, possess any strong motivational force. But if one also combines with it the concrete imaginary *picture* of oneself bursting into flames while handling benzine, in which frightful details predominate, one will be moved to be careful (Stern, 1938, p. 335).

Similar to the nature of human memory (Tulving, 1983), the human self-constraining system is built on the basis of construction and preconstruction (in fantasy or imagination) of episodes of one's encounters with the world. These episodes are organized by semiotic regulators (meanings), within which both the rational (cognitive) and affective sides create the constraining functions of the constructed devices. In Pierre Janet's empirical materials, the role of affect within the hierarchy of self-regulation devices includes numerous demonstrated versions of these phenomena (see chapter 4, and Valsiner and Van der Veer, 1997).

CONSTRAINING OF AFFECT ITSELF   The second role of feelings in the human personality system is to be the target of constraining themselves. Immediate affective phenomena have been of interest to psychology in a number of ways, from William James's (1890, 1894) and John Dewey's (1895, 1896) conceptualization efforts to present-day issues of "display rules" of facial action programs (Ekman, Friesen, and Ellsworth, 1972).

It is often the case that in the process of constraining the spontaneous affect, different meanings are socially evoked so as to canalize the affect toward some interpretation rather than another. In the case of the Inuit, for instance, the combination of meanings of *ihuma* (translated as mind, thought, memory, reason, sense) and *naklik* (protective concern for others—Briggs, 1975, p. 140; also Briggs, 1991) act as such canalizers. *Naklik* as promoted in childhood leads to the internalization of *ihuma*, so that adults are capable of deescalating their emotional reactions. The internalized *ihuma* feeds into externalized demonstrations of *naklik*, together with the meanings of fear (*ilira* = fear of being unkindly treated; *iqhi* = fear of being physically injured or killed). The result is a child socialization pattern that includes teasing and testing the child's understanding by countergoal demands (Briggs, 1979, 1991) so that the collective-cultural ideal of Inuit personality is being constructed. This has been described by Briggs as follows:

> A mature and good person is defined as one who is governed by reason and who demonstrates this by his consistently helpful, generous, considerate (naklik), permissive behavior toward everybody— not just his immediate family, but all Eskimos and whites as well. The value placed on protective concern (naklik) leaves no room for hostility; a person should never lose his temper, scold, or refuse a request— unless he can formulate the refusal itself as an act of concern: "You can't come, because you might hurt yourself," or, "I can't give it to you, because so-and-so needs it." (Briggs, 1975, pp. 141–142)

The meanings of specific emotiogenic situations are channeled to be different from their immediately evoked emotional content. Thus, anger- or fear-provoking situations may be translated into those of amusement, and laughter may accompany affectively difficult situations (Briggs, 1975; Rasmussen, 1993). The transformation of sorrow into its opposite (pride) can be demonstrated in situations where human beings are guided to identify their meanings of action with specific collective-cultural objectives (e.g., Sande, 1992).

Specific meanings that guide personal-cultural affectivity are often integrated into specific contexts of biological change. Therefore, it is not surprising that ontogenetic development that includes notable biological changes (e.g., menarche in girls) is a target for collective-cultural guidance efforts. The ritual of first menstruation in the context of different religious groups in Sri Lanka—Buddhist, Catholic, and Muslim—reveals a similarity in the sequence of symbolic actions (i.e., the newly menstruating girl is isolated for some days, bathed ritually, and then, with recognition of special status, returned to normal life—Winslow, 1980). However, the specific meanings used to organize this ritualistic activity context vary. In the Buddhist case, the organizing meaning of *killa* (pollution) was used to substantiate the girl's segregation from men in order to protect the latter. Specific actions within the context—like covering oneself when having to go outside during the seclusion period—were substantiated by the idea of protecting unwary males from female power.

In contrast, a similar seclusion ritual in a Catholic context was meant to be for the girl's own protection (rather than that of men). Paraphernalia of the Virgin Mary were introduced in the context. The meaning complex of the Virgin Mary is widespread in Catholic contexts everywhere (Maltz, 1978) and serves as a canalizer of the internalization/externalization process. Finally, Muslim girls in Sri Lanka, described by Winslow (1980, p. 611), are required to recite *kalima* ("There is no God but Allah, and Mohammed is his Prophet"). Notably, in all cases the very same biological novelty (menstruation) is marked by a separation/reintegration ritual, into which specific generic-religious meaning complexes, supported by specific action- or object-type paraphernalia, are embedded. Novel biological states in ontogeny necessarily provoke uncertainty in the personal lives of the children. That uncertainty can be organized by bringing into the situation a redundant cultural regulation system (coordinated meanings, objects, and action demands), which are expected to guide the general affective relations of the persons toward the given collective-cultural complex.

Persons within Societies: Understanding the Dynamics of Relationships

The phenomenon of interest in this chapter is human personality in its cultural-historical interdependence. Instead of the two usual directions in the theoretical explication of that interdependendence (i.e., the "upward" reductionism of personality to social entities; or "downward" reductionism of personality to the biological bases of human species), a third way is being used here. It entails elaboration of systemic relationships between the person and the social world in the course of human development within culturally organized life environments. As was claimed earlier, neither appropriation or internalization can capture the ontogeny of personality development. While emphasizing the fact of social origin of the psychological (in the case of appropriation) or the process of "making the social into one's own" (internalization), both fail to take into account the ways in which the social worlds might be organized, as well as the continuity of the personal construction of one's self through a never-ending variety of social situations.

Inescapable Heterogeneity of Social Environments

The general developmental perspective entails recognizing the irreversibility of time in human development and the highly redundant control over the cultural canalization processes. Different active participants (persons, social institutions, etc.) set up heterogeneous contexts for human development, which are filled with a polyphony of semiotically encoded messages ("social suggestions" or "voices," as will be described in chapter 3).

Human beings develop within an inherently heterogeneous and episodically inconsistent sociocultural world. They are surrounded by a variety of cultural texts (myths, narratives) and social suggestions that attempt to direct the developing person toward a future life course in accordance with the goals of the active "social others" who create or renarrate these social messages. The corpus of these messages is never complete; it entails the copresence of different versions of the same narrative, as well as the presence of *counter*narratives (e.g., as described by Ramanujan, 1991, who looked at heterogeneity of women's tales in South India). The person lives under conditions where tensions are created between different (contradictory) suggestions that are applicable to any given life situation and demand from the person an individual synthesis in conduct here and now. The situation of "Buridan's ass" (a hungry donkey unable to decide between two equal piles of hay) is the usual condition in which a developing person finds him- or herself in culturally structured environments. The latter are necessarily inconsistent and contradictory in their social expectations of the moment, as well as in their actual structural organization.

An example of the inherent ambiguity of culturally organized settings of a particular here and now can be taken from my investigation of toddlers' action canalization at mealtimes (Valsiner, 1987). Thus, a child (at around two years of age, no longer set up in a high chair but having lunch at a low table) accidentally drops some food on the floor. The mother, busy with other tasks, does not notice. The child climbs down from the chair, picks up the food from the floor, puts it in his mouth, and eats it. A similar episode recurs a few minutes later, but now the mother catches a glimpse of the food on the floor and intervenes actively, stopping the child from putting it into his mouth. When viewed from the child's point of view, a very consistent action-task situation (putting food into his mouth) is inherently unpredictable as to its cultural organization. Initially the mother does not intervene, yet at the next comparable moment she does (or might), and so on. Within her intervention is embedded a collective-cultural value (or a little cultural story)—which is beyond the explicit comprehension of the child—of the meanings of "germs" that "are there" on the food that has been "on the dirty floor." Nevertheless, exactly as the child is not yet understanding such stories, the heterogeneity of action contexts provides him with challenges for the personal construction of cultural understanding of situations that may never become explicitly instructed in his life. This *internalization of personal sense on the basis of actions (with or without explanations) of others* may be viewed as the core of the mechanism of observational or participatory learning.

Cultural settings where the main focus is on verbal communication (as it is distanced from the activity itself) are similarly heterogeneous in their depiction of social values. Through narrative perspective-taking, any human activity setting can be provided almost any meaning, which can then lead to constructive dilemmas in the internalization of personal sense. This openness of semiotic mediation (to be covered more fully in chapter 6) allows for both constant flexible reconstruction of the way in which a social setting is conceptualized by a person and persistent fixation of the situation's definition by way of concepts that lead to rigidity of understanding. In other words, human capacities to make sense of any situation—ranging from intolerable flexibility (e.g., Janet's description of "fear of action," which appears in chapter 4), to moderate flexibility of thinking and rethinking a situation, and on to fixed rigidity of thought—are all made possible by the same semiogenetic features of human psychology and complement the "irrational" heterogeneity of the organization of the world through collective-cultural narratives. Thus, the transitions of depicted actions of characters in a children's fairy tale (Bühler, 1918) or in a cultural myth (Menon and Shweder, 1994; also in chapter 4) are in their nature as flexible as their personal counterparts in the propensity to reinterpret a given here-and-now situation by a person.

Developing persons construct their own social roles in the middle of heterogeneous directionality of available social suggestions, and in ways that may range from extreme acceptance of some roles to equally extreme opposition to others. Such an actively co-constructive persons' role guarantees maintenance of their common cultural-historical heritage in all of its heterogeneity, by way of constructing their unique life courses. The heterogeneity of the collective-cultural and personal-cultural worlds is hierarchically (but dynamically) organized. Both persons (in their social roles) and "voices" within the collective discourse are at times dominant over their counterparts, yet at other times such dominance dissipates. As the hierarchical organization emerges and vanishes in the course of real-life personal lives, it is the mutual relationships *between* the differentiated components of the whole that guarantee the functioning of the psychological and social systems. In human development, hierarchies emerge with the ready propensity to disappear, and from the nonhierarchical (or undifferentiated) states in development, new hierarchies of a temporary nature are about to emerge. (For examples, see Raheja, 1990, who describes mutualities in the Indian caste system.) However, mutualities entail an inclusively separated form (see chapter 1), which is an alternative to the mutualism of Dewey and its neo-Gibsonian elaborations (Leudar, 1991; Reed, 1993, 1995). A consistently constraints-based view on personality is structural-dynamic in its core, rather than dismissive of hierarchical regulation principles.

Conclusions: Self-Regulation of Personality by Constraining

The theoretical model outlined here has extended the conceptualization of constraining as enabling (or empowering) partitioning of the world of actions to that of reflection. Both cognitive and emotional phenomena are jointly canalized by the constantly constructed and reconstructed constraint systems (or constraining fields) that operate concurrently and (at times) interdependently in the psychological system of the person. Ontogenetically, that personality system is socially suggested and personally constructed—by a process of co-construction between collective and personal cultures. Ontologically, the system of personality operates in ways that are functionally autonomous from the immediate social contexts of the here and now. Semiotic mediation at different levels of constraining fields allows for potentially infinite transcending of any here-and-now context by construction of personal senses and cultural meanings of different degrees of abstractness, and in terms of a differentiated and dynamic hierarchy of self-regulation. Yet the hierarchy is expanding (or constricting) as the needs for reflection upon the experiences happen to be organized. Semiotic constraining of acting, feeling, and thinking is an ongoing constructive process.

Constraining is viewed here as setting limits on the construction of action and semiotic mediating devices within fields of possibilities, which are dynamically reorganized by the complex of the zone of freedom of movement (ZFM) and the zone of promoted actions (ZPA). These two zone complexes operate in unity and at different parallel, mutually connected levels. The possible future extensions of their work to the future are conceptualized by the use of the concept of zone of proximal development (ZPD).

The crucial notion of the social nature of human personality is its *individual uniqueness* and *relative autonomy* of reflection and action—in any social context. These characteristics can emerge through the process of constructive internalization/externalization, which will be analyzed in chapter 3.

3

Appropriation, Internalization/Externalization, and Self-Construction

If human personality (or self) is a socially constituted—and yet personally relatively autonomous—dynamic system, then what processes of development have made such duality of the social and the personal possible? In sociogenetic discourse, these processes have received varied names, each of which has its own connotations: *appropriation, internalization, participation, sharing of experiences,* and so forth. Proponents of these concepts have entered into an active dispute about the social nature of human psychological functions, which centers around the feasibility or value of the "inner"-"outer" contrast. At times this contrast has been denied (in efforts to avoid creation of a "dualism") or emphasized as the necessary duality for any analysis of persons within their life environments.

Two Terminological Complexes: Appropriation and Internalization

The question of contemporary oppositions between two concepts—these of internalization and appropriation—provides a concrete example of the conceptual confusions emanating from the lack of distinction of the exclusive and inclusive separation models. Within contemporary sociocultural psychology and activity theory, metaphors of "fusion" between personal and social worlds abound (Rogoff, 1990, 1992, 1993; Rogoff, Chavajay, and Matusov, 1993). The contrast between appropriation with internalization has been brought into the open in psychologists' published disputes (Elbers, 1994; Góes, 1994; Goudena, 1994; Hoogsteder, 1994; Lacasa, 1994; Lawrence and Valsiner, 1993; Nossent, 1992; Orlov, 1992; Pino, 1994; Shotter, 1992, 1993b; Sinha, 1992; Wertsch, 1993). Yet most of these disputes remain argumentations in favor of one, and against the other, perspective. It is necessary instead to transcend the simple declara-

100

tion of authors' preferences for one or the other perspective, so that the possibilities that the two perspectives afford can be analyzed in a comparative way.

Two Core Conceptual Oppositions

The conceptual complication around the use of appropriation versus internalization terms seems to be explainable by way of two core oppositions. First (and foremost), it is the opposition between inclusive separation of the "inner" and "outer" personal worlds on the one hand and refusal to use that separation on the other. In the former case, talk about internalization (and externalization) has its place; in the latter, it is either actively denied (e.g., by insistence on the use of the appropriation term) or simply not necessary, since the *directionality* (from "out" toward "in," or vice versa) in the person-environment relation is not given a theoretical focus. In contrast, the preference for internalization (and externalization) terms entails focusing the investigator's attention exactly upon issues of directionality.

The second core opposition is that of the active versus passive role of the person in relation to the environment. Both internalization (and externalization) and appropriation can be viewed in either passive or active terms. If they are viewed in passive terms, the person is either "taking over" (appropriating) or "taking in" (internalizing) social messages as they exist. This perspective amounts to the acceptance of a unidirectional culture transmission model (Valsiner, 1989). The implications of such a model are actively denied by proponents of both appropriation (e.g., Wertsch, 1991, 1995a) and internalization (Lawrence and Valsiner, 1993; Winegar, 1993) terminologies. Both appropriation and internalization entail active participation by persons, a perspective that requires a bidirectional culture transmission model.

The Complex of Appropriation

The history of the use of the appropriation term (*Aneignung* in German, *prisvoenie* in Russian) goes back at least to Marxist thought, where (together with objectivation) it played a central role (Del Rio, 1994; Graumann, 1976, 1990; Leontiev, 1975; Pino, 1994). In its original (Hegelian-Marxist) form, the term meant that it is through human mental and physical activities that the world becomes "a truly human" environment, in which objects and events become "human things" and "affairs." On the other hand, it is the objective features of the material physical world that arouse, incite, foment, and "afford" environment-related human intentionality (Graumann and Kruse, 1997).

In its contemporary incarnation, appropriation has been used as a theoretical concept particularly since the 1970s, in parallel within environmental psychology and activity theories. It "means that the person is transformed in the process of appropriating the environment. Appropriation can take diverse forms, including *taking control over, becoming familiar with, investing with meaning, cultivating and caring for,* and *displaying identity* and *belonging with a place or object* . . . The term appropriation also connotes *mastery or efficacy,* such as when people exercise territorial control, and regulate use by others" (Werner, Altman, and Oxley, 1985, p. 5; emphasis added).

Clearly, the notion of appropriation has something to do with a person's relationship with the world. However, the dialectical mutuality of the earlier philosophical focus has been replaced by psychologists' usual emphasis on control and ownership themes. Hence it is not surprising that intellectual traditions that have emphasized the "socially situated" nature of human activities have made active use of the appropriation idea. The person is viewed as a contextualized actor in the texture of society, overwhelmed by the surrounding social phenomena and "shot through" by them.

How to Unite "the Social" and "the Personal": Unity by Construction

Oftentimes, talk about the social nature of the person is meant to deny the personal nature of such social person. It is as if "the social" and "the personal" are viewed within a Boolean logical scheme as opposites that cannot be true at the same time ("if the person is social then the person is not personal," and, conversely, "if the person is personal the person cannot be social"). Contemporary sociocultural perspectives in psychology are struggling to find a way out of this classical-logical thinking trap by frequent declarations that the person is both social and personal, or that the personality and society constitute each other. Yet these declarations are usually phrased in terms of abstract mediating terminology and are not translated into the language of concrete talk about personality.

A major theme used here to concretize the notion of sociality of the person is that of *constructivity*. Persons are constructors of their own development rather than mere recipients of "social influences" from others. Constructionist perspectives have had an important role in developmental psychology (Baldwin, 1906, 1908b, 1911, 1915) and genetic epistemology (Piaget, 1950). The developing person is constantly reassembling his or her psychological know-how on the basis of personal experience with the world. The latter, of course, is necessarily socially organized—as it entails the goal-oriented actions of other persons and meaningfully precoded physical environments in which the person's development takes place. The latter includes notions of "society" that are used by the thinkers themselves.

FOLK MODELS AS BASIS FOR THE COMMUNITY FOCUS IN NORTH AMERICAN VIEWS ON THE SOCIAL NATURE OF PERSONALITY   From early in this century, the constructive nature of personal takeovers has been recognized in North American social science discourse. For example: "A social mind is not a mere taking-over of the abstract individual contents a, b, c, etc., as blocks with a new external context. It means *a new volitional unity* which must be understood as such . . . we have a *unique creative synthesis* which must be appreciated as such and cannot be stated as merely an extension of our workaday unities" (Boodin, 1913, p. 43; emphasis added).

Boodin's focus on "volitional unity" and "creative synthesis" indicates the personalizing and constructive focus that the dependence of persons on social worlds entails. In his discussion of processes of education, the pragmatist John Dewey can be spotted at the origins of the use of appropriation concept in contemporary psychology. According to Dewey, the person "appropriates the purpose" of the human world (Dewey, 1980, p. 26). Dewey's educational ideals were built upon the focus on community and the notion of active participation.

The relevance of these two notions can be traced to the collective-cultural history of the United States, where the previously British model of community organization (within social class constraints) was elevated to a general social principle. In his analysis of the social role of community in U.S. history, George Herbert Mead pointed out: "When the colonies threw off their allegiance to the English crown and entered the family of independent nations, they had brought about a change which was even more profound than their political revolution . . . When they recognized themselves as citizens it was no longer as members of the English social hierarchy. For this they had substituted *a political national structure which was a logical development of the town meeting*" (Mead, 1930b, p. 212; emphasis added).

This community-centered unit of active participation (town meeting) is thus an outgrowth of the British community focus, under strict limits of social class boundaries. The focus on the given form of social organization is usually paralleled by an ideology that glorifies it—an example of semiotic regulation of the collective culture. Therefore, it is not surprising that the positive flavor of the community focus arrives in the thinking of North American sociocultural psychologists who assume an activity-theoretic position. They remain guided by the halo effects of community participation (Ratner, 1996).

The impact of these Anglo-American folk models of community-centeredness (and of individuals' "common union" with other persons as the basis for individual adaptation) can be found in many domains of social sciences. The wish to "restore the harmony" of relations between persons and societies through persuading persons that their desired state of being is that of active immersion within a community underlies many a scholarly effort in the contemporary social sciences. Exaggeration of such basic sublime moral agendas may hide some of the reality from the investigator. While it is undoubtedly a basic fact that human beings live within *some* form of communal social organization, it does not necessarily follow that the primary (or personally preferred) form of such organization is that of participatory community democracy. Efforts to assume that this is so may lead to basic oversights in the understanding of the "sociocultural other." Our reanalysis of Edward Banfield's "amoral familism," a label he applied to particular southern Italian forms of community organization, demonstrated how profound such interpretational oversights may become (Benigni and Valsiner, 1995).

RUSSIAN-MARXIST ACTIVITY THEORY OF A. N. LEONTIEV
Among the many activity-theoretic approaches that have emerged from the context of Russian psychology over the past century, that of Alexey N. Leontiev has undoubtedly been most emphasized within the context of appropriation discourse. In the context of psychology as it developed in the Soviet Union, the overlay of continental European psychological traditions by Marxist-based ideological discourse laid the foundation for the use of the appropriation term in Leontiev's activity theory (Leontiev, 1975, 1981). Largely following Marx, Leontiev saw the notion of labor as the starting point for the emergence of human psychological qualities

(Menschengattung). Through activity, human beings change their environments, and through that change they build up their own novel psychological functions. This relationship involves two directed, mutually complementary processes: objectification of the environment *(Vergegenständigung)* and appropriation (Russian: *prisvoenie,* German: *Aneignung*—Leontiev, 1981, p. 195).

Leontiev's focus on *prisvoenie* was a theoretical argument on his move from a general Marxist philosophical basis toward concrete psychology of activity. *Prisvoenie* built a bridge between the historical heritage of human beings and the process by which new generations take over that heritage. Interestingly, the terms he used to explain the contrast of the specifically human processes remain unclear:

> The main characteristic of the process of making-one's-own [*usvoenie*], "appropriation" [*"prisvoenie"*] or mastery [*ovladenie*] . . . is that it creates for the person new capabilities, new psychological functions. In this it differs from the learning process of animals. When the latter is a result of individual *adaptation* of the species-specific behavior to the conditions of survival, making-one's-own [*usvoenie*] is a process of *re-production* [*vosproizvedenie*] in the characteristics of the individual of the historically emerged characteristics and capabilities of the human species. (Leontiev, 1981, p. 420)

Leontiev's parallel use of the terms *usvoenie, prisvoenie,* and *ovladenie* creates a conceptual complication: each of these terms sets up a partial focus on the process of the person's "taking over" a historically formed heritage of the social world. More than mere nuances of word choice are involved here. Of the three terms, only *prisvoenie* refers to a two-sided process of taking over some external heritage. It entails the person's active effort to take over such heritage, in unity with that heritage (through its promoters) orienting itself to be taken over by the person. *Prisvoenie* refers to a person taking over (more exactly: assigning something to) oneself, as well as somebody else assigning something (or promoting something) to the person. In contrast, *usvoenie* refers to the person's active learning of some suggested models or skills, while *ovladenie* refers to mastery, or control, over the use of these models or skills. *Ovladenie* implies the usability of these skills in other contexts than those used for their formation *(usvoenie)*. Thus, the active person (involved in *prisvoenie* of the heritage of the human species to oneself) is learning the particular skills to a level of sufficiency *(usvoenie)*, as the latter result entails mastery *(ovladenie)* of these skills for their possible constructive transfer to novel contexts.

In the three terms used by Leontiev, the individual person is encoded as *the active agent who makes something that was not one's own into something new that belongs to the person,* albeit in a novel form. However, there is no notion of the "immersion" of the person's agentive role in the "community" of a *concrete* social context. Leontiev's story about the social heritage is general abstract talk about the cultural history of *Homo sapiens* as a whole, and not that of one or another kind of small community (e.g., participation in a town meeting—cf. Bronckart, 1995, p. 76).

The appropriated psychological functions, according to Leontiev, are internal—hence Leontiev's focus on the constructive nature of internalization process (Del Río, 1994, p. 22). Leontiev did not eliminate the directionality of the "internal" ↔ "external" contrast from his focus on the unity of the personal and the social. In fact, he stressed just the opposite— the process of appropriation can happen *because of* the "inner" ↔ "outer" contrast:

> Interiorization of the action, i.e., gradual transformation of external actions into internal, mental actions, is a process that necessarily takes place in human ontogeny. Its necessity is defined by the fact that the central contents of the child's development is the child's appropriation [*prisvoenie*] of the results of the historical development of mankind, including achievements of human thought, human cognition. These achievements appear in front of him in the form of external phenomena—objects, verbal meanings, knowledge. (Leontiev, 1981, p. 391)

Thus interiorization (or internalization) is the specific process in ontogeny through which appropriation takes place (also Leontiev, 1983, pp. 148–152). Yet at the same time this internalizaton extends forth to the realm of external activity—the active person brings his or her own psychological world to bear upon the world of objects. The "personality-sense" *(lichnostnyi smysl)*—which emerges in the internalization process—makes the person active in further encounters with the world.

APPROPRIATION IN MIKHAIL BAKHTIN'S WRITINGS   Much of contemporary sociogenetic and discursive thinking in psychology has relied on the Russian literary scholar Mikhail Bakhtin for substantiation of the turn toward complex socio-pragmatic psychological phenomena. It should be remembered that Bakhtin's target of investigation was literature (the novel, in particular), and not human psychological functioning in its everyday contexts.

While analyzing novels, Bakhtin certainly turned to wider issues of the role of language in social life. Such generalization has made it possible to apply some of Bakhtin's ideas to psychology. The most frequently quoted example of the notion of appropriation in Bakhtin's writings pertains to the role of "the word" (conceived widely as discourse) in the subjective worlds of language users. Bakhtin viewed "the word" (or discourse) as a "boundary phenomenon" that exists between the active person and the social world. From this standpoint,

> The word of language—is half alien [*chuzoye*—not belonging to me and unknown—in Russian] word. It becomes "one's own" when the speaker inhabits it with his intention, his accent, masters the word, brings it to bear upon his meaningful and expressive strivings. Until that moment of appropriation [*prisvoenie* in Russian] the word is not existing in neutral and faceless language (the speaker does not take the word from a dictionary!), but [it exists] on the lips of others, in alien contexts, in service of others' intentions: from here it has to be taken and made into one's own. (Bakhtin, 1934/35—see Bakhtin 1974/1975, p. 106)

Bakhtin's explicit emphasis on the active role of the person—who is the agent who makes the alien word to be one's own—restores the focus on duality to the study of persons' relations with their languages. The latter are not uniform (not taken from a dictionary) but represent *intentional, goal-oriented uses* of language for their own *personal* purposes. The use of the term *prisvoenie* guarantees the personally active, yet bidirectional, nature of the described processes. Appropriation takes place in the middle of heterogeneity of personal efforts by "social others" (see further in chapter 6). A number of contemporary investigators have transposed Bakhtin's focus on appropriation of languages to a more general understanding of communication (Shotter, 1993a). Nevertheless, there is some recognition of human personal agency in contemporary sociocultural perspectives, which leads one to reconsider how appropriation might be another form of internalization. For example,

> Identity is objectively defined as location in a certain world and can be subjectively appropriated only *along with* that world. Put differently,

all identifications take place within horizons that imply a specific social world. The child learns that he is what he is called. Every name implies a nomenclature, which in turn implies a designated social location. To be given identity involves being assigned a specific place in the world. As this identity is subjectively appropriated by the child ("I *am* John Smith"), so is the world to which this identity points. Subjective appropriation of identity and subjective appropriation of the social world are merely different aspects of the *same* process of internalization, mediated by the same significant others. (Berger and Luckmann, 1973, p. 152)

The irony of the dispute between proponents of appropriation and internalization terms in sociocultural theorizing is that the target phenomena for which these terms are coined are indeed "boundary phenomena"—existing in the process of transaction between the person and the social context. Both the realm of immediate activity and immediate (as well as postmediate and premediate) reflection about what is happening in these contexts exist at the same time. One of these realms—that of activities—can be easily viewed in its external (from my point of view, externalizing) form of conduct. Persons can be shown to "take over" specific forms of conduct from others and to create novel forms of conduct, thus demonstrating the constructive nature of the appropriation process. Yet this process exists only due to the mechanisms of internalization and externalization.

Contemporary Uses of the Appropriation Concept

Within much of the contemporary sociocultural tradition, the appropriation term is often used indiscriminately to refer to the whole of the human psychological system, including the intrapsychological realm of reflectivity—to "take over" (let it be constructively, with modifications and innovations) the indiscriminate world of collective culture, or social knowledge, or discursive practices, as a whole. It is here that the appropriation term tends to take on a general "umbrella role," creating an illusion of explanation of the processes involved in human development, with the side effect of blocking detailed inquiry.

A number of directions in contemporary sociocultural psychology have arrived at a preference for the appropriation concept over internalization. It is instructive to trace their reasons for such preferences.

PERSPECTIVES THAT RELATE TO DIFFERENT NOTIONS OF
ACTIVITY   Michael Cole's efforts to understand the social nature of
human psychological functions span more than the last two decades (Cole,
1975, 1981, 1990, 1992, 1995; Cole and Bruner, 1971; Laboratory of
Comparative Human Cognition, 1983). Cole's emphasis on socially organized transfer between contexts leads him to the use of the appropriation term (Newman, Griffin, and Cole, 1989, pp. 62–65). Culture
provides a range of cultural mediating devices (tools or signs) to the developing child in specific activity contexts; the child actively takes over (appropriates) those cultural means, reconstructing them in the process of
activity. For Cole, the main mechanism by which culture and person are
related is that of *mutual interweaving*. For example, Cole (1992, p. 26)
uses the metaphor of "intermingling of threads from two ropes"—those
of biological "modules" and cultural contexts. This notion of interweaving reflects the general process in which "the culture becomes individual
and the individuals create their culture" (Laboratory of Comparative Human Cognition, 1983, p. 349). In other words, culture and cognition are
mutually constituted, with the locus of this mutual constituting process
found in the concrete activities of everyday life (see Cole, 1985; Newman,
Griffin, and Cole, 1989). The cognitive processes that are established
within activity contexts can be transferred to other contexts under social
facilitation of such transfer.

CULTURAL "VOICES" IN (AND AROUND) THE MIND   James
Wertsch's emphasis on semiotic mediation of thinking persons (1985a,
1989, 1991, 1995b; Wertsch and Smolka, 1993) is built upon semiotic
(Vygotsky), activity-theoretic (Leontiev), and discursive (Bakhtin) bases.
Wertsch sets up the *dynamic process of situation redefinition* as the primary
means by which persons involved in a joint activity context guide one
another's development.

Interaction partners are constantly in some relation of intersubjectivity—they share similar situation definition—which they transcend by the
process of situation redefinition (Wertsch, 1984, pp. 7–13). Communication about the situation definition (and redefinition) takes place by semiotic means, and the structure of the activities involved guides that communication (Wertsch, Minick, and Arns, 1984). Wertsch unifies his
semiotically mediated activity approach with the wider sociolinguistic context (see Wertsch, 1985a; Wertsch and Stone, 1985). He has also combined that focus with Lotman's semiotic approach to communication and

with Tulviste's view on the heterogeneity of thinking processes (Tulviste, 1991; Wertsch, 1991). Bakhtin's legacy allows Wertsch to advance his theory of communication into the realm of conceptualizing *processual relations* between the components in a dialogue (i.e., different "voices").

Even as activity framing remains in the background of Wertsch's accounts, the main focus becomes the level of utterance as appropriate for analysis of the dialogue of "voices" in and around the mind. A "voice" is a label for a segment in the flow of semiotic reflection (word, utterance) upon experiencing by the person that is recognizable as "half somebody else's" (to use the widely quoted Bakhtinian description). The origins of a "voice" can be specifiable in personal (e.g., the person recognizes his or her mother's or father's "voice" in one's internal dialogue) or socio-institutional terms (e.g., recognition of a "social language" on the basis of some part of the utterance). The latter "voices" can come close to social representations (e.g., the case of "democracy"—Moody, Markova, and Plichtova, 1995) or become functional in terms of different models of "national history" that may be used as mediating devices in identity construction (Wertsch, 1997).

Wertschian discourse about "voices" makes creative use of the notions of dialogicality—any "voice" evokes its opposite counterpart ("counterword" or "countervoice"). Human reflexive processes make use of others' "voices" appropriated by oneself, in an always dialogic and often "multivoiced" manner:

> In parody a single concrete voice produces an utterance, but it incorporates the expressions of another voice in such a way that this second voice can be heard as well, resulting in a "multi-voiced" utterance. Thus if a speaker repeats the utterances of a well-known politician by producing these utterances with a different intonation or in contexts that differ from those in which the original utterances occurred, the parodic effect (be it humor, sarcasm, or whatever) derives from the simultaneous presence of *two* voices. Indeed, it is only if one hears both voices that a parodic effect is produced. (Wertsch and Smolka, 1993, p. 74)

The result of the multivoicedness of human reflection is an ambivalence among the systems of "voices" that are present in communicative messages—in the form of "polyphony of voices" or "heteroglossia" (Wertsch, 1985b, pp. 62–68). Different "voices" can be seen in the utterances in ways that "interanimate" or dominate each other in the act of speaking in

situated activity contexts. For instance, there can be a "privileging" relation between "voices" (i.e., the "foregrounding" of voice X while voice Y
is simultaneously "backgrounded"). Such construction of different kinds
of dialogic relationships between "voices" is a central issue for Wertschian
analysis of psychological phenomena (Wertsch, 1990, pp. 119–122).

The dynamic differentiation by way of temporary dominance relations
("privileging" one "voice" relative to another) makes Wertsch's theory
appreciative not only of the fluidity of mental phenomena but also of their
social-institutional and historical situatedness. In fact, we can see Wertsch
allowing for differentiation in the sphere of "voices" (e.g., different appropriated "voices" are distinct from one another and form dialogic relationships with one another), while the differentiation of the appropriation
process itself (in terms of allowing for the separation of the "mind" and the
"external social world") is left purposefully unclear. Wertsch consistently
emphasizes Bakhtin's notion that "word is always half somebody else's" as
the cornerstone for appropriation, yet he does not elaborate upon the
other half (i.e., the half that is presumably the person's "own").

Wertsch's theoretical perspective has been developed further in analyses
of voices explicated in educational settings (Pino, 1994; Smolka, 1994b;
Smolka, Góes, and Pino, 1995). Different dynamic forms of interplay
between voices have been demonstrated in classroom activities (Smolka,
1990, 1994b). Analyzing cultural voices within persons' situatedness in
activity contexts is linked with the emphasis on appropriation. The relationship between appropriated voices can be both polyphonic and dynamic
(e.g., different externalizations of different voices occurring at different
times), and synthesis of new meanings in the dialogue between the voices
has been demonstrated (Wertsch and Smolka, 1993).

ETHNOGRAPHY OF PARTICIPATORY APPROPRIATION   Bar-
bara Rogoff has been an active promoter of the cultural nature of situated
cognition over the recent decade (Rogoff, 1982, 1986, 1990, 1992, 1993;
Rogoff and Lave, 1984). Her own focus is mostly ethnographic, which
allows her to take into account intricacies of complexity of the culture-
embedded mentality in action. Rogoff is consistent in her emphasis on context linkage of all developmental processes all of the time (Rogoff, 1990,
1993). She provides an explicit solution to the problem of the context,
viewing it as the *sociocultural activity* that involves "active participation of
people in socially constituted practices" (Rogoff, 1990, p. 14) that acts as
the unit of analysis. The active (but not always persistent) guidance of the

developing person by the "social others" is complemented by the person's constructive role in his or her own development. The child is always an active apprentice who participates in the socially guided activity settings. The use of the metaphor of apprenticeship allows Rogoff to emphasize the active but subordinate role of the developing child in his or her ontogeny.

Rogoff prefers the concept of *appropriation* of culture (see Rogoff, 1993, pp. 139–141), explicitly relating it to the educational ideology of John Dewey (see Rogoff, 1993, pp. 126–127). Rogoff follows Dewey's lead in emphasizing the intermediary role of environment (as the totality of social conditions) and the union of the person with the community, within which appropriation takes place. Thus, Rogoff is indebted to Dewey's pragmatism.

Rogoff's notion of *participatory appropriation* entails acceptance of transformation of cultural forms into novel states (both by persons and by groups): "Participatory appropriation involves individuals changing through their own *adjustments* and *understanding* of the sociocultural activity" (Rogoff, 1993, p. 141; emphasis added). In a similar vein,

> *Participatory appropriation* refers to how individuals change through their involvement in one or another activity, in the process of becoming prepared for subsequent involvement in related activities. With guided participation as the interpersonal process through which people are involved in sociocultural activity, participatory appropriation is the personal process by which, through engagement in an activity, individuals change and handle a later situation in ways prepared by their own participation in the previous situation. This is a process of becoming, rather than acquisition. (Rogoff, 1995, p. 142)

It is obvious that the personal mental world is not denied (Rogoff, 1992) but merely left outside of the focus of empirical ethnographic analysis, while the main emphasis is put on individual change through activity through which participation takes place. This focus sets up description of persons' activities within local social settings as a positive methodological ideal.

Rogoff's emphasis on the creative (constructive) open-endedness of the appropriation process is relevant from the viewpoint of the appropriation versus internalization dispute, since it turns her theoretical system into a generative developmental framework. Culture in such a framework is never a given entity but is constantly changing by way of participating individuals who are involved in the appropriation process. However, it is the individuals who participate (rather than communities, which draw "automatic" participation from the individuals). The tension that was prominent in the creation of ideas in the case of Dewey, Cooley, and Mead (see chapter 4)—the tension between the belief in the goodness of community and distrust of any collectivity—seems to continue as an undertone in Rogoff's conceptualization of community participation.

From Appropriation to Internalization

The use of the appropriation term poses a number of difficulties, since it is an ideologically flavored complex meaning, a kind of "black box" that is utilized in theoretical constructions that actively avoid dualisms (and are about to lose dualities from their focus of attention). Appropriation is usually viewed as a constructive process (e.g., the appropriating person constructs new cultural phenomena—activities or discourses). How this personal side of construction takes place is not explicated by the use of the term; it is only claimed that it does.

When we look at the uses of the term internalization, it is not difficult to discover a similar tendency to construct a "black box" explanation (Winegar, 1993). However, in principle it might be possible to make the internalization (and its counterpart, externalization) concepts the core of making sense of person-society relations. This would be possible exactly due to the duality of the person and the (social) environment, and to locating the internalization/externalization processes between these parts of the dynamic whole.

Internalization and Externalization

The theoretical impasse of the appropriation notion is based on the inevitability of recognizing the unity of personal agency and social guidance worlds—that is, exactly the phenomena the appropriation term was supposed to cover. Thus, when "mutual constitution" of the person and the social world is discussed, it is the notion of self-regulation that emerges on the basis of interpersonal communication processes (Góes, 1994, p. 126). The process by which this self-regulation emerges is internalization/externalization. As a term, internalization has a long (and fuzzy) history of uses in psychoanalytic (Behrends and Blatt, 1985; Duindam, 1992) and developmental psychology (Goudena, 1994; Lawrence and Valsiner, 1993; Maier, 1992).

Selection and Construction

Human beings can be active in a number of ways. First, they can actively *select* from the myriad of fixed (pregiven) cultural messages. Any view of appropriation or internalization that defines the active role of a person as an agent who makes choices assumes this view on activity. The selection process may be active, but it is not constructive. The person as an active choice maker does not develop beyond the set of choices the social world has laid out in front of her or him. The notion of active role of the appropriating (or internalizing) person that would allow for development is that of a *constructor of new choices*—for oneself (in one's personal culture) and for others (by externalization and changing the collective culture). It is in this domain of theoretical thought where constructionist (e.g., Piaget) and co-constructionist perspectives in psychology coincide. This theoretical issue can be translated to a number of relevant questions:

1. Is the collective culture—heterogeneous as it may be at any moment—a fixed (even if rich) set of social suggestions, or is it an open system that develops in relationship with the appropriating or internalizing person?
2. Is the repertoire of psychological processes that are involved in appropriation or internalization a finite (even if large) set? Alternatively, is it assumed that novel psychological processes (that regulate the relation between person and environment) can emerge?
3. Are the systemic connections between the psychological processes fixed, or would the processes that participate in appropriation or internalization be amenable to dynamic reorganization of their structure?

"Selectionist" answers to these three questions would affirm the first part of each. The person actively selects from a large set of social suggestions, using some of the finite number of psychological functions as necessary means, and the structure of these functions (however complex it may be) is not altered in the process. A "constructionist" answers in the affirmative to the second alternatives. The person is viewed as reconstructing the set of social suggestions (by appropriating, or by internalizing and externalizing); within that process new psychological functions may emerge and new systemic relations between existing functions are constantly being formed.

Internalization and Externalization As Constructive Processes

The theoretical perspective that underlies the coverage of personality development in this book is straightforward. The main mechanism that organizes constructive interchange between collective and personal cultures is that of *internalization* and *externalization* (Lawrence and Valsiner, 1993; Orlov, 1992), both of which are conceptualized as mutually coordinated novelty-constructive processes. There exist both social and personal worlds, which are related by way of the internalization/externalization process. As was pointed out earlier, the duality (but not dualism) of the two worlds makes it possible to examine their mutual relations as a process.

Internalization and externalization involve a reciprocal cyclical process within which "personal sense" (in Vygotsky's sense, a complex of personally signified unique experiences) leads the construction of meanings, which are made available in the interpersonal domain. Internalization is the process by which meanings that relate to phenomena, and that are suggested for the individual by "social others" who pursue their personal goals while assuming social roles, are brought over into the individual's intrapsychological system. This "bringing-over" process involves constructive modification of the "brought-over" material by the person. The reciprocal process of externalization connotes activities by which the once-social—but now personal—set of meanings is constructively moved into novel contexts within the social environment (Valsiner and Lawrence, 1996).

Human beings are active subjects who relate to their surrounding world by way of constant construction of semiotically mediated intrapsychological (i.e., personal-cultural "stream of consciousness" à la William James) and extrapsychological (external forms of conduct and manufactured objects) psychological devices. The externalization process is constantly being culturally organized by the social expectations persons encounter in the sequence of varied activity settings that constitute their everyday lives. Inevitably, it leads to major methodological problems in the actual investigation of internalization/externalization processes (Hoogsteder, 1994; also see chapter 7).

The unity of internalization and externalization was most extensively worked out by George Herbert Mead (Valsiner and Van der Veer, 1997, chapter 6; also see chapter 4). In *both* the intrapersonal and interpersonal realms one can demonstrate human constructionism at work. While in the latter case this involves constant reconstruction of forms of everyday life in society, in the intrapersonal domain such construction entails a system of "me's" (to use Mead's terminology) or different semiotic means that allow the person different forms of psychological distancing from a given context.

Internalization and Psychological Distancing

Constructive internalization entails the establishment of hierarchically structured personal cultures that transcend the complex state of any collective culture of the given encounter context of the person and his or her society. The personal construction of such a system of personal culture builds up special psychological buffering devices that make *psychological distancing* possible in encounters with any immediate context. The person can regulate his or her own immediate perception and cognition through semiotic mechanisms of psychological distancing.

The notion of psychological distancing is not new in psychology (Bullough, 1912), and its uses continue in our present time (Sigel, 1993; Sigel, Stinson, and Kim, 1993). Its historical origins are linked with the question of *Einfühlung* (empathy, or sembling—see Wispé, 1987). In conjunction with the process of "feeling-in" with the world of others, the person constructs psychological distance relative to the object of "feeling-in"— perhaps to be labeled as "feeling-out." The person in a particular situation "feels outside" of that very situation, and through that feeling can survive and overcome the given situation. Construction of special intramental experiences that replace the actual here-and-now situation with some imaginary one, or creating a meaning for the given situation that neutralizes its relevance for the person, are two strategies of such "feeling-out."

Einfühlung and psychological distancing can be considered interdependent psychological construction processes of opposite direction—*Einfühlung* feeds into the construction of distancing, and psychological distancing allows for novel forms of *Einfühlung*. In human development, any event in the here-and-now situation that requires the person to act in accordance with the nonpresent or nonpalpable state triggers the processes of distancing (Sigel, 1970, pp. 111–112). Piaget's focus on progressing equilibration is built around the notion of a continuous flow of challenges that trigger distancing mechanisms, while the person is in some *Einfühlung* relation with the here-and-now situation. "Feeling-in" and "feeling-out" are mutually linked processes, with one creating the basis for the other and vice versa. Distancing is necessarily both the process and the product of development; in terms of differentiation and dedifferentiation processes (Werner, 1957), it is possible to find distancing in any situation where a psychological structure becomes hierarchically integrated (Sigel, 1993, p. 144).

Bullough's description of "psychical distance" illustrates the contrast between immediate relating with a context and the person's subjective separation from the context. Both immediacy and distancing are affect-laden; it could be said that thanks to the affective personal-sense construction it becomes possible for the person to achieve *both* immediacy and distancing: "Distance does not imply an impersonal, purely intellectually interested relation . . . On the contrary, it describes a *personal* relation, often highly emotionally coloured, but *of a peculiar character.* Its peculiarity lies in that the personal character of the relation has been, so to speak, filtered. It has been cleared of the practical, concrete nature of its appeal, without, however, thereby losing its original constitution" (Bullough, 1912, p. 91).

In terms of the present sociogenetic perspective on personality, such psychological distancing is made possible through human semiotic constructivity of the relations with the world. Distancing is possible thanks to the construction of hierarchically organized self- (and other-) regulation mechanisms—through meanings. One result of such hierarchical construction of levels of abstracted meanings is the emergence of aesthetic experience, which unites the immediacy and distance of the object of such experience into a novel affective whole (Baldwin, 1915; Cupchik and Winston, 1996).

Different persons in the same context necessarily construct their unique personal meaningfulness of the context, using semiotic means of different levels of generalization (as described in chapter 2 and will be covered in discussion of Bühler's "principle of abstractive relevance" in chapter 6). An illustration is provided by Bullough's example of a fog at sea:

For most people it is an experience of acute unpleasantness. Apart from the physical annoyance and remoter forms of discomfort such as delays, it is apt to produce feelings of peculiar anxiety, fears of invisible dangers, strains of watching and listening for distant and unlocalised signals. The listless movements of the ship and her warning calls soon tell upon the nerves of the passengers; and that special, expectant, tacit anxiety, and nervousness, always associated with this experience, make a fog the dreaded terror of the sea (all the more terrifying because of its very silence and gentleness) for the expert seafarer no less than for the ignorant landsman.

Nevertheless, a fog at sea can be a source of intense relish and enjoyment. Abstract from the experience of the sea fog, for the moment, its danger and practical unpleasantness, just as everyone in the enjoyment of a mountain-climb disregards its physical labour and its danger (though, it is not denied, that these may incidentally enter into the enjoyment and enhance it); direct the attention to the features "objectively" constituting the phenomenon—the veil surrounding you with an opaqueness as of transparent milk, blurring the outline of things and distorting their shapes into weird grotesqueness . . . note the curious creamy smoothness of the water, hypocritically denying as it were any suggestion of danger; and, above all, the strange solitude and remoteness from the world, as it can be found only on the highest mountain tops: and the experience may acquire, in its uncanny mingling of repose and terror, a flavour of such concentrated poignancy and delight as to contrast sharply with the blind and distempered anxiety of its other aspects. This contrast, often emerging with startling suddenness, is like a momentary switching on of some new current, or of the passing ray of a brighter light, illuminating the outlook upon perhaps the most ordinary and familiar objects. (Bullough, 1912, pp. 88–89)

Bullough's introspective example of the transformation of the immediate (i.e., dangers involved in the immediate action context) personal sense of a person on a ship's deck in a fog (or climbing a mountain) into an overwhelming feeling of aesthetic pleasure reflects the role of affective-semiotic processes in their constructive action. Both *Einfühlung* and distancing create a situation where the person simultaneously is a participant in the given context of action and transcends that context through affective-reflective abstraction processes.

The mechanism of distancing is seen as tension between what is and what is not. It is here that the "as-if" psychological construction mechanisms (à la Vaihinger) can be seen to be at work in human psychological worlds. Distancing entails comparison of the here and now with a desired ideal (future) state or with a hypothetical alternative (opposite) state. In the latter, mechanisms of distancing are the same as those of dialogic construction of novelty (through tension between opposites, between "voices" à la Bakhtin and Wertsch, or through dialogic overcoming of an opposition à la Markova).

Distancing allows for cognitive development. Thus, according to Sigel, "The discrepancy that emerges as a function of the distancing activities is thought to create an inner tension, which in turn sets cognitive activity in motion, thereby activating mental transformation, which ultimately influences the individual's representational system. Changes in the representational system provide learning experiences, which form the basis for subsequent awareness and understanding that experiences arc transformed into representations" (Sigel, 1993, p. 143).

Constructing representations is a semiotic process. It is made possible by the potentially infinite buildup of levels of generalization through semiotic mediating devices. Through these devices, a person can construct a wide variety of "personal sense" structures (à la Vygotsky) that allow for variability in distancing and its modulation over time.

Furthermore, semiotic mediating devices at different levels of generalization may enter into the regulation process of the given personality at any instant (e.g., Bullough's reference to "startling suddenness" of recognizing the given context, or Vygotsky's [1971] interest in the processes of "aesthetic synthesis" of novel feeling-meaning complexes while reading a short story). The hierarchical structure of mediating devices that create the distancing phenomena can be changed at an instant and be replaced by another constructed structure. The process of meaning-making (and re-making) entails constant change in the distancing process, from moment to moment.

MODULATION OF DISTANCING   The dynamic side of psychological distancing as a semiotic self-regulation device entails constant modulation of the person's relation with the given context—moving between various forms of immediacy and intermediacy. Across personal cultures—and within the realm of specific collective cultures—there exist large differences in the production and reception of human creations as ways of modulating psychological distance. Thus,

Many an artist has seen his work condemned, and himself ostracized for the so-called "immoralities" which to him were *bonâ fide* aesthetic objects. His power of distancing, nay, the necessity of distancing feelings, sensations, situations which for the average person are too intimately bound up with his concrete existence to be regarded in that light, have often quite unjustly earned for him accusations of cynicism, sensualism, morbidness or frivolity. The same misconception has arisen over many "problem plays" and "problem novels" in which the public have persisted in seeing nothing but a supposed "problem" of the moment, whereas the author may have been—and often has demonstrably been—able to distance the subject-matter sufficiently to rise above its practical problematic import and to regard it simply as a dramatically and humanly interesting situation. (Bullough, 1912, p. 95)

Undoubtedly it is the goal-oriented regulation of a person's internalization processes by "social others" that limits the person's immediate access to specific contexts of negatively flavored meanings. However, such external social regulation has its internalized counterpart. The person, though developing psychological distancing strategies through semiotic regulation of oneself, neutralizes different domains of experience within his or her personal culture and may use the distancing mechanisms to defocus his or her psychological orientation from the given side of the context (see Bullough's example of the person at sea).

Within each personal culture, the distancing function is a mechanism for regulating one's relationship with any particular new context. The mechanism can be built up to fit flexibly into a range of possible new settings. In context X a person can distance him- or herself from the immediate demands (through a reconstructed meaning); in the next context Y, he or she may unwillingly be "carried away" by the immediacy of a situation and the distancing mechanisms may not be brought into function; and when subsequently entering context Z he or she may again display extended distancing. Consider a person entering a church. She may effectively distance herself psychologically from the beggar asking for alms at the entrance, through an internal train of thought ("He is not real, he only pretends to be poor"); then get carried away by the priest's sermon (on the need to care for fellow human beings); and, after leaving the church, visit her friend for a coffee-table gossip (during which she may speak eloquently about the need for caring for the poor, and criticizing the government for not doing enough to eliminate poverty and beggars from the society). The person can flexibly move between different (more or less abstracted) forms of distancing—including that of "zero-distancing," or "fusion" of the self with the context. While the theoretical efforts to use the appropriation concept have emphasized the orientation of persons to become united with their sociocultural contexts, in the case of distancing mechanisms we can include "zero-distancing" among many other forms, made possible by the semiogenetic nature of human personality (see chapter 6). The person may be under external (contextual) expectations of operating within some specific range of distancing, yet the personal co-constructive nature of relating with any context can lead to renegotiation of that range, depending upon the personal culture and present goal orientations. This co-constructive process makes it possible for some persons to show their indignation at all the "pornography" of classic (yet "naked") Greek sculptures after visiting art museums and for others to enjoy a city's garbage dump as the most pleasing "aesthetic experience" of our postmodern over-industrialized consumer societies.

CONSTRUCTION OF DISTANCING IN PERSONALITY DEVELOPMENT   The following example taken from Carl Rogers's description of a patient indicates how distancing emerges within the structure of personality. A certain "Miss Har" expressed the following range of feelings about her father:

1. "I feel *nothing but hatred* for my father, and I am *morally right* in feeling this" [the father had left her mother]
2. "I have experienced dislike for my father in my contacts with him"
3. "I am like my father in several ways, *and this is shameful*" [Miss Har had also experienced positive feelings towards her father, in ways that looked inconsistent with the rest of her personality] (Rogers, 1951, p. 528; emphasis added)

This pattern of reported sentiments illustrates the use of signs in regulating one's feelings. First, by suggesting a boundless range of hatred ("nothing but"), together with claiming substantiation for such hatred by way of a general tautological claim ("I am morally right"), the patient seems to be attempting to canalize herself toward uniform negative feeling. Yet the recognition of similarity is there too—and semiotically marked as "shameful."

From this involved and ambivalent starting point, after sessions of psychotherapy, the following subpattern of Miss Har's personality emerged:

1. "I perceive that my mother hates my father and expects me to do the same"

2. "I dislike my father *in some ways and for some things*"
3. "And I also like him *in some ways and for some things,* and *both of these experiences are an acceptable part of me*" (Rogers, 1951, p. 530; emphasis added)

The person has moved from an immediate ambivalent ego-involved set of feelings to the construction of distance. This happens through the construction of meta-level personal sense, which allows the person to accept both the positive and negative sides of the father without being fused with either in her feelings. This feeling with distance allows for construction of stability in the personality system. It entails the construction of a new level of personal sense, which is distanced from the immediate feelings and therefore can regulate those feelings. It is interesting to note here the emergence of the awareness of the social suggestion attributable to the mother. It is in the realm of internalization processes that such distancing structures emerge—with or without external social support (e.g., psychotherapy, or social suggestions from social institutions or persons).

If we view internalization and externalization as a united bidirectional constructive process—leading to the construction of semiotic mechanisms of psychological distancing—we need to look for the particular process mechanisms that emerge. The immediate differentiation and dedifferentiation of semiotic control hierarchies constitute the microgenetic process of regulating any here-and-now setting. Symbol formation through such distancing can become long-lived in the ontogeny of personal culture, as well as in the collective culture (Ohnuki-Tierney, 1981).

It seems possible to reinterpret some very traditional concepts of personality organization from the viewpoint of semiotic distancing mechanisms. Let us consider the rich repertoire of "ego-defense" mechanisms as results of the internalization/externalization processes. These mechanisms function as relatively stable regulators of the functioning of the personality. Even as at first described (and labeled) in the psychoanalytic discursive context as mechanisms of defense, they can be equally well viewed as *ego-constructive* (as they emerge in ontogeny) and *ego-maintaining* (after their emergence). These mechanisms make it possible for the person to endure different challenges from the environment; thus they regulate the difference between the person's "open" and "closed" states for further developmental change. In order to understand how a person can undergo dramatic transformations in his or her life-course development, we need to understand the mechanisms that in parallel, limit such openness to developmental change, thus guaranteeing relative stability alongside a potential for change.

"Ego-Defense" Mechanisms As Means of Self-Construction

In the history of personality psychology, ego-defense mechanisms give us a good example of psychological phenomena of externalization. These mechanisms can be viewed as self-constructing structures, cocreated by the person and the world of social suggestions (as mediated via collective culture) that makes up the person's life-world. These mechanisms can be viewed as constraining the person's conduct in the movement from the present to the future. This focus on self-constraining extends the original focus of the psychoanalytic notion of defense mechanisms, which concentrated on connections between past traumatic experiences and the present. Defense mechanisms are not viewed as ways to "defend" the existing and persisting personality organization but as constructive mechanisms that guide the person's further development. These guidance mechanisms are generalized strategies of preemptive adaptation to *possible* next experiences (see Bergson's concept of adaptation in chapter 4). As such, they limit the future possible experiences of the person and lead the construction of their affective-semiotic nature (see chapter 6).

The notion of ego-defense mechanisms has been around since 1894, when Freud introduced it in the context of his developing psychoanalytic system. In the term's earliest meaning, mechanisms of unconscious defense were "an attempt to repress an incompatible idea which had come into distressing opposition to the patient's ego" (Freud, 1896/1962, p. 162). Freud axiomatically attributed such tensions to childhood sexual trauma, caused by persons close to the developing child. Freud's own defenses can be traced in his commentary upon the lives of his (middle-class Viennese) patients. Claiming to have analyzed thirteen cases, Freud commented:

> The childhood traumas which analysis uncovered in these severe cases had all to be classed as grave sexual injuries; some of them were positively revolting. Foremost among those guilty of abuses like these, with their momentuous consequences, are nursemaids, governesses, and domestic servants, to whose care children are only too thoughtlessly entrusted; teachers, moreover, figure with regrettable fre-

quency. In seven out of these thirteen cases, however, it turned out that blameless children were the assailants; those were mostly brothers who for years on end had carried on sexual relations with sisters a little younger than themselves. No doubt the course of events was in every instance similar to what it was possible to trace with certainty in a few individual cases; the boy, that is to say, had been abused by someone of the female sex, so that his libido was prematurely aroused, and then, a few years later, he had committed an act of sexual aggression against his sister, in which he repeated precisely the same procedures to which he himself had been subjected. (Freud, 1896/1962, pp. 164–165)

Freud's reliance on culturally constructed models of social roles (e.g., those of nursemaids and governesses), together with the folk model of male defense in relations between genders (e.g., uncontrollable male sex drives, triggered by female seduction) can be observed in this quote. The deductive focus of his (and other psychoanalysts') analyses has often followed such folk constructions as if they were axiomatic givens (see chapter 4 on Obeyesekere's overcoming of Freud's system and chapter 9 for alternative organizational forms of human sensuality). However, on the side of case presentations of ego defense, psychoanalytic discourse remains unsurpassed in drawing our attention to complex psychological realities.

Freud's Conceptualization of Primary and Secondary Defenses

For Freud, all obsessional ideas were seen as transformed self-reproaches that emerge from repression of prepubertal sexual-traumatic events (or fantasies). In the process of repression, the *primary defense mechanisms* are built up in ontogeny. Freud outlined two processes by which obsessional ideas emerge on the basis of traumatic experiences or fantasies. The first includes typical obsessional ideas,

in which the content engages the patient's attention and, as an affect, he merely feels an indefinite unpleasure, whereas the only affect which would be suitable to the obsessional idea would be one of self-reproach. The content of the obsessional idea is distorted in two ways in relation to the obsessional act of childhood. First, *something contemporary is put in the place of something past;* and secondly, *something sexual is replaced by something analogous to it that is not sexual.* These two alterations are the effect of the inclination to repress, still in force, which we'll ascribe to the "ego." The influence of the re-activated pathogenic memory is shown by the fact that the content of the obsessional idea is still in part identical with what has been repressed or follows from it by a logical train of thought. (Freud, 1896/1962, p. 170; emphasis added)

Through positing unidirectional replacement in service of repression (i.e., contemporary and nonsexual to replace past sexual trauma), Freud successfully narrowed his analysis to the sociomoral basis of his psychoanalytic movement. What became defocused was a possible *reverse* substitution—of present problems of any (not just sexual) kind by construction of narratives of past events (also nonsexual). Contemporaneous symbolic substitutions of present-day problems with present-day meaningful imagery (see chapter 4) were likewise eliminated from the investigator's field of attention.

The second mechanism of emergence of obsessional ideas was posited to include transformation of the affect of self-reproach into any other unpleasurable affect. This leads the substituted affect to become conscious: "*Self-reproach* (for having carried out the sexual act in childhood) can easily turn into *shame* (in case someone else should find out about it), into *hypochondriacal anxiety* (fear of the physical injuries resulting from the act involving the self-reproach), into *social anxiety* (fear of being punished by society for the misdeed), into *religious anxiety*, into *delusions of being noticed* (fear of betraying the acts of other people), or into *fear of temptation* (a justified mistrust in one's own moral powers of resistance), and so on" (Freud, 1896/1962, p. 171).

This multilinearity in the emergence of forms of primary defense indicates Freud's recognition of the open-systems nature of development (where multilinearity, leading to variability, is the norm). At the same time, it narrowed Freud's own search for predecessors to a single point of departure (self-reproach for sexual acts of the past), limiting psychoanalytic practices to the search for reverse connections from the outcome (manifested symptoms) to the axiomatically presumed antecedent. For instance, "religious anxiety" may be posited to also emerge on antecedent bases other than sexuality-based self-reproach—a possibility that would not be emphasized in the Freudian theoretical system.

For Freud, the *secondary defense* mechanisms emerge to protect the ego against obsessional ideas (as those have emerged in some form of primary defense). These take the form of obsessional actions—personal rituals performed without aggression, but as a necessary preemptive effort not to become subjected to the results of repression:

> Secondary defence against the obsessional ideas may be effected by a forcible diversion on to other thoughts with a content as contrary as possible. This is why *obsessional brooding*, if it succeeds, regularly deals with abstract and *suprasensual* things; because the ideas repressed are always concerned with *sensuality*. Or else the patient tries to make himself master of each of his obsessional ideas singly by logical work and by having recourse to his conscious memories. This leads to *obsessional thinking*, to a *compulsion to test things*, and to *doubting mania*. The advantage which perception has over memory in such tests at first causes the patient, and later compels him, to collect and store up all the objects with which he has come into contact. Secondary defence against obsessional *affects* leads to a still wider set of protective measures which are capable of being transformed into obsessional acts. These may be grouped according to their purpose: *penitential* measures (burdensome ceremonials, the observation of numbers), *precautionary* measures (all sorts of phobias, superstition, pedantry, increase of the primary symptom of conscientiousness); measures to do with *fear of betrayal* (collecting scraps of paper, seclusiveness), or to ensure *numbing* [of the mind] (dipsomania). (Freud, 1896/1962, p. 173)

When viewed from a co-constructionist viewpoint, the person can be seen to construct specific actions and meanings to reorganize the intial repression-based emergent defenses. Conflicting impulses set the defense mechanisms into action. The variety of specific mechanisms guarantees redundant protection of the personality, and the separation of primary and scondary mechanisms speaks of the active effort by the personality to regulate the world of substitutions for the initial traumatic events or fantasies. Both the intrapsychological and extrapsychological worlds can be the sources of unpleasure against which ego defense mechanisms are set into action. While acting, they transform both the function of these events and the personality system itself, thus participating in further development.

Multiplicity of Ego-Defense Mechanisms

Ever since the introduction of the concept of defense, psychoanalytic literature has prolifically described and labeled new defense mechanisms. This ever-increasing complexity of defense mechanisms is not merely an artifact of psychoanalysts' prolific publishing practices. Rather, the constructive nature of ego-defense mechanisms leads to the emergence of new versions of ego defense in the very process of psychoanalysis. This creativity has been well recognized by Therese Benedek: "We are always surprised at the versatility and inexhaustibility of psychic reactions. Again and again we find that the patient—like a child adjusting itself to the rules of adult education—will adjust himself to the rules of the analysis of resistance. Any interpretation, any attitude of the analyst, makes the patient expect a repetition, and the next defense-reaction will be more complicated by the reaction of this expectation" (Benedek, 1937, p. 118).

The explication of defense mechanisms is itself an object of defense—with the result that psychoanalysis has had to cope with the same methodological problems as are surfacing in the case of discursive or co-constructionst perspectives (see chapter 7).

The contribution of Anna Freud to the elaboration of the ego-defense system is classic in this context. Without accepting the psychoanalytic theoretical system, a careful analysis of the phenomena subsumed under the names of different mechanisms can widen the range of phenomena treated from a sociogenetic perspective.

DISPLACEMENT AND REVERSAL   A person can deny a painful fact and through fantasy turn it into its pleasurable opposite. Anna Freud provided an example of a seven-year old boy who, in his fantasy,

> owned a tame lion, which terrified everyone else and loved nobody but him. It came when he called it and followed him like a little dog, wherever he went. He looked after the lion, saw to its food and its comfort in general, and in the evening made a bed for it in his own room. As is usual in daydreams carried on from day to day, the main fantasy became the basis of a number of agreeable episodes. For example, there was a particular daydream in which he went to a fancy dress-ball and told all the people that the lion, which he brought with him, was only a friend in disguise. This was untrue, for the "disguised friend" was really his lion. He delighted in imagining how terrified the people would be if they guessed his secret. At the same time he felt that there was no real reason for their anxiety, for the lion was harmless so long as he kept it under control. (Freud, 1966, p. 74)

In the psychoanalytic interpretation of this case, we can observe a claim of substitution (the threatening father figure is assumed to be located behind the lion figure) and reversal (of the anxiety-producing animal by a tamed friendly one). However, from a sociogenetic perspective we can observe the semiotic construction of a field of symbolic action (see chapter 6); the construction of the "trickster" scenario indicates how personality organizes itself within an imaginary world.

RESTRICTION OF THE EGO   Human personality can preemptively restrict itself and avoid encounters with dangerous situations, in external reality as well as in fantasy. This avoidance is not inhibition but rather a developed form of conduct that selects out certain experiences that might be painful, following some previous unpleasurable experience. For instance,

> A little girl of ten went to her first dance, full of delightful anticipation. She fancied herself in her new frock and shoes, upon which she had expended much thought, and she fell in love at first sight with the handsomest and most distinguished-looking boy at the party. It happened that, although he was a total stranger, he had the same surname as she, and around this fact she wove a fantasy that there was a secret bond between them. She made advances on him but met with no encouragement. In fact, when they were dancing together, he teased her about her clumsiness. This disappointment was at once a shock and a humiliation. From that time on she avoided parties, lost her interest in dress, and would not trouble to learn to dance. For a little while she took some pleasure in watching other children dance, when she would look on gravely without joining in, refusing any invitation to dance herself. . . Having given up feminine interests, she set herself to excel intellectually and in this roundabout way she finally won the respect of a number of boys of her own age. (Freud, 1966, pp. 100–101)

The personality becomes involved in self-constraining (see chapter 2 for discussion of mechanisms) that guides the realm of potential experiences away from the range of unpleasurable ones. Self-constructed zones of free movement—for conduct and sense-making of the world—are goal-oriented. Yet the process of setting goals is one in which past experiences are constructively utilized to create one's own subjective world. These goal-setting processes may lead to the person's move to assume a stance of another. In psychoanalytic observations, it is the aggressive social other who is seen as the target of role assumption. However, even if such of role assumption is painstakingly visible, it is merely the "tip of the iceberg" in the realm of self-constructing assuming of others' roles (Oliveira and Rossetti-Ferreira, 1995; Rothbaum, Weisz, and Snyder, 1982; Weisz, Eastman, and McCarty, 1996—the concept of "secondary control").

IDENTIFICATION WITH THE AGGRESSOR   Through persistent imitation (or constructive, pretend play), a person can diminish the assumed dangers as the position of the danger source is assumed. The "aggressor" may be located within the realm of the social discourse of others or may be constructed by one's own fantasy.

At any time the collective culture suggests numerous appropriate "targets" for social stigmatization, and it is by way of turning these targets into objects of identification that some personalities solve the problem of defending themselves from those targets. Obviously, during World War II, the anti-German propaganda in the United States was exaggerated and extreme. Thus, in the context of pointed, intensive anti-Hitler social suggestions, cases of identification with the socially suggested aggressor could be described. Consider the following example:

Donald was an awkward, poorly coordinated youngster who, in spite of his obviously abnormal behavior, possessed charm. He was unable to maintain himself in groups because of his utter inability to defend himself against any aggression. He was unusually sensitive to any slight or trace of hostility, and it was inevitable that he should become the scapegoat and target of aggression in a group . . .

In 1943 Donald saw the motion picture "Hitler's children," and became a confirmed Nazi. When asked for his reasons, he became incoherent at times, but at other times said that he hated all Americans and wanted to see them bombed; he believed Hitler to be fond of children. It was amazing to see the consistency with which so disorganized a personality was able to adhere to a policy of determined anti-Americanism. Donald not only decorated his room and his person with swastikas, and announced to all and sundry that he was for Hitler, but he responded in what he thought the German manner to everyday situations. He rejoiced over German successes and became angry and depressed when the series of Allied victories set in, threatening that "we (the Nazis) will pay them back." He pleaded with people not to buy war bonds. Although unable to name any American airplane, he was able to identify most German types. Similarly he was unable to locate his home town of Topeka on the map, but could find Germany and its principal cities. (Escalona, 1946, p. 336)

This constitutes another example of the unity of a person's co-constructive strategies (in this case, oppositional reconstruction of social suggestions) and ego-defense mechanisms. The self-organizing nature of the identification with the "aggressor" is evident here, in the form of active—yet selective—buildup of a knowledge base, particularly in areas (geography) where the effectiveness of the boy's general education had been rather limited.

The "aggressor" can be—and is often suggested to be—an immaterial, ideally constructed image. These images are also suggested by the collective culture; the world of myths and fairy tales told to children abounds in ghost and spirit characters. These characters are often designated to be threatening, yet this may lead to co-constructive counteraction by the child, as in the following description of a seven-year old girl:

> At home, she was afraid to cross the hall in the dark, because she had a dread of seeing ghosts. Suddenly, however, she hit on a device which enabled her to do it: she would run across the hall, making all sorts of peculiar gestures as she went. Before long, she triumphantly told her little brother the secret of how she had got over her anxiety. "There's no need to be afraid in the hall," she said, "*you just have to pretend that you're the ghost who might meet you.*" This shows that her magic gestures represented the movements which she imagined ghosts would make. (Freud, 1966, pp. 110–111; emphasis added)

This girl's ritualistic conduct and its meaning illustrate the self-constraining functions of actions and semiotic devices, within the frames of ego-defense mechanisms. The self-constructed meaningful solution to the constructed problem (fear of ghosts) demonstrates the future-oriented nature of ego defense. Our understanding of these mechanisms is of course dependent upon the observation of their externalizations.

Externalization of the Internalized Material through Projection

Projection is probably the most widely known—and used—defense mechanism. Within the psychoanalytic tradition, projection has been viewed as a transfer of the causes for intrapsychological phenomena to the external world (Jelgersma, 1926, p. 353). Many cases of psychopathology—hallucinations, delusions, and so on—entail projection. Nevertheless, the mechanism of projection is a part of normal psychological existence, and its origins can be found in the difference between perceptual and thought processes:

> When we experience thought or any other mental process, if we can follow it more or less deeply to its origin we find either one or several other thoughts that have awakened the first. We discover in this way a series, varying in length, of inner mental processes, which precede the conscious thought. At the end we arrive at a perception which was projected into the external world.
>
> We cannot do the same for perception; in this case we are not able to indicate a series of mental processes that can be taken as the cause of perception. When we open our eyes or experience any other sense-perception, we have to see what is before our eyes, or feel what touches our skin. We are absolutely unable to influence our perceptions the same way as we influence our internal mental processes; these latter are partly subjected to our will, we have called them forth ourselves, and have them in our power, they are literally our possessions. (Jelgersma, 1926, p. 355)

Thus, the process of projection is a result of personal construction starting from the internalized personal-cultural world and ending in being transferred to the external world. In contrast, perception is the starting place for internalization as a constructive process.

While projection is a standard psychological mechanism involved in externalization, it can take different forms when its target is construction of personality-descriptive accounts. The most usual form that is recognized in the psychoanalytic literature is that of *direct projection*—"false perception and attribution"—in which one perceives characteristics of one's own in another person (in the case of whom these characteristics are absent). According to Allport (1979, pp. 387–388), it is "a means of solving one's conflict by ascribing to another person (or group) emotions, motives, and behavior that actually belong to the person who projects them, and not to the person who is blamed for them." Thus, the person's own existing characteristics are attributed, *as if they were perceived*, to the other, who demonstrably lacks such characteristics. This version of projection is linked with pathology (e.g., it may be involved in paranoid phenomena), yet it can be seen in the psychological world in realms as highly collective-culturally valued as politics.

In contrast, the "mote-beam" form of projection is a widespread part of normal personality organization (Ichheiser, 1947; Allport, 1979, chapter 24). It is universal in nature, as it not only is observable in individual personalities but also is collective-culturally canalized for them (Ichheiser, 1943). According to Ichheiser,

> We all tend to perceive (and to denounce) in others certain characteristics, e.g., prejudices or blind spots or ideologies or ethnocentrism, which, strangely enough, we ignore in ourselves. This lack of insight is obviously so widespread that its counterpart, namely, the ability of perceiving in ourselves those characteristics which we notice and disapprove in others, must be considered as a sign of an unusual detachment and almost "abnormally" keen insight. (Ichheiser, 1947, p. 131)

In contrast with direct, or "full" (or pathological), projection, in the case of the "mote-beam mechanism," "The *content* of the perception, *i.e., the perception of certain characteristics in other persons, is correct.* The prejudice, the ideology, the ethnocentrism are not 'projected' by us but are actually there in the other person who is the object of the given perception. And the *falsification* consists only in the *silent assumption that those characteristics are particular to the other person (or other persons) and that we ourselves are free of them*" (Ichheiser, 1947, p. 132).

As an externalization device, the "mote-beam mechanism" entails personal-cultural constraining of the given meaning (of personality term or personality characteristic X) to be applicable to the selected other person, and to be ruled out from consideration in one's own case. It is a constructive process built on some—usually not clear—perceived evidence from that other person. Since all persons are heterogeneous in their conduct, there can always be *some* facets of that conduct that legitimately afford the perception of *some* aspects of the phenomena subsumed under a particular character label. However, when the label is applied in the process of projection, the qualifiers of heterogeneity of the personality ("sometimes" the person is "somewhat" X) are eliminated, and what is constructed is the homogenized general statement "this person is X." The "mote-beam" projection is thus a process of other-oriented *overgeneralization* of the particular characteristic and creation of a homogenized *pars pro toto* erroneous picture of the other person (or persons). Since projection cannot take place without blocking of insight-oriented processes (i.e., the internalization process involving reconstruction of the meaning of the external object must be temporarily fixed), simultaneous blocking of the thought that such characteristics also exist in the case of the externalizer takes place.

A third mechanism is that of complementary projection, which is described by Gordon Allport as *"the process of explaining and justifying our own state of mind by reference to the imagined intentions and behavior of others.* To be a true instance of complementary projection, the description of the intention and behavior must be false" (Allport, 1979, p. 390). Thus, in Allport's example, "The timid housewife (who does not know the causes for her heavy burden of anxiety) fears tramps. She double-locks the doors against them, and regards all wayfarers with suspicion. She may also be an easy victim of bogey rumors" (Allport, 1979, p. 391).

The inference of the cause and effect is reversed in this attribution: from "they threaten/we fear" to "we fear/*therefore* they do threaten." Undoubtedly, this projection mechanism is powerfully controllable by any collective-cultural canalization process that simultaneously promotes the person's self-concept of vulnerability and creates the semiotic image of the "dangerous social other."

Collective-Cultural Guidance of the Development of Ego Defense

As externalized products of the personal-cultural processes, projections enter as newly constructed semiotic devices into the discursive practices of the collective culture. Overgeneralized characteristics that result from the projection ("pseudoconcepts" in Lev Vygotsky's terms) become canalization devices in the collective-cultural processes of society regulation. In ontogeny, one can observe a variety of ways in which the collective-cultural world provides input for the construction of defense mechanisms in the child. In fact, all of the "as-if" social suggestions that adults provide for children can be viewed as setting the stage for denial of the actual reality. To extend this point even further, from the sociogenetic standpoint, providing the child with challenging illusions at the given time (usually referred to as "creating the child's zone of proximal development") is a major way to assist the child's development. Thus, it is not surprising that every generation of adults creates models that are ahead of the children's current developmental status (and therefore constitute denial of reality):

> It is quite a common thing to tell even a small child "what a big boy" he is and to declare, contrary to the obvious facts, that he is as strong "as Father," as clever "as Mother," as brave "as a soldier," or as

"tough" as his "big brother." It is more natural that, when people want to comfort a child, they resort to these reversals of the real facts. The grown-ups assure him, when he has hurt himself, that he is "better now" or that some food which he loathes "isn't a bit nasty" or, when he is distressed because somebody has gone away, we tell him that he or she will be "back soon." Some children actually pick up these consolatory formulae and employ a stereotyped phrase to describe what is painful. For instance, one little girl of two years used, whenever her mother left the room, to announce the fact by a mechanical murmur of "Mummy coming soon." Another (English) child used to call out in a lamentable voice, whenever he had to take nasty medicine, "like it, like it"—a fragment of a sentence used by his nurse to encourage him to think that the drops tasted good. (Freud, 1966, p. 84)

The unity of the social suggestions→ internalization→ semiotic regulation of conduct sequence, with the complex structures of adaptation to life described as defense mechanisms, becomes clear in this example. The former constitute the basis for the latter, while the latter act as "frames" for any semiotic regulation of conduct.

The collective-cultural guidance of the construction of defense mechanisms has its limits—defined by the functioning of the personal-cultural defenses of the adults. The limited nature of such suggestions was well captured by Anna Freud:

When grown-up people consent to enter into the fictions whereby children transform a painful reality into its opposite, they invariably do so under certain strict conditions. Children are expected to keep the enacting of their fantasies within well-defined limits. A child who has just been a horse or an elephant, going about on all fours, neighing or trumpeting, must be prepared at a moment's notice to take his place at table and be quiet and well-behaved. The lion-tamer must himself be ready to obey his nursemaid, and the explorer or pirate must submit to be sent to bed just when the most interesting things are beginning to happen in the world of grown-ups. (Freud, 1966, p. 85)

The personal-cultural worlds of adults, in their turn, are guided by the heterogeneous system of cultural myths that guide their construction of personal cultures and entail similar foci on quick transformations (Boesch,

1983, 1991; see also chapter 6 for Bühler's analysis of fairy tales). Both the constructors of social suggestions (adults) whose externalizations make up collective cultures and the active recipients of these suggestions (children) construct their novel versions of understanding their selves and their worlds—all under conditions of mutual constraining.

Summary: Internalization and Externalization

A number of major points emerge from the discussion in this chapter. First, the two alternative terminological complexes of sociogenetic views on personality—those of appropriation and of internalization/externalization—differ relatively little in their functions. Both directions of thought entail explanation of the social nature of human psychological functioning. However, appropriation denies the usefulness of the "inner"-"outer" distinction, since that might retain a "dualism" of a kind that is dreaded in social sciences. The internalization/externalization viewpoint treats the subject-object distinction as a necessary construction of duality, upon which the assumptions of the existence of "inner" and "outer" psychological realms are built. If the latter distinction is made, then the use of internalization and externalization terminology becomes possible and necessary.

In this book, the duality of "inner" and "outer" realms of psychological functioning is axiomatically accepted, together with the assumption that these realms are interconnected through the bidirectional process of internalization/externalization. Nevertheless, both realms have established specific forms of existence that provide them with *relative autonomy* in respect of the immediate state of the other. The internalization/externalization process can be found to lead to establishment of self-construction processes (which in psychoanalysis have been called "ego-defense" mechanisms). From the present perspective, these mechanisms are organizational frameworks that canalize the development of personality. These mechanisms may have emerged in the personal culture on the basis of strenuous, or even traumatic, earlier experiences (not necessarily experiences based on sexuality), yet their function in human development is the organization of further development. These mechanisms are distinguished on the basis of the form of person-environment relation, while the specific meaningful contents is always context-specific.

II

HISTORICAL AND THEORETICAL FOUNDATIONS

4

Sociogenetic Perspectives on the Self

Any science begins its construction from some commonly available puzzling phenomenon and then proceeds beyond its manifest content in its efforts to explain it. The sociogenetic approach emerged at the turn of this century on the basis of public fascination in late-nineteenth-century Europe with phenomena of social suggestibility, "mesmerism," and hypnosis. The individual person obviously was not independent of the influences of others, nor was he a puppet run by the others. In terms of social ideological discourse, the person was neither "free" nor a "slave" in the psychological world. The person was at times viewed as both free and unfree, and at other times acting as if he were free, yet on occasions showing his full subservience to social demands.

The complexity of a person's relation with society led to a number of intellectual efforts to construct psychological accounts of human beings. The widespread interest in social suggestibility was functional at the conception of both the development of psychodynamic personality theories (e.g., of Freud), and to elaboration of the ideas of social influences (G. Tarde, G. Le Bon, E. Durkheim). Sociogenetic viewpoints on personality—perspectives that would accept the *social origins* of human personality, in ontogeny and in cultural history—emerge from the same collective-cultural background.

Hystericals, Mesmerists, and Psychiatrists: Ambivalence About Social Suggestibility

Access to the phenomena of social suggestion was most directly available to psychiatrists, who in the nineteenth century began to take interest in hypnosis as a method of curing mental illnesses (see Gauld, 1992, for a full historical overview). In the public sphere, different kinds of occult phenomena, publicized through the work of Franz Anton Mesmer (1734–1815), guided the public interest toward "mesmerism" (or "animal magnetism") and its puzzles. The phenomena of mind control led immediately to the fight between the occultist and scientific efforts to explain the exotic psychological events (see Janet, 1925). In the developing medical practice of psychiatry, hypnosis became usable as a therapeutic device, yet the whole nineteenth century shows inherent ambivalence—denial interspersed with fascination—toward phenomena of suggestion and hypnotism.

In France in the 1880s a new wave of interest in the titillating topics of the study of hypnotism in hysterical subjects led to the development of two decades of intense studies and fights between rival psychiatric traditions (Charcot in Paris, Bernheim in Nancy). This atmosphere of heightened intellectual quest for making sense of clinical phenomena of suggestibility, hypnosis, and its mechanisms created an intellectual background on the basis of which different sociogenetic ideas in psychology grew in the 1890s and afterward. Likewise, this intellectual atmosphere gave a basis for the development of different psychodynamic ideas, and the utilization of the notion of the unconscious in the explanatory schemes of psychology. Sigmund Freud spent four months at Charcot's clinic in 1885–1886, at the same time other relevant thinkers (Ribot, Binet, Janet) were involved with issues of hypnotism (Cairns, 1983, p. 59). His further work in psychoanalysis transposed the notions of hypnosis to similar issues without hypnosis (e.g., a person's childhood experiences creating implicit guidance for adulthood psychopathology). Likewise, James Mark Baldwin passed through Paris (and Nancy) in 1892 (Baldwin, 1892a, 1892b). France was *the* place to be for anybody interested in hypnotism in the last decades of the nineteenth century, similar to experimental psychologists' educational trips to Wundt's laboratory in Germany.

Hypnotic and Posthypnotic Suggestion

For the psychology of the end of the nineteenth century, the phenomena of hypnotic and posthypnotic suggestion constituted an interesting challenge. The fact that under hypnotic conditions it is possible to suggest to the patient something obviously untrue of the reality in the given actual context, which would not be remembered when the patient is awakened from the hypnotic sleep (i.e., hypnotic suggestion), was known in the psychiatric literature since the beginning of the century. Likewise, the phenomena of *delay* of execution of the suggestions made during the hypnotic sleep, but actualized after the patient is awakened (i.e., posthypnotic suggestion), were described around that time (Alexandre Bertrand in 1823; cf. Janet, 1925, pp. 153–154). Besides their clinical importance (e.g., the possibility of curing mental illness through the use of posthypnotic suggestion), these phenomena were of significance in the sociopolitical sphere. As with the possibilities for behavioral modeling in contemporary social learning theory, posthypnotic suggestion could be used by interested parties for making dramatic sociopolitical impacts. The dangers were serious: a person could be made into an assassin, even of a government leader or other public figure by suggesting to him or her under hypnosis to undertake the killing after waking up and to forget the fact that this course of action was suggested by the hypnotizer. If such scenarios were possible, much power for political change was suddenly in the hands of persons who could hypnotize others. Such a possibility could be both horrifying and appealing to people who occupied political positions.

It is therefore not surprising that many psychiatric demonstrations of posthypnotic suggestion were devoted to testing the limits of vulnerability to suggestion. That posthypnotic suggestion exists was not questioned, but whether a patient could be induced to act in *any* possible way was the issue for empirical testing—and of public demonstrations.

It was quite clear that posthypnotic suggestion indeed has its limits, which are related to some intrapsychological organization of the patient. Gilles de la Tourette described an incident that occurred at the clinic of Salpêtrière (Charcot's clinic) in the 1880s, during a public demonstration of the powers of hypnotic suggestion:

A number of persons of importance, magistrates and professors, had assembled in the main hall of the Salpêtrière museum to witness a great séance of criminal suggestions. Witt., the principal subject, thrown into the somnambulist state, had under the influence of suggestion displayed the most sanguinary instincts. At a word or a sign, she had stabbed, shot, and poisoned; the room was littered with corpses . . . The notables had withdrawn, greatly impressed, leaving only a few students with the subject, who was still in the somnambulist state. The students, having a fancy to bring the séance to a close by a less blood-curdling experiment, made a very simple suggestion to Witt. They told her that she was now quite alone in the hall. She was to strip and take a bath. Witt., who had murdered all the magistrates without turning a hair, was seized with shame at the thought of undressing. Rather than accede to the suggestion, she had a violent fit of hysterics. (Janet, 1925, p. 184)

The powers of hypnotic suggestion were thus found to have their limits, but the psychological mechanisms through which these limits were nego-tiable were not studied by the psychiatrists, who gained social capital in the society through showing their hypnotic powers to the powerful social others. Within the personality system of the patient, the act of undressing in the given system was powerfully blocked (see discussion of ZFM/ZPA complexes in chapter 2). However, the same patient could act out drama-tized "killings" in front of the celebrated audience. Anybody well versed in our contemporary language of "context dependency" of human action might nod approvingly: we know that human beings are context-bound. Yet what is the mechanism of such joint action of the context (of sug-gestions in the given situation) and the person's construction of his or her actions? That question remained hidden behind the dramatic demon-strations.

Social Suggestion and the Active Person: Joint Construction of Action

The demonstrations of the limits of posthypnotic suggestion led to the issue of the role of the target person in resisting and transforming these suggestions. Obviously, the earlier psychiatrists who used hypnosis were convinced of their hypnotic power over the patients. Nevertheless, the reality of posthypnotic suggestion phenomena proved that the patient played an active and constructive role in the actual realization of the sug-gestion (James, 1890, p. 605).

The role of the active person becomes even more obvious when we move from the demonstrations made in psychiatric clinics to real-life con-texts. Vladimir M. Bekhterev was a Russian psychiatrist with practical hyp-notic skills whose work on social suggestibility was of direct consequence for both clinical and social psychology (Bekhterev, 1922, 1994). Social suggestion in everyday life contexts was viewed by Bekhterev using the analogy with infectious diseases *(contagium vivum)* as a special kind of "psychological infection" *(contagium psychicum)*. Analogously to infection-carrying biological microorganisms, such psychological infection is carried by words, gestures, and other phenomena in social interaction—hence human beings are constantly receptive to social suggestions (Bekhterev, 1903, p. 5). Bekhterev's emphasis on the organism-environment interaction as the framework in which a "hidden reserve of energy" is being accumulated fits with the notion of psychological infections. Under social suggestions, different personalities accumulate the particular suggested "material" ("energy") in a way that later starts to look (from the perspective of others) as if it were the person's *own* willful act. Here we can observe an explanation of sociogenesis that builds on the model of taking in a seemingly materialistic yet indeterminate substance ("energy") that is supposed to create a person's autonomy. Both Bekhterev and Freud were clearly borrowing from the popular extensions of the concept of energy far beyond the realm of the physical sciences—a social movement initiated by Wilhelm Ostwald (see Hakfoort, 1992).

Bekhterev's view of the mechanisms of social suggestion (both in everyday life and under hypnosis) transcended the dilemma created by the traditional opposition of "self" versus "others' suggestion" *His notion of the active person led him to emphasize that in all cases of social suggestion the socially suggested material becomes related with the person's already existing "core" personality.* The latter, of course, was seen as a result of previous encounters with the world by the given person. Bekhterev viewed the implicit (we could call it "clandestine") process of everyday social suggestion as the normative context for development of personality:

> In essence, the involuntary suggestion and intersuggestion [*vzai-movnushenie*] as general phenomena, act everywhere in our everyday life. Without noticing it ourselves, we appropriate to some extent the feelings, superstitions, convictions, tendencies, ideas and even personality characteristics from persons around us, with whom we interact most frequently. That kind of inoculation of psychological states takes place mutually between people who live together, in other words, every personality to some or another degree inoculates the others with the peculiarities of his psychological nature, and in return takes from them one or another kind of psychological traits. (Bekhterev, 1903, p. 41)

The well-known clinical phenomena of folie à deux constitute a good example of these processes of mutual psychological contagion. However, even if Bekhterev viewed the main route of mutual social suggestion as taking place with minimal resistance from the person, he recognized the active role of the personality in the process of interpersonal psychological suggestion.

From his own experience with posthypnotic suggestion, Bekhterev could draw a number of instances where *the suggestion becomes transformed* on the basis of internal contradiction between the preexisting personality and the particular suggestion:

> The resistance to suggestion, if it occurs, is based on the critique, on the *discovery of the internal contradiction between the suggested ideas and the convictions of the person . . .* From here it becomes obvious that *suggestion in certain cases does not exclude even criticism* [of the suggested material by the person], *while it still does not cease to be suggestion.* This can be observed during hypnosis of mild levels when the personality or "I" that is not fully removed, still relates critically to all of the surroundings, including suggestion.
>
> I suggested to a person in hypnosis that when he wakes up he must take a postcard from the table. When he woke up, he almost immediately looked around on the table and his gaze became fixated on a certain spot. Do you see something—I asked. "I see a postcard." I said good-bye to him and prepared to leave, but he still keeps staring at the table. Don't you need to do anything?—I ask. *"I would like to take that card, but I do not need it!"*—answers the man, and leaves— not having fulfilled the suggestion and obviously fighting with it. (Bekhterev, 1903, p. 14; emphasis added)

This example of posthypnotic suggestion indicates how the person utilizes specific meanings ("I do not need it") in the active blocking of the previous suggestion made by the hypnotizer. The use of a semiotic device that repeats one's "needs" or "wants" is a flexible blocker or enabler of a range of actions (e.g., "I do X because I want to" and "it is tempting to do x but I don't want it"). In this case we see a semiotic device regulating the ZFM boundaries of a field of actions, within which the psychiatrist's suggestion has created a ZPA. Yet this circumscribed (by the psychiatrist) ZFM/ZPA complex is actively resisted by the patient—by a hierarchical control system of ZFM boundary at a meta-level. The whole incident may be described by the following scheme:

Level: Metareflection	Psychiatrist's suggestion:	Patient's co-construction: ZFM = needs vs. non-needs ("*don't need* the postcard")
		|
Reflection	instruction ("take postcard!")	ZFM = all situation ZPA = "*want* postcard"
		|
Action	ZFM = ZPA	no action

The boundary for ZFM at the metareflective level inhibits the accepted suggestion by the psychiatrist (which is transformed into an ego-centered form "I *want*"), so no action follows—even if the temptation is clearly visible in the process! This illustrates the basic notion of co-constructionism in person-society relationships: a person in a society, even if under the influence of various social suggestions, is at the same time an integrated self-system that processes these suggestions from his or her individual basis and arrives at novel actions that in this sense (of personal transformation of suggestions) are indeed his or her own.

French Sociological Traditions

Given the centrality of hypnotism and discourse about social suggestion in French society in the last quarter of the nineteenth century, it is not surprising that a number of thinkers outside of psychiatry took advantage of the collective-culturally established thought models. It was largely through the work of three major figures—Gustave Le Bon (see Moscovici, 1981a, 1985, chapter 4), Gabriel Tarde (1884, 1895a, 1895b, 1903), and Émile Durkheim—that the sociogenetic idea proliferated in the occidental social sciences.

Le Bon's (1841–1931) psychology of crowds (Le Bon, 1895) provides an example of the value-laden nature of any treatment of personality. The uncontrollable power of crowds haunted Le Bon, calling for explanation of the psychological mechanisms of the social suggestibility of persons in collective action. Le Bon's opposition to socialist ideas was profound (Mead, 1899). Le Bon was characteristically "sexist" (as our semiotic marking of the texts in the 1990s would go), yet perceptive, in his reflection upon the flexibility of the crowd, as Moscovici has described:

A crowd is a woman. A woman's supposedly emotional, capricious, temperamental, and fighty nature means that she is susceptible to suggestion, and her passivity, traditional submissiveness and capacity for endurance fit her equally well for devotion. She is the harlot and the housewife, a mistress to be conquered and a betrothed to marry. There was no need for Le Bon to invent the idea that there are strong links between the eternally feminine and the eternally collective. The crowds of the French Revolution were largely made up of women. (Moscovici, 1985, p. 110)

Le Bon belonged to the middle-class tradition, from whose standpoint his dislike of crowds led him to analyze their ways of being. Different kinds of structure of the social entities involved in human action may be differentially appealing and threatening to a person (including a researcher). The fear of *uncontrollability* of crowds' (and women's?) potential actions might have existed for Le Bon, as well as for others. Yet solutions to this uncontrollability may take different forms: avoidance of crowd formation by strict pregiven social role structure (British and Continental social systems have often attempted this) or through structuring of the protocrowd by the democratic rules of the "town meeting" (the North American approach). Both of these routes of social action might be seen as moving toward the same outcome—homogenization of the society by its masculinization. Contemporary "gender wars" fought on the battlefields of feminism may be far from the archetype of "eternally collective" feelings!

The Laws and Processes of Imitation

Processes of mutual imitation lead persons to lose their identity in a crowd. Gabriel Tarde's (1843–1904) systematic analysis of the laws of imitation stands out as one of the anchor works on sociogenetic personality models. For Tarde, the connection between society, imitation, and clinical examples of suggestibility was close yet not undifferentiated (Tarde, 1884). By imitation, he meant "every impression of an inter-psychical photography . . . willed or not willed, passive or active" (Tarde, 1903, p. xiv). Any social relation between two living beings includes imitation.

However, as Tarde emphasized, there are two ways of imitation: to act exactly like the model or to act exactly to the contrary (the case of *counterimitation*). Furthermore, Tarde considers counterimitation as clearly distinct from nonimitation and from invention (Tarde, 1903, p. xix). Voluntary nonimitation—such as a decision not to take over specific action patterns of some other person—is a way to disassociate from some part of society or personal influence, but it does not construct a novel form of society. Rather, it entails a "logical duel" between the model and the intentional nonimitator of the model. In contrast, counterimitation has the same role in the social transfer of social models, only with a reversal: "Men often counter-imitate one another, particularly when they have neither the modesty to imitate directly nor the power to invent . . . in doing or saying exactly the opposite of what they observe being done or said, they are becoming more and more assimilated, just as much assimilated as if they did or said precisely what was being done or said around them" (Tarde, 1903, p. xvii).

Tarde's emphasis on the universality of imitation entailed the interdependence of imitation *and* invention. While the imitation brings to the person the model in its "photographic" form, that process is constantly being modulated by the process of invention.

From Durkheim to Moscovici

Émile Durkheim's (1858–1917) multiple contributions to sociology include a specific facet that has been relevant for the sociogenetic view on personality. Durkheim's application of the notion of *collective representation* to issues of human religious sentiments was partly based on the philosophical notions of Henri Bergson and on William James's reflections upon thought processes. The fluidity of human psychological processes is tempered by the use of language, which is used to exchange concepts. It is the concepts as they are represented by words that act as mediators of collective representations:

> There is a great deal of knowledge condensed in the word which I never collected, and which is not individual; it even surpasses me to such an extent that I cannot even completely appropriate all its results. Which of us knows all the words of the language he speaks and the entire signification of each?
>
> This remark enables us to determine the sense in which we mean to say that concepts are collective representations. *If they belong to a whole social group, it is not because they represent the average of the corresponding individual representations;* for in that case they would be poorer than the latter in intellectual content, while, as a matter of fact, *they contain much that surpasses the knowledge of the average individual.* They are *not abstractions* which have a reality only in

particular consciousnesses, but they are as concrete representations as an individual could form of his own personal environment: they correspond to the way in which this very special being, society, considers the things of its own proper experience. (Durkheim, 1915, p. 435; emphasis added)

Through the "surplus cultural meaning" of concepts the possibility for heterogeneous construction of personal psychological phenomena is guaranteed within the knowledge system of the society. The individual makes use of collective representations to build up his personalized meaning system, and even may attribute to himself the authorship of the meanings, yet he remains dependent upon the collective representation. This idea is similar to the parallel direction of analysis of psychological phenomena in terms attributed to Mikhail Bakhtin.

Furthermore, for Durkheim the personal construction of meanings retains the dominant and deterministic role of society:

The individual at least obscurely takes account of the fact that above his private ideas, there is a world of absolute ideas according to which he must shape his own; he catches a glimpse of a whole intellectual kingdom in which he participates, but which is greater than he. From the moment when he first becomes conscious of these higher ideas, he sets himself to scrutinizing their nature . . . Thus the faculty of conception has individualized itself. But to understand its origins and function, it must be attached to the social conditions upon which it depends. (Durkheim, 1915, p. 437)

The prevailing image of the person who constructs his or her meanings is that of a discoverer of some "area" of the field of collective representation, who takes over (appropriates) the particularly discovered and individualized nuances of that source, including the constructed illusion of personal independence of construction.

Serge Moscovici's contemporary emphasis on social representations is a historical continuation of Durkheim's idea of collective representations (Farr, 1987; Jahoda, 1988), albeit in the direction of a narrower coverage of psychological phenomena. Moscovici (1981b, 1982, 1985, 1990, 1995) has actively created a social representation of his notion of social representation, framing the use of that concept in terms of an "upcoming era," expecting to redirect social psychology toward the study of structure and dynamics of such representations, and defending his direction quite vigorously (see Moscovici, 1988b). He expects social psychology to become "an anthropology of the modern world" (Moscovici, 1990, p. 169). Indeed, the concept of social representation has led to substantive research literature (see De Rosa, 1994; Flick, 1995a; Wagner, 1994), as well as to in-depth case analyses (Jodelet, 1991).

Theoretically, however, Moscovici's system of concepts has been developing much less intensively than his dialogue with social tendencies in psychology at large. A clear explanation of what social representations mean is hard to find in the literature (for exceptions, see Flick, 1995a, 1995b). When under criticism, Moscovici has elaborated different facets of the concept. Nevertheless, its actual theoretical elaboration has yet to take place, unless the "coming era of social representation" is to turn into a passing fashion in social psychology. As far as the collective sharing of the meaning of social representations is concerned, these representations entail the following:

(a) . . . theory-like structure of hierarchically organized propositions forming a central core and a set of peripheral elements . . .
(b) . . . metaphorical form as a figurative schema . . . which results
(c) from objectification . . .
(d) . . . function of anchoring new experiences . . .
(e) . . . being collectively shared (Wagner, 1994, pp. 212–213)

The common denominator of various kinds of reflections on social representations is that they are collectively shared between persons and socially elaborated in the communication process. In his conceptual construction, Moscovici considers social representations as entailing *performative* and *constructive* functions. The representation prescribes a socially shared definition of a social situation, thus creating a basis for enabling a social group to communicate and maintain shared concepts and images (Moscovici, 1988b, p. 230). People are *both* users and producers of social representations. This emphasis fits well with Moscovici's own claims of intellectual interdependencies with the work of Frederic Bartlett and Fritz Heider (see Moscovici, 1990, 1995).

Moscovici focuses on the dynamic side of the functioning of social representations in persons' encounters with their social worlds. The dynamic view leads to the question of actual construction of meaning by way of dialogic communication (Moscovici, 1994). Exploration of the intricacies of the presuppositions underlying specific terms reveals a number of zones of knowledge inherently coded into a particular conversational use of a term (e.g., statements like "John saw the man with two heads" or "Carol is a better linguist than Barbara" immediately provide the presupposition that there exist men with two heads, and that the unknown Barbara is a linguist—see Moscovici, 1994, p. 167). In cognitive psychology, the fashionable discussion of "heuristics" and "biases" (e.g., Kahneman, Tversky, and Slovic, 1982) may be viewed as an artifact of the functioning of social representations in the meaning-making process of persons who are asked projective questions about colors of taxicabs or bank tellers who are feminists. Most of those "heuristics" may be reflections of abductive inference as the core of human decision making (see description of C. S. Peirce's work in chapter 6). Social representations can thus be valuable as a concept if new social representations emerge from their use.

Moscovici's theory of social representations seems to circle between the need to view these representations as dynamic organizing entities while simultaneously implying the transformation of their holistic structure (see Flick, 1995a). Thus, he returns to the question that Gestalt psychology asked (and failed to answer) decades before: "Research on social representations shows that they are usually holistic. That is to say, the meaning of the 'whole' is, in a very intricate way, a function of the meaning of the parts. This should not lead one to believe . . . that all such meanings are of the same cognitive nature or expressed in the linguistic material. They are lying ready to be made explicit or derived when the conditions obtain" (Moscovici, 1994, p. 169).

The uncertainty of the nature of representations-language relations is evident here. As is demonstrated in chapter 6, a similar uncertainty can be observed in the linguistic counterpart of the social representations—Saussure's *langue* ↔ *parole* relation. Furthermore, the affective nature of the relation of social representations with the flow of experience leads to the constant valuation of the uses of such representations (see Krueger, 1928a, on the feeling-tone created by "striving for the whole," or violations of such striving). An effort to solve this complex problem via an emphasis on the hierarchical relations between meanings and actions has existed in the French intellectual traditions for about the last hundred years in the form of action theory of Pierre Janet.

Pierre Janet's Psychodynamic Action Theory

The role of Pierre Janet (1859–1947) as the major thinker of the sociogenetic background—as well as a careful investigator of complex psychological phenomena—is described in detail elsewhere (Gauld, 1992, chapter 17; Valsiner and Van der Veer, 1996; Van der Veer, 1994; Van der Veer and Valsiner, 1988). Janet's entrance into the study of human psychological processes took place under the general interest in French scientific and medical circles in the issues of hypnotism. It was by a lucky coincidence (see Janet, 1930b, p. 124) that he became involved with the analysis of Léonie while working in Le Havre (Janet, 1889). In 1889 Janet moved to Paris, where he became involved with the clinic of Charcot. He had begun teaching psychology at the Sorbonne in 1898 and was nominated professor of experimental psychology at the Collège de France in 1902 (see Brooks, 1993).

Janet was a "reserved, shy, scholarly and proud man, who made no attempt to found a school, and did not need constant reassurance from a chorus of admiring converts" (Gauld, 1992, p. 370). He was capable of uniting philosophical discourse with careful empirical analyses of case studies. The latter are the subject of most of his publications (Janet, 1889, 1898, 1926, 1928a). Janet himself was explicitly scornful of superficial interpretations of publicly displayed clinical cases (Janet, 1930b, p. 126); he developed his own empirical habits of meticulous recording of clinical experiments—his is the "psychology of the fountain pen," as he himself admitted.

Hierarchical Organization of Conduct

Janet's empirical interests in clinical cases had the general philosophical goal of understanding the basic functioning of the human mind. It is exactly the study of extreme (pathological) cases that can illuminate the dynamic side of normal psychological functions (Janet, 1905, pp. 115–116). Janet's *psychological analysis* (Janet, 1930a) entails the study of hierarchically organized (and constantly reorganized) psychological functions, where higher functions control their lower counterparts in specifiable ways.

As the hierarchical control system is dynamically set up and altered, at times it can provide examples of small, everyday anomalies of action. Many such "mishaps" of the hierarchical control system lead to actions that are quite ordinary, and their psychopathology can be demonstrated only through careful juxtaposition of the actions and the person's reflections upon those actions. Janet described cases of *uncritical and unchecked execution of actions,* triggered by—or not inhibited by—higher-level thought processes:

Nof. (m.,19) would from time to time pass into a very peculiar state in which he was unable to resist the tendencies aroused in him by certain impressions. Thus (the incident was reported by himself and was also watched by his relatives), when in this condition, one day, he happened to pass a hatter's shop. Thereupon he said to himself: "Hullo, there's a hatter's, a place where people buy hats," and he promptly went in to buy a hat for which he had no need. Another day, being in the same condition, he was passing the Gare de Lyon, and said to himself: "A railway station. This is the place one travels from." Thereupon he entered the station and, having read on a poster the name Marseilles, he took a ticket for that town, and set off by the Marseilles train. Not until he reached Mâcon did he come to himself, realise the absurdity of what he was doing, and quit the train. (Janet, 1925, p. 210)

Both of these examples indicate an alteration in the ways in which thinking and acting are (at least temporarily) related. The person who encounters the tension between action propensity and its thought reflection inevitably handles that tension in some way. For example, he may display *reversal of sentiments* (e.g., feeling X toward Y becomes transformed into its opposite, anti-X; "love" turns to "hate" or vice versa). Likewise, the aberrations in the thought-action relations can be prevented or repaired by setting up superordinate goals, or additional information imported into the given decision process, that would reorganize the structure. Thus, a person may preemptively block the tendency to travel to Marseilles (when seeing and naming Gare de Lyon as "railway station") by saying to oneself "this is a railway station . . . a place people travel from . . . *but I need to* go to the hatter's shop to buy a hat now." The earlier example of resistance to posthypnotic suggestion reported by Bekhterev shows how the general meaning of *"I don't need it"* blocked the person from executing the hypnotically suggested action (taking the card from Bekhterev's desk). In both cases there exists a superordinate ill-defined concept ("need" as evoked in the self-regulation process) that constrains (by way of enabling; see chapter 2) the specific relationship between thought and action. Many general-level concepts—"love," "hate," "interest," "justice," and so on—are necessarily vague and ill defined, and therefore are usable in the tension-regulation process (Valsiner, 1992). Or a person's beliefs become higher-level regulators of actions (Janet, 1926, 1928a, 1928b). It is through semiotic means—signs constructed by the person—that the

ZFM/ZPA complex for specific next actions (or for the blocking of any action) is set up.

TENSION AND PERSONAL SYNTHESIS   The ways in which persons—anybody in one's ordinary life, as well as Janet's psychiatric patients—deal with their intrapsychological regulation issues, are certainly highly variable. Nevertheless, what is universal is the emergence of tension in specific relationships between the parts of the psychological system. Every human being constructs some tension some of the time in some part of the psychological system, and becomes oriented toward that tension. Janet noted, in one of his general offhanded commentaries that are embedded in his elaborate descriptions: "The patients who are ill-satisfied with their action watch themselves and by dint of observations, through anxiety about themselves, they fall into a sort of perpetual auto-analysis. *They become psychologists; which is in its way a disease of the mind*" (Janet, 1921, p. 152; emphasis added).

Aside from being considered a derogatory remark upon psychologists as a whole (and surely Janet's comment was not meant to accomplish that grandiose objective), there is a simple universal principle embedded in it. Indeed, some issue that generates psychological tension becomes the target of action and reflection. Such efforts to resolve the tension necessarily lead to sensitization to (and differentiation of) that domain of experience. They also lead to the "vocational disease" phenomena, which are often visible: teachers tend to be hyperdidactic, brave heroes fearful of little everyday trivialities, and psychologists stuck in the analysis of the complexity of their phenomena.

The concept of psychological tension is present at all levels of Janet's thought-action hierarchy (see Sjövall, 1967, pp. 52–56). At the higher level of that hierarchy, the phenomena of personal will can be observed as the highest control mechanisms. Thus, will is not a mystical entity that stands outside of the regular action-control hierarchy and acts in opposition to it; instead, it is the highest-level part of the hierarchical system, a part that emerges through development.

A central tenet in Janet's conception of personality is the *personal synthesis* of experiences of one's past, in the personal present, through the use of language (Meyerson, 1947). This synthesizing process consists of the assimilation of new experiences into the existing schema, thus transforming the schema in the process. The focus on transformation of the schema in Jean Piaget's work is indebted to that of Pierre Janet. Furthermore, when this assimilation fails to happen—as in the case of traumatic memories of unassimilated events—the construction of neurotic symptoms can result (Janet, 1930a, p. 370). All in all, psychopathology can inform the study of basic psychological processes through empirical evidence of the outcomes of altered or broken-down systems.

GENERALIZATION FROM TENSION: FEAR OF ACTION   Janet encountered psychiatric cases that indeed allowed him to view psychopathological evidence as making reconstruction of normal psychological mechanisms possible. The examples reported previously (the buying of a hat and the trip to Marseilles) pertained to the *near-ordinary* situation of psychopathology of semiotic regulation of action. After all, any person has at times bought something that was not planned, under the immediate stimulation by some advertisement, or has altered his or her plan of movement when seeing an opportunity to take a different road. But Janet's patients included individuals in whom the hierarchical control system had lost its dynamic flexibility. The person can become hyperregulatory relative to his or her action. This can result in the *complete blocking of concrete action* by way of thought processes, as in the case of Sophie, one of Janet's patients:

> She has moments of lucidity during which I am able to persuade her to walk in the garden and to talk somewhat reasonably. She hesitates in her actions, she stops short and wails instead of acting brusquely and rapidly as she did in the observed activities of her delirium. When she thus stops short she is upset by fears and remorse of the strangest kind, "No, I should not have done that, it is precisely these few steps in this alley-way which were forbidden to me by Heaven. I give you death if I walk with you . . . I insult my mother if I eat as you desire . . . I am causing my father to suffer in his grave if I look on his photograph . . . I become a hideous monster if I speak to you . . ." *Each action is planned in its correct form by the patient* or undertaken with any self-consciousness or even a little reflection *presents itself with an appearance so strange and so odious that it awakens a thought of the most forbidden actions.* (Janet, 1921, p. 153; emphasis added)

Patients with anomalies of the semiotic regulatory system need not be in such a state all the time. Instead, they move in and out of such states, and at times are quite self-reflective about their own state. Thus Janet described the set of reported reflections by a woman named Flora (aged twenty-seven), resting in a sanatorium, where Janet recorded the following discussion with her:

> I think to please her in announcing that her brother's wife, of whom she is very fond, has borne a child, and that they intend bringing her the baby to have a look at him and kiss him. "Don't do that," she answers. "The automobile will dash into the trees by the street; my mother, the nurse, the child will be crushed, oh! what horror!" Another time I ask her: "Are you willing to see your mother and sister?" She: "It would be very painful for me to see them in mourning." I: "But the ladies are not in mourning." She: "If they must come and see me, my father and my brother will be dead, and they will come in mourning." And then she adds intelligently: "I cannot help this; it is a kind of catastrophic vision that is putting these things together. I lose my foothold, people wish me bad luck, mother scares me, everything is gloomy, the street looks gloomy, even the sun looks gloomy." (Janet, 1928b, p. 298)

This case is interesting because of the particular form of "running ahead" of time in imagining consequences of possible accident, and treating such consequences as if they were guaranteed to happen. A person in a far-off sanatorium, knowing that the road to the location may entail dangers, might similarly prefer not to see her relatives, but *would not preassume* the sad course of events to happen. In the terminology of the "zonological" system, Flora has ruled *out* from ZFM the event of relatives' visit at the level of action (see Figure 2.1.d. for the kind of ZFM: "anything but X"). This is accomplished at the reflection level by creating ZFM-boundary marking through a set of concepts *visit = death = mourning*, which are value-imbued through the general feeling of sadness and its avoidance, together with ego-involved feeling of participation: "At the bottom they all accuse themselves. Flora feels sure that she plays a part in the smashing of the automobile, for she adds: 'If they come to visit another person, the car would not run into the tree'" (Janet, 1928b, p. 299).

Thus, at the meta-level reflection, the idea of personal responsibility sets up the particular reflection-level meanings to mark the ZFM boundary for actions. If the meta-level notion were to be reorganized, the whole hierarchically generated phenomenon would immediately disappear (e.g., Flora's relatives could come to the same sanatorium *to visit others*). The example provided by Janet fits the multilevel control fields notion (developed after Bühler) depicted in Figure 2.3.

The example of Flora is also noteworthy because it entails construction of subjective feelings of reality by way of exaggerated, or double, "as-if" extrapolation mechanisms. Every human being at times operates with construction of possible ("as-if") scenarios for possible actions, in order to prepare for the action, avoid some consequences of action, or refrain from action altogether. In this respect, creating a "danger scenario" for a car trip to a far-off place is an "as-if" construction of possibilities that regulates our ordinary acting and thinking. Yet this kind of scenario building—the first-level "as-if" construction—can become supplemented by a second one that operates on it. Instead of considering the *possibility* that the car *might* run into a tree (and hence deciding to drive carefully), the person may construct the image "as if" the previous "as-if" scenario were already actualized. The fear is that simply thinking about a scenario like this may actualize it, and the future-oriented modeling of possible scenarios is viewed as if it already is actual. Without the fusion of the potential into the actual, Flora's case would be a perfectly ordinary, normal pattern. Janet warned his listeners against simple pathologizing of his psychiatric cases, as if those were something unordinary:

> Doubtless, veritable melancholia is a disease, but sadness in its most simple form is, after all, identical with melancholia and contains the same fear of action. There are families and, one might say, entire populations who are going through periods of discouragement, of sadness, and of recoiling from action. Let us also remember that those spells of sadness should not be called poetic, and they must not be cultivated. Sadness is always a sign of weakness and, sometimes, of a habit of living weakly. (Janet, 1928b, p. 309)

It is needless to add that specific meta-level general meanings are specifically cultivated by social suggestions to promote blockage of some actions, while enabling others. Any social suggestion that a person might "offend God" by doing X, Y, or Z is a socializing intervention, oriented toward creating the meta-level control systems in the person's internalized world.

Social Suggestions in Personality Development

Borrowing a metaphor from Charcot, Janet characterized suggestion as "a real parasite in thought" (Janet, 1901, p. 267). In the case of some persons it is possible to suggest the assimilation of ideas that install themselves in the mind and could be brought into function later. The process of suggestion can take many forms and has posed important definitional problems. Janet claimed: "Suggestion is a peculiar reaction to certain perceptions; the reaction consists in the activation, more or less complete, of the tendency aroused by the suggestion, in the absence of a completion of the activation by the collaboration of the remainder of the personality" (Janet, 1925, p. 280).

The person actively processes the suggestion. Whether a particular suggestion is accepted and immediately executed, or delayed, or accepted and executed in a different form (e.g., in an abbreviated one—Janet, 1901, p. 244), the possibility for a person's processing of suggestions sets the stage for the sociogenetic conceptualization of personality development.

Altogether, Pierre Janet can be considered the originator of both the psychodynamic and action-theoretic perspectives on human personality. His analysis of the *subconscious* as a part of the hierarchy of psychological tendencies parallels the Freudian use of the unconscious (but without the fixation upon the absolute centrality of sexuality). Likewise, Janet's emphasis on action has been the starting point for various versions of action theories (Boesch's, Basov's, Leontiev's, to say the least). His impact upon Piaget's genetic epistemology was likewise direct. Last but not least, his consistent emphasis on social suggestions and their role in human development was important for the development of Vygotsky's thought (Van der Veer and Valsiner, 1988). Furthermore, Janet's thinking was closely interdependent with that of his contemporaries—particularly Henri Bergson and James Mark Baldwin.

Sociogenetic Ideas in the New World

In the 1890s, a variety of productive sociogenetic thought traditions emerged in North America. This was a time of heightened social stress, marked by creativity in psychology and sociology (Bernard, 1929), all at the intersection of both intranational (rapid industrialization and tension between urban and rural lifestyles) and international contacts. The latter entailed intensive immigration (see Barry, 1968).

There has been an inherent tension within U.S. society—the contradiction between the action orientation that is hyperemphasized in politics and business, and the speculation-oriented interpretive tradition that stems from the nation's unique social-religious history. This contradiction has led to the unique form of independent dependence (Winegar, Renninger, and Valsiner, 1989) of U.S. social sciences on the society's immediate needs to quickly "fix" its problems, while replacing substantive theoretical analysis of social or psychological issues with undisciplined speculations grossly labeled "theories." Over the past century, this contradiction has not been resolved; it continues more or less along the lines described by George Mead, one of its participant actors: "America's native culture accepted the forms and standards of European culture. It was confessedly inferior, not different. It was not indigenous. The cultivated American was a tourist even if he never left American shores. When the American felt the inadequacy of the philosophy and art native to the Puritan tradition, his revolt took him abroad in spirit if not in person, but he was still at home for he was an exponent of the only culture the community possessed" (Mead, 1930b, p. 218).

Nevertheless, the creative social turmoil in U.S. society did produce substantial extensions of the basically European ideas of sociogenetic perspectives on human development. Most important, the pragmatist tradition was developing in a number of areas in psychology and sociology during the 1890s. In parallel, the idealist sociogenetic philosophy of Josiah Royce (1855–1916) played its role in interpreting the social nature of the person.

The Ego ↔ Non-Ego Dialectics of Josiah Royce

Royce's idealist Hegelian philosophy was a relevant input to American intellectual life at the turn of the century (Mead, 1917a). Combining his indebtedness to Hegel with influences from Spinoza, Fichte, and Schopenhauer (Royce, 1892b), Royce was interested in questions of selfhood and spirit in the context of community (see Collins, 1968). Royce's "loyal community," however, did not deny the centrality of the individual person; it emphasized the constructive nature of imitation as the main mechanism through which the individual develops his or her intricate self (Royce, 1893/1966; 1898). Royce's sociogenetic orientation borrows closely from Tarde and Baldwin. Given his background in Hegel and Baldwin, it is not surprising that Royce's philosophy of the self is explicitly developmental in its scope.

Royce set out his specific view on the self as a dialectical unity of self and nonself. The emergence of ego depends upon differentiation of the habits of guiding oneself, and remembering, from the flow of the stream of consciousness. The subject-object differentiation allows the person to construct his or her ego in contrast with its dialectical opposite (non-ego). There are different possibilities for such construction. According to Royce,

> If a man regards himself as this individual Ego, he always sets over against his Ego something else, viz.: some particular object represented by a portion of his conscious states, and known to him as his then present and interesting non-Ego. This psychological non-Ego, represented in one's conscious states, is of course very seldom the universe, or anything in the least abstract. And, for the rest, it is a very varying non-Ego . . . If I am in a fight, my consciously presented non-Ego is my idea of the opponent. Consequently I am then conscious of myself as of somebody fighting him. If I am in love, my non-Ego is thought of as my beloved, and my Self, however much the chord of it pretends . . . is the Self of my passion. (Royce, 1895c, p. 443)

The development of the self takes place through constructive imitation that builds new oppositions on the basis of social experiences. The origin of the process of differentiation of ego/non-ego is social, and its vehicle is the use of language (Royce, 1895c, p. 449). Internalization is the process by which the social experiences become functional in the self system, which always entails dialectical oppositions. For example: "If conscience is aroused . . . to act, one has, purely as a matter of social habit, a disposition to have present both the tendency to the action, and the disposition to judge it, standing to one another in the . . . relation of Ego and non-Ego. Which of them appears as the Ego, which the non-Ego, depends upon which most gets possession, in the field of consciousness, of the common sensibility" (Royce, 1895c, p. 454).

The flexibility of the distribution of roles of the ego and non-ego in Royce's self theory is crucial for development. This temporary tendency for one aspect of the self to dominate the other resembles quite notably our contemporary interest in discourse analytic views on the self, which apply Bakhtin's idea of "voices," their dialogue, and temporary prioritization of some voice over another (Wertsch, 1991). Such construction of asymmetrically dominant units in a pair guaranteed a dualistic view on the mental world (Royce, 1894b, p. 543), quite different from the antidualistic declarations of the "Chicago School" of thought (see later discussion).

For Royce, the phenomena of internal dialogue are certainly valuable sources of evidence for demonstration of his self system. Royce had access to the phenomena of self-work of a young student (reported in Royce,

1895c, pp. 574–584), which demonstrated richness of the internal dialogues, with self-analyzed different "selves" (or "voices") marked. For example,

> So I say to myself, I give myself up to you to make what use of it you can. *The personal self*—the narrowest—cries for recompense—*says I am foolish—even in saying this "foolish" foolish*—says I may be ridiculed—The *more impersonal steps in and says,* What then the difference? You (that is I) may be foolish but he (you, Professor Royce) makes use of it—and he understands—you wish to be understood—you have no object—not much object even in this—but let the writing go to him. (Royce, 1895c, p. 583; emphasis added)

This excerpt—reported by Royce as an "anomaly of self-consciousness"—is nevertheless usual for the intramental multivocality of "voices" and parallel descriptions of extramental voices in social interaction (Smolka, 1994a). Scenarios of different selves' *perspective taking* within the intrapsychological dialogue emerge in the stream of consciousness, the different "voices" begin to negotiate their relationships within the self, at times making reference to extramental (social) events. Differentiation of the perspectives of different selves amounts to the emergence of hierarchical organization, personally constructed meanings begin to act upon one another (e.g., the application of the *notion of "foolish"* upon *saying "foolish"* about anything else).

The emergence of meta-levels in the intraself discourse in principle has possibilities for "infinite progress" into ever-more-abstract and context-freed talking about the different perspectives, as well as value flavoring of any of those. This reflexivity of reasoning has rarely been considered in psychological analyses (for an exception, see Lefebvre, 1982; Litvinovic and Valsiner, 1993; Obeyesekere, 1990), yet it constitutes a relevant process in human symbolization, in both its adaptive and disadaptive (pathological) cases (e.g., a reanalysis of the religious fixation of John Bunyan—Royce, 1894a). As always, serious literary figures have provided psychology with rich intrapsychological dialogues, yet very few psychologists have made use of these, or have recognized literature as data, as Royce did (Royce, 1892a).

However, the sociogenetic nature of human self-reflection remains in force all through the human life course, requiring at least episodic embeddedness in the social world. Although Royce's main interest was in the intramental subjective world, he recognized its dependence upon the social realm: "Self-confidence is always a dependent affair. We can only choose whether our dependence shall be rational or capricious. Self-consciousness needs constantly renewed draughts of that water of life, the imitated authority of other minds" (Royce, 1894b, p. 541).

This notion of interdependency of the personal and social is an example of independent dependence (Winegar, Renninger, and Valsiner, 1989). Royce's emphasis on analytic units that contain dialectical oppositions entailed a clear anticategorizational stance, which one hundred years later is still rare in psychology (for exceptions, see the theme of intersubjectivity in chapter 1). Royce considered psychological terms as opposites united in the cycle of interdependency inside the mind, between the mind and society, and between social units within a society:

> It is only in abstraction that I can be merely egoistic. In the concrete case I can only be egoistic by being also voluntarily altruistic . . . I can aim, for instance, to be a political "boss." That appears to be a very egoistic aim. But the political "boss" exists by the suffrages of interested people, and must aim at their conscious, even if illusory, sense of advantage in so far as he wills them to be sincerely interested. I can will to be a flattering demagogue, admired for vain show by a crowd of fools. The end is selfish; but it also involves wishing to be agreeable in the eyes of many people. (Royce, 1895b, pp. 468–469)

Royce's dialectical unity-of-opposites focus provided numerous theoretical advantages, none of which were productively advanced in either American or international psychology. The former became the hostage to the avalanche of pragmatist thought as a social ideology, which culminated in the dominance of the cult of behaviorism in psychology. The latter had its own qualms with uses and abuses of dialectical thinking (Valsiner, 1988a), and Royce's philosophically framed excursions into the realm of psychological phenomena vanished into obscurity.

The Chicago School of Thought

Chicago, a rapidly growing industrial city at the turn of the century, was an unlikely location for a center of excellence of thought. In 1904, William James made a prophetic prediction:

> Chicago has a School of Thought!—a school of thought which, it is safe to predict, will figure in literature as the School of Chicago for

twenty-five years to come. Some universities have plenty of thought to show, but no school; others plenty of school, but no thought . . . Professor John Dewey, and at least ten of his disciples, have collectively put into the world a statement, homogeneous in spite of so many coöperating minds, of a view of the world, both theoretical and practical, which is so simple, massive, and positive that, in spite of the fact that many parts of it yet need to be worked out, it deserves the title of a new system of philosophy. (James, 1904a, p. 1).

James, of course, was referring to the philosophical orientation of pragmatism that through the activities of Dewey reached numerous areas of thought, ranging from education to psychology (including behaviorist movements—see Angell, 1961, p. 26) and sociology. Furthermore, James had his own reasons to hail the new school of thought, as he himself had moved his philosophical position further away from introspectionist psychology in the direction of glorifying experience (James, 1890, 1904b; Myers, 1986)

The "Chicago School of Thought" actually originated in Ann Arbor, at the University of Michigan, in the late 1880s. It remained there until 1894, when prominent members—Dewey himself, George Mead, and James R. Angell—moved to Chicago. Dewey's other disciples included James Tufts, Charles H. Cooley, Addison Moore, and E. S. Ames. Furthermore, the early pragmatist orientation at Chicago was paralleled by a substantial sociological tradition (Charles Henderson, Charles Ellwood, William E. Thomas, and Robert Park), to which the anthropological efforts of Edward Sapir were added in the 1920s (see chapter 6).

THE CORE OF THE "CHICAGO SCHOOL": JOHN DEWEY

John Dewey developed his version of pragmatist thinking by moving from his Hegelian roots to James's and Peirce's thought (Raphelson, 1973), and further freeing himself to be on his own (Cahan, 1992; Goetzmann, 1973; Mead, 1930b). His thinking in Ann Arbor, and then in Chicago, advanced the pragmatist philosophical stand and linked it with issues in psychology and education.

Dewey's pragmatism emerged in the course of the 1890s from neo-Hegelian roots, with the question of experience emerging at its center. Thus, in his early writings Dewey explained:

Experience begins when intelligence projects something of itself into sensations. We have now to recognize that experience grows, or gets more meaning, just in the degree in which intelligence reads more ideal content into it. The adult has more experience than the child—the Englishman than the Bushman—because he has more ideas in his intellect to bring to bear upon his sensations and thus make them significant . . . it is . . . the supplying of *meaning through sensations,* and not of sensations, that makes the experience more significant. (Dewey, 1887, p. 395)

The eclectic mixing of quantified notions of the process described ("experience . . . gets more meaning"; "adult . . . has more experience") with qualitative structural-dynamic process mechanisms (projection by "intelligence" onto "sensations," supplying "meaning through sensations") qualifies the still-Hegelian Dewey of 1887 as an American thinker. The collective-cultural model of quantifying the essentialistic common-sensical qualities (e.g., claims of "having"—"more" or "less"—of "experience," "intellect," etc.) that have plagued American social sciences by keeping them hostage to pseudo-empiricism (Smedslund, 1994, 1995) can be discerned in Dewey's ideas about experience. However, the qualitative process mechanism he implied to *generate* experience—the projection of intelligence upon sensations, through which meaning emerges—is a step in the direction of his emphasis on the pragmatic dynamics between the organism and the environment.

Dewey made a step forward in the direction of conceptualizing the process of development in his textbook *Psychology* (first published in 1886). Building upon the Hegelian notion of dialectical synthesis, Dewey claimed that "activity of mind never leaves sensuous elements isolated, but connects them into larger wholes" (Dewey, 1891, p. 90). The mechanism of such establishment of wholes of experience was seen as a unity of *integration* (of different present sensations) and *redintegration* ("extension of present sensory elements by distinct revival of past elements"—Dewey, 1891, p. 96). However, it is remarkable that the linkages between present and past sensations were conceptualized by Dewey in associationistic terms (similarity, contiguity), rather than building into the process of redintegration a Hegelian dialectical scheme. It could be claimed that Dewey was already on his way toward the pragmatist elimination of structural notions and emphasis on process over its participating components, which later became the key to his thinking. For example, he explicitly considered integration to be synonymous with fusion—the latter being clearly free from the notion of dialectical tension between opposites:

> We have . . . a continuous whole of sensation constantly undergoing modification and constantly expanding, but never parting with its unity. This process may be termed *fusion* or *integration,* to indicate the fact that the various elements are continually entering into the whole in which they lose their independent existence. Professor James illustrates this intimate union by the taste of lemonade. This does not retain unchanged the tastes of sugar and of lemon, but is itself a new sensation into which the old ones have passed as elements. What association gives us . . . is not a loosely connected aggregate of separable parts, but a new total experience. (Dewey, 1891, pp. 94–95)

James's example of the taste of lemonade indeed illustrates how fusion of substances leads to the holistic new taste as an outcome, rendering the process of the fusion itself into a de facto role of a "black box." Ironically, Dewey's constant insistence on the process nature of experiencing caused that process to be left out of the investigation itself.

By giving the process of entering into the whole of total experience a label *(integration),* and especially creating its synonym by the notion of *fusion,* Dewey successfully eliminated the process of emergence of that holistic experience (i.e., the process of synthesis) from the focus of investigation. Here we can trace an example of canalization of scientists' thought by the concepts they use. On the one hand, Dewey successfully ruled out an atomistic account of experience as a mere separated "count of elements" of the objective world or subjective state, and antedated the Gestalt psychological traditions in his youthful propagation of the primacy of the "experiential whole" (see Allport, 1951, p. 266). On the other hand, his emphasis on the fusion of the subject and object constrained his focus on intellectual fights with all kinds of "dualisms" and away from solving the conceptual problem of the processes that he successfully kept in focus by the fusion concept (see chapter 5). Dewey led the way for many sociogenetic theorists who came after him and who—willingly or not—took over the defocusing on emergence by emphasizing the fusion of the person and the social world (e.g., Rogoff, 1990; commentary in Valsiner, 1991a; Wertsch, 1991; also see the discussion on appropriation in chapter 3).

Dewey's efforts to fight dualistic concepts in psychology continued in the 1890s. His main criticism of the "reflex arc" concept followed from his dispute with William James on the issue of emotion concepts (Dewey, 1894, 1895; James, 1894). For Dewey, the reflex arc concept was important because it came close to his desired working model of a functionalist scheme yet carried the separation of parts of the functioning system ("center" versus "periphery") that he found to be unproductive. Hence his relabeling of the "reflex arc" as a "circuit" of "mediated experience" (Dewey, 1896, p. 363). The continuous unity of the process of acting does not allow separation of parts of the process into *independent* units but only to temporarily distinguished parts of the whole. The relations between thus inclusively separated (yet linked) parts were described as *coordinations*—another term referring to a process but turning the process into an entity through the labeling itself. For Dewey, experience is *seamless* (a descriptor also used in our contemporary descriptions of experience—see Rogoff, 1990); to be aware of oneself is to be merely a part of the total circuit of awareness (Allport, 1951, p. 269) and a participant in it. The theoretical paradoxes of the adoption of such a stand on the "seamless" nature of persons' relations with their worlds were obvious when they were first expressed (e.g. McGilvary, 1908) and remain so to the present time.

Although embracing pragmatism as a general label, Dewey's thought constituted a special version of it—one that emphasized dynamics of experience, its ethical and prospective side (see Dewey, 1908, p. 97), in contrast with James's person-focused and eclectic version of that general philosophy (James, 1907; also Allport, 1943b). Dewey's fight with dualisms in psychology seems to have resulted in the permanent disablement of psychologists' thinking in terms of dualities (i.e., inclusively separated parts of the system, between which functioning processes can be specified; see chapter 1). Dewey himself perhaps cannot be viewed as the sole producer of such casualty in ideas, as in conjunction with the notion of emergence traces of the notion of dialectical synthesis seem to come through:

> In any organized system . . . there is no dualism of self and world. The emergence of this duality is within the conflicting and strained situation of action; the activities which subtend purpose and intent define the "me" of that situation, those which constitute the interruptive factor define its "external world." . . . it is precisely the process of rationalization by which a brute practical acceptance-rejection gets transformed into *a controlled directed evaluated system of action,* in which the duality of me and object is again overcome. (Dewey, 1907, p. 255)

George Mead's Sociogenetic Quest

Dewey's close friend and collaborator George Mead made a lifelong effort to reconcile Dewey's pragmatic dynamicism with the emphasis on the subjective (yet socially embedded and interdependent) individual and the social world. Largely thanks to close contact with John Dewey, Mead's focus on the issue of unity of the social and the personal began to emerge (Cook, 1993, pp. 27–36). Nevertheless, that focus on unity did not stop Mead from recognizing the self of the person—who, while a participant in the social world and constantly interdependent with it, remains a reflexive system of his or her own. Linkages between Peirce's semiotic logic and Mead's perspective have been pointed out (see also chapter 6).

Starting from his personal search for social problems, Mead introduced a course on social psychology at the University of Chicago in 1900 (Cook, 1993, pp. 46–47). At first it was taught under the institutional labeling of "psychology" and later under "philosophy." It was Mead's increasing lack of fit with North American psychology in the early 1900s that led to both his minimal contribution to psychology and a notable role in sociology and philosophy. Ironically, it was the advent of behaviorist takeover in North American psychology that moved Mead's psychological system to the institutional realm of sociology or philosophy. The behaviorist creed can be traced to the pragmatism of the Chicago School (e.g., see Angell, 1961, p. 26), and it led to the displacement of psychologists' interests from human beings to laboratory rats. The ever-tentative expressions of Mead pertaining to the centrality of human phenomena were simply forgotten.

Similarly to Vygotsky (as described in Van der Veer and Valsiner, 1991), Mead was far more comfortable with speaking than with writing, and his course on social psychology was always new in its specific renderings. His intellectual interdependence was substantial (Valsiner and Van der Veer, 1988), and his contributions have only rarely received the in-depth analytic coverage they deserve (Cook, 1993; Joas, 1985; Dodds, Lawrence, and Valsiner, 1998).

Mead combined the intellectual heritages of Dewey, James, Wundt, and Bergson. His efforts to build his own theoretical understanding of the sociality of the person are evident in his definition of the psychical (Mead, 1903). Mead's emphasis on the centrality of gesture in interaction is closely related to the *Völkerpsychologie* of Wundt (Mead, 1903). His conceptualization of self results from the borrowing of the self-concept system of James (1890, chapter 10) but advances the ideas in the sociogenetic direction (Mead, 1908, 1909, 1910a, 1910b, 1912, 1913, 1918). Bergson's emphasis on the irreversibility of time also was of central importance to Mead (1907, 1925).

WILLIAM JAMES'S SYSTEM OF SELVES   Mead's self system was a slowly built theoretical construction, following the always eclectic (yet synthesis-oriented—Allport, 1943b, p. 112) system described by William James. Furthermore, other versions of self-conceptualizations that made use of the "self"-"other" distinctions were circulating in the 1890s (e.g., Baldwin's *ego* and *alii;* Royce's *self* and *not-self*).

James's conceptualization of self was all-inclusive (man's self is the "sum total of all that he can call his"—1890, p. 291). That totality was divided by James into its constituents (material, social, and spiritual selves, and "pure ego"), which lead to *self-feelings* and prompt actions (of *self-seeking* and *self-preservation*).

The *material self* expands the personal identity outward from one's body: "We all have the blind impulse to watch over our body, to deck it with clothing of an ornamental sort, to cherish parents, wife, and babes, and to find for ourselves a home of our own which we may live in and 'improve'" (James, 1890, pp. 292–293).

In terms of the present terminology, James's material self belongs to the part of the culturally constructed world called *personal culture.* Furthermore, James's *social self* entails recognition from other persons. As a personal reflection upon these relations, the person "has as many different social selves as there are distinct *groups* of persons about whose opinion he cares" (James, 1890, p. 294).

The internalized role-taking notion of Mead (see later discussion and also Dodds, Lawrence, and Valsiner, 1998) borrows from this notion. Furthermore, James's dependence on the community (groups), which has been a recurrent social representation among North American thinkers (see Mead, 1930b), surfaces here.

Examples of meanings-based personal identification with social-institutional organization of life constitute a relevant aspect of the social self. Thus, "A man's *fame,* good or bad, and his *honor* or dishonor, are names for one of his social selves . . . a layman may abandon a city infected with cholera; but a priest or a doctor would think such an act incompatible with his honor. A soldier's honor requires him to fight or die under circumstances where another man can apologize or run away with no stain upon his social self." (James, 1890, pp. 294–295).

The *spiritual self* for James was a felt-through reflection of the "inner sanctuary" of the personal subjective world. Recognizing the irreversible flow of experiencing, James charted out the relations between ME and NOT-ME as aspects of the process of reflection, as "objects which work out their drama together," but which do not yet include the contemplating of one's subjective being (James, 1890, p. 304).

The selves, according to James, entail their present-future differentiation:

> *In each kind of self, material social, and spiritual, men distinguish between the immediate and actual, and the remote and potential,* between the narrower and the wider view, to the detriment of the former and advantage of the latter . . .
>
> . . . the potential social self is the most interesting, by reason of certain apparent paradoxes to which it leads in conduct, and by reason of its connection with our moral and religious life. When for motives of honor and conscience I brave the condemnation of my own family, club, and "set"; when, as a Protestant, I turn Catholic; as a Catholic, freethinker . . . I am always inwardly strengthened in my course and steeled against the loss of my actual social self by the thought of other and better *possible* social judges than those whose verdict goes against me now. (James, 1890, p. 315)

James's elaboration of the structure of self and its time-bound functioning was one of the relevant thought models for Mead's conceptualization of the self. It has continued to fascinate modern investigators as well. For example, an outgrowth from the contextualist orientation in personality psychology of the 1970s, Hazel Markus's work starts from an empirical emphasis on the schematic self-descriptions (Markus, 1977) and continues in a theoretical direction where William James's notion of possible future selves becomes conceptualized in terms of subjective approach-withdrawal tendencies of a person who is facing possible futures (Markus and Nurius, 1986). Furthermore, the emphasis on "possible selves" constitutes a return to Allport's idea of hierarchical organization of personality (see chapter 5), and tentatively explains the role of the personally constructed "possible selves" in the regulation of personality development (e.g., Cross and Markus, 1991; Kato and Markus, 1993; Markus and Wurf, 1987). Although proceeding from self-personological roots, Markus creates a contrast between different collective cultures in terms of the opposition of *independence* versus *interdependence* notions that organize the selves (Markus and Kitayama, 1991).

FROM JAMES TO MEAD   The theme of heterogeneity of the self structure is present in Mead. Nevertheless, Mead went beyond James and utilized his closeness to Dewey's functionalism to create an emphasis on the *emergence of novel psychological phenomena* within the self system. Thus, in one of his earliest statements on the process structure of the self:

> There appears to be . . . a field of immediate experience within reflection that is open to direct observation, this does not have to be approached from the standpoint of parallelism . . . For this functional psychology an explicit definition of its subject-matter seems highly important. That suggested in this paper is as follows: that phase of experience *within which we are immediately conscious of conflicting impulses* which *rob the object of its character as object-stimulus,* leaving us in so far in an attitude of subjectivity; *but during which a new object-stimulus appears* due to the *reconstructive activity which is identified with the subject "I"* as distinct from *object "me."* (Mead, 1903, p. 35; emphasis added)

What Mead accomplishes is an act of internalization of the subject-object contrast into the whole of the self, setting those two components up in a constantly reverberating circuit of experience (cf. Dewey's criticism of the reflex arc), and making the I ↔ ME circuit generate novel subjective experiences, as well as new acts that transform the person's environment (cf. Mead, 1908, on the development of environments). Mead expressed his surprise at Bergson's unreadiness to view consciousness as an emergent phenomenon (Mead, 1907, p. 384), and made the usual sociogenetic declarations (e.g., "consciousness of meaning is social in origin"—Mead, 1909, p. 406). In criticizing Baldwin (for the latter's simplification of the *ego ↔ socius* relations), Mead claimed:

> There must be other selves if one's own is to exist. Psychological analysis, retrospection, and the study of children and primitive people give no inkling of situations in which a self could have existed in consciousness except as the counterpart of other selves. We can even recognize that in the definition of these selves in consciousness, the child and primitive man have defined the outlines and the character of the others earlier than they have defined their own selves. (Mead, 1909, p. 407)

Aside from the emphasis on internalization as construction of self in consciousness on the basis of social experience, the external world for the developing person depends upon the generalized other (Dodds, Lawrence, and Valsiner, 1998). Mead's criticism of the traditions of formal education—pointing out that the children's experiences and teachers' personalities are considered unimportant—is built on the assumption that the specific organization of the social experience serves as the basis of children's self-construction (Mead, 1910a). The process of interaction guides the process of intraself construction of consciousness. The "feel" of one's own attitude arises within the self spontaneously to meet the gesture of the other, in relation to the imagery of the change. As a result,

> Social conduct must be continually readjusted after it has already commenced, because the individuals whose conduct our own answers, are themselves constantly varying their conduct as our responses become evident. Thus our adjustment to their changing reactions takes place, by a process of our own responses to their stimulations. In these social situations appear not only conflicting acts with the increasing definition of elements in the stimulation, but also a consciousness of one's own attitude as an interpretation of the meaning of the social stimulus. *We are conscious of our attitudes because they are responsible for the changes in the conduct of other individuals . . .* Successful social conduct brings one into a field within which *a consciousness of one's own attitudes helps toward the control of the conduct of others.* (Mead, 1910b, p. 403; emphasis added)

The flow of social experiences in irreversible time (à la Bergson) makes it inevitable that the person is constantly confronted with the practical need to adjust to the changing conduct of other persons. This triggers self-reflexivity (consciousness of attitudes), which leads to further efforts to control the conduct of others. Language emerges in this two-sided process (oriented toward the consciousness of the self and toward the conduct of others) as a "highly specialized form of gesture" (Mead, 1910b, p. 404), or an instrument that makes both intra- and intermental acts possible in their human form. However, it is the intramental cyclical process of the *self's reflection upon one's own conduct toward* the gesture by the other, the strain of indeterminacy in that reflection, and its constructive openness that allow for the emergence of consciousness (Mead, 1910b, pp. 400–401).

In ontogeny, language develops from the "outer" toward the "inner" direction. *The person's inner speech creates the autonomy of the self,* through the capacity for imagination. Mead viewed development of the inner speech as passing through the state of self-oriented dramatization of conduct. It is in that conduct that the two parallel processes of communication—with oneself and with the other—participate in intrasubjective growth:

> The young child talks to himself, i.e., uses the elements of articulate speech in response to the sounds he hears himself make, more continuously and persistently than he does in response to the sounds he hears from those about him, and he displays greater interest in the sounds he himself makes than in those of others. We know also that this fascination of one's own vocal gestures continues even after the child has learned to talk with others, and that the child will converse for hours with himself, *even constructing imaginary companions, who function in the child's growing self-consciousness as the processes of inner speech—of thought and imagination—function in the consciousness of the adult.* (Mead, 1912, p. 403; emphasis added)

Thus, the self's movement through social roles plays a central part in coordinating the social and the personal in development (Mead, 1925, pp. 271–273). It is exactly through the *movement into, through, and out of the roles* of other selves that construction of inner autonomy becomes possible:

> Response to the social conduct of the self may be in the rôle of another—we present his arguments in imagination and do it with his intonations and gestures and even perhaps with his facial expression. In this way we play the rôles of all our group; indeed, it is only so far as we do this that they become part of our social environment—to be aware of another self as a self implies that we have played his rôle or that of another with whose type we identify him for purposes of intercourse. The inner response to our reaction to others is therefore as varied as is our social environment . . .
>   . . . the child can think about his conduct as good or bad *only as he reacts to his own acts in the remembered words of the parents. Until* this process has been developed *into the abstract process of thought,* self-consciousness *remains dramatic,* and the self which is a fusion of the remembered actor and this accompanying chorus is somewhat loosely organized and very clearly social. Later the inner stage *changes into the forum and workshop of thought.* The features and intonations of the *dramatis personae* fade out and the emphasis falls upon the meaning of the inner speech, the imagery becomes merely the barely necessary

cues. But the *mechanism remains social,* and *at any moment the process may become personal.* (Mead, 1913, pp. 377–378; emphasis added)

The process of internalization allows for the self to construct its own functioning structure, based on its social roots. The I ↔ ME structure entails the internally hidden nature of I that can be captured only by way of a (meta)-ME reflecting on another ME (Mead, 1913, pp. 374–375).

The inaccessibility of I in Mead's self system is based on the irreversibility of time: I addresses a ME, but as the latter becomes transformed as a result, any *reflection upon* that "by-I-transformed-ME" necessarily involves a new (meta)-ME emerging as a consequence. Hence, the reflection by the meta-ME upon the "by-I-transfomed-ME" occurs within a time lag that renders impossible any effort to "catch" the initially functioning I.

Mead's self-conceptualization thus leads to the constant construction of a dynamic structure of MEs, including some of those that are reflecting upon others (here I call them meta-MEs). The highly dynamic interactive process is paralleled by the constructive system within the self. In this, Mead synthesized both Dewey's insistence on the dynamics of relation with the world and James's differentiated self system. Mead's sociogenetic perspective on human subjective agency can be summarized in his own words:

> The order of the universe that we live in is the moral order. It has become the moral order by becoming the self-conscious method of the members of a human society. We are not pilgrims and strangers. We are at home in our own world, but it is not ours by inheritance but by conquest. The world that comes to us from the past possesses and controls us. We possess and control the world that we discover and invent. And this is the world of the moral order. It is a splendid adventure if we can rise to it. (Mead, 1923, p. 247)

MEAD AND HIS "SOCIAL OTHERS"   George Mead was certainly not the only North American thinker of his time who tried to conceptualize the social origins of human personality. It is merely his name that subsequently has been made into a "hero myth" as a result of the symbolic interactionist social movement (see Fine, 1993).

The atmosphere in North America at the turn of the century facilitated the play with sociogenetic ideas in a number of versions, a few of which are important here. The relevance of Charles Horton Cooley was emphasized by Mead (1930a) as well as by others (Perinbanayagam, 1975). For

Cooley, "self" and "social other" did not exist as mutually exclusive phenomena (Cooley, 1902, 1907). In his only adventure into the empirical study of human ontogeny (recording the emergence of a self-reflexive lexicon in the speech of his third child—Cooley, 1908), he demonstrates the intricate interdependence of the child and the social world. This interdependence led Cooley to favor thorough case analyses over mere accumulation of data (Cooley, 1929). His "sympathetic introspection" fits with his general theoretical stance.

As a master of the method of "sympathetic introspection," Cooley provided accessible narrative accounts of persons within their social worlds. The belief in the positive ideal of "sharing" within a community shines to the readers of Cooley's work:

> All mankind acknowledges kindness as the law of right intercourse within a social group. By communion minds are fused into a sympathetic whole, each part tends to share the life of all the rest, so that kindness is a common joy, and harshness common pain. (Cooley, 1925, p. 40)

> [The sentiment of mutual kindness] . . . flourishes most in primary groups, where . . . it contributes to an ideal of moral unity of which kindness is a part of. Under its influence the I-feeling becomes a we-feeling, which seeks no good that is not also good of the group. And the humanism of our time strives with renewed energy to make the we-feeling prevail also in the larger phases of life. (Cooley, 1925, pp. 189–190)

Cooley appropriated the notion of fusion of the person and the social world. George Mead's perceptive reflection on Cooley serves as a summary of his work: "His approach was that of objective introspection. The community that he discovered, so to speak from the inside, was a democracy, and inevitably an American democracy . . . Finding it in living, it was a process. Its organization was a manner of living. Its institutions were the habits of individuals" (Mead, 1930a, p. 694).

However, Cooley's notion of interdependence of person and society was not unstructured. He emphasized the importance of feelings of personal "ownership" of activities of the community in which the given person is a member, and he made a plea against applying economic thought to human values (Cooley, 1913). For Cooley, human knowledge was viewed as *both* behavioristic (i.e., viewing the world as it behaves) and sympathetic (empathizing with the world). Thus, the same person may at times treat another person as an external object (i.e., without any identification with him or her) and at other times move to share his or her internal selves, via empathic fusion (Cooley, 1926). The individual mind is a kind of *mental-social complex* that includes all the socially developed sentiments and understandings. At the level of social organization, a corresponding *social-mental complex* (or "group mind") can be conceptualized. The basis of common (shared) social perceptions is the general similarity of mental-social complexes throughout the human species. Persons become aware of this similarity by watching the behavior of others and realizing that such behavior can be attributed to sentiments that resemble one's own.

James Mark Baldwin's Sociogenesis of Self

The work of James Mark Baldwin was centrally relevant for the sociogenetic tradition of viewing personality as a socially constituted entity (Markova, 1990a; Valsiner, 1994e; Valsiner and Van der Veer, 1988). Baldwin's intellectual relations developed a clearly Francophilic focus from the 1890s onward, including among his closest intellectual partners Pierre Janet, Alfred Binet, Gabriel Tarde, Theodore Flournoy, Édouard Claparède, and Henri Bergson (Baldwin, 1926, 1930). Furthermore, his indebtedness to William James, C. S. Peirce, Josiah Royce, H. Osborn, A. R. Wallace, and C. Lloyd Morgan is notable. And, of course, the German models should not go unmentioned here. Like many American scholars of the 1880s, Baldwin made an educational trip to Germany in 1884–1885, spending a semester in Leipzig in Wundt's laboratory, another in Berlin with Friedrich Paulsen, and a third in Freiburg with Carl Stumpf.

PERSONALITY DEVELOPS THROUGH IRREGULAR SOCIAL ENCOUNTERS   The social world of the developing person is variable, particularly thanks to the personal constructivism of individuals who constitute that social world. Of course, there is sufficient regularity in that social world, but it is the constant encounter with changes that forces the person's persistently imitative processes to be ready for new challenges:

> The child begins to learn in addition the fact that persons are in a measure individual in their treatment of him, and hence that individuality has elements of uncertainty or *irregularity* about it. This growing sense is very clear to one who watches an infant in its second half-year.

Sometimes the mother gives a biscuit, but sometimes she does not. Sometimes the father smiles and tosses the child; sometimes he does not. And the child looks for signs of these varying moods and methods of treatment. Its new pains of disappointment arise directly on the basis of that former sense of regular personal presence upon which its expectancy went forth. (Baldwin, 1894b, p. 277; see also Baldwin, 1895, p. 123)

Again, Baldwin's close experiences with caring for his two daughters show their productive basis here. Elsewhere (Baldwin, 1897, pp. 37–39) he adds the structural-social context: not only are particular persons who make up the child's social environment irregular within their habits over time (and personal conditions), but the set of persons who make up the social environment is constantly changing (see also Simmel, 1908). From such heterogeneity of the person's social environment follows the need for selective treatment of that heterogeneity by the person. The previously established "schema" (see Baldwin, 1908a, p. 184) allows the person to become selective as to the variety of presently actual environmental inputs. According to Baldwin,

The individual *gradually builds up internally* the criteria of selection; and as his experience extends even more widely afield from the brute resistances, strains, and contacts with things, he becomes a more and more competent judge for himself of the value of variations in his thoughts. (Baldwin, 1898, p. 17)

He himself comes more and more to reflect the social judgment in his own systematic determination of knowledge; and there arises within himself a criterion of private sort which is in essential harmony with the social demand, because genetically considered it reflects it. The individual becomes a law unto himself, exercises his private judgment, fights his own battles for truth, shows the virtue of independence and the vice of obstinacy. But he has learned to do it by the selective control of his social environment, *and in this his judgment he has just a sense of this social outcome.* (Baldwin, 1898, pp. 19–20)

It is obvious that the social nature of a person is expressed in his or her personal individuality, rather than in the mere direct mirroring of the surrounding social world. The latter is already rendered impossible by its high heterogeneity (which triggers the need for "systematic determination" of the new knowledge by way of internalized selection mechanisms, or cognitive schemata—see Baldwin, 1898, p. 10). Baldwin saw the person-society relationship as a process of particularization (of general meanings by persons in specific contexts) on the one hand and generalization (of persons' thought variations by society) on the other (Baldwin, 1897, part 5). Society is thus a complex of various particularizations of general meanings by concrete individuals, and institutionalized generalizations of some of the ideas of some individuals.

Consistent with the rest of Baldwin's viewpoint, the person is capable of the intrapersonal selection of ideas by way of playful (i.e., persistently imitative) application of the knowledge (and its organizing meanings— Baldwin, 1908a, pp. 145–147) to new experiential contexts that are characterized by uncertainty (and heterogeneity). The self is mediated through the language-encoded inner experiences—judgments that are "already and always socialized" (Baldwin, 1908a, p. 145). The self is a bipolar entity, including "the ego" and "the alter," each of which constitutes the *socius* for the other (Baldwin, 1897, chapter 1).

At first glance, Baldwin's numerous statements about the social nature of psychological phenomena seem overwhelming in their declarative generality (e.g., of "personality-suggestion"—Baldwin, 1894b). For Baldwin, the "inner is not the outer" (Baldwin, 1906, p. 92), and the duality of the "inner" and the "outer" constitutes the source of development of both: "My sense of myself grows by imitation of you, and my sense of yourself grows in terms of my sense of myself" (Baldwin, 1894a, p. 42). "The child imitates the act of another, and in so doing what before he had only observed, comes to feel how the other feels. He thus learns to distinguish the arena of his direct feeling (the inner) from the larger range of presentative experience (the outer) from which this feeling was and may still be absent" (Baldwin, 1906, p. 87).

Clearly the imitation process leads to the creation of a personal psychological world that is rooted in the external experiences but is not an exact copy. Furthermore, neither are the objects in the external world psychologically separate from the person's already established (i.e., internalized) orientation toward them.

It can be argued that the key concept for understanding Baldwin's efforts toward making psychology both developmental and social is that of "persistent imitation." The reasons for Baldwin's need to create this concept can be discerned in his efforts to explain the future-oriented developmental processes at the level of the individual:

Suppose at first an organism giving random reactions, some of which are useful; now for development the useful reactions must be repeated, and thus made to outweigh the reactions which are damaging or useless. Evidently if there are any among the useful reactions which result in immediate duplication of their own stimulus, these must persist, and on them must rest the development of the organism. These are the imitative reactions. Thus it is that *a thing in nature once endowed with the reacting property might so select its stimulations as to make its relations to its environment means to its own progress:* imitative reactions, as now defined, being the only means to such selection. (Baldwin, 1894a, p. 29; emphasis added)

Here the need for inventing *some* notion of imitation becomes obvious as a deductively created object of study. Baldwin's functionalist and instrumentalist stance is clearly visible (e.g., reference to "usefulness" in general), and the developmental orientation helps to extend the sequence of a stimulus and reaction into a time-extended "circular reaction" in which the organism's reaction to a stimulus becomes the next stimulus for the organism, leading to the next reaction, and so on. The organism *begins to construct nonrandom experiences* on the basis of such circular reactions. The reactions become instruments, and thus begin to participate in the developmental process. Imitative reactions are the key to understanding the process of development. Baldwin's analyses of those reactions were based on his observations of his infant daughters' motor action (Baldwin, 1891, 1892a, 1892b) on the one hand and the conceptual distinctions of automatic versus perception-based copying of models on the other.

The interdependent nature of the "inner and outer" dualism leads to the development of other united oppositions ("self and not-self"—Baldwin, 1906, p. 91), thus being a first state in the differentiation of human personality. The dynamics of "inner-outer" relationships led Baldwin to two other relevant phenomena—those of play and art. He viewed play as having the function of "education of the individual for his life-work in a network of social relationships" (Baldwin, 1897, p. 148).

PROJECTION THROUGH SEMBLING   It was in the realm of discussing play and art that Baldwin related his theorizing with the *Einfühlung* of Theodor Lipps. Baldwin's translation of that term into English is a good example of his liking for terminological inventions; he translated

Einfühlung as *sembling* ("to semble" = to make like by imitation—Baldwin, 1906, p. 122). Of course, in the decades since Baldwin, the competing translation as *empathy,* suggested by E. B. Titchener and J. Ward (Baldwin, 1911, p. 167), has come to be used in psychology, albeit with all the confusions that *Einfühlung* brought with it at the beginning of the century.

Originally focusing on the "feeling-into" an object, Baldwin's version of sembling translates the *Einfühlung* into his imitation-centered conceptual system: "Broadly understood, the process of Sembling consists in the reading-into the object of a sort of psychic life of its own, in such a way that the movement, act, or character by which it is interpreted is thought of as springing from its own inner life" (Baldwin, 1906, p. 124).

Sembling thus entails projection upon another the oppositions that persist within one's own "inner"-"outer" relationships, as those are construed within the mind's "inner imitation." It was claimed to be present in both play and art. The "self sembles oneself"—the child takes on new roles, attaches one's personal understanding to their external demands, and that leads to further development of the self.

BALDWIN'S CONCEPTUALIZATION OF FEEL-FORWARD PROCESSES According to Baldwin, sembling is based on imagination, as viewed in his characteristic prospective way:

> The movement of imagination is of the greatest importance in the development of knowledge; it is the method of all genuine advance. We now find that it plays a corresponding role in the organization of interest. Indeed, we come here upon the fact that the sort of meaning known as ideal, due to an imaginative *feeling-forward,* has an essential place in the development of the affective life. The entire movement of cognition and feeling alike has not only the interest and intent to conserve its data and preserve its habits, but also the interest and intent to achieve, to learn, to adapt, to acquire, to *feel-forward.* (Baldwin, 1911, p. 125)

Sembling is thus a mechanism of the feeling-forward process—a certain construction in the present leads into the organism's readiness to encounter new situations (and act appropriately) in the future. The latter is always indeterminate, yet the developing person is oriented toward facing the future's real-life contexts by the feeling-forward notion of present actions. A similar psychological function was asserted by Baldwin to exist in art—as he moved to idealize the notion of "aesthetic synthesis" in his theory of *pancalism* (or "constructive affectivism"—see Baldwin, 1911, 1915). Yet he claimed that art differs from play in some ways:

> In art, the motives of the serious life are not reinstituted fragmentarily and capriciously, for mere recreation and amusement, as they are in play; but systematically and truthfully, in a system in which the judgments of value, appreciation, ideality, are semblantly reconstructed. Art thus becomes in its own sense serious. It is not a mere imitation of the actual; nor is it a caricature of it. It is a re-reading of the actual in the more systematic, perfect, and satisfying form which the abrogation of partial controls and the removal of their oppositions renders possible. The reality of the external is not lost; since the reconstructions preserve the gains of judgment and insight, both theoretical and practical. Nor is reality in the inner world lost or impaired; since the work of art is charged with its very spirit and life. (Baldwin, 1915, p. 243)

The notion of future-oriented adaptive readiness was a natural outgrowth of the theoretical context of organic evolution and was reflected in the constructive evolutionism of Henri Bergson.

BERGSON'S VIEWS ON ADAPTATION AND PERSONALITY   A central concept upon which Bergson's developmental thought was based was the notion of adaptation. That concept—popular as it was (and is)—can carry different meanings. First, it has been seen as a direct reaction to the conditions that are causing change—either "positive" (by way of giving rise to new variations) or "negative" (elimination of misfitting emerged variations). Bergson disagreed with both of these meanings (on the basis of their mechanistic elaboration—see Bergson, 1911, p. 63) and called for seeing adaptation in the process of emergence of novel mechanisms in ways *coordinated with* context demands (but not "molded" or "shaped" by those). Thus, in psychological development the psychological functions develop new organizational forms that make it possible for them to encounter new possible conditions in the future (as opposed to the idea of "fitting in" with the environmental demands at the present). The adaptations are organic (systemic) growths, oriented toward a set of future possibilities (which, as those do not exist in the present, cannot be precisely defined). Nevertheless, these new forms canalize the further encounters of the organism and the environment (see Bergson's [1911a] discussion of canalizing involved in vision—pp. 105–108; and the role of concepts in canalizing conscious processes—pp. 305–308). *In the case of creative adaptation, the organizational forms that emerge in adaptation go beyond the "fit with" the present state of the survival conditions and set the basis for facing the challenges of possible future demands.*

Bergson's focus of interest was primarily the world of human psychology, as his "intuitivistic" bases in understanding the world philosophically started from the highly personal act of introspection. Thus, his notion of becoming was expressed on the material of human personality in his characteristic way:

> Our personality, which is being built up at each instant with its accumulated experience, changes without ceasing. By changing it prevents any state, although superficially identical with another, from forever repeating it in its very depth [*En changeant, elle empêche un état, fût-il identique à lui-même en surface, de se répéter jamais en profondeur*]. That is why our duration is irreversible. We could not live over again a single moment, for we should have to begin by effacing the memory of all [*souvenir de tout*] that had followed . . .
>
> To foresee consists of projecting into the future what has been perceived in the past, or of imagining for a later time a new grouping, in a new order, of elements already perceived. But *that which has never been perceived, and which is at the same time simple, is necessarily unforeseeable.* Now such is the case with each of our states, regarded as a moment in a history that is gradually unfolding. . . It is an original moment of a no less original history. (Bergson, 1911a, pp. 8–9; emphasis added; French versions inserted from Bergson, 1907/1945, p. 23)

Undoubtedly there is a clear intellectual closeness between Bergson's ideas and James Mark Baldwin's "postulates of genetic science" (e.g., Baldwin, 1906, pp. 21–24). Indeed, Bergson relied on Baldwin's developmental ideas directly (e.g., Bergson, 1911a, p. 32). Furthermore, Bergson's emphasis on the role of acting upon one's environment as functional in development sets him up as a forerunner of our contemporary activity theories of different kinds. That role of Bergson's need not seem surprising, if we consider his reliance upon the actual forefather of activity theories—Pierre Janet (see Bergson, 1911b, pp. xix, 151, 229, etc.). Also, Bergson saw in action a parallel (in time) to perception (in space—cf.

Bergson, 1911b, p. 23: "Perception is master of space in the exact measure in which action is master of time").

SOCIOGENETIC EXPLANATIONS OF THE UNKNOWN   The major problem for any sociogenetic theory remains the explanation of a person's preparedness to act in any novel situation, and in ways that are always semiprepared for that situation. The person is *always* confronting novel situations (due to the irreversibility of time), and hence all psychological processes involved function in the process of this encounter with the still-somewhat unknown.

A mere reference to the past social experiences "transferring" to the present is not sufficient for an explanation, since the present always entails aspects of the situation that could not be predicted in the past. Thus, Morgan's (1892) question—how can a person decide to avoid *conduct* with which she or he has never had any previous direct experience—constitutes a theoretical problem for different sociogenetic views on persons-in-situations. (The same question is, of course, easily thrown into a "black box" by those personality theorists who attribute causality to personality traits or tendencies as causal personal agents—see chapter 5).

The main way to solve this problem within the sociogenetic orientation is to focus on constructive internalization (see Lawrence and Valsiner, 1993): persons transform their social experiences into an internal, semiotically coded "play of imagination," on the basis of which they can instantaneously and preemptively analyze scenarios of possible future encounters with the world, using these "play-out" intrapsychological phenomena for appraisal of possible conduct. Lev Vygotsky's theoretical contributions (see Van der Veer and Valsiner, 1991), as well as Jean Piaget's structuralistic thinking about knowledge construction in ontogeny and society (Piaget, 1965/1995), provide explanations for such personal, yet socially originated, future-oriented activity.

In addition to the intrapsychological work on possible futures, in the realm of social experiences constant construction and reconstruction of structures of social rules are taking place (Sherif, 1936; Sherif et al., 1961). The conduct rules are reconstructed in every new situation (i.e., constantly, since each situation is new!), with the immediate participation of real *or imaginary* "social others." The originators of the sociogenetic perspective—Baldwin, Mead, Janet, and Bergson—showed the intellectual courage to face the most difficult of all questions in understanding development—that of the constantly unknown nature of the to-be-known.

Contemporary Sociogenetic Approaches to Personality

Since the 1920s there have been very few productive efforts to advance the sociogenetic perspective on the development of personality. Different viewpoints were expressed in the 1950s and 1960s (Harry Stack Sullivan's interpersonal early social symbiosis notion—Sullivan, 1953; or John Bowlby's attachment concepts), which will not be analyzed here. It is with the reemergence of culture-oriented traditions in psychology (first of all in cross-cultural, and later cultural, psychology—Cole, 1975, 1981, 1990; D'Andrade, 1984; Krewer, 1990, 1992; Krewer and Jahoda, 1993; Paranjpe, 1989; Poortinga, 1992; Tulviste, 1991; Wertsch, 1991, 1995b) and in parallel with the proliferation of social constructionist tendencies in social psychology (Gergen, 1982, 1989, 1994, Gülerce, 1995; Harré, 1979; Shotter and Gergen, 1989; Youniss and Smollar, 1990) that the sociogenetic viewpoint has regained its vigor. Here it is only those tendencies among the manifold ones of our times that attempt to make sense of the self as a cultural phenomenon that are being considered.

Ernst Boesch's Semiotic Cultural Self-Psychology

Boesch's psychology can be characterized by its elegance, which is perfected in his analyses of the history and cultural construction of skilled action (see Boesch, 1983, 1993). By uniting an explicit account of acting with the symbolic meanings that emerge in that process, and beginning to organize that process, Boesch has laid the foundation for a semiotic cultural psychology of the individual. The relevance of the aesthetic is crucial for such a psychology (Allesch, 1993).

Building upon the ideas of Kurt Lewin and Pierre Janet, Boesch views the individuals' "action field" as organized by cultural meanings, which suggest the range of potential uses of objects by humans, as well as their symbolic value. The action field entails both objective and subjective domains, as well as polyvalence of goals. As an illustration, Boesch refers to an Alpine skier moving skillfully down a slope:

> We might say that his goal of sliding down the slope has two aspects: the one is the objective motion in space, the other are all the sub-

jective sensations related to it, the feeling of harmonious interplay of muscles, the sensation of speed, the impression of mastery. The skier might enjoy both "objective-instrumental" aspect of the action, i.e. mastering his skis, as well as the "subjective-functional" one, i.e., the proprioceptive experience related to it; at any rate, both are always simultaneously present: the action, by necessity, is "polyvalent." (Boesch, 1989, p. 42)

The developed introspective feeling at different levels (e.g., "bare" sensory experience not analyzable in a semiotic code, explicit reflection in speech, or generic discussion through language) guarantees the polyvalence of any human action. Furthermore, action processes are constantly changing—goals are set (and reset), different goals form dynamically changing goal hierarchies, and the person's consciously reflected goals may mismatch with the nonconsciously functioning set of subgoals. Individual action is thus highly heterogeneous, while culture defines the "zones of tolerance" of different ranges of actions rather than specific actions (Boesch, 1991, chapter 3). Furthermore, by way of semiotic mediation, all action possibilities are *redundantly overcontrolled*—there is more than one meaning system that could either set a particular pattern into action or block it from occurring.

Culture regulates action both in terms of limits on the physical execution of actions and by ideological rules. It opens some possibilities for acting, thinking, and feeling, while simultaneously closing others. Furthermore, cultural rules have a hierarchy of organization:

> The quality of a specific rule, such as prohibition to steal, derives from two sources. The first is the occurrence of specific events, such as jealousy, greed, and resulting thefts. The second source for a specific rule are general rules, such as . . . the right to private property. The rules of greeting derive from general rules of politeness, and those again from the ones of respect, social mutuality and social hierarchy. (Boesch, 1989, p. 45)

General cultural rules are partly coded in a variety of forms in the social environment—none of the environmental objects or social practices singularly represents a particular general rule, yet many allude to it in some partial form. Myths are constantly created in a society, while persons' private general idea frameworks (which are ill defined yet omnipresent—"fantasms" in Boesch's terminology) are the personal counterparts of the general rule systems in the self. The person is constantly in the process of structuring (and restructuring) his or her fantasms. Boesch demonstrates this constructive process in the development of Rainer Maria Rilke (Boesch, 1982). Myths constantly guide the construction of fantasms, and the externalization of fantasms leads to the active personal reorganization of the social myths (see Bartlett, 1920a).

Boesch emphasizes the embeddedness of any ontogenesis of action in its cultural-historical confines. The history of music provides a complex example of uniting the cultural history with personal self-motivation of the music maker to try making of new musical melodies—at the tension of experiencing beauty and being anxious to lose it (Boesch, 1993, p. 79). The personal field of a structure of valences is guided by the cultural field, yet it is the tension in the personal field that *can* lead to innovation in the cultural field.

Either painters' decisions to create extraordinary paintings (e.g., see Boesch's analysis of Picasso's *Guernica*—Boesch, 1991, pp. 279–294) or constant everyday modifications of our mundane actions, which we legitimate by boredom or adventure, indicate this locus of synthesis.

Gananath Obeyesekere's Cultural World of Personality

Obeyesekere has been working within a psychoanalytic paradigm, enriching it with his hermeneutic stance and diligently trying to reformulate its conceptual structure on the basis of empirical evidence from Sinhalese cultural contexts (Obeyesekere, 1963, 1968, 1975, 1976, 1977, 1981, 1984, 1990). He has also taken a look at encounters between cultures (Obeyesekere, 1993), revealing the "work of culture" as "the process whereby symbolic forms existing on the cultural level get created and re-created through the minds of people. It deals with the formation and transformation of symbolic forms, but is not a transformation without a subject as in conventional structural analysis" (Obeyesekere, 1990, p. xix).

The structure of personality becomes reorganized, in parallel with the cultural acceptance of that reorganized form (e.g., the aftermath of a woman's successful exorcism from demon possession—Obeyesekere, 1977). The work of culture is a developmentally progressive process in its main scope, even if it may include moments of temporary "regressions" in its course, such as a person's dissociation of the existing personality organization and being in turmoil for long periods of time (Obeyesekere, 1987, p. 104).

Cultural constraints set up conditions under which personal symbolic action takes place—be this the construction of women's pregnancy cravings in Sri Lanka (Obeyesekere, 1963, 1985) or sorcery for retribution (Obeyesekere, 1975). On the other hand, each person acts in unique ways and has a unique personal history; hence any "standard ritual" (e.g., that of exorcism of "demon dominance"—Obeyesekere, 1977) needs to accommodate a variety of specific conditions that may be characteristic of a particular person. Using his experience in South Asia, Obeyesekere emphasizes that it is not the presence or absence of private worlds (or "selves") that is at issue in the case of nonoccidental societies, but the phenomenon of constant movement back and forth between the public and private spheres (Obeyesekere, 1990, p. xix).

Obeyesekere uses the terms *objectification* and *subjectification* as complementary processes that link the personal and cultural symbolic worlds:

> The process by which personal meanings and deep motivations are canalized into public culture is objectification. The symbols that act as the vehicles for intrapsychic processes are personal symbols. Personal symbols are a part of a larger class of psychological symbols. Not all personal symbols need have personal intrapsychic significance, for some personal symbols may become *conventionalized* and lose intrapsychic significance. Other psychological symbols may be psychogenetic in origin but may not have personal significance in the context of a larger set of organized symbols and meanings . . .
>
> Cultural ideas are used to produce, and thereafter justify, innovative acts, meanings, or images that help express the personal needs and fantasies of the individuals. The vehicles that help canalize fantasies— burials, pyres—are *subjective images* and meanings . . . It is also likely that the genesis of the subjective image lies in the individual's fantasy life, but it ceases to be fantasy the moment it becomes justifiable through publicly accepted ideas. (Obeyesekere, 1981, pp. 136–137)

Furthermore, the heterogeneity of forms of personal symbols is already predetermined by the *variety of encounters* with different structured contexts. Thus only part of the cultural ideas becomes activated in the case of a particular person:

> While cultural ideas may be almost universally believed in, personal confrontation with these ideas is highly variable. I shall label that segment of culture that has relevance for experience as *operative cul-*

ture. In cultural analysis it is not sufficient to delineate the culture: it is also necessary to see how it *operates* in collective or individual experience. The belief in the Buddha is universal in Sri Lanka; it is also universally operative. The belief in incubi [male demons who have sexual intercourse with women] is also universal; yet it is operative only in rare cases. (Obeyesekere, 1981, pp. 139–140)

New kinds of encounters may be introduced by new social practices (e.g., proliferation of a religion previously unknown in the culture), which may lead to the construction of a projective system of ideas—constructed by persons in collective ways, projecting upon the the world (Obeyesekere, 1984, p. 481). A central place in this constructive process is given to subjective imagery:

Subjective imagery is often protoculture, or culture in the making. While all forms of subjective imagery are innovative, not all of them end up as culture, for the latter depends upon the acceptance of the subjective imagery by the group and its legitimation in terms of the larger culture. Subjective imagery, insofar as it is based on objective culture, has the potential for group acceptance, unlike fantasy or totally innovative acts, which have no prior cultural underpinnings. (Obeyesekere, 1984, pp. 169–170)

Culture for Obeyesekere consists of internalized ideas in the minds of persons, mediated by consciousness. Since consciousness is primarily personally constructed, the "sharing" of culture between persons can only be episodic and partial (see Obeyesekere, 1977; demon possession is a personal-psychological phenomenon that is not shared with others yet can be exorcised by cultural rules). Furthermore, specific sophistic readings of cultural texts by constructive persons can bring into being forms of conduct that seemingly deviate from cultural meanings yet are incorporated into those by special conditions (e.g., the making of "Buddhist eggs"—see Obeyesekere, 1968, p. 30).

Obeyesekere transcends the deterministic ethos of Freudian thought as he builds his theoretical composite terms (e.g., the notion of "work of culture" is an explicit opponent to the notion of "dreamwork"). In his analytic world of life dramas of Sinhalese ascetics and demons-possessed women, he views their process of the work of culture, as that moves them

into another level of reality that makes life not only bearable but transfigured and meaningful, and which is most interesting, utterly pleasurable—at least for most of them and for some of the time. It is this new level of reality that is now the crucial one: the mundane world where the Freudian reality testing takes place is left behind entirely or subordinated to the new reality. Yet what is striking about this new reality is that, unlike the mundane reality, it is in conformity with the pleasure principle. The virtuoso who undergoes trance . . . does so at the service of the ego; it is not regression, however, but progression. In spirit *attack* the priestess is overwhelmed by outside forces; after recovery she acts with autonomy to bring about divine possession. (Obeyesekere, 1990, p. 68)

Perhaps the most central innovation of the psychoanalytic thought that Obeyesekere introduces (and that moves him irreversibly away from orthodox occidental psychoanalytic explanations) is the move from *overdetermination of motive* (as emphasized by Freud and reflected in dream analysis) to *overdetermination of meaning* (Obeyesekere, 1990, p. 56). All events in human life occur in polysemic contexts, being framed by a variety of cultural meanings, operating simultaneously at different *levels of symbolic remove* from deep motivations. Some of the cultural meanings are closer to the motivations (events) that originally triggered the personal symbolization process, which utilized culturally available means. However, in human development, some levels of symbolization may lose all their connection with the initial "triggering event" and acquire symbolic life of their own in the individual's personality. This notion parallels the semiogenetic ideas of Lev Vygotsky (1971; see also Van der Veer and Valsiner, 1994) and other semiotic perspectives on human development (see chapter 6). Furthermore, Obeyesekere's theoretical transposition of the notion of overdetermination to the symbolic level eliminates an axiomatic impasse that had governed psychoanalysis since its inception:

"Symbolic remove" is based on the psychoanalytic idea that symbols in principle, if not always in practice, show infinite substitutionability. Related to this idea is another principle of the work of culture that psychoanalysis has not, and could not, consider seriously since it would threaten the isomorphism between symbol and symptom. And that is the principle of disconnection of the symbol from the sources of motivation. Substitution implies that symbol X related to motive Y can be replaced by symbols A, B, or C . . . n. A, B, C are all "isomorphic replacements" of X, related to motive Y in identical or similar manner. "Disconnection" questions the postulated isomorphism and suggests that A, B, C . . . n might exhibit degrees of symbolic remove from Y and might eventually lose its connection with Y . . . Admittedly, total disconnection is rare, but one can make a reasonable case that the more the symbol is removed from the sources of motivation the more it gets the attribute of arbitrariness, thus approximating the Saussurean idea of the arbitrary relation between signifier and signified. (Obeyesekere, 1990, p. 58)

Obeyesekere adds this constructive-disjunctive (of the symbol from the motive) dimension to the culture-work idea, thus liberating the psychoanalytic perspective from its expression-interpreting fate. This theoretical reconstruction leads Obeyesekere to accept the notion of multilinearity and equifinality in the symbolization process (Obeyesekere, 1987, p. 107). The *origins* of any cultural symbols in the ontogeny of a person become in principle untraceable retrospectively, yet the person's reconstruction of his or her self through the study of the culture-work process—moving from the personal present to the future—becomes a target of potential investigation. Obeyesekere thus finds a solution very similar to Baldwin's—the study of progressive developmental reorganization of the self—for his interest in making sense of the ascetics and the possessed in Sri Lanka. Furthermore, this innovation leads to a basic methodological criticism of existing traditions in psychology:

> The conventional cross-cultural method and cross-cultural tests of causal hypotheses pertaining to symbols are for the most part meaningless. Thus the hypothesis that if you have X, a certain motive, you would also have Y, a certain cultural symbol causally associated with it, is impossible to test on a random sample for the simple fact that Y may show degrees of symbolic elaboration ranging from the absence of Y in some societies to its fullest symbolic elaboration in others. Furthermore the notion of substitutionability of symbols implies that where X is related to Y in one society, X would be related to a substitute symbol Z in another society, rendering predictions either dubious or outright impossible. Third, the notion of disconnection implies that a postulated correlation between X and Y may not be a true causal relation insofar as Y has become disconnected from X . . . Finally, while X may exist, Y may not. (Obeyesekere, 1990, p. 62)

Obeyesekere's closeness to his empirical phenomenology puts him in a good position to extend the conceptual limitations of occidental myths that have been turned into a science. Thus, the Oedipus myth as the cultural vehicle for Freud in the development of his version of psychoanalysis could have been very different if Freud's place of origin and clinical practice had been Delhi instead of Vienna (Obeyesekere, 1990, pp. 86–87).

Obeyesekere's symbolic constructivism opens various novel possibilities for interdisciplinary scholarship in cultural history and developmental psychology (Stirrat, 1987). Historical case analyses of occidental materials—for instance, the religious conversion experiences of adolescents in medieval Europe (Bell, 1985; Weinstein and Bell, 1982)—display examples of the work of culture that have clear parallels with Obeyesekere's empirical analyses of aggression canalization (Obeyesekere, 1975), exorcism (Obeyesekere, 1977), or religious ritual performances (Obeyesekere, 1981). The definitive database for these studies is that of progressive case study of individuals in their cultural contexts. Furthermore, Pierre Janet's descriptions of persons' psychological organization in the case of sociopersonal tendencies in religious contexts (e.g, Janet, 1926, 1927, 1928a) are close in their interpretability in terms of culture work.

Shweder Within the Hindu World: Mutuality of Culture and Self

Starting from an anthropological background, Richard Shweder's claims of recent years have undoubtedly pointed to the need to consider culture in psychology as a primary constituting factor of the self (Shweder, 1984; 1991; Shweder and Much, 1987; Shweder and Sullivan, 1990, 1993). The cultural richness of India has certainly fascinated Europeans in many ways (see also chapter 9), but only rarely has occidental science attempted to provide in-depth analyses of the cultural constructions in the Hindu world.

It is through selectively positioned empirical themes that occidental science has penetrated the nonoccidental worlds. Much of the interest in the self has been triggered by questions of moral reasoning patterns in different societies. Surely this theme requires analyses of complex cognitive-affective worlds, in conjunction with their social practices. The domain of the field of culturally situated action is vast. Shweder's approach recognizes the heterogeneity and culture-inclusiveness of moral reasoning of human beings (Shweder, 1995; Shweder and Much, 1987; Shweder, Mahapatra, and Miller, 1987). Shweder returns to the emphasis of culturally constituted person as agents in both subjective and collective domains:

"To imaginatively conceive of subject-dependent objects (intentional worlds) and object-dependent subjects (intentional persons) interpenetrating each other's identities or setting the conditions for each other's existence and development, while jointly undergoing change through social interaction" (Shweder, 1990, p. 25).

The personal minds (object-dependent persons) construct mental and affective order out of the chaos of everyday events—hence, an illusory view of reality is constructed by persons, but on the basis of the culture. The latter facet led Shweder to reject the reconstructed versions of Piaget's ideas that circulated among American cognitive child psychologists.

The specific processes by which mental and cultural processes work become clarified by Shweder in his analyses of the construction of self in Hindu collective-cultural contexts. It has been argued that persons in India possess an alternative (to European or North American) postconventional moral code in which *interpersonal obligations are viewed as principled highest levels of moral reasoning*, rather than in terms of the decontextualized notion of abstract "justice" (Miller and Bersoff, 1992). This result from psychology's cross-cultural studies fits with occidental efforts to overcome dualisms as those are constructed in European or North American psychology. In most direct ways, the phenomenon of interpersonal interdependence being considered the highest principled level of moral reasoning refutes Lawrence Kohlberg's stage account of morality.

The cultural complexity and richness of Indian narrative and psychological traditions has fascinated many social scientists, who, however, have faced obstacles in their understanding due to their own cultural backgrounds (see Hiebert, 1983; Larson, 1990). The self in Hindu contexts has been a complex subject matter (Chatterji, 1985; Davis, 1983). Shweder's specific work on the organization of the self in Hindu collective-cultural contexts takes the form of elaboration of specific personal-cultural transformations of socially shared knowledge. Everyday conversations surrounding the developing person are filled with cultural suggestions for how to interpret the nature of experience in accordance with social representations (Moscovici, 1994). Shweder encountered specific collective-cultural organization of moral discourse in his efforts to apply Kohlbergian moral dilemmas in Hindu contexts in Orissa. His elaborate dispute with the informant Babaji (Shweder and Much, 1987, pp. 235–244; see also chapter 6) revealed how a Western collective-culturally shared "moral dilemma" (stealing or not stealing a drug when faced with a life-threatening illness of one's wife and a drug-owner's refusal to provide it by special arrangements) can be translated into a completely different personal-cultural issue (i.e., sinning versus not sinning by stealing for one's wife, even if the latter's life is in jeopardy). Most important, the Babaji interview reveals the *conditional setup of the boundaries* (see greater detail in chapter 2) of the realm of meanings applicable to the image of a given situation. By way of specific combination of collective-cultural meanings of "sin," "wife" (as "belonging to" the husband), "multiple lives," and "inevitability of death," a set of alternative personal-culturally allowable scenarios for the action of the person in a dilemma situation is being constructed.

Further information about the integration of the personal and collective cultures emerges in the study of how Oriya informants interpret an icon of the goddess Kali. Kali is the fierce goddess—bringing both birth and death—in the mythologies of the Hindu world (Kondos, 1986; Samantha, 1994). In the particular story used by Menon and Shweder, Kali is depicted stepping on the body of her husband Siva and displaying collectively shared emotional expression of *lajya* (usually translated as "shame"), expressed by the goddess's protruded tongue at the moment she discovers she is stepping on her own husband (Menon and Shweder, 1994).

Menon and Shweder demonstrated personally differential understanding of the particular cultural myth by their informants. Three "modules" of interpretation—*lajya* versus anger; destructive versus constructive role of women; and men-women relations—were differentially utilized by the informants. Furthermore, different cultural-historical traditions emerged in the interviews: the Tantric tradition of women's domineering role in social and psychological issues could be seen to be behind some of the personal reconstructions of the Kali/Siva story.

What emerges from Menon's and Shweder's analysis of the interpretations of the Kali/Siva story is the *intransitive relationship circle* that operates in the regulation of conduct in the collective culture and guides the personal cultural worlds through internalization (refer to theoretical elaboration in chapter 3). Thus, the goddess Kali (who is the wife of Siva and thus deferential to him) can transform into an all-powerful destructive agent who can kill anybody—human, deity, or demon. Yet her discovery of her own culturally inappropriate act *as the wife* (i.e., stepping on her husband, an act of ultimate nondeference) creates a basic ambivalence. While *in the role of the all-destructive demon hunter* Kali had been killing everybody on her way, based on her rage (Menon and Shweder, 1994), now her discovery that she is about to breach a major social rule triggers the emotion that is interpretable from the viewpoint of its contrast with a *counter-*

role (see Oliveira and Valsiner, 1996). Kali's *lajya* emerges at the moment of personally recognized tension between the roles of wife and destroyer.

Intransitivity in dynamic social relations and intrapersonal psychological flow may be the rule, rather than exception (as was remarked in chapter 3). In a substantive reanalysis of the Hindu caste system (Das, 1982b, p. 69), gift-giving decisions in kinship network context (Das, 1976a), and an analysis of role relations in the temple (Appadurai and Appadurai-Breckenridge, 1976), a similar picture of intransitive temporal relations seems to emerge. What has been looked at (by Western views) as an impenetrably *fixed strict hierarchy* (i.e., one characterized by transitivity: A>B and B>C, therefore A>C) of Indian social relations may in reality be a hierarchy organized in time by intransitive logical relations (as was described in chapter 3). Evidence for this exists in Shweder's work on three major themes of moral discourse in Orissa: autonomy, community, and divinity (Shweder et al., 1993).

In summary, it can be argued that in South Asia—as well as everywhere else (as is shown in this book)—a dynamic organization of interdependent self (or inclusively differentiated self) can be found. In this case, "the individual is seen as constantly being transformed by his transactions with others since he can convey the essence of his nature and receive the essence of others by entering into relationships of transaction" (Das, 1992, p. 89).

The emphasis on constant transformation of the self is obviously a link between the developmental mind-set and dynamically oriented accounts of personality. A modern return to the analysis of selves occurs in the contemporary rhetoric and hermeneutic traditions, at least as an effort.

Rhetoric and Hermeneutic Sociogenetic Perspectives

The penetration of "postmodernist" ideologies from the social discourses of occidental societies into the social sciences that have grown in their midst is an inevitable growth of a fragile scientific enterprise that is caught between a quest for basic knowledge and the inherent ideological inclinations of the knowledge seekers (see Mead, 1930a, 1930b). The rhetorics-oriented views of the self that have flourished in recent decades have certainly restored some phenomenological openness to the study of the self, thus transcending the triviality of the traditions of unbounded uses of rating scales, with the resulting overgeneralization of the findings. Building on the intersection of ideological values of cultural relativism, belief in the social nature of the mind, and belief in the ethics of the unity of the person with the society (or its texts), the rhetoric approaches have actively deconstructed methodological assumptions of traditional psychology (Gergen, 1982, 1985, 1988, 1989, 1990, 1994; Gergen and Gergen, 1988; Harré, 1970, 1974, 1979, 1980, 1984b; Shotter, 1990, 1993a). However, in the chorus of loud "voices" in favor of these ideologies, and in the calls for socially situated perspectives on personality, the historical (and therefore developmental) focus can become lost, in all of its facets (culture-genetic, ontogenetic, and microgenetic):

> Whether we look back to the less individualistic Middle Ages or across cultures to Japan, India, or the remnants of unlettered societies, our natural tendency to take our own perspective on self and world as the only right and true perspective is challenged. Both approaches raise the challenge of relativism, although somehow *my students turn out to be extreme cultural relativists without the slightest sense of historical relativism:* They forgive the Buga-Buga everything, except maybe infanticide and clitoridectomy, but they hold their forebears morally responsible for extreme benightedness. (Smith, 1994, p. 406; emphasis added)

The unevenness in the proliferation of the meaning of ideological equality of cultures in the discourse of occidental social scientists is itself a collective-cultural construction (see chapter 5). Paradoxically, the *de*construction of traditional psychology's perspectives on the self in society from a rhetoric perspective has guaranteed an intellectual impasse of the critical effort, since replacing the focus on the individuated self with a focus on the socially situated one moves scientists' thinking into the realm of sociological reductionism. The latter orientation is exactly equal (in its inability to provide *re*constructive possibilities) to the perspective that it has been making the target of its insinuations (e.g., the "positivist" or "individual-fixed" or "dualistic" psychology).

The focus on language use in accounting for personality has led contemporary scholars to the understanding of wide possibilities of the common languages to provide almost any explanation for human conduct (see empirical demonstration in Gergen, Hepburn, and Fisher, 1986). Such wide semiotic constructivity is exactly at the heart of the functioning of language in human mental processes (see chapter 4), and is predicated upon the *omniscopous* (i.e., "all-seeing" or everything-interpreting) nature of language that has been used productively by fortune-tellers (Aphek and Tobin, 1983, 1990) as well as (possibly) by psychologists (Siegfried, 1994).

The omniscopous nature of language has triggered numerous efforts to find out the limits of its applicability to the study of human action and personality (Heider, 1958; Semin, 1994). In its very liberal application, the omniscope of language makes it possible to view persons *as if* they were cultural texts. *Any* description of personality can be constructed by the use of language. From here it follows that *many* different scenarios—built along the lines of demands of communicative process, or on the basis of cultural scenarios—are encountered in laypersons' self-descriptions or in psychologists' narratives. The "truthfulness" of such accounts cannot be established, since the self-descriptive scenarios are themselves culturally constructed particulars that depend upon the given person in the situation (Gergen, 1988). Neither would the empiricistic methodological traditions in psychology allow for construction of adequate knowledge within this field of heterogeneous social construction (Gergen, 1986, 1990).

The heterogeneity of language use in the construction of self leads to the investigation of the *kinds of cultural constraints* that regulate the omniscopous use of language. Such organizational constraints—narrative structures—have provided a basis investigating temporal structures of the social construction (Gergen and Gergen, 1984, 1986, 1988). In a further extension of the communicational constructivist position, John Shotter (1990, 1994) emphasizes social construction of psychological phenomena in the context of situated activity. These contexts—"the sphere of diffuse, sensuous or feelingful activity, this unordered hurly-burly or bustle of everyday social life" (Shotter, 1990, p. 7)—are supposed to lead persons to act in responsive ways and to develop their ways of *knowing from within a situation*. It is in the process of that knowing "from within" (or "practical-moral knowledge") that social rhetorics constitute the process of meaning-making. Ways of talking are rooted in the background world of socially organized everyday activities, yet what is constructed by way of communication can restructure the person's understanding of the "bustle of life." Shotter situates psychology among "moral sciences," with a respective centrality in the inquiry attributed to moral concepts (e.g., "citizenship") and the scientist's embeddedness in the social field (Shotter, 1990). Much of this kind of language-based social constructionism borrows from the work of Ludwig Wittgenstein, makes overtures toward a sociocentric interpretation of the work of Lev Vygotsky and Mikhail Bakhtin, and yet is importantly continuous with the work of Rom Harré.

Rom Harré's Sociophilosophical Perspective on the Self

Harré's long-range efforts to reformulate psychology's focus (Harré, 1970, 1979, 1980, 1981a, 1981b, 1981c, 1981d, 1984b, 1989) have resulted in a view on personality that builds on the sociogenetic generic thought model by way of rich dramaturgical metaphors. Human action is a temporal process, and hence its regulation depends upon the actor's immediate interpretation of an interpersonal setting in terms of a hierarchical rule system. In his earlier work, Harré used the everyday phenomenon of hesitant or inappropriate hand-shaking to illustrate the notion of rule hierarchies as constraining social action:

> Sometimes the person wonders why the hand of the interactor has been put forward. Is it the opening move in a greeting ritual? Is it the beginning of a request for something? Are we about to wrestle? . . . Choice of definition calls forth a certain set of rules and the appropriate episode develops. Sometimes the person realizes that a hand has been put forward as the opening of some greeting ceremony but does not know what to do with it, that is the beginning of a greeting ritual has been identified, but the rule for proceeding is unclear. Are they Anglo-Saxons, expecting a firm grip? Are they Orientals expecting a limp touch? Are they Royalty expecting a kiss? . . . The next stage of this study will involve the construction of scenarios and the acting out of various action-possibilities, and the collection of further accounts from the actors, which in turn will lead to refinements in the scenarios. (Harré, 1974, p. 160)

The functioning of rules is viewed as excluding different action options at each node (decision moment in time). For instance, in ontogeny the rule system is established through partial encounter: children discover "what is right" only by experiencing their own (or someone else's) running up against clearly prohibited actions (rather than acquiring long lists of "acceptable" actions). Different rules interact (under time pressure) in ways that provide for a wide variety of interpretations and corresponding actions. This variety of possible actions is regulated by "dramaturgical constraints"—maxims of style of conduct (Harré, 1974, p. 181). By presenting socially authentic selves, persons transform their selves into novel structural forms—which nevertheless remain social in nature. The dramaturgical constraints affect the cultural organization of gender roles and sexuality (Harré, 1981a), as well as psychologists' enacting the puritan rituals of experiments (Harré, 1981b, 1981d; Moghaddam and Harré, 1992; see also chapter 9) and regulation of feelings (Harré, 1981c, 1984a, pp. 123–140).

Harré's conceptualization of the socially organized physical environment is analogous with von Uexküll's *Bedeutungslehre* (see also chapter 5). In borrowing von Uexküll's terminology (of *Umwelt*), Harré sets up the social context for a person in terms of a social topography: "As we pass through space and time we are continually adjusting ourselves to a complex social topography. Some regions are closed to us, some open. For some various keys or magic passwords are required, such as 'Oh, yes, I'm a member here.' Looking at this ethogenically, we must ask how these barriers are established and promulgated, how they are maintained, how legitimately crossed, how their accidental violation is remedied" (Harré, 1979, pp. 194–195).

The social world sets up the structure of the topographic world for the person to relate with. Rituals—different in different societies, and at different age levels within a society (see Harré, 1979, pp. 219–220)—are markers of value at entrance points. After entrance to a field, rituals exist in different parts of the field, and are usable for its maintenance. Social roles charted out on that field are supported by the reframing of the person's body (through costumes and uniforms, or social expectations for clothing styles), including permanent modifications (e.g., tattoos, ear piercing) or cultural regulation of exposure or modification of specific aspects of the body (e.g., cultural dramas around body hair—Delaney, 1994; Hershman, 1974; Olson, 1985).

As a result of the social construction of the *Umwelt,* the person "is not a natural object, but a cultural artefact" (Harré, 1984a, p. 20). Harré distinguishes the person (as an empirical concept, in contrast with a collective) and the self (as a socially constructed theoretical self-reflection). Harré's "personal being" consists of a sense of personal identity, self-consciousness (self-awareness and self-attention), and agency. The latter—usually seen in personal-causal ways in psychology—is reinterpreted by Harré as socially guided. Even the agency for a particular act, attributed to some god by a person, is part of that person's "personal being" (see Harré, 1984a, pp. 26–30).

Harré reaches a relatively extreme view of the socially embedded nature of the person by claiming that no psychological mechanisms exist, other than persons' social practices (Harré, 1989, pp. 27, 34). While the reason for such dramatic claims is explainable as a rhetorical step to counteract the individualistic assumptions of cognitive science in favor of the study of discourse (see also Harré, 1992; Harré and Gillett, 1994), the dispute resembles the one between Dewey and his disciples on the one hand and the "mentalistic" cognitive science of the 1890s. Thus, in an almost direct parallel to Dewey, claims such as the following are being made:

> Discursive phenomena, for example, acts of remembering, are not manifestations of hidden subjective, psychological phenomena. They *are* the psychological phenomena. Sometimes they have subjective counterparts; sometimes they do not. There is no necessary shadow world of mental activity behind discourse in which one is working things out in private. This viewpoint amounts to a fundamental denial of the Cartesian view of human beings, not least because it denies that the workings of the mind are inaccessible. The workings of each other's minds are available to us in what we jointly create conversationally, and if our private mental activity is also symbolic, using essentially the same system, then we can make it available or not, as the situation seems to require it. (Harré and Gillett, 1994, p. 27)

The process orientation in Harré's perspective (like Dewey's of a century earlier) provides for a reasonable starting point for the conceptualization of psychological processes. That focus on dynamicity is shared by other followers of the discursive, narrow, and treacherous path to the mountaintop of knowledge; it provides some rationale for the uses of discourse-analytic schemes applied to novels (Bakhtin, 1934/1975) in the case of psychological investigation (Wertsch, 1991; Smolka, 1994b). The same is true of perspectives emanating from dynamic systems theory (Fogel, 1993) or from the observations of early construction of semiotic means (Lyra and Rossetti-Ferreira, 1995).

Conclusions: Ambivalence of Person and Culture in the Sociogenetic Perspectives on Personality

Sociogenetic perspectives on personality have struggled over the past century in an effort to overcome the ambivalence in our reflections upon the social nature of the person. There have been only a few ways to solve the problem. The simplest—outright *denial* of the social nature (or social origins) of human personality—would of course be unavailable to those thinkers who are here loosely grouped under the sociogenetic label. From the outset, their efforts ruled out denial as a solution.

The second widespread strategy of sociogenetic thinkers is that of viewing personality as reducible to some social explanatory principle. Talk of "persons *as* texts" or "persons *as* social roles" may indicate traces of such social reductionism. In its nature, the reduction of the psychological processes to their social backgrounds effectively gets rid of the issue of persons' *relations with* the social world. If the persons are mere socially embedded puppets—even if biologically separate from one another—then it is sufficient to study the social world as such and see it merely mirrored in the conduct of individuals. The social reductionist stance is thus a more complicated denial strategy—by *avoidance*. It is one in which the focus of attention is changed in order to avoid the difficulties of a major conceptual problem.

Third, we encounter social reductionist versions that solve the problem of person-society relations by *labeling* it—for instance, as fusion (of the person with the social context) or coordination (see earlier discussion on Dewey). Here the existence of a relationship is presumed—albeit in ways that deny further study of it. Once a dynamic process is labeled by a convenient term, it may replace the actual analysis of the process it refers to with the illusion that the semantic field of the term clarifies the process. Thus, in a curious way, different sociogenetic perspectives that are about to make sense of the person's social nature become hostages to the very social nature (of language semantics) on which they depend.

As will be shown in the next chapter, there is considerable overlap between the sociogenetic and personological approaches to personality. It will also be obvious that the conceptualization difficulties of the person-social world relations are very similar to the ones outlined here for the personological approaches. The social nature of human personality proves to be teasing the social scientists through the hidden assumptions of their language games.

5

Personological Constructions of Personality

The central focus of personalistic perspectives is parallel to that of socioge-netic ones—an emphasis on person-environment relationships as the basis for personality development. The basic difference between these perspec-tives is in the particular accent of dominance in these relationships. For personology the subjective, lived-through experience constitutes the do-main in which personality develops, while for the sociogeneticists the focus is on the social suggestions that have control over the personal experiences that lead in personality development.

Despite this differential focus, the two perspectives do not lose track of each other. The personological thinkers find ways to make sense of the per-son living within the sociocultural world: the unique personal experience itself is socially organized. Similarly, socioculturally minded researchers cannot overlook the relative psychological autonomy of the person from any given social context. The social nature of human development results in personal subjectivity, which allows for relative autonomy in personal conduct. It is in fact the presence of such relative personal autonomy from any particular cultural context that is the ultimate proof of the sociogenetic perspective on human development.

Experience: Personal and Constructed

It is not surprising that the sociogenetic and personological perspectives share their locus of interest—that in the phenomena of human experi-ence—yet explain these phenomena from axiomatically different positions. It is the *human* nature of experience that provides both perspectives with sufficient possibilities to expand their analyses. Yet often these perspectives are viewed in terms of "either/or" opposites, separated (exclusively) from each other. The sociogenetic thinkers may be considered to be the "opposite camp" to the personological thinkers. Such a presentation is clearly counterproductive for further advancement of both sociogenetic and personological ideas.

In reality, it is not problematic to unite the seeming opposites, which consider human experience as either "inherently social" or "phenomenologically personal." They are united in the central role of the experiencing person in any psychological phenomena. Without assuming the presence of such person, neither perspective can exist. The experiencing person develops in irreversible time (Bergson, 1911a; Krech, 1950; Prigogine, 1987) and is necessarily the locus of origin of one's subjectively experienced universe (Bühler, 1990). This person has developed possibilities to reflect subjectively upon real, remembered, or imaginary experiences in the space of "here and now," and to transcend the context of the latter to think, feel, and desire some state of "there and then." The experiencing person is simultaneously embedded in some sociocultural context and free from it. The latter is made possible by personal construction of semiotically mediated subjectivity (see chapter 6).

William James's Captivation of the *Psyche*

William James's emphasis on pragmatism (Myers, 1986) can be viewed as a conceptual effort to coordinate the personal-experiential and physical aspects of human experience. If one considers a person in a room, looking at a book, then the perceiving and acting person treats the book (and the room) in ways that imply the presence of characteristics not limited to the physical ones. The (physically) same object is not the same in being interpreted by a person. How can the unity of same and not-same be conceptualized? In an analogy with geometry, James claimed:

> The puzzle of how the one identical room can be in two places is at the bottom just the puzzle of how one identical point can be on two lines. It can, if it be situated at their intersection; and similarly, if the "pure experience" of the room were a place of intersection of two processes, which connected it with different groups of associates respectively, it could be counted twice over, as belonging to either group, and spoken of loosely as existing in two places, although it would remain all the time a numerically single thing. (James, 1904b, p. 481)

James was trying to overcome dualisms in psychological conceptualization, and hence was eager to find ways to show the united but relatively autonomous nature of the subjective ("conscious") and objective sides of personal experience. He both borrowed from the European traditions of the nineteenth century (particularly from Franz Brentano) and fed into the development of Edmund Husserl's phenomenology (see analysis by Herzog, 1995), which in its turn has given rise to numerous psychological traditions.

By belonging simultaneously to opposite but united contexts, James tried to replace the habit of *exclusive* separation of the person and the environment (or "consciousness" and "reality") with its *inclusive* form (see chapter 1). Thus, in the example of the room, two processes are simultaneously present:

> One of them is the reader's personal biography, the other is the history of the house of which the room is part. The presentation, the experience, the *that* in sort (for until we have decided *what* it is it must be a mere *that*) is the last term of a train of sensations, emotions, decisions, movements, classifications, expectations, etc., ending in the present, and the first term of a series of similar "inner" operations extending into the future, on the reader's part. On the other hand, the very same *that* is the *terminus ad quem* of a lot of previous physical operations, carpentering, papering, furnishing, warming, etc., and the *terminus a quo* of a lot of future ones, in which it will be concerned when undergoing the destiny of a physical room. The physical and the mental operations form curiously incompatible groups. As a room, the experience has occupied that spot and had that environment for thirty years. As your field of consciousness it may never have existed until now. (James, 1904b, pp. 481–482)

The two histories—that of the subjectivity of the person and of the objectivity of the room—are united in the act of their mutual encounter. The two are *not* fused. They do not lose their separate being, yet they are closely intertwined in the person's living through of the given present. However, their separate origins lead to different pragmatic possibilities for the experiencing person:

> As a room, attention will go on to discover endless details in it. As your mental state merely, few ones will emerge under attention's eye. As a room, it will take an earthquake, or a gang of men, and in any case a certain amount of time, to destroy it. As your subjective state, the closing of your eyes, or any instantaneous play of your fancy will suffice. In real world, the fire will consume it. In your

mind, you can let fire play over it without effect. As an outer object, you must pay so much a month to inhabit it. As an inner content, you may occupy it for any length of time rent-free. (James, 1904b, p. 482)

The intersection of the objective and the subjective allows for personal construction of experiences that are unique yet interdependent with context. Furthermore, the subjective process of experiencing makes it possible to construct abstracted and retained encodings of previous (real or imaginary) experiences that are actualized in novel immediate contexts. The basis for such reflexive adaptation of the psychological processes may be social (as claimed by the sociogenetic traditions, described in chapter 4), yet their actual functioning in any setting is centered on the constructive activity of the personal subjective world. It is in the traditions of thought that have emphasized the centrality of personal psychological worlds in the context of experiencing—the personologies of William Stern and Gordon Allport—where we can look for the complementation of otherwise overly deterministic sociogenetic claims.

William Stern's Personology

Louis William Stern's (1871–1938) contributions to psychology have recently become the focus of interest and revival (Deutsch, 1991; Hoppe-Graff and Mäckelburg, 1991; Kreppner, 1992; Lamiell, 1981, 1987, 1991, 1992; Reinert, Boné, Heil, Kindermann, and Zeimet, 1980). Despite the eminent availability of Stern's theoretical work in English (Stern, 1938) and its explanations by Stern himself (Stern, 1930) as well as by others (Allport, 1937b; Eyferth, 1976; Grossmann, 1986; Hardesty, 1976; Werner, 1938), for a long time his basic contributions to psychology were left to the collection of ideas in history of psychology.

Forgetting Stern is not difficult for contemporary psychology, which is dominated by classifications of "theories and systems," focuses on empirical research, and is historically myopic. Stern's holistic Weltanschauung—which included both empirical and philosophical sides in an inseparable multiple unity—defies any classification efforts. Thus, it is not surprising that Stern usually is mentioned for specific contributions (e.g., as the originator of differential psychology, as the inventor of the "intelligence coefficient," or for his early studies of children as witnesses). Or he can be conveniently considered a "personologist" within the "systems and theories" classification system. However, the intellectual reasons that led Stern to all of these areas—even as those are explicated by Stern himself (see Stern, 1930)—have rarely been analyzed.

Escape From Philosophy Through Creating It: Stern's Life Course

Stern's early autobiography (Stern, 1930) gives us a vivid account of his formative years. Born in 1871, Stern began his studies at the University of Berlin in 1888, first showing an interest in philology, then in philosophy, then finally creating his own solution to his intellectual needs in his specific way of unifying philosophy and empirical psychology. Interestingly, in his studies of philosophy, Stern acknowledged the role of Friedrich Paulsen (almost singularly among his teachers in Berlin). It is noteworthy that the whole cohort of his age-mates who moved through Berlin as students in the 1880s were similarly grateful to Paulsen, who was mentioned in similar terms by James Mark Baldwin and George Herbert Mead, among others. Stern also studied with Hermann Ebbinghaus, who emphasized the need for careful empirical investigations in parallel with general philosophical elaborations.

Stern's retrospect of the studies of philosophy in German universities (especially in Berlin) at the end of the nineteenth century is anything but complimentary:

> The collapse of speculative philosophy after the death of Hegel had had a paralyzing effect, the triumphal procession of natural science a downright hypnotic one. The professional representatives of philosophy were for the most part content to evade the situation by turning their gaze backwards: either to the history of philosophy in general, or particularly "back to Kant." Some saw the essence of philosophy in its history, others in epistemology. Some thought to attain the objective spirit of history through the utmost suppression of their own point of view, others found in epistemology essentially a justification for not having any opinion on ultimate, i.e. metaphysical questions. . .
>
> . . .Under such conditions, the mental and educational intellectual influences of philosophy instructors upon their students were rather pathetic. Among the students, the hatred of metaphysics took the form of simple hatred toward all philosophy; that anyone who did not for reasons of academic credit have to attend philosophy lec-

tures should do so from choice was almost unthinkable. (Stern, 1930, pp. 336–337)

Stern lived through similar ambivalence toward philosophy and saved his soul through engagement in empirical psychology—yet asking questions of metaphysical relevance. Thus, in his own words, "I have never, like so many other experimental psychologists, become 'scientificated.' The connection with philosophy and the humanities was always evident for me" (Stern, 1930, p. 340).

Perhaps it was exactly the resistance to dogmatic philosophizing (as well as to the equally dogmatic belief in the saving grace of psychological experimentation) that made it possible for Stern to construct his personological system, benefiting from (but not being slave to) his meticulous empirical investigations. He developed his system after his move to Breslau (in 1897), where—instead of surroundings of philosophical dogmatism—Stern found philosophical isolation. In the context of having nobody but himself to dialogue with on philosophical matters, he constructed the philosophical system of personalism —in 1900–1901 (Stern, 1930, p. 351). The resulting "fifty theses" were used in his seminar with students, who, unlike from his colleagues, were eager to enter into substantive dialogues. The exposition of the personalistic system over the following years was mostly an elaboration of the system as conceived in these years. Stern's close contact with his relative Ernst Cassirer—who also worked in Breslau and was later brought by Stern to Hamburg—left the human sciences with an interesting parallel of ideas. Stern's focus on "concrete subjectivity" has intellectual parallels in Cassirer's fundamental contribution to the issue of life organization via "symbolic forms" (which was partly an anchor point for Lev Vygotsky's sociogenetic ideas).

Stern recognized different sources of intellectual interdependency of his system with those of his predecessors: Fechner's focus on hierarchical organization, Wundt's on activity, Hartmann's on teleology, and Dilthey's on the concreteness of personality. However, none of these played more than a supportive role in Stern's own task. Stern confessed that he "had to find a dialectic solution, which would not be a compromise, but a genuine radical synthesis of teleology and mechanism: and this was the concept I undertook to develop critically, the concept of *personality*" (Stern, 1930, p. 353). The system was developed over the course of three relevant monographs entitled *Person und Sache* (Stern, 1906, 1919, 1924).

At Hamburg University: The Intellectual *Umwelt* and Advancement of Ideas

In 1915, Stern moved to Hamburg, where he was instrumental in the establishment of both the University of Hamburg (in 1919) and its Psychological Institute. In the 1920s, the Psychological Institute in Hamburg was one of the three major centers of construction of new directions in psychology (together with Berlin, the center of Gestalt psychology, and Leipzig, where *Ganzheitspsychologie* traditions were being advanced— Sander and Volkelt, 1962).

In Hamburg, the intellectual environment expanded remarkably in the 1920s, largely facilitated by Stern's administrative actions. He turned his Psychological Laboratory into the Psychological Institute in 1919 and established a close group of intellectually active coworkers. Stern participated in the advancement of the whole University of Hamburg. He brought over Ernst Cassirer in 1919. Heinz Werner became privatdozent at the institute in 1920. Among the researchers at the institute were others who later became well known in different areas of psychology (Heinrich Klüver, Marta Muchow, Fritz Heider, and Curt Bondy). The advancement of the university's intellectual excellence continued until the mid-1930s, when the Nazi takeover forced Stern to escape to America, where his life ended at Duke University in Durham, North Carolina, in 1938.

Hamburg was an important intellectual center for German academic life in the 1920s. Johann Jakob von Uexküll established the Institute of Environmental Study at the university in 1926. von Uexküll's contributions to theoretical biology took the form of emphasizing organism-environment mutualities of adaptation. His *Umwelt-lehre* (study of phenomenological worlds of species) constituted an alternative to the atomistic conceptualizations of biological adaptation that flourished in evolutionary thought. Instead, species can be conceptualized as creating their specific *Umwelten* in their ecological niches or biological meanings (von Uexküll, 1926, 1957, 1980).

Personality As a Philosophical Issue: Ernst Cassirer's Conceptualization

Cassirer's role in twentieth-century philosophical and psychological thought is perhaps similar to that of Henri Bergson. Cassirer created a synthesis of his contemporary psychological know-how, using that creatively to develop his own philosophical system of "symbolic forms." Discussion of personality issues was an inevitable part of the elaboration of the issues of symbolic forms. Furthermore, Cassirer's thought moved largely in parallel with the emerging speech-theoretical thought of Karl Bühler (e.g., Cassirer, 1929/1957, p. 110), and benefited from the developmental thought of Heinz Werner and William and Clara Stern, and from the neuropsychology of Kurt Goldstein.

Hence Cassirer's philosophy of personality was built around developmental lines. When trying to make sense of the role of cultural myths in personality development, Cassirer basically accepted Werner's differentiation notion:

> The individual feeling and consciousness of self stand not at the beginning but at the end of the process of development. In the earliest stages to which we can trace back this development we find the feeling of *self* immediately fused with a definite mythical-religious feeling of community. The I feels and knows itself only insofar as it takes itself as a member of a *community*, insofar as it sees itself grouped with others into the unity of a family, a tribe, a social organism. (Cassirer, 1926/1955, p. 175)

The issue of fusion/differentiation between person and community (see chapter 3 for more contemporary discussion) was important for Cassirer's view on human development. He saw the role of myths in mediating the differentiation of the self out of the state of fusion with the social world. Yet the most important aspect in the growth of the consciousness of personality is practical action: "All true action is *formative* in a twofold sense: the I does not simply impress its own form, a form given to it from the very outset, upon objects; on the contrary, it acquires this form only in the totality of the actions which it excerts upon objects and which it receives back from them. Accordingly, the limits of the inner world can only be determined, its ideal formation can only become visible, if the sphere of being is circumscribed in action" (Cassirer, 1926/1955, p. 200).

From action the person moves on to the schema, or representation. This symbolic representation is possible in the human species, who is a willful subject:

> Only a being who wills and acts, who reaches into the future and determines the future by his will, can have a "history"; only such a

being can know of history because and insofar as he continuously produces it. Thus true historical time is never a mere time of events; rather, its specific consciousness radiates as much from will and accomplishment as from contemplation. . .

. . .Symbolic representation is no mere looking back on . . . reality as something finished, but becomes a factor and motif in its unfolding. It is this form of symbolic vision that specifically distinguishes the cultural, historical will from the mere will to live, mere vital instinct. (Cassirer, 1929/1957, p. 182)

The *person's world is always pregnant with the future* (Cassirer, 1929/1957, p. 202). Symbolic functioning makes it possible to make the future into the present. Human language is actively utilized by persons in this process (see also Karl Bühler's similar viewpoints in chapter 6). Cassirer's focus echoes the widely developed theme in the human sciences of the 1920s—the focus on the linkages between present and past, and present and future.

Personality As a Philosophical Issue: Stern's Views

Similarly to Cassirer, for Stern the question of personality was first and foremost philosophical. However, since Stern himself needed an empirical counterpart to keep himself balanced in the middle of philosophical discourses in Germany at the turn of the century, he moved from philosophical issues to psychological investigations. Nevertheless, it is the philosophy of Stern's personalism that is supported by empirical work.

THE QUESTION OF THE CONTINUOUS PRESENT   For Stern, the psychological "now" contains within itself duration and organization. The psychological event necessarily spans time, and thus consciousness is necessarily a *temporally extended* phenomenon. Stern's concerns paralleled those of Bergson. That extension makes it not merely possible but necessary for the past to participate in the construction of the future (see later discussion of the "historifying" nature of experience).

The question of "psychological present" had interested Stern since his Breslau years (Stern, 1897). The flow of time sets up conditions for integration of lived-through experiences. Stern returned to the question of here and now toward the end of his career (Stern, 1935b). Similarly to

Karl Bühler (see chapter 6), he emphasized the person-centered nature of all subjective space and time.

PERSON AND THING—HETEROGENEITY OF PERSONALITY

From the beginning of the development of his personalistic worldview, Stern emphasized the contradictory unity of persons and things (Stern, 1906, p. 16). The person as a multifaceted, functioning whole *(unitas multiplex)* is spontaneously active relative to the things around; yet the organization of both the person and the things has structure, which is constantly in the process or reorganization (by the goal-orientedness of the active person). The structure of the person (in contrast with that of things) entails dynamic construction of systemic complexity, and its constant reorganization. In contrast, things have structure in terms of passive conglomerates of elements (Stern, 1919, p. 8). Things are not functioning wholes (even if they are structured), while persons are.

The *unitas multiplex* notion leads Stern to reject associationistic views of the person: "The world is to be comprehended neither through a process of refining out its ultimate elements, nor by joining elements together into complexes, but only through a *coordination* of everything that appears to us as elements and aggregates, with real, original, closed totalities, into which they resolve themselves, and through which they may be understood" (Stern, 1930, p. 371).

For Stern, the *dialectic of the concrete* (in contrast with Hegel's dialectics of the abstract) took the form of examining the unity of experience. Each individual has his or her own relevant "personal world"—a world of the person's own construction (Stern, 1935a, p. 126). Such a world is constructed by two parallel processes: by *participation in the world* (the centrifugal direction, or spontaneous actions guided by the material character—Stern, 1938, p. 388) and by the *world's impression upon the person* (centripetal direction or reactions to the demand characteristics of the world). The constructed personal world serves as a further guide in development, leading to the emergence of (albeit limited) novelty by way of the person's role in co-construction:

However great the power exerted by the world to make the individual fall in with its trend, he nevertheless continues to be a "person" and can react to its influence only as a person, thereby modifying and deflecting its very tendency. And vice versa, however strikingly novel and penetrating the effect of the impress by which the genius of an artist, the founder of a religion, a statesman, puts a new face upon the world; since this modified world has no creative genius, it can absorb novelty only in a diluted, simplified form; and since it meanwhile follows its own laws and is subject to other influences, it perforce modifies all acquisitions. (Stern, 1938, p. 90)

The personal world affords both continuity and change within the person. The active person constructs his or her personal world, making use of surrounding cultural messages. The person's assimilative/accommodative processes transform the semiotically encoded information from/about the world into internalized personal knowledge. At the same time, the focus on volition and personal agency retains its central place.

In Stern's explanation of personal volition, the core of psychology's unsolved ground problem finds its sophisticated elaboration. The notion of "entelechy," or "goal-directedly unified personal causality" (Graumann, 1960, p. 129), maintains volition in the center of his psychological system.

THE PROCESSES OF TENSION   Stern's theoretical system is process-oriented, as is reflected in his *hierarchy* and *convergence* principles (Stern, 1919, pp. 8–10). The person is constantly living through (experiencing) relations with the external world, which entails simultaneously separation (*Spaltung*) of and tension (*Spannung*) between different facets of the wholeness of experience (Stern, 1935a, p. 103). This process is very similar to Piaget's reliance on the unity of assimilation and accommodation, although in the case of Stern's personalism it is given in the context of the heterogeneous totality of person-world relations rather than in relation to incoming information into the cognitive system.

Stern's notion of *unitas multiplex* focused on hierarchy within the system of the person. Hierarchical order is the necessary outcome of the separation–tension–overcoming of tension sequence, in the case of converging reorganization of the whole. The whole is multiply determined by convergence of inner and outer conditions of human existence. Different kinds of heterogeneous factors converge in concrete personal life (Stern, 1918, pp. 34–49).

Experiencing the separation and tension not only occurs in the realm of actions is transformed to the realm of subjective symbol formation. In human imagination, the "weakness of nonobjectivity" becomes "strength of subjectivity":

The imaginative individual sets up in his consciousness a world of his own, which, precisely because he shares it with no one else, informs inner experience as an extension of his individual personality and at the same time serves as its protective covering; for without it he would be delivered up to the harshness of the objective world. We now perceive that imagination is not a special power . . . but a mode of inner experience growing out of the depths of personal striving and fed by these depths in both form and substance. *A man is what he imagines,* that is, he is at least brought under a definite perspective as a creature of desire and uneasiness, as the shaper of his intramental world in accordance with his needs, impulses, fears, and ideals. (Stern, 1938, p. 327)

THE ROLE OF THE PAST IN THE PRESENT, WHILE MOVING TOWARD THE FUTURE   Stern's personalistic philosophy made use of his focus on the notion of the present (Stern, 1897, 1935b). Thus, the notion of "historious" (or "historifying") referred to "intrinsic personalistic unities of super-individual character, which produce their own history, namely the way their self-determination is realized in the course of time. A characteristic of historiousness (as opposed to mere 'development' is the 'dually directed temporality'; for not only does the past function progressively, into the future, but every present reaches back into the past, relates the latter to the life-unity and *thereby is constantly remaking it*" (Stern, 1930, p. 385).

Stern's solution to the issue of personal duration is close to what has been emphasized recently by Cole (1992, 1995; see also chapter 4). It differs in construction from C. S. Peirce's notion of tension between a never-meeting past and future (see chapter 6). The role of value provides historifying processes with direction (by participating in the teleological creation of personal worlds).

STERN'S SCHEME OF INNER-OUTER RELATIONS   Aside from conceptualizing the constructive nature of the making of the personal future, Stern also utilized the notion of space in making sense of personality. He claimed regularly that his conceptualization of spatiotemporal relations of the person was value-neutral (Stern, 1950, p. 133).

Figure 5.1 provides Stern's depiction of the inner-outer relationships in person-world relations. In Figure 5.1 we can observe a number of theoretical components that are of heuristic interest. First, in both ends of the process—that of the person and that of the world—the end states are left to be indeterminate ("*Innere Unendlichkeit,*" or inner infinity, in the person; "*Äussere Unendlichkeit,*" or outer infinity, in the case of the world).

Leaving both ends of the scheme defined by infinity marks Stern's concern for the processes that take place at the contact area between the person and the world (see Figure 5.1). The steps marked by Stern in either direction from the personal present (*"Personale Gegenwart"*) in the direction of inner world—surface (*"Oberfläche"*) and deep (*"Tiefe"*) phenomena; and in the direction of the outer world—proximity (*"Nähe"*) and distant (*"Ferne"*) "zones of the world"—constitute simultaneous movement of lived-through experience in both space and time simultaneously.

The personal present is a structured field—it involves the whole personal experience field in the (temporal) "now" and (spatial) "here" setting. What a person encounters in the immediate personal present entails the immediate field of perceived objects and their potential functions. The latter are based on the person's making of the relevance for the objects— that is, the objects obtain that relevance through the subjectivity of the person who encounters them.

Stern had relatively little to say about the inner direction of the person-world contact. In contrast, he explained the outer direction of near and distant "world zones" as entailing movement from the definite (i.e., the present) to the realm of multiple possibilities, from the actual to the possible, in the direction of "outer infinity." The "personally near zone" links

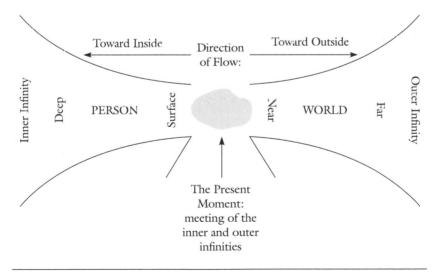

Figure 5.1. Schematic representation of William Stern's view of person ←→ world relations (from Stern, 1950, p. 132).

the present with the next possibilities, via personal meanings, and creates readiness for further contact with new areas of the world. It depicts the goals that are set up by the person in the present and provides direction for the action that moves the person from the present to the near future. The function of this "world zone" bears a clear resemblance to Vygotsky's notion of "zone of proximal development," particularly as that notion was narrowed in the present book (as described in chapter 2).

Beyond the threshold of the "personally near zone" exists the "personally distant world zone," which includes possible events that have not yet been made personally meaningful (their personal relevance is lacking). However, some of the material from the "distant zone" can be moved to the "near zone" (and vice versa), so through the construction of the personal value of the environment the person changes him- or herself. The person creates a personal life-world by extending his or her system of values to the environment, changing the environment accordingly, and thus changing the self.

CONSTRUCTIVE ROLE OF IMAGINATION   The teleological nature of personality is made possible through the constructive uses of imagination and fantasy, and the constructing symbols in that process. A person creates a fantasy by projection of a personal state of being onto the particular realm of the outside world (see chapter 3 on externalization, as the counterpart to internalization, in the present theory). By means of fantasy,

> The individual can impart to this personal world (or to various strata of it) *different orders of reality!* By means of fantasy he is able to insinuate into the unyielding and narrow reality of sense and immediate action a world that is equally "real" in terms of inner experience without being objectively consistent. He is able to merge the two worlds into one (especially in the primitive magical and mythological stage of development); he can also enjoy shifts and flights between them (as may be observed very frequently in children's play); finally, he may set the two worlds into sharp opposition and flee into the world of fancy in order to remove himself at least for the time being (this obtains especially in the enjoyment of art) from the robust, pragmatic world. (Stern, 1938, p. 329)

This process of differentiation and dedifferentiation of the personal worlds of acting and fancying was meant to be productive and constructive (rather than an indication of pathological escape). Stern can be found to assume a position very similar to that of sociogenetic thinkers (e.g., George Herbert Mead) when he explained the processes whereby imagination functions:

> Fantasy produces *new objectivity as its product.* It proves to be a psychophysically neutral process, for what is produced does not remain lodged in the subject's consciousness, but *alters reality* and becomes "creation."
>
> The effect of imagination upon the building of personality is to be regarded as creative. The protective and wishful nature of imaginative activity operates so that the individual *transforms himself* and recasts his relation to the world. Don Quixote, imagining himself to be turned into the "last wandering knight," *acts* accordingly and thereby interferes with the objective course of events. Much the same thing obtains, of course, when the individual transforms his life by means of imagination in a normal rather than a delusive manner.
>
> But the imaginative individual also has a direct need for the *external projection* of his intramental experience; in answer to it he tends to replace simple imagery with movement, expression, and production . . . At the same time there is progressive *detaching* of the product of imagination from its maker, and its transfer into the objective patterns of play, art and myth-making. (Stern, 1938, p. 330)

Taking meaningful social roles, the imaginative person reorganizes the external world in ways that jointly create new objectivity and subjectivity. The process of "external projection" as described here is another version of externalizaton and "detachment"—that of "distancing" (see chapter 3). The process of "detachment" necessarily brings the differentiating system into some form of hierarchical organization. Heinz Werner's consistently developmental perspective grew out of Stern's personology. Likewise, Stern's general system was the source of inspiration for the personality theory of Gordon Allport.

Gordon Allport: A Developmental Interactionist

Gordon Allport has been recognized as a classic author in personality psychology and a fundamental contributor to our knowledge in social psychology (Clark, 1979), yet his actual contributions to the study of mechanisms of human development have remained relatively underemphasized. Having studied with Stern in Hamburg in 1923 for a semester (Allport, 1924b, 1967; Evans, 1981, p. 18), Allport served as an active reviewer of the German ideas for the American psychological scene (Allport, 1927, 1940a; Allport and Vernon, 1930). He also summarized new tendencies in North American psychology for the German audience (Allport, 1924a). In his own scientific credo, Allport represents a case of continuity with Continental thinking before World War II (Allport, 1937b). These complex ideas remained visible, albeit outside of the mainstream, for psychologists in the United States after World War II (see Allport, 1962, 1967). The methodological implications of Allport's thinking about personality were threatening to the socially constructed organizing concepts of "objectivity" and "behavior" in mainstream American psychology.

Allport's experiences in Europe in the 1920s (see Allport, 1967, pp. 9–10) set the stage for his lifelong interest in the autonomous psychological functioning of persons who are active participants in their lives. This focus borrows directly from a number of German sources—Edward Spranger's *Lebensform*-perspective, Gestalt psychology, William Stern's personology (Allport, 1937b), and Kurt Lewin's field theory (Allport, 1968b). Of these traditions, Allport found the personal life experience–oriented ideas of Spranger and Stern most congenial to his own self. He was highly resistant to efforts to idealize the role of the social group in regulating the creativity of persons that from time to time surface in North American public and psychological discourse (Allport, 1925). Likewise, he pointed to the idealization of the notion of social participation in American social discourse (Allport, 1945). Instead, he saw the European emphasis on persons as intertwined with society and yet personally autonomous as a realistic starting point of his inquiry. *Social participation becomes personality-relevant only if it is ego-involved*—hence the primacy of the personal over the social in psychological analysis.

Ambivalence in American retrospects on Allport is not surprising. By locating his efforts within the *verstehende Psychologie* tradition (he himself suggested its translation as "interpretative psychology"—Allport, 1929b, p. 15), Allport made himself into a socioinstitutionally recognized "maverick" of American psychology of the middle of the twentieth century. He moved consciously against the dominant social tendencies that prevailed in of American psychology at the time (Allport, 1940c). He propagated the centrality of single-case study as the basis for making psychology more (rather than less!) scientific (Allport, 1929b, p. 17; see also chapters 1 and 7).

Personality and Its Systemic Organization

For Allport, personality is not a distinctly finished product but *a structure of features that is continually undergoing change* (Allport, 1955, p. 19). In most general terms, Allport defined personality as "the dynamic organization within the individual of those psychophysical systems that determine his unique adjustment to his environment (Allport, 1937c, p. 48)

Here the notion of dynamic organization entails its opposite (i.e., dynamic *dis*organization) of the system of determining tendencies for ongoing action. The meaning of unique adjustment entailed creative action (rather than passive, reactive adaptations to the environment as given). From the very beginning of outlining his personality conception, Allport had to face the prevailing tendencies in North American psychology toward quantification of elementaristic units of analysis of psychological phenomena. The available models of "intelligence measurement" were indeed an obstacle for establishing qualitative (structured) accounts of personality—a feature explicitly recognized in the very beginning of Allport's efforts to conceptualize personality (Allport and Allport, 1921, p. 8). Personality is not a bagful of haphazardly discovered features but an organized and self-organizing system.

Ontogenetically, the development of personality entailed the construction of increasingly general functional organizers of conduct. It is in this respect that Allport proceeded beyond the (then usual) reductionist talk of attributing the organizing functions to low-level (but behavioristically clarified) notions of "habit" or conditional reflex (or—in case of pregiven organization—"instinct"). It was in his effort "to escape the deceptive snares of pseudophysiology" (Allport, 1937c, p. 141) that his trait concept dealt with the issue of personality integration beyond habits and reflexes. In one of his schemes, Allport expressed his notion of personality integration at different hierarchical levels over ontogeny (see Figure 5.2).

Total personality is here seen as emerging as an organizer of high integrative value in the life course. At the same time, the total personality structure entails moments of disintegration within itself: some traits or selves can vanish over the life course, others can emerge, and so on.

The core of Allport's personality theory is the emphasis on the uniqueness of personal being, both across persons at any time and within persons across time. In this we can see clear continuity with William Stern's and Henri Bergson's ideas, from the early years of Allport's remarkable productivity (Allport, 1924a, p. 134). Likewise, the role of Henry Murray's ideas (1938, 1959) in the advancement of Allport's thinking should not be underestimated.

In his search for the unit of analysis of personality, Allport decided to utilize the notion of trait as a sufficiently generalized mechanism. Traits are "derived drives" or "derived motives" (based on habits) that—as generalized "form qualities" (Allport, 1924a)—act as preorganizers of the person's actions in new contexts. They emerge in the person's life course and, once formed, direct the person's responses to stimuli into characteristic channels (Allport, 1931, p. 369).

The Nature and Role of Psychological Traits

The key to understanding Allport's (1931, 1966) trait theory is its dynamic-systemic focus. The person's traits are organized into a dynamic trait hierarchy that is likely to contain contradictory and mutually oppos-

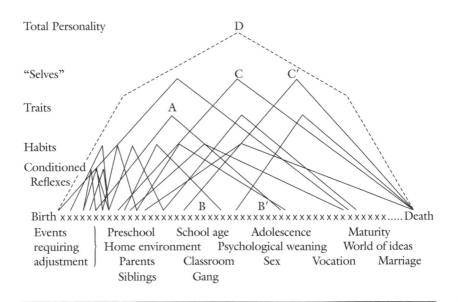

Figure 5.2. Schematic representation of integration of personality over the life course (from Allport, 1937c, p. 141).

ing traits (e.g., combination of *ascendance* and *submission*—Allport, 1928, p. 121). For example, the same individual may have traits of both *neatness* and *carelessness,* which are organized within the trait hierarchy so that one is usually—but not always—dominant over the other. Consider Allport's description of "Dr. D.," who is:

> always neat about his person and desk, punctilious about lecture notes, outlines, and files; his personal possessions are not only in order but carefully kept under lock and key. Dr. D. is also in charge of the departmental library: in this duty he is careless; he leaves the library door unlocked, and books are lost; it does not bother him that dust accumulates. Does this contradiction in behavior mean that D. lacks traits? Not at all. He has two opposed stylistic traits, one of orderliness and one of disorderliness. Pursuing the case further, this duality is explained by the fact that D. has *one* cardinal (motivational) trait from which these contrasting styles proceed. The outstanding fact about his personality is that he is self-centered egotist who never acts for other people's interests, but always for his own. This cardinal trait of self-centeredness (for which there is abundant evidence) *demands* orderliness for himself, but not for others. (Allport, 1937c, p. 331)

The heterogeneity of conduct is thus easily explainable by a hierarchical control mechanism (of a cardinal trait, or *radix*) that activates one of the mutually opposed traits under different conditions. This situation is described schematically in Figure 5.3. What Allport's scheme leaves unclear here is the set of conditions under which the general control mechanism *(radix)* activates one of the opposing traits and blocks the other. However, in the example of "Dr. D.," the contextual differentiation (things for oneself versus things for others) is seen as making that distinction. The specific context—interpreted through the person's ego involvement— guides the heterogeneity of functions controlled by traits. Through his emphasis on the hierarchical control systems in human personality, Allport gave a concrete elaboration to Kurt Lewin's imperative for the use of conditional-genetic analysis (Lewin, 1927) in psychology. The main methodological issue is that of demonstrating what particular outcomes *can* develop out of the present state of affairs, under a combination of specific conditions, rather than mere description of these present states of affair. Thus, under the condition of a personal sense of situation X that "this situation belongs to me," the trait of "neatness" is activated, and "Dr. D." shows one kind of conduct—just the opposite of what would emerge when the personal sense of a situation Y indicates "this is another public setting," not linked with "Dr. D's" personal culture. This model of thinking is prevalent in contemporary protein genetics (where the main issue is the set of conditions that regulate gene expression). Elaboration of experimental methods for the causal-genetic study were elaborated by the research tradition of *Aktualgenese* (Sander, 1927) on the basis of the theoretical notion of the formation of structural wholes in human psychological life (Sander and Volkelt, 1962).

RECOMBINATIONAL AND EMERGENT CONSTRUCTION OF COMPLEXITY   From Allport's point of view, personality is a dynamic process in two ways. First, it is dynamic in its constant activation (and disactivation) of mutually oppositional traits, through the higher control of these via cardinal traits (and, further, by the selves). This guarantees the heterogeneity of human conduct in different situations. Seemingly opposite conduct forms can be generated by the same hierarchical personality system that has already emerged. Second, the whole hierarchical organization of personality is a transient process that is constantly involved in the emergence of new traits and their higher-order organizational forms

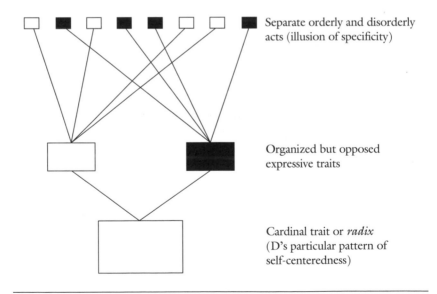

Separate orderly and disorderly acts (illusion of specificity)

Organized but opposed expressive traits

Cardinal trait or *radix* (D's particular pattern of self-centeredness)

Figure 5.3. Illustration of congruence within personality through the view of basic dynamic systems (from Allport, 1937c, p. 358).

(Allport, 1955, p. 19). The eternally becoming structure was that of intra-mental regulating means of relative stability. That structure is personally constructed yet at the same time culturally guided by the available meanings in the language.

Traits and Trait-Names

The detection of traits in self- and other-observation is made possible by the encoding of specific enduring personal characteristics in the language (by way of trait-names). Allport's "trait theory" not only was dynamic in its emphasis but also recognized sociogenetic roots in its secondary focus. For reasons of social opposition of his own (to the prevailing behavioristic reduction of social influences on development to the "shaping" of personality by culture), Allport de-emphasized the interdependence of the person and the social world in his trait-based account of personality (see a description of Allport's explanation of this in Smith, 1993, p. 58). Nevertheless, in one of its earlier formulations, the nature of trait-names is quite explicitly given in what (given the context of the present book) amounts to language use that recognizes semiotic regulation of oneself:

> Trait-names are symbols socially devised (from a mixture of ethical, cultural and psychological interests) for the naming and evaluation of human qualities. Some of these terms are obviously censorial and as such have little utility for the psychologist. The non-censorial terms, however, are significant, for *their common usage establishes a presupposition that some human beings possess actual dispositions or traits roughly corresponding to these symbols.* There are, however, many more traits than any list of single names would indicate, for we often find neologisms, phrases, and metaphors called upon where trait-names are insufficient. (Allport and Odbert, 1936, p. 20; emphasis added)

The classic study of personality-descriptive lexicon in the English language produced a thesaurus of 17,953 terms (Allport and Odbert, 1936), yet the most important feature for making sense of this unbearable richness of human language is the openness to allow for construction of new terms or phrases to denote personal characteristics. The crucial nature of such constructed devices (semiotic means, as one is tempted to label them in our present vernacular) is their interdependence with the life of the person (Allport, 1929b, p. 16), the result of which is their fuzziness of meaning (Allport understood this long before any application of the fuzzy set theory to semantics) and the idiosyncratic nature of their actual uses in real contexts: "A trait-name is a range-name. Although traits are real enough entities, trait-names are essentially blankets, covering one trait in one person and other (similar) traits in other people. Though perceived as similar and labelled identically the trait is never, strictly speaking, in two different human beings exactly the same" (Allport and Odbert, 1936, p. 21).

The "trait" ↔ "trait-name" relation as presented here has interesting parallels with the Vygotsky-Paulhan "personal sense" ↔ "meaning" relation (Van der Veer and Valsiner, 1991). Similarly to the role of meanings in guiding personal sense, Allport viewed culture to be of great relevance in guiding the person to interiorize its contrasts in the dynamic structure of personality (Allport, 1937c, p. viii). However, personality constructs its distance—or relative autonomy—from the demands of the surrounding world. This can be observed in the heterogeneity of political attitudes (Allport, 1929a), as well as in personal relations (Allport, 1965).

The Question of Functional Autonomy

Allport's answer to the question of the organization of personality was to assume a rich variety of person-specific intramental constructs (traits, motives, etc.) that become hierarchically organized and are constantly reorganized in the process of living. Such hierarchies operate as self-regulating systems (Allport, 1937a, 1937c, 1943), which develop into states of functional autonomy in relation to their antecendents. Thus, he considered adult motives

> as infinitely varied, and as self-sustaining, *contemporary* systems, growing out of antecedent systems, but functionally independent of them. Just as child gradually repudiates his dependence on his parents, develops will of his own, becomes self-active and self-determining, and outlives his parents, so it is with motives. Each motive has a definite point of origin which may possibly lie in instincts, or, more likely, in the organic tensions of infancy. Chronologically speaking, all adult purposes can be traced back to these seed-forms in infancy, but as the individual matures the tie is broken. Whatever bond remains, is historical, not functional. (Allport, 1937a, p. 143; see also Allport, 1937c, p. 194)

Aside from arguing against psychoanalytic excesses of discovering supposed direct causal links between a person's present and early-childhood past, Allport *emphasized the constructivity in the ever-developing intramental regulatory systems.* Assumptions about the *inflexible projections* of psychological phenomena from childhood to adulthood in terms of continuity of form (or "problem-status") that have been widespread in child psychology are ruled out by Allport. In conjunction with that emphasis on developmental constructivity, he was accused of accepting the concept of ontogenetic emergent evolution (e.g., Bertocci, 1940, pp. 518–519), with which Allport himself readily concurred (Allport, 1940b, p. 541). New motives emerge constructively in the course of a person's living interdependently with the environmental structure, and old motive hierarchies are transformed into novel forms. Some old motives are transformed to the extent of unrecognizability relative to their parent form (these could be viewed as *supplanted*—see Allport's answer to Bertocci in Bertocci, 1940, p. 526); others may maintain recognizable historical connections with the previous ones. Functionally, the whole motive hierarchy *is always contemporaneous* with ongoing living process (Allport, 1937a, p. 144).

Allport's notion of emergent functional autonomy of motives is similar to Vygotsky's talk about "fossilized behavior"—the loss of the forms of conduct that were relevant in the process of development but that vanished from the organism's repertoire once a particular function had developed. Allport's emergent autonomy notion of motives (similar to Vygotsky's notion of novel control forms) within the personality structure was an easy target for misinterpretations. As pointed out in chapter 2, nonstrict hierarchy notions are not common in psychology's conceptual repertoire. Yet it is exactly the notion of dynamic hierarchical reintegration of the structure of motives (with granting relative autonomy—but no dissociation—to some parts of the hierarchy) that Allport contributed to our understanding of personality (Allport, 1946b, 1953).

DEVELOPMENT THROUGH PRODUCTION OF NOVELTY

Allport emphasized the role of constructive imitation in human psychological development—in ways very similar to the persistent imitation notion of James Mark Baldwin (as described in chapter 4). His observations and their interpretation reveal his clear grasp of the microlevel phenomena of development. At age eight months, twenty-eight days, "little Andrew"

> watches intently father smoking his pipe. When father offers A. the pipe (properly cleaned), A. puts the stem into his mouth and *blows* vigorously.

According to the theory of conditioning, Andrew should have *sucked* the stem (as he would a nipple or pacifier). Actually Andrew imitated the father blowing out the smoke. The resemblance of his action to the puff of smoke he had been watching demands explanation in terms of insight—a deliberate attempt to reconstruct or to duplicate the stimulus-situation as *understood* (Allport, 1937c, p. 157)

Human development proceeds in accordance with introception (borrowed from Stern—Allport, 1937c, p. 217), as the child constructively incorporates the experiences of others into his or her own life. The "raw material" for personality development is the sociocultural world.

Culture in Guidance of Personality

Allport was not a sociogenetic theorist. In fact, he made it a point to reject the efforts to translate personality to its social frames (e.g., Allport, 1943a, p. 465; 1955). Nevertheless, he considered the culturally organized world as the input system for the developing person—one that, *under some conditions,* becomes instrumental at the level of individual personality—yet always mediated by the intramental regulatory hierarchies (of traits, interests, motives, dispositions, etc.). The social input can become part of the personal world only *if it becomes ego-involved,* and in forms that may differ vastly from that input as it is. This viewpoint clearly parallels that of our contemporary discussion of the bidirectional nature of cultural transmission (see Valsiner, 1994b, 1994c), even if Allport phrased it in traditional personality terminology. Thus, human attitudes have roots that are biological and that are based on cultural influences as they are constructed—and yet the motive to construct them is personal (Allport and Schanck, 1935, p. 205). Likewise, quick transformations of social contexts can trigger a range of psychological adaptations to the changes, where *personal resistance* dominates over conformity (Allport, Bruner, and Jandorf, 1941, p. 7).

Allport's emphasis on functional autonomy as an emerging state of organization carried over to his view of internalization processes. Personality develops via constructive internalization that guarantees both the "fit" and "misfit" of different persons with their cultural surroundings: "What culture does is to offer models both for common adaptive acts and for styles of expressive behavior. These models the individual may or may not adopt. In so far as he adopts them he fits the 'cultural type'; in so far as he does not, his personality is sharply etched against the contrasting cultural ground. No personality is an exact replica of prevailing cultural norms, but to understand the deviating as well as the relatively typical cases, knowledge of these norms is indispensable" (Allport, 1937a, p. 372).

Importantly, the criterion of ego involvement as the final determiner of what aspect of the cultural input to personality becomes actually used by the person leads to the episodic and casual nature of personally significant encounters with the cultural world. Thus, children are not "taught" prejudices by their parental environments where such prejudices exist, but the children themselves create their novel prejudices on the basis of occasional encounters within prejudice-infested social atmospheres (Allport, 1979, pp. 299–300). Allport's data on the memories of personally significant teachers among college students (Allport, 1968a) show exactly that personal-constructive nature of significant encounters. As a critic of the U.S. educational system as of the early 1960s, Allport was not shy in locating the implications of the oversight of the primacy of personal construction:

> The problem, as I see it, is one of interiorizing motivation. To put it in a student's words: "I am fed up with having everybody else cheer me on. I want to work to please myself rather than others, but I don't know how to do it . . ." In school, the child is rewarded and punished by good grades and bad grades. Even in college, As and Bs are pats on the back, Ds and Fs are punishments. To gain love, the student must read books and toe the academic line. Finally he obtains his degree (which is a symbol of academic love) and is freed from his external form of motivation. What then happens?
>
> We know that a shockingly high percentage of college graduates rarely or never read another book after receiving their bachelor's degree. Why should they? Their love now comes from their employer, their wife, their children, not from the approval of parents and teachers. *For them, intellectual curiosity never became a motive in its own right.* External rewards are appropriate props in early childhood. But we educators, being limited by our current inadequate theories of learning, do not know how to help the student free himself from the props of reward and develop a functionally autonomous zeal for learning. With our slavish dependence on reinforcement theory, I think it surprising that we arouse as much internal motivation as we do. (Allport, 1968a, pp. 177–178; emphasis added)

Writing on education surely brings out the necessary recognition of the role of the sociocultural guidance of human development. Allport preserves the primary focus on the self-development of the person yet recognizes the cultural input to it, both in terms of age-appropriate canalization of motivation (i.e., the frequent nonemergence of internalized intellectual curiosity motives is blamed on the absence of its social guidance) and in terms of educators' appropriation of the behavioristic ideology as the basis for education. In the context of their goal-oriented activities within social institutions, some persons (e.g., teachers) construct their elaborate personal credos about teaching on some socioculturally suggested basis (e.g., the global truthfulness of reinforcement theory across ages) and externalize this credo in actual conduct (i.e., teaching). Such *personal* conduct in a social-institutional setting *becomes the sociocultural organizer* of the development of other persons (students). It guides their personal constructions of their selves toward the emergence of some (e.g., dependency upon external motivation, based on love withdrawal as a cultural practice—see Benigni and Valsiner, 1995, for a contrast), rather than other (e.g., intrinsic "zeal for intellectual curiosity"), versions of the personal structure of motives. Through *active self-construction* by the person, then, a situation can emerge where the person *wants* to act in accordance with intrinsic motivation but has *personally blocked its construction* as specified by cultural guidance. The resulting personal confusion and helplessness guide the person to actively seek out further extrinsic motivation sources, but unless the sociocultural blocking of interiorization of those into a novel personal intrinsic motivation source is eliminated, the cycle may repeat itself all through the person's life. The active person is guided by the sociocultural world through its "independent dependence" upon that world (Winegar, Renninger, and Valsiner, 1989).

By now, it should become evident that the sociocultural world is underemphasized in Allport's system of thought for a good reason. He rejected the unidirectional culture transmission model used by most of his contemporaries (see Allport, 1955, pp. 81–82), while he was not ready to provide a fully elaborate alternative that would specify exactly *how* the sociocultural world serves as the basis for personal construction of the self. Perhaps in the case of his concept of "proprium" we get closest to Allport's effort to provide such an account, fragile and incomplete as it remained.

PROPRIUM AND ITS DYNAMICS   For Allport, the holistic emphasis on unique personality led to the need to conceptualize the person-in-context, thus (at least partially) taking the context into account. By introducing the concept of "proprium," he attempted exactly such unity: "Personality includes . . . all the regions of our life that we regard as peculiarly ours, and which for the time I suggest we call the *proprium*. The proprium includes all aspects of personality that make for inward unity" (Allport, 1955, p. 40).

It is clear that Allport's proprium is otherwise close to the notion of life space as found in the work of Kurt Lewin. The proprium includes personal bodily sense (coenesthesis), self-identity, self-seeking, ego extension, rationalizing, self-image, propriate striving, and the self-reflecting knower. Allport's listing of these features was meant to coincide with an ontogenetic sequence of human development. It is the affective tone of a person's extensions of ego to the environment that distinguishes the boundaries of the proprium:

> Coenesthesis, self-identity, ego-enhancement—are relatively early developments in personality, characterizing the whole of the child's proprium. Their solicitations have a heavily biological quality and seem to be contained within the organism itself. But soon the process of learning brings with it a high regard for possessions, for loved objects, for ideal causes and loyalties. We are speaking of whatever objects a person calls "mine." They must at the same time be objects of importance, for sometimes our sense of "having" has no affective tone and hence no place in the proprium. A child, however, who identifies with his parent is definitely extending his sense of self, as he does likewise through his love for pets, dolls, or other possessions, animate or inanimate.
>
> As we grow older we identify with groups, neighborhood, and nation as well as with possessions, clothes, home. They become matters of importance to us in a sense that other people's families, nations, or possessions are not. Later in life the process of extension may go to great lengths, through the development of loyalties and of interests focused on abstractions and on moral and religious values. (Allport, 1955, p. 45)

The development of the person starts from a strong personal externalization orientation and extends its subjectively valued flavor to the lived-in world. Proprium can be seen as Allport's version of the notion of personal culture, constructed through his focus on the externalization process. In parallel, his focus on the role of constructive internalization constituted the complement to the buildup of the proprium. The person-centeredness of the proprium fits with the central importance of single-case (systemic) analysis.

Morphogenic Science

Allport's identification with the emphasis on the idiographic research orientation has been prominent from the very beginning of his intellectual contributions (Allport, 1924a), proceeded through his vigorous defense of that orientation (see Allport, 1946b), and continued to the very end of his productive research career (Allport, 1962). His own reflections upon his life (Allport, 1967, pp. 8–9) indicate that for him the interest in the human lived-through experience was as much a personal quest as was the restoration of lost harmony in persons' relations with the world for Piaget (see Chapman, 1988; Vidal, 1993) or the urge to reach aesthetic synthesis for Vygotsky (see Van der Veer and Valsiner, 1991).

Like Stern, Allport tried to overcome the breach between the exclusively separated nomothetic and idiographic perspectives in psychology's methodology. On the one hand, he persistently called for combining the varied approaches (Allport, 1937c, p. 22), pointing to the benefit for each of the approaches from the other. At the same time, without any doubt it was the systemic single-case analysis of dynamic personality (as process more than product—see earlier) that was considered the definitive database for Allport's theoretical elaborations on personality.

Allport's way of combining populational and single-case analyses was to view interpersonally common traits as possible targets to which the interindividual reference frame (Valsiner, 1989, chapter 2) can be applied. While recognizing that "no two people have precisely the same trait" (Allport, 1937c, p. 299), he still compromised with the research traditions of using existing "trait scales" in populational application contexts. Interestingly, in this compromise Allport may have fused his differentiation of the meanings of trait-names (as range-meanings, see earlier) and traits themselves.

Nevertheless, Allport consistently insisted upon the primacy of idiographic analysis over its nomothetic counterpart. When the focus of research is on the *organization* of the personality as a whole, surely the systemic analysis of the single case is the only reasonable analytic stand (Thorngate, 1986, 1992). When the focus of investigation is on the *abstracted characteristics of* personality that are distributed among persons within a population, the study of individual personality organization is of course no longer the goal. However, in the latter case, the population of persons (who carry different traits) becomes the system that is being analyzed. In other terms, sample-based studies involving persons are not studies of persons but constitute a single-case study of the population. It is the population—however ill-defined its boundaries may be—that becomes the single subject under investigation, while persons are viewed as its parts.

It becomes evident that the goal of science is always the systemic under-standing of the single (generic) case—be that of the person, social group, community, society, or human species as a whole. Most of the contro-versy in psychology concerning the nomothetic versus idiographic analysis (see Valsiner, 1986) is merely a result of direct mapping of the nomo-thetic label upon sample-based (and statistically analyzed) empirical stud-ies, while delegating the idiographic label to cover the clinical single-case understanding of persons. Unfortunately, Allport himself participated in the construction of this shared misunderstanding in most direct ways. Nevertheless, if we see through his numerous rhetoric endorsements of the idiographic orientation in contrast with the nomothetic one, we can see that his analytic focus was in the growth of form in the development of personality. Hence his relabeling (toward the end of his life) of his idiog-raphic emphasis as morphogenic reflects more than a mere label change (see also Lamiell, 1987, pp. 12–13).

THE MEANING OF MORPHOGENIC ANALYSIS   Allport utilized a directly biological model—that of embryology—for his propagation of the morphogenic analysis:

> Molecular biology takes common elements and finds that almost all life is made up of the same basic elements. The parallel dimension in psychology would be dimensional or differential or trait psychology. Morphogenic biology, however, is a little further behind as a science. We know very little about embryology, how organisms take a form and arrive at the peculiar structures they have. In psychology it's a particularly difficult problem as well because we're not trying to ex-plain a species, but we're trying to explain the uniqueness of the person. That's what I call a morphogenic problem. (Evans, 1981, p. 25)

The focus on morphogenic emergence is more fundamental than mere relabeling of the term *idiographic*—despite Allport's frequent fussing about the need for such a change because of "students' misspelling" of the latter term (e.g., "idiographic" versus "ideographic"). Namely, the em-phasis on the uniqueness of emerging novel forms makes it impossible to rely upon previous observation(s) of similar forms. Uniqueness of per-sonality exists both across persons and across time: "A murderer seldom commits more than one murder. Therefore, we cannot reason from his previous behavior that when conditions are thus and so, he will commit murder. The act is a one-time happening. Although no frequencies are involved, the deed is *determined* and scientifically speaking, lawful. It should then be predictable" (Allport, 1942, p. 158).

The unique onetime happening has its form, and that form has to be explained through morphogenic analysis—which recognizes the uniqueness of the occasion yet considers general (morphogenic) lawfulness in the explanation. In the case of morphogenic analysis, the general and the unique are taken into account together. Hence, what Allport was suggesting was not a mere relabeling of psychologists' uses of the term *idiographic* but *another kind of science of the emergence of structure* that is closer in emphasis to the conceptual models of those sciences in our times that explicitly deal with the emergence of forms (e.g., genetics—Crick, 1988; immunology—Löwy, 1992; or thermodynamics—Prigogine, 1987). Any particular personality—for instance, "Bill" (see Allport, 1962)—constructs its own organized form in the course of living. That form is idiosyncratic in its product, yet the processes by which each of the idiosyncratic forms is generated can be generic. In a way, Allport's call for morphogenic psychology is not different from Chomsky's generative grammar epistemology— in which case all the uniqueness of the possible speech utterances is generated by the same general rules.

PREDICTABILITY IN SINGLE-CASE STUDIES   Allport was faced with the myriad of challenges that pointed to the difficulty of predicting the future development of any particular person. Since prediction was (and still is) supposed to link an area of investigation to the symbolic status of science, these challenges were of more than peripheral importance.

Given the principled open-endedness of personality development, Allport recognized the impossibility of automatized exact predictions and concentrated on the notion of *range* of possible futures:

It is not, of course, the *exact* response of an individual that is predictable. It is only the *range* of his response. Rarely can we foretell the precise words our friend will use in expressing pleasure at the gift we have brought him, but that he will like it we are sure. With just what movements an aggressive person will show his nature in a given situation we do not know, but that he will be aggressive in some way we can safely wager. In other terms, we predict the operation of a *trait,* but allow for a fairly wide range of equivalent responses that will be called forth by other determinants prevailing at the time the behavior takes place. (Allport, 1937c, p. 353)

Allport's emphasis on the predictability of ranges of possible psychological phenomena may counter the challenges of his opponents, but they nevertheless indicate a certain inconsistency in his argumentation. If personality operates as a *dynamic system of traits* (leading to situation-adjusted action), then predictability of a single range of possible events on the basis of any *single* trait (even if it is a dominant one within the personality structure) may be unrealistic. Instead, a given structure of trait relations may give rise to a number of ranges of psychological phenomena of different content (direction). This would follow from the control of traits by the radix (see Figure 5.3). Allport's inconsistency here is probably a result of the heterogeneity of the psychological discourse in which he was involved, rather than his actual theorizing. His proof of the irrelevance of normal distributions in understanding psychological phenomena could be taken as an example of his clear emphasis on the complexity of prediction.

USES OF NORMAL DISTRIBUTION IN PSYCHOLOGY'S METH-ODOLOGY   Allport saw the intellectual mediocrity of his contemporaries' blind trust in the normality of the normal distribution curves. While recognizing the possibility that biological phenomena may be normally distributed, he saw the cultural world setting up constraints for psychological phenomena that lead to asymmetrical (J-curve type) distributions (Allport, 1937c, pp. 332–337). As personality traits depend upon cultural and directionally pointed input to the developing person, their distributions can most easily deviate from the normal distribution, and it is exactly those deviations that can tell us about the functioning of the real cultural constraints in personality development. Allport's emphasis on the functioning of traits as a hierarchically organized system made it possible for him to think of normal distribution of data being an artifact of the constraints generated by mutually complementary yet opposed traits. Thus, two mutually complementary traits may lead to a conjoint (but opposite) J-curve type distribution, the result of which may easily *look as if* it were a Gaussian distribution.

Here Allport followed the intellectual lead of his older brother, whose classic paper on J-curves (F. Allport, 1934) had been published some years prior to *Personality*. Demonstrating interpersonally variable ways of responding to social conformity demands, Floyd Allport reached the notion of constraint systems that can be viewed as generating approximately normal-looking distributions in data—yet ones in which the explanations for different parts of the distribution can be attributed to different mechanisms. The probabilistic belief system that has glorified the normality of the normal distribution (which has been the basis for most of psychology's accepted inferential practices) is itself unacceptable for an interactionist account of personality.

From Allport to Modernity (and Beyond)

Reception of Allport's theoretical contributions in the discourse of North American psychology has been overshadowed by the ideological opposition between the discourse voices of "hard" and "soft" psychologies. The exclusively separated opposition of nomothetic and idiographic orientations within psychology has become mapped upon the previous ideological segregation of psychologies by psychologists, which has essentially led to a lack of appreciation of Allport's theoretical contributions to personality psychology. Despite being heralded as a "classic" of personality psychology and the study of prejudice (Katz, 1991), his actual theoretical contributions are rarely noted in the literature (Zuroff, 1986). Or, when "neo-Allportian" labels are used to capture the attention of the modern public (e.g., Funder, 1991), the systemic and morphogenic focus of Allport's theory, as well as its developmental implications, have become lost in the discourse about empirical methods. It is as if Allport's resistance to the takeover of psychology by narrow-minded empiricism has been forgotten—purposefully, one might add—on behalf of the latter.

Contemporary Person-Centered Approaches

Many personality psychologists claim to follow Allport, yet it is rare that his contributions are really analyzed and further advanced (e.g., Lamiell, 1981, 1987). The prominence of cognitive psychology has resulted in efforts to view personality in mentalistic terms (Mischel, 1979; Mischel and Peake, 1982). In the domain of personality analysis that follows from George Kelly's "personal construct theory," a number of Allport's ideas are put into practice (Fransella, 1981). Nevertheless, it is curious that Allport's basic morphogenic approach to personality has become largely lost in contemporary psychology.

The personological tradition has been retained in a number of specific research tendencies, like those of personal strivings (Emmons, 1986) or personal projects (Little, 1989). The dynamic facets of personality as a system have been emphasized by meaning-centered conceptualizations of self (Baumeister, 1986, 1989; Larsen, 1989; Thorne, 1989) and pointed to its relativity in different social structures (Ryff, 1987). A case of special attention in this context is to be given the life-course traditions in the study of lives (Elder, 1974; Caspi, 1987, 1989). These approaches move between sociological analyses (of age and shared-experiences cohorts—e.g., persons who at a specific age period in their personal development experienced a major socioeconomic event, such as the Great Depression or a war) and assumptions about psychological effects of such life experiences. An interactionist—but not systemic or developmental—perspective is assumed by the life-course researchers.

The interactionist perspective on personality—a synthesis of personological and situationist views—got its strong impetus from the reanalysis of issues of personality as intertwined with its context (Ekehammar, 1974; Endler and Magnusson, 1976; Magnusson and Endler, 1977; Magnusson and Bergman, 1990). The person was viewed as intricately related with the context (Nuttin, 1973, 1977). This *person-oriented research approach* has found a new beginning over the last two decades in a number of forms. The first approximation of this orientation amounts to turning into analysis of homogenized subgroups of heterogeneous samples: "In *person-approach* analysis, the questions are asked and answered in terms of individuals. In operationalization, individuals are grouped in homogeneous categories with reference to similarities in their profiles based on values for variables relevant to the problem under consideration" (Magnusson and Cairns, 1996, p. 25).

Surely this movement away from population-type generalizations toward profile-type categorizations of individual personal phenomena is a step toward a morphogenic science (in Allport's sense), but certainly it misses an important characteristic. The dynamic interaction of the person and the environment is yet to be reflected in this individual-profile kind of description. Despite the limitations of contemporary returns to the recognition of complexity of the person-environment relations, after the devastating effects of the occupation of methodology by the "empire of chance" (see Gigerenzer et al., 1989), the result of recent advancement of interactionist perspectives on personality is a return to the developmental focus of personologists and sociogenetic thinkers. Thus, the systemic dynamics of human personality includes the individual's mental system and world-view (Magnusson, 1990, 1995; Magnusson and Törestad, 1993, pp. 447–448), as well as an emphasis on the self-constructing nature of the self (e.g., Schwalbe, 1991). Nevertheless, whether the self and personality are viewed as self-organizing dynamic systems or as systems of traits in some order, the question of unity of personality within the diversity of contexts remains as a challenge to person-centered and interactionist or contextual perspectives (Graumann, 1960).

Summary: Personalistic Views and Sociogenesis

In this chapter, some largely forgotten aspects of personalistic views on personality have been brought back to theoretical focus. What has been slowly lost from the psychology of personality over the past hundred years is the recognition of the phenomena of the "stream of consciousness" that characterized William James's method of making sense of phenomena. Personality psychology has become dominated by standardized methods, and the phenomenological focus has become lost. The result of such historical change is that the "tail" of the "personality-dog" (i.e., consensually approved methods) "wags the body" (i.e., personality theories) of that "dog." The resulting historical and theoretical myopia in personality psychology has led to overlooking of the promising theoretical texture that different personological theories had been building up in the past. Still, the myopia of hyperempiricism can be corrected by a new look at the old ideas. A number of theoretical implications follow from the reanalysis of personological approaches.

First, the personalistic perspectives of William Stern were crucial for the advancement of focus on personality in psychology. In conjunction with the philosophy of Ernst Cassirer, Stern's focus on personology of lived-through worlds was an anchor point for unification of sociogenetic and personological perspectives in psychology. Stern's contribution entailed a prominent developmental focus. This was taken over by Gordon Allport and carried forward to the domain of viewing personality is an organized whole that transforms itself dynamically in response to the needs present in any context. Sometimes it constructs its own subparts that acquire a relatively autonomous status (e.g., Allport's "functional autonomy" notion). In our extension of this notion (see chapter 6 and Conclusion), it becomes "filled in" with the notion of semiotic mediating devices. The human personal culture constructs its own self-regulation devices, semiotic mediators, which make it possible for the person's conduct to be "functionally autonomous."

Second, the personalistic perspectives outlined here recognize the sociogenetic embeddedness of the developing personality. To be more exact, that embeddedness is *recognized* but not directly investigated. Nevertheless, the exclusive separation of sociogenetic and personological viewpoints appears to be an artifact, since each needs the other for an adequate account of their subject matters. Sociogenetic thinkers cannot avoid positing *some* kind of personal agency (as was shown in chapter 4), and personologists cannot—and do not—overlook the sociogenetic nature of personality development.

However, what both personological and sociogenetic perspectives have failed to emphasize in full is the semiogenetic (sign-constructing) nature of human personality. It is through human language that persons construct themselves (and participate in the development of others). Human personality is a semiotic phenomenon, as will be shown in the next chapter.

6

Semiotic Regulation of
Psychological Processes

Human existence is organized by socially constructed and personally inter-nalized semiotic means—signs of different kinds. Signs become presenta-tions of some aspect of the experienced phenomena as they are being constructed by a person for the needs of communication—with others and with oneself. Thus, signs are the vehicle for cultural mediation of any psychological functions that entail reflection upon any aspects of the ongo-ing flow of experience.

The aspect of signs that I emphasize in this book is that of sign construc-tion (or *semiogenesis*), rather than that of appropriation and use of already existing signs. This focus is not meant to de-emphasize the reliance of hu-mans upon collective-culturally available "ready-made" signs, but merely to emphasize the functional context of signs in the regulation of ever-novel phenomena of experience. By the process of turning some aspect of human conduct—be it sound or gesture—to stand in for some other aspect, hu-man beings *create* the world of signs. This constructive act is always per-sonal, requiring an active human being who relates his or her personal culture with the collective culture via the process of internalization and externalization. Signs—as these are externalized—become maintained in the collective-cultural realm and are utilized by others for further recon-struction of the signs. The reciprocal movement between the personal culture and the collective culture entails constant reconstruction of the semantic fields of the signs.

Semiosphere As Human Environment: Meaningful Contexts

How do signs emerge in the flow of conduct? The image of human beings as "talking apes" is not unreasonable. In a generic sense, the human nature of *Homo sapiens* makes the species to be *animal symbolicum* (Ivic, 1978)—

an animal species that is involved in excessive construction of semiotic means in order to organize their lives. The result of such constructivity of signs is that the human environment—in contrast to that of most non-human species—becomes a *semiosphere* (Lotman, 1992), a bounded field of heterogeneous structure of semiotic mediating devices that are constructed and guided by human actors.

The use of the notion of semiosphere entails a recognition of the signs-"infested" nature of all human environment. Not surprisingly, it is in the realm of environmentally oriented areas of psychology that the notion of signification has become accepted in productive ways (Csikszentmihalyi and Rochberg-Halton, 1981; Fuhrer, 1993; Kopytoff, 1986; Lang, 1992b, 1993c, 1995; Slongo et al., 1995; Werner, Altman, and Oxley, 1985).

Semiosphere is a product of semiogenesis. It is a totality of constructed and reconstructed versions of semiotic devices that both *represent* a lived-through experience and *present* the represented experiences to others and oneself, facing the always indeterminate experiential future. The process of semiogenesis is contemporaneous with the experiencing itself; it is a parallel process that allows the person to regulate his or her experiential process. Semiogenesis creates human preadaptations—social regulators—in the form of signs. The person's ability to highlight (see Lyra and Rossetti-Ferreira, 1995) some aspects of the flow of experience and to make those aspects into signs that represent and present that selected aspect is the root of all semiogenesis (Werner and Kaplan, 1984). This is possible thanks to the availability of acting in an "as-if" relation to the actual situation—any act of pretend play of children, imagination of adults, or play with established meanings by actors, writers, or politicians is an example of the meaning-making process (see reflections by Bruner, 1990). The possibilities of transcending on individual's objective here-and-now situation make psychological regulation by invented mediating devices possible (Cole, 1995; Vygotsky and Luria, 1930/1994). Yet the nature of such devices, their emergence and functioning, require a special analysis.

Semiogenesis as a Process of Sign Production and Transformation

As was shown in chapter 4, sociogenetically oriented perspectives in psychology have not tired of repeating ad infinitum that "human psychological functioning is social." Such voices of the developing sociocultural science are based on recognition of the meaningful organization of personal and social worlds. Undoubtedly that is made possible by semiotic mediation. However, there is an inherent problem in these claims—namely, any claim about the semiotic nature of something else is itself part of a semiotic mediating process. This autocatalytic feature of semiosis sets up specific limits upon techniques of empirical research in psychology (see further discussion in chapter 7). However, it also leads to the developmental question about the emergence of sign mediation in the personal-cultural worlds of human beings.

It is remarkable that traditional semiotics—as a science of signs—has largely ignored the issue of the dynamic process of its construction of the phenomena it attempts to reflect. In symbolic anthropology, the study of time-based transformation of cultural symbols has been largely missing (see analysis of that oversight by Ohnuki-Tierney, 1981). Likewise, at the level of personal cultures, the sense-making and sense-changing process is largely unstudied. This lack was pointed out by Frederick Bartlett some time ago (Bartlett, 1924, p. 279), and the situation has remained in this state in psychology ever since.

Bartlett's own effort to highlight the semiogenesis process included a focus upon different systems of "reaction tendencies" in the human psychological whole to enter into specific relations with one another, thus making one of the tendencies to produce symbols for the other. He posited a general mechanism of the emergence of symbols in the sphere of mental processes:

> Material arouses a given tendency, is attended to, and *put into relation with other material* to help to *form a particular mental system*. At the same time *another tendency comes into play*, and by it *the same material gains different relations and a place in a different mental system*. Mental systems, however, are not normally isolated. They *are linked together*, first, because they share common materials, and secondly because among all the tendencies which take a share in their formation, one or two are always masterful. The masterful tendencies set the systems migrating, so to speak, and the watchword of the growth of symbols in the individual mental life is the *"contact of mental systems."* (Bartlett, 1924, p. 281; emphasis added)

Bartlett's (self-admittedly clumsy) effort to provide an account of the psychological processes involved in semiogenesis is actually very contemporary. It entails *simultaneous input* from some experiential event (A) into two (or more) parts of a hierarchically organized psychological system ("tendencies" that are "not normally isolated"): X =>>= Y (where >> indicates the previous dominance relation in the holistic system). By way of A relating to Y, it becomes related to X, and integrated into the hierarchical structure, letting the latter be transformed (similarly to the assimilation/accommodation notion of Piaget). It would then be a question of how the new material (A) becomes seen *as if* it represents the dominant tendency. Thus, any oblong-shaped object (A) in the psychoanalytic field of meaning construction could be viewed as a symbolic representation of the penis (Y), because of the dominant tendency of the complex of sexuality (X) already linked with the notion of penis. As Bartlett himself remarked,

> If we are considering the growth of symbols in the *individual* life, the most important clue to the whole process is to be found in the fact that, in the case of any individual, there are always certain tendencies, or groups of tendencies, which take the leading place, and dominate the others . . . The master tendencies of an individual always determine the direction along which his own symbolism proceeds. It may be said that, in general, two groups of tendencies have, in the past, stood out as master impulses of an individual life more frequently than any others. They are the religious group and the sex group; and as a result there is scarcely anything that a human being can attend to that has not at some time or another served as a religious or a sexual symbol. (Bartlett, 1924, p. 281)

The flexibility of the system that dominates the semiogenetic process can be seen in the reversibility of the dominance relations described by Bartlett. Thus, sexual conduct can become meaningful in a religious context (see chapter 9), similarly to religious conduct becoming interpretable under the dominance of sexuality, or power, discourses (refer to Obeyesekere's reconstruction of psychoanalysis in chapter 4). More important, the process of semiogenesis entails generalization of the meaning in terms of general feeling-tone. Such symbolic feeling is not describable in elementaristic terminology—and can be described in abstract fuzzy general terms (e.g., an American young student, returning from weeks of trekking in the Himalayas, glimpses a U.S. Marine guard in front of the U.S. Embassy in Kathmandu and reports the feeling of "being at home, at last"). Such generalized semiotic feeling is a global phenomenon that was the target of analysis for *Ganzheitspsychologie* (Krueger, 1926, 1928a) and has remained largely out of focus in later approaches to persons' construction of sense—largely due to the overcognitivization of psychology (after its behaviorization). It is in the context of Heinz Werner's "organismic-holistic" framework that such phenomena have been considered.

Semiogenesis as Construction of Subjective Order

Werner's developmental starting point on symbol formation is based on the assumptions of *holism* (i.e., any activity is dependent upon the context or field—a whole of which it is a constitutive part) and *directiveness* (i.e., an organism's activities are oriented toward realization of ends immanent in the activity of the whole organism). It is obvious that both of these assumptions have been actively rejected in much of psychology of the recent half century: while the assumption of holism "smells vagueness" in many a view of it, the notion of directivity entails a clear teleological stance. Psychological theory constructors have usually tried to avoid assumptions of teleology, thus making it difficult for themselves to conceptualize development.

In line with the "orthogenetic principle" (Werner, 1957; see also chapter 5), the process of semiogenesis involves differentiation of the experiencing subject and the semistructured object fields:

> The man, destined to conquer the world through knowing, starts out with confusion, disorientation, and chaos, which he struggles to overcome. This struggle is a never-ceasing process, continuing throughout life: man's objects are always touched with a coefficient of indeterminacy and, as long as he is open to new environments and experiences, they are constantly in the process of transformation, changing in their significance. One may indeed say that man lives constantly in a world of becoming rather than in a world of being. Now it is our contention that in order to build up a truly human universe, that is, a world that is known rather than merely reacted to, man requires a new tool—an instrumentality that is suited for, and enables the realization of, those operations constituting the activity of knowing. (Werner and Kaplan, 1984, p. 13)

This instrumentality is a symbol—distinct from a sign, signal, or thing. Signs or signals are mere elicitors or inhibitors of action, whereas a symbol rises above these in the form of generalized meaning. Symbol formation takes place through dynamic schematization that entails a *double form-*

building process (Werner and Kaplan, 1984, p. 22): the meaningfulness of objects (referents of the symbol-in-the-making) is being constructed in parallel—and interdependently—with the articulation of expressive meaning (the vehicle of the meaning—the symbol). Signs and symbols develop as the experience with objects proceeds, and through that the objects are transformed in their meanings. This process is utilized in Vygotsky's elaboration of the "method of double stimulation" (Vygotsky and Luria, 1930/1994), in the differentiation of stimulus-objects and stimulus-means.

Dynamic schematizing is a differentiation process in the course of irreversible time. As an example, consider a person

> confronted by a configuration which he apprehends as possessing a "sitting tone": that is, the configuration instigates in him a postural-affective state which is organized schematically as "something there to move towards and sit down on." It is this schematizing activity and the ingredient organismic state that leads the individual to apprehend the configuration as "chair" rather than, for example, a "table" (even though the same configuration, considered physically, for example, a "tree stump," might be articulated—depending of course on organismic states—as either "chair" or "table").
>
> Now we assume that the vocable *chair*, in an English-speaking individual, issues forth from the same schematizing activity: as an essentially dynamic, intonationally molded sound stream—not as a static sonic configuration—the material, phonemically unique sequence, *ch-ai-r*, is articulated into a production whose expressive features parallel those ingredient in the percept "chair." As a mere sound configuration, the utterance *chair* functions as a sign or label (as it actually is for one learning a foreign language). Only when the vocable has become embedded in an organismic matrix, regulated and directed by an activity of schematizing or form-building, does it enter into a semantic correspondence with the object (referent) and does it become transformed from the status of sign to that of symbolic whole. (Werner and Kaplan, 1984, pp. 24–25)

Werner and Kaplan's symbol formation process thus entails distancing of the subject from the object of referencing, through the construction of the symbol. The first level of making of the subject-object relationship (represented by the "sitting tone" of the object "out there," or by "affordances" that relate the person to the structured object—Reed and Jones,

1984, part 4.9) differentiates the actor and the object of action, and gives rise to the reflection in terms of the sign ("chair"). The word ("vocable") is taken over from language to be "populated" by the person's intentions (see discussion of Bakhtin in chapter 3). As such, it operates as a sign, without generalization—it is only when the latter process takes place that it becomes a symbol.

The making of a symbol involves distancing in a number of ways. First, there is distancing of the object (referent) from the generalized meaning field of the constructed symbol. Second, there is distancing of the person's domain of contemplation (symbolic discourse within oneself) from the realm of actions. Finally, there is the distancing of the positions of addressor and addressee in the act of communication—use of generalized symbols allows for the creation of illusionary intersubjectivity (through generalized symbols) while the particular referents of the symbols can be interpersonally unshared). For Werner and Kaplan, the move toward abstraction and generalization of symbols constitutes an important step in the *autonomization of symbols* from their contexts, thus leading to "development toward a system of vehicles which enables a person to communicate adequately with an audience psychologically quite distant from the addressor. In other words, the greater the interpersonal distance between individuals involved in a communication situation, the more autonomous must be the symbolic vehicles in order to be understood, that is, the more communal and the less egocentric, idiosyncratic, and contextualized must the vehicles become" (Werner and Kaplan, 1984, p. 49).

Here we find the crucial opposition that emerges in the process of semiogenesis. On the one hand, the construction of increasingly abstracted, generalized, and hence decontextualized signs and symbols creates possibilities for the signs-making and signs-using person to distance him- or herself from any immediate context of here and now. The growth of the system of semiotic mediators is "vertical," so to speak; it entails building ever-new levels of generalization and abstraction beyond the experiences of the here-and-now setting.

On the other hand, the generalized and abstracted mediating devices can operate only in some here-and-now setting, since the person who uses them (for addressing others or oneself) is necessarily embedded in this setting. The use of the most highly abstracted and generalized semiotic devices is always concrete—even if not meant to have an immediate impact upon actions. The "alienation" between the acting, thinking, and generalized feelings is a necessary outcome from the notion of semiogenesis, and from the sociocultural focus on semiosphere. The tension emerging from such "alienation" may make it possible for the person to intentionally alter the here-and-now settings, *both* by acting differently within these and by reorganizing his or her feelings (and personal sense systems) about those settings.

It is obvious that Werner and Kaplan, as well as Bartlett, were considering the notion of symbol not as one type of sign (e.g., Peirce's icon-index-symbol typology for signs) but as a meta-level sign that can be used to reflect upon other signs due to its generalized and abstracted nature. Bartlett's and Werner's accounts of symbol formation are in line with the systemic focus on semiotic mediational structures that the constraining-based theoretical scheme that is outlined in the present book. The notion of signs in general, and symbols as a subtype of signs, as constraints upon the fields of action and reflection is further supported by a reanalysis of selected traditions from semiotics. Semiotics—the general science of sign mediation—is based on the parent disciplines of logic and linguistics. The initial formulation of semiotics is often attributed to Charles S. Peirce.

Peirce's World of Logic Through Signs

Charles Sanders Peirce (1839–1914) was an American scholar whose impact upon philosophy, logic, and semiotics has been profound, despite his limited and tumultuous relations with the official academic system (see Deledalle, 1990). Peirce was interested in the general systematization of sciences, using logic as a central discipline. Logic was the desired "gold standard" of nineteenth-century thought, and the desire for logical rationality prevailed in the social discourse. It is possible that the emphasis on logical rationality was a countertheme to the esoteric fascinations that raged in European societies and that forced a number of logic-oriented scholars to reveal their illogicality.

In 1865, Peirce posited the relations between different parts of logic:

Logic is objective symbolistic.
Symbolistic is the semiotic of symbols . . .
Semiotic is the science of representations.
Representation is anything which is or is represented to stand for another and by which that other may be stood for something which may stand for the representation. (Peirce, 1982, p. 303)

Semiotics was of central importance in the science of logic, where the issue of substitution by a representation of an object was of the essence. A sign, according to Peirce, was "something which stands for another thing to a mind" (1873, cited in Peirce, 1986, p. 82). Later (ca. 1897), Peirce gave a more elaborate explanation: "A sign, or *representamen,* is something which stands for somebody for something in some respect or capacity. It addresses somebody, that is, creates in the mind of that person an equivalent sign, or perhaps a more developed sign. That sign which it creates I call the *interpretant* of the first sign. The sign stands for something, its *object.* It stands for that object, not in all respects but in reference to a sort of idea, which I have sometimes called the *ground* of the representamen" (Buchler, 1955, p. 99).

That the interpretant is possibly a "more developed sign" than the representamen opens Peirce's sign concept for a consistently developmental standpoint. The interpretation of the sign is a constructive process—an idea that echoes the developmental thinking of Peirce's contemporary James Mark Baldwin (see chapter 4). The dynamic-constructive nature of Peirce's semiotic thinking has been emphasized by many who claim to follow him (Bonfantini, 1988; Jappy, 1989; Ponzio, 1985; Robinson, 1985; Short, 1988).

Peirce's system of signs is perhaps best known by his trichotomy of icon–index–symbol differentiation, even though his classification of signs was actually much richer. He emphasized the dynamic nature of signs, thus claiming: "Symbols grow. They come into being by development out of other signs, particularly from icons, from mixed signs partaking of the nature of icons and symbols. We think only in signs. These mental signs are of mixed nature; the symbol-parts of them are called concepts. If a man makes a new symbol, it is by thoughts involving concepts. So it is out of symbols that new symbols can grow" (Buchler, 1955, p. 115).

All signs are viewed by Peirce as dynamically transforming and transformable. For him, the creation and use of signs permeate the human existence—in both its intramental and interpsychological domains. A sign maker makes the created sign available to others—and in the case of those others some of the signs are supposed to excite in the intrapsychological world familiar images, based on their memories of past life experiences. Still, the images are sufficiently detached from their original occurrences in the past that they can be attached to new occasions. Peirce used a selection of the nineteenth-century U.S. social realities to explain such sign mediation: "Tramps have the habit of carrying bits of chalk and making marks on the fences to indicate the habits of the people that live there for the benefit of other tramps who may come on later. If in this way a tramp leaves an assertion that the people are stingy, he supposes the reader of the signal will have met stingy people before, and will be able to call upon an image of such a person attachable to a person whose acquaintance he has not yet made. (Peirce, 1896, p. 28)

Thus it is through signs that personal past experiences can guide one's own and others' future conduct. Peirce recognized the special case that the irreversibility of time brings to the functioning of the human mind. Its focus on the present is crucial, as is evident in Figure 6.1, which illustrates Peirce's attempt to describe the "insistency" of past ideas for the present, and of the present's relevance for the immediate future. Different life experiences of the past—the more recent ones more than the more distant ones—insist upon framing the person's way of making sense of the present. At the same time, the imagery of the possible future—from most immediate to most distant—creates the contrasting "pull" for the sense of the present. This tension is depicted by the two equilateral hyperbola, which create a permanent tension at any present moment. It is the present that affects the future through personal semiotic construction:

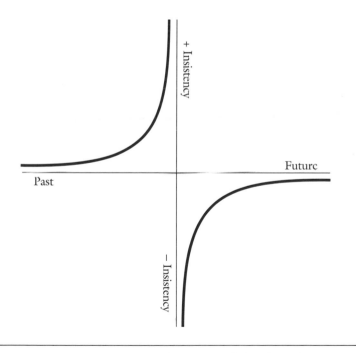

Figure 6.1. C. S. Peirce's description of insistency of ideas from the past to the present, and from the present toward the future (from Peirce, 1935, p. 104).

Feeling which has not yet emerged into immediate consciousness is already affectible and already affected. In fact, this is habit, by virtue of which an idea is brought up into present consciousness by a bond that had already been established between it and another idea while it was still *in futuro*.

the affected idea is attached as a logical predicate to the affecting idea as subject. So when a feeling emerges into immediate consciousness, it always appears as a modification of a more or less general object already in the mind. The word suggestion is well adapted to expressing this relation. The future is suggested by, or rather is influenced by the suggestions of, the past. (Peirce, 1935, pp. 104–105 [6.141 and 6.142])

Time flow guarantees the constantly active novelty of semiotic processes. Therefore, for Peirce, the sign could not be something repetitive— each time it is taken up it appears in a new act of semiosis (Ponzio, 1985, p. 16). The constant construction of novelty in the act of semiosis à la Peirce leads to the emphasis on the main cognitive process of inference— that of abduction.

Abduction As Constructive Inference

Abduction, induction, and deduction are three forms of inference. Deduction proves that something *must be,* induction shows that something *actually is* operative, and abduction just suggests that something *may be* (Deledalle, 1990, p. 60). Since all time-bound life experiences link some past experiences with future possibilities, a concept that allows us to make sense of this process of construction is necessary. The future is not merely a deduction from general premises (built on the basis of past experiences), nor is it induction from those past experiences (by way of their transfer to the present). Both deduction and induction lack the moment of construction of novelty, and hence are not fit for explanation of semi-open developmental processes. Abduction can be seen as the process whereby the thinker "leaps" from the field of possible inferences (that what "may be") to a definite new construction. Hence abduction is a process for going beyond the information given.

Peirce's solution to the problem of how new knowledge is being created (on the basis of the observed facts of the present) entailed the notion of hypothesis and its construction. Hypothesis is a supposition about proposed truth, which *at the time of setting up the hypothesis* is not available. Hence there has to be semiotic constructivity without an immediate—inductive or deductive—basis. The constructed hypothesis can subsequently be put to the test. All invention of new knowledge, that is, inventions before they might become proven—entails the construction of uncertain possible signs. The process of setting up hypotheses is that of abductive inference: "The first starting of a hypothesis and the entertaining of it, whether as a simple interrogation or with any degree of confidence, is an inferential step which I propose to call *abduction*. This will include a preference for any one hypothesis over others which would equally explain the facts, so long as this preference is not based upon any previous knowledge bearing upon the truth of the hypotheses, nor any testing of any of the hypotheses, after having admitted them on probation" (Peirce, 1935, p. 358 [6.525]).

In other writings Peirce also referred to abduction as "inference *a posteriori*" (or retroduction). The crucial characteristic of abductive inference (inference *a posteriori*) is its enablement of further possibilities (Peirce, 1982, p. 181) that are not entailed by either inductive or deductive (a priori) inference. Enablement of further possibilities is always uncertain, thus bringing into the reasoning process both openness and indeterminacy. Richard Shweder has detected in Peirce's thought of abductive reasoning a valuable direction for our contemporary cultural psychology, because

> Transcendent realities can be imagined but never seen or deduced, for they are constructions of our own making, which sometimes succeed at binding us to the underlying reality they imagine by giving us an intellectual tool—a metaphor, a premise, an analogy, a category—with which to live, to arrange our experience, and to interpret our experiences so arranged. In other words, the abductive faculty is the faculty of imagination, which comes to the rescue of sensation and logic by providing them with the intellectual means to see through experience and leap beyond empty syllogisms and tautologies to some creative representation of an underlying reality that might be grasped and reacted to, even if that imagined reality cannot be found, proved, or disproved by inductive or deductive rule following. (Shweder, 1990, p. 38)

Peirce's abductive inference notion is undoubtedly a productive line of theorizing for modern cognitive psychology as well. All the attention received (since the 1970s) by the myriad of "cognitive heuristics" that have been dramatically displayed (e.g., Kahneman, Slovic, and Tversky, 1982)—or disputed—as basic "errors of rationality" of human reasoning can easily be seen as rather simple demonstrations of abductive inference in practice. The "magic" show point of the cognitive heuristics tradition has been the demonstration that ordinary human beings do not operate on the basis of the rules of inductive inference, when the task given to them primes them for abductive inference (Gigerenzer, 1991; Sovran, 1992). That they indeed do not—and in fact cannot—was obvious to Peirce a century ago. It is the embeddedness of human semiotic activity within the irreversible time of existence, and the inevitable interdependence with any here-and-now context, that render inductive (and deductive) inference strategies defective for the problem solver and turns the future-oriented abductive inference strategies into the most appropriate cognitive adaptation. Abductive inference is the necessary strategy, given time and information limitations of the cognitive process, and is paralleled by the satisficing strategy in real-life decision processes (see discussion of Herbert Simon's idea in Valsiner, 1987, pp. 28–30).

ABDUCTION AS A PROCESS OF SIGN CONSTRUCTION   Karl-Otto Apel has provided an example of the procedure of identification of the flow of experience in Peircean terms, which includes symbols, linguistic indices, and icons, and demonstrates the coordination of different signs in the process of meaning construction:

> *This* thing *over there*—under the big tree in the foreground—looks *so and so* (to be specified by describing the perceptible qualities and relations of qualities that make up the phenomenal structure). On the basis of these perceptible qualities, I don't know how to determine *what* it is (i.e., under which general concept it could be subsumed). That is, I find it impossible *at present* to provide a conceptual subsumption of the given stuff on the basis of an *abductive inference* of the form: "This there is so and so; what is so and so might be an exemplar of A." Hence, in order to provide for the possibility of a later determination on the basis of re-identification, I will give it a name: I *hereby* baptize the given stuff by the name of "baboo." I thereby define the extension of "baboo" as "being everything that is the same as this over there which *now* causes my present experience by presenting the following phenomenal structure (to be specified by a picture or by a list of phenomenal qualities)." (Apel, 1989, p. 42)

Apel's example points to the way in which abductive inference and naming (i.e., symbol invention) are coordinated. Abduction can take place in the form of an extension of an existing category boundary, marked by a general meaning (category name that already exists). Yet blockage of the possibility for such abductive incorporation into a preexisting category can lead to the *naming* ("baptizing") of the discordant phenomenon, which creates a new category of named objects. The naming allows for further abductive inference—from the "baptized" label "baboo," the generalizing process leads to making the given object a core of the general category "baboo," and the sign construction has succeeded in creating new meaning.

In contrast, easy availability of the symbolic denotation of "this thing over there" would immediately lead to abductive category-including constructions: if "this thing over there" looks like "A," and *perhaps is* "A," then X, Y, and Z can be inferred. Of course the process of discovery of "this thing over there" is guided by the social roles of the discoverer (and of the social suggestions entailed in the discovery process).

BASIS FOR ABDUCTION: DISEQUILIBRATION   What makes abduction possible? The dynamic activity of the sign-constructing mind has to be explained in some way. Peirce's solution to this issue turned out to be fittingly contemporary for both his time and ours—a century later! Thus, he explained:

> Everybody knows that the long continuance of a routine or habit makes us lethargic, while a succession of surprises wonderfully brightens the ideas. Where there is motion, where history is a-making, there is the focus of mental activity, and it has been said that the arts and sciences reside within the temple of Janus, waking when that is open, but slumbering when it is closed. Few psychologists have perceived how fundamental a fact this is. A portion of mind abundantly commissured to other portions works almost mechanically. It sinks to the condition of a railway junction. But a portion of mind almost isolated, a spiritual peninsula, or *cul-de-sac,* is like a railway terminus. Now mental commissures are habits. Where they abound, originality is not needed and is not found; but where they are in defect, spontaneity is set free. (Peirce, 1893, p. 187)

Peirce's simile of the operation of railway connections as an example of different kinds of mental processes brings out the focus on the linkage of abductive inference with *history in the making*. Recognizing that the developmental process constantly undermines automatisms and habits in conduct (and borrowing from James Mark Baldwin in this), Peirce formulated in generic terms what in our time could be recognized as a law of development through disequilibration (or the widespread "order out of chaos" idea, following the thermodynamics of Ilya Prigogine). Thus,

> Protoplasm is in an excessively unstable condition; and *it is the characteristic of unstable equilibrium, that near that point excessively minute causes may produce startlingly large effects.* Here, then, the usual departures from regularity will be followed by others that are very great; and the large fortuitous departures from law so produced, will tend still further to break up the laws, supposing that these are of the nature of habits. Now, this breaking up of habit and renewed fortuitous spontaneity will, according to the law of mind, be accompanied by an intensification of feeling. The nerve-protoplasm is, without doubt, in the most unstable condition of any kind of matter; and consequently, there the resulting feeling is the most manifest. (Peirce, 1892, p. 18; emphasis added)

Thus it is through the constant process of disequilibration—taking place in irreversible time (à la Bergson, 1911a, and Prigogine, 1987)—that conditions are created for the living organisms to construct new preadaptational forms. In the case of psychological phenomena (i.e., "nerve-protoplasm," as Peirce uses here), the semiotic innovation proceeds via *affective* instabilities (which lead the process of sign reconstruction).

It may be this focus of Peirce's that deserves elaboration in the present context. The duality of cognitive and affective sides can be posited to be present in any sign constructed (see discussion in chapter 3). Hence within each sign there is already encoded a tension between those sides. Regulation of that tension through efforts to maintain some equilibrium—which at times fail and lead to disequilibration—would serve as the basis for further sign construction.

Social Role Relations As Guiding Abductive Inference

Peirce's notion of abductive inference warrants being put into a wider context. Since abduction is a "weak" kind of argument—in its openness to suggestions from the past—its process can be guided both through the personal experiences encoded semiotically from the past and through similarly encoded social suggestions at the present. The openness of abduction to creative construction makes it a target for the social canalization processes in society that are based on the power (dominance) roles of different social agents. From birth onward—all through ontogeny—human beings are provided with specific social role models and construct their own models on their basis (Oliveira, 1995; Oliveira and Valsiner, 1996). This assuming of social roles is not a passive takeover of static roles as preprovided (i.e., a popular misreading of Theodore Sarbin's "role theory"—for reality see Sarbin, 1950, 1952); rather, these roles are always personally co-constructed on the basis of the collective-cultural constraint structures, in accordance with the person's goal-oriented aspirations. The latter are always embedded within a hierarchically organized—yet dynamic—social system. This system constrains role-constructive activity through constructing its own differentiation by semiotic means (e.g., by naming to create social classes and their oppositions—Bourdieu, 1985). In the process of semiotic construction of the social structure, the constraint systems for personal constructions of social roles are being set up within the symbolic field (see chapter 2 for an analysis of Pierre Bourdieu's field theory).

The differentiated hierarchical nature of social organization creates the basis for semiotic mediating devices to be means of negotiation of power between the persons enacting different roles. This enacting has double historicity (see Bourdieu and Wacquant, 1992, p. 139); through the dispositional structure of habitus, active persons reconstruct both the social structure and their own selves in irreversible time. This takes many forms—for instance, the roles of "experts" or "professionals" relative to those of "laypersons" (Bourdieu, 1991), roles of lower-level officials in bureaucracies (e.g., Bourdieu, 1981, pp. 312–315), social (re)presentations of academic activities (through images of time "expenditures" and social power-role labeling—see Bourdieu, 1988), or discourses about prioritizing languages in multilanguage contexts (Goke-Pariola, 1993)—are all semiotic constraining devices for human development over the life course. Peirce's emphasis on the dynamic nature of sign construction processes is applicable at both psychological and sociological levels of analysis.

Peirce's Semiotic Developed: Alfred Lang's Semiotic Ecology

There are very few efforts in contemporary psychology to borrow basic ideas from Peirce's semiotics (e.g., Moro and Rodriguez, 1994). Among these, the developmental-*semiotic ecology* of Alfred Lang constitutes a basic effort to reconceptualize psychology through a systematic focus on semiotic processes that are involved in the dynamic relation between the person and the world.

Lang's theoretical system has three roots. First, von Uexküll's focus on the unity of organisms and their environment *(Umwelt)* gives Lang's solution to the problem of human psychology a dynamic quality. Using von Uexküll's functional circle *(Funktionskreis)*, Lang overcomes the problem of dualism in person-world relations. The functional circle operates as an ongoing relation between the organism and the *Umwelt,* so by focusing on the relation the dualism between the opposites (which is a result of exclusive separation) becomes a duality (or: a result of inclusive separation). This solution is similar to John Dewey's (1896) suggestion that the reflex arc be changed into a reflex circle—which led to the emphasis of the processes that proceed within that circle.

However, the focus on the functional circle is not sufficient by itself for placing semiotic processes into human psychological systems. It merely creates a basis for doing so. The second root of Lang's theoretical account is Kurt Lewin's theoretical heritage—particularly the notions of experiencing any environment as imbued by meaning, and development along different lines *(Genesereihe)*. Lang started from the need to build a developmental ecological psychology (Lang, 1988) as a solution to the problems that psychology's nondevelopmental and environment-dismissive traditions had brought to light. The support for this solution is amply present in Lewin's field-theoretic and (especially in the 1920s) developmentally oriented ideas (Lang, 1991, 1992a). As a partial result of the integration of Lewinian ideas and the insistence of dynamic relationships-based closeness of the person and the world, Lang arrives at the notion of simultaneous existence of psychological phenomena inside of the psychological system as well as outside. The external psychological structures—the "external soul" (Lang, 1992b, 1993a, 1993b) is culturally encoded psychological construction. In this step, there is a similarity between the conceptual reasons for creating the notion of the "external soul" in Lang's theoretical system, and that of the "external brain" in the thinking of Pablo del Río (Del Río, 1994; see also the "flexible architectures" notion in Del Río and Alvarez, 1995b, and the elaborations of "zone of syncretic representation" in Del Río and Alvarez, 1995a).

However, the developmental and relational view on human psychological phenomena is not yet cultural. For that final step, Lang brings into psychology Peirce's focus on triadic (rather than dual) structures. This has made it possible for Lang to find his solution to the question of how to avoid "the Cartesian split" between the subjective and objective worlds (Lang, 1993b, p. 142). Surely that would not happen via theoretical assumptions of "full merging" of persons with cultural contexts: to claim that the persons *are* such contexts or that persons *are* "cultural texts" would amount to a solution of no theoretical return to make sense of the complexity of psychological phenomena. Similar problems await the elimination of person-context "boundaries" in other ways (see chapter 3).

Lang's advancement of a semiotic perspective makes use of Peirce's semiotics as the way to "fill in" the content into the functional circle of person-environment relations. The functional circle, according to Lang, entails four mutually linked semiotic processes, two at the relation between the person and environment (perceptual processes: *IntrO-Semiosis;* action processes: *ExtrO-Semiosis*) and the other two within each of the parts of the united system (in the person: psychological processes or *IntrA-Semiosis;* in the environment: cultural processes or *ExtrA-Semiosis*). All four processes are semiotic in their nature and their mutual feed-in in a cyclical fashion (e.g., IntrO→ IntrA→ ExtrO→ ExtrA→ IntrO . . . and so on—cf. Lang, 1993b, p. 144; Lang, 1993d, p. 79). This guarantees the linking of person and environment in inclusively separated, yet dynamically mutually intertwined, processual, and *constantly sign-constructing* fashion. Each of the four semiotic processes involves construction of signs, and the whole cycle can be studied via juxtaposition of each of the processes, using different empirical tactics (see Slongo et al., 1995).

The sign-constructing process can be viewed at each junction of the functional cycle, which—given the irreversibility of developmental time—functions as a helix that moves constantly toward the future, never repeating its previous constructions of signs. The formation of such sign construction is a structure-building process, or *Anaformation:* previously existing structures relate to new material and form a new sign structure (Lang, 1992c, p. 670). The crucial feature of Lang's semiotic ecology is the focus on the *constant process of restructuring* of the world of signs. He solves the problem of reconciliation of the perennial tension between structure and function in the development of organisms—at the human level—by way of letting a hyperdynamic process (of the *Funktionskreis*) generate different by-products (sign structures) as it proceeds in its cyclical-helical unity. These by-products—sign forms—are the vehicles (structural ones) that further guide the functioning of the helix in time.

Empirical investigation can bring out specific results of such construction of sign forms at multiple levels (e.g., the constructions of the object "door" can be traced to the user in action, to an architect or builder, or to anybody in an abstracted and generalized ways—see Lang, 1993d, pp. 56–58; similar issues are reflected in Boesch, 1993, and Ohnuki-Tierney, 1987, 1993). However, more elaborated semiotic constructions can be obtained from persons' complex relations with specific objects in their environments. Such objects are not "pregivens" (for the psychological world of the person). They may arrive under largely coincidental conditions yet become well established through the anaformation process. The following passage from the work of Daniel Slongo provides an interesting example.

THE CASE OF THE "DIRTY CLOTHES CHEST" In an interview with a young married woman, the woman (S.), when asked about "some important things" in the apartment, selected a "dirty clothes' chest" and reported that this object had appeared in the environment as she had "reluctantly bought it" from her sister. She proceeded to elaborate:

> The interesting thing, now, with that Chest that stands in the sleeping room, is that *it pleases me highly,* it's in fact *almost like a sea trunk,* that's what it is to me, you can stow away something like the used clothes of 3 weeks or so. *I don't really like* to do the laundry, and if I have to, I like to have the machine full; and this is the only thing [from my sister] which I have considered, *I wouldn't like to give it back* to her. Because this *chest stands for comfort,* on the one hand [laughs], that is, there is a mad lot of clothes going in. I can hide the things inside, I can make them disappear, and then, on the other side, it's *decorative,* too. And then, the chest in addition *takes charge* of R. [the husband]. When *he has no shirts left, you don't notice,* because everything is inside the chest, he only sees it in the cupboard. Earlier, we had a smaller basket, it was overflowing already after one week, so you had to do something against, you just had to go somewhere with the dirty clothes. And then, since we live here and have this large chest, it is R. who does the laundry most of the time, not me [laughs!].
>   . . . I believe, it has something to do with the capacity of the chest, of what goes in there, there is connection, that we did the laundry less often since then, and that *we did not participate in the washing-day schedule that reigns the house.* In this house, people do their laundry every week, each party has one fixed day, and when the people in this apartment left, then everybody in the house assumed we would take

over their fixed day, but we didn't. And that's for me *a kind of sign
that I do not participate* in the Swiss washing-day philosophy.
. . . Well, this chest, I would not like to give it back, it's *kind of
freedom for me,* well, a kind of *revolt.* (Lang, 1993b, p. 140; emphasis
added)

This example from a person's self-report about the functional-psycho-
logical history of the chest is illustrative in a number of ways. First, it
brings out phenomena from different parts of the ongoing functional
circle: perception (of the chest), personal sense construction ("my freedom," "revolt," "comfort"), action (how things are put into the chest,
and when laundry is done, and by whom), and culturally featured environmental aspects (chest is "decorative"). Note that the reported excerpt is
the present-past self-report, so the explication of all parts of the functional
circle indicates its reality.

Second, the reported sign phenomena indicate the restructuration of
the whole process of doing laundry, beginning with the appearance of the
new physical object (the chest). The previous arrangement ("a smaller
basket, it was overflowing already after one week") that evoked a clear
psychological tension ("you had to do something *against*") was restruc-
tured by the new chest by eliminating the previous tension and letting the
chest become a sign of "freedom" from the need to do laundry, as well as
"revolt" against the "Swiss washing-day philosophy." The physical object
(chest) made it possible to reorganize the action field (doing laundry),
which was organized by specific social rules (of sharing the week between
families in the house for washing), leading to the meanings of "revolt" and
"freedom." The physical object now became a sign for these general meanings. The personal perception of the chest stands for these meanings, so
that it (as a sign) constrains the set of possible actions (ruling out—or at
least making it unlikely—that she would agree to get rid of the chest).

Finally, the excerpt indicates the use of signs as constraints upon the field
of meanings that regulate actions. S's use of "you" includes an indeterminate complex of herself, the husband, and any understanding hearer ("he
has no shirts left, *you* don't notice" or "*you* had to do something against,
you just had to go somewhere" versus "everybody in the house assumed *we*
would take over *their* fixed day"), while most of the rest of the story is
narrated in the "I" form (see further elaborations of this phenomenon in
the discussion of Karl Bühler's sematology).

Lang's semiotic functional circle notion can gain further support from other real-life situations where new physical objects are introduced into the person-*Umwelt* system (e.g., introduction of oral contraceptives to women in Jamaica—MacCormack and Draper, 1987; introduction of baby formula in infant feeding in Africa—Meldrum, 1982; or introduction of an encyclopedia into the life of a Jewish Orthodox girl—Lawrence, Benedikt, and Valsiner, 1992). Similarly, specific unexpected events that happen in the course of ritualistically organized activities (e.g., a fire-walking ceremony that fails—Freeman, 1981) force the functional circle to construct new semiotic solutions to the experienced events. Or in its concrete and established form, the functional circle can work between actions and signs to maintain the desired status quo of an interactive context (e.g., the semiotic organization of gynecological examinations—Henslin and Biggs, 1978).

Peirce's starting base (in logic) led him to search for general laws of human semiotic constructivity. Lang's elaboration brings these general laws to bear upon the complexity of everyday life, where little details of action and reflection tell us a big story of the functional interdependence of the concrete and the general. Semiogenesis makes it possible to transcend any established sign system.

Ferdinand de Saussure's Semiology

Ferdinand de Saussure (1857–1913) was a Swiss linguist whose efforts to create a science of signs—*semiology*—became celebrated as a social reconstruction after his death (Gadet, 1989). As Saussure was made to fit into the role of the "father" of modern structuralist linguistics, the static and arbitrary nature of signs in their synchronic mutual relations usually was emphasized in references to or borrowings from Saussure's difficult-to-access works.

Fatherhood of a scientific tradition is a difficult role to bear; so perhaps it was of some relief for Saussure that he was fitted into that role after he could no longer participate in the activity contexts of the linguists who came to respect his efforts. Since the beginning of this century, Saussure's emphasis on the use of signs as constituting human reality has been hailed as revolutionary science (Tobin, 1990), and its impact in our thinking about the sign-mediated nature of human psychological functions was amplified by the Prague Linguistic Circle (Gadet, 1989, pp. 120–123). He has also been criticized by the more sociologically oriented semioticians for his reliance on static forms of economic rationality (Ponzio, 1990).

The story of the social construction of Saussure's fame resembles greatly that of George Herbert Mead and Lev Vygotsky. Saussure never wrote a book—in fact, he had immense psychological difficulties facing writing tasks at all (Culler, 1986, pp. 23–24). Yet he is credited for his classic text—*Cours de linguistique générale*—which was compiled from his students' lecture notes only after his death and first published in 1916 (Saussure, 1916/1949). Although the compiled product is estimated to be generally adequate (Culler, 1986), even a cursory look at the careful tracing of how the compilation was actually made (available in Engler, 1968) indicates that much of the original richness of the oral presentation (Saussure gave his course at the University of Geneva in three years: 1907, 1908–1909, 1910–1911) has been lost in the process.

Neither was Saussure without his clearly specifiable predecessors. The influence of the German neogrammarians, especially that of Hermann Paul (1846–1921), upon Saussure can be traced to his university years spent in Leipzig in the 1870s. Like theirs, the role of the American linguist William D. Whitney and his book *The Life and Growth of Language* (Whitney, 1875) was referenced explicitly by Saussure in his lectures (Engler, 1968, p. 15). The work of Georg von der Gabelentz also has been discussed as providing sources for Saussure's thought (Bierbach, 1978; Koerner, 1988). It was clear for Saussure that issues of language needed to be studied in their synthetic unity, including historical, structural, and social manifestations (Engler, 1968, pp. 47–48). Saussure's *semiology*—study of the life of signs in the social life (Saussure, 1916/1949, p. 33)—was a rebellious undertaking for linguistics of his time.

For Saussure, the social nature of human sign-related activities was a central ideological axis around which different analytic efforts were built. He introduced a threefold analytic scheme (the translation of which into English has posed substantial problems—see Gadet, 1989, chapter 2)— *langage, langue,* and *parole.* According to Saussure,

(1) *Langage* is simultaneously a social institution (e.g., such as French language) and human possibility (e.g., a capability of a person to utilize the language). In this respect, *langage* constitutes a duality between social and linguistic structures;

(2) *Langue* refers to the domain of signs as those serve as linkages between thought and speaking activity; those signs are collective models taken over from langage by persons and stored in memory, and which become the basis for constructivity in the speech sphere.

Langue operates as a system of constraints (in the restrictive sense) upon the speaking activity.

(3) *Parole* is the constructive activity of speaking, constrained by the person's *langue*-limits but expressing novel sentiments at each moment. It is a personal, incidental speaking act that reflects the acts of will and intelligence, and leads to re-constitution of langue. (Saussure, 1916/1949, chap. 3)

Relations between the three concepts are not clearly provided in the compiled edition of Saussure's *Cours* but are more discernible from its sources (see Engler, 1968, p. 41). In Figure 6.2 we can see the unity of passive, resultant collectivity of *langue* within the person, oppositionally and inseparably linked with the active process of *parole*.

We can see how *langage* (as a structure existing independently of the individual) encompasses the opposition of *langue* and *parole* within a person. When viewed from the perspective adopted in this book (as was outlined in chapter 2), the structures of *langue* constrain the production of *parole*, while the act of speaking may participate in the reconstruction of these structures. Unfortunately, Saussure's pictorial depiction (through the diagonal separation of *langue* and *parole* within a person's sign-

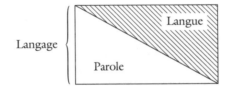

Saussure's contrasts between *langage, langue,* and *parole* (Engler, 1968, p. 41)

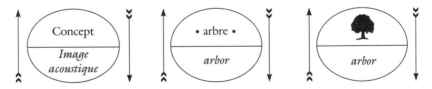

Example of *signifié* (concept) and *significant* (acoustic image) (Saussure, 1949, p. 99)

Figure 6.2. Basic concepts of Saussure.

mediated activity) fails to bring out the mutually constraining nature of the two. Instead, his figure depicts some additive relation between *langue* and *parole*, as if their sum were to make up *langage*.

EXTENSION OF SAUSSURE'S DUALITY   In line with the theoretical perspective outlined in chapter 2, as well as with Saussure's own claims, the processes of "dialogue" between *langue* and *parole* are to be seen in terms of constrained fields. In Figure 6.3, a redrawn version of Saussure's initial scheme (Figure 6.2) illustrates that focus.

In this scheme, different contexts within which *langage* can be used by the person differ in the extent of the "ready organization" of the given speech effort by *langue*. On the one extreme (C), *langue* provides easily usable organizational forms for *parole*, and the speaking process is either automatic (i.e., the use of automatized expressions, freed from linkage to content). Here the *langue* executes the maximum constraining role (ZFM and ZPA coinciding) upon *parole*. The novelty-constructive role of the *parole* is minimal under these circumstances. In this area of Figure 6.3 we can observe internalized patterns of *langage* (into *langue*) to determine the form *parole* takes. At this end of the range of speaking contexts, constraining of *langue* by *parole* can be completely absent. Here also belong cases of "empty talk" (see chapter 3), in which a person may produce

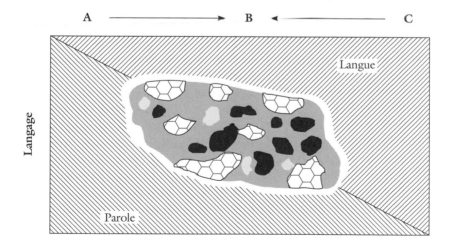

Figure 6.3. Modified view of Saussure's *langue-parole* relations.

elaborate speech—free of any substance—in accordance with all the rules of grammar.

On the other extreme (A), the person's speaking efforts can be abandoned by the constraining role of the *langue,* and the processes involved in *parole* are creating their own new organizational forms. Speaking situations in which uncertainty of speech generation reigns, or which are filled with unknown or emotiogenic aspects, are of such kind. A person is searching for a way to express oneself, and it is in this process of difficulty (due to absence of support from *langue* patterns) that *parole* reorganizes the given context. This "open field" leads to establishment of constraints by *parole* upon the construction of *langue.*

These two extremes—*langue*-determined and *parole*-challenging contexts—are special cases in the field. Usually, we can see the active speaker trying to escape from this overconstrained situation by creating innovations in *parole* that reconstruct the context in the direction of a semiconstrained state (indicated by arrow A→ B). In an opposite movement, the speaking person attempts to reconstruct *langue* via constraints of *parole,* so that the uncertainty of the speaking situation becomes semiclosed (indicated by arrow C→ B).

Thus, the posited tendency in *langue-parole* relations is to mutually structure each other through constraining. This semi-open state is described in locus C, where the field of *parole* is set up by *langue* and the boundaries of *langue* are set up by *parole.* It is in this "boundedly indeterministic" field of sign construction that new signs are made by the active speaker (who tries to "make sense" of an uncertain situation). The relation between *langue* and *parole* can be viewed as a dialogic process that exists due to the unavoidable uncertainty in any speaking context. Each context is filled with the tension between the new and the known.

SYNCHRONIC AND DIACHRONIC PERSPECTIVES   It is important to point out that Saussure emphasized the separation of synchronic and diachronic views to be applicable to *langue* (rather than *langage*—see Engler, 1968, p. 224; Saussure, 1916/1949, p. 139). *Langue* has two facets—static and evolutive—which lead innovation in each other.

Saussure understood the difficulties of translating this three-part scheme into other languages. For example, in German *Sprache* fails to distinguish *langue* and *langage* (while *Rede* fits—not well—with *parole,* amended to be "mais sens spécial de 'discours'"—Engler, 1968, p. 42, column 2, extract 249). These translation difficulties parallel those into the English language.

Saussure's ideas addressed the important question of production of a large variety of speech forms on the basis of relatively stable linguistic structures. By *langue*'s constraining of *parole,* the relative conservatism of human communication is preserved. One can view the process of such constraining as filled with opposition between the constraint rules and the multitude of speech intentions of a person at any moment (see chapter 2). Saussure's focus on the actual process of language use by socially situated persons has led to the "Saussurian paradox": if *langue*—as social entity—exists in the brains of all people using the given *langage,* it should be available for analysis by materials from any one person (including the linguist oneself). However, it is the personal identity that can be actually revealed by way of *parole,* in its social contexts (see also Labov, 1970). The social nature of the personal speech and the social nature of the *langue* "hidden" within the person create an epistemological paradox that is very similar to the difficulties encountered by contemporary researchers of "voices in the mind" (e.g., Wertsch, 1991, after Bakhtin). Likewise, the study of "social representations" repeats this paradox (as was shown in chapter 4).

The Double Nature Sign and Its Characteristics

Saussure introduced the notion of semiology in the context of writing about the social nature of *langue* (Engler, 1968, pp. 44–52). For Saussure, the linguistic sign is a two-faced psychological entity, which includes the concept *(signifié)* and the acoustic image or signifier *(signifiant*—Saussure, 1916/1949, p. 99). The psychological (rather than material) character of the acoustic image of the concept becomes clear in the case of speaking to oneself (e.g., reciting verses within oneself). Similarly to the united opposition between *langue* and *parole,* that of *signifié* and *signifiant* is that of interdependence (see Figure 6.1.B)

Signs have two fundamental characters—arbitrariness and the linear nature of the signifier (Saussure, 1916/1949, pp. 100–103). Arbitrariness guarantees relative freedom from dependency upon time and context of the sign use. Thus the idea of "sister" (or *"soeur"*) is not given by the sequence of sounds produced to utter the word. The signifier of a concept—or of an object—in actual speech can take different forms in different languages (*Ochs* versus *boeuf*).

THE QUESTION OF THE ARBITRARINESS OF SIGNS   Arbitrariness provides the signs with the possibility for uniting similar life experiences of persons across unrepeatable life contexts. Whereas the reality of life is possibly always novel, through arbitrary encoding of it through signs we can pretend that it is relatively stable. Thus, the *actual* identity of "Genève-Paris 8 h. 45 evening express" train (see Engler, 1968, p. 245) may be always new. The train may consist of different railway cars and engines every day, the train personnel may change, and the train may leave not at 8:45 but later. Yet through the arbitrary encoding it remains "the 8:45 express" (*even if* it is delayed until the scheduled departure of a later train!). This arbitrariness of signs permits continuity across time and circumstances, forcing the sign user to abstract from any particular context.

In linguistics, discussions about arbitrary encoding of the world by signs have often overlooked the limits on this arbitrary encoding process. These limits exist even in the example of "the 8:45 express train": it is train (rather than airplane), and if it were consistently late in its departure it may become "formerly 8:45, now 12:45 train." Arbitrariness of signs—in the sense used in the present book (and not necessarily in Saussure's terms)—entails a limited field of possible versions of reality that can still be encoded by the same sign. In this sense, arbitrariness is another depiction of the fuzzy-set depiction of meanings. It becomes possible thanks to the differentiation of levels of action, reflection, and metareflections, and constitutes a temporary autonomization of the given level from the others. That this separation is not full or permanent can be demonstrated by phenomena of "phonemic symbolism" and the physiognomic nature of words in general (Werner and Kaplan, 1984).

LINEARITY OF SIGNS AND MULTIPLICITY OF MEANINGS
The linear character of the signifier allows for linear discernible associative chains to emerge in the course of speaking. These associative chains can proceed in different directions (see Figure 6.4)

In Figure 6.4, the notion of *quadruplex* can lead the constructing mind along two lines of associative chains (*quadru-pes; quadr-ifrons; quadra-ginta;* or: *simplex; triplex; centuplex,* etc.). This syntagmatic organization (at the level of *langue,* where it is passively encoded in memory, yet in multiple chains) provides the constraints for the generation of speech (*parole*). The word summons (in a nonconscious way) ideas that lead to one or another stream of thought. Thus (see Figure 6.4.B), the word *enseignement* (teaching) can evoke numerous directions of associations from the pool of *langue,* each of which would carry the line of discourse in a different direction (e.g., teach—*enseigner;* apprenticeship—*apprentissage;* armament—*armement;* see Engler, 1968, p. 289).

Linearity of signs allows for a multilinearity in the process of constructing a context. Each sign can have a set of multiple trajectories for its interpretation. Each of those trajectories may be triggered by specific assumptions about the given speech situation, that the speaker takes in a here-and-now situation. The relation of the speaker with his (or her) im-

A. The example of QUADRUPLEX (p. 178)

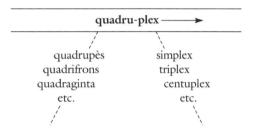

B. The example of ENSEIGNEMENT (p. 175)

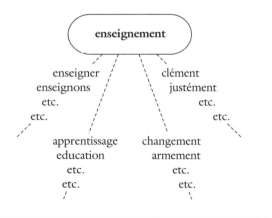

Figure 6.4. Bifurcation of associative chains, possibly proceeding from a word (Saussure, 1916/1949).

mediately and subjectively interpreted context creates the choice moments between alternative trajectories of sign uses, which are possible because of the linearity of the sign. Yet the decision to proceed along one or another interpretational trajectory depends upon a decision at the meta-level (relative to the choice of these trajectories) and is itself based on a symbolically oriented view of the person. This realm of multiple interpretations of the world, by the use of the same sign, guarantees the process of disequilibration within the intersubjectivity of interlocutors, which can lead to construction of higher levels of semiosis.

Semiological Constraining by the Person

Saussure's efforts to make sense of sign construction in *parole,* guided by *langue,* allow us to look at how personality regulates itself in specific speaking situations. Thus, an active speaker—in a condition of relative uncertainty of *langue-parole* relations (such as depicted in Figure 6.3)— may guide him- or herself to utilize one (rather than another) associative chain that can follow from a specific word. The person constructs elaborations of the sign and its associative neighbors in the process of speaking. These constructed elaborations may either open a new way of thinking about what the person is currently trying to speak or close some other ways of thinking. Examples of the constraining of ways of thinking by use of meanings were given in chapters 2 and 4. Saussure's terminology—extended to viewing the *langue-parole* relation and the linearity and arbitrariness of signs—allows for an analysis of personality development in the act of speaking.

Karl Bühler's Sematology

Karl Bühler (1879–1963) can be seen as one of the thinkers in psychology whose work was of profound programmatic value for other disciplines— linguistics and philosophy of language in his case (Eschbach, 1987; Wetterstein, 1988). As is usual in such cases, the contributions of productive thinkers are carried on by a small group of persons, while the social processes operating upon the main streams of the discipline leave the ideas involved for the historians—to be classified into convenient categories and often forgotten through that classification process. The fact that Bühler's intellectual input was of great relevance for some later famous philosophers (Karl Popper), or that he can be considered the originator of "speech act" theory (Searle, 1969, 1989) may at times be mentioned, but the historical continuity of his contributions is often forgotten.

Bühler's intellectual life course (described in detail in Lebzeltern, 1969) was interrupted by the course of European social history (see Eschbach, 1990, pp. 120–121). Bühler had a deep interest in overcoming psychology's narrow focus on either mental phenomena or behavior. His contribution was such which nowadays we are apt to label "interdisciplinary" and hail their ideological value. The domain of language and speech was considered the crucial organizer of human higher psychological functions. Not surprisingly, Bühler's efforts in that direction have been shown to parallel those of Vygotsky (Innis, 1988; Pléh, 1988). The years of production of their major contributions even run in parallel: Bühler's version of the analysis of the crisis in psychology (Bühler, 1926, 1927/1978) took place at exactly the same time as Vygotsky's (see chapter 7 in Van der Veer and Valsiner, 1991). Both published their main collections of ideas on the role of semiotic mediation in the human psyche in the same year—1934 (Bühler, 1934/1965; Vygotsky, 1934). Finally, both failed to surpass their theoretical syntheses of that year—Vygotsky by way of his death, Bühler in connection with his emigration.

Bühler's intellectual heritage brings forth the best traditions from the Würzburg School of thought of Oswald Külpe (Eschbach, 1990; Wetterstein, 1988) and combines these with the intellectual input from the Prague Linguistic Circle of the 1920s, in which Bühler was an active participant (see Bühler, 1931). Last but not least, the intellectual environment of Vienna (including the empirical developmental psychological work by Charlotte Bühler and her coworkers) provided for numerous possibilities to attempt a solution for theoretical problems that had challenged psychology. Furthermore, Edmund Husserl's philosophy has been interpreted as one of the sources for Bühler's thought (Eschbach, 1987; Smith, 1988). Bühler likewise appreciated various aspects of Saussure's thought (available to him in the 1916 *Cours*, as well as through the Prague Circle—Koerner, 1988, pp. 115–136).

The Organon Model

Bühler's organon model is the central concept of all his language philosophy (Bühler, 1934/1965, pp. 24–33; 1990, pp. 34–39; see also Graumann, 1988). It is based on his idea of the three functions that language use accomplishes:

1. Expression—of sender's subjective understanding (*Kundgabe* or *Ausdruck*). The sender constructs the message through expressing oneself; thus the starting point for communication is expression of personal subjectivity, and the result is a constructed message.
2. Appeal—the impact of the message to the receiver (*Auslösung* or *Appell*). For Bühler this label was a nice extension from the American talk of "sex appeal" to that of "speech appeal" (see Bühler, 1932, p. 106). The receiver cannot avoid the message, encoded in signs. It is there to be received—yet by a process that entails active reconstruction.
3. Representation—of the state of affairs of what is being reflected by language (*Darstellung*). The sender refers to some external world, which can also be perceived by the receiver. However, given the nonsameness of these two positions (sender, receiver), the same objective world can never be the same from two different personal standpoints.

These three functions are depicted in Bühler's triangular scheme of the organon model (see Figure 6.5). In Bühler's own words,

> The circle in the middle symbolizes the concrete acoustic phenomenon [*Schallphänomen*]. Three variable factors in it go to give it the rank of a sign in three different manners. The sides of the inscribed triangles symbolize these three factors. In one way the triangle encloses less than the circle (thus illustrating the principle of abstractive relevance [*Prinzip der abstraktiver Relevanz*]). In another way it goes beyond the circle to indicate that what is given to the senses always receives an apperceptive complement [*apperzeptive Ergänzung*]. The parallel lines symbolize the semantic functions of the (complex) language sign. It is a *symbol* by virtue of its coordination to objects and states of affairs, a *symptom* (*Anzeichen, indicium:* index) by virtue of its dependence on the sender, whose inner states it expresses, and a *signal* by virtue of its appeal to the hearer, whose inner or outer behaviour it directs as do other communicative signs [*Verkehrszeichen*]. (Bühler, 1990, pp. 34–35; 1934/1965, p. 28)

It can easily be seen that Bühler transcends both Saussure's and Peirce's kinds of semiotics, by introducing both the abstracting and apperceptive moments into the center of his model. In the tension between the versions of the message—as those are constructed by the sender and the receiver from the standpoint of their ego perspectives—the meanings of the signs can grow in the direction of novel abstractness. In fact, Bühler's figure needs complementation into the third dimension—it is at the intersection of the triangle and circle in Figure 6.5 where new meanings and metameanings are being constructed. The central question of how far (in the third, i.e., vertical, dimension) the sematological process of abstraction and generalization might proceed remains open. Bühler pointed to its relevance and illustrated it by his notions of representational fields (see later discussion and also Figure 2.3), but the full extent of the theory of sematological regulation of human meaning construction under uncertainty of communicative contexts remains to be developed.

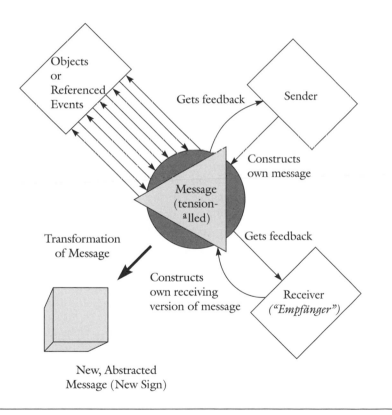

Figure 6.5. Karl Bühler's organon model of communication (from Bühler, 1932, p. 106).

EGO-CENTEREDNESS OF COMMUNICATION   The only anchor point in human communication is the self's perspective, which can never be *exactly* the same as that of another person. Hence the inevitable negotiation of intersubjectivity (as covered in chapter 2) and the potential for construction of abstract signs. Furthermore, the speaker can constantly modulate the boundaries of inclusion/exclusion of specific meaning fields. Even as the inevitable anchor point of reference is the center of the ego (see also William Stern's emphasis on personal center in chapter 5). It can be mediated by signs to include domains extended far beyond that center. Thus, even as a speaker's only vantage point while speaking is "I," he or she can revert to the use of "we." The extensions (and constructions) of the field indicated by such modulation can be observed in the following example:

> *I* (i.e., the author of this book) claim that *we* (i.e., I as the author, and you as the reader) should look at personality from a sociogenetic perspective, so that *we* (i.e., all psychologists and laypersons who take an interest in this subject) could benefit from this perspective, which could lead *us* (humankind in total) to better understanding of how human psychology works, which in turn is essential for *our* (psychologists') professional standing in society, and *our* (*you* as the reader and *I* as the author) present encounter, which is instigated by *my* way of writing this book.

This example of gradual expansion ("I"→ "we" of different extensions) and constriction (from all humankind to the "I") of the field of meaning of "we" indicates the way in which sematological limits regulate human thought (see also the example given above for Lang's functional circle—the "dirty clothes chest"). The ways in which these limits are regulated are constrained by collective-cultural rules. For instance, psychologists and other scientists avoid using the active voice in some parts of their writing or speaking but not in others (Rodman, 1994).

RELEVANCE AND NATURE OF ABSTRACTION   The problem of abstraction was seen by Bühler to take a key position in his sematology (Bühler, 1990, pp. 52–54). The principle of abstractive relevance *(Prinzip der abstraktiven Relevanz)* was necessary to set up a possible dominance relation in the coordination of different fields. By arbitrary consensus, obvious differences within one sign-field can be purposefully overlooked, under the control of an abstracted aspect. In Bühler's terms, "the perceptible here and now need not enter the semantic function. Rather, it may be only that this or that abstract factor is relevant for its calling to function as a sign" (Bühler, 1990, p. 52). The abstract convention can be set up to overrule the emergence of complex nuances of understanding. It can be posited that the personal understanding and the abstractness of the signs involved in its process are in constant tension, which may lead to novel construction of both abstract meanings (from extension of the previous semantic field of the abstract sign to the invention of a new one) and new personal (intuitive-looking) understandings of subjective overgeneralization. One is reminded of Vygotsky's fundamental problem: how can a writer in a short story create a generalized subjective feeling in the reader by inserting a specific sentence in a specific context? (see Van der Veer and Valsiner, 1991, chapter 2).

Construction of abstract concepts is not well represented in Bühler's scheme—it would require a move into the third dimension (above the page) at the intersection of the triangle and the circle. The sign is constantly under tension of the discrepancies of expression and interpretation, which of course are guided by social constraints upon the communicative process (e.g., the assumption of intersubjectivity). Language as structured instrument sets further constraints upon the process of communication. Nevertheless, Bühler successfully avoided the trap of assuming a unidirectional determinist stance, as he stated that "we claim only that the receiver's own constructive thought *cannot be eliminated* and that it is *innocuous* within wide limits, indeed that it is highly *conducive* to most goals of language" (Bühler, 1934/1965, p. 172; also in Bühler, 1990, p. 195). The constructionist focus on the actions of the person in speech contexts complements that of general social guidance. The person transcends the immediate suggestions by the appealing sign through constructing one's understanding that transcends the here-and-now nature of the concrete speech act.

Bühler's organon-model can be viewed as an example of co-constructionist thinking that emphasized varied fields (with their specifiable boundaries) that guide all three functions of speech. The field of possible sounds that allows for phonemic patterns or relations has specific limits, within which different languages structure their phonemic structures differently. Given the high variability of possible combinations of speech-sign elements—phonemes—the semantic relevance can further constrain the speech forms (Bühler, 1931). On the side of the speaker, the spheres of meaning carried by a specific range of linguistic structures are based on the experiencing of (what has seemed to be) successful communication. The remarkable freedom of personal expression via signs is still outwardly constrained by preexisting sentence structures with "empty lots" *(Leerstellen)* for expansion (Innis, 1988, p. 82). Physiological factors play their constraining role in determining the range of possible sound forms upon which meaningful communication in all its richness can be built. Distinguishing his approach from other versions of semiotics, Bühler introduced the term *sematology* (1990, p. 42) to refer to the meanings of signs emerging from the coordination of relations between different representational fields.

Bühler's Hierarchy of Three Fields *(Darstellungfeld)*

Bühler could not accept the usual linguistic talk about "arbitrary encoding" of the language signs in relation to their referents (Bühler, 1990, p. 210). This should not be surprising, given his interest in the pragmatics of the communicative process, where signs are instruments in the texture of accomplishing some objects, rather than entities in themselves. Thus all signs must be "fieldable" *(feldfähig*—Bühler, 1934/1965, p. 187) in order to be usable in the given field. Surely there are limits to such "fieldability"—for instance, musical note symbols are not "fieldable" upon a geographical map (and, conversely, geographical symbols are not "fieldable" upon music paper). Formal logical symbols are "fieldable" only within the narrowly defined field of the logician, and their function for the purposes of logic is exactly in such narrow evocation of the field.

Bühler (1928) separated three levels of representational fields *(Darstellungsfeld)* for speech signs. These three fields can be seen as mutually interdependent, in the sense of phenomena that are "fielded" within one setting up constraints for the other fields.

The *primary* representational field is the field—or the place—that the speech sign "brings with itself," so to say, when it is actualized. The sign—given its form—evokes a particular field of relations within which its meaningfulness can be further constructed by the interpreter. Bühler's example is that of a geographical map—a reference to some city or route evokes (as its necessary context) the whole reference system of the map (with all its representational parts). Any answer to a specific geographical question can be given only within this reference system. Likewise, speech signs evoke a rich conglomerate of experiences.

The *secondary* representational field entails the field of personal memories and productive fantasies that the speech act evokes in the co-constructive hearer. This representational field frees the construction of the hearer's understanding from the immediate here and now, and leads to the development of the internalized control functions of the speech signs in the personal world of the hearer. This focus brings in Bühler's emphasis on the role of history (Bühler, 1990, pp. 65–66). The person brings one's past experiences to the personal senses that are fielded within the secondary field.

Finally, the *tertiary* representational field entails the syntactic schemata that are evoked by a specific speech act. The speaker is intentional and encodes a particular message within a field of goal-oriented possible meanings.

Bühler's three fields can be illustrated by the stock example of speech act theory—the utterance "Can you pass me the salt." Obviously, in its context of the tertiary field, that utterance is a goal-directed request and, if treated like that, leads to the utterer's receiving of the desired object from the other person. However, if we consider the same utterance fielded within the secondary field, we may observe rather anxious reactions from the other person (e.g., "Why are you always exploiting me!?"—as the request is fielded within some personal life history episode of the past, interpreted in terms of "exploitation"). Furthermore, if fielded within the primary field, the response (without action) could be "yes, I can" (the receiver interprets the utterance as if it was a question about his or her abilities). If the request is interpreted simultaneously within the framework of the three hierarchical fields, it depends which version of "fielding" becomes dominant in this interpretation.

Extension of Bühler's Hierarchy of Fields

Undoubtedly Bühler's system of fields for signs constitutes a concise starting point for our contemporary concerns with "context." In fact, the different fields that provide a reference frame for the sign constitute their contexts. The interdependence of the three fields can be conceptualized in terms of mutual constraining (see chapter 2 and Figure 2.3). Each higher field in the hierarchy creates the set of constraints for its lower counterparts. Furthermore, in some situations, some fields are assumed (rightly or wrongly) not to be present, or there may be efforts to neutralize their role.

Psychology's methodological quests provide ample evidence for how efforts are made to regulate the relations between the three fields (as elaborated in chapter 7). As an example let us consider an Ebbinghaus-type memory experiment, which makes use of nonsense syllables. In such an experiment, efforts are made to neutralize the possible role of the secondary field of the subject (i.e., the rationale for the use of nonsense materials is exactly to eliminate the linkage with past experiences, which may "bias" the results) and to assume a fixed representation of the experimental task of remembering at the tertiary field level (i.e., assuming that the subject is, and continues to be through the experiment, oriented toward the goal of trying to learn and later recall the given materials). In other words, the experimenter needs to assume a certain structure of the relations of the three fields, in order for the experiment to make sense. The failure to succeed in superimposing the experimenter's representation upon the subject's would render the whole memory experiment useless.

However, what follows from Bühler's organon-model is that the communicator (in this case the experimenter) cannot, in principle, succeed. The recipient (subject) necessarily "fields" the given experience in one's own hierarchy of fields. Thus, the use of nonsense materials in psychological experiments only reduces (or masks) the subject's linking of the materials with past experiences (i.e., the secondary field cannot be eliminated). Furthermore, at any moment the subject can change the conditions of the tertiary field and turn from a cooperating to a noncooperating subject.

In general, we can look at the hierarchy of fields in terms of mutual constraining of the ZFM/ZPA structures within each field. A specific meaning at the primary field level (e.g., a word "water" may evoke the reference system of chemical formulae of the substance, bounded from other substances) may simultaneously become fielded at the secondary level (and, for instance, bring back a specific memory of happy play in the water, on a seaside in a past summer), which in its turn constrains the fielding at the tertiary level (e.g., making plans for a vacation trip). In the reverse sequence, the newly emerged plans for the vacation may now become fieldable in terms of "what if I went to the Alps now, in the wintertime" (primary field), with a further evocation of personal life experiences in feeling cold in the snow (secondary fielding). The ZFM/ZPA system can be evoked in parallel at adjacent fields, and the constraining process may move between the fields, resulting in novel and (seemingly) surprising outcomes (e.g., in our example, from water to winter holiday in mountains).

Furthermore, the *flexibility* of moving the self-constraining system between the hierarchically organized fields is the main mechanism for human psychological functioning. Psychologists usually "field" that for them-selves as if it is "inconsistency"—which indeed is a major phenomenon with which psychologists feel helpless to deal. However, the world of human psychological functions has not emerged in order to simplify the tasks of the scientists who study it. It is exactly that flexibility—expressed in the evasiveness of any research procedure—that needs to be conceptual-ized.

In his pragmatic scheme, Bühler dealt with both action- and sign-fields. While ontogenetically these fields at first could be viewed as overlapping, human semiotic functioning gradually moves out of the obligatory control by the action-fields and continues in the ideational sphere of sign-fields. This process entails a focus on abstraction.

SEMATOLOGICAL GUIDANCE OF THINKING AND ITS DE-VELOPMENT: THE CASE OF FAIRY TALES   Bühler's explanation of the ways in which fairy tales guide human development is a good description of how the communication process works in forms that en-tail fantasy, exaggeration, and disconnected lines of reasoning—all charac-teristics of fairy tales. Bühler's analysis of the social guidance function of fairy tales derives from the analysis of fairy tales by Charlotte Bühler (1918) and leads to a "theorem" that is quite close to the co-constructionist ideas expressed in this book: "Certain achievements of the imagination are definitely encouraged by the fairy tale, which is adapted to them as to no other type of literature; others are called into play by it only very slightly; a third group is almost completely ignored" (Bühler, 1930, p. 101).

Thus, fairy tales create some domains of actively promoted imagination while bypassing other possible domains of thought. Thus, the *rapid and varied changes in the image content* are highly exaggerated in fairy tales, whereas *simultaneous combination* of ideas belongs to the domain of ig-nored possibilities. The fairy tale avoids all thinking that is in any way complicated, and it replaces complications by exaggerations of temporal transformations of unexplained nature.

The Functioning of Language

The three somewhat different versions of sign-centered views on psycho-logical processes—Saussure's semiology, Bühler's sematology, and Peirce's semiotics—lead to a number of productive means of constructive depiction of how semiotic processes operate at both personal and interpersonal levels. Each of the three perspectives chose their specific focus of interest, yet they all shared the belief that adequate explanation of human psychological processes requires a central focus on language and other semiotic processes. Since language is the main source of semiotic constraints upon the self, its role as such has been examined in linguistics and psychology over centuries.

Nature of Language Constraints

The branches of semiotics outlined earlier were all situated in the context of cultural history, within which interest in the role of language was present long before the explicit emergence of the different semiotic orientations. The role of language in the organization of human thought occupied the forefather of modern linguistics, Wilhelm von Humboldt (1767–1835), all through his multifaceted intellectual career. Largely in conjunction with Humboldt's intellectual heritage, issues of language continued to be of interest to German *Völkerpsychologie* (Heyman Steinthal and Moritz Lazarus—see Jahoda, 1993, chapter 9) and other European (e.g., Aleksandr Potebnya in Russia—Potebnya, 1989) language philosophers of the nineteenth century.

Wilhelm von Humboldt's Legacy

Humboldt's efforts to understand the relationships between persons (their "spirit," or *Geist*) and society, mediated through languages, ranged from 1790s to the publication—a year after his death—of his *Diversity of Human Language-Structure and Its Influence on the Mental Development of Mankind* (Humboldt, 1836). Humboldt's philosophical efforts have been claimed to take a direction (with an emphasis on *Bildung*) parallel to (and surpassing) that of his contemporary post-Kantian dialectician Georg G. W. Hegel (see Ramishvili, 1985). Humboldt's relevance for a number of philosophers of the twentieth century is profound—the language philosophies of Georgii Shpet, Hans-Georg Gadamer, Ernst Cassirer, and Karl Bühler have been his intellectual beneficiaries.

In his *Plan for a Comparative Anthropology* (dated to 1795), Humboldt addressed the question of formation of human character within its surroundings. The constant capacity for thinking and experiencing (*Thätigkeit der Gedanken und Empfindungen*—Humboldt, 1903, p. 386) creates the building of the specific features of the character and leads (via nonuse) to the disappearance of others. Humboldt pointed to the fact that a person cannot understand the world outside of his or her own perceptual experiences. In a similar vein, the person cannot be in any form for which there is no concept ("aber man kann auch nichts seyn, wovon man gar keinen Begriff hat, wozu die Form fehlt"—Humboldt, 1903, p. 386). The language set us specific limits upon the possible ordering of the subjective experiences of the *Geist*.

The role of language is to guide the process of experiencing in two forms—that of heightening the capacity for language *("erhöhete Sprach-fähigkeit")* and formation of a special worldview (*"eigenthümliche Weltan-sicht"*—see Humboldt, 1905a, p. 428). The capacity for language use develops in practice. In the process of speaking, the person becomes capable of expressing thoughts better and more reliably, making the origins of the thoughts unavailable by retaining only their final verbal expression. Speech becomes quick in coordinating the language constraints and the process of thought. The construction of a new worldview takes place at the same time. While the mastery of language use is obtained, simultaneously we can see the constructive role of language. It acts as the creator and organizer that gives form to unclear thoughts and brings the thinking processes of the person to novel ways of understanding (Humboldt, 1905a, p. 428).

In Humboldt's ideas we can see the origins of Bühler's three-part organon model. Like Bühler over a century later, Humboldt emphasized the relevance of three functions of language. First, it mediates the process of understanding, as it triggers the demands of expressional clarity *(Klarheit)* and resoluteness *(Bestimmtheit)*. Second, it gives feeling to expression *(Ausdruck)*. Third, it gives the basis for new thoughts on the basis of the already communicated ones and demands further actions from the soul *(Geist)* (Humboldt, 1905a, p. 431). These three functions could be viewed as parallels to Bühler's representation, expression, and appeal functions (see earlier text).

In sum, Humboldt set the stage for consideration of the mutuality of the person and language in the process of speaking and thinking. With his emphasis on development (in his version of *Bildung*), he treated language as a vehicle that assists in the process of human improvement. His view was not that of one-sided linguistic determinism upon thought but rather a two-sided organic process where language use leads the construction of thought and its expression, and thus participates in persons' construction of their worldviews. The migration of Humboldt's ideas to North America has fostered a growing view that resembles Continental treatments of language-person relations.

The "Sapir-Whorf Hypothesis"

Humboldt's ideas on the role of language in guiding human psychological functioning have proceeded in different directions in Europe and North America. In the former, these ideas have led to a wealth of philosophical elaborations around issues of speech, many of which constituted part of the intellectual environment of the early sociogenetic theorists (see chapter 4). In North America, notions of linguistic relativity were evident in the work of anthropological linguist Edward Sapir (1884–1939) and that of Benjamin Lee Whorf (1897–1941).

The roots of the North American version of the linguistic relativity hypothesis can be found in German thought of the nineteenth century. Thus, Sapir's master's thesis (on Herder's *Roots of Language*—Sapir, 1907), as well as the influence of Franz Boas in North America, led Sapir to develop a person-centered view on the functioning of language in thought (Sapir, 1921, 1924). Having performed a number of classic studies on American Indian languages, and inspired a cohort of graduate students at the University of Chicago and Yale, Sapir's own direct contributions to the (later) canonized version of the "Sapir-Whorf hypothesis" may be doubted (e.g., Kroeber, 1984, p. 136). It was primarily the work of Whorf, which became more widely known only after 1956, that led to the discourse about linguistic relativity in North American psychology and anthropology. Whorf's direct scientific relation with Sapir dates to years after 1928 (and especially after 1931). Aside from highly specialized studies of American Indian languages (Hopi, in particular), Whorf prepared a number of popular articles, including "Language, Mind, and Reality" (Whorf, 1942/1956, pp. 246–270; originally published in *Theosophist* in Madras in 1942).

In its popularized form, the "Sapir-Whorf hypothesis" is shown as starting from a unidirectional culture transmission model. It has been taken to imply that human understanding of the environment and thinking are *determined* by language. The originators of the hypothesis might not agree with this unidirectional translation of the psychological dependence upon language into a deterministic account. The dominance of language over mental processes constitutes a linguistic constraint system:

The forms of a person's thoughts are controlled by inexorable laws of pattern of which he is unconscious. These patterns are the unperceived intricate systematizations of his own language—shown readily enough by a candid comparison and contrast with other languages, especially those of a different linguistic family. His thinking itself is in a language . . . And every language is a vast pattern-system, different from others, in which are culturally ordained the forms and categories by which the personality not only communicates, but also analyzes nature, notices or neglects types of relationship and phenomena, channels his reasoning, and builds the house of his consciousness. (Whorf, 1942/1956, p. 252)

Of course, Whorf's between-languages comparisons reveal basic differences in which any particular language structure *canalizes individual users toward differentiation of some aspects of the world and ignorance about others.* The issue of thinking of persons is a question of a three-part sequence of guidance. First, the language guides the generation of speech of its users in specific situations. Second, the speaking process itself is interlinked with reasoning. In this sequence the dependence upon language in concrete situations is far from overly dominating the process of thinking. Instead, the thinking process may interact with the speaking decisions, leading to the creation of novelty in the given speech context (Maturana, 1978).

Furthermore, aside from language per se, the person's general world orientation sets up constraints upon the canalization of reasoning by the structure of language concepts and norms (von Bertalanffy, 1955). The language user is constantly being constrained by the rules of the language—yet that constraining makes it possible to express some of the complex sentiments in communicable form (Bloom, 1981; Lardiere, 1992; Lee, 1976).

Transcending Linguistic Relativity

Deterministic interpretations of the "Sapir-Whorf hypothesis" have not prevailed in interpretations of language uses, even if episodically such a focus may be assumed. It is not difficult to see how speaking and acting by a person can lead to innovation in language, beginning from its sociolinguistic and semantic domains. The process of language use is *open-ended and constructive*—human beings speak while acting in specific culturally organized settings, and through that work on reconstructing language. In other terms:

> Languages do bring with them world-views, categories of thought, grammatical structures which exhibit certain embedded ontologies. But they do not imprison us. They do not imprison because they come not with one world-view but with several, which compete, and also with problems of each world-view. When solved these problems might yield not only a modified world-view but novel concepts, and even, sometimes, new categories of thought. The need to improve our understanding of the world is a continual one . . . Language, moved by this force, is constantly changing its concepts and its categories, even if we ignore the influence of contact with new people. (Hattiangadi, 1987, p. 172)

Our language use is an open-ended generative enterprise where we introduce subtle novelty into the very instrument that we use in that process. Language use in everyday contexts is constantly oriented toward going beyond its own confines, constituting a case of boundary renegotiation at the level of personal cultures.

Language performs a dual function. On the one hand, it generates self-reflexive stability by eliminating the real "flow" of irreversible personal experience through translating it into symbols reflecting stability. On the other hand and exactly because of its stability-constructing role—it makes it possible for human consciousness to transcend the present here-and-now context, and reconstruct memories of the past (as well as transfer reflections of the present to a new context). Language liberates the person from the confines of lived-through experiences of here and now:

> Without language, intelligence would probably have remained riveted to the material objects which it was interesting in considering. It would have lived in a state of somnambulism, outside itself, hypnotized on its own work. Language has greatly contributed to its liberation. The word, made to pass from one thing to another, is, in fact, by nature transferable and free. It can therefore be extended, not only from one perceived thing to a recollection of that thing, from the precise recollection to a more fleeting image, and finally from an image fleeting, though still pictured, to the picturing of the act by

which the image is pictured, that is to say, to the idea. (Bergson, 1911a, p. 175)

Language is thus a tool that is used to act upon the immediate dynamic experiences and transform those in the process of experiencing—or enduring, to use Bergson's terminology. Specific generalizations that emerge from language use perform further canalizing functions in regulating both subjective and intersubjective realms of activity.

Lev Vygotsky on the Unity of Thinking and Speech

Human beings are involved in constant construction and reconstruction of collective-cultural meanings and personal-cultural senses of the experienced world. This process constitutes the universal psychological basis for all cultural phenomena in society and personality. The present emphasis on semiotic constructivity as the universal of human psychological functioning follows the lead of Lev Vygotsky's ideas. In his emphasis on the dynamic interplay of cultural meanings and personal senses, Vygotsky's distinction of meaning *("znachenie")* and sense *("smysl")* was expressed with an emphasis on the dynamic nature of psychological processes:

A word's sense is the aggregate of all the psychological facts that arise in our consciousness as a result of the word. Sense is a dynamic, fluid, and complex formation which has several zones that vary in their stability. Meaning is only one of these zones of the sense that the word acquires in the context of speech. It is *the most* stable, unified, and precise of these zones. In different contexts, a word's sense changes. In contrast, meaning is a *comparatively* fixed and stable point, one that remains constant with all the changes of the word's sense that are associated with its use in various contexts. Change in the word's sense is a basic factor in the semantic analysis of speech. The *actual meaning of the word is inconstant.* In one operation, the word emerges with one meaning; in another, another is acquired . . . Isolated in the lexicon, the word has only one meaning. However, *this meaning is nothing more than a potential that can only be realized in living speech, and in living speech meaning is only a cornerstone in the edifice of sense.* (Vygotsky, 1934, p. 305; also in Vygotsky, 1987, pp. 275–276; emphasis added).

Vygotsky viewed the relationship between meaning and sense in dynamic terms—both are changing entities, but their change is different in the time frame. The relatively slower rate of changing the meaning is obtained by inserting the previous meaning into a novel speech context (realizing the *potential* of the meaning by turning it into the "actual meaning"—the unity of sense and meaning in the given context). The dynamic, fluid personal sense makes use of potential meanings encoded in language and constructs ever-imprecise semiotic devices (actual meanings), which nevertheless fit the task of reduction of experiential uncertainty the person faces in the given situation. It can be said that the great power of human language in guiding human meaning-making is in the vagueness of the actual meanings that are constructed by persons in uncertain situations. One can detect Saussure-like parallels of *langue-parole* in Vygotsky's *znachenie-smysl* pair.

COMPLEXES, CONCEPTS, AND PSEUDOCONCEPTS   The contrast between "thinking in complexes," "thinking with concepts," and their intermediate forms was emphasized by Lev Vygotsky. Development of reasoning is characterized by the unification and abstracting generalization of the multiplicity of relations, arriving at a general abstract feature that unites the objects in the given set. The difference between "complex" and "concept" was seen by Vygotsky to be in the principles of organization:

> The complex, like the concept, is a generalization and unifier of concrete varied objects. However, the tie with which this generalization is built, can be of most different type. *Any* kind of link can lead to the inclusion of a given object in a complex, if it only practically exists— and the characteristic feature of the complex is exactly that. When linkages of unified type—logically equivalent to one another—are at the foundation of the concept, very varied factual linkages that often have nothing in common with one another, are the bases of a complex. In the concept, objects are generalized by one characteristic, in a complex—by most varied practical bases. That is why in the concept the relevant, unifying link and relationship between objects finds its reflection, while in a complex—practical, occasional, concrete [relations are reflected]. (Vygotsky, 1931, p. 250)

The process of differentiation and hierarchical integration in the movement from complexes to concepts was viewed by Vygotsky as entailing an important transitional form—that of *pseudo-concept*. This is a form of reasoning that at the outside looks like concept (i.e., seems organized by an abstract, unitary relation between objects) but in reality remains a complex (i.e., entails a multitude of relations between objects—Vygotsky, 1931, p. 256). For example, in an experimental setting a person selects from all available materials all triangles. This operation could be accomplished on different bases—on that of a generalized "idea of triangle" (concept) or on the basis of a myriad of associative ties between the similar-looking objects of triangular shape, without any use of generalization (i.e., reasoning on the basis of a complex). In the case of concept use, the deductive process is applied; in the case of a complex, the inductive generalization.

Vygotsky and his colleagues (Luria would be the closest example) attributed an overly idealized role to the role of concepts in human reasoning. This role fitted with his emphasis on the hierarchy of mental functions (i.e., higher mental functions regulating lower ones), yet by this exaggerated emphasis the focus on the process of semiogenesis is actually diminished. In contrast, it could be claimed that pseudo-concepts (i.e., specific unified conglomerates of concept and complex qualities) are the core (and highest form) of human psychological functioning. This claim would fit with the unity of representational fields (of Karl Bühler, described and extended earlier) and with the central focus of abduction (rather than induction or deduction) in the process of making sense (along the lines of Peirce).

Mikhail Bakhtin and the Multivoicedness of Discourse

The importation of the literary scholarship of Mikhail Bakhtin to sociogenetic psychology and social sciences at large has already been described in specific areas (see the question of appropriation in chapter 3). In a certain sense, the notion of appropriation (for which Bakhtin gets credit) is applicable to the takeover of Bakhtin's own work in psychology. Bakhtin's ideas are half foreign to psychology, and, once they are taken over, need to be inhabited by the intentionality of the appropriators.

Bakhtin's intellectual heritage can be located in continental European thought of the beginning of the twentieth century. His "dialogue of cultures" notion was borrowed from the philosophy of Oswald Spengler, Theodor Lipps, Wilhelm Wundt, Hermann Cohen, and Nikolai Lossky (Babich, 1994; Bonetskaia, 1994; Kalganov, 1994). From the 1940s until his death, Bakhtin's ideas were moving in lines parallel to the development of the German hermeneutics of Hans-Georg Gadamer.

Bakhtin carried over to the notion of culture the systemic, holistic focus that has characterized German philosophical views on personality. Thus, culture became a living organism, heterogeneous and contradictory within itself, and coordinating itself in goal-oriented ways. It could be said that his object of investigation—the novel (rather than the functioning person)—allowed him to treat the multivoicedness of discourse. In the novel, the reader can have access to all of the depicted story in the course of reading, discovering ever-new nuances of the text. In contrast, the immediate interaction of human beings would not easily allow for such backward referencing.

Speaking of the novel, Bakhtin explicated the multivoicedness due to different social languages as woven into the text by the author. Thus,

> The internal multi-layeredness of the unified national language into social dialects, group styles, professional jargons, languages of genre, languages of generations and age cohorts, languages of [ideological] directions, languages of experts, languages of groups of people and passing fashions, languages of social-political days and even hours (every day has its own slogan, its own lexicon, and accents)—this internal multi-layeredness of each language at each moment of its historical existence—is the necessary assumption of the genre of the novel. (Bakhtin, 1934/1975, p. 76)

What characterizes novels may also fit society at large. The heterogeneity of the collective culture can be viewed as a dynamic hierarchy of social languages. Within this heterogeneous whole, opposite forces—toward unification of the whole and toward its fragmentation—are assumed to be operating. Such centripetal and centrifugal tendencies (see Bakhtin, 1934/1975, p. 85) lead to individualized heteroglossic speech. Hence in speech we have "internal dialogicity"—different "voices" of different languages of the whole are in dialogue with one another. Furthermore, this dialogicality entails movement toward the future in irreversible time. In each dialogue, "While fitting in the atmosphere of what is already said, the word at the same time is defined by what is not yet said, but what is already implied and already expected by the word of response" (Bakhtin, 1934/1975, p. 93).

By focusing on what might be about to be said, Bakhtin makes his view of dialogue open for further developments. The actual meaning of an utterance is generated on the background of language, through the encounter of the myriad experiences of the person. The person actively encounters the word of the others, and creates his or her own personal understandings. Understanding is created in the process of responding in a dialogue.

General Conclusion: Semiotic Mediation and Sociogenetic Personology

Semiotic mediation is a subjective preadaptation for encountering always indeterminate futures, which is made necessary by the irreversibility of time. Semiosis is a process of construction and use of signs of different kinds—unified into complexes (and pseudoconcepts)—that guides the person's development. The process of semiotic self-constraining is constant and unending. The person is in parallel involved in *both* external and internal dialogues, which feed into each other to allow for the making of personal sense through semiotic mediation.

By pointing to the semiotic regulation of the self it is possible to arrive at a synthesis of sociogenetic and personological perspectives (reviewed in chapters 4 and 5, respectively). For three central figures of semiotics— Peirce, Saussure, and Bühler—the role of the sign-constructing active person was present. All semiotic phenomena are possible due to the subjective constructivity of persons, extended to the realm of signs. Yet such subjective construction is part and parcel of the constant circular process that unites human beings with their environments (Lang's semiotic *functional circle*). Such unity constantly produces diversity—first of all, at the level of action (as human beings reorganize their environments), but simultaneously and interconnectedly in the signs that are constructed.

In the context of the present book, such extensions are presented in terms of canalization. A particular sign sets up some bounded field of meanings (at different levels of the hierarchy of fields—primary, secondary, and tertiary, in Bühler's terms). The limits upon that field (ZFM), as well as subareas of the field chosen for special suggestions (ZPA) guide the person's making of the personal-cultural reflection upon the world. Semiotic mediation is a way to subjectively transcend the experience within the present context. Semiotic constructivity is thus viewed as future-oriented construction of subjectively meaningful possibilities (which may, but need not, become actualized). On the basis of collective-cultural canalization by language and social practices—which take place in one or another social encounter of the person with the culturally organized world—the personal experiences become the site for constant construction of personal culture.

This constant construction of personal novelty sets up rather intricate constraints upon psychology's methodological activities. It is quite clear that most of the conventional rules of empirical research in psychology need a major overhaul. Claims about the meaningful and sign-constructive nature of human beings—at a theoretical level—cannot be coordinated by empirical research rules and practices that eliminate the meanings from the phenomena under study. Psychology cannot already be "the study of behavior" because the notion of "behavior" entails a whole hierarchy of semiotic constructions that need clarification as to how these function in the personal cultural systems of the investigators—in addition to their functioning in the conduct of research participants. Part III of the present book provides a forceful excursion into issues of methodology and empirical practices of possible sociocultural study of personality.

III

FROM THEORY TO INTERPRETATIONS OF PERSONAL WORLDS

7

Semiosis and Methodology: Implications for Psychological Research Practices

> Science always has a world of reality by which to test its hypotheses,
> but this world is not a world independent of scientific experience,
> but the immediate world surrounding us within which we must act.
> Our next action may find these conditions seriously changed, and
> then sciences will formulate this world so that in view of this
> problem we may logically construct our next plan of action.
>
> (MEAD, 1917B, P. 226)

Mead's methodological credo as expressed here obviously follows from his general epistemological perspective (see chapter 4). It leads to the inevitable recognition that any research procedure is *itself part of the context for the phenomena* that are being studied. Since these phenomena are context-interdependent (as any open system would be), research procedures inevitably trigger change in the phenomena. This is our main general problem of methodology, viewed as a generic cycle of knowledge-constructive relationships between basic assumptions, theory, methods, phenomena, and, finally the data (Branco and Valsiner, 1997; Kindermann and Valsiner, 1989; Winegar and Valsiner, 1992). The crucial feature of this methodology circle is the interdependence of the data derivation (or construction) tactics with the theoretical and phenomenological sides of the research process.

Within prevailing empirical research practices, the data have often become glorified in their decontextualized form, as if they stand alone as givens. It is the relevant counterposition to that practice, exposed here, that the data are crucial within the methodology circle of a particular research project and are not simply exchangeable across projects (Valsiner, 1997b, chapter 3). Given this context specificity, aggregation of data across different research contexts into meta-analytic summaries is an intellectual impasse that cannot cure psychology's disease of inconclusiveness of most of the empirical evidence (Valsiner, 1995b). Instead, a solution to

285

the problem is suggested via explicit coordination of all parts of the methodology circle (see Figure 7.1).

The basic assumptions accepted by an investigator set up constraints
upon how he or she views the realm of phenomena, as well as the intellectual direction in which theory building might proceed. Surely the relationship of the assumptions and theory and data is two-sided: the constraining
by a set of assumptions can be modified from the side of experiencing of
the phenomena or from some construction decision about the theory.
However, as is presented in Figure 7.1, the form of the methodology circle
accepted here involves an asymmetrical dominance relationship between
the parts: ASSUMPTIONS dominate over THEORY, and PHENOM-

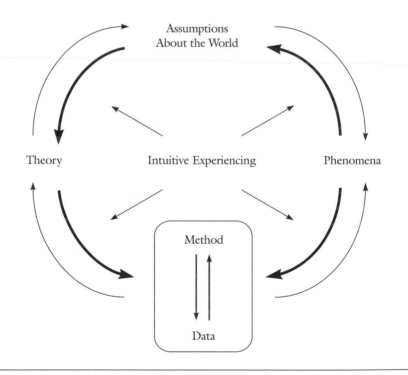

Figure 7.1. The methodology circle that unites empirical and nonempirical sides
of the research process (from Branco and Valsiner, 1997). Methodology is
depicted as a circle (or cycle) that unites all sides of research, as well as the
subjective world of the researcher (who intuitively experiences all of the sides).
The relative strength of the oppositely directed arrows at each connection
indicates the dominance of the role of one direction of inferential "movement"
over its opposite counterpart.

ENA over ASSUMPTIONS; THEORY dominates over METHOD ↔ DATA relation (with subdominant feedback from the latter to the former), and the same is true for PHENOMENA (dominating over METHOD ↔ DATA relation). The whole circle is functional as a process of research, where generalizing activities (of making theories and adjusting assumptions) are viewed as dominant over the empirical enterprise. Furthermore, the form of the methodology circle accepted here has a clear phenomenological focus.

In the center of the methodology circle is the active and subjective scientist, who—similarly to any artist—feels *into* the phenomena, creates and accepts assumptions, constructs theories, and creates methods for the derivation of the data. This intuitively operating experiencer is a human being first and a scientist second. As a result, the psychological processes involved in scientific knowledge construction are similar to everyday knowledge construction in its main feature—semiotic mediation.

Empirical Research in Psychology As Semiotically Mediated Construction of Meaningful Knowledge

Psychological research as an epistemological activity constitutes a meta-level reflection upon the particular psychological phenomena that are selected by the investigator as objects of attention. The researcher operates simultaneously as a reflective agent upon the psychological phenomenon as a layperson, and as the reflective agent in the role of the "researcher," whose look at the reflective and acting layperson has gone through some process of social-institutional canalization. Thus, an adult researcher looking at "attachment" of a twelve-month-old child is simultaneously feeling into the issue as a person who has constructed some personal-cultural sense complex about "bonding," "attachment," or "human relationships," and at the same time attempting to take the perspective of the accepted view of "attachment theory" and act in accordance with it. The activity of a researcher always entails a dialogue between different levels of semiotic construction.

Levels of Semiotic Mediation in the Process of Psychological Inquiry

The semiotic nature of psychological inquiry exists at three levels. First, at the level of *basic phenomena*—the sign-mediated nature of most human psychological functioning—psychologists cannot but take into account the meaningful and meaning-transforming nature of their object of investigation. Second, at the level of *psychological conceptualizations,* any statement about human psychological functioning is encoded semiotically. Undoubtedly that encoding takes place in numerous ways, yet its sign-mediated nature is a necessary given, rather than an optional decision about language choice. Finally, at the *metapsychological* level, all of the epistemological activities of psychologists who study their objects of investigation (human or animal) are guided by semiotic constructions erected within the social world. At all of these levels, the semiotic processes are dynamic and constructive—use of specific mediating devices can emerge in an instant, and novel forms of mediating devices are constantly being created. The first two of these levels were analyzed in chapter 6.

THE ISSUE OF COORDINATION BETWEEN LEVELS   The different levels can become semiautonomous from one another. Semiotic organization of human conduct constitutes a level of control that is superior to that of immediate actions. It not only entails regulation of these actions but also affords linking of the memory of the experiences of the personal past with personal imagination of possible future experiences (see chapters 2 and 6). The result of such possibility guarantees the *principled uncontrollability*—by the experimenter—of any research settings where human subjects are studied. The subjects can always distance themselves from the given research context, either explicitly (by refusing to enter the role of "subject") or implicitly (through invisible noncooperation by changing one's participation intensity).

The function of sign-based mediation can be seen in going beyond the person's immediate lived-through action contexts. Methodologically, this means that for the investigator's purposes much of the psychological activity under study necessarily remains transcendent to the specific events observed. What is the savior for the subject (i.e., the possibility of "leaving the immediate field" through sign-mediated reflection) is a devilish trick for any researcher, leading one to recognize the limits of direct knowing and (in some cases) to become tormented by the flames of never-ending hermeneutic possibilities for understanding.

Psychologists habitually strive to avoid the use of ordinary language exactly because of its great flexibility and potential richness. They invent novel terminology that may be set up to refer to a restricted range of phenomena and may be considered (by the psychologists themselves) to "explain" the phenomena. Not surprisingly, that habit regularly leads to frustration with the alienation of psychological scientific language from the "real life" (Siegfried, 1994) and to a recognition that the causality-implying theoretical talk of psychology may lead scientists to illusory generalizations. Simultaneously, a psychologist is a constructive language user and the target of such use—nobody who tries to make sense of our language use can do so outside of that language use itself (Smolka, 1994). Semiosis is part and parcel of development: "The semiotic approach is ruled by a sort of *indeterminacy principle:* in so far as signifying and communicating are social functions that determine both social organization and social evolution, to 'speak' about 'speaking,' to signify signification or to communicate about communication cannot but influence the universe of speaking, signifying and communicating" (Eco, 1976, p. 29).

The resistance of psychology to the complexities of semiotic mediation is a good example of the functioning of sign-mediated social guidance of whatever is labeled science by social institutions (and individuals with their personal internalized versions of the value-laden signs). Whole domains of inquiry (e.g., that of intramental psychological phenomenology) have been temporarily rendered inaccessible to psychology by semiotic stigmatization of the available methods (e.g., labeling of introspection as subjective and hence untrustworthy).

Social Context for a Focus on Methods: Instrument Construction As Semiosis

Mead's quote also refers to the macrosocial aspect of social sciences. After a scientist has studied a changing phenomenon in one context (and participated in its change), the findings may lead to some social intervention in the same (but changed) context, or in another context viewed as similar to it. But because the phenomenon has changed, the intervention plan devised on the basis of previous investigation may already be missing the point. This has been a persistent problem in the case of replication of specific studies in the social sciences (see Valsiner, 1994f).

This macrosocial aspect leads to a general rule: any applications of the results of social sciences (even if minimally transformed by the ideology of the applier) are discordant with the phenomena to which they are applied. Each effort to investigate a phenomenon that is previously autonomous from the investigator becomes interdependent with the very act of investigation, as well as with its produced outcomes. The latter—when they enter the collective cultural domain of both the researchers and their research participants—become new meanings that regulate the collective-cultural world of phenomena. This feature of research makes it possible for the researchers to produce knowledge that changes the phenomenon—studying a topic phrased as "a social problem" renders results that intensify the collective-cultural attention to the given issue *as a "problem,"* possibly making it the battlefield of different ideologies that fight one another with a given society.

Piaget's notion of disequilibration can be put to work to explain the mechanism of such applications. A "problem" for empirical investigation may emerge on the basis of theoretical constructions of an investigator (e.g., that of children's mealtime conduct—Valsiner, 1987, 1997b) or from some applied "social expectation." The latter may include studies of "adolescents' aggression" in U.S. schools in the 1990s, or questions of "prevention" of "at-risk" phenomena such as adolescents' childbearing, or infants' cutting the upper teeth before their lower counterparts (see Beidelman, 1963, p. 56). The specific "problems" for which the appropriate experts—diviners, fortune-tellers, or social scientists—are consulted are, of course, phrased in the meaning system of the laypersons of the given society at the given time, and thus vary greatly across societies and over history. Yet the process of semiotic construction of an external specialist's knowledge, the latter's actions upon the phenomena that result in such knowledge, and the reintroduction of the knowledge as semiotic material into the communication system of the society remain the same.

This model of knowledge construction allows for different scenarios for the development of human understanding of phenomena. On the one extreme, it allows for alienation of a particular common-language meaning—valued by its collective-cultural insertions of positive importance—in the process of investigation. The constructed knowledge becomes "fielded" within its own field of meanings and enters into the world of everyday life only in specifically limited ways. In psychology, the uses of the concept of "intelligence" constitute a good example: the term that is used and positively valued in everyday life became a target of investigation, leading to the construction of methods ("intelligence tests"), which led to the creation of a field of meanings of psychologists about the tests and their results. The semiotic constructivity in this field continues as different new "offspring" of "intelligence tests" are constructed and used, and the results of such uses are discussed in specialized psychological literature. The knowledge from that literature enters into ordinary life contexts in conjunction with practical uses of the methods (as persuasive vehicles to legitimize such uses, by reference to symbolic status of "validity," "standardization," and "reliability" of the tests). At times, the semiotic devices from the field of "intelligence testing" meanings domain are brought to public attention in conjunction with other meanings-overdetermined themes (e.g., those of white-black racial differences in U.S. society), leading to the escalation of already existing disputes (and not to constructive solutions of the issues that are unsolved for the notion of "intelligence" itself). The scientific notion of "intelligence" has become stabilized by the constructed method, and the system of meanings within which that method is "fielded": the "intelligence test" is an *indexical* sign (in Peirce's sense) of the nondefinable "property" of "persons' intelligence," and psychologists' term "intelligence" is a *symbol* of the indexical sign. The symbol is stabilized by the index, and stabilizes the index (psychologists' concept of "intelligence" leads to further construction of "intelligence tests," which lead back to further differentiation of the field of the symbol "intelligence"). These two signs are thus related in a symbiotic and mutually beneficial relationship, which is alienated from the issues subsumed under the ordinary-language meanings of "intelligence." As a result, no new knowledge about the latter can emerge from the practices of "intelligence testing"—the latter has lost touch with the phenomena of initial meaning-focus of everyday life. That the scenario of "loss of phenomena" (Cairns, 1986) exists in different areas of psychology is not surprising; the creation of methods outside of the realm of consistency of all of the methodology circle (Branco and Valsiner, 1997) is a historical tendency of recent decades. It applies similarly to the myriad of traditions of empirical "measurement of personality."

This picture is very different from one painted in popularizations of science, in which a clever scientist using the "right methods" always discovers new facts (or at least accumulates reliable ones), which lead to constant improvements in human life. Such nice descriptions of how social sciences are beneficial (and benevolent) may be necessary in societal communication, yet they are far from the collective-cultural construction of the sciences as such. After all, the very existence of science is possible as a result of externalization of meanings by persons who set their goals in the difficult to define areas of human existence of understanding how the world at large is organized. The world of human psychology provides the further difficulty in the form of inevitable relatedness of the personality of the scientist with the science of personality.

Semiotically, then, psychology's overconcern with the construction of methods is an example of sign construction. Methods become indexical signs for something—which is not studied, yet leads to the indexical "marks" that research participants leave on the medium on which the sign construction is prescribed. Whether the methods involve letting subjects leave marks on paper (e.g., on rating scales or response sheets), on audiotape (taped interviews), or in a computer file (in computerized experiments), the traces left by the subjects amount to as limited an index of the whole as a footprint in asphalt is of the person who walked on there when the substance was still hot. Only a limited part of the whole phenomenon becomes represented in such "traces"—which, when labeled "the data," acquire a value of their own (Valsiner, 1995b).

The penetration of semiotic thinking into psychology is both irresistible and resisted—the latter being the tendency of psychology's behavioristic and cognitivistic mainstreams to avoid the perils of interpretative "softness" that any analysis of multimeaningful signs may bring to the discipline. Of course, such resistance itself is semiotic and is based on the guidance of psychology's self-construction by general meanings such as the opposition between "soft" and "hard" sciences (e.g., equating the meaning of quantification with "hard" sciences—Hornstein, 1988; Porter, 1992). In a similar vein, the meaning of "objectivity" has been a major semiotic canalizer of psychologists' thought and action (Valsiner, 1997b, chapter 3). Psychology has been ambivalent toward the centrality of the role of semiotic means in human intrapsychological and extrapsychological existence. This ambivalence exists both at the level of ordinary people's personality organization and at that of psychology's own scientific terminology (Valsiner, 1994g). Psychologists are caught by the richness of the mediating devices that (among other pleasures) make psychology itself possible. On the one hand, the richness of encoding of nuances of phenomena that our ordinary language affords sets up the possibility for a rich and complex description of persons' selves. This possibility is always a temptation that might make the work of psychologists inherently interesting. However, it constitutes a trap because the use of ordinary language for descriptive purposes can easily lead to thinking that this description equals understanding these phenomena. Generalized knowledge does not immediately emerge from such understanding, and the possibility of such generalized knowledge can even be doubted. Yet if a theoretical perspective in a science is aimed at getting at generalized knowledge, the possibility of creating such knowledge needs to be preassumed. The question then becomes in what particular ways can specific evidence from empirical studies reflect the general knowledge, rather than merely be an indexical sign of something that is left by particular research participants.

Social Construction of Objectivity: A Historical Look

That objectivity in psychological research is not guaranteed by the use of "right methods" should be obvious—except, of course, if the meaning of "objectivity" becomes circularly defined as "the use of 'the right' methods." However, the idea (or ideal) of the "objectivity of the data" remains a powerful meaning internalized by psychologists and constraining their construction of the structure of knowledge. The discursive dialogue between "objectivity of the data" and "social construction of psychological knowledge" continues in the 1990s (Gergen, 1994).

DIFFERENT CONSTRUCTED MEANINGS OF "OBJECTIVITY"
The question of objectivity is itself an example of cultural-historical construction. Three kinds of perspectives on what objectivity means might be outlined.

First, there is *personal-perspectival objectivity,* which emphasizes the actively objectivity-constructing nature of specially educated persons, who are well acquainted with the phenomena and therefore can reach an understanding of how these phenomena function. Objectivity is reachable exactly because a person devotes his or her observational and inferential powers toward creating it. Undoubtedly persons of this kind can come up with inadequate conceptualizations, and disputes between scientists are widespread. Yet it is believed that the active person is the locus where new understanding emerges. The person's individual perspective is as important as her view of the phenomena. C. Lloyd Morgan's focus on "two inductions" (see later discussion) provides another description of this kind of objectivity.

The personal-perspectival model of objectivity prevailed in eighteenth- and early nineteenth-century natural sciences (Daston, 1992). In psychology it survived to the end of the last century, especially in the case of introspection experiments, where the authorship for the studies was legitimately attributed to the introspecting subjects (Danziger, 1985).

In contrast, by the second half of the nineteenth century the model of aperspectival objectivity became an accepted social norm in the natural sciences. Instead of communicability between specialists (i.e., disputes between personal perspectives of specialists), the *commonality* of perspectives became emphasized. This model grew from the social processes of accounting for different social phenomena (as well as economic resources) (see Porter, 1992). The specially skilled persons became replaced by a controllable collective of research. It was as if science moved from an artisan's workshop to a factory floor in the manufacture of objectivity:

> Aperspectival objectivity was the ethos of the interchangeable and therefore featureless observer—unmarked by nationality, by sensory dullness or acuity, by training or tradition; by quirky apparatus, by colorful writing style, or by any other idiosyncrasy that might interfere with the communication, comparison and accumulation of results . . . Subjectivity became synonymous with the individual and solitude; objectivity, with the collective and conviviality. (Daston, 1992, p. 609)

The dominance of the aperspectival model of objectivity can be detected in scientists' selectively impersonal writing styles (e.g., Rodman, 1994). Furthermore, the linkage of objectivity with average or prototypical cases within a population stems from this model of objectivity. In psychology, this model is evoked every time researchers carefully train their so-called blind observers to apply their not-so-"blind" categorization systems to complex phenomena, demonstrate some conventionally accepted level of intercoder agreement (e.g., 70 or 80 percent or more), and assume that this exercise of conformity training adds reliability to their substantive claims. Conversely, if the personal-perspectival objectivity model were to be evoked, the researchers would overcome their own blindness (about the "blindness" of trained observers), educate their observers to understand the theoretical perspective from which the object phenomenon is analyzed, and then proceed to look carefully at the instances of interobserver disagreements (i.e., the 20 or 30 percent or fewer of the cases), since a dialogue about disagreements would be heuristically valuable. Instead, conditions of illusionary intersubjectivity (as described in chapter 1) are socially constructed for purposes of communication between researchers (and groups of researchers).

Third, by the end of the twentieth century we can observe the spreading of *corporationistic objectivity* models. These models establish control over the objectivity of scientific production by setting up specific generic "brand names" of quality and operating at the level of comparison of such brand names (e.g., "data from research group X are more adequate than from research group Y"). A version of this kind of objectivity can be seen in presentations of results of research from well-established groups, which may include almost tachistoscopic presentations of data of any form on slides, without any explanation of their meaning. The function of such presentations is the same as of TV commercials, where the value of a "brand name" is propagated in ways that purposefully limit access to the actual data, their methods of construction, and actual explanations, while creating an illusion of public access to the objective data. The data presented by a representative of a research corporation are assumed to be objective because of the "brand name." No critical insider in the corporation is allowed to question the data (and/or their construction methods), and relevant aspects of the data construction processes may even become legally protected against rival groups trying to replicate the studies (e.g., see the rhetoric construction of the "cold fusion" case—Taylor, 1991).

Demonstrating the cultural-historical construction of models of objectivity is merely an effort to demonstrate how the basic evaluative meanings that operate as social canalizers of science are themselves culturally constructed. Actual objectivity of research is always based on some perspective—either implicit or explicit in the philosophical and theoretical systems of the scientists. These perspectives are linked with the wider sociocultural perspectives of the societies these scientists inhabit, yet these contexts do not determine (but merely constrain) the intellectual creativity of the scientists (e.g., on Vygotsky's case, see Van der Veer and Valsiner, 1991; an analysis of Hans Spemann—Rinard, 1992; the emerging social psychology in the United States—King, 1990). Analysis of the discourse of science, and about science, remains a valuable vehicle for the analysis of processes that canalize sciences both toward breakthroughs and to intellectual impasses.

Perhaps the notion of "objectivity" that helps to transcend the limits of each of the three folk models is that of genetic epistemology (Piaget, 1950). It is a characteristic of knowledge that is constructed by purposeful actions of meaning-making investigators in their contacts with the target phenomena, as an outcome (rather than the "starting datum") of the research process. From this perspective, "objectivity" is a characteristic that may emerge within the research process (Piaget, 1977, pp. 30–31) but is not automatically guaranteed by any special emphasis upon one or another part of the methodology circle. Such emphases are often marked by power assertions to insert the halo value of "objectivity" into some part of the methodology cycle. Thus, psychologists at times claim "objectivity" on the basis of their use of so-called standardized methods (see also Porter, 1994, on the use of the "rhetoric of standardization" at large). Similarly, field anthropologists may claim "objective" status for their descriptions because they have direct experience with the community they describe. Yet both of these assertions of "objectivity" are merely examples of symbolic meta-scientific disputes, rather than examples of emergence of "objectivity" as integrity between theoretical, methodical, data, and phenomena qualities.

Social sciences are open to different ideological orientations that at times may be involved in "paradigm clashes." The major symbolic theme around which metascientific "wars" are being fought in psychology is the legitimacy (or lack of it) of quantification of qualitative phenomena in the process of data derivation. On the one hand, the world of psychological phenomena consists of entities that are systemically related with one another. On the other hand, psychology's analytic schemes are mostly built around the axiom of quantifiability of structured phenomena.

The Question of Quantification

When psychology approaches complex phenomena, it becomes a hostage to its own traditions. In particular, it is the tradition of quantification and reliance on inferential statistics that creates a curious situation where many complex psychological phenomena have been left out of the focus of investigation. The focus on quantification as a guarantee of objectivity is historically not a borrowing from the "hard sciences" (as widespread rhetoric in the social sciences often claims), but follows from the social organization of developing industrialized societies. As Porter has indicated, the developing U.S. democracy made use of quantified knowledge and calculatory practices as a means to organize social life in the new society:

> Those whose authority is suspect, and who are obliged to deal with an involved and suspicious public, are much more likely to make their decisions by the numbers than are those who govern by divine or hereditary right. It is not by accident that the authority of numbers is linked to a particular form of government, representative democracy. Calculation is one of the most convincing ways by which a democracy

can reach an effective decision in cases of potential controversy, while simultaneously avoiding coercion and minimizing the disorderly effects of vigorous public involvement. (Porter, 1994, p. 206)

Aside from being a vehicle for governance, quantification offers the possibility of constructing ways to bring values—material or social—into a system of numbers-mediated comparability (see Kvale, 1983, on quantification in education). This is part and parcel of the economic system, which easily carries over to these areas of human reasoning where it is usually not considered appropriate to make such comparisons (i.e., in my present terms, an alteration of ZFM/ZPA complex of how value comparisons are socially regulated). Thus, it seems to strike nobody as an odd suggestion when an administrative official of an university in the present-day United States) suggests openly to a faculty member to apply for academic positions elsewhere, so as to find out his or her "market value" (in the form of the salary offer from another institution). The similarity of this suggestion to similar (maybe more publicly visible!) testing of "market value" of slaves in U.S. history seems to pass without a comment. In a wider domain of applications, parents may insure their lives for certain sums of money, yet they would find it inappropriate if somebody suggested to them that the value of their beloved children may be stated in monetary terms (e.g., "My life is insured for $1 million, my three-year-old daughter—who is nice and always eats well—has a monetary value of $23,545, while my two-year-old son's value is only $18,454").

When it comes to quantification of psychological characteristics, the knowledge constructive role of such quantifications has been suspect. Complex forms of personality organization surely are little known thanks to the obligatory quantification that has proliferated in psychology—in conjunction with aperspectival objectivity models.

The Rule of Quantification as a Device of Social Canalization

Whereas the social history of quantification in psychology has been studied (Gigerenzer et al., 1989; Hornstein, 1988), it is the clear recognition of the constraining role of consensual transformation of quality into quantity that deserves analysis. First, we can see social canalization of research process in action. It is a subjective confidence game, played with and around the meaning of "objectivity." It was the institutionalized science that fixed the meaning of "objectivity" to be affectively linked with quantification. Once such linkage was made, and internalized by psychologists, the very operation of quantification has become accepted without question:

> The mere fact that complex phenomena could now be represented in some kind of numerical form conferred a degree of objectivity on the results of psychological research that qualitative findings appeared to lack. But beyond the use of numbers in and of themselves, quantification made it possible to objectify aspects of decision making that would otherwise be seen as clearly subjective. The conduct of research requires that one make a whole variety of choices: which groups to compare and how to compare them, how to measure the phenomenon of interest, what to count, how to count it, what data to include and what to ignore as error or artifact, which statistical tests to use, how to represent the findings graphically, which findings to stress and which to discount, and so on. *By providing ways to "package" these choices, quantification transformed the experience of the researchers into one of merely applying various standardized techniques, rather than having to make a series of complex choices.* (Hornstein, 1988, p. 23; emphasis added)

QUANTIFICATION AS A SOCIAL CONSTRAINT It is possible to view the social regulation of psychology's knowledge construction in terms of constraining—in this case, constraining of the activities and thinking patterns of a professional group by the group itself. The "zonological" notions (outlined in chapter 2) are applicable here as well. Psychology as a social institution (profession) creates its own system of ZFM/ZPA/ZPD at multiple levels: actions (empirical investigatory acts), theory construction, and metapsychological discourse about "new" and "old," "progressive" and "regressive" directions in the discipline, as well boundaries of what is admissible within the "science" of psychology (e.g., LISREL analysis and factor analysis are within ZFM, while their counterparts of palm reading and parapsychology are clearly beyond the ZFM boundaries). In "practical" psychology some tactics (e.g., single-case analysis, qualitative descriptions via "clinical method") are within ZFM, while in the "science" side these very same tactics are either outside of ZFM or involved in boundary negotiation to be "inside." Some parts of the psychoanalytic belief system are allowed to the ZFM of the "scientific" psychology (e.g., energy-based models of personality, ego-defense mechanisms), while other meanings are either made into a nonmentionable entity or actively defended against (e.g, "penis envy").

Along similar lines, semiotic construction of quantification as immediate "guarantee" of objectivity has led to the ZFM/ZPA complex for researchers, where the boundaries of how to (and how not to) quantify the phenomena (to turn them into data) are constantly set and reset. Within these boundaries, different specific data-treatment tactics could be outlined (as ZPA) from time to time. These tactics may change over time, yet all come to the field the ZFM boundaries of which are fortified by the "quantification = objectivity" construct. Such negotiation of the ZFM boundary has been going on in parallel, of course (and reaches a climax currently with the proliferation of "qualitative methods" à la ethnographic approaches). It has led to symbolic segregation of in-group/out-group relations (e.g., psychology that in the United States was labeled "humanistic" was excused from the "sin" of not using normative quantitative methods but of course was considered to be "unscientific"). At times such segregation is temporarily overcome—in the form of carnival-type events such as national conventions—yet the boundary maintenance of social group relationships within the profession remains in full power (Hurme, 1997).

Boundary markers of institutionalized science usually utilize semiotic markers to make (or break) ZFM boundaries. Thus, any talk about "being" (or "not being") "scientific" is semiotic activity at the ZFM boundaries of the charting of a given discipline as an ideational and social entity. Thus, all the following possible statements are equal in their function of constructing the ZFM boundaries of psychology:

1. "Humanistic psychology is not scientific because it refuses to use quantitative methods" (ZFM boundary defense: meaning of "quantification" is utilized as semiotic marker of the boundary).
2. "Interdisciplinary approaches in psychology provide the discipline with a way to benefit from other sciences" (ZFM enlargement, rhetorically based on the meaning of "benefit": it enlarges ZFM for psychology to allow other disciplines to be talked about on equal terms).
3. "Marxist psychology is not scientific because it is based on a dogma" (ZFM boundary defense—itself making use of "dogma" by making its own dogmatic assertion look undogmatic; compare with a statement "Behaviorist psychology is not scientific because it is based on a

dogma," or "Any statement that psychology X is not 'scientific' because it is based on a dogma, is based on (another) dogma itself").

4. "Use of analysis of variance is not scientific because it assumes summativity of variance, which is not fitting with the gestalt nature of the phenomena" (a possible ZFM boundary defense for gestalt psychology—here excluding a "received" specific technique use).

5. "Cognitive psychology is not scientific because it utilizes computer metaphors" (another ZFM boundary defense).

Most probably we all have heard (and made) comments like statements 1 through 3, and even reading statements 4 and 5 may trigger in us an emotional reaction of some kind. It could be "How on earth could any-body say such things!" or "It is good somebody dares to state this!" or possibly an internal response somewhere in between. These reactions illustrate my point of each of them pertaining to the affective-conceptual "working through" of the ZFM boundary of psychology as science—albeit at the level of metascientific argumentation.

Quantification and the Study of Developmental Phenomena

The story of quantification is even more clearly told within developmental psychology. This subpart of psychology is really an outsider in all of psychology. As it was historically developed on the basis of embryology, the notion of qualitative structure, its transformation, and its irreducibility to its elements was never fully lost in that area (as described in chapters 4 and 5).

James Mark Baldwin made it clear that unsubstantiated quantification of phenomena is a theoretical error in psychology. He understood the futility of the transfer of quantitative methodology to psychology:

The . . . quantitative method, brought over into psychology from the exact sciences, physics and chemistry, must be discarded; for its ideal consisted in reducing the more complex to the more simple, the whole into its parts, the later-evolved to the earlier-existent, thus denying or eliminating just the factor which constituted or revealed what was truly genetic. Newer modes of manifestation cannot be stated in atomic terms without doing violence to the more synthetic modes which observation reveals. (Baldwin, 1930, p. 7)

Similarly, there is not much value in behaviorist analyses of "objective" phenomena (Baldwin, 1930, p. 29). Needless to add, in both of these evaluations (made after his active work in psychology had ended more than a decade previously), Baldwin's criticisms paralleled those of Vygotsky and Bühler.

It is clear that reduction of qualitative structured phenomena to arbitrarily quantified linear "variables" eliminates the complexity of the phenomena under study. Such complexity can never be reassembled later through different "multivariate" means (see Kindermann and Valsiner, 1989; Lamiell, 1987, 1990). The notion of "variables" creates a theoretical impasse for psychology at large, and for any study of personal complexity in particular. Recent talk about the need to return to person-centered approaches (e.g., Magnusson and Cairns, 1996) reflects the recognition of the knowledge-acquisition deficit of contemporary psychology.

Multivoiced Nature of Knowledge Construction: From "Measurement" of Characteristics to Logics of Transformation

Modern social sciences are hostages to the sociomoral demand characteristics of the very societies within which they were created. Whether for the sake of progress or morality (or any other general concept used in a society for its self-organization), the scope of theoretical orientations and empirical research practices is selectively limited by extrascientific guidance, ranging from the inevitable embeddedness within common sense to explicit embracing of social ideologies by the social scientists. This should not be surprising, since sciences include their own multivoicedness of discourse (à la Bakhtin) and make use of various languages. The issue is how are these languages within science organized? And how is heteroglossia within a science coordinated with its counterparts within the given society?

Fusing of social ideologies and psychological languages in communication at the level of common sense has rendered psychology largely a part of the collective culture of the persons who create the discipline. When immediate practical issues dominate the discourse in a given society, and that discourse flows into the languages of psychology, we get a fusion of meanings where psychological terminology and everyday language uses are indistinguishable (Gusfield, 1976). The history of other sciences (so-called hard ones) may reveal similar situations in the past. An alchemist's sincere wish to make gold out of other substances was undoubtedly a socially desirable goal, and theories of how that could happen may be similar to our contemporary applications of psychology to improve human beings and their society. In comparison with the history of chemistry, it can be claimed that psychology is still in a state similar to that of alchemy, but perhaps with some hopes for developing into a substantive science if its cultural self-blinders are rethought.

The need for reconceptualization of the "variables-oriented approach" in personality psychology has been voiced in the pertinent literature (Magnusson, 1988; Magnusson and Törestad, 1993). The full implication of such calls entails a basic reorganization of psychology's accepted folk models of how to build its formal scientific language system. Currently—and via a historical social construction—such models have relied on the notion of classical physics' measurement of simple physical characteristics. From that point of view, human personality might be characterized as a conglomerate of values on parameters that are supposed to be linear and labeled by common-language terms. The latter would afford too many possibilities (see Allport's lexicon analysis in chapter 5), all of which remain within the system of meanings of the ordinary language use. Consider the following two statements:

a. "Mr X. is a domineering, mean, and humorous person."
b. "Mr. X has high scores on dominance, meannness, and humor dimensions."

These statements do not differ in their meanings—the first has been expressed in ordinary language, the second, in ordinary language with the addition of reference to measurement procedures. In both cases the description of personality is given by the ordinary language meanings, and thus statement (b) is pseudoempirical (see Smedslund, 1994). The classical physics folk model (of measurement) is transformed into a commercial ("price" à la "value") model; it is no surprise that psychology's research practices can be observed to fit the accounting model of the world (Porter, 1992).

Physical or accounting models are by no means necessarily definitive for psychology. There are numerous alternatives. For instance, one could borrow a basic model from chemistry. Following an old metaphor (introduced in 1820 by Thomas Brown—see Woodworth, 1948, p. 35), psychology can be formally close to being a "chemistry of the mind"—based on formal qualitative systems that allow psychologists to analyze both the relative stability and the dynamic transformations of the generic structures. Such structuralistic focus was discussed (but not fully implemented) at the turn of the twentieth century, again primarily in developmental psychology (Krueger, 1913b), and mostly in German psychology between the two world wars.

Reconstructing the Unity of Methodology *and* Methods

One blinder is the social construction of the separation of psychological methods from their philosophical and general-theoretical assumptions. As was pointed out previously, the received practice in contemporary psychology is to treat methods are if they were free of the theoretical contexts within which they were conceived. That this is a social construction of recent decades has been demonstrated by a number of thinkers (Danziger, 1990; Gigerenzer, 1993; Gigerenzer et al., 1989). In parallel, we can observe the making of equivalence of the terms "method" and "methodology." De facto the use of these terms in English-language psychology has become fused, and the empirical research enterprise separated from its theoretical underpinnings. This has been captured well by Obeyesekere:

> The dominant Anglo-American tradition of social science believes that true knowledge can be achieved by *method*. Hence epistemology is the key to the social sciences: and ontology is to be shunned. I think the reverse is true: the human sciences *(Geisteswissenschaften)* are essentially ontological and any attempt to divorce ontology from epistemology cannot succeed but can only produce a shallow ontology. We have only a few philosophically well developed ontologies in the human sciences, a good example being Cassirer's philosophy of symbolic forms or Heidegger's Dasein. Yet incipient or partially developed ontological assumptions underlie such notions as "species being," "cultural relativism," "economic man," "pleasure principle" and so forth. (Obeyesekere, 1987, p. 109)

Obeyesekere's call for reuniting ontological (i.e., basic assumptions) analysis with that of methods-linked epistemology is undoubtedly crucial for the advancement of ideas in any science (not just in human sciences) yet is easily blocked by ideological constraints (see later discussion of models of objectivity). In the context of the present book, methodology entails the unity of the epistemological process.

Hermeneutics of the Research Process

The function of research methods in the evocation of the emergence of novelty makes co-constructivist methodology close to the concerns of hermeneutically oriented researchers. In the hermeneutic process of knowledge construction, the moments of sudden mutual divergence of communication between experimenter and subject may give rise to the relevant phenomena to be investigated (Hermans, 1991, 1996; Hermans and Bonarius, 1991a, 1991b; Hermans and Kempen, 1995; Hermans, Kempen, and van Loon, 1992). This hermeneutic process is dialogic in nature—irrespective of whether that dialogue takes place within the intra- or interpersonal communication process. It entails constant construction of semiotic differences, which include repetitively new versions of phenomena. The treatment of repetition as novelty fits the reality of irreversible time, while it cannot be detected on the basis of time-freed assumptions of classical logic. For example, let us consider two phrases

> that are completely identical, "life is good" and again "life is good."
> In terms of Aristotelian logic, these two phrases are related in terms of
> *identity*; they are, in fact, one and the same statement. From a dialogical point of view, however, they may be considered as two remarks
> expressed by the voices of two spatially separated people in communication, who in this case entertain a relationship of *agreement*. The two
> phrases are identical from a logical point of view, but different as
> utterances: the first is a statement, the second a confirmation. In a
> similar way the phrases "life is good" and "life is not good" can be
> elaborated. In terms of logic, one is a *negation* of the other. However,
> as utterances from two different speakers, there is a dialogical relation
> of *disagreement*. (Hermans, 1995, p. 378)

It is the temporal structure of the phenomena that makes the relationships of agreement or disagreement. In either case, duality-based relations are constructed in time, and by active goal-oriented (and goal-orienting) persons. When this approach is applied to the process of experimenter-subject relations, the objectivity of any research effort is a result of a hermeneutic process—not pregiven by starting conditions (of "objective methods," etc.).

AN EXAMPLE OF THE CONSTRUCTION OF KNOWLEDGE
The person who takes the role of a "subject" in the research process is constantly creating novelty, the emergence of novel psychological phenomena embedded in the fuzzy nature of the person's concrete interaction—or co-construction—with the context. An example from a study of the acceptance and meanings of amniocentesis by pregnant women in New York contexts may provide a further example:

When I interviewed a 36-year old Honduran UPS package inspector in a run-down neighborhood of Queens . . . she seemed to have accepted an amniocentesis without great introspection. As the mother of two teenage boys from a former marriage, she "just wanted everything to be all right." During the course of an hour's home interview, my tape was filled with her disinterested answers, interrupted by the flamboyant and sonorous testimony of her fervently Pentecostalist husband. He described his vivid visions of the infant Jesus protecting his own infant-to-be, swore that the prayers of his co-congregants had already healed all manner of potential problems the child might have faced, and used the occasion of my visit to witness the benefits of faith . . .

Later, Mari-Carmen walked me back to the subway, and without the pressures of husband or tape recorder told me that Pentecostalism was saving her husband, who had twice been jailed on drug charges, and from whom she had separated because of his infidelities. Her chief worries centered on her older sons, both having problems in school, one involved with a neighborhood gang. If "having baby for him" would stabilize the family, she would accept the pregnancy, and the amniocentesis, and any other advice the doctor gave her, just as she had accepted the Pentecostalist congregation. *Without the benefit of this shadow interview, I might have well coded Mari-Carmen's answers as "medically compliant," an instance of a working-class Spanish-speaker accepting the authority of medicine rather passively. I might also have coded her husband's intense Pentecostalist presentation as "Hispanic."* (Rapp, 1994, pp. 223–224; emphasis added)

Joint construction of interview results—as indicated in this passage—thus exemplifies the active role of the interviewee. This happens first by letting the interviewer gain access to the personal culture, and second in the construction of a particular view of that personal culture. The interviewer may facilitate (or block) that active role of the interviewee, yet cannot eliminate it.

The co-constructional nature of the use of any psychological method is similar. The declared "objectivity" of "factual evidence" in the study of human beings is not the starting point of investigation (as shown earlier), but the result of a joint construction process in which both the investigator and the investigatee are involved. This process proceeds along the lines of interpersonal and intrapersonal constraining of meanings, their externalizations (by the investigator), constructive interpretation, goal-oriented transformation, and reexternalization (by the investigatee). This flow of the research process sets up the logic of knowledge construction in case of developmental sciences in a very different way from the usual actions by researchers (of hypothesis testing, for instance).

Baldwin's "Genetic Logic" and Its Implications

James Mark Baldwin's efforts to advance a system of "genetic logic" are worth reconsidering, given the paucity of efforts to advance this direction of formalization of psychology (see also Valsiner, 1997b, chapter 3; 1995b). For Baldwin, the main metatheoretical contrast for him was between genetic (developmental) and a-genetic (nondevelopmental) science. The former had to develop its own theoretical system and could not rely upon the latter: "We must be free from all constructions drawn from the strictly a-genetic sciences in which the causal sequence is the typical one. The birth of a new mode in the psychic life is a *'progression' from an earlier set of conditions, not the effect of these conditions viewed as cause;* and this is equally true of any new genetic mode, just so far as the series in which it appears is really genetic at all" (Baldwin, 1906, p. 29; emphasis added).

Baldwin here recognized the difference within the phenomena—between nonliving and living systems. If traditional models of causality apply to the former, they cannot apply to the latter. He also formulated four "axioms" for the methodology of developmental science (1902, p. 323; 1906, p. 20), which fortified the irreducibility of the developmentally more complex phenomena to their preceding (less complex) counterparts.

In Baldwin's postulates, the notion of hierarchical organization of developmental phenomena and their dynamic transformation are made into the central focus of science:

> First, the phenomena of science at each higher level show a form of synthesis that is not accounted for by the formulations which are adequate for the phenomena of the next lower level. By lower and higher I mean genetically before and after.
>
> Second, the formulations of any lower science are not invalidated in the next higher, even in cases in which new formulations are necessary for the formal synthesis which characterizes the genetic mode of the higher.

Third, the generalizations and classifications of each science, representing a particular genetic mode, are peculiar to that mode and cannot be constructed in analogy to, or a fortiori on the basis of, the corresponding generalizations or classifications of the lower mode.

Fourth, no formula for progress from mode to mode, that is, no strictly genetic formula in evolution or in development, is possible except by direct observation of the facts of the series which the formulation aims to cover or by the interpretation of other series which represent the same or parallel modes. (Baldwin, 1906, p. 20)

The phenomena to which these postulates can be applied are those of biology and history. The postulates set up constraints against reductionism (explanation of higher-level phenomena by lower levels), as well as against the opposite tendency (of using higher levels for explaining lower ones). On the basis of these axioms, Baldwin derived two "postulates of method": "*First*. The first or negative postulate: *the logic of genesis is not expressed in convertible propositions.* Genetically, A = (that is, becomes, for which the sign = is now used) B; but it does not follow that B = (becomes) A. *Second*. The second or positive postulate: that series of events is truly genetic which cannot be constructed before it has happened, and which cannot be exhausted backwards, after it has happened" (Baldwin, 1906, p. 21).

The first postulate specifies the realm of possible relations that are allowable among the formulae of "genetic logic"—namely, *each proposition includes a temporal directionality vector.* It is the second postulate that seems more problematic, as it possesses an agnostic flavor. If a developmental phenomenon cannot be explained before it takes place, nor afterward, then when and how can the "genetic science" explain anything? It seems appropriate to interpret the second postulate as an *imperative for the study of developmental events as those unfold* (i.e., concurrently). This interpretation maintains the productivity of the "genetic science."

Baldwin tried (e.g., Baldwin, 1908b) to develop a formalized system for his genetic logic but was unsuccessful. There may be numerous explanations for his failure, ranging from his life moving in the direction of academic administration (which never helps scholarly productivity) to his choice of an unfortunate parent model (logic) for his pursuits. His direction of pursuits remains underdeveloped, which is a major issue in methodology (see also chapter 1, on cogenetic logic).

Developmental Structuralism: The Geneva Tradition of Genetic Epistemology

Aside from Baldwin's earlier theoretical efforts, the developmental orientation in the 1920s gave the science of psychology examples of creating methods for studying novel formations in part-whole relationships in human development. The tradition of child study advanced in Geneva, first by Édouard Claparède and then by Jean Piaget (Chapman, 1988), is notable for its concentration on the development of part-whole relations in human psychological phenomena (Piaget, 1965, 1970). Piaget's focus on developmental processes with structure was close to that of the "Second Leipzig School" (see later discussion), even if it grew out of different intellectual roots (James Mark Baldwin's "genetic logic" and Henri Bergson's "creative evolution"). The result of his theoretical development was the system of genetic epistemology—the study of the construction of knowledge structures in general (Piaget, 1965, p. 31) yet based on the analysis of empirical phenomena in their qualitative complexity.

Such qualitative complexity required qualitative tactics for data derivation. Piaget achieved this through his version of the "clinical method," which was well coordinated with his focus on how a child constructs novel psychological structures, and which changed together with his interests (Vinh-Bang, 1966). It involved a mixture of experimental manipulation of the conditions of the participant observation (by the investigator) of the conduct of a young child and active introduction of "tricky" action tasks into interviews with children.

Piaget's observations of his own children's early development provided him with a basis to discuss the formation of holistic action schemes from previously established part-schemes. His own interaction with the children was a relevant part of the method, as can be seen from the following example:

> At 1 [year]; 1 [month] (15 [days]) J.[acqueline] watched me when I made a long nose at her. She *first put her fingers on her nose, then her forefinger only.* A series of repetitions produced no new reaction.
>
> Later on, in the evening of the same day, *I put my thumb in my mouth,* at the *same time raising my fingers.* J. at once *put her thumb in her mouth* and moved her fingers until they reached a fairly correct position. I then *took my thumb out of my mouth,* and put it to my nose without changing the position of the fingers, thus again making a

long nose. J. succeeded in doing the same thing. Thus *by merely separating the operations involved in making a long nose,* I had made it possible for her to imitate correctly. (Piaget, 1962, pp. 56–57; emphasis added)

Piaget's description of this encounter illustrates his focus on the emergence of structure in the child's action. A specific combination of the actions of the model makes it possible for the child to imitate, while another combination creates interferences. The description constitutes molar qualitative data that maintain relation to the phenomena. The sequential order in the emergence of the child's answer is described here. It is further evident in the continuation of the "long nose" theme two months later:

At 1 [year]; 3 [months] (7) [days] I again put my thumb in my mouth, with the fingers raised, but this time I sucked my thumb noisily. J., who had in the meantime forgotten the model and how to imitate it, broke up the movement in the following way. She began by blowing a kiss (to produce the sound), then she put her thumb in her mouth, with her forefinger on her nose (without making any sound), and finally raised her other fingers. She thus perceived the model in terms of various schemas of assimilation (the sound of a kiss, the action of sucking her thumb, and that of raising her finger, and then accommodated these schemas to the model. (Piaget, 1962, p. 57).

Piaget can detect the parts that would become integrated into the whole only thanks to their sequential expression. By looking at how a child arrives at an imitative act, he takes the stand oriented toward progressive study of emerging phenomena. This focus brings him close to the traditions of *Ganzheitspsychologie* in looking at the development of holistic units.

Developmental Holism: *Ganzheitspsychologie* of the "Second Leipzig School" and Its Methodological Contributions

The methods of step-by-step formation of a holistic structure (nowadays best known under the label "microgenetic methods"—see Draguns, 1984) were basically developed within the German tradition of *Ganzheitspsychologie,* which was led by the efforts of Felix Krueger (1874–1948), the successor of Wilhelm Wundt in Leipzig. Krueger's focus was on the development of holistic units (gestalts), although his perspective differed from the more widely known Gestalt psychology tradition of Wolfgang Köhler and his colleagues. Krueger criticized Gestalt psychology for its lack of developmental and historical focus on holistic units (Krueger, 1926, 1928a, 1928b).

Aside from Wundt, the predecessors of *Ganzheitspsychologie* were Hans Cornelius and Theodor Lipps, with the romantic contributions by Johann Wolfgang Goethe and Wilhelm Dilthey creating the basis for the development of a holistic and developmental perspective within which generalized feeling *(Gefühl)* was of central relevance. The totality (holistic unit) can be lived through in terms of that generalized feeling. This continued the tradition of Goethe—his *Lebensereignis* referred to the irreducible medium through which human beings grasp the phenomena of the world in a complex of "feelable" and "reflectable" knowledge (see Koerner, 1993, p. 485). This complex was seen by Goethe as individual-specific personal experience. Later, through the intermediaries of Georg W. Hegel and Wilhelm Dilthey (see Makkreel, 1992), this notion reached into twentieth-century science in the form of the focus of experience *(Erlebnis),* where it found its centrality in the personology of William Stern (see chapter 5) and in other person-oriented approaches, including *Ganzheitspsychologie.*

Krueger's early theoretical credo echoes the ideas expressed by Baldwin:

> The ever changing *genetic* conditions of all psychic processes and the intimate fusion of their effects with those of actual circumstances, constitute a characteristic trait of all psychic life. Herein lies the essential reason why the psychic can not be reduced to constant and qualitatively equal elements such as physical atoms, but only to a system of purely functional relations and ultimately of functional laws . . . The genetic structure of human consciousness is really an historical one . . . fundamentally dependent upon every individual's interrelations with *other* individuals and upon the past of their civilization. These social-genetic and cultural conditions admit still less of experimental method than do those of the individual. (Krueger, 1913b, pp. 260–261)

Krueger's interest in the emergence of psychological forms led the *Ganzheitspsychologie* tradition into the focus on successive gestalts (or time-gestalts). This fit well with the axiomatic assumption of the tradition—viewing in any psychological phenomenon an inherent "tension" that leads toward construction of holistic units (gestalts) in irreversible time. Much of the empirical work within the tradition of the "Second Leipzig School" was devoted to the demonstration of how such striving-toward-wholeness takes place in perception (Fw Tarng Dun, 1939; Hausmann,

1935; Johannes, 1939), thinking (Lichtenberg, 1933), feeling (Klemm, 1937, 1938), and action (Krueger, 1913a; Rüssel, 1944). The focus within this tradition upon structures of the whole transcended the traditions of gestalt psychology—for *Ganzheitspsychologie*, all gestalts were psychological wholes *(Ganzen)*, with all the assumed characteristics of the tendency toward further structuring. The reverse was not the case. Not all wholes, especially those that lacked well-ordered structure (e.g., the whole-quality in the notion of "chaos"), could be considered gestalts (Sander, 1928/1962, p. 75). The "Second Leipzig School" took very seriously the need to maintain the holistic integrity of psychological systems, without giving up efforts at careful empirical analysis. The latter mostly demonstrated concrete conditions of the process of the formation of the wholes.

THE CONSTRUCTIONIST ORIENTATION OF *GANZHEITSPSY-CHOLOGIE* In its theoretical buildup and assumptions focusing on the making of holistic units, the tradition of Krueger and his associates was clearly developmental in its focus. From a developmental perspective, all developing psychological structures are time-gestalts, which are constantly in the process of formation as their duration becomes extended in actuality (Krueger, 1926; Wellek, 1954). Hence a better-fitting term might be *process-Gestalt* (cf. *Verlaufsgestalt*—Volkelt, 1959/1962, p. 148).

The need for empirical study of process-gestalts led to the development of an orientation of methods construction that was labeled *Aktualgenese* by its major inventor, Friedrich Sander (Sander, 1927, p. 187). The roots of this notion were historically grounded in the morphogenetic theorizing of Johann W. Goethe (see Kuhn, 1987, for an analysis of Goethe's notions of development). Goethe's term *Realgenese* perhaps could have been usable, since the translation of *Aktualgenese* into English has been difficult. There also has been substantial difficulty with understanding Sander's methods-constructive orientation in English-speaking psychology. Sander's early English translation rendered *Aktualgenese* as "genetic realization" (Sander, 1930, p. 193), which overlooks the constructive, personal feelings-inserting nature of the emergence of the psychological whole. The whole was not a rationally completed gestalt (as the Berlin gestalt psychologists would have preferred to think), nor merely a personal positional view (or *Anschauung*, as Werner [1927, p. 443] claimed while developing a parallel method of microgenesis). The whole emerges in its fullness of personal subjectivity—the person "inhabits it" (to use an oft-quoted phrase from Bakhtin) with his or her subjective world—general feeling, personal-cultural sense, or other "fillers" of such kind. The emerging process-gestalt is always a subjective, personal whole that can come into existence due to psychological relation of the active-constructive person and the environment.

The tactics of experimentation in the *Aktualgenese* tradition entailed modifications of the active person's access to objects in the environment. Since most of the experiments within this framework were devoted to perception and action, it was easy to modify the stimulus field so that the process of whole formation would be rendered gradual and stepwise. Thus, visual stimuli were presented at short exposure time, with gradual lengthening of the exposures, requiring subjects to explain what they saw. Or figures could be presented in extreme miniature forms, or under insufficient lighting, and gradually taken to normal conditions. The perceptual processes that ordinarily take place quickly were thus slowed down, and the step-by-step formation of the whole could thus be described as a sequence of stages ("pre-wholes" or *Vorgestalten*). Without doubt, Piaget's habit of distinguishing stages in every psychological process he viewed (both in ontogeny and in immediate problem-solving process) was similar to the tactic of *Aktualgenese*.

The theoretical status of the "pre-wholes" in the *Aktualgenese* methodology circle is important. These formations were viewed as potentially "richer" than the final gestalt would be:

> The peculiar mode of presentation of these prefigurations that are simplified relative to some final form is in no wise comparable to that of final forms of similar outline; *it is considerably richer in quality.* Their regular formation is only one trait of these closed self-sufficient constructs, which unfold with well-ordered regularity, without exhausting themselves in these characteristics. The evolution of these unitary, still unmembered constructs into significant forms with increasing membral differentiation *is not something that the observer follows with cool objectivity, but all metamorphoses are engulfed in a maximally emotional process of pronouncedly impulsive and tensor nature,* and take place through an intense participation of the whole human organism. Every formation is experienced as a satisfactory fulfillment of some inner urge, possessing the whole consciousness with dull compressed feelings, an *urge for formation of the formless, significance of the meaningless.* What passes here in the sphere of perception is repeated in exaggerated measure in the higher realm of

artistic or intellectual formulation. (Sander, 1930, p. 194; emphasis added)

Sander's method-constructive orientation as described here fits well with the focus on dialogicality (see chapter 1). The "dialogue" involved in the "urge of formation of the formless" or "significance of the non-significant" gives rise to the construction of novel forms, which happen to be "pre-wholes" relative to the given "final" whole only from the perspective of the experimenter (who knows the expected outcome form) but not from the viewpoint of the subject (who acts prospectively and constructively). Sander's *Aktualgenese* is perhaps the best existing tactic of method construction that fits with James Mark Baldwin's call for the direct investigation of the process of development (see earlier discussion of Baldwin's "second postulate" of developmental science).

The *Ganzheitspsychologie* tradition was certainly not without its contemporaries in the efforts to devise adequate methods for the study of development. Aside from Piaget's adoption of the "clinical method," similar efforts were given approximate formulation by Vygotsky in his focus on the "method of double stimulation" (Vygotsky and Luria, 1930/1994; Valsiner, 1989, chapter 3), based on the observational studies by the research group of Mikhail Basov (1931). However, the unity of the methodology circle was not fully elaborated in Vygotsky's or Basov's cases. A parallel version to Sander's *Aktualgenese* was developed by Heinz Werner based on his physiognomic theoretical standpoint (Werner, 1927) and on the perceptual experiencing of micromelodies (Werner, 1926, 1940b) and the role of speech in human understanding (Werner, 1931, 1956; Werner and Kaplan, 1984).

Summary: Developmental Methodology Circle Requires Analysis of Processes of Transformation

The efforts to reintegrate methods into the methodology circle reported here lead to a relatively simple conclusion: the assumptions of the investigation and the grasp of the phenomena guide the ways in which particular methods are constructed to derive data from the phenomena. If the assumptions are developmental and structuralist (as in the case of Piaget, Vygotsky, Werner, and the *Ganzheitspsychologie* tradition), the tactics necessary for methods construction (as well as the nature of "the data" derived with these methods) are cardinally different from the usual construction of quantified analogues for qualitative phenomena in the data. General analysis of developmental processes can include relevant empirical data only if the data are adequate reflections of the phenomena of such processes. Calls for abandonment of quantification in psychology (in their extreme case) or for recognizing the limits of quantification (in the case of ordinary reasoning of psychologists) are not subversive strategies of "non-scientific extremists" (as ZFM boundary-defense efforts may lead it to be phrased) but merely expressions of the need to reflect upon what researchers are actually accomplishing if they blindly follow social rules of data construction.

The semiotic perspective elaborated in the present book lets us look at different methods used in psychology as signs. In this perspective, the question of the referents of the signs remains crucial for science. One can narrow the criteria for what "scientific" means—always determinable within the field of metascientific discourse. *Psychological methods create scientific data only if the selected original facets of the phenomena are retained in the data* (i.e., the data represent the selected side of the phenomena) and when the *theoretical focus and the nature of the data fit one another* in their basic assumptions.

Methodology of Constraining: Different Methods As Derivatives From Basic Observation

Psychology is filled with rhetoric statements about methods. Usually these statements are evaluative and classificatory. Here I will try to organize this talk of methods a bit differently, looking at different methods as transformations of the core epistemological activities of human beings. Human personality is the researcher who—on the basis of one's personality system—enters into encounters with realities singled out for scientific analyses. In this respect, knowledge construction in science is a socially guided yet personalistic process (as described in previous chapters). It takes place from the standpoint of a wide heterogeneity of motives of unique personalities entering into similar kinds of social roles (see Devereux, 1961).

Starting from sociogenetic personalism, observation in general—particularly introspective observation—is the core of *all* psychology's methodological construction efforts (James, 1890, p. 185). Introspection as a scientifically adequate methodological direction needs to be rehabilitated within the "scientific method" in psychology. Over the twentieth century, that direction has been stigmatized as "soft" or "subjective" psychology, and its early users caricatured as nonobjective "soul searchers" for whom "scientific rigor" was a foreign word. Nothing can be further from the actual state of affairs (see Danziger, 1980, 1985; Danziger and Shermer, 1994).

TWO INDUCTIONS Morgan wrote about "two inductions" involved in the process of constructing knowledge:

> Our conclusions concerning the mental processes of beings other than our own individual selves are . . . based on a two-fold induction. First the psychologist has to reach, through induction, the laws of mind as revealed to him in his own conscious experience. Here the facts to be studied are facts of consciousness, known at first-hand to him alone among mortals; the hypotheses may logically suggest themselves, in which case they are original so far as the observer himself is concerned, or they may be derived—that is to say, suggested to the observer by other observers; the verification of the hypotheses is again purely subjective, original or derived theories being submitted to the touchstone of individual experience. This is the one inductive process. The other is more objective. The facts to be observed are external phenomena, physical occurrences in the objective world; the hypotheses again may be either original or derived; the verification is objective, original or derived theories being submitted to the touchstone of observable phenomena. Both inductions, subjective and objective, are necessary. Neither can be omitted without renouncing the scientific method. (Morgan, 1894, pp. 47–48)

Morgan's emphasis on the unity of the two inductions was lost in twentieth-century psychology. Largely because of the advent of a behavioristic mind-set and a focus on hypothesis testing (rather than hypothesis construction), psychology has constrained the intricacy of the research process to examination of "the other" (be that "other" a rat or another person). Perhaps the inclusion of the researcher in the process was too close for comfort (see Devereux, 1967) for the persons conducting the research. In any case, psychologists have constrained themselves toward exclusion of their personal lived-through experiences from the research process.

If we were to include scientists' lived-through (and imagined) personal constructions into the methodology circle (Figure 7.1), we would immediately change our focus from methods (and data) to the contents of our hypotheses (or assumptions) about the phenomena and would ask questions along the lines of how a particular method becomes constructed for the given purposes as created by the scientist. The set of methods thus is a product of the methodology process, rather than a pregiven "toolbox" from where ready-made (and often copyrighted) methods are merely taken (or purchased). Different methods are tools in the making, as those are constructed by the scientist and related to the phenomena—to lead to the construction of data.

Methods as Constraint Structures

Specific methods are transformations of the basic observation by one observer of the other. Thus, the psychologist claims to observe—by introspection or extrospection—an "other." The "other"—usually labeled "subject" or "research participant"—is involved in a simultaneous process of counterobservation. The latter process cannot be eliminated in psychological studies; in fact, it is purposefully regulated by different kinds of constraints that the psychologist sets up for the subjects, via the particular method.

Obviously, the very first act of constraining is that of the psychologist getting the other to take the role of the subject. In other words, the other person is brought "into the field" of the given study, persuaded (or coerced or bought) to stay in that field for the time it takes to conduct the study and to follow the guidance of the psychologist. This ZFM/ZPA structure is set up differently for different methods.

Beyond the setting of the study situation, different methods entail constraining different sides of the extra- and intrapsychological activities of the subject. Thus, the use of introspective methods may entail efforts to structure a "deep" intramental processes that only the subject can access. However, the introspective method is also used in its minimalist version—that of a rating scale. Here the subject be instructed to respond "at the first feeling" to the given task. The ZFM/ZPA complex canalizes the subject toward an immediate and superficial "flash" of introspection. The actual process that goes on within the subject who makes a mark on a rating scale interests nobody; the outcome—the mark itself—becomes the basis for further interpretations. Rating scales are thus a method that guarantees scientists lack of access to psychological processes from the outset by speeding up the responding process. In contrast, traditional "deep"-introspectionist methods worked on the basis of recording medium-speed intrapsychological processes or by slowing them down for recording.

Experimental Methods

Experiment also entails assumed relations to two domains of reality, made via generalization (Moghaddam and Harré, 1992). First, whatever happens in an experiment can be viewed in terms of the pretense that persons act *as if* they would, under similar circumstances in the "real world" (i.e., the world outside of the experimental context). Second, the experiment could be related to the "could if" function—by demonstrating the kinds of conduct that *could* occur in "real life," *if* certain conditions were met.

By its nature, experimental method constitutes a purposeful distortion of the ordinary reality, in order to provoke phenomena that may allow us to test some generic aspects of human reality as a whole. This nature of *purposeful* distortion of reality for the purposes of knowledge construction has become confused with *substitutional* distortion of reality (i.e., cases where artificially created experimental contexts render data that are made to substitute the reality—Prinzhorn, 1933). Criticisms of the latter (e.g., Harré, 1970, 1980, 1981b) are actually criticisms of the confusion of relationships between methods, data, theories, and phenomena (see Branco and Valsiner, 1997). The construction of previously non-existing conditions in an experiment is an "as-if" construction—the experimenter alters the situation through the setup of ZFM/ZPA boundaries. In a classical experimental setting (such as a psychophysical or reaction time experiment) the situation is constrained by ZFM to the specific position of the subject (e.g., attached to a chair), and to the set of possible actions (e.g., touching surfaces at arm's length), together with ZPA of "instruction" to act in way A in case X, and in way B in case Y. The subject certainly has different ways to reorganize his or her actions within that ZFM/ZPA structure, such as not acting, or acting in ways undesired by the psychologist. Furthermore, the subject can reconstruct the meaning of the instructed action, possibly undermining the whole experiment (e.g., in a reaction time experiment, turning the ZPA of "act as quickly as you can" into "I act as quickly as is comfortable for me").

In versions of the experimental method where this constructive activity of the subject is made into a relevant part of the experiment (such as Vygotsky's "method of double stimulation"—Valsiner, 1989, chapter 2) the notion of investigator's control of the setting via a ZFM/ZPA complex remains the same. Only the ZFM includes more possible options, around a ZPA (or instruction), and it is exactly the subject's construction of conduct on the background of the ZFM/ZPA complex that is being studied.

The Interview

The interview is a method of dialogic coordination of two externalized introspective processes. The interviewer sets up a ZFM/ZPA complex by each question that is asked. The interviewee interprets the questions from his or her personal-cultural standpoint and answers not the asked but the introspectively transformed question. The whole sequence of the interview entails the process of counterobservation and counterinterpretation by the subject.

For example, consider the following dialogue (inspired by Ericsson and Simon, 1993, p. 20) between the investigator and the subject:

1. *Investigator:* Why did you buy this book?
2. *Subject:* Because I happened to have money and could buy it, instead of stealing it.
3. *Investigator:* Why did you buy this book?
4. *Subject:* Because it is on a topic that interests me.
5. *Investigator:* Why did you buy this book?
6. *Subject:* Because I did not want to buy anything else.

Despite the identical wording of all (same) questions by the investigator, the subject creates his own specific interpretation of the question (projecting emphasis on either "buy," "this," or "book") and generates answers that fit this co-constructed introspective image of the subject. In terms of Sander's *Aktualgenese,* what we have here is a sequence of pregestalts, each of which emerges on the basis of a different interpretation of the question. The interview question constrains the realm of investigation to the field of the content material mentioned, and at the same time evokes novel interpretations. Interestingly, it is exactly the nonleading way of asking of questions in an interview that enhances the projecting role of the subject. For example, if the investigator in our example provided paralinguistic emphasis on that of the three words he wanted to be emphasized (i.e., paralinguistic leading cue), then the range of possible interpretations by the subject would have been narrowed.

Furthermore, the impossibility of asking nonleading questions in an interview is proven if we examine the social roles assumed by the interviewer and the interviewee during the interview. In fact, the "scientist" and "subject" role differentiation (which is usually taken for granted by psychologists) may be sufficiently well defined in a European or North American middle-class context, but not in the case of other social classes or other collective-cultural contexts (see the example from Babaji interview of Shweder, in chapter 2). Nevertheless, the subject can co-construct the role of the interviewer in the very process of the interview. Thus, let us consider the following possible hypotheses of the subject in the preceding dialogue, each time after the same question is asked:

After #1: This person really is working for the police, and may know of my shop-stealing bouts when I was an adolescent.

After #3: Maybe this is some kind of an educational survey.

After #5: Probably some marketing survey, it seems.

Once a particular intrapsychologigal determination of the role of the interviewer is reached, the same interview question becomes answered in accordance with the role scenario just constructed. This process is explainable by the functioning of the three levels of representational fields of Bühler and their extension in terms of constraining by meanings (see chapter 3). The first afterthought is "fielded" within the secondary representational field (linking the personal past with the present question), while the second and third entail "fielding" on the tertiary level (i.e., making hypotheses about the implied intentionality of the interviewer, based on his assumed role).

Certainly these examples could be described as cases of "misunderstanding"—the researcher is "honestly" asking questions, trying to keep those as nonleading as possible. It is the interviewee who "misunderstands" the intentions of the interviewer. However, the communication process can be viewed as that of overcoming misunderstanding (Robinson, 1988). The interviewer-interviewee "intersubjectivity" is the unity of two separate but united subjectivities (as described in chapter 1) rather than a guaranteed fusion of the interviewee's definition of the context with that of the interviewer.

Examples of such discrepancies of interpretation abound in the social sciences. From this perspective, it is not surprising if U.S. anthropologists in Africa have been perceived to be CIA agents, or that in Asian contexts the tendencies of subjects to "please the interviewer" by providing what are assumed to be expected answers, have been described.

It is thus not surprising that for coordination of interpretations of each other's worlds of meanings, the interviewer and the interviewee may benefit from a known history of a mutual relationship. Usually, information about that history is not reported in psychology or anthropology, although there are notable exceptions (Obeyesekere, 1981, pp. 10–11).

For analysis of complex psychological phenomena, informants or subjects may become friends, sharing background interests, without consensus on special issues.

Observation: Unconstrained but Self-Constraining

Surely the most extrospection-based method of all is observation. The observed subjects' intrapsychological processes are not queried here—although they undoubtedly exist. This is similar to traditional experimentation, where the focus is on the outcomes of the processes, not on the processes themselves. At the same time, the method allows access to the process of externalized conduct.

Given the centrality of observation in any constructed method, the habitual contrast between "field" and "laboratory" research becomes eliminated, by way of treating the laboratory as a special case of the field (Valsiner and Benigni, 1986; Valsiner, 1994g). Likewise, any specific constraints introduced in the field contexts to the phenomena under study operate in reality as laboratory interventions. The actual nature of the study context—its "naturalness" or "artificiality"—remains in the hands of the research participants. They attach these labels to different settings they traverse, in accordance with the perception and goal orientations of the investigators. Thus, even if the observation situation is minimally constrained externally (by the observer's introduction of novel conditions), its loosely organized ZFM/ZPA for the subjects' action field is complemented by the subjects' construction of their own ZFM/ZPA complexes of meanings that self-regulate their conduct in a given setting. Observation can reveal only the external results of such self-constraining, not its generation process. This is obvious in any case where a particular subject in an observation situation is given a possibility to act "freely" and elects to not act at all, remaining in a motionless position for the whole observational period. Or, alternatively, the observed subjects may be acting within particular social role constraints that they have assumed for the given setting, interpreted by themselves as fitting. If an observation of the persons at a party is made, its interpretability on the basis of observational evidence alone is misleading. Consider the following self-report of possible subjects:

> We are a bright, young, elegant, cosmopolitan married couple, good conversationalists and financially secure. As a result, a large part of our

life is spent at social gatherings. People vie to invite us, and we must frequently choose between one party and another . . .

And yet . . . we abhor gatherings, we hate parties. Moreover, we are actually shy, contemplative individuals given to silence and solitude . . . people who despise crowds, dances, loud music, frivolity, small talk, and forced smiles . . .

On our way to a party, we're submerged in gloomy thoughts, bitter tribulations, and painful guilt feelings. But once we enter into the noisy whirlwind of the throng, the voices, faces, smiles, and jokes all make us forget the annoyance of being there against our will.

But then, home once again, how it hurts us to consider how fragile our personality is! How painful our feeling of helplessness! How horrible to see ourselves always obliged to be the life of the party! (Sorrentino, 1988, pp. 110–111)

The possibility of dissociation of the reflection field and action field, given the assumed social roles, limits the ability of direct observation of human behavior to gain access to the organization of the conduct of the persons involved. In the case of a multilevel system of constraints, the investigative methods need to be coordinated between levels. This may provide a basis for a multimethod approach—yet if such an approach is not organized within a methodology circle, mere additive "piling up" of methods cannot provide a solution.

Summary: Methods As Constrained Meaning-Construction Fields

As this brief overview of the usual classes of methods (experiment, interview, observation, rating scales) shows, all methods stem from the same basic process of meaning construction (by the investigator) on the basis of some encounter with the investigatees. There is unity of introspection and extrospection in this process. First (and foremost), all research questions necessarily are based on the investigator's introspection (and, of course, related with extrospection). As long as research is done by human investigators (in contrast with programmed robots), the hypotheses are personal constructions within a semiotic field of the notions of the given science. Psychologists would set up their personally constructed hypotheses within the semiotic sphere of psychology, and at times its "allied disciplines," and not in other fields. For example, a psychologist's hypothesis that "Mars is more aggressive than Venus"—fielded in astronomy—would be either pathological or humorous; while a comparable statement "Miguel is more aggressive than Verena"—or, in a more usual vein, "Estonians are more gregarious than Bantus"—can be easily accepted as part of psychological discourse.

Second, each of the methods entails selective constraining of its conditions. We see maximum constraining of the subject's introspection in the case of experiments and rating scales. On the other extreme, we see minimum constraining of the subject's externalizations in observation, paralleled by the constraining of the researcher's externalization (of the focus of observation). In the interview, we saw mutual, complementary constraining of both internalization and externalization processes. Leaving open the constraints of the meanings used in formulating a question requires complementary constraining of the question by the personal culture of the interviewee. The intended nonleading question necessarily becomes a leading one—by the necessity of answering it. The nonleading questions are actually leading—since they can be answered only through the interviewee's co-constructive interpretation.

Third, the co-constructive nature of all methods leads to the inevitable result that all methods necessarily produce interindividual variability in the data that are constructed through their use. Not only is the reality (the phenomena) interindividually variable, the very act of persons' involvement in research through some method amplifies that interindividual variability. Thus the usually great variability that can be seen in the data is a by-product of the application of the methods, and may actually reflect some general universality.

General Conclusions

The aim of this chapter has been to outline the major themes of methodology that are necessary for derivation of data from various phenomena. It was demonstrated that the single systemic case is the basis for empirical investigation in its process of relating to the context. This unifies analysis of developing personality with the analysis of any social system in its history. The cultural-historical perspective on personality is thus both historical and cultural—in the latter case, through semiotic constructivity.

Methodology in psychology was presented as a process of relations between phenomena, methods, data, theories, underlying assumptions, and researchers' socialized subjective constructions. The research process entails construction of different forms of intersubjectivity around the particular methods that are used, which set up limits upon the kind of data, and eventually—knowledge—that may be constructed in these settings.

No matter which particular phenomena we may take an interest in, the general methodological questions remain the same. These phenomena may at times be limited to verbal expressons in the course of communication (as will be analyzed in chapter 8) or removed from us by events in historical time (chapter 9). The crucial unity of these examples is the embeddedness of the person in a semiotically overdetermined collective-cultural context. Within that context, the person actively constructs her or his life course, filled with endurance, and miseries, as well as happiness. All these subjective phenomena are culturally organized, yet personally constructed—in all their complexity.

8

The Subjective World of Jenny:
A Case of Caring Suffocation

Analysis of personal culture—the sociogenetic equivalent of "personality"—can certainly proceed in many ways, some of which are immediate and involve direct contact of the investigator with the person and others are mediated through others' (or the self's) externalizations. At first glance it may seem that immediate contact with the person is necessarily preferable for an analysis. However, both immediate and mediated forms of investigation encounter the same set of difficulties in the form of the personal culture being always only *partially* and *episodically* externalized. Whether that partial externalization occurs in the context of an immediate encounter with the researcher (even in the context of a maximally thorough interview) or becomes available through mediated information sources (e.g., personal documents, self-narratives in the case of autobiography) does not eliminate the concrete episodic nature of this information. All information that is available—directly or indirectly—is incomplete, either by design (i.e., the person presenting some aspects of the internalized world at externalization, rather than others) or by coincidence.

All empirical evidence is episodic, partial, and incomplete. Any externalization of personal culture is constructed by the person in some specific here-and-now context, and in accordance with his or her personal sense of that context, personal goal orientations at the time, and the medium in which that externalization takes place. A psychologist is necessarily faced with the same inferential problems that plague sciences that deal with faraway (e.g., astrophysics) or long-ago existing (e.g., paleoanthropology) phenomena, access to which is inevitably limited. For instance, as was elaborated in the previous chapter, the seemingly cooperating person who interacts with the psychologist in a face-to-face situation can be taken for the guarantee of access to the complexity of personality. In reality, that seemingly cooperating person may be involved in goal-oriented self-presentation strategies, and hence numerous aspects of his or her personal culture may remain closed to the investigator—no matter how extensive is the contact or how cooperative the person may seem.

Empirical analysis makes sense when situated within the general methodology framework described in the previous chapter. Any return to previous analyses by other investigators serves as a way to demonstrate how the difference of methodological perspectives of the investigators gives us different kinds of highlighting of relevant phenomena. I have chosen the single empirical analysis of personal documents by Gordon Allport for such demonstration—a set of letters. Letters are obviously the most episodic of all forms of communication—when, for what purpose, and under what conditions the letters were written would not necessarily be available from the letters themselves. Of course our interpretation can project specific—again, theory-based—goal orientations into the materials. Allport's reasons for his analysis of the set of letters was demonstrably different from the use of the letters in this book. While Allport tried to characterize the personality via a system of characteristics in their functional relationships, my goal here is to use the case to illustrate how different semiotic organizers of the person's self—both within the self and in its presentation to others—are created, communicated, and used. Thus, the present reanalysis effort is both continuous with Allport's efforts (to demonstrate how the morphogenic analysis of personal documents might proceed) and discontinuous with it. In the latter direction, I will pay attention to specific semiotic devices that are used in the letters to organize one or another general understanding of the described situation, rather than to arrive at a description of the author of the letters as being of some kind of personality type.

Background of the *Letters from Jenny*

The case history of Jenny plays an important part in the history of personality research. This case has been the primary target for Gordon Allport's analysis of single cases using personal documents (Allport, 1965; Baldwin, 1942). In fact, it constitutes Allport's main case study, analyzed by him over long period of time (from the early 1940s until the mid-1960s). The reanalysis attempted here is meant to build historical continuity between Allport's work (outlined chapter 5) and the present sociogenetic perspective (outlined in chapters 2, 3, and 6).

The case of Jenny is remarkable because of Allport's personal connection with the case. In fact, the reported correspondents of Jenny's—identified in the letters as "Glenn" and "Isabel"—were Allport himself and his wife. The correspondence lasted from 1926 (when Jenny was fifty-eight years old) until her death, at age seventy, in 1937. After Jenny's death, Allport was remarkably slow in publishing the correspondence. Even though he had secured Jenny's agreement for the public use of the letters before her death (Allport, 1965, p. vi), it was only in 1946 that a selection of the letters appeared (Anonymous, 1946). Further publication—also not full—occurred only in 1965 (Allport, 1965). All in all, the correspondence is reported to have included 301 letters.

Despite the slowness of publication, Allport used the letters extensively in his teaching. He noted:

> I may say that I have found the Letters the most effective case material I have ever encountered for provoking fruitful class discussions of theories of personality. I have sometimes asked myself why they should be so stimulating and pedagogically so effective. Much credit must go to Jenny and her flair for clear and forceful expression of her perceptions and feelings. But there is a deeper reason. Every male reader is himself a son; every female reader is a mother or a potential mother. Therefore the bitter dilemma of Ross and his mother often seems to echo the reader's own personal (but usually milder) problem. Like a Greek tragedy the Letters have a universal appeal. (Allport, 1965, p. vi)

The challenge of the case of Jenny may be further accentuated by the limited access to the materials that Allport's contemporaries—especially of psychoanalytic persuasion—would have needed for making sense of the personality of the woman. The letters do not reveal any substantial or systematic evidence about Jenny's childhood—which was (and is) the assumed realm of relevance for personality development from psychodynamic perspectives. In fact, Allport's application of psychodynamic explanations to the letters (see Allport, 1965, chapter 7) indicates how any interpretation of these kinds necessarily becomes a retrospective reading-in of different psychodynamic explanatory terms into the assumed childhood of Jenny. Retroactive inference from materials produced at age fifty-eight (and more) to early childhood is more than questionable, especially as it is paired with the reverse causal statement from the projected childhood phenomena back to the personality of the elderly woman.

Allport's own analytic orientation took him to the extraction of specific personality trait structures from the letters, and efforts to describe the structure of meanings of persons and life events in Jenny's personal culture. The first explicit effort of this kind was Alfred Baldwin's "personal structure analysis," which was applied to early letters (1926–1927). It constituted a thematic contingency analysis of co-occurring emotional themes and persons (Jenny herself, Ross, etc.). Later, a fuller content analysis of the letters was performed by Jeffrey Paige (see Allport, 1965, pp. 199–205). From his perspective of trait analysis, Allport had relatively little difficulty arriving at a consensually shared picture of Jenny's personality. His thirty-six readers of Jenny's letters suggested 198 trait names, which clustered into larger groupings. Allport reported the results of that effort, indicating a certain ambivalence:

(a) Nearly all judges perceive as most prominent in the structure of Jenny's personality the traits of suspiciousness, self-centeredness, autonomy; and the majority remark also her dramatic nature, her aestheticism, aggressiveness, morbidity, and sentimentality. (b) While there may be disagreement concerning the classification of any given trait name, the main clusters are not difficult to identify. (c) The *reader, however, feels that these clusters are not independent of one another; they interlock; thus her sentimentality and her artistic nature seem somehow tied together, and her quarrelsomeness is locked with her aggressiveness.* For this reason we cannot claim by the trait-name approach to have isolated separate radicals in her nature. (Allport, 1965, pp. 194–195; emphasis added)

By the 1960s Allport may have arrived at the contradiction between exclusive and inclusive separation of phenomena (as described in chapter 1). The statistical tactics used for content analyses of the letters did bring out the general structure of personality traits (and their clusters), but these methods could not reveal the inherent connectedness between the phenomena assumed by the traits. Thus, despite consensual validation of the set of traits attributed to Jenny, the processual aspect of her personality could not be recovered from these analyses. In some respect, Allport's methods failed to be in line with his own theoretical developmental emphasis (as it was described in chapter 5). The difficulty of the empirical analysis efforts was that the analysis ended up with detection of different personality traits, while the theoretical system emphasized the functioning of the emerging traits (and radii) in the personality system.

The Life Course of Jenny

Allport (1965) provided a thorough analysis of Jenny's life course, complementing the letters with evidence from his own observations and with those of his wife. Here is the case description as it was reported in the very first publication on the materials:

> Jenny Gove Masterson was born in Ireland, the first child in the family, but was taken to Canada when she was very young. When Jenny was eighteen her father died. His death forced her to leave school to help support the rest of the family. She worked for nine years until all her siblings were able to take their places in the world before she resigned her job to get married. Because her husband had been previously married and divorced, Jenny's family strongly disapproved of her marriage to him. She married him in spite of their disapproval and after a quarrel which separated her from her family for several years.
>
> Her married life was boring to Jenny because she was not accustomed to be a passive housewife instead of an active breadwinner. Perhaps the care of her son would have reconciled her, but a month before he was born, her husband died. Jenny became a telegrapher in Ohio, living in the same building in which the office was located so that she could keep Ross, her son, with her constantly. When he was old enough to go to school, Jenny obtained employment as a librarian and later as a housemother in a girls' school so that she could be near Ross.
>
> Their relation was a close and happy one. She taught him to enjoy luxury by providing him with an expensive private-school education and ample spending money. Furthermore, she taught him that he owed her no gratitude for her sacrifice because she was responsible for bringing him into this sad and miserable world.
>
> When Ross was old enough to go to college, she sent him to Princeton, but she herself remained in Chicago as a librarian. She lived on an absolute minimum in order to provide him with suitable clothes and sufficient funds for luxuries. His college career, although interrupted by the war, was completed satisfactorily. Following college, he was rather poorly adjusted. He joined the marines for a year because he was unable to find steady employment. Jenny moved to

New York to be near him when he returned to civilian life, but their relation was no longer smooth and unperturbed. Jenny was very jealous of Ross's girl friends. She had conceived an intense hatred for the wife of one of Ross's professors, who she thought was immorally interested in Ross. During the period when she and Ross were both in New York they quarreled continually about girls in whom Ross was interested. When Ross was married, he hid it from his mother for a time, but she eventually discovered the fact by a little smart detective work. This discovery let to a serious quarrel, ending with Jenny's threat to have Ross arrested if she ever saw him again.

Since she seemed to need some contact with Ross's friends, she wrote to the boy who had been Ross's roommate in college. His name was Glenn and his wife's name was Isabel . . . Glenn and Isabel's correspondence with Jenny was very desultory at first, but began in earnest with a series of four letters from Jenny explaining her recent history, her desires for the future, and her fear that she would die at any moment. She requested Glenn and Isabel to act as her executors, to dispose of her body, and to receive her property if she should die.

The story is much more detailed from this time on because the letters recounting it month by month are available. Briefly, Jenny showed many symptoms of maladjustment. She couldn't stay in one town for long; she worked in a department store, in art shops, in a children's home, and in a hospital. Finally she communicated with Ross, partly through necessity, partly through desire. Ross and she were very friendly, had neighbouring apartments, and bought a car in partnership.

Their troubles had not ceased, however, but only recessed. Ross and his wife were divorced, but Jenny bitterly resented Ross's interest in other women. She found numerous defects in the character of each likely candidate for Ross's affection. A number of girls entered the scene, each to be succeeded by the next in line. Vivian, the last and most prominent, was not disliked at first but her interest in Ross made her thoroughly hated. Vivian and Ross became very friendly. He established her in an apartment and went on a vacation to the beach with her. During that vacation Ross contracted a mastoid infection which resulted in his death.

Following Ross's death Jenny tried several types of jobs, attempted to live in Montreal with her sister, but at last entered an old ladies' home in New York where she was to spend the rest of her life. Immediately following Ross's death she and Vivian had almost gone to court in a quarrel about Ross's belongings, but Jenny apparently won without an actual trial. She carried Ross's ashes with her in a box, never letting them leave her possession, until at last, in a constant fear of death, she took them to the beach to scatter them dramatically into the ocean.

In the old ladies' home, Jenny was at first happy and contented, but not for long. Distrust and suspicion led her to reject the other inmates and to rebel against the authority of the home. She ran away once, but was unable to enter Canada and had to go back to the home again. She lived there five years before she died, suddenly and dramatically, as she was entering the dining-room. (Baldwin, 1942, pp. 164–165)

Both Ross and Jenny had strong tempers, yet Jenny had the stronger will and temper, and a deep capacity for hatred. Ross tolerated her domination in his life to a point, beyond which he escaped to different relations with women (which only escalated the dilemma of caring domination by Jenny). After each of his amorous escapade—except the one at the time of his death—Ross returned to Jenny. Ross was

handsome, somewhat passive, charming and attractive to women. On social occasions we saw him as courteous and considerate of his mother, agreeable to her wishes . . . To Jenny Ross's sex needs and sex involvements were the big flaw in his nature, exploited by greedy and designing women. To us as outside observers Ross seemed essentially normal, surprisingly so, given his abnormally close relation to his mother until his college years. His weakness was rather one of ego and character structure, taking the easy way out, accepting what was given him without much feeling of obligation. (description by Isabel—in Allport, 1965, p. 149)

Ross was described as "neurotically in love with his mother" (Allport, 1965, p. 149). The difficult process of negotiating the individuation from his mother was made impossible by Jenny's counteractions. It is here that the divergence of goal orientations gives rise to maintenance of ambivalent conflictual states in personal relationships. We will examine in greater detail the period of March 1928 to November 1929, when the theme of reflecting on Ross's relationships with other women was the major theme in the letters.

MAKING OF DISTINCTIONS In the examples from Jenny's correspondence, an effort is made to demonstrate how Jenny organizes her thinking and feeling process. The transformation process in relationships is necessarily filled with ambivalences, yet these can be reconstructed through semiotic means. Thus, Shi-xu (1995) has demonstrated how Dutch travelers in a foreign society maintain their collective-cultural self-identity through "self"-"other" distinction via discourse. Viewing "the other" as inferior in some meaningful (to the self) ways says little about "the other" and much about the needs of the self's personality processes. No surprise that human interaction is filled with gossip, competitive comparisons, and stigmatization—and that parents of adult children can be viewed complaining about their children's ways of living. Fussing of mothers-in-law (not to speak of their more active ways of complicating the lives of their children and children's spouses) is a common theme in folklore and everyday life. Jenny's case is certainly one of these.

Episodes of Jenny's Construction of Her Self Through Others

The sequence of letters involved in the present application of the constraint notions is necessarily merely a narrow selection of the material (relative to Allportian analyses). What is selected here is the sequence of letters that gives Jenny's self-*presentation* (to the Allports) of her conceptualization of her son, Ross. My focus here—quite differently from Allport's—is on how Jenny *constructed her self-presentation* through semiotic devices that set up ZFM/ZPA field organization of the meanings she used to communicate her ambivalences with the inevitable loss of her "child"— first to other women and then to death. March 9, 1928: "The only *real thrill* I have ever experienced in my whole life was when I held Ross's tiny hand in mine and knew him to be *mine*. There isn't any experience in life that can compare with motherhood—every other experience can be duplicated, or counterfeited, but not motherhood" (Allport, 1965, p. 48).

Jenny's self-presentation involves mapping of the constrained field (via "the *only real*" ZFM boundary built between the set of *"real"* and *"other"*) of positively valued designation (*"thrill"*) on the maximally widened meaning field (*"ever* experienced . . . in my whole life"), then linked with the focus (via ZPA) on the personal ownership (as an interpretation of very specific nuance of the mother-child interaction). This is followed by linking the personal ownership with *"motherhood"* (a generalized meaning field—fielding the experience of *"holding tiny hand"* which meant *"he is mine"* within the glorification of motherhood in general: "there isn't *any* experience"). Furthermore, the boundaries of the positively marked "motherhood" meaning are immediately protected by comparison with "every other" experience (maximum open meaning field: "motherhood" versus "every other experience") by specifying what events ("duplication," "counterfeiting") cannot occur related to "motherhood."

The *modulation of the boundaries constructed within the fields of meanings* is a notable way of constructing the self-presentation here. Jenny moves from a general meaning field to a specific feature (holding the boy's hand) and back to general fields of "mine" and "motherhood." The latter makes it possible to give the former the flavor of collective-culturally legitimate and valued acceptance of the feelings of personal ownership. Hence cases of possessiveness and overprotection of children by parents are easily presentable as examples of devoted and "good" parenting. It may be of interest to contrast Jenny's words with those of Ross, who wrote to Glenn (on April 21, 1929): "Mother has entrenched herself behind truths, half-truths, and utter fabrications concerning my limitations as the ideal son, and there is no dislodging her. No amount of even demonstrating my presence will change her constant reiteration that I am entirely bad and have cast her off in her old age . . . Day and night, Mother recites her own good deeds to her family, her friends, her husband, her son, and how each in turn failed to pay her back" (Allport, 1965, p. 64).

The actual sequence of Jenny's self-presentational treatment of Ross's "problems" ranges from August 1928 to Jenny's ritualistic scattering of Ross's ashes in the ocean in 1932. Not every letter that is published includes pertinent material. That is quite reasonable, since the need for self-presentation to the given recipients (Glenn and Isabel) could emerge in Jenny's personal world episodically, sometimes triggered by a specific event (e.g., discovering some aspect of her son's amorous affairs), but at other times in the middle of other life experiences: August 28, 1928: "It isn't money that stands between Ross and me—not by any means—it's *women*—more women (My writing is awful—I'm all nerves). Sometimes I wonder if Ross is a trifle off balance—sex mad" (Allport, 1965, p. 51). "Now, my dear ones, I do not want you to misunderstand. I *do not* object to Ross's marrying, and said so, he is so made sexually that he *ought* to marry. But I won't be a party to *a lie*. If Ross wants to marry either Marie or any other prostitute, all right, I will help to make a plan, and be agreeable, but I refuse to take part in a lie. Ross is the *greatest liar* I have ever known" (p. 52).

For Jenny, the meanings of Ross's girlfriends either start from considering them "prostitutes" or change from an initial depiction of *"nice girl"* to that of *"prostitute."* The strategy of modulation of meaning fields is relatively simple—utilization of collective-cultural "prostitute" image guarantees the ZFM boundary in the presentation along the lines Jenny needs (i.e., projection of any negatively flavored characteristic to Ross's girlfriends via the use of the "prostitute" image). More important here is the setup of the contrast "I'M ALL NERVES" versus "WOMEN." Further coverage of the contrasted meaning fields by "diagnosing" the "problem" ("ROSS SEX MAD") with a qualification ("trifle"). Furthermore, Jenny uses the strategy of counterpositing her case ("I do not want you to misunderstand") and claims that she does not object to Ross's marriage (but—under the condition of her "making plain"—and promising to "be agreeable"—and under the notion that "he is so made sexually"). Jenny immediately uses the generalized meaning of "lie" (in reference to Ross's withholding of information from her, not described in the quoted excerpt), invalidating her previous self-presentational "generosity" ("I'll not be part of lie") and diagnosing Ross as "the greatest liar." Also it is here where the meaning fields of "prostitute" and "marriage" are set up in a relation that creates the cycle MARRY ("PROSTITUTE") → MEN SEXUALLY MADE → MOTHER CAN COOPERATE → BUT MAN LIES → HOW CAN HE DO SO→ MAN LIAR AND SEX-MAD → HOW CAN I COOPERATE (under these circumstances: as he wants to "marry a prostitute"). This discourse cycle allows Jenny to present herself as if she were flexible and accepting of Ross's personal life decision, yet immediately semiotically block her just-presented nominal acceptance by overriding it through general meanings of "liar" and "sex-mad." This episode is close in its semiotic organization to the use of semiotic means to create "fear of action" in one of Pierre Janet's psychiatric patients (see chapter 4): August 30, 1928: "The woman is merely a she-dog to me—the way she has crowded herself on Ross is, to me, a disgrace . . . He has had enough experience with women to last him for a year or so, and maybe by that time he may meet a woman who is decent—there must be some decent women, even in 1928, but up to this time he has evidently not met any of them (Allport, 1965, p. 54).

Jenny's construction of the world of Ross's women here is built upon a sequence of PERSONAL STATEMENT ("she-dog to me") → SPECIFIC (yet not informative in details!—"the way she has crowded herself on Ross") → another PERSONAL STATEMENT ("disgrace") → ELABO-

RATION → EXTENSION (to reflect—in parallel—on Ross's "experience" and "women [decent ones] even in 1928").

January 10, 1929:

If Ross intends to marry I should not be sitting here waiting, and wishing to die. I should have my teeth fixed—they need it badly—*rest,* not mope, get myself and my wardrobe in good shape, and when the spring comes, find a job.

Ross would be much healthier, and happier, if married. He should marry. We would not need to quarrel over it—it is not now in Ross's power to hurt me. He broke my heart long ago. We could make an arrangement, and if he is ever going to marry the woman it's about time. She can hardly be said to be in her first youth. To have people standing around waiting for me to die, is terrible. If I do not die fast enough they may be tempted to hurry me along, and that would indeed be tragic. (Allport, 1965, p. 57)

February 1, 1929:

The fact is that I am a sick lady—my heart is decidedly on the rocks, and the chances are that Ross won't have to wait so very long until he has the pleasure of sending me to the crematory . . .

Ross has a new affinity. She appears to be a very nice girl, he has brought her to the house several times. She is a combination of American-Irish-Scotch and has the very romantic name of Vivian Vold. She is in the Art Department of T. H. Co. (with Ross) designs silk patterns, combines colors, etc. She graduated from the art school here. She is a blond, very pretty, refined, and quite a lady in manner of bearing—very New York.

If he marries Vivian (they are quite intimate—he has known her a year or so) I feel quite sure he would urge me to remain with them—do the washing and cooking and the dishes, and cleaning, etc. Vivian isn't a lady to do much housework; but nothing doing—that won't ever happen. No matter who the lucky lady may be she will have to go it alone as far as I am concerned. (Allport, 1965, pp. 59–60)

After hearing of the accidental death of her sisters and a brother in Canada, Jenny sent Ross to help with the situation and meanwhile wrote (on February 23, 1929), "Vivian, *the nice girl I mentioned to you,* is stopping with me until Ross returns" (Allport, 1965, p. 61). By April 18, her expression is changed ("When Ross marries *his present dumb-bell,* if he is not already married to her, I shall . . ." and "She has no intellect. Ross does not care of people of intellect" (p. 62). The letter of the next day (April 19, 1929—compare with Ross's letter of April 21, cited earlier) allows the reader a glimpse of a narrative of self-explanation: "I am not a charming person—not beautiful—not clever, but what of that? I carried him in my body for 9 mos., was good to him for many years (you know that) altho' he says I wasn't—that it was all *selfishness* on my part—but even granting all that to be so—I am still *his* Mother. Oh! what is it that's so wrong? Be patient with me—I try you sadly—but I'm alone, and it's awful to be in the dark, and be alone" (pp. 63–64).

By May 31, 1929 Jenny's story continues:

> No, things have not improved for me. Ross's chip-lady (Vivian) is all settled-down in their apartment, about 15 minutes walk from our house, and Ross spends most of his time there—most of his nights certainly for he is seldom in this apt. until 4 or 5 A.M. . . . Ross is so unbelievably unprincipled unfeeling and almost inhuman, that—there is just nothing to be said . . .
>
> I have not spoken 10 words to him, or to anyone, in weeks . . . Ah! Glenn, my dear, Ross is not a good son, nor is he a decent fellow. Ross is sex-mad.
>
> The Chip is the flapper-type—assumes Baby ways, and that sort of nonsense. She might be called pretty, but has no intellect.
>
> There are times when I positively *hate* Ross—he is a contemptible cur. (Allport, 1965, p. 65)

Ross's side is depicted in his letter to Glenn (from July, 6, 1929):

> I am sorry not to have something cheerful to say about Mother and me. Our lives seem constant problems—so constant that I am lost in their maze and see neither right nor wrong nor any solution.
>
> Last night I was told that I am mad. And that appears to be a reasonable explanation, though it solves no difficulty.
>
> In a word, this is the situation. Ever since last summer I have returned home to be nagged about Marie. The artist friend, Vivian Vold, whom Mother adopted for four months, helped for a while to dampen the recriminations about Marie. Then Mother decided I stayed out too late with Vivian. Then Vivian moved into a flat, and Mother began throwing my meals at me . . . She never talked. She would not ride in the car. Whenever she broke silence at all it was to

call Vivian a whore, prostitute, rat, etc., and immediately bring in Grace and Marie.

And this has lasted since April first. Mother sometimes switches to threats . . . Meanwhile I am worried about my job which seems shaky, and my life which seems futile.

Meantime I can discuss nothing with Mother who will not talk— nor go anywhere with me. Every attempt boils down to a horrible scene, in which my various sexual debauches are described in the minutest details . . .

If anything except the passage of time were being accomplished, I would not object. But I get nowhere, have no fun, do nothing, live in struggle preserving enough sanity to continue supporting Mother and me, and trying to think out a means of living. (Allport, 1965, pp. 66–67)

Jenny's presentation continued (letter from August, 12, 1929): "Did I tell you that he has had the prostitute-woman in an ap't near us since May 1? He has practically lived with her all the time since. Well, now they are away some place on a vacation. They have been gone two weeks—I am quite alone. Sometimes I think that Ross is mentally unbalanced. There is no reason why he cannot marry the creature if he is fond of her, and if he is not fond of her why act this way?" (Allport, 1965, pp. 67–68).

As a result of the beach vacation, Ross developed an illness that necessitated surgery and a stay at a hospital. Immediately the power conflict between Jenny and Ross's girlfriend developed around the issue of who was considered to be "in charge" from the viewpoint of the hospital. Jenny wrote on September 10, 1929:

The "Chip" is there—morning, noon and night. She is entered in the ofc. as being "in charge of the case." I am nobody at all. When one of the Drs. told me that he couldn't explain the case to everyone and anything I wanted to know about it I must find out from "the young woman in charge" I nearly died. Ross assures me that he *is not* married, but it is quite evident that he wants the Chip to do everything for him and that I must be ignored. I do not recognize the Chip when there, but turn and walk out, and Ross seems to think that's as it should be. (Allport, 1965, pp. 68–69)

After discharge from the hospital, Ross was cared for by his girlfriend. Jenny's letter (of November 6, 1929) reflects her projection:

On hearing that he is living with that woman, and eating her bread—lying in bed mornings when *she* hustles out to work—I was in despair. Of course anyone (except Ross) could see why she does it. She must cajole him into a marriage ceremony—merely to protect *herself*—and then—well! then she will tell him what she thinks of him (and who could blame her), just as his first wife did . . .

. . . My plan is this—Ross acknowledged that he would not marry the chip at this time only that he is under a financial obligation to her, and feels that he *owes* her a marriage ceremony. I say, all right, marry her, but not now. Today he has nothing at all to offer her. Leave her and announce to her Father and friends that she is his fiancee, and that he is going to *make a home* for her. Then go, get a job—get himself in good physical condition, insure his life *for her*—have some money ahead, and then say "now here's the home I have made for you" and return to N.Y. and marry her. (Allport, 1965, p. 71)

Ross died of medical complications two days later, on November 8, 1929. The two women—Jenny and Vivian—met at the funeral, where Jenny did her best to attack the latter: "On the way to the crematory Glenn sat between Jenny and the 'chip' in the limousine. While the latter was decently silent Jenny kept sending barbed verbal darts across Glenn to her" (Isabel, in Allport, 1965, p. 153).

In her subsequent letters to Glenn and Isabel, Jenny expressed her feelings of safety for Ross (March 6, 1930: "Nobody can injure Ross now—Ross is safe, and is all mine as of yore—I don't have to share him with anybody" July 27, 1930: and "Now Ross is safe with his Mother again—nothing can separate us now—Ross is safe"—Allport, 1965, pp. 79, 85). Finally, in a symbolic break with Ross, Jenny decided to throw his ashes into the ocean. Fear of her own death (a recurrent theme in her letters) led Jenny to dramatize her departure from Ross's remains. On October 27, 1932, she wrote to Glenn:

I, too, may drop out suddenly—my affairs are not in good shape. Ross's ashes was still on the top shelf of my closet—those people here would probably fling it into the garbage box—it would be all my fault. I must dispose of it myself. . .

. . . It rained on Oct. 12 and 13. I put on storm rubbers, took the ashes, and went. Rain. Rain. On reaching the end of pier I found *8 or 10 men fishing*. The boardwalk was deserted. There were some beachcombers on the beach but not many—I wandered on, intending to select a breakwater, climb out on the stones to deep water and then— On standing at the rail to look around, a beachcomber—a dirty, filthy-looking ragged fellow made signs to me and pointed under the boardwalk. I actually leaned over the rail to look, feeling sure there must be someone needing help there, maybe dead, or dying—but alas, no. This dirty, filthy ragged brute evidently wanted *me* to go down. There wasn't a policeman anywhere. Certainly I could not now get to a breakwater. And then a man came on the walk. I followed him—he was a respectable looking man—wore good clothing, gloves, carried an umbrella. It was growing late. I touched the man on the arm, he looked at me in surprise; I said "Are you a decent man?" Well, he said that depends on what one calls decent, he tried to be. I asked if he believed in cremation; he said on principle he did, but his wife and family did not, and so he supposed that he would be buried—*but,* he added, what difference does it make when one is dead. He had a strong, nice voice. I told my trouble and asked if he would stand on the beach, hold my purse and umbrella, and protect me from beach-combers while I climbed out on the breakwater. He thought a while, looked grave, and finally said Yes, if I gave my word *not to commit suicide*. The stones were very slippery—green with slime—the tide was coming in and the waves dashed over me, but I went on. The man shouted what stones I should grab. It was done—ah Ross. But I had gone out pretty far—and it was easier to go out than get back. I slipped badly. The man shouted to *sit down*—for God's sake *sit down*. As I knew I could not hold a footing I sat down. The tide dashed over me. The man shouted that I was now wet as I could be and to step down, lift up my skirts and walk in—I did.

He walked to the station with me—helped me wring out my jacket and skirt . . . We shook hands—he hoped I would not get pneumonia—but I said that people like me do not die—a young mother with children dependent on her would get pneumonia, but not I. He was gentleman enough not to ask my name, or a thing about me, nor tell his. Now it's done, it is well. (Allport, 1965, pp. 105–106)

ALLPORT'S ANALYSES OF JENNY   Surely the multifacetedness of mother love is expressed in Jenny's self-presentations of her relations with her son in ways that defy simple analysis. Allport paraded the explanatory systems of his time—existentialist, Freudian, Jungian, ego-psychological, and so on—in front of the readers of the letters. Each of these systems of explanation *could* be applied to *some* aspects of the materials from the letters, yet none could provide a systematic explanation of Jenny's personality. Allport's own structural-dynamic approach (Allport, 1965, chapter 8) continued along the lines of his personological theory (see chapter 5) and ended up with a clustering of personality descriptors. In his final word, Allport claimed, "Eclecticism in personality theory is no doubt necessary, but it is the task for the future to blend the approaches so that a *systematic* eclecticism, a true synthesis of theories, will emerge" (Allport, 1965, p. 211).

However, a systematic eclecticism may mean a new theoretical organization of a view on personality, rather than synthetic combination of existing theories. Jenny's letters included creative use of language in all its richness, which only some psychologists have dared to analyze in its everyday form (Heider, 1958).

Jenny's Uses of Semiotic Canalization Devices

Jenny's letters reveal a sequence of self-canalization and recanalization of her self-presentations to her recipients. Through coordination of ZFM/ZPA structures of specific meanings that she used, Jenny could build up a discourse of accusing Ross of a set of different wrongdoings (as well as try to make him look "mad" or "ill"), while sustaining her positive mother's role as a caring and helpful person—even through the rhetoric use of self-denigration strategies (e.g., "I am X, but this is as I am Y, which is legitimate, since . . .").

Surely the case of Jenny is no extreme in the wide world of overcontrolling mothers and jealous persons. Its analysis reveals more or less the "tip of the iceberg" of the semiotic processes that were taking place within the personality system during the episodes described by Ross (about their everyday interaction) or Isabel (about Jenny's conduct at the funeral). The specific tactics of semiotic constructions of the presentations included structures of ZFM/ZPA, which are modulated in ways that rule out undesirable interpretations—sometimes blocking them through some collective-culturally accepted meanings, at other times through suggesting the undesirables and then blocking the suggested train of reasoning by overriding opposite meanings. Elaboration of general forms of such social regulation of human conduct is a question for basic knowledge—albeit supportable from systemic single-case data and applicable to further individual cases.

Strategic Communication Through Semiotic Means

Jenny's examples can provide us with a lead-in to the variety of complex forms of regulation of personal culture. Personal culture becomes externalized in specific contexts, embued with strategic overtones created by goal orientation. In those externalizations, the constraint systems simultaneously perform the function of guiding one's own and others' views of the self. Complex structures of ZFM/ZPA-ZPD can be utilized for such a task.

It would be interesting to try to synthesize the constraining-perspective expressed in this book with other traditions of analysis of personal meanings. Here, Wierzbicka's action-descriptive semantics (Goddard, 1995; Wierzbicka, 1992, 1995) and Smedslund's psycho-logic (Smedslund, 1988) could be considered as models of generalized analysis of tactics of self-presentation. All these forms are examples of coordination of primary, secondary, and tertiary representational fields of Karl Bühler (as described in chapter 6; see also Figure 2.3). The dynamic flexibility of the human semiotic constraining process is visible in the coordination of deductive and inductive flows of reasoning in social role–based conduct (Litvinovic and Valsiner, 1993). Schemes of flexible canalization are observable through dialogic approaches to human meaning-circumvention strategies (Josephs and Valsiner, 1996). An elaboration of some forms of semiotic self-regulation devices in their generic forms may be of use here.

Examples of Generic Strategic Forms of Constraint Structures

DIRECT SETUP OF A ZFM/ZPA SYSTEM WITH RECURRENCE In this case the person sets a goal G. The field of usable meanings is set up in accordance with G, in conjunction with repeated (or variable) uses of meanings from the ZFM-defined field as ZPAs. For example:

G =   to persuade the interlocutor that "I am a good person"
ZFM =   include all positively flavored self-descriptive terms, and block
            the possibility to access negatively flavored ones.

ZPA = create a subset of terms to which to refer in a sequential manner, with or without contextualization of each through linking it with episodes of experience.

The following texts could be generated by this ZFM/ZPA structure:

Text 1: "I am a good person. I am honest. I help others. I always want to make life nice for others," and so on. [The text is generated by highlighting different subparts of the ZFM-defined field, with no repetitions.]

Text 2: "I am a good person, I am honest even when I see others not being honest. Even when I know others are immoral I remain honest," and so on. [The text is generated with repetition of the selected ZPA, linking the ZPA with contrasting cases of "the others."]

Text 3: "I am a good person. I am honest. Let me tell you [story about some concrete episode of honesty]," and so on. [The text is generated through repetition of the same ZPA linked with different described episodes, i.e., contextualized use of the ZPA term.]

SETUP OF ZFM/ZPA SYSTEM WITH BLOCKING COUNTER-MEANINGS This is a more complex general form of externalization. Here, too, the ZFM/ZPA complex is set up as in the previous form, but the opposite suggestions are used to protect the ZFM boundaries, as well as accentuate the ZPA:

G = to persuade the interlocutor that "I am a good person"

ZFM = include all positively flavored self-descriptive terms and block the possibility to access negatively flavored ones; countermeanings to mark ZFM boundaries; include the opposites of the ZFM-included meanings, marked by immediate affective-declarative denial of their truthfulness

ZPA = create a subset of terms to which to refer in a sequential manner, with or without contextualization of each through linking it with episodes of experience; contrasting ZPA concepts create the subset of opposites of the ZPA terms, together with their discounting devices

The previous text examples would look different if generated by this form. For instance, consider a modulation of Text 1: "I am a good person.

You may think that I am not—but I am! I am honest. Surely *bad people may tell you* this is not true, but it is! I help others. People are so prejudiced and do not notice people who help others. I always want to make life nice for others. Maybe you don't believe that, but in all honesty—I like to make it nice for others," and so on. This text is generated by highlighting different subparts of the ZFM-defined field, introducing counterclaims that are immediately overridden by the author. There are no repetitions, except the last return to the "I am honest" kind.

STRATEGIC "TRAPS" IN SELF-PRESENTATION The third form of externalization works on the principle of presentation of the opposite in order to prove the point.

G = to persuade the interlocutor that "I am a good person"—via external presentation of the opposite "I am a bad person," providing the interlocutor with expectation of denial and reverse persuasion of the person

ZFM = include all negatively flavored self-descriptive terms, and promote the possibility of accessing positively flavored ones

ZPA = create a subset of terms that facilitates the interlocutor's rejection of the self-presentation and evokes the opposite meanings

The following is an example of a dialogue generated by this setting of traps:

Person: I am such an awful person: a liar, I cheat others, etc.
Interlocutor: Hmh . . . well, surely you do not lie all the time.
Person: No, I do, almost all the time . . . and I am not nice with others.
Interlocutor: Well, nobody can always be nice with others.
Person: You are too good to me . . . I also have bad wishes for others.
Interlocutor: Maybe they deserve it, etc.

Surely these forms of modulation of externalization of ZFM/ZPA complexes do not exhaust the human repertoire of self-expression. Neither would they cover the complexity of Jenny's case, even if some of these forms can be located in her letters. The microgenetic process of externalization can constructively create new forms, combine others, and face new presentations in the immediate future. Goal orientation is a necessary starting point of such externalizations. Psychology has tried to avoid teleological assumptions in its theoretical core, but when we analyze persons' externalizations, we cannot but notice the teleogenetic (goals-constructing) nature of human psychological processes.

Conclusions: Learning From Jenny

The present small reanalysis of some of Allport's materials demonstrates the great richness of the tactics through which a person's self-presentations (to others and to his or her own self) are set up. Jenny's constantly changing feelings about the women in Ross's life were communicated by way of discursive means that set up *loci of dramatizations*. Such loci are *complex structures of self-presentation* in specific contexts (or about such contexts, as Jenny's letters indicate). Such structures are dynamically constructed, filled in with general feeling-tone (see chapter 7—the focus of the "Second Leipzig School"), and altered—possibly diametrically, and to an opposite general set of claims and feeling-tone. Such quick restructuration possibilities exist due to the tension generated by the A ↔ non-A tensions (see chapter 1); they indicate that human semiotic self-constraining possibilities exist in a flexible form. In other words, the widely acclaimed human tendencies of moving from love to hate, or from war to peace, by way of quick transitions that often are surrounded by "memory loss" of the previously dramatized opposites, is a reflection of the dualities-based semiotic organization of human systems of meaning (Gupta and Valsiner, 1996). Specific constraint systems emerge from the tensions within such structured fields of meanings, ready for regulation of the person's immediate conduct, as well as for their own transformation should the immediate context trigger it.

Surely such personal-cultural flexibility is itself constrained—via collective-cultural meaning systems that set up their own constraints for personal cultures. In chapter 9, a case of one such constraining system from the history of India is presented. The structured contexts for the life courses of Hindu temple dancers over the last fourteen centuries—even without much direct personal evidence—provide an elucidation of the guided nature of self-guiding psychological systems.

9

Personality Dancing in the Temple: Cultural Constraining and Sensuality

Human development entails personal construction of subjectivity under specific collective-cultural constraining processes. These processes are dynamic, taking place in irreversible time and within structured contexts of real life. These contexts are meaningful, as their structure is organized semiotically. Since subjectivity primarily entails a constant stream of operations upon the intrapersonal feelings field, the semiotic constraining operates at the levels of both emotional connotations and mental constructions (as outlined in chapters 2 and 3). Many of those connotations belong to the areas of personal culture that are closed to outside observation. Human sensuality is certainly an area where psychology at large has had little direct access. At the same time, psychological discourse is filled with theoretical constructions and episodic allusions to the powers of sexuality (and sensuality).

Dialogues with Psychoanalysis

The issue of sexuality has certainly been given much consideration within psychoanalysis, although from a perspective that may have built a theoretical castle on the uneasy grounds of *pars pro toto* error of generalization. The facts about the relevance of sexuality-linked imagery and dreams that psychoanalysts have diligently interpreted remain beyond challenge, yet their interpretation can be challenged on the grounds that there is no compelling reason that *all* psychological phenomena of adults must follow from *some* psychosexual problem in childhood (see Obeyesekere's 1990 criticism of psychoanalytic thought in chapter 4). Undoubtedly many psychological problems of most of Freud's patients could have arisen on a psychosexual basis, but the latter was intricately canalized (in the sense of the constraining theory outlined in chapter 2) by the collective culture of the middle-class Viennese (and other European) social role expectations. The received view on sexuality in psychoanalysis has been that of its constraining by society in directions that force the "sexual energy" to transform into different forms. Hence, an analysis of those forms was assumed to trace their origins in psychosexual problems.

In the present theoretical system, it is assumed that the relation between sexuality (and sensuality) with social worlds is *not* unidirectional (i.e., the arrow of causality does not run from SEXUAL ISSUES → PSYCHO-LOGICAL PROBLEMS), nor is it uniform (i.e, there exists no single normative relation between sexuality and psychological phenomena). Rather, human collective-cultural meaning construction can constrain the meanings of sexuality in human psychological lives in different ways. Under some circumstances, early traumatic psychosexual events can be viewed as leading to later psychological problems. However, this is posited to happen under specific ways in which collective culture charts out human life course models. Alternatives to such a model—even if it has been glorified by psychoanalysis as *the* model for life course—may entail interesting possibilities. For example, a collective-cultural meaning system may guide laypersons (including psychologists) to look at early psychosexual events as mere coping tasks for the developing person (i.e., the core of development is an "active coper" who faces challenges—including psychosexual traumas—and overcomes them). On the other extreme, the axiomatic arrow of direction of influences can be reversed. Some psychological life problem— a psychological "trauma"—may lead to problematic rearrangements in the sphere of sexuality.

Positing multiple relations between sexual and psychological domains is not (yet another) deconstruction effort of psychoanalytic explanatory systems. That task has been attempted by many and done successfully by few (Janet—see chapter 4; Obeyesekere, 1990). Instead, the goal here is to demonstrate how the complexity of the organization of personal culture through collective cultural constraining can produce versions of personality organization where psychological, social role, and sexual/sensual aspects of existence are tied together in ways by far more complex than any direct linear causality scheme would assume (e.g., see an analytic effort by Giles, 1994). This complexity entails examples of intransitive hierarchical power relations (as described in chapter 2) and is built around the redundant unity of ritualistic action systems (social roles in the Hindu temple activities) and collective-cultural meanings (of the role of female sexual powers, different meanings of love, and corresponding texts).

The case of Hindu temple dancers *(devadasis)* is a domain of sociocultural and psychological phenomena that could provide contemporary cultural-historical psychology evidence about the constructive processes between collective and personal cultures. These women represented a relevant cultural-institutional profession throughout the history of Hindu temple contexts (Chatterjee, 1945; Kersenboom, 1984). They were (and, wherever the tradition survives, continue to be) agents of promotion of the unity of personal-cultural and collective-cultural worlds, which is the main role carried by the temples in society (Beck, 1976; Desai and Mason, 1993; Schnepel, 1993). As will be shown, even if the cultural history of the *devadasi* tradition is declining, traces of that history may prevail in the personal culture of individuals.

The Cultural Worlds of the Temple Dancers

The Hindu temple is an architectural construction that semiotically mediates interpersonal relations (Appadurai, 1985; Dayalan, 1992). Socially prescribed roles within the temple create contexts in which visitors undergo relevant psychological work upon their personal cultures (Obeyesekere, 1981, 1990). Within this context, "the *devadasi* herself is a very expressive semiotic unit signifying the mythical-aesthetic-cum-ritual object residing in the collective consciousness of Hindu tradition . . . [That semiotic unit consists of] . . . the signifier being her own person and the signified being the Hindu tradition in which she functions" (Kersenboom, 1984, pp. 4, 300).

The social context of the dancers was semiotically overdetermined in its cultural history. The dancers' roles in the temple entailed dynamic social and personal complexity, a result of their religious and sensual facets being unified in one psychological complex.

The Meaning of *Devadasi*

The term denoting a Hindu temple dancer—*devadasi*—literally means "servant to the God"; the temple dancers also were referred to as "heavenly courtesans" (*swargabesya* or *apsaras*—Marglin, 1985, p. 91). The latter designation links the temple dancers with the socially highly relevant roles of courtesans in history, including that of the complex social world of India (Hasan, 1983; Oldenburg, 1984, 1990). The *devadasis* were "ever-auspicious women" *(nitya-su-mangali)* who were ritually married to the deity and never formed a caste (Kersenboom, 1984).

The dancers' main role was to perform specific ritual dances at ceremonies, as well as being involved in other duties in and around the temple. Yet it was the meaning of these activities, rather than the externally observable behavior per se, that defined the cultural role of the *devadasis*. The opposition of life-enhancing and life-destroying forces has a central role in Hindu meaning systems (see Menon and Shweder, 1994, also described in chapter 4; and Much and Mahapatra, 1995). These two forces must be kept in balance, which is the theme of many temple rituals. In that context, "The *devadasi-nityasumangali* was extremely important as a person who is guaranteed 'danger proof': she should be present in those critical moments of balancing the auspicious and the inauspicious. She was to remove the accumulated destructive force of evil eye" (Kersenboom, 1984, p. 9).

The *devadasis* were of critical relevance in the world of devotion to deities. Not only did they become skilled ritual specialists themselves, but their role included providing social guidance of the visitors to the temple toward higher forms of religious devotion. The history of the special social role of *devadasis* in Hindu temples is closely linked with the development of *bhakti* (devotional) religious movements in southern India (Hardy, 1983). As such, the social role of the *devadasis* united the public role of display of sensuality in the context of temple rituals with specific forms of sexual conduct that were ruled out for married Hindu women and specific power roles linking deities and local rulers.

Social Construction of a Stigma: How *Devadasis* Were Cast As Prostitutes

The history of human societies is rich in acts of colonization and stigmatization. Sociomoral dominance over the devotion and loyalty of persons go hand in hand with political control in societies. After the British colonized India, most of the reflections upon the *devadasi* system have been made under the influence of modern European tendencies to view the world through the lens of economic commoditization (see Kopytoff, 1986). The social role of the *devadasis* who united their personal sensuality with devotional religion made them an ambiguous target for Westerners' description and evaluation.

A culture's semiotic units are often viewed from the ideological standpoint of an outside interpreter. It is exactly the *devadasi* semiotic role in society that has proven difficult for the social sciences to analyze, since those sciences are guided by the ideologies of occidental societies that were linked with the sociopolitical practices of colonialism. Furthermore, processes of building and maintaining self-identity operate within persons when they encounter "cultural others" (see Shi-xu, 1995), which further complicates the understanding by outsiders of semiotic units such as the *devadasi* in the Hindu temple context. Westerners project their available meanings upon the cultural complex of "the other" (society), together with their (Western) ambivalences and (de)valuations. As a result, a cultural complex of another society becomes the far-off battleground for cultural fights of the interpreting one.

The complexity of the *devadasi* role has been impossible to unravel in terms of the exclusively separated Western dichotomy of "morality" versus "immorality." As a result of British colonial superimposition of such dichotomies upon Hindu cultural traditions, the temple dancers (as well as women's other religious-sensual social roles in other countries throughout history) have been socially stigmatized by the application of the value-laden label "prostitutes." Even if that translation of the *devadasi* tradition into the nineteenth-century English meaning system has sometimes been qualified (e.g., calling the *devadasi* "sacred prostitutes" or "temple prostitutes"), the cross-cultural translation of the unit into a Western worldview has succeeded in blocking inquiry into the unit itself. As a result, at least ignorance (and at most social stigmatization) about the complexity of the dancers' social roles, as well as of their personal lives, has been produced in the pertinent social sciences.

Aside from the British cultural outsiders, many representatives of social movements in India (Heggade, 1983; Raghuramaiah, 1991; Ranjana, 1983) have also labeled the *devadasis* "temple prostitutes," in line with the unclear but negative connotation that the term "prostitute" has acquired in social discourse in the Western world (Davis, 1937). Within that social discourse, the repressive, Christianity-based conceptualization of female sexuality has flavored most understanding of women in their many social roles (see Foucault, 1980, 1986). Thus it has been easy—from the power position of modern colonial powers—to stigmatize the widespread traditions of women's sensuality-linked participation in religious institutions all over the ancient world of pre-Christian times (e.g., Lerner, 1986). Social stigmatization through collective-cultural meanings of immediately emotiogenic connotations is a widely used semiotic vehicle for goal-oriented canalization of personal interpretations and knowledge in socially desired directions. For the social sciences aimed at reaching general knowledge, such stigmatization constitutes a phenomenon to be explained rather than a starting point for any knowledge construction.

Powers of Social Representations

Ever since Durkheim, social scientists have paid attention to the relevance of collective or social representations as organizers of human interaction and thought (see also chapter 4). What usually remains de-emphasized in discussions of social representations is the goal-oriented use of such representations in social practices. Any use of social representations entails the user's goal-oriented discourse, which starts from a specifiable orientation. By evoking a specific social representation as a general meaning, the evoker sets up a direction, a meaning-based perspective from which to interpret a particular target event. The boundaries of the meaning field of the given social representation set up the ZFM stage for the range of various interpretations. Within that range, ZPAs can be specified to further guide the thinking about the target issue.

When we observe the *devadasi* being referred to as "temple prostitutes" (e.g., Chatterjee, 1945; Heggade, 1983; Ranjana, 1983; Raghuramaiah, 1991), a collective-cultural interpretation is being set up in one way. When, alternatively, in treatises of ancient Indian dance or temple contexts one would find quite different representations (e.g., that of professional dancers—Ismail, 1984; Kersenboom, 1984; Khokar, 1979; Marglin, 1985), our interpretive framework is set up in a clearly different direction. Surely which framework is set up (which social representations are evoked as organizing meanings) depends upon the ideological goal-orientedness of the persons (or institutions) doing the orienting.

In short, ideological positioning sets up the frame for making sense of the cultural complexity of "the other." Protection of some social roles can be seen as the basis for creating social stigmas through evoking social representations. Thus, in the middle of the nineteenth century, the way in which prostitution was explained is clearly linked with collective-cultural construction of male (and female) sexuality. Occidental moralization seems to be behind many explanations of prostitution, as in the following: "There appear to have been in every age men who *did not avail themselves of the marriage covenant,* or who could not be bound by its stipulations, and their *appetites created a demand for illegitimate pleasures,* which *female weakness* supplied. This may be assumed to be the real origin of prostitution throughout the world, though in particular localities this first cause has been assisted by *female avarice or passion,* religious superstition, or a *mistaken sense of hospitality*" (Sanger, 1859, p. 35). The added emphases here indicate the semiotic encoding of the sociomoral connotations of the author (and the ideologies circumvented through him). The *active* male role was assumed to break social rules, and the *emotionality and other "weaknesses"* of the female *psyche* to complement that breakage. A number of historical studies have pointed to the historically constructed nature of male/femaleness (e.g., Foucault, 1986; Rossiaud, 1985) in the Western meaning systems, which have acted as axiomatic bases for most of the social sciences.

Early Western descriptions of the *devadasi* custom built upon the moralistic orientations of the travelers to India on the one hand and the existing historical narratives about "temple prostitution" on the other (e.g., Herodotus, 1954, pp. 121–122). Thus, the French priest Dubois (who stayed in Madras and Mysore in the late eighteenth century) has provided an account of the temple dancers that indicates the heteroglossia between his "moral Christian" and "traveller's fascinating voices." On the one hand, he spared no words to indicate his moral disapproval of the custom (e.g., calling the *devadasis* "lewd women," viewing temples as "converted into mere brothels"), while on the other hand he recognized the dancing and singing as educational and "appearance decency" (Dubois, 1905, pp. 585, 586). The *devadasi* as a cultural phenomenon is a puzzle for European minds.

Occidental Meanings of "Prostitution"

Despite excessive efforts to clearly define it, the term *prostitute* remains ill defined, in ways that may emphasize undefinable terms, such as "emotionally indifferent selling of sexual favors on a promiscuous basis" (May, 1935, p. 553). The monetary exchange and (assumed) emotional indifference facets of the phenomena of prostitution have been repeatedly emphasized. Alternatively, social responsibilities have been made into the anchor point: "By *prostitutes* I mean *individuals generally of the female sex, who use their sex for the purpose of making a living.* Looked from the standpoint of man's feeling of kinship, prostitution is an occupation based upon the fact that *instead of insisting upon the manifold and fundamental responsibilities contained in sexual intercourse, it treats it on the analogy of trade as a monetary equivalent*" (Adler, 1924, p. 327).

Adler's explanation—from a Eurocentric viewpoint—proves nicely how the *devadasi* example *cannot* be viewed as a case of prostitution. It is clear that the *devadasis* (in the case of Jagannatha temple, described later) did not "use their sex for the purpose of making living"; instead, they were provided for by the temple, and only accepted additional gifts from their admirerers. The *devadasis* were keen at "insisting upon the manifold and fundamental responsibilities contained in sexual intercourse" (which, in the case of Puri, amounted to devotional relations with the deity and his representatives), and under no circumstances was *devadasi* activity an "analogy of trade" involving "monetary equivalent."

Thus, Alfred Adler's culturally and historically specific definition leads us to the basic uncertainty about what prostitution is semiotically made to be. In societies, it is a service profession of high ambivalence in the meaning system of collective culture—it is both accepted and symbolically rejected. This semiotic ambivalence is reflected in the definitional difficulties—segregating phenomena that come under prostitution from the conditions of any human service occupation have been pointed out (e.g., Hirschi, 1962). In fact, a narrow definition of prostitution seems possible only in narrow sociomoral terms of Western societies, where an effort is made to stigmatize the phenomenon by defining it. Such definitions end up being useless for social sciences, as Kingsley Davis has pointed out:

> We cannot . . . define prostitution simply as the use of sexual responses for an ulterior purpose. This would include a great proportion of all social behavior, especially that of women. It would include marriage, for example, wherein women trade their sexual favors for an economic and social status supplied by men. It would include the employment of pretty girls in stores, cafes, charity drives, advertisements. It would include all the feminine arts that women use in pursuing ends that require men as intermediaries, arts that permeate daily life, and, while not generally involving actual intercourse, contain and utilize erotic stimulation.
>
> . . . The basic element in what we actually call prostitution—the employment of sex for non-sexual ends within a competitive-authoritative system—characterizes not simply prostitution itself but all of our institutions in which sex is involved, notably courtship and wedlock. Prostitution therefore resembles, from one point of view, behavior found in our most respectable institutions. (Davis, 1937, p. 746)

In a similar vein, the resemblance of prostitution and other service professions has been socially overlooked (see Hirschi, 1962, for a penetrating analysis). In our day, we hear numerous moralistic stories about AIDS risks

in contacts with prostitutes, but we overlook comparable health risks involved in automobile accidents in a hired taxicab. Once societal discourse
has rendered a particular meaning to bear negative connotations, the definitional and social representational means utilized will guide the discourse
along those lines (see ZFM/ZPA complexes as described in chapter 2).
The functionality of the connotationally flavored phenomenon within the
society and personal-cultural worlds remains overlooked. It can be documented that the notion of "temple prostitution" emerged in conjunction
with the "vice wars" in England (see also Mitter, 1977, chapter 11). Social
scientists are servants to the temple of sociomoral discourses of a society,
and their socialization in this predicament may be as overdetermined as
that of the *devadasis.*

Overcoming the Stigma: Historical Background of the Devadasi *Custom*

Although primarily known in southern Indian contexts, the practice of
young women's dedication to temple service was spread widely across
India's diverse culture (see Patil, 1975; Shankar, 1990). The earliest record
of the *devadasi* custom dates back to the second century B.C. and has
been discovered at Jogimara cave in Ramgarh Hill in central India (Desai,
1985, p. 107). The institution of *devadasis* started to gain prominence
around the seventh to eighth centuries (Dayalan, 1992), reached its most
advanced state by the eleventh to twelfth centuries (Prasad, 1990), and
has continued even under sociolegal attacks up to the present time
(Tarachand, 1991).

There is substantial heterogeneity within the specific semiotic and activity organization of the roles of *devadasis* (Bradford, 1983; Patil, 1975).
This heterogeneity stems from the highly heterogeneous nature of the set
of traditions in Indian religious practices that typically have been subsumed under the label of "Hindu religion" yet constitute a myriad of very
different (even if overlapping and interdependent) collective-cultural
meanings and practices (Kolenda, 1983; Preston, 1983). The emergence
of the term *Hinduism* in the social sciences has its own peculiar history
(Frykenberg, 1989). Contrary to the desires of Eurocentric scientists who
are used to thinking in terms of homogeneous classes, the label is best
treated as a depiction of a heterogeneous class (Beteille, 1965; Von Stietencron, 1989). It is in the context of recognition of heterogeneity that
psychological phenomena can be adequately conceptualized. Further-

more, the heterogeneous "Hinduism" is present in all aspects of human life. It flavors all aspects of living, and as such is particularly difficult to describe in any canonical form.

Actual descriptions of the *devadasi* custom reflect a similar heterogeneity. In various regions they are named differently (e.g., *maharis* in Kerala; *jogatis* or *basavis* in Karnataka; *natis* in Assam; *bogams* in Andhra Pradesh; *muralis* in Maharashtra; *padiyilar* and *devaradiyar* in Tamil Nadu—Ismail, 1984; Patil, 1975; Shankar, 1990). *Devadasis* could be encountered in rural or urban temples, and the rules that delimit their possibility to take on a marital status vary from strictly unmarriable with human males (since they were married to the deity), to married (Tarachand, 1991). They could be of highly varied caste backgrounds, and may have entered religious service via a number of routes (Bradford, 1983)—intergenerational transfer of the dancer's role, adoption by a *devadasi* as a child, dedication by parents to the temple as gratitude for deity's good deeds, or for need of money. Once within the temple service, the young girls were to remain as *devadasis* all of their lives (even if the actual dancing roles may have ended in their middle age). The temple provided the *devadasis* with basic means of subsistence (land, salary), to which gifts from visitors to the temples added further resources. The *devadasis* were economically well-established ritual specialists in temple service whose role was recognized as positive, honorable, and necessary for the whole of society.

The conditions for the emergence of the *devadasi* profession were economic as well as religious. The sociohistorical role of Hindu temples was that of places for social regulation of dramas of power or devotion, as well as of economic interchanges (Appadurai, 1981a). The accumulation of wealth generated by the feudal economic system led to a wave of temple construction in South India by the seventh to eighth centuries. The temples emerged as symbolic places within which unity of the powers of religious deities of various functions and kinds, the local kings (viewed as both rulers and servants of the deities—Appadurai and Appadurai-Breckenridge, 1976; Schnepel, 1993), and people of various castes and psychological needs was maintained and renegotiated semiotically (Pandian, 1983). In the case of religious practices in South India, such renegotiation entailed the unification of erotic *(akam)* and heroic *(puram)* folk models: "The world of eros *(akam)* came to include not only the emotional world between two human beings but, due to the influence of Brahmanic speculation, it became an emotional rapport with the divine, personified by the heroic god" (Kersenboom, 1984, p. 52).

The needs of the local social system were linked with the differentiation of ritual functions to be performed by specifically designated personnel of the temple. Dance in the context of a Hindu temple is a form of prayer, as it brings into motion relevant religious myths. It was in the context of dance that the erotic and heroic worlds of mythology were displayed in interdependent ways and the worlds of gods and kings were marked to be fused. Furthermore, it was through the services of ever-auspicious women of the temple—whose symbolically erotic function was part of the religious purification—that visitors to the temple could destroy their sins (Kersenboom, 1984, pp. 94–95). Dancing and recital of the religious texts required designated, well-prepared specialists, who were deserving of their special status in the temple context. Given the role of the erotic facet in religious unification, and the belief in female sexual powers, only girls could be assigned such important roles. However, in order to make them semiotically enabled to take these roles, their personal life courses had to be redirected away from the usual female roles. Thus they became married to a deity, freed from adhering to specific caste rules, yet their conduct became regulated through new social role expectations.

Devadasis became one category of the religious functionaries attached to medieval Hindu temples; other categories included priests, dancing masters, drummers, and pipers. By specific accounts, the number of dancing girls in the medieval Hindu temples was by far the highest, at times making up two-thirds of the entire servant group (Prasad, 1990, pp. 29–30). The girls underwent extensive training in dance and education in religious texts; because of their special flexible status in the generally hierarchical social world, they were the most educationally sophisticated women in medieval India. Their elevated status was both produced and protected by their circumscribed social role in the temple context.

The social context of the proliferation of the *devadasis* changed under the British colonial rule. In accordance with the European intolerance of the Hindu traditions of linking religious and sensual worlds of human existence (see Mitter, 1977), the *devadasi* traditions became stigmatized as a "vice" to be eradicated. Hence a number of legislative actions since the late 1800s have led to the legal downturn in the *devadasi* system. In Madras in the 1890s, British colonizers and Indian moralists joined efforts in the "anti-nautch campaigns" ("nautch" = anglicized version of words for dance—see Marglin, 1985, pp. 6–7), which spread over all of India. Between 1910 and 1955, the *devadasi* custom was outlawed in a number of states (Henriques, 1963, pp. 194–195). Nevertheless the practice is deeply connected with the socioeconomic texture of the society; it be-comes transformed under changes in economic conditions (Marglin, 1985) and continues within rural contexts (Tarachand, 1991). Changes in the social meaning of the dance forms are related to changes in institu-tional roles of the local kings who control the temples. Moving the dance traditions out of the temple context into an art form has been a socially guided effort to secularize classical Indian dance, which nevertheless is continuous with the narrative tradition of the collective culture (Khokar, 1979; Kothari and Pasricha, 1990).

Sensuality, Sexuality, and Cultural Canalization

Human sexuality has always been an object of projection of social con-cerns by way of discourse (Foucault, 1980, 1986), as well as a vehicle for organizing and reorganizing social life (Mageo, 1994). Historically, the functions of sexual conduct have been closely intertwined with religious belief systems. This was a rather usual state of affairs in Indian (Siegel, 1978), Japanese (Ohnuki-Tierney, 1993), and Western (e.g., Flandrin, 1985) contexts. Undoubtedly the specific forms of linkage between sexual and religious domains were different, covering a wide range from exclu-sion of sensual bodily functions from the realm of religion and their intrap-sychological repression, to their explicit and collective-culturally meaning-ful inclusion in the public contexts of religious events. The former has been the case in the Christianity-dominated Eurocentric world, where such repression developed slowly over fourteen centuries, to reach its cul-mination in the eighteenth and nineteenth centuries. It was exactly at the culmination of that cultural-historical process that psychology as a disci-pline separated from philosophy and Freud built his system of psychody-namic theorizing upon the culturally formed but deeply personal psycho-logical problems of his patients.

The opposite direction was maintained in the cultural history of the role of the *devadasis*. Their ritual functions in the temple made explicit use of their sensuality—in full accordance with the religious texts their dances represented. Sensuality in the Hindu context is culturally emphasized by the numerous Radha and Krishna stories that circulate within the collective culture (Kakar, 1986, 1989). Hence there was nothing particularly exotic in the unity of sensuality, sexuality, and temple services in the case of the *devadasis*. It merely continued (in a highly ritualized temple context) the indigenous beliefs in the magical fertility-bringing role of female sexuality in regulating human relations with the world at large (Desai, 1985, chapter 6). That world entailed the crucial role of local kings who (while being local rulers) were simultaneously servants *(cevarti)* of the deities (Appadurai and Appadurai-Breckenridge, 1976).

In order to serve the deities of the temple, the kings were dependent upon the symbolically constructed female powers of the *devadasis*—particularly in the public symbolism of granting fertility of the area (by evoking rain). While being the servants of the deity, and the "representatives" of the deity in the form of the king, the *devadasis* were nevertheless uncontrollable autonomous agents in their devotional use of their female powers in service of the common social good. The social status of the *devadasis* can be viewed in terms of an intransitive relation KING → TEMPLE SERVANTS → *DEVADASIS* → KING (see description of intransitive hierarchies in chapter 2).

Much of South Indian temple history is linked with Tantric religious traditions. That tradition within Hinduism built its social power on the unification of sensual and devotional experiences (Allen, 1982). The emergence and proliferation of the *devadasi* system can be seen as a case of collective-cultural guidance of such beliefs to a highly sophisticated socioreligious practice, and employment of such practices for the purposes of social regulation of roles in a complex feudal state. *Devadasis'* roles in the temple context were multiple and complex, including maintenance of the ceremonial environments. Many jobs were to be accomplished by the *devadasis*. Besides dancing and singing, they were active in sweeping and cleaning the temple floors, putting oil in sacred lamps, fanning the deity figure during worship, carrying sacred lamps during processions, and so forth (Patil, 1975). As responsible for culturally crucial ritual duties, the *devadasis* were also the only women in medieval India who could become literate (Dubois, 1905, p. 337), in contrast with the confinement of regularly married women to secluded lifestyles and illiteracy.

The Devadasis *in a Temple Context*

Most of the following analysis is based on evidence reported from the Jagannatha temple contexts in Puri, Orissa (Marglin, 1982a, 1982b, 1985, 1990; Siegel, 1978). That context has been described in greater detail than others (Geib, 1975) because Puri is one of the most famous locations for religious pilgrimages. The historical background of the Jagannatha temple, built in the twelfth century (Kulke and Rothermund, 1986, p. 137; Tripathy and Tripathy, 1992), blends the religious and secular history of power, making use of the collective-cultural constructions of local tribes. Jagannatha ("Lord of the World") was made the state deity (identified with Vishnu) by the king of Orissa in the thirteenth century, with the social function of blending the king's secular and the deity's sacral power roles. The Orissa empire declined in power as it was conquered—first by the Muslims in 1568 and later by the British in 1803 (Marglin, 1990, p. 214). In terms of local organization, however, relatively little changed. The local Hindu king remained the head of the Jagannatha temple (until the 1960s, when the state government of Orissa took over the administrative control) and retains a ritual role in the temple context to the present.

In terms of its complex of meanings, the Jagannath religious tradition is a result of a historical combination of a variety of aspects. Thus, it has absorbed tribal, Buddhist, Tantric, Saivite, and Vaisnavite moments into its complex structure (Preston, 1983). It reflects the high syncretism of religious belief systems that proliferate within Orissa. Undoubtedly, the religious-devotional functions of the town—its approximately seventy thousand regular inhabitants encounter about three to four times as many pilgrims who visit the holy town, especially during major rituals of the chariot *(rathayatra)* and candan *(candanyatra)*—create a unique social context.

Devadasis As Special Servants: Powers and Limitations

The important aspect is the ritualistic status of the *devadasis*—they are not fitted into any special caste in the Indian tradition, as they are honored in specific ritual. The *devadasis,* like the musicians (*bajantari*—see Marglin, 1982a, p. 159), are the only temple servants who are also considered servants in the king's palace. In the temple context, the *devadasis* are considered to be the "walking goddesses" (in parallel with the king, who is "walking Vishnu"). Thus,

> The *devadasis* embodying the female aspect of divine sovereignty are considered in most contexts to be living embodiments of the goddess *Lakshmi,* the consort of Lord Jagannatha. As such, the *devadasis* can have sexual relations with all the men who share in the sovereignty of their divine husband, the ultimate sovereign. . . . The active sexuality of the *devadasis* ensures the fertility of the land through timely and sufficient rain; therefore. it ensures the prosperity of the kingdom.

The king's function of bringing good rains and good harvests depends on a specifically female life force concretely materialized in female sexual fluid. This life force can be conceptualized as the female aspect of sovereignty, and the *devadasis* represent it in this world. Among normal married women, this life force is carefully channeled toward the continuity of their husband's lineage as well as to the welfare and well-being of the entire family including the ancestors; thus, married women are enjoined to be faithful to their husbands. By renouncing family ties, the *devadasis* make their life force available for the welfare and well-being of the whole kingdom. (Marglin, 1990, p. 216)

The collective-cultural linking of female sexual functions with mythological belief in (and production of) fertility—beyond the direct aspect of producing offspring—is a widespread tradition in human cultural history (Desai, 1985). In fact, the *devadasis* could perform their social role in the temple because they were of the female gender. In cases where their dance has come to be performed by boys who dress themselves as females (*gotipuas*—see Kothari and Pasricha, 1990, pp. 44–48), the same emphasis on the female power role is maintained. The social role of *devadasis (maharis)* is based on the powerful feminine meanings that have been maintained all though the history of Hindu mythology and entail unity of creative and destructive roles (Kolenda, 1981).

A girl could enter the social role of the *devadasi* in many ways. The role could be inherited through affinal kinship, by parents' decisions to dedicate one of their daughters to the deity, by a young woman's wish to serve the deity, and so on (Bradford, 1983; Marglin, 1985; Tarachand, 1991). The central meaning of such dedication was the attainment of married status with the deity (an example of theogamy), and establishment of sensual but nonpermanent relations with persons representing the deity (e.g., local king, temple priests).

The ceremony of dedication of temple servants—male or female—is the same: "sari tying." From that day on, the *devadasis* consider themselves married to Jagannatha. For the *devadasi* dedicated before menarche, a puberty ceremony is performed at the first menstruation ("seeing menstrual blood for the first time"—*pratama raja darsana*). It consists of her defloration by either the king or a person of comparable ritualistic roles (which could include a temple servant, by the king's permission). Subsequently, the *devadasi* could accept more or less temporary male partners from among the allowable categories (i.e., temple servants, local higher-caste persons, but no outsiders, such as pilgrims to Puri).

Rituals in the Temple

The *devadasis* participated in two daily rituals at the Jagannatha temple. They danced at the midday ritual (the *Sakal Dhupa*), which takes place during the morning/midday meal and carries the meaning of royal offering of food to the deity (Kothari and Pasricha, 1990, p. 42). At the evening ritual involving putting the deity to sleep *(Bada Singar)*, the *devadasis (maharis)* performed a similarly important but symbolically slightly different role. A more detailed account of these two rituals is necessary to outline the semiotic functions of the *devadasi* role in the sacred and profane world of human relations with the cultural world of the deities.

THE MORNING/MIDDAY RITUAL   The general specifics of the midday ritual are described elsewhere (Marglin, 1982a, pp. 157–158; 1990, pp. 216–225) as "royal offering" of food to the deity. The important aspect of the *devadasi* social role in this context is that (1) they *do not* actually participate in the food offering to the deity (which is performed by priests in the inner sanctum of the temple, to which *devadasis* have no right of access on this occasion), and (2) the ritual dance is *oriented outside*—toward pilgrims and visitors. It is supervised by the high official *(rajaguru)*, who is a high-class Brahman and the representative of the king in the course of the midday ceremony (he does not participate in the evening ceremony—Marglin, 1982a, p. 158).

While observing the *devadasi* dancing, the pilgrims and visitors can simultaneously face Jagannatha and the dancing girls. At the end of the dance some pilgrims were reported taking the dust from the *devadasi*'s feet or rolling their entire body on the area where she had danced, to collect on their whole body the dust of her feet (Marglin, 1985, p. 109). By semiotic construction that dust comes to "contain" special "sacralizing" powers, attainable only through female powers for bringing good luck in the generalized sense of fertility.

The special dance of the *devadasis* (*nritta*—a family tradition of the *devadasis*) relates food, dust, and *srngara rasa* (a complex of erotic feelings that entails sensual experiencing of specific settings of interpersonal closeness—Marglin, 1990, pp. 212, 219; also Siegel, 1978, p. 200) into one devotional experience. In an explanation provided to Marglin, the *ra-jaguru* insisted that "the sole purpose of the dance is the production by the dancer's movements of female sexual fluid *(raja)* which falls on the ground. According to his interpretation when the devotees roll themselves on the dancing floor they pick up dust and *raja*. Another meaning of the word *raja* is dust (or dirt), and this reinforces the link between the dust of the dancer's feet and her sexual fluid" (Marglin, 1990, p. 218).

The sacralized functions of the female sexual fluid that is assumed to be emitted during the *devadasi* dance (and also secreted during regular sexual intercourse) are central in the context of the midday ritual. The *devadasi* here represents the fertile power embodied in her sexual functions, and the visitors and pilgrims recognize her superior status in this context (e.g., taking the dust from a person's feet or washing the person's feet and then sipping the water expresses the superiority of the person).

After the *devadasi* dance ritual, the pilgrims and visitors receive a food offering. Hence the divine food offering and the *devadasi*'s dust production are ritually integrated within the same thought complex:

> The act of picking up the leftovers of *Sakti* [= female life force and Tantric god] is the spectators' partaking in the goddess's *srngara rasa;* a physical-emotional-cognitive experience. The transformation, spoken of in Hindu India as an experience of tasting *(rasana, asvada, bhoga)* an essence or a juice *(rasa)*, is rooted in the physical experience of food and eating . . .
>
> The source of tasting of an emotional essence is the divinized dancer. The *bhava* [= a separably manifest part of the dance; postural and gestural gestalt in dance] of erotic love *(srngara)* dominated the midday dance ritual, which is erotic love in action; it is a way of relating and communicating with another person, an activity at once physical, emotional, *and* cognitive. The mobile goddess is married to the god, and in their cosmic intercourse they produce a sexual leftover that fertilizes the land and produces well-being in the people. The dance is a divine sexual intercourse . . . The *bhava* of the dancer arouses in the spectators traces of their own erotic sensations that are constituted emotionally as *srngara rasa*. Should a spectator directly lust for the dancer, the performative efficacy of the ritual would have failed, and the erotic sensation would not be experienced as *srngara rasa* but simply as lust. (Marglin, 1990, p. 224)

The social function of *srngara rasa* in the temple ritual complex is to grant symbolic empowerment for the persons participating, and rain for the region, which is an important task of the king. Much of the Puri ritual activity is related to water as a life-sustaining resource (Geib, 1975; Marglin, 1985).

THE EVENING RITUAL   The evening ritual in the Jagannatha temple (Marglin, 1982b, 1985, 1990) takes place just before the deities "go to sleep" for the night and the temple is closed. A *devadasi* stands on the threshold of the inner sanctum and signs verses from *Gitagovinda*. The evening ritual brings the deity close to the audience—a transition that is possible through the *devadasi*'s singing:

> The deity comes close to his devotees; in other words, he responds to their devotion as expressed by the *devadasi,* the ideal devotee. Through her dance and song as well as her nonattached social status she is able to extract the essence of devotion, total absorption in Krishna and single-minded centering of emotion, thought, and physical love for him. The essence of her devotion is *srngara rasa* which is aroused in her audience who, unlike that of the midday ritual, is the deity, not the visitors. The deity in this temple is conceived to be a real person with authority, ownership of lands, needs, and desires . . .
>
> As for the audience of visitors to the temple, the outward manifestation of an inward transformation is their taking of the leftovers of the deity: flower and flame. If, as for the midday ritual, one takes these as tangible signs of an inward emotional-mental transformation, one must conclude that the source of this transformation is the divinity, not the *devadasi*. The *devadasi* as the embodiment of refined and single-minded devotion is instrumental in bringing the deity closer to the devotees . . . By coming close to them the deity arouses in his devotees renewed and intensified love and devotion. (Marglin, 1990, p. 230)

The emphasis on unity of the male and female is a major theme in the songs at the evening ritual. The *devadasis* are not expected to enter into sexual relations within the times of their ritual performance in the temple (i.e., from morning until evening).

Semiotic Direction by Collective-Cultural Meaning Complexes

Any historically pervasive sociocultural practice is built upon semiotic bases that persons have constructed and constantly reconstructed over generations. The Indian context is perhaps one of the best examples in the world where folklore texts organize personal lives (Kakar, 1981, 1989; Roland, 1988). It is in the process of intergenerational transfer of folklore texts that the collective-cultural knowledge base is maintained (with modifications) and personal-cultural understandings of the world are channeled in their general directions.

Role of Folkloric Texts in Collective Culture

Folklore texts entail meaning complexes that weave together general and concrete know-how, marked specifically by connotational implications. The inclusion of moments foreign to everyday life experiences (e.g., transformations of persons into animals, monsters, and vice versa) allows for high flexibility to bring collective-culturally relevant focal meanings. The texture of folkloric complexes guides the persons toward collective-culturally fitting interpretations of their relations with the world. Such semiotic constraining performs the function of *symbolic empowerment* of the person—in the activity of construction of personal culture, the person can use folkloristic "anchor ideas" to assemble his or her personal understanding with high flexibility in symbolic construction (Obeyesekere, 1981, 1990). Folklore does not merely reflect collective culture; it participates in the development of persons within it. The heterogeneity of *genres* in folklore texts allows for collective-cultural acceptance of multiplicity of personally constructed cultural solutions to human cognitive and affective tasks (Ramanujan, 1991). The multitude of versions of Krishna stories in India that have proliferated over centuries have guided personal cultures toward synthesizing different facets of human experiences.

Jayadeva's *Gitagovinda*

Jayadeva was a professional court poet. His *Gitagovinda* (composed around A.D. 1200) is a major cultural text that, by way of retelling the Krishna-Radha legend, guides patterns of internalization/externalization processes in respect to devotion and sensuality (Siegel, 1978). The legend itself takes many forms in Indian folklore (Kakar, 1986). Jayadeva's version carries traces from a variety of folkloric traditions in Orissa of the previous centuries (Hindu Tantrism, *Bhagavata purana*—Hardy, 1983). It takes to poetic perfection the unification of sensual and devotional-religious experiences: "The sexual experience was equated with the yogic experience in the attainment of the state of non-ego, vacuity, the suspension of thought-process and self-consciousness. The internal physiological process by which the state of vacuity was achieved was analogous to the union of the man and the woman and symbolized by the thunder entering the lotus" (Siegel, 1978, p. 40).

Importantly, Jayadeva's version of the Krishna legend became institutionalized in the Jagannatha temple as an obligatory text on which all ritual dancing and singing of the *devadasis* was based from the sixteenth century onward (Siegel, 1978, p. 229). In accordance with the collective-cultural regulation of women's relations with their bodily functions, the dedicated *devadasi* were expected to live according to the sensual patterns of loving the deity, culturally encoded in *Gitagovinda*. Within the text of the epic, the well-known encounter of Krishna with cowherdesses *(gopis)* is important from the standpoint of collective-cultural canalization of sensuality.

The *Gopis* and Their Symbolic Relevance

The *gopis* were important female characters in the myriad of legends involving Krishna and Radha. Numerous encounters of Krishna with the *gopis* (e.g., Krishna stealing the *gopis'* clothes; Krishna's dance and amorous play with the *gopis*) have been retold in various versions all over India (Archer, 1957; Hardy, 1983; Singer, 1966). In Jayadeva's *Gitagovinda* the *gopis* appear in the context of sensual role presentation for Krishna, whose sensuality is imbued with the liberation from phenomenal existence (song 2, stanza 21—Siegel, 1978, p. 244). Krishna's "eye is a spotless lotus petal," he is both lover (of Janaka's daughter Sita) and destroyer of enemies in battle (note the unification of erotic and heroic sides of the role). He is both a person and a god. The active role of the *gopis* in the sensual play is reflected, in conjunction with highly symbolic descriptions of the trees, birds, and springtime. The following excerpt from the fourth song illustrates the rhetorical presentation in the *Gitagovinda*:

39. [He has] a forest garland and a yellow garment on his sandal-smeared, blue body and laughter on his cheeks which are adorned with jewelled ear-rings shaking in play; here Hari plays in the coquettish and playful flock of artless [*mugdha:* lovely, beautiful, innocent] women.
40. Passionately embracing Hari with the massive weight of her swollen breasts a certain herdsman's wife sings a resounded fifth note [*pancama-raga:* a love cry made during or before coition to signify pleasure]; here Hari plays . . .
41. Another artless woman continually contemplates the lotus-face of the

Killer-of-Madhu, [the face-lotus] produced love on account of the quivering of his eyes rolling about seductively [*vilasa:* in a love-play with amorous gesture]; here Hari plays . . .

42. Another [woman] with beautiful buttocks, came-up to say something into his ear and sweetly kissed the beloved on the surface of his cheek which was obliging [*anukula:* obliging by showing his pleasure—an ironic element here] with bristling-hairs; here Hari plays . . .

43. And another, with eagerness for the arts of love-play, on the bank of the Yamuna's waters, with her hand on his robe, pulled him who was in the beautiful cane grove; here Hari plays . . .

44. While his sweet-toned flute is sounded, rows of bracelets shake on their clapping hands; in the enjoyment of the *rasa* [pastoral circular dance] a deer-like young-girl, intent on dancing with him, praised him; here Hari plays . . .

45. He embraces one, kisses one, sexually-pleases some sexually-pleasing one, he sees yet another beauty more charming still on account of her smiles and he chases her; here Hari plays . . .

46. May this song of Sri Jayadeva, the secret of marvelous Kesava's love-play, lovely and famous in the Vrndavana forest, spread-abroad prosperities! here Hari plays. . . (Siegel, 1978, pp. 248–249)

Much of the *Gitagovinda* is dedicated to the expression of Radha's jealousy and love at a distance, and women's desire for sensual relation with Krishna. The complexity of Krishna's feelings about his leaving of Radha and longing for her are likewise narrated (song 7—Siegel, 1978, pp. 254–256). All through the *Gitagovinda,* Jayadeva highlights the process of sensual experiencing, either in the Krishna's encounter with the *gopis* or in his feelings about Radha. However, all of that experiencing is related with the devotional sentiment, which is generated by ambiguities of the feelings. The women are depicted as devotedly active, with explicit recognition of their erotic *(srngara)* feelings. It is clear that the Hindu *bhakti* context empowers women in religiously context-bound ways (see Ramanujan, 1982, p. 316). The role of the *Gitagovinda* in the cultural canalization in the context of Hindu life is to provide meaning bases for personal-cultural reconstruction of the self's sensual sphere. That sensual sphere is linked with the cultural complex of powers of balancing "heat" and "cool" (Kersenboom, 1984), for which the special role of ever-auspicious women was culturally necessary.

Basic Meanings: Collective-Cultural Differentiations

The conceptual complexes that guide the organization of human development are undoubtedly difficult to translate directly from one semiotic code to another (Wierzbicka, 1992). Furthermore, the basic organizational schemes of concepts show how collective-cultural differentiation patterns guide our reasoning. Furthermore, it is not only the cognitive domain that is semiotically mediated. The domain of human feelings is likewise under collective-cultural guidance. In the context of India, the contrast with most assumptions taken by psychology is perhaps the greatest: "In the Western cultural formulation emotion is conceived as an inherently irrational aspect of life and talked about in metaphors that center on ideas of chaos. In contrast, Hindu metaphors for emotion center on food and semantic similarities between emotion as an experience and the bodily experiences of eating and nurturing" (Toomey, 1990, p. 174).

The personal-cultural world of the *devadasis* provides an example where our usual concepts are inadequate. A major conceptual opposition that proves to be an obstacle for our understanding of the *devadasis* is the Western social sciences' culturally constructed exclusive separation (as discussed in chapter 1) of the "sacred" and "profane" domains of human existence. It has been repeatedly pointed out that the use of binary oppositions in making sense of Indian cultural complexity brings social science to an impasse (Das, 1976b, 1992; Kakar, 1981, 1989; Siegel, 1978). The same ("sacred" and "profane," or any other) opposites can be viewed as separated but linked (by way of inclusive separation), in which case different forms of the linkage between them are potentially open for investigation. This perspective allows for the coverage of interdependencies between the distinguished opposites and the formulation of different multiple (rather than binary) interdependent oppositions between cultural meanings.

In the domain of making sense of the *devadasis*' role, inclusive separation is necessary for viewing the difference and unity of two distinct Hindu concepts—*auspiciousness (manga* or *subha* or *kalyan)* and *inauspiciousness (amangal* or *asubha* or *akalyan)*. While being opposite terms, these concepts are linked in ways that allow for a particular event or act (under some conditions) to move from one state to another in time (Samantha, 1992). Thus, the "forever-auspicious" state of the *devadasi* (Kersenboom, 1984) sets up the semiotic basis for the *devadasis* to act upon either auspicious or inauspicious social events, repairing the imbalances between the two sides by rituals and unifying the opposites in ways that lead to new potential imbalances. This dialectical view on the Hindu auspiciousness/inauspiciousness opposition transcends the usual view of seeing those terms as irreconcilable opposites. In some sense, the cultural construction of the *devadasi* role in Indian cultural history indicates the need for unification (and continuous regulation) of the complex of these opposites. Thus, the *mangal/amangal* complex is not equivalent to the widely used pure-impure contrast (Madan, 1991; Raheja, 1988, chapter 2).

However, common sense does operate with exclusively separated opposites. Most of Hindu social organization is based on the reading of good "signs" of the *mangal* and avoidance of the bad omens of *amangal*. *Mangal* assumes a special "well-being" relationship between devotees and feminine powers. The *devadasis* are clearly semiotically marked by belonging to the world of *mangal* (Marglin, 1985, p. 98). Their auspicious nature creates their special status, both by setting up constraints (against undermining their auspiciousness by inauspicious conduct) and by promotion of their freedoms of action (in their auspiciousness they are close to the king). Furthermore, their auspicious status guides their semiotic organization of sensuality.

Conceptualizing Desire: Relations of *Kama* and *Prema*

The concept of *kama* (both sensual desire and desire for any object) belongs to the core of Hindu organizing concepts, together with *dharma* (religious duty), *artha* (wealth), and *moksa* (renunciation). These four constituents of the true purpose of existence can be viewed in different mutual relations (Das, 1982a). Of the four, *kama, artha,* and *dharma* belong together under the term *bhoga,* which "is derived from the verbal root bhuj, which means enjoy, use, possess, eat, consume, exhaust, use up, have sexual intercourse with . . . All three of these goals were subsumed under the single notion of enjoyment" (Inden, 1982, p. 100).

The meaning complex of enjoyment thus sets the stage for making sense of *kama*. *Kama* is the procreative power that is claimed to "magnify the ego" yet be paradoxical and transcendable (Siegel, 1978, pp. 64–67). Pursuit of *kama* has been sanctified since the Upanishads as the foundation of human existence, as it unites in itself two different (yet interdependent) domains of sexuality—for procreation and pleasure on the one hand and for mystical and magical power on the other (Jha, 1979, p. 7). However, in its wider meaning, *kama* entails *any* kind of desire (Malamoud, 1982).

Kama exists between husband and wife, involves relinquishing seed, and leads to childbearing. In contrast, *prema* (devotional love) involves a sensual-emotional love relation that is continuous, free of hierarchical social relations (e.g., those between Krishna and the *gopis*), and hence an integrated emotion complex: "*Prema* cannot be classified as either ascetic or erotic but seems to partake of both sides of the opposition . . . the absence of *kama* does not mean chaste, platonic love. Krishna and the *gopis* fondle, caress, embrace each other with abandon and show all the signs of sensual pleasure. What the absence of *kama* specifically refers to is the fact that in his love-making Krishna does not spill his seed" (Marglin, 1982b, p. 306).

The possibility for conceptualizing *prema* is thus based on the historical-cultural constraint by the meanings of semen loss, which is widespread in Indian folk theories (Bottéro, 1991; Kakar, 1989, pp. 118–120). Sensual experiences paired with the avoidance of semen loss in nonprocreative contexts might allow the meaning of *prema* to emerge on the foundation of *kama*. In devotional religious contexts, cultural guidance for the personal construction of a distinctive, elaborate, and formalized attitude of devotion by sharing of the emotions of *prema* (as divine love) combined with joy (*ananda*) can lead to a generalized new feeling (Bennett, 1990).

The experiencing of the positive emotionality in sensuality is enabled by the meaning of *prema,* while *kama* dominates in specific (husband-wife) role relationships. It is viewed as selfish (and hence at times presented as an opponent to be overcome) and, through its inherent oppositionality, can become *prema.* In the transition to *prema,* the sensual focus of *kama* is not lost but becomes integrated into a new whole and subsumed within the dominant scheme of *prema.* Both *kama* and *prema* involve a sensual component but are distinguishable on the basis of everyday-life (procreational) and mystical-sensual functions. Yet where there is "true love," *kama* is involved (Pandey, 1965).

Prema in the Lives of *Devadasis*

The highly specific collective-cultural role of the *devadasi* leads to the construction of a personal-cultural system in ways that may defy the usual Western models of understanding. The *devadasi* case provides us with a sophisticated picture of cultural organization of personal life courses. The crucial personal-cultural construction starts from seeing one's own self in terms of *prema:*

The *devadasi* is not married and therefore lacks a married woman's feeling of possession toward a husband. As Haripriya, a *devadasi,* said to me, "A wife says 'I have a husband,'" a statement that bespeaks ego feelings (ahankara). When Haripriya spoke to me of her own life, she told me about an important liaison she had had in which there was no feeling of attachment . . . On a different occasion, Sasi, another *devadasi,* told me: "We don't marry. We don't have children; we don't have a household; devotion is the one important thing for us." . . . Haripriya herself explained to me at great length the nature of the erotic and passionate love of the *gopi-devadasi* for Krishna while all the time contrasting it to the attached eroticism of the married woman. Conjugal eroticism is never separated from procreative considerations, whereas the erotic love between the *gopis* and Krishna is completely separated from procreation. (Marglin, 1990, p. 227)

By way of the highly symbolic social role, a woman creates for herself a personal life-world mediated by the general meaning of devotion to deity, which entails (as a meaning complex) *prema* and allows her to construct her marital self-definition in terms different from those of usual wives (who, in the Hindu context, bear children within a hierarchical dominance network within the joint family).

The collective-cultural meanings that were used to organize the *devadasis'* personal worlds constitute a flexible and nonstrict hierarchy. The status of being symbolically married to the deity constrains the *devadasis* both in their actions (within their role performance in the temple) and in their personal lives with men who in some sense are linked to the deity. This constraining by the meaning also gives the *devadasis* special status in an otherwise status-conscious social world. Their particular internalized reconstructions of their marital status provide a variety of forms (Marglin, 1985, chapter 1), all of which led the *devadasis* to not enter the role of a traditional Hindu wife.

Furthermore, the meaning of *prema* (and the *devadasis'* perceived similarity with the *gopis*) makes it possible to develop a personal-emotional relationship with the world that transcends the usual role relations of the wider society. The special status of the *devadasis* enables them, while also constraining their spheres of activity (e.g., childbearing). They can be stigmatized by the wider society, yet they have made themselves free by their semiotic self-constraining.

*Implications for Theory: Cultural Process As Basis
for Personality*

The case of the *devadasis* leads to a number of questions about psychology's time-honored assumptions about the role of sexuality in human personality. Sexuality has undoubtedly been the favorite topic of psychologists since Freud. Although psychoanalytic uses of sexuality have been widely criticized (as well as defended) in psychological discourse, new basic assumptions need to be made about the ways in which sexual, sensual, and higher mental-affective functions are related within the human self. As is emphasized by Kakar, "As a 'depth psychology,' psychoanalysis dives deep, but in the same waters in which the cultural river too flows. Preeminently operating from within the heart of the Western myth . . .—from myths of ancient Greece to the 'illusions' of the Enlightenment—psychoanalysis has had little opportunity to observe from within, and with empathy, the deeper import of other cultures' myths in the working of the self" (Kakar, 1989, p. 139).

Myths can be seen as collective-cultural constraining devices than channel personal cultures toward reconstruction not only of the knowledge transferred via those but also of the affective marking. By way of acting about myths (as recipients, retellers, etc.), persons bring their personal cultures to bear upon modification of the collective culture. Collective-cultural narrated texts allow both disjunctive and conjunctive constructions to emerge in human subjective worlds. For example, both the separation (disjunction) and unification (conjunction) of the worlds of religious devotionalism and physioaffective sensuality are granted by the same internalization/externalization processes (see also Das, 1982a; Gandhi, 1982) and can coexist in diametrically opposite personal forms within the same society at the same time.

Collective-cultural texts are both the starting datum and the product of the internalization/externalization process. The texts lead to subjectification of the personal lived-through experiences (Obeyesekere, 1981, p. 137). The person uses the collective-cultural meanings to produce and justify innovative acts, which become objectified and conventionalized in social communication. The latter may lead to an ontological misattribution in the social sciences; a semiotically encoded feature that is created in conjunction with a goal of the encoder may be made into a characteristic of the reality. Thus, various efforts to present the *devadasi* custom as a case of prostitution may have reflected the investigators' socioinstitutional goals and/or discomfort with the collective-culturally sanctioned unity of religiosity and sensuality in the Indian context (see Devereux, 1967, on researchers' psychological projections).

It becomes clear that psychology cannot posit the existence of basic motivating substances (such as libido) that has emerged as a result of collective-cultural synthesis in some areas of the World, as the universal basis for psychological functioning. The intrasubjective field of persons in any society includes domains of sexuality, sensuality, and so on, yet none of these domains is to be viewed a priori as the basis for building a personality theory. Rather, the universal human process of semiotic mediation can create a number of substance-like subjective fictions, and interpersonal communication using such fictions is treacherously simple. It is nevertheless misleading, as it *substitutes the fundamental process by its specific outcomes.* The foundation for psychology's conceptualization of personality (or self) can be set up in that process—sign construction, reconstruction, and meaning-making are the core of human personality. The semiotic mediation *process* is the most fundamental mechanism of human functioning and development, generating a variety of forms of meanings that are but specific outcomes of the process. The cross-societal universal of human psychology is the generative mechanism that allows for the construction of a variety of Krishna, Oedipus, or other myths—and that makes it possible to modify these myth families as particular conditions of living-through experiences trigger such novel constructs. In an analogy with modern genetics, it is not "the genes" that cause the synthesis of specific proteins but the translation of the information encoded in the genes into the actual construction of proteins.

This theoretical view on human development leads to the necessity for multisided consideration of lived-through experiences and their cultural organization. The case of temple dancers—even if distant from the scope of coverage of psychology by historical, cultural, and disciplinary boundaries—provides a glimpse into a realm of psychological reality where human sensuality becomes semiotically canalized in the direction of socially relevant goals. This is accomplished by a system of higher-order cultural organizer terms (auspiciousness, *kama, prema,* etc.), specific narrated myths (Krishna's social interaction with the *gopis*), and conduct constraints for specific settings in the everyday lives of the *devadasis* in the temple and outside.

A fundamental culturally canalized outcome is discernible in the two-thousand-year history of the Hindu temple dancers: the specific form of relating sensuality and religious devotion. Social stigmatization of their roles for any sociomoral discourse purposes cannot overshadow their psychological achievements. *Devadasis* were unique women not only in their role in their society but also in the form of synthesis of their selves in that role. The collective culture created the directed set of suggestions, which the personal cultures of the dedicated girls internalized and reconstructed in their personally idiosyncratic (and therefore solidly continuous) ways.

Personal Culture of Devadasis

The guidance of the personal culture of the *devadasis* was a lengthy process, not different in kind (only in content) from socialization of girls not dedicated to temple service. The emphasis on sensuality was highlighted by way of promoting *affective* involvement through religious practices:

> In their youth, within the ninth year, instruction should be given in sexual intercourse . . . , of practicing the skills of Rambha [one of the heavenly courtesans known for love art skills], and bringing out charm. It is necessary that they possess all *laksanas* (diagnostic features) of exemplary bearing, a body with proper limbs, excessive beauty that shines like lightning, breath with good fragrance, speech like the peacock, capacity for *ciksai* (lessons of music and dance) with emotional involvement, general education and *bhakti* in the shrine of Sakti. (Kersenboom, 1984, p. 319)

The following personal retrospect (a case from Telugu-speaking areas in southern India) gives an idea of the meaning context in which a girl named Malli became dedicated to temple service:

> I was born in Mughalkode village in Karnataka. On the very day that I came into this world, my parents betrothed me to the goddess Yellamma. They believed that by giving away their children to the goddess they would find a place in heaven. . . This is our tradition— our way to go to heaven. Yellamma is a *jagrat devata* (wakeful deity). You have only to ask for a thing, and she gives it. She cures the sick. She gives children to barren women. Our *vamsa* (family and clan) grows in strength because of her. But we have to give her *dasis* in return. We must propriate her, for her wrath is terrible. It will bring upon us leprosy—all kinds of misery. Some people give their daugh-

ters to Yellama to fulfil a vow. To beget children, a childless couple would promise to offer her their first-born. Both boys and girls are offered to Yellama. They are called *jogtis* and can't marry because they are already married to Yellama. Once a girl is dedicated to the goddess she can be regarded as a boy. She has a share of the family property like her brothers. She can even perform the funeral rites of her parents. This is one reason why people without sons marry their daughter to Yellama. (Kersenboom, 1984, p. 329)

The activities of *jogtis* contained mostly begging (at a minimum of five doors per day) and sexual services. However, the meaningful context of the lives of *jogtis* entailed religious servitude. According to Malli: "On Tuesday and Friday (days sacred to Yellamma) *jogtis* go out begging with their *jag*, a brass pitcher which is the symbol of Yellamma. It also has an image of the goddess with a halo of peacock feathers. The *jag* has to be worshipped every day. The *jag* of Yellamma is handed down from generation to generation and the flame must be kept burning before the *jag*. We call it 'passing on the family light'" (Kersenboom, 1984, p. 330).

Surely a semiotic complex that includes linkages with the world of deities and dedication of persons to such linkages is not different from phenomena often talked about in occidental psychology as issues of "identity formation." When seen from this angle, the *devadasi* custom can be considered one of formation of identities not only of the girls involved but also of their families and the communities the girls served through assuming their roles.

Subjective Regulation in Personal Culture: Contemporary Cases

The lives of *devadasis* were regulated by semiotic and action constraint systems that operated conjointly—creating redundant control over action by affective meaningfulness, and over affective meanings through ritually prescribed meaningful action. Personal-cultural constructions entail constraints on feelings that canalize action and thought.

The *devadasi* example is generalizable beyond the Hindu context. Devotionalism of any kind—religious, political, or any other—is built on these internalization/externalization mechanisms. Practices of affective tying of personality to a specific culturally constructed illusionary object (general meaning: ideal, value, etc.) is a widespread practice in human socialization. Its mechanisms, however, entail the ruling out and ruling in of different ways of feelingful ideas, setting up acceptable combinations of those and thus constraining the stream of personally lived-through experiences (as emphasized in chapters 3, 5, and 6)

In our time, psychological phenomena similar to the *devadasi* cases can be found in any society. A contemporary Indian therapy case illustrates this well.

The Case of Shakuntala

The case history of a Hindu woman named Shakuntala, reported by Roland (1988, pp. 154–174), provides us with a pattern of personal-cultural reorganization of the self by the self, through internally reconstructed rule and value systems of the collective culture. Shakuntala was a college lecturer in the humanities in Bombay, who entered into an unintensive psychoanalytic therapy encounter with Alan Roland, after dissatisfaction with another—more orthodoxly Freudian—therapeutic effort that had failed through her personal-cultural resistance (see Roland, 1988, p. 155).

The central conflict in Shakuntala's life (as interpreted by Roland) was the dilemma between her family's (particularly her mother's) pressure to arrange a marriage for her and Shakuntala's own constructed devotion to her long-term intimate feelings toward the husband (Kumar) of her friend Veena. Shakuntala had been a close friend of Veena and Kumar for the previous ten years, although the emotional dynamics of the relationship had its subtleties, as reported by Shakuntala and interpreted by Roland:

> Shakuntala senses that Veena is very uneasy about Shakuntala's relationship with Kumar. Shakuntala feels Veena is acting in a very subtle way to edge her out. In front of Kumar, Veena enthusiastically invites Shakuntala over, but she then conveys to Kumar privately that Shakuntala doesn't really want to visit, thus slowly manipulating matters to cut off the relationship. In the past, Veena had subtly alienated Kumar from his favourite niece because the latter tended to be too exclusively involved with Kumar. Shakuntala, on the other hand, goes out of her way to be a close friend of Veena. In fact, Shakuntala sees all of them as her second family, is very attached to Veena and the children as well as to Kumar, and so is both disturbed and angry over what she senses Veena is doing, though she realizes that Veena sees her as a rival. (Roland, 1988, p. 157)

However, Shakuntala's network of close relationships was not related only to the arranged marriage versus feelings of intimacy toward Kumar and his family. It was further complicated by suggestions made by her favorite aunt, who had wanted Shakuntala to marry her son (a marriage that was blocked by Shakuntala's father because of the social norm not allowing first cousins to marry). After becoming widowed (in her thirties), the aunt turned to religion and became a respected guru. She was trying to persuade Shakuntala to come to her ashram, or at least to get married. Joining the ashram would have been opposed by Shakuntala's mother. Thus, being "pulled" by three different possible life-course directions, Shakuntala was in a situation of inner conflict—personally constructed yet in terms of the collective-cultural meaning systems (marriage, ashram, devotion).

A collective-culturally appropriate direction to solve part of the internalized conflict was provided by Kumar, who (with his wife, children, and Shakuntala) went on a pilgrimage to a temple of a highly revered, deceased holy man, of whom he was an ardent devotee. The aftereffects of this pilgrimage for Shakantula included further support for her close relation to Kumar, albeit in a way mediated by collective-cultural belief systems: "Although she had never been a devotee of this holy man, Shakuntala exprienced visions of him and his presence for at least two months after they returned to Bombay. Shakuntala was absolutely convinced that she and Kumar had been connected to each other in past lives through their relationship with this holy man, that she was simply living through her past attachments *(samskaras)* to Kumar, and that when these were eventually satisfied, the relationship would end (not necessarily in this life)" (Roland, 1988, p. 160).

Through interpreting her relation with Kumar in its status quo (of his being married and not changing that status) in the meaning system of the collective culture, in conjunction with the semiotic mediation of the pilgrimage (and the image of the holy man), Shakuntala could reconstruct her personal-cultural sense of her relation with Kumar through the collective-cultural meanings (which include irresistible attachment between persons in their present lives, if their involvement in their past lives is implicated). However, the contradiction about her marriage (versus unmarried) status, as well as the issue of a personally and collective-culturally fitting marriage partner, remained unsolved. A suitor (a Christian by religion) appeared at this time, but Shakuntala rejected his offer of marriage. Not only Shakuntala but both her parents were against the marriage. Yet in

Roland's psychotherapeutic encounter, this episode of rejecting a suitor on the basis of loyalty to one's parents' customs dependency revealed the presence of a marriage ceremony some years earlier—a ceremony that led to a collective-cultural solution to personal-cultural ambivalence. Shakuntala revealed to Roland that

> six years previously an excellent marriage had been arranged for her. The wedding date had been set after consultation with the family priest and everyone was invited. Somehow, two days before the wedding, Shakuntala managed to wriggle out of the arrangements. The *priest, however, judged it was important that she be married then,* as it was an extremely auspicious time. *Two days later she went through the full marriage ceremony,* circling the sacred fire seven times, and *was married to one of the most important gods in the Hindu pantheon.* (Roland, 1988, pp. 162–163; emphasis added)

The merging of collective-cultural action prescriptions and meanings created here a persevering context where the girl was married to a deity following her ambivalence toward her actual suitor. Both the acceptance and rejection of arranged marriage are here intertwined in an interesting way; marriage to a deity (collective-culturally) makes the individual's personal culture both socially legitimate and personally free—at least in the subjective world of the person. Two years later, when Roland met Shakantula again in Bombay, her life situation revealed some modification:

> Her parents had left Bombay because of a not unusual mother-in-law/daughter-in-law conflict, but, more unusually, with the son siding with his wife. Her parents decided to sell their house in Lucknow and provide for Shakuntala's security by buying her a flat in Bombay. Her aunt, in the meanwhile, had died. Shakuntala had recently visited the ashram, very much wanting to stay, but had returned to Bombay for Kumar. In spite of the ups and downs of this relationship, Shakuntala now accepted its inevitability, and was living with and enjoying it . . .
> . . . Although her colleagues saw her as a social butterfly, *inside she felt highly traditional; in fact, she felt practically married to Kumar. But the one she really felt married to was the god.* For the first time, Shakuntala elaborated that girls from her north Indian community are married to this god . . . as a ritual to offset bad planetary influences, in order to make it easier to get married . . . Shakuntala had always taken

the marriage to the god seriously and as inevitable, and was unwilling to discuss it in any detail. (Roland, 1988, p. 170; emphasis added)

Shakuntala's case brings together the explanation of intrapsychological constraining of relevant complex feelings and the collective-cultural organization of varied social roles for women in the history of Hindu society. As Obeyesekere has claimed,

> According to Brahmanic norms the wife is expected to treat her husband as a god. This Brahmanic injunction is not simply a product of the sexism of the Puranas and Dharmasastras; it is also, I believe, importantly related to the fantasy life of Hindu women. The husband as god is based on the *model* of the man that the woman possesses in her own unconscious, and this in turn is based on her perception of her own father . . . It is likely that she would want her husband to fit that model, to be an idealized and loving figure, almost a god. It is very unlikely that any woman consciously believes this parallelism will hold true . . .
>
> . . . In Hindu society the husband-wife tie can be very strong, but this bond is not primarily sexual. The husband can be loved and tolerated only if he is, or rather can be, viewed as a god—that is, an approximation of the woman's model of her father . . . it is very likely that in a large number of instances the husband can never match his wife's ideal of the male . . . Hence sensitive females must search elsewhere for loving surrogate male figures, which in Hindu society are the guru and the idealized god (generally Krisna in the North and Skanda-Murukan in the South), toward whom a woman can direct her love, her bhakti, a combination of eroticism and devotionalism. The loving god and the beloved guru are sublimations of the father imago, and they are transformed many times over in the symbolic universe of Hindu life. For some women it is one way out of the harsh realities of the Hindu joint family. (Obeyesekere, 1984, pp. 434–435)

Let us here note the emphasis on flexibility within the systemic organization of personal culture. The full functioning of the human body is constantly being *directionally presented* (to the self and to others) through the social suggestions encoded in metaphors, myths, and images of social roles (Kirmayer, 1992). The set of such social suggestions is heterogeneous (e.g., including both folktales and countertales—Ramanujan, 1991), incomplete (new suggestions are constantly being constructed), and re-dundantly encoded (similarly directed messages coexist in various forms). The use of devotionalism in conjunction with the *devadasi* role construc-tion in Hindu cultural history is merely an example of how part of this personal-cultural flexibility of construction can be utilized for the con-struction of specifically constrained life courses. The processes of personal identity formation within "ordinary" Hindu joint families are not different in principle from those on which the *devadasi* social role construction was based. Only in the latter case, we see the constraining of female sensuality and identification in the direction that fitted with the social role and, in fact, constituted the role. *Devadasis* can be viewed (in their respective context) as highly skilled experts, the buildup of whose expertise is set up socially to start sufficiently early.

Social systems are the birthplace of specific forms of social organization (by way of participation of active persons, a co-constructionist position would imply). These forms set up social role expectations and meaning systems that regulate the boundaries of these roles. Persons constructively internalize these constraining meanings and re-present the meanings to themselves as *the* ways of organizing their lives. Finally, social scientists borrow the externalized versions of those meanings and use them as axi-oms in their research. Here the question of whether "pair bonding" can be axiomatically assumed provides an example: "I myself believe that this aspect of pair bonding has been grossly exaggerated by the present-day Western definitions of marriage and family life in terms of sexuality and the (initial) erotic bond between man and woman. What is crucial is not only the mutual sexual attractiveness, but also, in the human scheme of things, the sense of the helplessness of the infant and the empathy with the mother-child bond that evokes pity, love, and a sense of caring in the male" (Obeyesekere, 1990, p. 95).

Sexuality As a Means to Cultural Ends

The *devadasi* case was important in its unity of collective- and personal-cultural facets: through the collective cultural system of meanings, embed-ded in the architectural, textual, and ritual scripts' knowledge base, per-sonal-cultural construction of the social roles was accomplished in terms of particular women's individual relations to the social worlds. We could also see how the same personal-cultural semiotic mechanisms (e.g., the construction of the personal sense of "being married to a deity") could emerge in the Hindu context in social loci quite distant from the historically disappearing contexts of the *devadasi*. The meaning systems constructed by (and for) collective-cultural processes serve as inputs for personal-cultural constructions, which can proceed in similar directions at different times and places. Thus, Christian Protestant devotionalism has canalized women's selves toward identification with the church via the "bride of Christ" meaning system (see Maltz, 1978). A number of religious sects in the history of the United States (e.g., the Oneida Community of John Noyes in the nineteenth century) have redefined forms of sexuality in conjunction with the goals of the given social institution. Last but not least, the history of the European Catholic Church reveals episodes of making use of believers' sexual practices for the purposes of linking them with the church (Rossiaud, 1985).

The picture that emerges points to human sexuality and sensuality being human personal "material" for collective-cultural canalization of personal cultures. Women's sensuality in the case of the *devadasi* was utilized by the collective culture for collectively salient purposes. Sensuality was made into a means for collective-cultural canalization of the relations of persons with religious and social institutions.

Transcending the Biological Body: Culture's Playgrounds

This turn of a biological function (like sexuality) into a cultural means for achieving social-semiotic ends should not be surprising if we consider the possibility that *any* human bodily function can become a cultural tool of some kind. First and foremost, the traditions of cultural modifications of human bodies as such (e.g., tattooing—Barker and Tjetjen, 1990; Govenar, 1982; Steiner, 1990; ear piercing—Jevons, 1896, p. 172; scarification—Bohannan, 1956) have been utilized for a number of cultural aims (including those of personal cultural construction—see Sanders, 1989; Strathern, 1979). The strenuous or at times painful nature of such modifications has usually only added to the personal-cultural value of such undertakings (Obeyesekere, 1981). Modifiability of external characteristics of the human body (e.g., body hair—Basow, 1991; Hope, 1982; scalp hair—Getz and Klein, 1994) or cultural paraphernalia (clothing—from uniforms to meaningful holey jeans), as well as hygienic procedures of a sensual nature (bathing—Bushman and Bushman, 1988; Wilkie, 1986;

eating—Appadurai, 1981a) have all been utilized for cultural organization of psychological and social functions. Bodily functions may at the same time be the bases for, and the targets of, cultural construction processes. Biological and cultural processes are not opposed to one another but converge in ways that the biologically essential functions (e.g., alimentation, elimination, sleep, sexuality, body appearance, care of offspring) are also made to bear cultural functions whose role goes beyond that of biological ones.

Thus, the *devadasis'* cultural-semiotic role of empowerment of the community and its members through their fertility functions in ritualistic contexts is but one specific example of cultural uses of human sensuality. That it was accompanied by a cross-cultural perceptual construction of occidental attribution of the "prostitute" role to them adds a meta-level analysis to the specific history—the roles of the *devadasis* were reconstructed culturally by India's occidental colonizers for the purposes of their own social identity construction as such (i.e., the owners of the colonized lands).

The unity of the history of the *devadasi* role and personal cultures in construction (e.g., the case of Shakuntala) is reemphasized when persons reconstruct collective-cultural practices. Thus, a recent report in the *Times of India* announced a case of five women—all educated and in their thirties—turning up at the offices of the Jagannatha temple in Puri, asking to be dedicated to the temple as *devadasis* ("Five turn up . . .," 1995). The event created a sociojournalistic interest in the issue of the *devadasis,* yet the crucial part of the effort of the women to dedicate themselves as *devadasis* was personal-cultural: they had formed a religious group and considered themselves to be married to Jagannatha. The starting point of externalization of personal-cultural construction led to the public ceremony of application for the time-honored role in the temple.

From Female to Male Worlds: Cultural Construction of Heterosexual Differentiation Through Homoerotic Practices

Interestingly, the examples used so far pertain to the collective-cultural canalization of females' construction of personal cultures. This is but a coincidence here. Similar cases of uses of male sexual functions for cultural purposes can be observed in many cultural contexts. Let us consider one example: Sambia male "temporary homosexuality" as part of the cultural canalization of young boys to strict heterosexual orientation, social identity as warriors, and bonding with their age sets.

Semiotic Construction of "Discovery" of "Ritual Homosexuality"

The case of the Sambia in New Guinea has been described by Gilbert Herdt (1980, 1982, 1987, 1990). The collective culture canalizes male social identities in ontogeny through the emerging sexual functions of boys, and through secret ritual homoerotic practices, both male identities as warriors and their heteroerotic orientation toward regular marriage emerge.

The "discovery" of practices of "adolescent homosexuality" in many Pacific societies by occidental anthropologists in the early 1980s was certainly facilitated by the semiotic construction of open discourse of homosexuality in the anthropologists' societies of origin (Knauft, 1994). There seems to be an analogy between the use of Western social representations of the *devadasi* case on the one hand and New Guinea "homosexual societies" (or "sperm cultures") on the other. Anthropologists may project social discourse emphases from their own society onto the societies they study, using the latter as if the empirical evidence supported some of the ideological positions in the social negotiations at home. The "social other" of anthropologists' study is necessary for their own self-negotiations (Penuel and Wertsch, 1995a; Shi-xu, 1995). Thus, at colonial times, the tribes of New Guinea were viewed as "savages," while later they became viewed (as a result of the prevailing ideology of cultural relativism) as equal—or even better—"others" in terms of culture preservation. And when homosexuality became an open topic in Europe and North America, the "ritual homosexuality" in New Guinea was brought to the attention of the consumers of anthropological knowledge. This amounted to the highly selective pairing of a fashionable Western topic of talk and the complexity of cultural practices of the society investigated (Appadurai, 1986). Such construction of research themes has overlooked parallel issues in the society under study (e.g., the presence of "ritual heterosexuality" in New Guinean societies where "ritual homosexuality" is being "discovered"), and in the history of the investigators' own societies. Contemporarily in social sciences, "New Guinea has become what ancient Greece used to be for the discussion of sexual behavior between adult and adolescent males" (Schiefenhövel, 1990, p. 395).

In contrast, a closer look reveals that the so-labeled "ritual homosexuality"—as a collective-cultural practice—has little to do with homosexuality as such and very much to do with the semiotic construction of intergender boundaries in the social lives, and of male group cohesion. Homoerotic practices are utilized in the canalization of the development of exactly the opposite (heterosexual) orientation, and are made sense of in the meaning fields of "feeding" and "growth."

Sambia Male Initiation: Sexuality in Service of Gender Role Construction

The Sambia are a group in the Eastern Highlands of New Guinea. Their not very numerous society (estimated poulation, two thousand persons) is dispersed over a wide region. Men are hunters (and warriors), both women and men garden. In terms of gender-role socialization, the Sambia assume qualitatively different trajectories for men and women:

> Maleness is thought to depend on the acquisition of semen—the stuff of "biological" maleness—for precipitating male anatomic traits *and* masculine behavioral capacities (e.g., prowess). Femaleness rests on the creation and circulation of blood, which is held, in turn, to stimulate the production of menstrual blood, the menarche, and final reproductive competence . . . In the native model . . . the femaleness is a natural development leading into feminine adulthood; maleness is not a naturally driven process but rather a personal achievement of which men wrest control through ritual initiations to ensure that boys attain adult masculine competence. (Herdt, 1982, p. 195)

The initiation rituals for boys include stages, at each of which the boy is brought into the secret male know-how and practices. Among the Sambia, gender groups are segregated from each other through boundaries based on gender-specific knowledge. In line with this, social relations between the sexes are not only polarized but also hostile. Boys are brought out from women's care and gradually initiated into the male secret world; their primary identification is expected to be with other men—loyalty to age set and respect for men older than they.

The intergender social boundaries are internalized with the help of semiotic organizing concepts such as "shame." For example, Sambia men avoid mentioning words such as "menstrual blood" or "vagina" because such mention is linked with promoting shame (Herdt, 1981, pp. 166–

167; compare with the uses of "zero signifiers" in chapter 3). While creating across-gender separation at the internalized level, shame clearly does not regulate homoerotic and heteroerotic contacts in the practice of fellatio in male adult–adolescent boy relations, or in boy-girl relations. The canalizing role of shame is overrun by the notion of "food." What for outsiders looks like a homoerotic practice—fellatio—in the Sambia context is an act of gender-specific nutritional practice that cannot be accomplished in other ways. For boys of Sambia, the notion of semen as a necessary food for growth leads to the acceptance of fellatio in the case of relations with older peers and adult males. Despite the ease with which this can be labeled "homosexual practice" in the meaning field of occidental societies (and of the social sciences), its emic cultural function is not that of overoccupation with issues of sex but regulation of collective-culturally organized growth of male personality. Once this function is fulfilled (and adolescent boys have been initiated into full manhood), the need for such a regulator disappears. Young males marry, and their sexual functions proceed fully within the realm of ordinary procreational heterosexual practices (even though exceptions do occur—see Herdt, 1980). Their meaningful concern with semen loss now becomes displaced into another secret male realm (of drinking tree sap for the "replacement" of semen lost to women in regular intercourse). Thus, the meaning of semen as a crucially powerful source of energy is retained in the self-system, but by now its collective-cultural role is different.

Conclusions: Semiotic Regulation of Human Lives As Redundant Control by Collective and Personal Cultures

The material analyzed in this chapter reveals a double-level semiotic canalization in the case of the Hindu temple dancers. First, the actual lives of the women who entered temple service as a lifelong career were brought into this situated activity context through a *semiotically overdetermined* organization of their everyday life environments, and of meaningful activities within these environments. *Devadasis'* conduct was jointly regulated by the collective-cultural organization of their roles and their personal-cultural sense systems. Both kinds of regulators supported the functioning of the other, thus creating a stable regulatory system that allowed for many compensatory possibilities.

The *devadasi* historical case challenges the axiomatic assumption of psychoanalysis (of the primacy of sexual experiences in relation to psychological constructions) by pointing to the possibility of reverse translation of experiences (the primacy of collective-cultural meanings—internalized by personal cultures—that lead to sexual experiences). That the *devadasi* cases—extreme in their collective-cultural canalization as those may be seen—are not so different from our ordinary personality organization was demonstrated by pointing to similar uses of semiotic self-regulation devices in our contemporary cases (e.g., that of Shakuntala). The Sambia case of "semen feeding" from men to boys constitutes an example of how male sexuality is culturally set up in service of social objectives.

The second level of semiotic canalization involves the regulation of the social scientists' orientation toward phenomena that entail sensual-sexual facets. Depiction of the *devadasis* as "temple prostitutes" has been a rhetorical device that has ruled out some possibilities of understanding the cultural and personal histories of the practice and its practitioners. Similarly, the construction of the notion of "homosexual societies" is a semiotic means for social negotiations of issues of sexuality in the investigators' own societies. Empirical research entails a hierarchy of canalized meanings: first the field of meanings of the investigator constrains the realm of meaning-making of the phenomena (as those are translated into the data—described in chapter 7). Certain aspects of the phenomena remain unmentionable (as outside of the ZFM), others are mentioned but not emphasized, and still others are made into the focus of investigation (ZPA). As a result, empirical research in the social sciences necessarily is value-laden and selectively interpreted as to its "social relevance." The researcher's knowledge of these semiotic self-constraints would not change this, but would clarify the conditions under which some aspect of general knowledge was created.

However, the constraining mechanisms are at work at both levels—the persons whose personal worlds are studied constrain their own relations with their selves through semiotic mediation. This personal-cultural canalization is interdependent with collective-cultural constraining. Therefore, on many occasions the persons who are studied demonstrate some form of intersubjectivity with the investigator. An investigator who casts a *devadasi* as a "prostitute" may encounter at least some women in the role of the *devadasi* who also utilize that meaning in their personal-cultural system. This may happen to mark the opposition to its implications (e.g., "they consider us prostitutes but we are servants to the deity"), or acceptance and escalation of the suggestion ("I am a prostitute and this is shameful"), or many other personal co-constructed versions of meanings. Undoubtedly, what follows from this is the necessity to know *all three* components of semiotically mediated research process: the investigator's constructions of meanings of the issues under study (and the reasons for studying it), the collective-cultural orientation of the issues as viewed from different institutional perspectives, and the persons' own semiotic self-constructions. Discrepancies among these components are not only expected but valuable for our general knowledge. The latter needs to be *ideologies-recognizing* rather than ideological in itself (Valsiner, 1995a).

In other terms, a relevant part of general knowledge in the social sciences is the recognition of the areas of ignorance, some of which are canalized by the ideological setup of ZFM boundaries by the investigators themselves. Within the ZFM boundaries of the field of research, the question of "pseudoempiricism" in psychological studies that has been consistently raised by Smedslund (1988, 1994, 1995) reveals another subdomain of meaning construction (e.g., accepting all empirical evidence as evidence and claiming the need for new evidence in previously unstudied areas; or considering only that empirical evidence that forces us to change our conceptual constraints system).

It is the triangulation of researcher–researchee–collective-culture perspectives that gives rise to knowledge that is simultaneously both particular and general. Psychology's theoretical constructions could benefit from making this triangulation explicit, choosing to make use of it rather than let it be a cultural convention that motivates our efforts, creates problems of misunderstanding, and at times leads us to general conclusions of temporary social value.

Conclusion: The Guided and (Self-) Guiding Mind

This book has brought together a wide variety of intellectual traditions from psychology, anthropology, sociology, and history. Its focus has been on interdisciplinary synthesis—an effort to cast the question of human personality into a theoretical framework that borrows from the traditions of personality psychology yet does not become a hostage to the limits of that tradition. Hence most of the ordinary discourse about personality in psychology—discussions of personality types or "measurement"—does not occupy a relevant part in this book. Instead, the central focus is on the emergence and functioning of different semiotic devices that act as social regulators within the personal-cultural constructions of conduct regulation systems. These systems set up constraints upon persons' acting, thinking, and feeling within concrete life-experiencing contexts, as those flow within irreversible time.

The human personality is socially guided and also guides itself through the construction and use of semiotic mediating devices. All human personality originates in social relationships that are organized by human use of semiotic systems. This form of organization guides—but *does not determine*—the development of personality by way of constructive internalization/externalization mechanisms. It sets the stage for the person's directed, suggested, and in all ways canalized movement toward the future—yet in that movement the person is actively constructing his or her personal world (personal culture). Assumptions of the social determinacy of human personality that have dominated the sociocultural viewpoint for decades, and similar assumptions of internal determinacy that are at times projected into the notion of "personality," are better replaced by a view of *jointly negotiated co-(in)determinacy* of human personality development.

385

Personal Uniqueness Is Autonomous, Yet Social

The result of this co-indeterministic view on personality is the recognition of the *increased autonomy of the self* in relation to other persons and social circumstances over one's life course. Personality is socially constituted exactly as it is relatively independent of the immediate social demands or expectations in any particular situation. In other terms, personality is *dependently independent* (or independently dependent) in relation to its social world (Valsiner, 1984a; Winegar, Renninger, and Valsiner, 1989). This independent dependence is recognized by the notion of *bounded* indeterminacy of development: development is simultaneously "free" for emergence of novel forms and bounded by the conditions (of both the developing organism and its environment) within which it proceeds.

At first glance, this claim of autonomy as proof of social embeddedness of personality seems paradoxical, since it contradicts the traditional notion of "causal influences." According to the latter, if the social world is relevant for personality, it must have "an effect" on the latter. Thinking in terms of "effects" is borrowed from our common sense and is exemplified by the model of one passively moved object (e.g., a billiard ball) having impact ("effect") upon another, setting the latter into motion. In more usual terms of stimulus-response sequences, the latter ("response") is "caused by" the former ("stimulus"), rather than set into motion by itself. To talk about the "self-generated active role" of a "response" (or of a "stimulus") would lead a psychologist to the "danger zone" of being accused of personification of strictly inanimate entities, or to straight animistic thinking. To continue with the billiard balls example, it is as if each of the billiard balls had its own "internal engine" that rolls it in different directions—to avoid being hit by another, to counterhit the hitting ball, or to merely withstand the hit without any movement. Surely a game of billiards with such (self-guiding) balls would be a very different game. The same is true of the study of human development—notions of simple linear causality, borrowed from the world of inanimate objects, are not applicable. Rather, the open-systemic world of development operates in terms of conditional (catalyzed) systemic causality (Valsiner, 1987, 1989).

The developing systems acquire relative autonomy—relative to their immediate environmental demands—to preemptively prepare themselves for the future. Human personality is a self-organizing system that constantly reconstructs itself (i.e., is autopoetic—Maturana, 1980). The social environment is to be viewed as making it possible for the personality system to rearrange itself in many unique forms, not necessarily along the lines of social expectations of any particular setting. Thus, the social origins of human personality can be demonstrated by the seeming lack of "social influences" within the personality at a given time or context. A person who actively resists current demands for "group conformity," "social suggestibility," "fashion," and the like demonstrates the sociogenetic origins of personality as well as (or better than) another who happens to follow current social demands.

Another result of the general tendency toward autonomization of personality is its principled individual uniqueness. Each person is unique in his or her co-construction of the personality system, yet all personalities are constructed through general developmental mechanisms. There is unity in diversity in the personal uniqueness—well recognized by William Stern (1911) and at times recognized anew in systemic treatises on human beings. For example:

> We should conceive of systems not only in terms of global unity . . . but in terms of *unitas multiplex* . . . The whole is effectively a macro-unity, but the parts are not fused or confused therein; they have a double identity, one which continues to belong to each of them individually (and is thus irreducible to the whole), and one which is held in common . . . More than that, . . . a system is not only a composition of unity out of diversity, but also a composition of internal diversity out of unity. (Morin, 1992, p. 373)

It is exactly that internal unified diversity that provides human personality with its multifaceted and context-dependent nature. The intricacies of loving and hating persons have been well described by novelists, and sometimes psychologists have given the structural complexity of personality its due through individual-case-focused, consideration (e.g., Scheerer, Rothman, and Goldstein, 1945).

The intellectual efforts made in this book are directed against increasing fragmentation of knowledge in the social sciences, and toward making sense of the *context specificity* of human conduct and its development. Numerous empirical demonstrations of how such conduct varies in different situations—termed "contexts"—or from one society to another (as found in cross-cultural psychology) have led to a lack of interest in the universality of the general principles that might exist behind the dynamic heterogeneity of "context effects." In our modularization of the complexity of human beings we may have lost an explanatory focus, failing to see the "the forest behind trees."

The discourse in this book is itself a good example. Both personological and sociocultural views on the person have had to accept the variability of the person's life organization over time. Indeed, the multitude of personality traits (or sociocultural contexts or semiotic mediating devices) is potentially infinite. However, behind this potentially infinite proliferation of specificity can exist universal generative mechanisms that make it possible for individual persons to create novel meaningful situations, enter into those, let themselves be guided by those, and distance oneself from those and break with the "situated activity contexts." If we see the function of semiotic mediation as preadaptation to possible future happenings, the actualization of which is to be worked out by the person's own acting and thinking—then the capacity for production of a large variety of psychological phenomena is a relevant achievement of human evolution.

Preadaptation Through Semiotic Mediation, and Needs for Theory

This break—the capability to transcend a present situated activity context and create a new one—is made possible by the human capacity for semiotic regulation of one another and of oneself. The necessity for such constant transcending of the here-and-now contexts is created by the irreversibility of life processes. The living and experiencing person is not merely "adapting" to the "environment" as the latter exists in any present state but is constantly *preadapting* to possible future encounters with new environments. The latter may *resemble* some of the previously lived-through settings in some ways, yet in their constitution they are necessarily new in their totality. The developmental course has a helical structure, where the curves of the helix may look similar to previous turns, yet the whole process of development moves in a spiral fashion from the past toward the future—never stopping in the human lifetime, never repeating a previously traversed curve. Persons are thus always incompletely "fitted in" with the demands of any present context, since human conduct is oriented toward expected (but not predictable) sets of future conditions and thus only partly fits with the present state of person-environment relations.

This latter feature of human psychological development sets up unique demands for psychological theory. Theory of human psychological development needs to be formulated in terms that relate the personal present with the expected (yet unpredictable) future, while at the same time allowing it to benefit from the experiences of the past. The notion of bounded indeterminacy was designed to serve as the general conceptual basis for such theorizing (Valsiner, 1987, 1997b). It entailed using a third way to look at the determinacy/indeterminacy issue of human development, bringing together both deterministic (constraints) and indeterministic sides (actual actions) of developmental phenomena (as elaborated in chapter 2).

Human personality is regulated by constraints in two domains—those of action and reflection. In both domains, constraints are set up in two areas—interpsychological (i.e., in communication and joint action between people) and intrapsychological (i.e., within the internal psychological system of the person). Constraints are *not* "repressors" or "suppressors" of human "unlimited freedom," as commonsense thinking within occidental societies may present those. Instead, *constraints are partitions of the field of possibilities* that are set (and reset) dynamically. The notion of constraining is ideologically neutral; it merely indicates that at every moment, construction of structural regulating devices of the ongoing process of development takes place.

The "zone" concepts elaborated in this book (see chapter 2) are specific ways to describe the processes involved in constraining. These concepts come from the history of field-theoretic constructions in the history of psychology. In an earlier version of the present theory, the system of "zones"—ZFM/ZPA and ZPD—was applied to early childhood development in everyday life contexts. In this book, thinking in terms of these zone concepts was applied to adult personality development.

Of course, the general organismic focus on personality that has been used in the present approach is not new. Most of the "primary propositions" advocated by Henry Murray (1938) for the study of personality are in agreement with the basic assumptions used here. However, a novel emphasis in the psychology of personality is that of persons' constraining their own development by semiotic mediating devices of various kinds. Human development entails construction of signs. The signs can be of different levels of abstractedness (relative to a here-and-now situation), and as such these signs set up constraints on the construction of holistic meaning complexes within any particular setting.

Based on signs, human beings have developed different *relatively* stable ways of relating their personality with the social world (see discussion of "ego-defense" mechanisms in chapter 3). Such general functions of signs make it possible for human personality to operate on the basis of materials that can be labeled variously as "social representations," "beliefs," "values," "truths," and so on. Each particular meaning that is labeled to be of the status of these concepts sets up specific boundaries within which a particular situation can be made meaningful for the person. Signs operate as *cultural organizers* of the human personality system.

Cultural Organizers of Psychological Functions: A Parallel Thought Model to Protein Synthesis

In this book, culture in personality is addressed from a semiotic perspective. The notion of cultural organizers is introduced here in direct analogy with the notion of regulator genes in modern genetics of protein synthesis. In the latter, specific systemic relations between regulator genes make it possible (or impossible) for a particular protein structure to be built. It can be argued that in human psychological functioning, the role of regulation of the generative possibilities of the human mind takes precedence over charting out the full set of human semiotic possibilities. Given the propensity toward constructing ever-new signs and changing the specific meanings of existing ones, as well as the flexibility of operating simultaneously (as well as successively) at various levels of abstraction, the human psychological processes can be inherently infinitely open to new ways of reflecting upon any situation. This excessive openness is a necessary result of future-oriented adaptation efforts, which follow from the inevitability of irreversibility of time. Each here-and-now situation in the life of a human being is inevitably unique and novel, and it is through the construction of the system of cultural organizers—semiotic devices—that the personality can function with remarkable coherence across these unique situations.

Cultural organizers (or regulators) are a system of meanings that regulate reflection (both cognitive and affective) and action. These meanings are *constructed by the person's psychological system,* under the constraining guidance on behalf of various agents that represent the collective culture in the personal world of the constructor. That guidance can be simultaneously oriented toward variable (often opposing) objectives, putting the constructing person in the middle of ambivalent interpretations of a given situation, or in dilemmas that cannot be solved. This picture differs cardinally from one where the society—harmoniously and homogeneously—

"socializes" persons in the direction of desired states of personality. The reality of collective culture is always heterogeneous, changing, and filled with unclarities, redundancies, and illogicalities of the guidance the "social others" provide for the developing persons. It is though cultural organizers of such a potpourri of the collective-cultural suggestions that the developing person can construct his or her personality.

Cultural organizers are thus *intrapersonal* phenomena—products of the internalization/externalization process. They are future-oriented functional products; as constructed, they regulate the development of a here-and-now state into its next version in time. Simultaneously they become functional in longer-term feed-forward processes: they can be constructively evoked at times in the more distant future to organize a specific impending encounter with the (always) novel conditions of the environment. Human development thus entails overproduction of cultural organizers in order to be ready for a variety of possible future situations.

Cultural regulators form different kinds of hierarchical systems (transitive, intransitive, and mixed, as described in chapter 2). Cultural regulators can include "empty domains" in their structure ("zero signifiers"), as well as "overextended" ones (e.g., the use of excessive—yet normative— "empty talk" as a regulator of lack of access to the underlying phenomena). The fact that *Homo sapiens* has developed the means for speaking does not mean that all representatives of this species use it for information exchange. Alongside the transfer of knowledge exists the separation of some of the information into the realm of nontransferability. Furthermore, the communication channels may be overflown by substituted materials that create the desired illusion of information being exchanged, while in reality becoming a sign that represents information by its surrogates. This may be an extension of general separation of the producers (creators) of goods and their users (consumers) in society (see Del Río, 1996).

The notion of cultural organizers is not a new label to personality traits—no assumption is made regarding the existence of these organizers "in" the personality. The organizers are constructed in the process of forward-oriented adaptation and can become extinct when not needed. If they are maintained, then that process constitutes a steady-state maintenance of an open system. Through the functioning of cultural regulators, the personality system can modulate its active participation in any given setting. It can move itself "out" of the given setting through increased distancing or "into" the given situation by semiotically guiding one's actions to become "fused" with the given social situation. In other terms, psychological mechanisms of both phenomena of "trance" and "alienation" are the same—distancing through the system of cultural regulators that are set up to canalize the person in either of the two opposite states.

Through cultural regulators, human personality becomes a teleogenetic (goal-setting and goal-oriented) system. Constraining through cultural regulators sets up future objectives for which the personality in the present is guided to strive. Surely these objectives can be immediately changed— the system need not imply long-term goal-following—yet the general orientation at all times is toward some future objective. On the basis of such an orientation, strategic goal-oriented acting and thinking become possible.

Communication, Intersubjectivity, and Subjectivity

One of the greatest difficulties in the usual sociogenetic view on personality is to make sense of *subjectivity* of persons as individuals, and *intersubjectivity* of persons' encounters with one another (as described in chapter 1). A solution that was provided in this book fits with the unification of sociogenetic and personological approaches. First of all, phenomenologically the only psychological reality we can possibly consider to exist is the subjective one. It is accessible to each unique person directly through introspection, and secondarily through interpersonal communication. In the latter, semiotic means of communication challenge the construction of the understanding of the other communication partner's view of the world.

Karl Bühler's organon model (analyzed in chapter 6) is used to emphasize the mutuality of intersubjectivity and subjectivity—the former creates the context for construction of the latter. Thus, intersubjectivity leads personality away from "sharing" with others and toward increasing construction of unique personal forms of subjective reflection and affection toward the world. The social world orients the developing person toward life-course options that are collective-culturally appropriate. Nevertheless, the active person can resist, neutralize, revolt against, as well as (obviously) accept, such canalization efforts. Hence the social guidance and personal active construction of one's self are jointly involved in the construction of the life course. The mind—to paraphrase the title of this book—is guided both by one's own subjectivity at any given time and by the collective-cultural world (with its intersubjective moments) which the person inhabits.

Functions for the Breaking of Assumed Intersubjectivity

Probably the major implication of this emphasis is the acceptance of the idea that most of human development takes place through *active ignoring and neutralization of most of the social suggestions* to which the person is subjected in everyday life. In order to guarantee relative stability of the personality system, it has to be well buffered against immediate social suggestions. The latter may be filled with dramatisms, hurtful efforts, or declarations of love or hate (or both), yet the likelihood of such single episodes having "long-term effects" of any direct kind need not be taken for granted. Hence, what is usually viewed as "socialization efforts" (by social institutions or parents) necessarily counteracted by the active recipients of such efforts, who can neutralize or ignore a large number of such episodes, aside from single particularly dramatic ones. This helps us recognize human ontogeny of personality as a slow and conservative process, where the loci of openness to social input are largely made available by the intrasystemic organization of the personality. It is the emerging system of personal culture that allows some of the incoming social suggestions to be accepted as "input" for further construction of the personality, while dismissing others with the help of various buffering strategies.

On the side of the collective culture, permeated by "social others'" efforts at creation of the "socialization effects," one can observe adaptation to this autonomously selective nature of the developing personality. The "social others" are constantly involved in excessive construction of various kinds of social suggestions, especially in areas highlighted by their relevance for the collective-cultural system (e.g., issues of "morality," "success in life," "patriotism"). In this respect—looking at the collective culture—the present semiotic perspective on personality builds upon the previous efforts to unify culture and personality (e.g., Kluckhohn and Murray, 1948).

Compensation by the Social World for Personal Resistance: Overproduction

The social world around a developing person is involved in massive overproduction of social suggestions for the person, whereas the latter has constructed his or her own strategies of neutralization, ignoring, transforming, and evaluation of those masses of suggestions. Thus, no "economic rationality" can be involved in the socialization efforts that target developing personality: the overproduction of suggestions takes place all through the human life course, even if it may be particularly overdetermined at some periods of childhood.

Psychologists tend to borrow nondevelopmental models from other disciplines. One of these is the prevailing tendency to consider rationality of calculable solutions to be an axiomatic norm. As a result, we get "cost-benefit" analyses applied in different areas of modeling psychological phenomena. Yet the maximization-oriented notion of "economic rationality" may be an untenable concept even in the field of economics (Simon, 1957). To expect it to be present in human development—a phenomenon far more sophisticated than economic processes—might be a naive effort to insist upon illusory simplicity of the human psyche. The latter striving is certainly fortified by social consensus of psychologists regarding methodology. It goes without saying that the theoretical system elaborated here has some profound implications for psychology's empirical practices.

General Methodology and Implications for Empirical Studies

If the theoretical perspective outlined in this book is taken as a starting point, a number of implications for what kind of empirical investigations of human personality make sense follow suit. The co-constructionist nature of personality development would make the *negotiation* process between the active person and the complex of collective-cultural suggestions the object of direct investigation. This relocation of the focus of investigation away from presuming the existence of intrapersonal entity-like components of personality (such as "traits"), and from the mere documentation of the folk models of human personality that exist in the given society, fits the open-systemic axiom of development. If we are interested in the study of development, the process by which the person relates to the world—in this case that of negotiation with the diverse suggestions from the collective culture—needs to be studied. This negotiation process is *open-ended:* it can entail the construction of previously unencountered actions and reflective devices (cultural organizers).

Primacy of the Individual Case, Studied Systemically

Developmental investigation involves the study of negotiation as a process—preserving the time involved in the process. Repeated efforts to construct a meaningful solution for the personal culture at the intersection of specifiable contrasting collective-cultural suggestions are thus the field of phenomena where human personality can be studied as a process. It is therefore natural that the *definitive empirical source for data derivation is the single case: a particular personality studied in its negotiation process with the collective culture.*

In this perspective, generalizations are made from single cases to the generic functioning of the personality system. The empirical task of the researcher is first to analyze the systemic functioning of single personality and then to aggregate knowledge of the ways in which the system works, across persons, into a generic model (Thorngate, 1992). The process of such postanalysis aggregation is that of reapplication of the generic model (created on the basis of a single case) as a hypothetical pattern, to new selected single cases. The latter may be selected on the basis of information about the standing of the case within a sample (thus leading to a combination of case-based and sample-based information—still with the primacy of the former). In fact, selection of cases from different ranges of the sample (i.e., using information about interindividual differences)—from extreme ends and from the middle of the distribution—may help the inductive side of the generalization process. If the hypothesized generic model of the single case (and based on one single case, say, drawn from the middle range of the sample distribution) is demonstrated to function in those who are extremes in the distribution, the researcher is on her or his way toward basic knowledge. This strategy is well known in linguistics, where adequacy of a theoretical proposition is tested on singular examples from language, testing for extreme cases that may refute the proposition. Finding such single countercases forces the theoretical system to reconstruct, or at times may lead to the abandonment of the system.

Multiplicity of Generic Models

Nevertheless, generalization from single case to generic models, and testing the latter on other single cases, introduces a conceptual difficulty that brings the issue of deductive and inductive knowledge generation paths back into focus. Namely, the story is reasonable when we can be sure that there can be only one adequate generic model, and we have a hard time reconstructing it only on the basis of our thinking and empirical evidence. This was true for Watson and Crick when they were playing with different possible models of DNA yet being safe in their assumption that only one model can describe *the* structure of DNA. However, if we consider processes of biological or psychological development, we have good reasons to doubt an assumption that there is only one model. The reasons for such doubt stem from the open-systemic nature of development. In open systems, *redundancy* of control mechanisms is theoretically expected. This means that different models of systemic regulation coexist, even if one of them may "do the job" at a given time. Furthermore, they coexist within the single case, and if one of them (the currently dominant or "visible" one—A, as opposed to non-A) becomes used in the derivation of the generic model, the inductive information basis for this generalization is already at fault. If such a model is now tested on the basis of another single case where it fails to be demonstrable (the non-A becomes demonstrated instead), then the researcher is left with the need to consider two opposite models (A and non-A). This would mean that systematic inductive inquiry about new models may lead us to an ever-expanding list of such models (for example, see discussion of "ego-defense" mechanisms in chapter 3).

It is clear that unbounded reliance on inductive generalization from single cases needs to be constrained by deductive theoretical argumentation (Van Geert, 1994). It is the direction of experimental theoretical psychology—which tests the range of outcomes generated by a posited model (or set of models)—that may bring the study of human development out from under the menace of "galloping empiricism" (to use Allport's term). A return to the notion of methodology as a circle that links general assumptions, phenomena, theories, methods and data in one knowledge-construction process (as outlined in chapter 7) may afford establishment of reasonably balanced contributions of the empirical and theoretical sides of knowledge construction. Psychology has done itself a major disservice, over recent decades, by being hyperactively empirical in its ideological stance.

A Co-Constructionist Perspective on "Variables"

For purposes of labeling convenience, the perspective outlined in this book can be called co-constructionist—since it emphasizes the role of both the person and the "social others" in the negotiation of the course of development. The co-constructionist focus does not introduce any new specific methods but rather provides an interpretive framework for existing ones. Thus, experiments cannot be viewed as entailing simple changing of "independent" variables to check their "effect" upon the "dependent" ones. In fact, there cannot be "variables" in the strict sense of this term (i.e., quantitative entities that can be varied at will, independently from one another). Instead, the experimental situation is constructed (and reconstructed) by the experimenter in its total structure, which is expected to elicit in the subject a process of acting and thinking. The latter processes would be the targets of analysis—equivalents of the traditional talk of "dependent variables." Clearly the folk model of "quantification as objectivity" (see Valsiner, 1987, chapter 5; 1997b, chapter 3) disappears from use in the case of this modification of the experimental method, and certain (usually termed "old") traditions of experimentation used by Gestalt or *Ganzheit* psychologists come back into vogue.

Possibilities for empirical investigations transcend the realm of traditional psychological methods in the case of the present constraining theory of personality. The use of personal documents (proposed long ago by Gordon Allport) and historical materials about personal lives in different social roles at other historical periods provides an adequate basis for present co-constructionist reconstructions. Undoubtedly the difficulties of inference remain in the case of such applications, yet it must be pointed out that such difficulties are similar in traditional methods of psychology in a contemporaneous research practice. The mere possibility that the subject who is sitting in front of us here and now can at any moment internally construct distance from this situation (and become, in our usual vernacular, uncooperative) creates interpretational hurdles comparable to those of putting together an account of vanished (or vanishing) sociocultural life courses (such as the case of the *devadasis*, as analyzed in chapter 9).

History in Contemporary Theory-Building

A key feature of the present theoretical coverage of human personality is the integration of historical know-how into the construction of a contemporary perspective. Studies in the history of psychology and language provide us with a number of efforts to solve basic problems.

Usually, history is exclusively separated from contemporary theorizing, and treated as if it were a museum of many failures and few successes. It is often de facto removed from the advancement of science, being considered a record of the failures of science rather than a source for new ideas. Yet all the ideas that have been tried out to solve a given problem— whether successfully or not—were novel efforts at their time. An analysis of the history of ideas is as relevant for our understanding of a science as the analysis of human development is for understanding personality. The history of psychology constitutes "a privileged ground for an exercise of reflexivity" (Rosa, 1994, p. 164), rather than a mélange of ideas that are old and useful merely for classification purposes of collectionists.

Here I treat ideas coming from history as cultural organizers of the present construction of a view on personality. Thus, the heritage of Charles S. Peirce, James M. Baldwin, Pierre Janet, Karl Bühler, William Stern, Gordon Allport, and others is utilized here on the basis of the value of their specific conceptual innovations to capture the functioning of human personality. This amounts to the inclusive separation of these historical ideas from our present construction efforts: surely we recognize their past contexts of intellectual interdependency, while at the same time these ideas are treated as equals to any contemporary theoretical construction. History of psychology is thus a fertile source for constructing new perspectives in our present time, and not a separate area of interest (for those few who "take interest" in history).

Collective Culture and Personal Culture: Contextualized Personality

As has been emphasized throughout this book, the collective culture is the heterogeneous system of meanings, meaningful objects, environmental settings, ritualized action contexts, and direct social suggestions that serve as goal-oriented "input" into the development of the personality—that is, of the personal culture. The person actively constructs the latter through the internalization/externalization process. Hence the personological viewpoint on personality has its focus confirmed when viewed through a sociogenetic prism: *the central role of the person lies in the constant construction of his or her self as a semiotic system.*

In this construction process, abductive inference (C. S. Peirce, as described in chapter 6) dominates in the construction of personal culture. This is a necessary condition if we consider the construction of personal culture as a bidirectional transmission process (Valsiner, 1989) in which collective culture is not directly "transmitted" (or given over) to the personal culture. Instead, the specific communicative messages of the collective culture are disassembled by the active person and reassembled in novel forms in the personal culture. Personal culture construction entails emergence of ever-new personal nuances of abstracted feelings and reflections (i.e., it operates according to Bühler's principle of abstractive relevance; see chapter 6). This makes it possible for the personality to move quickly between being immersed in a here-and-now situation to being distanced from it. Such *modulation of distancing* constitutes a flexible resource for the personality as the latter is *simultaneously* part of the given situation (as he or she is necessarily in *some* here-and-now setting) and not part of that setting (i.e., distanced from it through personal-cultural means). This modulation may have its role in constructive adaptation of the personality in terms of emergence of new distancing strategies (e.g., as was described under "ego-defense" mechanisms in chapter 3).

What does all this have to do with personality? This is a rather legitimate question, especially from the vantage point of occidental common sense, where personality has established its meaning as an independent intrapersonal entity. It is exactly the abandonment of this concept (and of the occidental common sense) that has been attempted in this book. The static and entified implications of the notion of "personality" and its characteristics ("traits," "types," etc.) are theoretically unproductive. Personality, when viewed as a process of constant construction and reconstruction of the subjective totality of reflections upon the world, cannot be phrased in terms of static entities. As Josef Nuttin has expressed it:

> At each moment human personality is creating itself, partially in new and unknown ways. The stereotyped behavior patterns in which the individual expresses himself, and the fixed traits of character in which his fellow man tries to catch his personality, do not exhaust the ever-new life that at each moment bubbles up at the source of consciousness. What is most "personal" and "new" at each moment of human life is experienced in one's own intimacy and is unattainable to others and situated far behind the conventional forms of personality expression. In this inexhaustible and creative intimacy, the attractive mystery of human personality finds its origin and its continous supply. (Nuttin, 1950, p. 347)

In the present conceptualization, the notion of personal culture replaces the notion of personality as it focuses on the interdependence between the person and the collective culture. This interdependence is captured in the constructive process of internalization and externalization. The tandem concept—personal and collective culture—is of heuristic value only as a set of terms to guide psychologists' interest in the ubiquitous processes between the person and the social world. Nevertheless, human beings develop through their life courses in their personally unique but generically uniform ways. This variability constitutes the strength of human lives, which can endure dramatic changes in their habitats, invoked by themselves or others, while retaining their selves in contexts as divergent as stock exchanges, executive board meetings, looking for surviving relatives in one's hometown after an air raid, or watching a glorified journalistic account of the latter in the comfort of one's peaceful living room.

The personality prevails under different circumstances. Yet what on the side of our usual commonsense depiction is an entity in its own standing is actually a constant process of internalization/externalization that is guided by cultural organizers. The science of personality cannot proceed through treating personality (or self) as a static entity, as its open-systemic nature haunts psychologists at every step. Yet recognition of that ghost of openness requires a major methodological turn in the discipline. The "birth pangs" of such a turn—much discussed and still little accomplished—continue to make psychology a challenging arena for our intellectual efforts.

References

Adler, A. (1924). The individual-psychology of prostitution. In A. Adler, *The practice and theory of individual psychology* (pp. 327–338). New York: Harcourt, Brace.

Allen, M. (1982). The Hindu view of women. In M. Allen and S. N. Mukherjee (eds.), *Women in India and Nepal* (pp. 1–20). Australian National University Monographs on South Asia, No. 8. Canberra: Australian National University Press.

Allesch, C. G. (1993). The aesthetic as a psychological aspect of man-environment relations, or: Ernst E. Boesch as an aesthetician. *Sweizerische Zeitschrift für Psychologie, 52,* 2, 122–129.

Allport, F. H. (1934). The J-curve hypothesis of conforming behavior. *Journal of Social Psychology, 5,* 141–183.

Allport, F. H., and Allport, G. W. (1921). Personality traits: Their classification and measurement. *Journal of Abnormal and Social Psychology, 16,* 6–40.

Allport, G. W. (1924a). The study of the undivided personality. *Journal of Abnormal and Social Psychology, 19,* 132–141.

——— (1924b). Die theoretische Hauptströmungen in der amerikanischen Psychologie der Gegenwart. *Zeitschrift für pädagogische Psychologie und experimentale Pädagogik, 25,* 129–137.

——— (1925). Book review of M. Follett, *Creative experience. Journal of Abnormal and Social Psychology, 19,* 426–428.

——— (1927). Concepts of trait and personality. *Psychological Bulletin, 24,* 284–293.

——— (1928). A test for ascendance-submission. *Journal of Abnormal and Social Psychology, 23,* 118–136.

——— (1929a). The composition of political attitudes. *American Journal of Sociology, 35,* 220–238.

——— (1929b). The study of personality by the intuitive method: An experiment in the teaching from *The locomotive god. Journal of Abnormal and Social Psychology, 24,* 14–27.

——— (1931). What is a trait of personality? *Journal of Abnormal and Social Psychology, 25,* 368–372.

———— (1937a). The functional autonomy of motives. *American Journal of Psychology, 50,* 141–156.

———— (1937b). The personalistic psychology of William Stern. *Character and Personality, 5,* 231–246.

———— (1937c). *Personality: A psychological interpretation.* New York: Henry Holt.

———— (1940a). Foreword to H. Werner, *Comparative psychology of mental development* (pp. ix–xii). New York: Harper and Brothers.

———— (1940b). Motivation in personality: Reply to Mr. Bertocci. *Psychological Review, 47,* 533–554.

———— (1940c). The psychologist's frame of reference. *Psychological Bulletin, 37,* 1–28.

———— (1942). The use of personal documents in psychological science. *Social Science Research Council Bulletin,* no. 49.

———— (1943a). The ego in contemporary psychology. *Psychological Review, 50,* 451–478.

———— (1943b). The productive paradoxes of William James. *Psychological Review, 50,* 95–123.

———— (1945). The psychology of participation. *Psychological Review, 52,* 117–132.

———— (1946a). Geneticism versus ego-structure in theories of personality. *British Journal of Educational Psychology, 16,* 57–68.

———— (1946b). Personalistic psychology as science: A reply. *Psychological Review, 53,* 132–135.

———— (1951). Dewey's individual and social psychology. In P. A. Schlipp (ed.), *The philosophy of John Dewey* (pp. 265–290). New York: Tudor.

———— (1953). The trend in motivational theory. *American Journal of Orthopsychiatry, 23,* 107–119.

———— (1955). *Becoming: Basic considerations for a psychology of personality.* New Haven, Conn.: Yale University Press.

———— (1962). The general and the unique in psychological science. *Journal of Personality, 30,* 405–422.

———— (1965). *Letters from Jenny.* New York: Harcourt, Brace and World.

———— (1966). Traits revisited. *American Psychologist, 21,* 1–10.

———— (1967). Gordon W. Allport. In E. G. Boring and G. Lindzey (eds.), *A history of psychology in autobiography.* Vol. 5 (pp. 3–25). New York: Appleton-Century-Crofts.

———— (1968a). Crises in normal personality development. In G. W. Allport, *The person in psychology* (pp. 171–183). Boston: Beacon Press. [First published in 1964 in *Teachers College Record.*]

———— (1968b). The genius of Kurt Lewin. In G. W. Allport, *The person in psychology* (pp. 360–370). Boston: Beacon Press.

———— (1979). *The nature of prejudice.* 25th anniversary edition. Reading, Mass.: Addison-Wesley.

Allport, G. W., Bruner, J. S., and Jandorf, E. M. (1941). Personality under social catastrophe: Ninety life-histories of the Nazi revolution. *Character and Personality, 10,* 1–22.

Allport, G. W., and Odbert, H. S. (1936). Trait-names: A psycho-lexical study. *Psychological Monographs, 47* (whole no. 211), 1.

Allport, G. W., and Schanck, R. L. (1935). Are attitudes biological or cultural in origin? *Character and Personality, 4,* 195–205.

Allport, G. W., and Vernon, P. E. (1930). The field of personality. *Psychological Bulletin, 27,* 677–730.

——— (1933). *Studies in expressive movement.* New York: Macmillan

Alvarez, A. (1994). Child's everyday life: An ecological approach to the study of activity systems. In A. Alvarez and P. Del Río (eds.), *Explorations in socio-cultural studies.* Vol. 4, *Education as cultural construction* (pp. 23–38). Madrid: Fundación Infancia y Aprendizaje.

Angell, J. R. (1961). James Rowland Angell. In C. Murchison (ed.), *A history of psychology in autobiography.* Vol. 3 (pp. 1–38). New York: Russell and Russell.

Anonymous [G. W. Allport] (1946). Letters from Jenny. *Journal of Abnormal and Social Psychology, 41,* 315–350, 449–480.

Apel, K.-O. (1989). Linguistic meaning and intentionality: The compatibility of the "linguistic turn" and the "pragmatic turn" of meaning-theory within the framework of a transcendental semiotics. In G. Deledalle (ed.), *Semiotics and pragmatics* (pp. 19–70). Amsterdam: John Benjamins.

Aphek, E., and Tobin, Y. (1983). On image building and establishing credibility in the language of fortune-telling. *Eastern Anthropologist, 36,* 287–308.

——— (1990). *The semiotics of fortune-telling.* Amsterdam: John Benjamins.

Appadurai, A. (1981a). Gastro-politics in Hindu South Asia. *American Ethnologist, 8,* 494–513.

——— (1981b). *Worship and conflict under colonial rule: A South Indian case.* Cambridge: Cambridge University Press.

——— (1985). Gratitude as a social mode in South India. *Ethos, 13,* 236–245.

——— (1986). Theory in anthropology: Center and periphery. *Comparative Studies in Society and History, 28,* 356–361.

Appadurai, A., and Appadurai-Breckenridge, C. (1976). The South Indian temple: Authority, honour and redistribution. *Contributions to Indian Sociology, 10,* 187–211.

Archer, W. G. (1957). *The loves of Krishna.* London: George Allen and Unwin.

Arima, M. (1991). Creative interpretation of the text and the Japanese mentality. In Y. Ikegami (ed.), *The empire of signs: Semiotic essays on Japanese culture* (pp. 33–55). Amsterdam: John Benjamins.

Avrahami, J., and Kareev, Y. (1994). The emergence of events. *Cognition, 53,* 239–261.

Babich, V. V. (1994). Lossky and Bakhtin: A comparison. *Dialogue, Carnival, Chronotope, 4,* 34–46.

Bakhtin, M. M. (1934/1975). Slovo v romane [Discourse in the novel]. In M. Bakhtin, *Voprosy literatury i estetiki* (pp. 73–232). Moscow: Khudozhestvennaya Literatura. [In English translation in Bakhtin, 1981.]

——— (1942). Personal structure analysis: A statistical method for investigating single personality. *Journal of Abnormal and Social Psychology, 37,* 163–183.

——— (1946). The study of individual personality by means of the intraindividual correlation. *Journal of Personality, 14,* 151–168.

——— (1981). *The dialogic imagination.* Austin: University of Texas Press.

Baldwin, A. L. (1940). The statistical analysis of the structure of a single personality. *Psychological Bulletin, 37,* 518–519.

Baldwin, J. M. (1891). Suggestion in infancy. *Science, 17,* no. 421, 113–117.

——— (1892a). Among the psychologists of Paris. *The Nation, 55,* no. 1413, 68.

——— (1892b). With Bernheim at Nancy. *The Nation, 55,* no. 1415, 101–103.

——— (1894a). Imitation: A chapter in the natural history of consciousness. *Mind,* n.s., *3,* 26–55.

——— (1894b). Personality-suggestion. *Psychological Review, 1,* 274–279.

——— (1895). *Mental development in the child and the race.* New York: Macmillan

——— (1897). *Social and ethical interpretations in mental development.* New York: Macmillan

——— (1898). On selective thinking. *Psychological Review, 5,* 1–24.

——— (1902). *Fragments in philosophy and science.* New York: Scribner.

——— (1906). *Thought and things: A study of the development and meaning of thought, or genetic logic.* Vol. 1, *Functional logic, or genetic theory of knowledge.* London: Swan Sonnenschein.

——— (1908a). Knowledge and imagination. *Psychological Review, 15,* 181–196.

——— (1908b). *Thought and things: A study of the development and meaning of thought, or genetic logic.* Vol. 2, *Experimental logic, or genetic theory of thought.* London: Swan Sonnenschein.

——— (1911). *Thought and things: A study of the development and meaning of thought, or genetic logic.* Vol 3, *Interest and art being real logic.* London: Swan Sonnenschein.

——— (1915). *Genetic theory of reality.* New York: Putnam.

——— (1926). *Between two wars 1861–1921.* 2 vols. Boston: Stratford.

——— (1930). James Mark Baldwin. In C. Murchison (ed.), *A history of psychology in autobiography.* Vol. 1 (pp. 1–30). New York: Russell and Russell.

Barker, J., and Tjetjen, A.-M. (1990). Women's facial tattooing among the Maisin of Oro Province, Papua New Guinea: The changing significance of an ancient custom. *Oceania, 60,* 217–234.

Barry, R. M. (1968). A man and a city: George Herbert Mead in Chicago. In M. Novak (ed.), *American philosophy and the future: Essays for a new generation* (pp. 173–192). New York: Scribner.

Barthes, R. (1979). *Elements of semiology.* New York: Hill and Wang.

Bartlett, F. C. (1920a). Psychology in relation to the popular story. *Folk-Lore, 31,* 264–293.

—— (1920b). Some experiments on the reproduction of folk-stories. *Folk-Lore*, *31*, 30–47.

—— (1924). Symbolism in folk lore. In *Proceedings and papers of the Seventh International Congress of Psychology, Oxford, 1923* (pp. 278–289). Cambridge: Cambridge University Press.

—— (1932). *Remembering*. Cambridge: Cambridge University Press.

Basov, M. (1931). *Obshchie osnovy pedologii*. Moscow-Leningrad: Gosudarstven-noe Izdatel'stvo.

Basow, S. A. (1991). The hairless ideal: Women and their body hair. *Psychology of Women Quarterly, 15*, 83–96.

Basso, K. H. (1970). "To give up on words": Silence in western Apache culture. *Southwestern Journal of Anthropology, 26*, 213–230.

Baumann, R. (1983). *Let our words be few: Symbolism of speaking and silence among 17th century Quakers*. Cambridge: Cambridge University Press.

Baumeister, R. F. (1986). *Identity: Cultural change and the struggle for self*. New York: Oxford University Press.

—— (1989). The problem of life's meaning. In D. M. Buss and N. Cantor (eds.), *Personality psychology: Recent trends and emerging directions* (pp. 138–148). New York: Springer.

Beck, B. E. F. (1976). The symbolic merger of body, space and cosmos in Hindu Tamil Nadu. *Contributions to Indian Sociology, 10*, 213–243.

Behrends, R. S., and Blatt, S. J. (1985). Internalization and psychological development throughout the life cycle. *Psychoanalytic Study of the Child, 40*, 11–39.

Beidelman, T. O. (1963). Kaguro omens. *Anthropological Quarterly, 36*, 43–59.

Bekhterev, V. M. (1903). *Suggestion and its role in the social life*. 2d ed. St. Petersburg: K. L. Rikker. [In Russian.]

—— (1922). *Kollektivnaia refleksologia*. Berlin.

—— (1994). *Collective reflexology*. Commack: NOVA Science Publishers.

Bell, R. M. (1985). *Holy anorexia*. Chicago: University of Chicago Press.

Bem, D., and Allen, A. (1974). On predicting some of the people some of the time: The search for cross-situational consistencies in behavior. *Psychological Review, 81*, 506–520.

Bem, D., and Funder, D. (1978). Predicting more of the people more of the time: Assessing the personality of situations. *Psychological Review, 85*, 485–501.

Benedek, T. (1937). Defense mechanisms and the structure of the total personality. *Psychoanalytic Quarterly, 6*, 96–118.

Benigni, L., and Valsiner, J. (1995). "Amoral familism" and child development: Edward Banfield and the understanding of child socialization in southern Italy. In J. Valsiner (ed.), *Child development within culturally structured environments*. Vol. 3, *Comparative-cultural and constructivist perspectives* (pp. 83–104). Norwood, N.J.: Ablex.

Bennett, P. (1990). In Nanda Baba's house: The devotional experience in Pushti Marg temples. In O. M. Lynch (ed.), *Divine passions: The social construction of emotion in India* (pp. 182–211). Berkeley: University of California Press.

Berger, P. L., & Luckmann, T. (1973). *The social construction of reality*. Middlesex, England: Penguin.

Bergson, H. (1906). L'Idée de néant. *Revue Philosophique, 62,* 449–466.

——— (1907/1945). *L'Evolution créatrice.* Geneva: Éditions Albert Skira.

——— (1911a). *Creative evolution.* New York: Henry Holt.

——— (1911b). *Matter and memory.* London: George Allen and Unwin. [English translation of Bergson, *Matière et mémoire.* Paris: Felix Alcan, 1896.]

Bernard, J. (1929). The history and prospects of sociology in the United States. In G. Lundberg, R. Bain, and N. Anderson (eds.), *Trends in American sociology* (pp. 1–71). New York: Harper and Brothers.

Bertalanffy, L. von (1950). The theory of open systems in physics and biology. *Science, 111,* 23–29.

——— (1955). An essay on the relativity of categories. *Philosophy of Science, 224,* 243–263.

Bertocci, P. (1940). A critique of G. W. Allport's theory of motivation. *Psychological Review, 47,* 501–532.

Beteille, A. (1965). Social organization of temples in a Tanjore village. *History of Religions, 5,* 74–92.

Bierbach, C. (1978). *Sprache als "Fait social."* Tübingen: Max Niemeyer Verlag.

Bloom, A. H. (1981). *The linguistic shaping of thought.* Hillsdale, N.J.: Erlbaum.

Boesch, E. E. (1982). Fantasmus und Mythos. In J. Stagl (ed.), *Aspekte der Kultursoziologie* (pp. 59–86). Berlin: Dietrich Reimer Verlag.

——— (1983). *Das Magische und das Schöne: Zur Symbolik von Objekten und Handlungen.* Stuttgart: Frommann.

——— (1989). Cultural psychology in action-theoretical perspective. In Ç. Kagitçibasi (ed.), *Growth and progress in cross-cultural psychology* (pp. 41–51). Lisse: Swets and Zeitlinger.

——— (1991). *Symbolic action theory and cultural psychology.* New York: Springer.

——— (1993). The sound of the violin. *Schweizerische Zeitschrift für Psychologie, 52,* 70–81.

Bohannan, P. (1956). Beauty and scarification amongst the Tiv. *Man, 56,* 117–121.

Bonetskaia, N. K. (1994). On the philosophical inheritance of M. Bakhtin. *Dialogue, Carnival, Chronotope, 4,* 5–18.

Bonfantini, M. A. (1988). Semiosis and history. *Cruzeiro semiotico,* no. 8, 88–95.

Boodin, J. (1913). The existence of social minds. *American Journal of Sociology, 19,* 1, 1–47.

Bottéro, A. (1991). Consumption by semen loss in India and elsewhere. *Culture, Medicine and Psychiatry, 15,* 303–320.

Bourdieu, P. (1981). Men and machines. In K. Knorr-Cetina and A. W. Cicourel (eds.), *Advances in social theory and methodology: Toward an integration of micro- and macro-sociologies* (pp. 304–317). London: Routledge and Kegan Paul.

———— (1985). The social space and the genesis of groups. *Social Science Information*, *24*, 195–220.

———— (1988). *Homo academicus*. Stanford, Calif.: Stanford University Press.

———— (1991). *Language and symbolic power*. Cambridge, Mass.: Harvard University Press.

Bourdieu, P., and Wacquant, L. J. D. (1992). *An invitation to reflexive sociology*. Chicago: University of Chicago Press.

Bradford, N. J. (1983). Transgenderism and the cult of Yellamma: Heat, sex, and sickness in South Indian ritual. *Journal of Anthropological Research*, *39*, 307–322.

Branco, A., and Valsiner, J. (1997). Changing methodologies: A co-constructivist study of goal-orientations in social interactions. *Psychology and Developing Societies*, *9*, 1, 35–64.

Briggs, J. L. (1975). The origins of nonviolence: Aggression in two Canadian Eskimo groups. *Psychoanalytic Study of the Child*, *6*, 134–203.

———— (1979). The creation of value in Canadian Inuit society. *International Social Science Journal*, *31*, 393–403.

———— (1991). Expecting the unexpected: Canadian Inuit training for an experimental lifestyle. *Ethos*, *19*, 259–287.

Bronckart, J.-P. (1995). Theories of action, speech, natural language, and discourse. In J. V. Wertsch, P. Del Río, and A. Alvarez (eds.), *Sociocultural studies of mind* (pp. 75–91). Cambridge: Cambridge University Press.

Bronfenbrenner, U. (1977). Toward an experimental ecology of human development. *American Psychologist*, *32*, 513–531.

———— (1979). *The ecology of human development*. Cambridge, Mass.: Harvard University Press.

———— (1989). Ecological systems theory. In R. Vasta (ed.), *Annals of child development*. Greenwich, Conn.: JAI Press.

———— (1993). The ecology of cognitive development. In R. Wozniak and K. Fischer (eds.), *Development in context* (pp. 3–46). Hillsdale, N.J.: Erlbaum.

Bronfenbrenner, U., and Ceci, S. J. (1994). Nature-nurture reconceptualized in developmental perspective: A bioecological model. *Psychological Review*, *101*, 568–586.

Brooks, J. I., III (1993). Philosophy and psychology at the Sorbonne, 1885–1913. *Journal of the History of the Behavioral Sciences*, *29*, 123–148.

Bruner, J. S. (1990). *Acts of meaning*. Cambridge, Mass.: Harvard University Press.

Buchler, J. (ed.). (1955). Philosophical writings of Peirce. New York: Dover.

Bühler, C. (1918). Das Märchen und die Phantasie des Kindes. *Beihefte zur Zeitschrift für angewandte Psychologie*, *17*, 1–82.

———— (1968). The integrating self. In C. Bühler and F. Massarik (eds.), *The course of human life* (pp. 330–350). New York: Springer.

Bühler, K. (1926). Die Krise der Psychologie. *Kant-Studien*, *31*, 455–526.

—— (1927/1978). *Die Krise der Psychologie*. Frankfurt am Main: Ullstein.

—— (1928). Die Symbolik der Sprache. *Kant-Studien, 33*, 405–409.

—— (1930). *The mental development of the child*. New York: Harcourt, Brace.

—— (1931). Phonetik und Phonologie. *Travaux du Cercle Linguistique de Prague, 4*, 22–53.

—— (1932). Das Ganze der Sprachtheorie, ihr Aufbau und ihre Teile. In G. Kafka (ed.), *Bericht über den XII Kongress der Deutschen Gesellschaft für Psychologie* (pp. 95–122). Jena: Gustav Fischer.

—— (1934/1965). *Sprachtheorie*. Jena: Gustav Fischer.

—— (1990). *Theory of language: The representational function of language*. Amsterdam: John Benjamins.

Bullough, E. (1912). "Psychical distance" as a factor in art and an aesthetic principle. *Journal of Psychology, 5*, 87–118.

Bushman, R. L., and Bushman, C. L. (1988). The early history of cleanliness in America. *Journal of American History, 74*, 1213–1238.

Cahan, E. D. (1992). John Dewey and human development. *Developmental Psychology, 28*, 205–214.

Cairns, R. B. (1983). The emergence of developmental psychology. In P. H. Mussen (ed.), *Handbook of child psychology*. Vol. 1 (pp. 41–102). New York: Wiley.

—— (1986). Phenomena lost. In J. Valsiner (ed.), *The individual subject and scientific psychology* (pp. 97–111). New York: Plenum.

Calil, E. (1994). The construction of the zone of proximal development in a pedagogical context. In N. Mercer and C. Coll (eds.), *Explorations in socio-cultural studies*. Vol. 3, *Teaching, learning, and interaction* (pp. 93–98). Madrid: Fundación Infancia y Aprendizaje.

Caspi, A. (1987). Personality in the life course. *Journal of Personality and Social Psychology, 53*, 1203–1213.

—— (1989). On the continuities and consequences of personality: A life-course perspective. In D. M. Buss and N. Cantor (eds.), *Personality psychology: Recent trends and emerging directions* (pp. 85–98). New York: Springer.

Cassirer, E. (1926/1955). *The philosophy of symbolic forms*. Vol. 2, *Mythical thought*. New Haven, Conn.: Yale University Press.

—— (1929/1957). *The philosophy of symbolic forms*. Vol. 3, *The phenomenology of knowledge*. New Haven, Conn.: Yale University Press.

Chapman, M. (1988). *Constructive evolution*. Cambridge: Cambridge University Press.

Chatterjee, S. (1945). *Devadasi (temple dancer)*. Calcutta: Book House.

Chatterji, R. (1985). The voyage of the hero: The self and the other in one narrative tradition of Purulia. *Contributions to Indian Sociology, 19*, 95–114.

Clark, K. (1979). Introduction. In G. W. Allport, *The nature of prejudice* (pp. ix–xi). 25th anniversary edition. Reading, Mass.: Addison-Wesley.

Cole, M. (1975). An ethnographic psychology of cognition. In R. W. Brislin, S.

Bochner, and W. Lonner (eds.), *Cross-cultural perspectives on learning* (pp. 157–175). New York: Wiley.

——— (1981). Society, mind, and development. In F. S. Kessel and A. W. Siegel (eds.), *The child and other cultural inventions* (pp. 89–123). New York: Praeger.

——— (1985). The zone of proximal development: Where culture and cognition create each other. In J. V. Wertsch (ed.), *Culture, communication, and cognition: Vygotskian perspectives* (pp. 146–161). Cambridge: Cambridge University Press.

——— (1990). Cultural psychology: A once and future discipline? In J. Berman (ed.), *Nebraska Symposium on Motivation*. Vol. 37 (pp. 279–336). Lincoln: University of Nebraska Press.

——— (1992). Context, modularity and the cultural constitution of development. In L. T. Winegar and J. Valsiner (eds.), *Children's development within social context*. Vol. 2, *Research and methodology* (pp. 5–31). Hillsdale, N.J.: Erlbaum.

——— (1995). Culture and cognitive development: from cross-cultural research to creating systems of cultural mediation. *Culture and Psychology, 1,* 25–54.

Cole, M., and Bruner, J. S. (1971). Cultural differences and inferences about psychological processes. *American Psychologist, 26,* 867–876.

Collins, J. (1968). Josiah Royce: Analyst of religion as community. In M. Novak (ed.), *American philosophy and the future* (pp. 193–218). New York: Scribner.

Cook, G. A. (1993). *George Herbert Mead: The making of a social pragmatist.* Urbana: University of Illinois Press.

Cooley, C. H. (1902). *Human nature and the social order.* New York: Scribner.

——— (1907). Social consciousness. *American Journal of Sociology, 12,* 675–687.

——— (1908). A study of early use of self-words by a child. *Psychological Review, 15,* 339–357.

——— (1913). The sphere of pecuniary valuation. *American Journal of Sociology, 19,* 188–203.

——— (1925). *Social organization: A study of the larger mind.* New York: Scribner.

——— (1926). The roots of social knowledge. *American Journal of Sociology, 33,* 59–79.

——— (1929). The life-study method as applied to rural social research. *Publications of the American Sociological Society, 23,* 248–254.

——— (1930). *Sociological theory and social research.* New York: Henry Holt.

Crick, F. (1988). *What mad pursuit.* Harmondsworth, England: Penguin.

Cross, S., and Markus, H. (1991). Possible selves across the life span. *Human Development, 34,* 230–255.

Csikszentmihalyi, M., and Rochberg-Halton, E. (1981). *The meanings of things: Domestic symbols and the self.* Cambridge: Cambridge University Press.

Culler, J. (1986). *Ferdinand de Saussure*. Rev. ed. Ithaca, N.Y.: Cornell University Press.

Cupchik, G. C., and Winston, A. S. (1996). Confluence and divergence in empirical aesthetics, philosophy, and mainstream psychology. In M. P. Friedman and E. C. Carterette (eds.), *Handbook of perception and cognition: Cognitive ecology.* 2d ed. (pp. 61–85). San Diego: Academic Press.

D'Andrade, R. (1984). Cultural meaning systems. In R. A. Shweder and R. A. LeVine (eds.), *Culture theory: Essays on mind, self and emotion* (pp. 88–119). Cambridge: Cambridge University Press.

Danet, B. (1980). Baby or fetus?: Language and the construction of reality in a manslaughter trial. *Semiotica, 32,* 187–219.

Danziger, K. (1980). The history of introspection reconsidered. *Journal of the History of the Behavioral Sciences, 16,* 241–262.

———— (1985). The methodological imperative in psychology. *Philosophy of the Social Sciences, 15,* 1–13.

———— (1990). *Reconstructing the subject.* Cambridge: Cambridge University Press.

Danziger, K., and Shermer, P. (1994). The varieties of replication: A historical introduction. In R. Van der Veer, M. H. Van IJzendoorn, and J. Valsiner (eds.), *Reconstructing the mind* (pp. 17–36). Norwood, N.J.: Ablex.

Das, V. (1976a). Masks and faces: An essay on Punjabi kinship. *Contributions to Indian Sociology, 10,* 1–30.

———— (1976b). The uses of liminality: Society and cosmos in Hinduism. *Contributions to Indian Sociology, 10,* 245–263.

———— (1982a). Kama in the scheme of purusarthas: The story of Rama. In T. N. Madan (ed.), *Way of life: King, householder, renouncer* (pp. 183–203). New Delhi: Vikas.

———— (1982b). *Structure and cognition: Aspects of Hindu caste and ritual.* Delhi: Oxford University Press.

———— (1992). Reflections on the social construction of adulthood. In S. Kakar (ed.), *Identity and adulthood* (pp. 89–104). Delhi: Oxford University Press.

Daston, L. (1992). Objectivity and the escape from perspective. *Social Studies of Science, 22,* 597–618.

Davis, K. (1937). The sociology of prostitution. *American Sociological Review, 2,* 744–755.

Davis, M. (1983). The individual in holistic India. In G. R. Gupta (ed.), *Religion in modern India* (pp. 49–77). New Delhi: Vikas.

Dayalan, D. (1992). *Early temples of Tamilnadu.* New Delhi: Harman.

Delaney, C. (1994). Untangling the meanings of hair in Turkish society. *Anthropological Quarterly, 67,* 159–172.

Deledalle, G. (1990). *Charles S. Peirce: An intellectual biography.* Amsterdam: John Benjamins.

Del Río, P. (1994). Extra-cortical connections: The sociocultural systems for living. In J. Wertsch and J.-D. Ramirez (eds.), *Explorations in socio-cultural studies*. Vol. 2, *Literacy and other forms of mediated action* (pp. 19–30). Madrid: Fundación Infancia y Aprendizaje.

——— (1996). Building identities in a mass-communication world. *Culture and Psychology, 2,* 159–172.

Del Río, P., and Alvarez, A. (1992). Tres pies al gato: Significado, sentido y cultura cotidiana en la educación. *Infancia y Aprendizaje, 59–60.*

——— (1995a). Directivity: The cultural and educational construction of morality and agency. *Anthropology and Education Quarterly, 26,* 384–409.

——— (1995b). Tossing, praying, and reasoning: The changing architectures of mind and agency. In J. V. Wertsch, P. Del Río and A. Alvarez (eds.), *Sociocultural studies of mind* (pp. 215–247). Cambridge: Cambridge University Press.

De Rosa, A. S. (1994). From theory to metatheory in social representations: The lines of argument of a theoretical-methodological debate. *Social Science Information, 33,* 273–304.

Desai, D. (1985). *Erotic sculpture of India: A socio-cultural study.* New Delhi: Munshiram Manoharlal.

Desai, V. N., and Mason, D. (eds.). (1993). *Gods, guardians, and lovers: Temple sculptures from North India A.D. 700–1200.* Middletown, N.J.: Grantha Corporation.

Deutsch, W. (ed.) (1991). *Über die verborgene Aktualität von William Stern.* Frankfurt am Main: Lang.

Devereux, G. (1961). Two types of modal personality models. In B. Kaplan (ed.), *Studying personality cross-culturally* (pp. 227–241). Evanston, Ill.: Row, Peterson.

——— (1967). *From anxiety to method in the behavioural sciences.* The Hague: Mouton.

Dewey, J. (1887). Knowledge as idealisation. *Mind, 12,* 382–396.

——— (1891). *Psychology.* New York: American Book Company.

——— (1894). The theory of emotion. I. Emotional attitudes. *Psychological Review, 1,* 553–569.

——— (1895). The theory of emotion. II. The significance of emotions. *Psychological Review, 2,* 13–32.

——— (1896). The reflex arc concept in psychology. *Psychological Review, 3,* 357–370.

——— (1907). The control of ideas by facts. *Journal of Philosophy, Psychology and Scientific Methods, 4,* 253–259.

——— (1908). What does pragmatism mean by practical? *Journal of Philosophy, Psychology and Scientific Methods, 5,* 85–99.

——— (1980). *The middle works, 1899–1924.* Vol. 9. Carbondale: Southern Illinois University Press.

Dodds, A., Lawrence, J. A., and Valsiner, J. (1998 in press). The personal and the social: Mead's theory of the "generalized other." *Theory and Psychology.*

Doi, T. (1985). *The anatomy of self.* Tokyo: Kodansha International.

Douglas, M. (1966). *Purity and danger.* London: Routledge and Kegan Paul.

Draguns, J. (1984). Microgenesis by another name . . . In W. D. Froelich, G. Smith, J. Draguns, and U. Hentschel (eds.), *Psychological processes in cognition and personality* (pp. 3–17). Washington, D.C.: Hemisphere.

Drijvers, H. J. W. (1994). The saint as symbol: Conceptions of the person in late antiquity and early Christianity. In H. J. W. Drijvers, *History and religion in late antique Syria* (pp. 137–157). Aldershot, England: Variorum.

Dubois, J. A. (1905). *Hindu manners, customs and ceremonies.* 3d ed. Oxford: Clarendon Press.

Duindam, V. (1992). Internalization and the sociologising of psychoanalysis. In R. Maier (ed.), *Internalization: Conceptual issues and methodological problems* (pp. 113–123). Utrecht: ISOR.

Dumont, L. (1980). Postface toward a theory of hierarchy. In L. Dumont, *Homo hierarchicus: The caste system and its implications.* Complete revised English edition (pp. 239–245). Chicago: University of Chicago Press.

Durkheim, É. (1915). *The elementary forms of religious life: A study in religious sociology.* London: George Allen and Unwin. [French original published in 1912.]

Eco, U. (1976). *A theory of semiotics.* Bloomington: Indiana University Press.

Ekehammar, B. (1974). Interactionism in personality from a historical perspective. *Psychological Bulletin, 81,* 1026–1048.

Ekman, P., Friesen, W. V., and Ellsworth, P. C. (1972). *Emotion in the human face.* Oxford: Pergamon Press.

Elbers, E. (1994). Internalization and the child's contribution to development. In A. Rosa and J. Valsiner (eds.), *Explorations in socio-cultural studies.* Vol. 2, *Historical and theoretical discourse* (pp. 65–72). Madrid: Fundación Infancia y Aprendizaje.

Elder, G. H., Jr. (1974). *Children of the great depression.* Chicago: University of Chicago Press.

Elias, N., and Scotson, J. (1965). *The established and the outsiders.* London: Cass.

Emmons, R. A. (1986). Personal strivings: An approach to personality and subjective well-being. *Journal of Personality and Social Psychology, 51,* 1058–1066.

Endler, N., and Magnusson, D. (1976). Toward an interactional psychology of personality. *Psychological Bulletin, 83,* 956–979.

Engler, R. (1968). *Ferdinand de Saussure Cours de linguistique générale: Édition critique.* Wiesbaden: Otto Harrassowitz.

Escalona, S. (1946). Overt sympathy with the enemy in maladjusted children. *American Journal of Orthopsychiatry, 16,* 333–340.

Eschbach, A. (1987). Edmund Husserl (1859–1938) und Karl Bühler (1879–1963). *Kodikas, 10,* 301–315.

———— (1988). The characteristics of Karl Bühler's pragmatically integrated theory of signs. In G. Deledalle (ed.), *Semiotics and pragmatics: Proceedings of the Perpignan symposium* (pp. 117–129). Amsterdam: John Benjamins.

———— (1990). Denken: Der semiotische Ansatz der Würzburger Schule. *Kodikas, 13,* 119–130.

Evans, R. I. (1981). *Dialogues with Gordon Allport.* New York: Praeger.

Eyferth, K. (1976). The contribution of William and Clara Stern to the onset of developmental psychology. In K. F. Riegel and J. A. Meacham (eds.), *The developing individual in a changing world.* Vol. 1 (pp. 9–15). The Hague: Mouton.

Farr, R. (1987). Social representations: A French tradition of research. *Journal for the Theory of Social Behaviour, 17,* 343–369.

Festinger, L., Riecken, H., and Schachter, S. (1956). *When prophecy fails.* Minneapolis: University of Minnesota Press.

Fine, G. A. (1993). The sad demise, mysterious disappearance, and glorious triumph of symbolic interactionism. *Annual Review of Sociology, 19,* 61–87.

Fisher, H. (1995). Whose right is it to define the self? *Theory and Psychology, 5,* 323–352.

Fite, W. (1911). *Individualism: Four lectures on the significance of consciousness for social relations.* New York: Longmans, Green.

———— (1913). The social implications of consciousness. *Journal of Philosophy, Psychology and Scientific Methods, 10,* 365–374.

Five turn up in Puri to become devadasis (1995). *Times of India,* September 12.

Flandrin, J.-L. (1985). Sex in married life in the early Middle Ages: The Church's teaching and behavioural reality. In P. Ariès and A. Béjin (eds.), *Western sexuality* (pp. 114–129). Oxford: Basil Blackwell.

Flick, U. (1995a). Social representations. In J. A. Smith, R. Harré, and L. Van Langenhove (eds.), *Rethinking psychology* (pp. 70–96). London: Sage.

———— (ed.) (1995b). *Psychologie des sozialen.* Reinbek: Rohwolt.

Fogel, A. (1993). *Developing through relationships.* Chicago: University of Chicago Press.

Fogel, A., Lyra, M. C. D. P., and Valsiner, J. (eds.) (1996). *Dynamics and indeterminism in developmental and social processes.* Hillsdale, N.J.: Erlbaum.

Ford, D. H., and Lerner, R. M. (1992). *Developmental systems theory.* Thousand Oaks, Calif.: Sage.

Foucault, M. (1980). *The history of sexuality.* Vol. 1, *Introduction.* New York: Vintage Books.

———— (1986). *The history of sexuality.* Vol. 3, *The care of the self.* New York: Random House.

Fransella, F. (1981). Personal construct psychology. In F. Fransella (ed.), *Personality: Theory, measurement and research* (pp. 147–165). London: Methuen.

Freeman, J. M. (1981). A firewalking ceremony that failed. In G. R. Gupta (ed.), *The social and cultural context of medicine in India* (pp. 308–336). New Delhi: Vikas.

Freud, A. (1966). *The writings of Anna Freud.* Vol. 2, *The ego and the mechanisms of defense.* New York: International Universities Press.

Freud, S. (1896/1962). Further remarks on the neuro-psychoses of defence. In J. Strachey (ed.), *The Standard Edition of the complete psychological works of Sigmund Freud.* Vol. 3 (pp. 162–185). London: Hogarth Press.

Frykenberg, R. E. (1989). The emergence of modern "Hinduism" as a concept and as an institution: A reappraisal with a special reference to South India. In G. D. Sontheimer and H. Kulke (eds.), *Hinduism reconsidered* (pp. 29–49). New Delhi: Manohar.

Funder, D. C. (1991). Global traits: A neo-Allportian approach to personality. *Psychological Science, 2,* 31–39.

Fwu Tarng Dun (1939). Aktualgenetische Untersuchung des Auffassungsvorganges chinesischer Schriftzeichen. *Archiv für die gesamte Psychologie, 104,* 131–174.

Gadet, F. (1989). *Saussure and contemporary culture.* London: Hutchinson Radius.

Gandhi, R. (1982). Bhahmacarya. In T. N. Madan (ed.), *Way of life: King, householder, renouncer* (pp. 205–221). New Delhi: Vikas.

Gauld, A. (1992). *A hystory of hypnotism.* Cambridge: Cambridge University Press.

Geertz, C. (1975). On the nature of anthropological understanding. *American Scientist, 63,* 47–53.

Geib, R. (1975). *Indradyumna-Legende: Ein Beitrag zur Geschichte des Jagannatha-Kultes.* Wiesbaden: Otto Harrassowitz.

Gergen, K. J. (1982). *Toward transformation in social knowledge.* New York: Springer.

———— (1985). The social constructionist movement in modern psychology. *American Psychologist, 40,* 3, 266–275.

———— (1986). Correspondence versus autonomy in the language of understanding. In D. W. Fiske and R. A. Shweder (eds.), *Metatheory in social science* (pp. 136–162). Chicago: University of Chicago Press.

———— (1988). If persons are texts. In S. B. Messer, L. A. Sass, and R. L. Woolfolk (eds.), *Hermeneutics and psychological theory* (pp. 28–51). New Brunswick, N.J.: Rutgers University Press.

———— (1989). Social psychology and the wrong revolution. *European Journal of Social Psychology, 19,* 463–484.

———— (1990). Metaphor, metatheory, and the social world.. In D. E. Leary (ed.), *Metaphors in the history of psychology* (pp. 267–299). Cambridge: Cambridge University Press.

———— (1994). *Realities and relationships.* Cambridge, Mass.: Harvard University Press.

Gergen, K. J., and Gergen, M. M. (1986). Narrative form and the construction of psychological science. In T. R. Sarbin (ed.), *Narrative psychology: The storied nature of conduct* (pp. 22–44). New York: Praeger.

———— (1988). Narrative and the self as relationship. In L. Berkowitz (ed.), *Advances in experimental social psychology.* Vol. 21 (pp. 17–56). New York: Wiley.

Gergen, K. J., Hepburn, A., and Fisher, D. C. (1986). Hermeneutics of personality description. *Journal of Personality and Social Psychology, 50,* 1261–1270.

Gergen, M. M., and Gergen, K. J. (1984). The social construction of narrative accounts. In K. J. Gergen and M. M. Gergen (eds.), *Historical social psychology* (pp. 173–189). New York: Plenum.

Getz, J. G., and Klein, H. K. (1994). The frosting of the American woman: Self-esteem construction and social control in the hair saloon. In K. A. Callaghan (ed.), *Ideals of feminine beauty* (pp. 125–146). Westport, Conn.: Greenwood Press.

Gigerenzer, G. (1991). How to make cognitive illusions disappear: Beyond "heuristics and biases." In W. Stroebe and M. Hewstone (eds.), *European review of social psychology*. Vol. 2 (pp. 83–115). Chichester, England: Wiley.

——— (1993). The superego, the ego, and the id in statistical reasoning. In G. Keren and C. Lewis (eds.), *A handbook for data analysis in the behavioral sciences: Methodological issues* (pp. 311–339). Hillsdale, N.J.: Erlbaum.

Gigerenzer, G., Swijtink, Z., Porter, T., Daston, L., Beatty, J., and Krüger, L. (1989). *The empire of chance*. Cambridge: Cambridge University Press.

Giles, J. (1994). A theory of love and sexual desire. *Journal for the Theory of Social Behaviour, 24,* 339–357.

Giordano, P. (1989). Sons reflecting upon their fathers: Reconstruction of ambivalence in their relationships. Ph.D. diss., University of North Carolina at Chapel Hill.

Giordano, P., and Valsiner, J. (1998 forthcoming). *Ambivalence in father-son relationships: Subjective transformations of the self.* New York: Plenum.

Goddard, C. (1995). Conceptual and cultural issues in emotion research. *Culture and Psychology, 1,* 289–298.

Góes, M. C. R. (1994). The modes of participation of others in the functioning of the subject. In N. Mercer and C. Coll (eds.), *Explorations in socio cultural studies*. Vol. 3, *Teaching, learning, and interaction* (pp. 123–128). Madrid: Fundación Infancia y Aprendizaje.

Goetzmann, W. H. (1973). Introduction: The American Hegelians. In W. H. Goetzmann (ed.), *The American Hegelians* (pp. 3–18). New York: Knopf.

Goke-Pariola, A. (1993). Language and symbolic power: Bourdieu and the legacy of Euro-American colonialism in an African society. *Language and Communication, 13,* 219–234.

Gottlieb, G. (1976). The roles of experience in the development of behavior and the nervous system. In G. Gottlieb (ed.), *Neural and behavioral specificity* (pp. 25–54). New York: Academic Press.

——— (1992). *Individual development & evolution: The genesis of novel behavior.* New York: Oxford University Press.

——— (1997). *Synthesizing nature-nurture.* Mahwah, N.J.: Erlbaum.

Goudena, P. (1994). Vygotsky's concept of internalization: Its strength and its limitations. Poster presented at the Thirteenth Biennial Meeting of the Society for Research in Child Development, Amsterdam, June 28—July 2.

Govenar, A. B. (1982). The changing image of tattooing in American culture. *Journal of American Culture, 5,* 1, 30–37.

Graumann, C.-F. (1960). Eigenschaften als Problem der Persönlichkeits-Forschung. In P. Lersch and H. Thomae (eds.), *Handbuch der Psychologie*. Vol. 4, *Persönlichkeitsforschung und Persönlichkeitstheorie* (pp. 87–154). Göttingen: C. J. Hogrefe.

——— (1976). The concept of appropriation *(Aneignung)* and modes of appropriation of space. In P. Korosec-Serfaty (ed.), *Appropriation of space* (pp. 113–125). Strasbourg: Université Louis Pasteur.

——— (1988). Aspektmodell und Organonmodell: Die Problematik des Verhältnisses zwischen Sprachwissenschaft und Psychologie bei Karl Bühler. In A. Eschbach (ed.), *Karl Bühler's theory of language* (pp. 107–124). Amsterdam: John Benjamins.

——— (1990). Aneignung. In L. Kruse, C. F. Graumann, and E. D. Lantermann (eds.), *Ökologische Psychologie* (pp. 97–104). Munich: Psychologie Verlags Union.

Graumann, C.- F., and Kruse, L. (1997). Children's environments: The phenomenological approach. In D. Görlitz, H. J. Harloff, G. Mey, and J. Valsiner (eds.), *Children, cities, and psychological theories: Developing relationships*. Berlin: Mouton de Gruyter.

Groeben, N., and Christmann, U. (1995). Lesen und Schreiben von Informationstexten. In C. Rosebrock (ed.), *Lesen im Medienzeitalter* (pp. 165–194). Weinheim: Juventa.

Grossmann, K. E. (1986). From idiographic approaches to nomothetic hypotheses: Stern, Allport, and the biology of knowledge, exemplified by an exploration of sibling relationships. In J. Valsiner (ed.), *The individual subject and scientific psychology* (pp. 37–70). New York: Plenum.

Gülerce, A. (1995). Culture and self in postmodern psychology: Dialogue in trouble? *Culture and Psychology, 1,* 141–159.

Gupta, S. (1995). The role of myths in psychological meanings construction. Poster presented at the European Conference of Developmental Psychology, Krakow, August.

Gupta, S., and Valsiner, J. (1996). Myths in the hearts: Implicit suggestions in the story. Paper presented at the Second Conference for Socio-Cultural Research, Geneva, September 14.

Gupta, S.N. (1895). Nature of inference in Hindu logic. *Mind, 4,* 159–175.

Gusfield, J. (1976). The literary rhetoric of science: Comedy and pathos in drinking driver research. *American Sociological Review, 41,* 16–34.

Habermas, J. (1992a). Peirce and communication. In J. Habermas, *Postmetaphysical thinking: Philosophical essays* (pp. 88–112). Cambridge, Mass.: MIT Press.

——— (1992b). Toward a critique of the theory of meaning. In J. Habermas, *Postmetaphysical thinking: Philosophical essays* (pp. 57–87). Cambridge, Mass.: MIT Press.

Hage, P., Harary, F., and Milicic, B. (1995). Hierarchical opposition. *Oceania, 65,* 347–353.

Hakfoort, C. (1992). Science deified: Wilhelm Ostwald's energeticist world-view and the history of scientism. *Annals of Science, 49,* 525–544.

Hamel, J. (1992a). The case method in sociology. *Contemporary Sociology, 40,* 1–15.

———— (1992b). On the status of singularity in sociology. *Contemporary Sociology, 40,* 99–119.

Hardesty, F. P. (1976). Louis William Stern: A new view of the Hamburg years. *Annals of the New York Academy of Sciences, 270,* 31–44.

Hardy, F. (1983). *Viraha-bhakti: The early history of Krisna devotion in South India.* Delhi: Oxford University Press.

Harkness, S., and Super, C. M. (1994). The developmental niche: A theoretical framework for analyzing the household production of health. *Social Science and Medicine, 38,* 217–226.

Harré, R. (1970). *The principles of scientific thinking.* Chicago: University of Chicago Press.

———— (1974). Some remarks on "rule" as a scientific concept. In T. Mischel (ed.), *Understanding other persons* (pp. 143–183). Totowa, N.J.: Rowman and Littlefield.

———— (1979). *Social being: A theory for social psychology.* Oxford: Basil Blackwell.

———— (1980). Making social psychology scientific. In R. Gilmour and S. Duck (eds.), *The development of social psychology* (pp. 27–51). London: Academic Press.

———— (1981a). The dramaturgy of sexual relations. In M. Cook (ed.), *Bases of human sexual attraction* (pp. 251–274). London: Academic Press.

———— (1981b). The positivist-empiricist approach and its alternative. In P. Reason and J. Rowan (eds.), *Human inquiry* (pp. 3–17). Chichester, England: Wiley.

———— (1981c). Psychological variety. In P. Heelas and A. Lock (eds.), *Indigenous psychology* (pp. 79–103). London: Academic Press.

———— (1981d). Rituals, rhetoric and social cognitions. In J. P. Forgas (ed.), *Social cognition* (pp. 211–224). London: Academic Press.

———— (1984a). *Personal being: A theory for individual psychology.* Cambridge, Mass.: Harvard University Press.

———— (1984b). Psychology as moral rhetoric. *Behavioral and Brain Sciences, 7,* 595–596.

———— (1989). Language games and texts of identity. In J. Shotter and K. J. Gergen (eds.), *Texts of identity* (pp. 20–35). London: Sage.

———— (1992). Introduction: The second cognitive revolution. *American Behavioral Scientist, 36,* 5–7.

———— (1995). The necessity of personhood as embedded being. *Theory and Psychology, 5,* 369–373.

Harré, R., and Gillett, G. (1994). *The discursive mind.* London: Sage.

Hasan, A. (1983). *Palace culture of Lucknow.* Delhi: B. R. Publishing Corporation.

Hattiangadi, J. N. (1987). *How is language possible?* La Salle, Ill.: Open Court.

Hausmann, G. (1935). Zur Aktualgenese räumlicher Gestalten. *Archiv für die gesamte Psychologie, 93*, 289–334.

Heggade, O. D. (1983). A socio-economic strategy for rehabilitating Devadasis. *Social Welfare, 39*, 10, 26–28.

Heider, F. (1958). *The psychology of interpersonal relations.* New York: Wiley.

Henriques, F. (1963). *Prostitution and society.* New York: Citadel Press.

Henslin, J. M., and Biggs, M. A. (1978). Dramaturgical desexualization: The sociology of vaginal examination. In J. M. Henslin and E. Sagarin (eds.), *The sociology of sex* (pp. 141–170). New York: Schocken Books.

Herbst, D. P. (1995). What happens when we make a distinction: An elementary introduction to co-genetic logic. In T. Kindermann and J. Valsiner (eds.), *Development of person-context relations* (pp. 67–79). Hillsdale, N.J.: Erlbaum.

Herdt, G. (1980). Semen depletion and the sense of maleness. *Ethnopsychiatry, 3*, 79–116.

———— (1981). *Guardians of the flutes.* New York: Columbia University Press.

———— (1982). Sambia nosebleeding rites and male proximity to women. *Ethos, 10*, 189–231.

———— (1987). *Sambia: Ritual and gender in New Guinea.* New York: Holt, Rinehart and Winston.

———— (1990). Secret societies and secret collectives. *Oceania, 60*, 360–381.

Hermans, H. J. M. (1991). The person as co-investigator in self-research: Valuation theory. *European Journal of Personality, 5*, 217–234.

———— (1995a). The limitations of logic in defining the self. *Theory and Psychology, 5*, 375–382.

———— (1995b). Voicing the self: From information processing to dialogical interchange. *Psychological Bulletin, 119*, 31–50.

———— (1996). Opposites in a dialogical self: Constructs as characters. *Journal of Constructivist Psychology, 9*, 1–26.

Hermans, H. J. M., and Bonarius, H. (1991a). The person as co-investigator in personality research. *European Journal of Personality, 5*, 199–216.

———— (1991b). Static laws in a dynamic psychology? *European Journal of Personality, 5*, 245–247.

Hermans, H. J. M., and Kempen, H. J. G. (1993). *The dialogical self: Meaning as movement.* San Diego: Academic Press.

Hermans, H. J. M., Kempen, H. J. G., and van Loon, R. J. P. (1992). The dialogical self: Beyond individualism and rationalism. *American Psychologist, 47*, 23–33.

Herodotus of Halicarnassus (1954). *The histories.* Harmondsworth, England: Penguin.

Hershman, P. (1974). Hair, sex and dirt. *Man, 9*, 274–298.

Herzog, M. (1995). William James and the development of phenomenological psychology in Europe. *History of the Human Sciences, 8*, 29–46.

Hiebert, P. G. (1983). Indian and American world views: A study of contrasts.

In G. R. Gupta (ed.), *Religion in modern India* (pp. 399–414). New Delhi: Vikas.

Hirschi, T. (1962). The professional prostitute. *Berkeley Journal of Sociology, 7,* 33–49.

Ho, D. Y. F. (1995). Selfhood and identity in Confucianism, Taoism, Buddhism, and Hinduism: Contrasts with the West. *Journal for the Theory of Social Behaviour, 25,* 113–139.

Hochschild, A. R. (1983). *The managed heart: Commercialization of human feeling.* Berkeley: University of California Press.

Holland, D. C., and Eisenhart, M. A. (1990). *Educated in romance: Women, achievement, and college culture.* Chicago: University of Chicago Press.

Hoogsteder, M. (1994). Socio-cultural theory and methodology of adult-child interaction. In N. Mercer and C. Coll (eds.), *Explorations in socio-cultural studies.* Vol. 3. *Teaching, learning, and interaction* (pp. 37–52). Madrid: Fundación Infancia y Aprendizaje.

Hope, C. (1982). Caucasian female body hair and American culture. *Journal of American Culture, 5,* 93–99.

Hoppe-Graff, S., and Mäckelburg, B. (1991). Phantasie und Illusion beim Spielen. *Zeitschrift für Entwicklungspsychologie und Pädagogische Psychologie, 23,* 115–131.

Hornstein, G. A. (1988). Quantifying psychological phenomena: Debates, dilemmas and implications. In J. G. Morawski (ed.), *The rise of experimentation in American psychology* (pp. 1–34). New Haven, Conn.: Yale University Press.

Hughes, P. (1906). The term ego and the term self. *Psychological Bulletin, 3,* 289–291.

Humboldt, W. von (1836). *Ueber die Verschiedenheit des menschlichen Sprachbauses und ihren Einfluss auf die geistige Entwicklung des Menschengeschlechtes.* Berlin.

———— (1903). Plan einer vergleichenden Anthropologie. In A. Leitzmann (ed.), *Wilhelm von Humboldts Gesammelte Schriften.* Vol. 2 (pp. 377–410). Berlin: B. Behr's Verlag.

———— (1905a). Ueber den Nationalcharakter der Sprachen. In A. Leitzmann (ed.), *Wilhelm von Humboldts Gesammelte Schriften.* Vol. 4 (pp. 420–435). Berlin: B. Behr's Verlag.

———— (1905b). Ueber die Aufgabe des Geschichtschreibers. In A. Leitzmann (ed.), *Wilhelm von Humboldts Gesammelte Schriften.* Vol. 4 (pp. 35–56). Berlin: B. Behr's Verlag.

Hurme, H. (1997). Psychological concepts, their producers and consumers. *Culture and Psychology, 3,* 115–136.

Hurrelmann, K. (1988). *Social structure and personality development.* Cambridge: Cambridge University Press.

Ichheiser, G. (1943). Misinterpretations of personality in everyday life and the psychologist's frame of reference. *Character and Personality, 12,* 145–160.

———— (1947). Projection and the mote-beam mechanism. *Journal of Abnormal and Social Psychology, 42,* 131–133.

Ignjatovic-Savic, N., Kovac-Cerovac, T., Plut, D., and Pesikan, A. (1988). Social interaction in early childhood and its development. In J. Valsiner (ed.), *Child development within culturally structured environments.* Vol. 1, *Parental cognition and adult-child interaction* (pp. 89–153). Norwood, N.J.: Ablex.

Inden, R. (1982). Hierarchies of kings in early medieval India. In T. N. Madan (ed.), *Way of life: King, householder, renouncer* (pp. 99–125). New Delhi: Vikas.

Innis, R. (1988). The thread of subjectivity: Philosophical remarks on Bühler's language theory. In A. Eschbach (ed.), *Karl Bühler's theory of language* (pp. 77–106). Amsterdam: John Benjamins.

Ismail, K. (1984). *Karnataka temples: Their role in socio-economic life.* Delhi: Sundeep Prakashan.

Ivic, I. (1978). *Covek kao animal symbolicum.* Belgrade: Nolit.

Jahoda, G. (1988). Critical notes and reflections on "social representations." *European Journal of Social Psychology, 18,* 195–209.

——— (1993). *Crossroads between culture and mind.* Cambridge. Mass.: Harvard University Press.

James, W. (1890). *Principles of psychology.* New York: Holt.

——— (1894). The physical basis of emotion. *Psychological Review, 1,* 516–529.

——— (1904a). The Chicago school. *Psychological Bulletin, 1,* 1–5.

——— (1904b). Does "consciousness" exist? *Journal of Philosophy, Psychology and Scientific Methods, 1,* 477–491.

——— (1907). *Pragmatism: A new name for some old ways of thinking.* New York: Longmans, Green.

Janet, P. (1889). *L'Automatisme psychologique: Essai de psychologie expérimentale sur les formes inférieures de l'activité humaine.* Paris: Félix Alcan.

——— (1898). *Névroses et idées fixes.* Paris: Félix Alcan.

——— (1901). *Mental state of hystericals: A study of mental stigma and mental accidents.* New York: Putnam.

——— (1905). Mental pathology. *Psychological Review, 12,* 98–117.

——— (1921). The fear of action. *Journal of Abnormal Psychology and Social Psychology, 16,* 2–3, 150–160.

——— (1925). *Psychological healing.* Vol. 1. New York: Macmillan.

——— (1926). *De l'angoisse a l'extase: Un délire religieux la croyance.* Vol. 1. Paris: Félix Alcan.

——— (1927). L'Excitation sociale dans les sentiments religieux. In *Proceedings and papers of the 8th International Congress of Psychology* (pp. 94–98). Groningen: P. Noordhoff.

——— (1928a). *De l'angoisse a l'extase: Un délire religieux la croyance.* Vol. 2, *Les Sentiments fondamentaux.* Paris: Félix Alcan.

——— (1928b). Fear of action as an essential element in the sentiment of melanchonia. In M. L. Reymert (ed.), *Feelings and emotions: The Wittenberg symposium* (pp. 297–309). Worcester, Mass.: Clark University Press.

———— (1930a). L'Analyse psychologique. In C. Murchison (ed.), *Psychologies of 1930* (pp. 369–373). Worcester, Mass.: Clark University Press.

———— (1930b). Pierre Janet. In C. Murchison (ed.), *A history of psychology in autobiography*. Vol. 1 (pp. 123–133). Worcester, Mass.: Clark University Press.

Jappy, A. (1989). Peirce's sixty-six signs revisited. In G. Deledalle (ed.), *Semiotics and pragmatics* (pp. 143–153). Amsterdam: John Benjamins.

Jelgersma, G. (1926). Projection. *International Journal of Psychoanalysis, 7,* 353–358.

Jevons, F. B. (1896). *An introduction to the history of religion*. London: Methuen.

Jha, A. (1979). *Sexual designs in Indian culture*. New Delhi: Vikas.

Joas, H. (1985). *G. H. Mead: A contemporary re-examination of his thought*. Cambridge, Mass.: MIT Press.

Jodelet, D. (1991). *Madness and social representations: Living with the mad in one French community*. Berkeley: University of California Press.

Johannes, T. (1939). Der Einfluss der Gestaltbindung auf das Behalten. *Archiv für die gesamte Psychologie, 104,* 74–130.

Josephs, I. E., and Valsiner, J. (1996). How does dialogue work? Coordinating the mundane and the miraculous in religious understanding. Paper presented at the Second Conference for Socio-Cultural Research, Geneva, September 11.

Kahneman, D., Slovic, P., and Tversky, A. (eds.) (1982). *Judgment under uncertainty: Heuristics and biases*. Cambridge: Cambridge University Press.

Kakar, S. (1981). *The inner world*. 2d ed. Delhi: Oxford University Press.

———— (1986). Erotic fantasy: The secret passion of Radha and Krishna. In V. Das (ed.), *The word and the world: Fantasy, symbol and record* (pp. 75–94). New Delhi: Sage.

———— (1989). *Intimate relations: Exploring Indian sexuality*. New Delhi: Penguin.

Kalganov, A. A. (1994). Where did Bakhtin come from? *Dialogue, Carnival, Chronotope, 4,* 122–128.

Kato, K., and Markus, H. (1993). The role of possible selves in memory. *Psychologia, 36,* 73–83.

Katz, D. (1928). The development of conscience in the child as revealed by his talks with adults. In A. L. Reymert (ed.), *Feelings and emotions: The Wittenberg symposium* (pp. 332–343). Worcester, Mass.: Clark University Press.

Katz, I. (1991). Gordon Allport's *The nature of prejudice*. *Political Psychology, 12,* 125–157.

Kersenboom, S. C. (1984). *Nityasumangali: Towards the semiosis of the devadasi tradition of South India*. Utrecht. [Published Ph.D. dissertation, no. 52.]

Khokar, M. (1979). *Traditions of Indian classical dance*. London: Peter Owen.

Kindermann, T., and Valsiner, J. (1989). Strategies for empirical research in context-inclusive developmental psychology. In J. Valsiner (ed.), *Cultural context and child development* (pp. 13–50). Toronto: C. J. Hogrefe and H. Huber.

King, E. G. (1990). Reconciling democracy and the crowd in turn-of-the-century American social-psychological thought. *Journal of the History of the Behavioral Sciences, 26*, 334–344.

Kirmayer, L. J. (1992). The body's insistence on meaning: Metaphor as presentation and representation in illness experience. *Medical Anthropology Quarterly, 6*, 323–346.

Klemm, O. (1937). Die ganzheitspsychologische Theorie der Gefühle. In *Rapports et comptes rendus de Onzieme Congrès International de Psychologie, Paris, 1937* (pp. 306–307). Agen: Imprimerie Moderne.

——— (1938). Gedanken über seelische Anpasung. *Archiv für die gesamte Psychologie, 100*, 387–400.

Kluckhohn, C., and Murray, H. (eds.) (1948). *Personality in nature, society, and culture.* New York: Knopf.

Knauft, B. M. (1994). Foucault meets South New Guinea: Knowledge, power, sexuality. *Ethos, 22*, 391–438.

Koerner, K. (1988). *Saussurean studies/Etudes Saussuriennes.* Geneva: Editions Slatkine.

Koerner, L. (1993). Goethe's botany: Lessons of a feminine science. *Isis, 84*, 470–495.

Kolenda, P. M. (1981). Pox and the terror of childlessness: Images and ideas of the smallpox goddess in a North Indian village. In P. Kolenda, *Caste, cult and hierarchy* (pp. 198–221). Meerut: Folklore Institute.

——— (1983). The mother-goddess complex among North Indian sweepers. In G. R. Gupta (ed.), *Religion in modern India* (pp. 215–228). New Delhi: Vikas.

Kondos, V. (1986). Images of the fierce goddess and portrayals of Hindu women. *Contributions to Indian Sociology, 20*, 173–197.

Kopytoff, I. (1986). The cultural biography of things: Commoditization as process. In A. Appadurai (ed.), *The social life of things* (pp.64–91). Cambridge: Cambridge University Press.

Kothari, S., and Pasricha, A. (1990). *Odissi Indian classical dance art.* Bombay: Marg Publications.

Krech, D. (1950). Dynamic systems as open neurological systems. *Psychological Review, 57*, 345–361.

Kreppner, K. (1992). William L. Stern, 1871–1938: A neglected founder of developmental psychology. *Developmental Psychology, 28*, 539–547.

Krewer, B. (1990). Psyche and culture: Can a culture-free psychology take into account the essential features of the species "homo sapiens"? *Quarterly Newsletter of the Laboratory of Comparative Human Cognition, 12*, 24–36.

——— (1992). *Kulturelle Identität und menschliche Selbsterforschung.* Saarbrücken: Breitenbach.

Krewer, B., and Jahoda, G. (1993). Psychologie et culture: Vers une solution du "Babel"? *International Journal of Psychology, 28*, 3, 367–375.

Kroeber, A. L. (1984). Reflections on Edward Sapir, scholar and man. In K.

Koerner (ed.), *Edward Sapir: Appraisals of his life and work* (pp. 131–139). Amsterdam: John Benjamins.

Krueger, F. (1913a). Magical factors in the first development of human labor. *American Journal of Psychology, 24,* 256–261.

—— (1913b). New aims and tendencies in psychology. *Philosophical Review, 22,* 251–264.

—— (1926). Über psychische Ganzheit. *Neue Psychologische Studien, 1,* 1–121.

—— (1928a). The essence of feeling. In M. L. Reymert (ed.), *Feelings and emotions: The Wittenberg symposium* (pp. 58–86). Worcester, Mass.: Clark University Press.

—— (1928b). Das Wesen der Gefühle. *Archiv für die gesamte Psychologie, 65,* 91–128.

Kuhn, D. (1987). Goethe's relationship to the theories of development of his time. In F. Amrine, F. J. Zucker, and H. Wheeler (eds.), *Goethe and the sciences: A reappraisal* (pp. 3–15). Dordrecht: D. Reidel.

Kuklick, H. (1991). *The savage within: The social history of British anthropology, 1885–1945.* Cambridge: Cambridge University Press.

Kulke, H., and Rothermund, D. (1986). *A history of India.* London: Croom Helm.

Kurtines, W. M., Berman, S. L., Ittel, A., and Williamson, S. (1995). Moral development: A co-constructivist perspective. In W. M. Kurtines and J. L. Gewirtz (eds.), *Moral development: An introduction* (pp. 337–376). Boston: Allyn and Bacon.

Kvale, S. (1983). The quantification of knowledge in education: On resistance toward qualitative evaluation and research. In B. Bain (ed.), *The sociogenesis of language and human conduct* (pp. 433–447). New York: Plenum.

Laboratory of Comparative Human Cognition (1983). Culture and cognitive development. In W. Kessen (ed.), *Handbook of child psychology.* Vol. 1, *History, theory and methods* (pp. 295–356). New York: Wiley.

Labov, W. (1970). The study of language in its social context. *Studium generale, 23,* 30–87.

Lacasa, P. (1994). Piaget and Vygotsky: A convergent approach to "consciousness," "activity," and "word." In A. Rosa and J. Valsiner (eds.), *Explorations in socio-cultural studies.* Vol. 2, *Historical and theoretical discourse* (pp. 85–96). Madrid: Fundación Infancia y Aprendizaje.

Lamiell, J. T. (1981). Toward an idiothetic psychology of personality. *American Psychologist, 36,* 276–289.

—— (1987). *The psychology of personality.* New York: Columbia University Press.

—— (1990). Explanation in the personality psychology. In D. N. Robinson and L. P. Mos (eds.), *Annals of theoretical psychology.* Vol. 6 (pp. 153–192). New York: Plenum.

—— (1991). Great psychologists resurrected: William Stern. Paper presented at the Ninety-ninth Annual Convention of the American Psychological Association, San Francisco, August.

———— (1992). Personality psychology and the second cognitive revolution. *American Behavioral Scientist, 36,* 88–101.

Lang, A. (1988). Die kopernikanische Wende steht in der Psychologie noch aus! Hinweise auf eine ökologische Entwicklungspsychologie. *Schweizerische Zeitschrift für Psychologie, 47,* 93–108.

———— (1991). Was ich von Kurt Lewin gelernt habe. In K. Grawe, R. Hänni, N. Semmer, and F. Tschan (eds.), *Übre die richtige Art, Psychologie zu betrieben* (pp. 121–135). Göttingen: Hogrefe.

———— (1992a). Die Frage nach den psychologischen Genesereihen—Kurt Lewins grosse Herausforderung. In W. Schönpflug (ed.), *Kurt Lewin—Person, Werk, Umfeld* (pp. 39–68). Frankfurt am Main: Peter Lang.

———— (1992b). Kultur als "externe Seele"—eine semiotish-ökologische Perspektive. In C. Allesch, E. Billmann-Mahecha, and A. Lang (eds.), *Psychologische Aspekte des kulturellen Wandels* (pp. 9–30). Vienna: Verlag des V.w.G.Ö.

———— (1992c). Eine Semiotik für die Psychologie: Eine Psychologie für die Semiotik. In L. Montada (ed.), *Bericht über den 38, Kongress der Deutschen Gesellschaft für Psychologie in Trier, 1992.* Vol. 2 (pp. 664–673). Trier.

———— (1993a). The "concrete mind" heuristic: Human identity and social compound from things and buildings. In D. Steiner, C. Jaeger, and M. Nauser (eds.), *Human ecology: Fragments of anti-fragmentary views of the world* (pp. 249–266). London: Routledge.

———— (1993b). Non-Cartesian artefacts in dwelling activities: Steps towards a semiotic ecology. *Schweizerische Zeitschrift für Psychologie, 52,* 138–147.

———— (1993c). Das Semion als Baustein und Bindekraft—eine einhentliche Semiosekonzeption von Struktur und Prozess, welche Zeit konstituieren und analysieren kann. Paper at 7. Internationale Kongress der Deutschen Gesellschaft für Semiotik, October, 6.

———— (1993d). Zeichen nach innen, Zeichen nach aussen: Eine semiotisch-ökologische Psychologie als Kulturwiessenschaft. In P. Rusterholz and M. Svilar (eds.), *Welt der Zeichen—Welt der Wirklichkeit* (pp. 55–84). Bern: Paul Haupt.

———— (1995). Hat oder is wird man Person? Eine evolutive Person-Kultur-Konzeption in der semiotische Ökologie. Paper at Gemeinschaftsseminar der philosophiosche-historischen Fakultät der Universität Bern, June 8–10.

Lardiere, D. (1992). On the linguistic shaping of thought: Another response to Alfred Bloom. *Language in Society, 21,* 231–251.

Larsen, R. J. (1989). A process approach to personality psychology: Utilizing time as a facet of data. In D. M. Buss and N. Cantor (eds.), *Personality psychology: Recent trends and emerging directions* (pp. 177–193). New York: Springer.

Larson, G. J. (1990). India through Hindu categories: A Sāmkhya response. *Contributions to Indian Sociology, 24,* 237–249.

Lawrence, J. A., Benedikt, R., and Valsiner, J. (1992). Homeless in the mind: A case history of personal life in and out of a close orthodox community. *Journal of Social Distress and the Homeless, 1,* 157–176.

Lawrence, J. A., and Valsiner, J. (1993). Conceptual roots of internalization: From transmission to transformation. *Human Development, 36,* 150–167.

Lc Bon, G. (1895). *Psychologie des foules.* Paris: Félix Alcan.

Lebzeltern, G. (1969). Karl Bühler: Leben und Werk. *Österreichische Akademie der Wissenschaften, Philosophisch-historische Klasse Sitzungberichte, 265,* Bd. 3, 7–70.

Lee, D. (1976). Freedom and social constraint. In D. Lee, *Valuing the self* (pp. 65–76). Englewood Cliffs, N.J.: Prentice-Hall.

Lefebvre, V. (1982). *Algebra of conscience.* Dordrecht: D. Reidel.

Leontiev, A. N. (1975). *Deiatel'nost, soznanie, lichnost'.* Moscow: Politizdat.

——— (1981). *Problemy razvitia psikhiki.* 4th ed. Moscow: Izdatel'stvo Moskovskogo Universiteta.

——— (1983). *Izbrannyie psikhologicheskie issledovania.* Vol. 2. Moscow: Pedagogika.

Lerner, G. (1986). The origin of prostitution in ancient Mesopotamia. *Journal of Women in Culture and Society, 11,* 236–254.

Leudar, I. (1991). Sociogenesis, coordination and mutualism. *Journal for the Theory of Social Behaviour, 21,* 197–220.

Lewin, K. (1927). Gesetz und Experiment in der Psychologie. *Symposion, 1,* 375–421.

——— (1933). Environmental forces. In C. Murchison (ed.), *A handbook of child psychology.* 2d ed. (pp. 590–625). Worcester, Mass.: Clark University Press.

——— (1935). *A dynamic theory of personality.* New York: McGraw-Hill.

——— (1943). Defining the "field at a given time." *Psychological Review, 50,* 292–310.

Lichtenberg, W. (1933). Über das physikalisch-kausale Denken bei Hilfsschüler. *Archiv für die gesamte psychologie, 87,* 447–531.

Lightfoot, C., and Valsiner, J. (1992). Parental belief systems under influence: Social guidance of the construction of personal cultures. In I. Siegel, J. Goodnow, and A. McGillicuddy-De Lisi (eds.), *Parental belief systems.* 2d ed. (pp. 393–414). Hillsdale, N.J.: Erlbaum.

Linell, P. (1992). The embeddedness of decontextualization in the contexts of social practices. In A. H. Wold (ed.), *The dialogical alternative: Towards a theory of language and mind* (pp. 253–271). Oslo: Scandinavian University Press.

Lipps, T. (1903). Einfühlung, innere Nachahmung, und Organepfindungen. *Archiv für die gesamte Psychologie, 1,* 185–204.

——— (1923). *Ästhetik: Psychologie des schönen und der Kunst.* 3d ed. Leipzig: Leopold Voss.

Little, B. R. (1989). Personal projects analysis: Trivial pursuits, magnificient obsessions, and the search for coherence. In D. M. Buss and N. Cantor (eds.), *Personality psychology: Recent trends and emerging directions* (pp. 15–31). New York: Springer.

Little, P. E. (1992). One event, one observer, two texts: Analyzing the Rio earth summit. Reports of Universidade de Brasilia, Serie Antropologia, No. 134.

Litvinovic, G., and Valsiner, J. (1993). Process mechanisms in the construction of culture. Paper presented at the Twelfth Biennial Meetings of the International Society for the Study of Behavioural Development, Recife, Pernambuco, Brazil, July 19–23.

Lotman, J. M. (1992). O semiosfere. In J. M. Lotman, *Izbrannye stat'i*. Vol. 1, *Stat'i po semiotike i tipologii kul'tury* (pp. 11–24). Tallinn: Aleksandra.

Löwy, I. (1992). The strength of loose concepts—boundary concepts, federative experimental strategies and disciplinary growth: The case of immunology. *History of Science, 30,* 90, part 4, 376–396.

Lucy, J. (1992). *Language diversity and thought: A reformulation of the linguistic relativity hypothesis.* Cambridge: Cambridge University Press.

Luria, A. R. (1976). *Cognitive development.* Cambridge, Mass.: Harvard University Press.

Lutz, C. A. (1988). *Unnatural emotions: Everyday sentiments on a Micronesian atoll and their challenge to Western theory.* Chicago: University of Chicago Press.

Lyra, M. C., and Rossetti-Ferreira, M. C. (1995). Transformation and construction in social interaction: A new perspective of analysis of the mother-infant dyad. In J. Valsiner (ed.), *Child development in culturally structured environments.* Vol. 3, *Comparative-cultural and constructivist perspectives* (pp. 51–77). Norwood, N.J.: Ablex.

MacCormack, D. B., and Draper, A. (1987). Social and cognitive aspects of female sexuality in Jamaica. In P. Caplan (ed.), *The cultural construction of sexuality* (pp. 143–165). London: Tavistock.

Madan, T. N. (1991). Auspiciousness and purity: Some reconsiderations. *Contributions to Indian Sociology, 25,* 287–294.

Mageo, J. M. (1994). Hairdos and don'ts: Hair symbolism and sexual history on Samoa. *Man, 29,* 407–432.

Magnusson, D. (1988). *Individual development from an interactional perspective: A longitudinal study.* Hillsdale, N.J.: Erlbaum.

——— (1990). Personality development from an interactional perspective. In L. Pervin (ed.), *Handbook of personality* (pp. 193–222). New York: Guilford Press.

——— (1995). Individual development: A holistic integrated model. In P. Moen, G. H. Elder, and K. Luscher (eds.), *Linking lives and contexts: Perspectives on the ecology of human development.* Cambridge: Cambridge University Press.

Magnusson, D., and Bergman, L. (1990). A pattern approach to the study of pathways from childhood to adulthood. In L. Robins and M. Rutter (eds.), *Straight and devious pathways from childhood to adulthood* (pp. 101–115). Cambridge: Cambridge University Press.

Magnusson, D., and Cairns, R. B. (1996). Developmental science: Toward a unified framework. In R. B. Cairns, G. H. Elder, and E. J. Costello (eds.), *Developmental science* (pp. 7–30). New York: Cambridge University Press.

Magnusson, D., and Endler, N. S. (eds.) (1977). *Personality at the crossroads.* Hillsdale, N.J.: Erlbaum.

Magnusson, D., and Törestad, B. (1993). A holistic view of personality: A model revised. *Annual Review of Psychology, 44,* 427–452.

Maier, R. (1992). Internalization in cognitive development: An examination of Piaget's theory. In R. Maier (ed.), *Internalization: Conceptual issues and methodological problems* (pp. 71–91). Utrecht: ISOR.

Makkreel, R. A. (1992). *Dilthey: Philosopher of the human studies.* Princeton, N.J.: Princeton University Press.

Malamoud, C. (1982). On the rhetoric and semantics of purusartha. In T. N. Madan (ed.), *Way of life: King, householder, renouncer* (pp. 33–54). New Delhi: Vikas.

Maltz, D. N. (1978). The bride of Christ is filled with his spirit. In J. Hoch-Smith and A. Spring (eds.), *Women in symbolic and ritual roles* (pp. 27–44). New York: Plenum.

Marglin, F. A. (1982a). Kings and wives: The separation of status and royal power. In T. N. Madan (ed.), *Way of life: King, householder, renouncer* (pp. 155–181). New Delhi: Vikas.

—— (1982b). Types of sexual union and their implicit meanings. In J. S. Hawley and D. M. Wulff (eds.), *The Divine Consort: Radha and the goddesses of India* (pp. 298–315). Berkeley, Calif.: Berkeley Religious Studies.

—— (1985). *Wives of the god-king: The rituals of the Devadasis of Puri.* Delhi: Oxford University Press.

—— (1990). Refining the body: Transformative emotion in ritual dance. In O. M. Lynch (ed.), *Divine passions: The social construction of emotion in India* (pp. 212–236). Berkeley: University of California Press.

Markova, I. (1990a). The development of self-consciousness: Baldwin, Mead, and Vygotsky. In J. E. Faulconer and R. N. Williams (eds.), *Reconsidering psychology: Perspectives from Continental philosophy* (pp. 151–174). Pittsburgh, Pa.: Duquesne University Press.

—— (1990b). A three-step process as a unit of analysis in dialogue. In I. Marková and K. Foppa (eds.), *The dynamics of dialogue* (pp. 129–146). Hemel Hempstead, England: Harvester.

—— (1994). Mutual construction of asymmetries. In P. van Geert and L. Mos (eds.), *Annals of theoretical psychology.* Vol. 10. New York: Plenum.

Markus, H. (1977). Self-schemata and processing information about the self. *Journal of Personality and Social Psychology, 35,* 63–78.

Markus, H., and Kitayama, S. (1991). Culture and the self: Implications for cognition, emotion, and motivation. *Psychological Review, 98,* 224–253.

Markus, H., and Nurius, P. (1986). Possible selves. *American Psychologist, 41,* 954–969.

Markus, H., and Wurf, E. (1987). The dynamic self-concept: A social psychological perspective. *Annual Review of Psychology, 38,* 299–337.

Maturana, H. (1978). Biology of language: The epistemology of reality. In G. Miller and E. Lenneberg (eds.), *Psychology and biology of language and thought* (pp. 27–63). New York: Academic Press.

——— (1980). Autopoiesis: Reproduction, heredity and evolution. In M. Zeleny (ed.), *Autopoiesis, dissipative structures, and spontaneous social orders* (pp. 45–79). Boulder, Colo.: Westview Press.

May, G. (1935). Prostitution. *Encyclopedia of the Social Sciences.* Vol. 12. New York: Macmillan.

McGilvary, E. B. (1908). The Chicago "idea" and idealism. *Journal of Philosophy, Psychology and Scientific Methods, 5,* 589–597.

McGuire, W. J. (1984). Search for the self: Going beyond the self-esteem and the reactive self. In R. A. Zucker, J. Aronoff, and A. I. Rabin (eds.), *Personality and the prediction of behavior* (pp. 73–120). New York: Academic Press.

Mead, G. H. (1895). Review of *An introduction to comparative psychology* by C. L. Morgan. *Psychological Review, 2,* 399–402.

——— (1899). Review of *The psychology of socialism* by Gustave Le Bon. *American Journal of Sociology, 5,* 404–412.

——— (1903). The definition of the psychical. *Decennial Publications of the University of Chicago.* First series. Vol. 3, *Investigations representing the departments* (pp. 3–38). Chicago: University of Chicago Press.

——— (1907). Social evolution. Review of *L'Évolution créatrice* by H. Bergson. *Psychological Bulletin, 4,* 379–384.

——— (1908). The philosophical basis of ethics. *International Journal of Ethics, 18,* 311–323.

——— (1909). Social psychology as counterpart to physiological psychology. *Psychological Bulletin, 6,* 401–408.

——— (1910a). The psychology of social consciousness implied in instruction. *Science, 31,* no. 801, 688–693.

——— (1910b). Social consciousness and the consciousness of meaning. *Psychological Bulletin, 7,* 397–405.

——— (1911). Review of *Individualism: Four lectures on the significance of consciousness for social relations* by Warner Fite. *Psychological Bulletin, 8,* 323–328.

——— (1912). The mechanism of social consciousness. *Journal of Philosophy, 9,* 401–406.

——— (1913). The social self. *Journal of Philosophy, 10,* 374–380.

——— (1917a). Josiah Royce: A personal impression. *International Journal of Ethics, 27,* 168–170.

——— (1917b). Scientific method and individual thinker. In *Creative intelligence: Essays in the pragmatic attitude* (pp. 176–227). New York: Henry Holt.

——— (1918). The psychology of punitive justice. *American Journal of Sociology, 23,* 577–602.

——— (1923). Scientific method and the moral sciences. *International Journal of Ethics, 33,* 229–247.

——— (1925). The genesis of the self and social control. *International Journal of Ethics, 35,* 251–277.

——— (1930a). Cooley's contribution to American social thought. *American Journal of Sociology, 35,* 693–706.

——— (1930b). The philosophies of Royce, James, and Dewey in their American setting. *International Journal of Ethics, 40,* 211–231.

——— (1932). *The philosophy of the present.* Chicago: Open Court.

——— (1934). *Mind, self and society from the standpoint of a social behaviorist.* Chicago: University of Chicago Press.

——— (1938). *The philosophy of the act.* Chicago: University of Chicago Press.

Meldrum, B. (1982). Psychological factors in breast feeding versus bottle feeding in the Third World. *Bulletin of the British Psychological Society, 35,* 229–231.

Menon, U., and Shweder, R. A. (1994). Kali's tongue: Cultural psychology and the power of "shame" in Orissa. In S. Kitayama and H. Markus (eds.), *Emotion and culture* (pp. 237–280). Washington, D.C.: American Psychological Association.

Meyerson, I. (1947). Pierre Janet et la théorie des tendances. *Journal de Psychologie, 40,* 5–19.

Miller, J. G. (1994). Cultural psychology: Bridging disciplinary boundaries in understanding the cultural grounding of self. In P. K. Bock (ed.), *Handbook of psychological anthropology* (pp. 139–170). Westport, Conn.: Greenwood Press.

Miller, J. G., and Bersoff, D. M. (1992). Culture and moral judgment: How are conflicts between justice and interpersonal responsibilities resolved? *Journal of Personality and Social Psychology, 62,* 541–554.

Mischel, W. (1979). On the interface of cognition and personality. *American Psychologist, 34,* 740–754.

Mischel, W., and Peake, P. K. (1982). Beyond déjà vu in the search for cross-situational consistency. *Psychological Review, 89,* 730–755.

Mitter, P. (1977). *Much maligned monsters: History of European reactions to Indian art.* Oxford: Clarendon Press.

Moghaddam, F. M., and Harré, R. (1992). Rethinking the laboratory experiment. *American Behavioral Scientist, 36,* 22–38.

Moll, L. C. (1990). Vygotski's zone of proximal development: Rethinking its instructional applications. *Infancia y Aprendizaje, 51–52,* 157–168.

Moody, E., Markova, I., and Plichtova, J. (1995). Lay representations of democracy: A study in two cultures. *Culture and Psychology, 1,* 423–453.

Morgan, C. L. (1892). The law of psychogenesis. *Mind, 1,* 72–93.

——— (1894). *An introduction to comparative psychology.* London: Walter Scott.

Morin, E. (1992). From the concept of system to the paradigm of complexity. *Journal of Social and Evolutionary Systems, 15,* 371–385.

Moro, C., and Rodriguez, C. (1994). Prelinguistic sign mixity and flexibility in interaction. *European Journal of Psychology of Education, 9,* 301–310.

Moscovici, S. (1981a). *L'Âge des foules: Un traité historique de psychologie des masses.* Paris: Fayard.

——— (1981b). On social representations. In J. P. Forgas (ed.), *Social cognition* (pp. 181–209). London: Academic Press.

——— (1982). The coming era of representations. In J.-P. Codol and J.-P. Leyens (eds.), *Cognitive analysis of social behavior* (pp. 115–150). The Hague: Martinus Nijhoff.

——— (1985). *The age of the crowd: A historical treatise on mass psychology.* Cambridge: Cambridge University Press.

——— (1988a). Crisis of communication and crisis of explanation. In W. Schönpflug (ed.), *Bericht über der 36. Kongress der Deutschen Gesellschaft für Psychologie in Berlin.* Vol. 2 (pp. 94–109). Göttingen: Hogrefe.

——— (1988b). Notes towards a description of social representations. *European Journal of Social Psychology, 18,* 211–250.

——— (1990). Social psychology and developmental psychology: Extending the conversation. In G. Duveen and B. Lloyd (eds.), *Social representations and the development of knowledge* (pp. 164–185). Cambridge: Cambridge University Press.

——— (1994). Social representations and pragmatic communication. *Social Science Information, 33,* 163–177.

——— (1995). Geschichte und Aktualität sozialer Repräsentationen. In U. Flick (ed.), *Psychologie des sozialen* (pp. 266–314). Reinbek: Rohwolt.

Much, N. C., and Harré, R. (1994). How psychologies "secrete" moralities. *New Ideas in Psychology, 12,* 291–321.

Much, N. C., and Mahapatra, M. (1995). Constructing divinity. In R. Harré and P. Stearns (eds.), *Discursive psychology in practice* (pp. 55–86). London: Sage.

Murray, H. (1938). *Explorations in personality.* New York: Oxford University Press.

——— (1959). Preparations for the scaffold of a comprehensive system. In S. Koch (ed.), *Psychology: a study of science.* Vol. 3, *Formulations of the person and the social context* (pp. 7–54). New York: McGraw-Hill.

Myers, G. E. (1986). *William James: His life and thought.* New Haven, Conn.: Yale University Press.

Naraindas, H. (1996). Poisons, putrescence and the weather: A genealogy of the advent of tropical medicine. *Contributions to Indian Sociology, 30,* 1–35.

Neisser, U. (1991). Two perceptually given aspects of the self and their development. *Developmental Review, 11,* 197–209.

Nersessian, N. J. (1984). Aether/or: The creation of scientific concepts. *Studies in History and Philosophy of Science, 15,* 175–212.

Newman, D., Griffin, P., and Cole, M. (1989). *The construction zone: Working for cognitive change in school.* Cambridge: Cambridge University Press.

Nossent, S. (1992). On internalization as a mechanism of psychogenesis. In R. Maier (ed.), *Internalization: Conceptual issues and methodological problems* (pp. 93–111). Utrecht: ISOR.

Nuttin, J. R. (1950). Intimacy and shame in the dynamic structure of personality. In M. Reymert (ed.), *Feelings and emotions: The Mooseheart Symposium* (pp. 343–352). New York: McGraw-Hill.

———— (1955). Consciousness, behavior, and personality. *Psychological Review, 62,* 349–355.

Nuttin, J. R. (1973). Das Verhalten des Menschen: Der Mensch in seiner Erscheinungswelt. In H. Gadamer and P. Vogler (eds.), *Psychologische Anthropologie.* Stuttgart: Thieme.

———— (1977). A conceptual frame of personality-world interaction. In D. Magnusson and N. S. Endler (eds.), *Personality at the crossroads* (pp. 201–206). Hillsdale, N.J.: Erlbaum.

Obeyesekere, G. (1963). Pregnancy cravings (*Dola-Duka*) in relation to social structure and personality in a Sinhalese village. *American Anthropologist, 65,* 323–342.

———— (1968). Theodicity, sin and salvation in a sociology of Buddhism. In E. R. Leach (ed.), *Dialectic in practical religion* (pp. 7–40). Cambridge: Cambridge University Press.

———— (1975). Sorcery, premeditated murder, and the canalization of aggression in Sri Lanka. *Ethnology, 14,* 1–23.

——— (1976). The impact of Ayurvedic ideas on the culture and the individual in Sri Lanka. In C. Leslie (ed.), *Asian medical systems: A comparative study* (pp. 201–226). Berkeley: University of California Press.

———— (1977). Psychocultural exegesis of a case of spirit possession in Sri Lanka. In V. Crapanzano and V. Garrison (eds.), *Case studies in spirit possession* (pp. 235–294). New York: Wiley.

———— (1981). *Medusa's hair.* Chicago: University of Chicago Press.

———— (1984). *The cult of the goddess Pattini.* Chicago: University of Chicago Press.

———— (1985). Symbolic foods: Pregnancy cravings and the envious female. *International Journal of Psychology, 20,* 637–662.

———— (1987). Reflections on Pattini and Medusa. *Contributions to Indian Sociology, 21,* 99–109.

———— (1990). *The work of culture.* Chicago: University of Chicago Press.

———— (1992). *The apotheosis of Captain Cook: European mythmaking in the Pacific.* Princeton, N.J.: Princeton University Press.

Obeyesekere, G. (1993). *The apotheosis of Captain Cook.* Princeton, N.J.: Princeton University Press.

O'Brien, M. (1994). The managed heart revisited: Health and social control. *Sociological Review, 42,* 393–413.

Ohnuki-Tierney, E. (1981). Phases in human perception/conception/symbolization process: Cognitive anthropology and symbolic classification. *American Ethnologist, 8,* 451–467.

———— (1987). *The monkey as mirror: Symbolic transformations in Japanese history and ritual.* Princeton, N.J.: Princeton University Press.

—— (1993). *Rice as self: Japanese identities through time.* Princeton, N.J.: Princeton University Press.

—— (1994). The power of absence: Zero signifiers and their transgressions. *L'Homme, 34,* 2 (whole no. 130), 59–76.

Oldenburg, V. T. (1984). *The making of colonial Lucknow 1856–1877.* Princeton, N.J.: Princeton University Press.

—— (1990). Lifestyle as resistance: The case of the courtesans of Lucknow, India. *Feminist Studies, 16,* 259–287.

Oliveira, Z. M. R. (1995). The concept of "role" and the discussion of the internalization process. In B. Cox and C. Lightfoot (eds.), *Sociogenetic perspectives on internalization.* Hillsdale, N.J.: Erlbaum.

Oliveira, Z. M. R., and Rossetti-Ferreira, M. C. (1996). Understanding the co-constructive nature of human development. In J. Valsiner and H.-G. Voss (eds.), *The structure of learning processes* (pp. 177–204). Norwood, N.J.: Ablex.

Oliveira, Z. M. R., and Valsiner, J. (1996). Play and imagination: The psychological construction of novelty. In A. Fogel, M. Lyra, and J. Valsiner (eds.), *Dynamics and indeterminism in developmental and social processes.* Hillsdale, N.J.: Erlbaum.

Olson, E. A. (1985). Muslim identity and secularism in contemporary Turkey: "The headscarf dispute." *Anthropological Quarterly, 58,* 161–170.

Orlov, A. B. (1992). Only internalization? *Journal of Russian and East European Psychology, 30,* 28–32.

Overton, W. F. (1997). Developmental psychology: Philosophy, concepts, and methodology. In R. M. Lerner (ed.), *Handbook of child psychology.* Vol. 1, *Theoretical models of human development.* 5th ed. New York: Wiley.

Pandey, S. M. (1965). Mirabai and her contributions to the bhakti movement. *History of Religions, 5,* 54–73.

Pandian, J. (1983). The sacred symbol of the mother goddess in a Tamil village: A parochial model of hinduism. In G. R. Gupta (ed.), *Religion in modern India* (pp. 198–214). New Delhi: Vikas.

Paranjpe, A. C. (1989). Towards a pluralist approach to psychology: A metatheoretical critique of the unity of science model. In D. M. Keats, D. Monro, and L. Mann (eds.), *Heterogeneity in cross-cultural psychology* (pp. 41–53). Lisse: Swets and Zeitlinger.

Parish, S. M. (1994). *Moral knowing in a Hindu sacred city.* New York: Columbia University Press.

Patil, B. R. (1975). The devadasis. *Indian Journal of Social Work, 35,* 377–389.

Peirce, C. S. (1892). Man's glassy essence. *The Monist, 2,* 1–22.

—— (1893). Evolutionary love. *The Monist, 3,* 176–200.

—— (1896). The regenerated logic. *The Monist, 7,* 19–40.

—— (1935). *Collected papers of Charles Sanders Peirce.* Vol. 6. Cambridge, Mass.: Harvard University Press.

—— (1982). *Writings of Charles S. Peirce.* Vol. 1. Bloomington: Indiana University Press.

―――― (1986). *Writings of Charles S. Peirce*. Vol. 3. Bloomington: Indiana University Press.

Pellerey, R. (1989). Thomas Acquinas: Natural semiotics and the epistemological process. In U. Eco and C. Marmo (eds.), *On the medieval theory of signs* (pp. 81–105). Amsterdam: John Benjamins.

Penuel, W., and Wertsch, J. (1995a). Dynamics of negation in the identity politics of cultural other and cultural self. *Culture and Psychology, 1*, 343–359.

―――― (1995b). Vygotsky and identity formation: A sociocultural approach. *Educational Psychologist, 30*, 83–92.

Perinbanayagam, R. S. (1975). The significance of others in the thought of Alfred Schutz, G. H. Mead, and C. H. Cooley. *Sociological Quarterly, 16*, 500–521.

Petrilli, S. (1993). Signs and values: For a critique of cognitive semiotics. *Journal of Pragmatics, 20*, 239–251.

Piaget, J. (1950). *Introduction a l'épistémologie génétique*. 3 vols. Paris: Presses Universitaires de France.

―――― (1962). *Play, dreams and imitation in childhood*. New York: Norton.

―――― (1965). Psychology and philosophy. In B. B. Wolman and E. Nagel (eds.), *Scientific psychology* (pp. 28–43). New York: Basic Books.

―――― (1965/1995). *Sociological studies*. London: Routledge. [Original: *Études sociologiques*. Geneva: Droz.]

―――― (1966). Genèse et structure en psychologie. In M. de Gandillac, L. Goldman, and J. Piaget (eds.), *Entretiens sul les notions de genèse et de structure* (pp. 37–61). Paris: Mouton.

―――― (1970). *Structuralism*. New York: Basic Books.

―――― (1977). The role of acting in the development of thinking. In W. Overton and J. McCarthy Gallagher (eds.), *Knowledge and development*. Vol. 1 (pp. 17–42). New York: Plenum.

Pino, A. (1994). Public and private categories in an analysis of internalization. In J. Wertsch and J.-D. Ramirez (eds.), *Explorations in socio-cultural studies*. Vol. 2, *Literacy and other forms of mediated action* (pp. 33–40). Madrid: Fundación Infancia y Aprendizaje.

Platt, J. (1992). "Case study" in American methodological thought. *Current Sociology, 40*, 19–48.

Pléh, C. (1988). Two conceptions on the crisis of psychology: Vygotsky and Bühler. In A. Eschbach (ed.), *Karl Bühler's theory of language* (pp. 407–413). Amsterdam: John Benjamins.

Ponzio, A. (1985). Semiotics between Peirce and Bakhtin. *Kodikas, 8*, 11–28.

―――― (1990). *Man as a sign: Essays on the philosphy of language*. Berlin: Mouton de Gruyter.

Poortinga, Y. H. (1992). Towards a conceptualization of culture for psychology. In S. Iwawaki, Y. Kashima, and K. Leung (eds.), *Innovations in cross-cultural psychology* (pp. 3–17). Lisse: Swets and Zeitlinger.

Porter, T. M. (1992). Quantification and the accounting ideal in science. *Social Studies of Science, 22*, 633–652.

———— (1994). Objectivity as standardization: The rhetoric of impersonality in measurement, statistics, and cost-benefit analysis. In A. Megill (ed.), *Rethinking objectivity* (pp. 197–237). Durham, N.C.: Duke University Press.

Portes, P. R., Smith, T., and Cuentas, T. E. (1994). Cross-cultural parent-child interactions in relation to concept of development: Structure and processes in the ZPD. In A. Alvarez and P. Del Río (eds.), *Explorations in socio-cultural studies.* Vol. 4, *Education as cultural construction* (pp. 97–108). Madrid: Fundación Infancia y Aprendizaje.

Potebnya, A. A. (1989). *Slovo i mif.* [Word and myth.] Moscow: Pravda.

Prasad, A. K. (1990). *Devadasi system in Ancient India.* Delhi: H. K. Publishers.

Preston, J. J. (1983). Goddess temples in Orissa: An anthropological survey. In G. R. Gupta (ed.), *Religion in modern India* (pp. 229–247). New Delhi: Vikas.

Prigogine, I. (1973). Irreversibility as a symmetry-breaking process. *Nature, 246,* 67–71.

———— (1978). Time, structure, and fluctuations. *Science, 201,* no. 4358, 777–785.

———— (1987). Exploring complexity. *European Journal of Operational Research, 30,* 97–103.

Prigogine, I., Allen, P. M., and Herman, R. (1977). Long term trends and the evolution of complexity. In E. Laszlo and J. Bierman (eds.), *Goals in a global community* (pp. 1–63). New York: Pergamon Press.

Prinzhorn, H. (1933). The value and limits of the experimental method in psychology. *Character and Personality, 1,* 251–258.

Raghuramaiah, K. L. (1991). *Night birds: Indian prostitutes from Devadasis to call girls.* Delhi: Chanakya Publications.

Raheja, G. G. (1988). *The poison in the gift.* Chicago: University of Chicago Press.

———— (1990). Centrality, mutuality and hierarchy: Shifting aspects of inter-caste relationships in North India. In M. Marriott (ed.), *India through Hindu categories* (pp. 79–101). New Delhi: Sage.

Ramanujam, B. K. (1992). Toward maturity: Problems of identity seen in the Indian clinical setting. In S. Kakar (ed.), *Identity and adulthood* (pp. 37–55). Delhi: Oxford University Press.

Ramanujan, A. K. (1982). On women saints. In J. S. Hawley and D. M. Wulff (eds.), *The divine consort: Radha and the goddesses of India* (pp. 316–324). Berkeley, Calif.: Berkeley Religious Series.

———— (1991). Toward a counter-system: Women's tales. In A. Appadurai, F. J. Korom, and M. A. Mills (eds.), *Gender, genre, and power in South Asian expressive traditions* (pp. 33–55). Philadelphia: University of Pennsylvania Press.

Ramishvili, G. V. (1985). From comparative anthropology to comparative linguistics. In W. von Humboldt, *Yazyk i filosofia kul'tury* (pp. 309–317). Moscow: Progress. [In Russian: Language and philosophy of culture.]

Ranjana (1983). Devadasis: The girls dedicated to temples. *Social Welfare, 39,* 10, 24–25.

Raphelson, A. C. (1973). The pre-Chicago association of the early functionalists. *Journal of the Behavioral Sciences, 9,* 115–122.

Rapp, R. (1994). Women's responses to prenatal diagnosis: A sociocultural perspective on diversity. In K. Rothenberg and E. J. Thomson (eds.), *Women and prenatal testing: Facing the challenges of genetic technology* (pp. 219–233). Columbus: Ohio State University Press.

Rasmussen, S. J. (1993). Joking in researcher-resident dialogue: The ethnography of hierarchy among the Tuareg. *Anthropological Quarterly, 66,* 211–220.

Ratner, C. (1996). Activity as a key concept for cultural psychology. *Culture and Psychology, 2,* 407–434.

Reed, E., and Jones, R. (eds.) (1984). *Reasons for realism: Selected essays by James J. Gibson.* Hillsdale, N.J.: Erlbaum

Reed, E. S. (1993). The intention to use a specific affordance: A conceptual framework for psychology. In R. H. Wozniak and K. W. Fischer (eds.), *Development in context* (pp. 45–76). Hillsdale, N.J.: Erlbaum.

———— (1995). The ecological approach to language development: a radical solution to Chomsky's and Quine's problems. *Language & Communication, 15,* 1, 1–29.

Reinert, G., Boné, E., Heil, F. E., Kindermann, T., and Zeimet, U. (1980). William Stern: Eine Titelbibliographie seiner Werke. *Trier Psychologische Berichte, 7,* 4.

Ribeiro, G. L. (1994). The condition of transnationality. Working Papers No. 173, Série Antropologia, Universidade de Brasilia.

Rinard, R. G. (1992). Hans Spemann: Cultural factors in the rejection of an engineering stance in embryology. *Synthese, 91,* 73–91.

Robinson, D. (1985). Intentions, signs, and interpretations: C. S. Peirce and the dialogic of pragmatism. *Kodikas, 8,* 179–193.

Robinson, J. A. (1988). "What we've got here is a failure to communicate": The cultural context of meaning. In J. Valsiner (ed.), *Child development within culturally structured environments.* Vol. 2, *Social co-construction and environmental guidance in development* (pp. 137–198). Norwood, N.J.: Ablex.

Rodman, L. (1994). The active voice in scientific articles: Frequency and discourse functions. *Journal of Technical Writing and Communication, 24,* 309–331.

Rogers, C. (1951). *Client-centered therapy: Its current practice, implications, and theory.* Boston: Houghton Mifflin.

Rogoff, B. (1982). Integrating context and cognitive development. In M. Lamb and A. Brown (eds.), *Advances in developmental psychology.* Vol. 2 (pp. 125–170). Hillsdale, N.J.: Erlbaum.

———— (1986). Adult assistance of children's learning. In T. E. Raphael (ed.), *The contexts of school-based literacy* (pp. 27–40). New York: Random House.

———— (1990). *Apprenticeship in thinking.* New York: Oxford University Press.

———— (1992). Three ways of relating person and culture. *Human Development, 35,* 316–320.

———— (1993). Children's guided participation and participatory appropriation in sociocultural activity. In R. H. Wozniak and K. W. Fischer (eds.), *Development in context* (pp. 121–153). Hillsdale, N.J.: Erlbaum.

——— (1995). Observing sociocultural activity on three planes: Participatory appropriation, guided participation, and apprenticeship. In J. V. Wertsch, P. Del Río, and A. Alvarez (eds.), *Sociocultural studies of mind* (pp. 139–164). Cambridge: Cambridge University Press.

Rogoff, B., Chavajay, P., and Matusov, E. (1993). Questioning assumptions about culture and individuals. *Behavioral and Brain Sciences, 16,* 533–534.

Rogoff, B., and Lave, J. (eds.) (1984). *Everyday cognition.* Cambridge, Mass.: Harvard University Press.

Rojas-Drummond, S., and Rico, J. A. (1994). The development of independent problem solving in pre-school children. In N. Mercer and C. Coll (eds.), *Explorations in socio-cultural studies.* Vol. 3, *Teaching, learning, and interaction* (pp. 161–175). Madrid: Fundación Infancia y Aprendizaje.

Roland, A. (1987). The familial self, the individualized self, and the transcendent self: Psychoanalytic reflections on India and America. *Psychoanalytic Review, 74,* 237–250.

——— (1988). *In search of self in India and Japan.* Princeton, N.J.: Princeton University Press.

Rommetveit, R. (1979a). On common codes and dynamic residuals in human communication. In R. Rommetveit and R. Blakar (eds.), *Studies of language, thought and verbal communication* (pp. 163–175). London: Academic Press.

——— (1979b). On negative rationalism in scholarly studies of verbal communication and dynamic residuals in the construction of human intersubjectivity. In R. Rommetveit and R. Blakar (eds.), *Studies of language, thought and verbal communication* (pp. 147–161). London: Academic Press.

——— (1992). Outlines of a dialogically based social-cognitive approach to human cognition and communication. In A. H. Wold (ed.), *The dialogical alternative: Towards a theory of language and mind* (pp. 19–44). Oslo: Scandinavian University Press.

Rosa, A. (1994). History of psychology as a ground for reflexivity. In A. Rosa and J. Valsiner (eds.), *Explorations in socio-cultural studies.* Vol. 1, *Historical and theoretical discourse* (pp. 149–167). Madrid: Fundación Infancia y Aprendizaje.

Rose, N. (1996). *Inventing our selves: Psychology, power, and personhood.* Cambridge: Cambridge University Press.

Rossiaud, J. (1985). Prostitution, sex and society in French towns in the fifteenth century. In P. Ariès and A. Béjin (eds.), *Western sexuality* (pp. 76–94). Oxford: Basil Blackwell.

Rothbaum, F., Weisz, J. R., and Snyder, S. (1982). Changing the world and changing the self: A two-process model of perceived control. *Journal of Personality and Social Psychology, 42,* 1, 5–37.

Royce, J. (1892a). The outlook in ethics. *International Journal of Ethics, 2,* 106–111.

——— (1892b). *The spirit of modern philosophy.* Boston: Houghton Mifflin.

——— (1893/1966). The two-fold nature of knowledge: Imitative and reflective. *Journal of the History of Philosophy, 4,* 326–337.

——— (1894a). The case of John Bunyan. *Psychological Review, 1,* 22–33, 134–151, 230–240.

——— (1894b). The external world and the social consciousness. *Philosophical Review, 3,* 513–545.

——— (1895a). Preliminary report on imitation. *Psychological Review, 2,* 217–235.

——— (1895b). Self-consciousness, social consciousness and nature. *Philosophical Review, 4,* 465–485, 577–602.

——— (1895c). Some observations on the anomalies of self-consciousness. *Psychological Review, 2,* 433–457, 574–584.

——— (1898). The psychology of invention. *Psychological Review, 5,* 113–144.

Rüssel, A. (1944). Das Wesen der Bewegungskoordination. *Archiv für die gesamte Psychologie, 112,* 1–22.

Rychlak, J. F. (1995). A teleological critique of modern cognitivism. *Theory and Psychology, 5,* 511–531.

Ryff, C. D. (1987). The place of personality and social structure research in social psychology. *Journal of Personality and Social Psychology, 53,* 1192–1202.

Saada-Robert, M. (1994). Microgenesis and situated cognitive representations. In N. Mercer and C. Coll (eds.), *Explorations in socio-cultural studies.* Vol. 3, *Teaching, learning, and interaction* (pp. 55–64). Madrid: Fundación Infancia y Aprendizaje.

Samantha, S. (1992). *Mangalmayima, sumangali, mangal:* Bengali perceptions of the divine feminine, motherhood, and "auspiciousness." *Contributions to Indian Sociology, 26,* 1, 51–75.

——— (1994). The "self-animal" and divine digestion: Goat sacrifice to the goddess Kali in Bengal. *Journal of Asian Studies, 53,* 779–803.

Sande, H. (1992). Palestinian martyr widowhood: Emotional needs in conflict with role expectations. *Social Science and Medicine, 34,* 709–717.

Sander, F. (1927). Ueber Gestaltqualitäten. *Proceedings of the 8th International Congress of Psychology, 1926* (pp. 183–189). Groningen: P. Noordhoff.

——— (1928/1962). Experimentelle Ergebnisse der Gestaltpsychologie. In F. Sander and H. Volkelt (eds.), *Ganzheitspsychologie* (pp. 73–112). Munich: C. H. Beck.

——— (1930). Structure, totality of experience, and gestalt. In C. Murchison (ed.), *Psychologies of 1930* (pp. 188–204). Worcester, Mass.: Clark University Press.

——— (1932). Gestaltpsychologie und Kunsttheorie. *Neue Psychologische Studien, 4,* 321–346.

Sander, F., and Volkelt, H. (1962). *Ganzheitspsychologie: Grundlagen, Ergebnisse, Anwendungen.* München: C. H. Beck.

Sanders, C. R. (1989). *Customizing the body: The art and culture of tattooing.* Philadelphia: Temple University Press.

Sanger, W. W. (1859). *The history of prostitution*. New York: Harper and Brothers.

Sapir, E. (1907). Herder's *Ursprung der Sprache*. *Modern Philology, 5,* 109–142.

—— (1921). *Language: An introduction to the study of speech*. New York: Harcourt and Brace.

—— (1924). Culture, genuine and spurious. *American Journal of Sociology, 29,* 401–429.

Sarbin, T. R. (1950). Contributions to role-taking theory: I. Hypnotic behavior. *Psychological Review, 57,* 255–270.

—— (1952). A preface to a psychological analysis of the self. *Psychological Review, 59,* 11–22.

Saussure, F. (1916/1949). *Cours de linguistique générale*. Paris: Payot.

Scheerer, M., Rothman, E., and Goldstein, K. (1945). A case of "Idiot Savant": An experimental study of personality organization. *Psychological Monographs, 58,* 4 (whole no. 269), 1–63.

Schegloff, E. A. (1987). Some sources of misunderstanding in talk-in-interaction. *Linguistics, 25,* 201–218.

—— (1989). Reflections on language, development, and the interactional character of talk-in-interaction. In M. H. Bornstein and J. S. Bruner (eds.), *Interaction in human development* (pp. 139–153). Hillsdale, N.J.: Erlbaum.

—— (1991). Conversation analysis and socially shared cognition. In L. B. Resnick, J. M. Levine, and S. D. Teasley (eds.), *Perspectives on socially shared cognition* (pp. 150–171). Washington, D.C.: American Psychological Association.

—— (1992). Repair after next turn: The last structurally provided defence of intersubjectivity in conversation. *American Journal of Sociology, 97,* 1295–1345.

Schiefenhövel, W. (1990). Ritualized adult-male/adolescent-male sexual behavior in Melanesia: An anthropological and ethological perspective. In J. R. Feierman (ed.), *Pedophilia: Biosocial dimensions* (pp. 394–421). New York: Springer.

Schnepel, B. (1993). Die Schutzgöttinnen: Tribale Gottheiten in Südorissa (Indien) und ihre Patronage durch hinduistische Kleinkönige. *Anthropos, 88,* 337–350.

Schütz, A. (1982). *Life forms and meaning structures*. London: Routledge and Kegan Paul.

Schütz, A., and Luckmann, T. (1973). *The structures of the life-world*. Evanston, Ill.: Northwestern University Press.

Schwalbe, M. L. (1991). The autogenesis of the self. *Journal for the Theory of Social Behaviour, 21,* 269–295.

Searle, J. R. (1969). *Speech acts: An essay in the philosophy of language*. Cambridge: Cambridge University Press.

—— (1989). Individual intentionality and social phenomena in the theory of speech acts. In G. Deledalle (ed.), *Semiotics and pragmatics: Proceedings of the Perpignan symposium* (pp. 3–17). Amsterdam: John Benjamins.

Semin, G. (1994). The linguistic category model and personality language. In J.

Siegfried (ed.), *The status of common sense in psychology* (pp. 305–321). Norwood, N.J.: Ablex.

Sewertzoff, A. (1929). Direction of evolution. *Acta Zoologica, 10,* 59–141.

Shankar, J. (1990). *Devadasi cult: A sociological analysis.* New Delhi: Ashish Publishing House.

Sherif, M. (1936). *The psychology of social norms.* New York: Harper and Brothers.

Sherif, M., Harvey, O. J., White, B. J., Hood, W. R., and Sherif, C. W. (1961). *Intergroup conflict and cooperation: The Robbers Cave experiment.* Norman, Okla.: University Book Exchange.

Shi-xu (1995). Cultural perceptions: Exploiting the unexpected of the Other. *Culture and Psychology, 1,* 315–342.

———— (1996). Cultural representations: Understanding Chinese and Dutch discourse about the other. Ph.D. diss., University of Amsterdam.

Short, T. (1988). The growth of symbols. *Cruzeiro semiotico,* no. 8, 81–87.

Shotter, J. (1990). *Knowing of the third kind.* Utrecht: ISOR.

———— (1992). Vygotsky and Bakhtin: On internalization as a boundary phenomenon. In R. Maier (ed.), *Internalization: Conceptual issues and methodological problems* (pp. 147–174). Utrecht: ISOR.

———— (1993a). *Conversational realities: Constructing life through language.* London: Sage.

———— (1993b). Vygotsky: The social negotiation of semiotic mediation. *New Ideas in Psychology, 11,* 61–75.

———— (1994). Is there a logic in common sense? The scope and the limits of Jan Smedslund's "geometric" psychologic. In J. Siegfried (ed.), *The status of common sense in psychology* (pp. 149–168). Norwood, N.J.: Ablex.

Shotter, J., and Gergen, K. J. (eds.). (1989). *Texts of identity.* London: Sage.

Shweder, R. A. (1984). Anthropology's romantic rebellion against the enlightenment, or there is more to thinking than reason and evidence. In R. Shweder and R. A. LeVine (eds.), *Culture theory: Essays on mind, self and emotions* (pp. 27–66). Cambridge: Cambridge University Press.

———— (1990). Cultural psychology: What is it? In J. W. Stigler, R. A. Shweder, and G. Herdt (eds.), *Cultural psychology* (pp. 1–43). Cambridge: Cambridge University Press.

———— (1991). *Thinking through cultures.* Cambridge, Mass.: Harvard University Press.

———— (1995). The confessions of a methodological individualist. *Culture and Psychology, 1,* 115–122.

Shweder, R. A., and Bourne, E. J. (1984). Does the concept of person vary cross-culturally? In R. A. Shweder and R. A. LeVine (eds.), *Culture theory: Essays on mind, self and emotions* (pp. 158–199). New York: Cambridge University Press.

Shweder, R. A., Mahapatra, M., and Miller, J. G. (1987). Culture and moral development. In J. Kagan and S. Lamb (eds.), *The emergence of morality in young children* (pp. 1–83). Chicago: University of Chicago Press.

Shweder, R. A., and Much, N. (1987). Determinations of meaning: Discourse and moral socialization. In W. M. Kurtines and J. L. Gewirtz (eds.), *Moral development through social interaction* (pp. 197–244). New York: Wiley.

Shweder, R. A., Much, N. C., Mahapatra, M., and Park, L. (1993). The "big three" of morality (autonomy, community, divinity), and the "Big Three" explanations of suffering. In A. Brandt and P. Rozin (eds.), *Morality and health*. Stanford, Calif.: Stanford University Press.

Shweder, R. A., and Sullivan, M. A. (1990). The semiotic subject of cultural psychology. In L. Pervin, (ed.), *Handbook of personality* (pp. 399–416). New York: Guilford Press.

—— (1993). Cultural psychology: Who needs it? *Annual Review of Psychology*, *44*, 497–523.

Siegel, L. (1978). *Sacred and profane dimensions of love in Indian traditions as exemplified in the Gitagovinda of Jayadeva*. Delhi: Oxford University Press.

Siegfried, J. (1994). Commonsense language and the limits of theory construction in psychology. In J. Siegfried (ed.), *The status of common sense in psychology* (pp. 3–34). Norwood, N.J.: Ablex.

Sigel, I. E. (1970). The distancing hypothesis. In M. Jones (ed.), *Effects of early experience* (pp. 99–118). Coral Gables, Fla.: University of Miami Press.

—— (1993). The centrality of a distancing model for the development of representational competence. In R. R. Cocking and K. A. Renninger (eds.), *The development and meaning of psychological distance* (pp. 141–158). Hillsdale, N.J.: Erlbaum.

Sigel, I. E., Stinson, E. T., and Kim, M.-I. (1993). Socialization of cognition: The distancing model. In R. H. Wozniak and K. W. Fischer (eds.), *Development in context* (pp. 211–224). Hillsdale, N.J.: Erlbaum.

Simmel, G. (1906). The sociology of secrecy and of secret societies. *American Journal of Sociology*, *11*, 441–498.

—— (1908). Vom Wesen der Kultur. *Österreichische Rundschau*, *15*, 36–42.

Simon, H. (1957). *Models of man*. New York: Wiley.

Singer, M. (ed.) (1966). *Krishna: Myths, rites, and attitudes*. Honolulu: East-West Center Press.

Sinha, C. (1992). Vygotsky, internalization and evolution. In R. Maier (ed.), *Internalization: Conceptual issues and methodological problems* (pp. 125–146). Utrecht: ISOR.

Sjövall, B. (1967). *Psychology of tension*. Nordstets: Svenska Bokförlaget.

Skinner, D., Valsiner, J., and Basnet, B. (1993). Singing one's life: An orchestration of personal experiences and cultural forms. *Journal of South Asian Literature*, *26*, 1 and 2, 15–43.

Slongo, D., Schär-Moser, M., Richner, M., Billaud, C., Schläpp-Schreiber, .S., and Lang, A. (1995). Über die Regulation psycho-sozialer Systeme durch architektonische und alltagsdingliche Kultur. *Forschungsberichte aus dem Psychologischen Institut der Universität Bern*. No. 2.

Smedslund, J. (1988). *Psycho-logic*. New York: Springer.

—— (1994). What kind of propositions are set forth in developmental research? Five case studies. *Human Development*, *37*, 280–292.

—— (1995). Psychologic: Common sense and the pseudoempirical. In J. A. Smith, R. Harré, and L. van Langenhove (eds.), *Rethinking psychology* (pp. 196–206). London: Sage.

Smith, B. (1988). Materials towards a history of speech act theory. In A. Eschbach (ed.), *Karl Bühler's theory of language* (pp. 125–152). Amsterdam: John Benjamins.

Smith, M. B. (1993). Allport and Murray on Allport's *Personality:* A confrontation in 1946–1947. In K. H. Craik, R. Hogan, and R. N. Wolfe (eds.), *Fifty years of personality psychology* (pp. 57–65). New York: Plenum.

—— (1994). Selfhood at risk: Postmodern perils and the perils of postmodernism. *American Psychologist, 49,* 405–411.

Smolka, A. L. B. (1990). School interactions: An analysis of speech events in a Brazilian public school setting. Paper presented at the Boston University Conference on Language Development, Boston, October.

—— (1994a). Discourse practices and the issue of internalization. In A. Rosa and J. Valsiner (eds.), *Explorations in socio-cultural studies.* Vol. 2, *Historical and theoretical discourse* (pp. 75–84). Madrid: Fundación Infancia y Aprendizaje.

—— (1994b). Examining multiparty interactions: Approaching knowledge and meaning elaboration in the classroom. Paper presented at the Thirteenth Biennial ISSBD Meeting, Amsterdam, July, 2.

Smolka, A. L. B., Góes, M. C., and Pino, A. (1995). The constitution of the subject: A persistent question. In J. Wertsch and B. Rogoff (eds.), *Sociocultural studies of the mind.* Cambridge: Cambridge University Press.

Sorrentino, F. (1988). The life of the party. In F. Sorrentino, *Sanitary centennial* (pp. 110–122). Austin: University of Texas Press.

Sovran, T. (1992). Between similarity and sameness. *Journal of Pragmatics, 18,* 329–344.

Steiner, C. B. (1990). Body personal and body politic. *Anthropos, 85,* 431–445.

Stern, W. (1897). Psychische Präsenzzeit. *Zeitschfrift für Psychologie und Physiologie der Sinnesorgane, 13,* 325–349.

—— (1906). *Person und Sache: System der philosophischen Weltanschauung.* Leipzig: J. A. Barth.

—— (1907). Grundfragen der Psychogenesis. *Zeitschrift für Pädagogische Psychologie, Pathologie und Hygiene, 9,* 77–80.

—— (1908). Tatsachen und Ursachen der seelischen Entwicklung. *Zeitschrift für angewandte Psychologie, 1,* 1–43.

—— (1911). *Differentielle Psychologie.* Leipzig: J. A. Barth.

—— (1918). *Grundgedanken der personalistische Philosophie.* Berlin: Reuther and Reichard.

—— (1919). *Person und Sache.* Vol. 2, *Die menschliche Persönlichkeit.* 2d ed. Leipzig: J. A. Barth.

—— (1922). Das Psychologische Laboratorium der Hamburgischen Universität. *Zeitschrift für Pädagogische Psychologie, 23,* 161–196.

—— (1924). *Person und Sache.* Vol. 3, *Wertphilosophie.* Leipzig: J. A. Barth.

——— (1930). William Stern. In C. Murchison (ed.), *A history of psychology in autobiography*. Vol. 1 (pp. 335–388). Worcester, Mass.: Clark University Press.

——— (1932). Das Kind und die Welt. Presentation at the introduction of Kurt Lewin's film at Hamburg Urania, February 12.

——— (1935a). *Allgemeine Psychologie auf personalistischer Grundlage*. Den Haag: Martinus Nijhoff.

——— (1935b). Raum und Zeit als personale Dimensionen. *Acta Psychologica, 1,* 220–232.

——— (1938). *General psychology from the personalist standpoint*. New York: Macmillan

——— (1950). *Allgemeine psychologie*. 2d ed. Den Haag: M. Nijhoff.

Stirrat, R. L. (1987). A view from Britain. *Contributions to Indian Sociology, 21,* 67–75.

Strathern, M. (1979). The self in self-decoration. *Oceania, 49,* 241–257.

Sullivan, H. S. (1953). *The interpersonal theory of psychiatry*. New York: Norton.

Tarachand, K. C. (1991). *Devadasi custom: Rural social structure and flesh markets*. New Delhi: Reliance Publishing House.

Tarde, G. (1884). Qu'est-ce qu'une société? *Revue Philosophique, 18,* 489–510.

——— (1895a). *La Logique sociale*. Paris: Félix Alcan.

——— (1895b). *Les Lois de l'imitation*. 2d ed. Paris: Félix Alcan.

——— (1903). *The laws of imitation*. New York: Henry Holt.

Taylor, C. A. (1991). Defining the scientific community: A rhetorical perspective on demarcation. *Communication Monographs, 58,* 401–420.

Thommen, E. (1994). Internalization and acquisition of concepts: Adolescent thinking from the point of view of Piaget and Vygotsky. In A. Rosa and J. Valsiner (eds.), *Explorations in socio-cultural studies*. Vol. 2, *Historical and theoretical discourse* (pp. 98–104). Madrid: Fundación Infancia y Aprendizaje.

Thorne, A. (1989). Conditional patterns, transference, and the coherence of personality across time. In D. M. Buss and N. Cantor (eds.), *Personality psychology: Recent trends and emerging directions* (pp. 149–159). New York: Springer.

Thorngate, W. (1986). The production, detection, and explanation of behavioural patterns. In J. Valsiner (ed.), *The individual subject and scientific psychology* (pp. 71–93). New York: Plenum.

——— (1992). Evidential statistics and the analysis of developmental patterns. In J. Asendorpf and J. Valsiner (eds.), *Stability and change in development* (pp. 63–83). Newbury Park, Calif.: Sage.

Tobin, Y. (1990). *Semiotics and linguistics*. London: Longman.

Toomey, P. M. (1990). Krishna's consuming passions: Food as metaphor and metonym for emotion at Mount Govardhan. In O. M. Lynch (ed.), *Divine passions: The social construction of emotion in India* (pp. 157–181). Berkeley: University of California Press.

Tripathy, G. M., and Tripathy, B. (1992). *Sri Jagannath Puri*. Bhubaneswar: Banita Publications.

Tulving, E. (1983). *Elements of episodic memory*. New York: Oxford University Press.

Tulviste, P. (1991). *The cultural-historical development of verbal thinking.* Commack, N.Y.: Nova Science Publishers.

Vaihinger, H. (1920). *Die Philosophie des als ob: System der theoretischen, praktischen und religiösen Fiktionen der Menschheit.* 4th ed. Leipzig: Felix Meiner.

Valsiner, J. (1984a). *The childhood of the Soviet citizen: Socialization for loyalty.* Ottawa: Carleton University Press.

——— (1984b). Two alternative epistemological frameworks in psychology: The typological and variational modes of thinking. *Journal of Mind and Behavior, 5,* 449–470.

——— (ed.) (1986). *The individual subject in scientific psychology.* New York: Plenum.

——— (1987). *Culture and the development of children's action.* Chichester, England: Wiley.

——— (1988a). *Developmental psychology in the Soviet Union.* Brighton, England: Harvester.

——— (1988b). Ontogeny of co-construction of culture within socially organized environmental settings. In J. Valsiner (ed.), *Child development within culturally structured environments.* Vol. 2, *Social co-construction and environmental guidance of development* (pp. 283–297). Norwood, N.J.: Ablex.

——— (1989). *Human development and culture.* Lexington, Mass.: D. C. Heath.

——— (1991a). Building theoretical bridges over a lagoon of everyday events. *Human Development, 34,* 307–315.

——— (1991b). Integration of theory and methodology in psychology: The legacy of Joachim Wohlwill. In L. Mos and P. Van Geert (eds.), *Annals of theoretical psychology.* Vol. 7 (pp. 161–175). New York: Plenum.

——— (1992). Interest: A metatheoretical perspective. In K. A. Renninger, S. Hidi, and A. Krapp (eds.), *The role of interest in learning and development* (pp. 27–41). Hillsdale, N.J.: Erlbaum.

——— (1994a). Bidirectional cultural transmission and constructive sociogenesis. In W. de Graaf and R. Maier (eds.), *Sociogenesis reexamined* (pp. 47–70). New York: Springer.

——— (1994b). Co-constructionism: What is (and is not) in a name? In P. van Geert, L. P. Mos, and W. J. Baker (eds.), *Annals of Theoretical Psychology.* Vol. 10 (pp. 343–368). New York: Plenum.

——— (1994c). Culture and human development: A co-constructionist perspective. In P. van Geert, L. P. Mos, and W. J. Baker (eds.), *Annals of Theoretical Psychology.* Vol. 10 (pp. 247–298). New York: Plenum.

——— (1994d). Irreversibility of time and the construction of historical developmental psychology. *Mind, Culture, and Activity, 1,* 25–42.

——— (1994e). James Mark Baldwin and his impact: social development of cognitive functions. In A. Rosa and J. Valsiner (eds.), *Explorations in sociocultural studies.* Vol. 1, *Historical and theoretical discourse* (pp. 187–204). Madrid: Fundación Infancia y Aprendizaje.

——— (1994f). Replicability in context: The problem of generalization. In R. Van der Veer, M. H. Van IJzendoorn, and J. Valsiner, (eds.), *Reconstructing the mind: Replicability in research on human development* (pp. 173–182). Norwood, N.J.: Ablex.

———— (1994g). Uses of common sense and ordinary language in psychology, and beyond: A co-constructionist perspective and its implications. In J. Siegfried (ed.), *The status of common sense in psychology* (pp. 46–57). Norwood, N.J.: Ablex.

———— (1995a). Editorial: Discourse complexes and relations between social sciences and societies. *Culture and Psychology, 1,* 412–421.

———— (1995b). Meanings of "the data" in contemporary developmental psychology: Constructions and implications. Gastvorträg am *12.* Tagung der Fachgruppe Entwicklungspsychologie der Deutschen Gesellschaft für Psychologie, Leipzig, September 27.

———— (1997a). Constructing the personal through the cultural: Redundant organization of psychological development. In K. A. Renninger and E. Amsel (eds.), Hillsdale, N.J.: Erlbaum.

———— (1997b). *Culture and the development of children's action.* 2d ed. New York: Wiley.

Valsiner, J., and Allik, J. (1982). General semiotic capabilities of the higher primates: Some hypotheses on communication and cognition in the evolution of human semiotic systems. In M. R. Key (ed.), *Nonverbal communication today: Current research* (pp. 245–257). Berlin: Mouton.

Valsiner, J. and Benigni, L. (1986). Naturalistic research and ecological thinking in the study of child development. *Developmental Review, 6,* 203–223.

Valsiner, J., and Cairns, R. B. (1992). Theoretical perspectives on conflict and development. In C. U. Shantz and W. W. Hartup (eds.), *Conflict in child and adolescent development* (pp. 15–35). Cambridge: Cambridge University Press.

Valsiner, J., and Lawrence, J. A. (1996). Human development and culture across the life span. In J. W. Berry, P. R. Dasen, and T. S. Saraswathi (eds.), *Handbook of cross-cultural psychology.* Vol. 2, 2d ed. (pp. 69–106). Boston: Allyn and Bacon.

Valsiner, J., and Van der Veer, R. (1988). On the social nature of human cognition: An analysis of the shared intellectual roots of George Herbert Mead and Lev Vygotsky. *Journal for the Theory of Social Behaviour, 18,* 117–135.

———— (1993). The encoding of distance: The concept of the zone of proximal development and its interpretations. In R. R. Cocking and K. A. Renninger (eds.), *The development and meaning of psychological distance* (pp. 35–62). Hillsdale, N.J.: Erlbaum.

———— (1996). From gesture to self: George Mead's construction of a socio-psychology. In D. Paez Rovira and A. Blanco (eds.), *Social psychology and sociocultural theory: Current perspectives* (pp. 63–74). Madrid: Fundación Infancia y Aprendizaje.

———— (1998 in preparation). *The social mind.* New York: Cambridge University Press.

Van der Veer, R. (1994). Pierre Janet's relevance for a socio-cultural approach. In

A. Rosa and J. Valsiner (eds.), *Explorations in socio-cultural studies*. Vol. 1, *Historical and theoretical discourse* (pp. 205–209). Madrid: Fundación Infancia y Aprendizaje.

Van der Veer, R., and Valsiner, J. (1988). Lev Vygotsky and Pierre Janet: On the origin of the concept of sociogenesis. *Developmental Review, 8,* 52–65.

——— (1991). *Understanding Vygotsky: A quest for synthesis.* Oxford: Basil Blackwell.

——— (eds.) (1994). *The Vygotsky Reader.* Oxford: Basil Blackwell.

Van Geert, P. (1994). Vygotskian dynamics of development. *Human Development, 37,* 346–365.

Van Stolk, B., and Wouters, C. (1987). Power changes and self-respect: A comparison of two classes of established-outsider relations. *Theory, Culture and Society, 4,* 477–488.

Vasconcellos, V. M. R., and Valsiner, J. (1995). *Perspectiva co-constructivista na psicologia e na educação.* Pôrto Alegre, Brazil: Artes Medicas.

Vegetti, S. (1994). Activity theory and historical cultural psychology: A comparative explanation of learning. In A. Alvarez and P. Del Río (eds.), *Explorations in socio-cultural studies.* Vol. 4, *Education as cultural construction* (pp. 168–179). Madrid: Fundación Infancia y Aprendizaje.

Vidal, F. (1993). *Piaget before Piaget.* Cambridge, Mass.: Harvard University Press.

Vidyabhusana, M. S. C. (1970). *A history of Indian logic (ancient, mediaeval and modern schools).* Delhi: Motilal Banardisas.

Vinh-Bang (1966). La Méthode clinique et la recherche en psychologie de l'enfant. In *Psychologie et épistémologie génétiques* (pp. 67–81). Paris: Dunod.

Volkelt, H. (1959/1962). Simultangestalten, Verlaufungsgestalten und "Einfühlung." In F. Sander and H. Volkelt (eds.), *Ganzheitspsychologie* (pp. 147–158). Munich: C. H. Beck.

Von Baer, K. E. (1828). *Über Entwicklungsgeschichte der Thiere: Beobactung und reflexion.* Königsberg: Bornträger.

Von Stietencron, H. (1989). Hinduism: On the proper use of a deceptive term. In G. D. Sontheimer and H. Kulke (eds.), *Hinduism reconsidered* (pp. 11–27). New Delhi: Manohar.

Von Uexküll, J. J. (1926). *Theoretical biology.* New York: Harcourt, Brace.

——— (1957). A stroll through the worlds of animals and men. In C. H. Schiller (ed.), *Instinctive behavior: The development of a modern concept* (pp. 5–80). New York: International Universities Press.

——— (1980). The theory of meaning. *Semiotica 42,* 25–82.

Von Wright, G. H. (1986). Truth, negation, and contradiction. *Synthese, 66,* 3–14.

Vygotsky, L. S. (1931). *Paedology of the adolescent.* Moscow: Gosudarstvennoe uchebno-pedagogicheskoe izdatel'stvo.

——— (1934). *Myshlenie i rec'* . Moscow: Gosudarstvennoe Sotsialnoeknomicheskoe Izdatel'stvo. [In Russian.]

——— (1971). *Psychology of art.* Cambridge, Mass.: MIT Press.

———— (1987). *Thinking and speech.* New York: Plenum.

Vygotsky, L. S., and Luria, A. R., (1930/1994). Tool and symbol in child development. In R. Van der Veer and J. Valsiner (eds.), *The Vygotsky reader* (pp. 99–174). Oxford: Blackwell.

Waddington, C. (1966). Fields and gradients. In M. Locke (ed.), *Major problems in developmental biology* (pp. 105–124). New York: Academic Press.

Wagner, W. (1994). Fields of research and socio-genesis of social representations: A discussion of criteria and diagnostics. *Social Science Information, 33,* 199–228.

Weinstein, D., and Bell, R. M. (1982). *Saints and society: The two worlds of Western Christendom, 1000–1700.* Chicago: University of Chicago Press.

Weissert, T. P. (1995). Dynamical discourse theory. *Time and Society, 4,* 111–133.

Weisz, J. R., Eastman, K. L., and McCarty, C. A. (1996). Primary and secondary control in East Asia. *Culture and Psychology, 2,* 63–76.

Wellek, A. (1954). Die genetische Ganzheitspsychologie der Leipziger Schule und Ihre Verzweigunge. *Neue Psychologische Studien, 15,* 1–67.

Werner, C. M., Altman, I., and Oxley, D. (1985). Temporal aspects of homes: A transactional perspective. In I. Altman and C. M. Werner (eds.), *Home environments* (pp. 1–32). New York: Plenum.

Werner, H. (1926). Über Mikromelodik und Mikroharmonik. *Zeitschrift für Psychologie, 98,* 74–89.

———— (1927). Ueber Physiognomische Wahrnehmungsweisen und Ihre experimentell Prüfung. In *Proceedings and papers of the 8th International Congress of Psychology, 1926, Groningen* (pp. 443–446). Groningen: P. Noordhoff.

———— (1930). Die Rolle der Sprachempfindung im Prozess der Gestaltung ausdrückmässig erlebter Wörter. *Zeitschrift für Psychologie, 117,* 230–254.

———— (1931). Das Prinzip der Gestaltschichtung und seine Bedeutung im kunstwerklichen Aufbau. *Zeitschrift für angewandte Psychologie,* Beiheft 59, 241–256.

———— (1938). William Stern's personalistics and psychology of personality. *Character and Personality, 7,* 109–125.

———— (1940a). *Comparative psychology of mental development.* New York: Harper and Brothers.

———— (1940b). Musical "micro-scales" and "micromelodies." *Journal of Psychology, 10,* 149–156.

———— (1948). *Comparative psychology of mental development.* New York: International University Press.

———— (1954). Change of meaning: A study of semantic processes through the experimental method. *Journal of General Psychology, 50,* 181–208.

———— (1956). Microgenesis and aphasia. *Journal of Abnormal and Social Psychology, 52,* 347–353.

———— (1957). The concept of development from a comparative and organismic point of view. In D. B. Harris (ed.), *The concept of development* (pp. 125–147). Minneapolis: University of Minnesota Press.

Werner, H., and Kaplan, B. (1956). The developmental approach to cognition: Its relevance to the psychological interpretation of anthropological and ethnolinguistic data. *American Anthropologist, 58,* 866–880.

——— (1984). *Symbol formation.* 2d ed. Hillsdale, N.J.: Erlbaum.

Wertsch, J. V. (1979). From social interaction to higher psychological processes: A clarification and application of Vygotsky's theory. *Human Development, 22,* 1–22.

——— (1981). The concept of activity in Soviet psychology: An introduction. In J. V. Wertsch (ed.), *The concept of activity in Soviet psychology* (pp. 3–36). Armonk, N.Y.: Sharpe.

——— (1983). The role of semiosis in L. S. Vygotsky's theory of human cognition. In B. Bain (ed.), *The sociogenesis of language and human conduct* (pp. 17–31). New York: Plenum.

——— (1984). The zone of proximal development: Some conceptual issues. In B. Rogoff and J. V. Wertsch (eds.), *Children's learning in the "zone of proximal development"* (pp. 7–17). New Directions for Child Development, no. 23. San Francisco: Jossey-Bass.

——— (1985a). Adult-child interaction as a source of self-regulation in children. In S. R. Yussen (ed.), *The growth of reflection in children* (pp. 69–97). Orlando, Fla.: Academic Press.

——— (1985b). The semiotic mediation of mental life: L. S. Vygotsky and M. M. Bakhtin. In E. Mertz and R. J. Parmentier (eds.), *Semiotic mediation: Sociocultural and psychological perspectives* (pp. 49–71). Orlando, Fla.: Academic Press.

——— (1989). Semiotic mechanisms in joint cognitive activity. *Infancia y Aprendizaje, 47,* 3–36.

——— (1990). The voice of rationality in a sociocultural approach to mind. In L. C. Moll (ed.), *Vygotsky and education* (pp. 111–126). Cambridge: Cambridge University Press.

——— (1991). *Voices of the mind.* Cambridge, Mass.: Harvard University Press.

——— (1993). Commentary [on Lawrence and Valsiner, 1993]. *Human Development, 36,* 168–171.

——— (1995a). The need for action in sociocultural research. In J. V. Wertsch, P. Del Río, and A. Alvarez (eds.), *Sociocultural studies of mind* (pp. 56–74). Cambridge: Cambridge University Press.

——— (1995b). Sociocultural research in the copyright age. *Culture and Psychology, 1,* 81–102.

——— (1995c). Vygotsky: The ambivalent Enlightenment rationalist. *Heinz Werner Lecture Series.* Vol. 21 (pp. 39–62). Worcester, Mass.: Clark University Press.

——— (1997). Narrative tools of history and identity. *Culture and Psychology, 3,* 1–25.

Wertsch, J. V., Minick, N., and Arns, F. J. (1984). The creation of context in joint problem-solving. In B. Rogoff and J. Lave (eds.), *Everyday cognition: Its devel-*

opment in social context (pp. 151–171). Cambridge, Mass. : Harvard University Press.

Wertsch, J. V., and O'Connor, K. (1992). The cognitive tools of historical representation: A sociocultural analysis. Paper presented at the First Socio-Cultural Studies Conference, Madrid, September.

Wertsch, J. V., and Smolka, A. L. B. (1993). Continuing the dialogue: Vygotsky, Bakhtin and Lotman. In H. Daniels (ed.), *Charting the agenda: Educational activity after Vygotsky* (pp. 69–92). London: Routledge.

Wertsch, J. V., and Stone, C. A. (1985). The concept of internalization in Vygotsky's account of the genesis of higher mental functions. In J. V. Wertsch (ed.), *Culture, communication, and cognition: Vygotskian perspectives* (pp. 162–179). Cambridge: Cambridge University Press.

Wetterstein, J. (1988). Külpe, Bühler, Popper. In A. Eschbach (ed.), *Karl Bühler's theory of language* (pp. 327–347). Amsterdam: John Benjamins.

Whitney, W. D. (1875). *The life and growth of language: An outline of linguistic science.* New York: D. Appleton.

Whorf, B. L. (1942/1956). Language, mind, and reality. In J. B. Carroll (ed.), *Language, thought and reality: Selected writings of Benjamin Lee Whorf* (pp. 246–270). Cambridge, Mass.: MIT Press.

Wierzbicka, A. (1992). *Semantics, culture, and cognition.* Oxford: Oxford University Press.

—— (1995). *Culture and Psychology, 1,* 227–258.

Wikan, U. (1989). Managing the heart to brighten the face and soul: Emotions in Balinese morality and health care. *American Ethnologist, 16,* 294–312.

—— (1990). *Managing turbulent hearts: A Balinese formula for living.* Chicago: University of Chicago Press.

Wilkie, J. (1986). Submerged sensuality: Technology and perceptions of bathing. *Journal of Social History, 19,* 649–664.

Winegar, L. T. (1993). Can "internalization" be more than a magical phrase? Paper presented at the meeting of the Society for Research on Child Development, New Orleans, March.

Winegar, L. T., Renninger, K. A. and Valsiner, J. (1989). Dependent independence in adult-child relationships. In D. A. Kramer and M. J. Bopp (eds.), *Movement through form: Transformation in clinical and developmental psychology* (pp. 157–168). New York: Springer.

Winegar, L. T., and Valsiner, J. (1992). Re-contextualizing context: Analysis of metadata and some further elaborations. In L. T. Winegar and J. Valsiner (eds.), *Children's development within social context.* Vol. 2, *Research and methodology* (pp. 249–266). Hillsdale, N.J.: Erlbaum.

Winslow, D. (1980). Rituals of first menstruation in Sri Lanka. *Man, 15,* 603–625.

Wispé, L. (1987). History of the concept of empathy. In N. Eisenberg and J. Strayer (eds.), *Empathy and its development* (pp. 17–37). Cambridge: Cambridge University Press.

Woodworth, R. S. (1948). *Contemporary schools of psychology*. Rev. ed. New York: Ronald Press.

Wouters, C. (1987). Developments in the behavioural codes between the sexes: The formalization of informalization in the Netherlands, 1930–85. *Theory, Culture and Society, 4,* 405–427.

Wozniak, R. (1986). Notes toward a co-constructive theory of the emotion-cognition relationship. In D. J. Bearison and H. Zimiles (eds.), *Thought and emotion: Developmental Perspectives* (pp. 39–64). Hillsdale, N.J.: Erlbaum.

——— (1993). Co-constructive metatheory for psychology. In R. Wozniak and K. Fischer (eds.), *Development in context* (pp. 77–92). Hillsdale, N.J.: Erlbaum.

Young, K. (1942). Variations in personality manifestations in Mormon polygynous families. In Q. McNemar and M. A. Merrill (eds.), *Studies in personality* (pp. 285–314). New York: McGraw-Hill.

Youniss, J. (1987). Social construction and moral development: Update and expansion of an idea. In W. M. Kurtines and J. L. Gewirtz (eds.), *Moral development through social interaction* (pp. 131–148). New York: Wiley.

Youniss, J., and Smollar, J. (1990). Self through relationship development. In H. Bosma and S. Jackson (eds.), *Coping and self-concept in adolescence* (pp. 129–148). Heidelberg: Springer.

Zuroff, D. C. (1986). Was Gordon Allport a trait theorist? *Journal of Personality and Social Psychology, 51,* 993–1000.

Index

451